Physical Memory Analysis Fundamentals

Dmitry Vostokov
Software Diagnostics Services

Published by OpenTask, Republic of Ireland

OpenTask books and magazines are available through booksellers and distributors worldwide. For further information or comments send requests to press@opentask.com.

A CIP catalogue record for this book is available from the British Library.

ISBN-13: 978-1-906717-15-5 (Paperback)

First printing, 2014

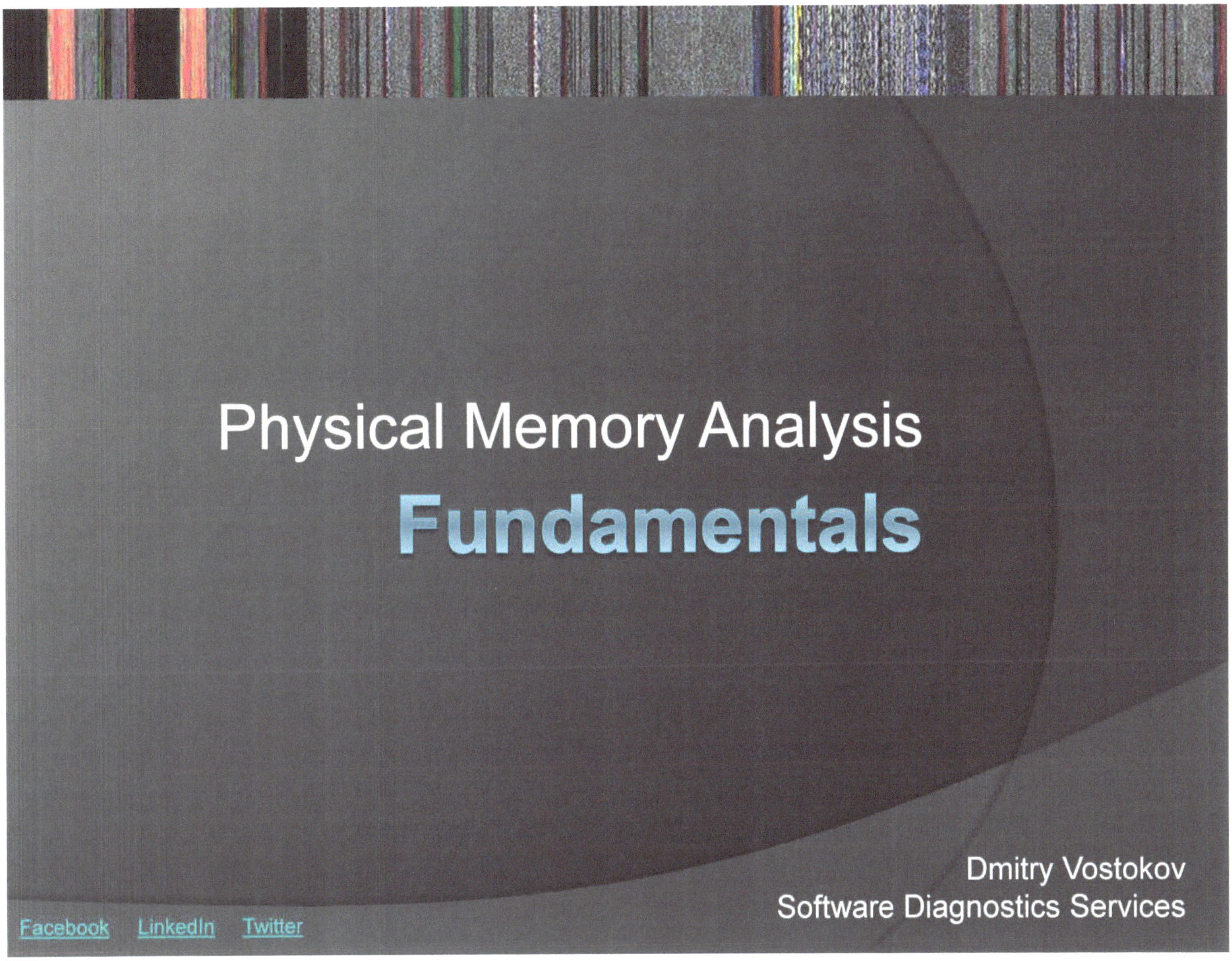

Hello everyone! More than two years have been passed since I presented the second version of Complete Crash and Hang Memory Dump Analysis webinar and more than three years since its first version. Before that time I found this topic a bit neglected so I had decided to summarize it and make a presentation. Many new memory dump analysis patterns have been identified since that time and new training courses became available so I decided to make a revision.

Facebook:
http://www.facebook.com/SoftwareDiagnosticsServices

LinkedIn:
http://www.linkedin.com/company/software-diagnostics-services

Twitter:
http://twitter.com/DumpAnalysis

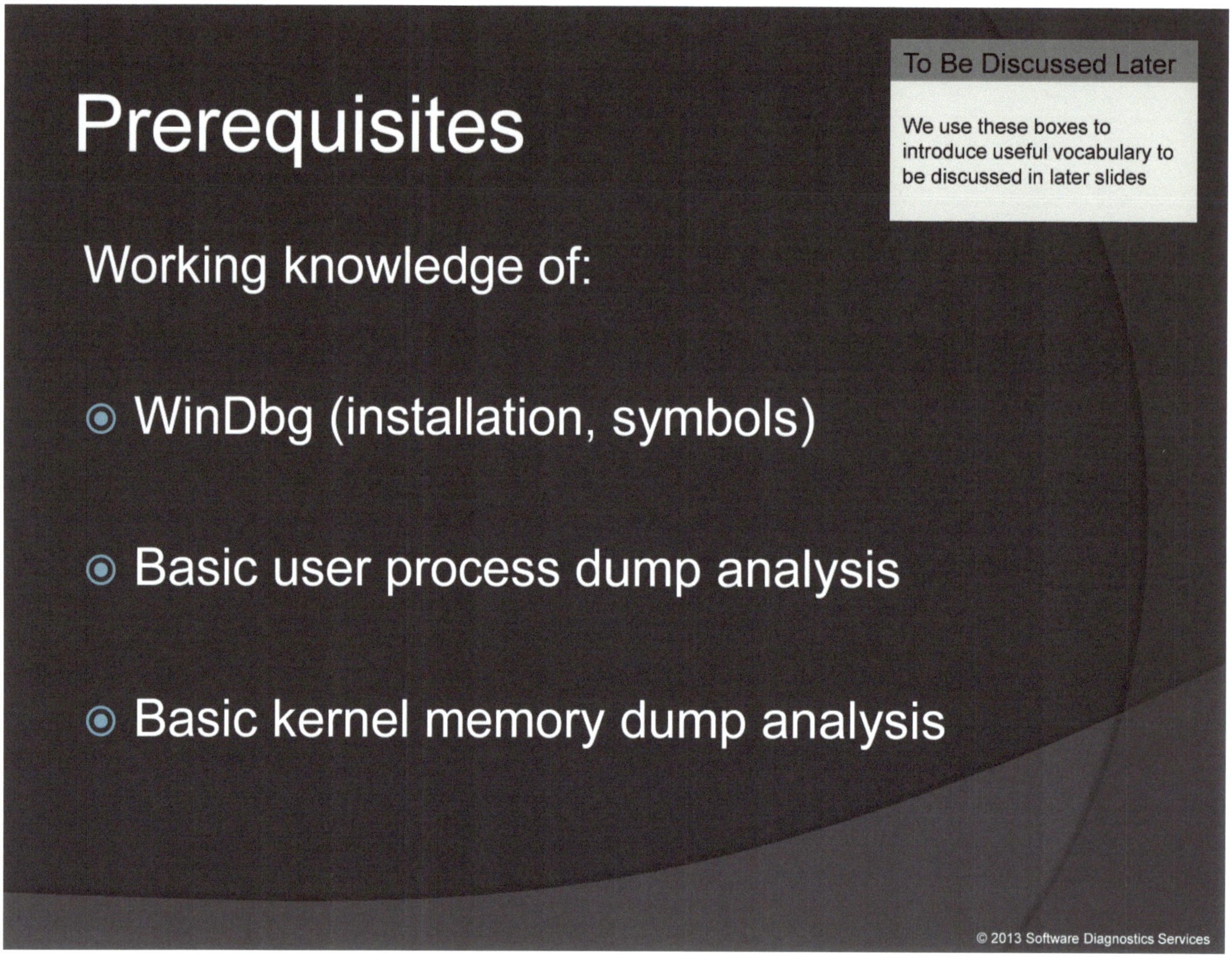

This is a big topic and I assume you already know what kernel, process, physical and virtual spaces are, how to set up and use symbols files, basic WinDbg commands to get stack traces and list loaded modules and their information.

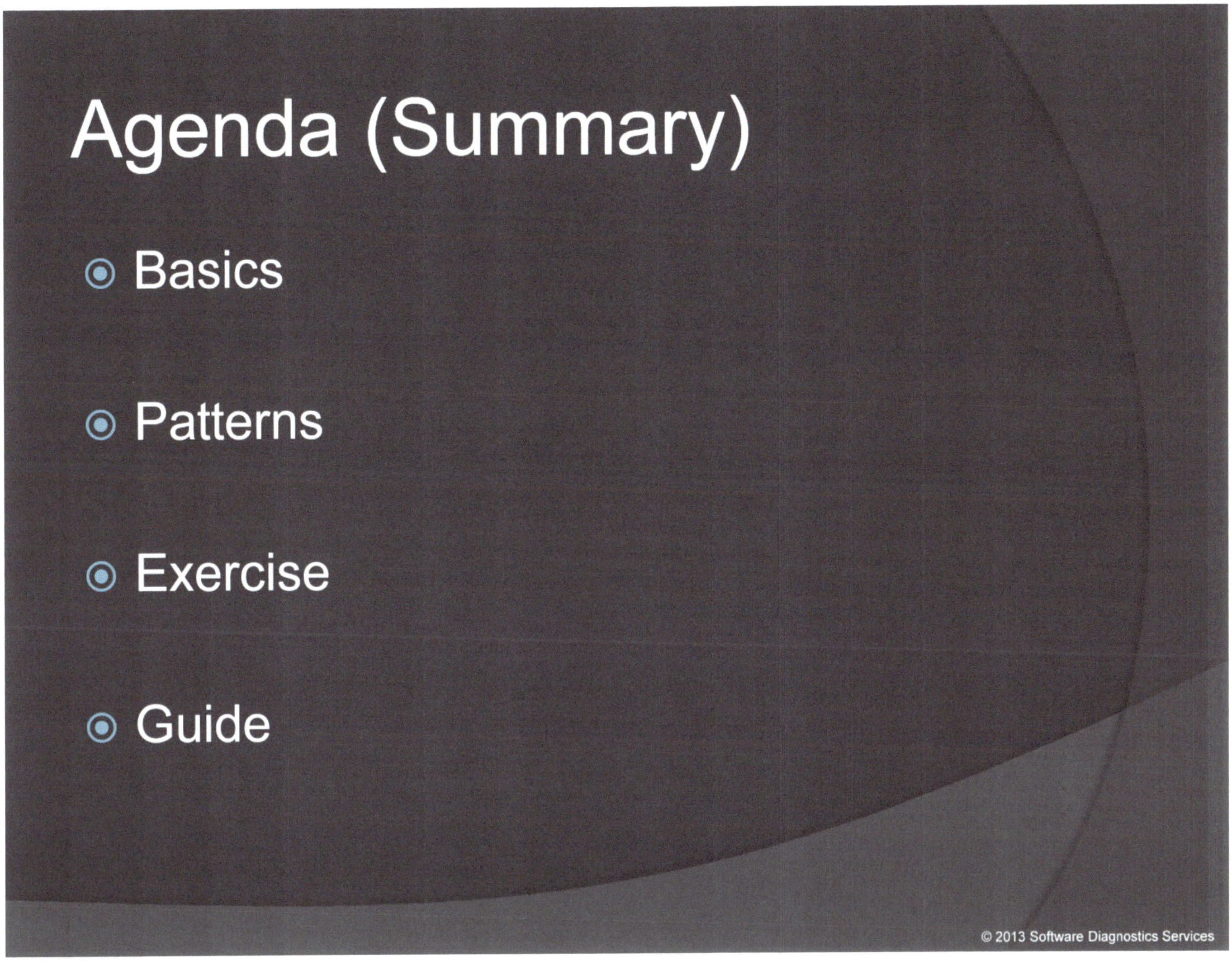

First, I remind you and discuss the very basic concepts like what a physical memory space is and how it relates to what we see in WinDbg debugger when we open a complete memory dump. Then I discuss a pattern language to communicate memory dump analysis findings. Next, I do a quick hands-on demonstration and finally provide a short incomplete guide. You can type your questions and I do my best to answer them either at the end of the Webinar or publish them later on a special page for this revision.

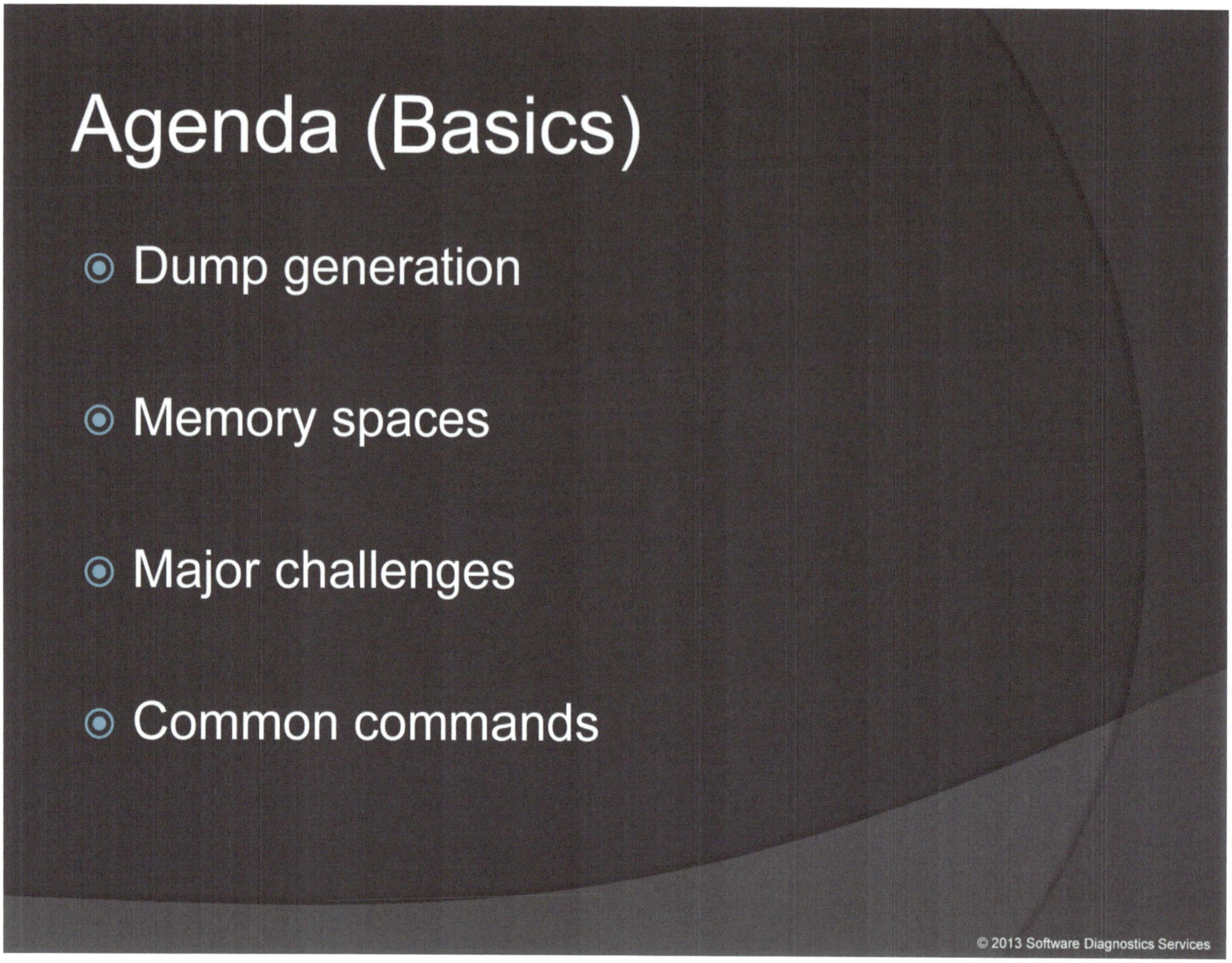

Here I talk about the need for complete or physical memory dumps and how to force them; the differences between various memory spaces; major challenges we face when we start looking at them and common WinDbg commands absolutely essential to know.

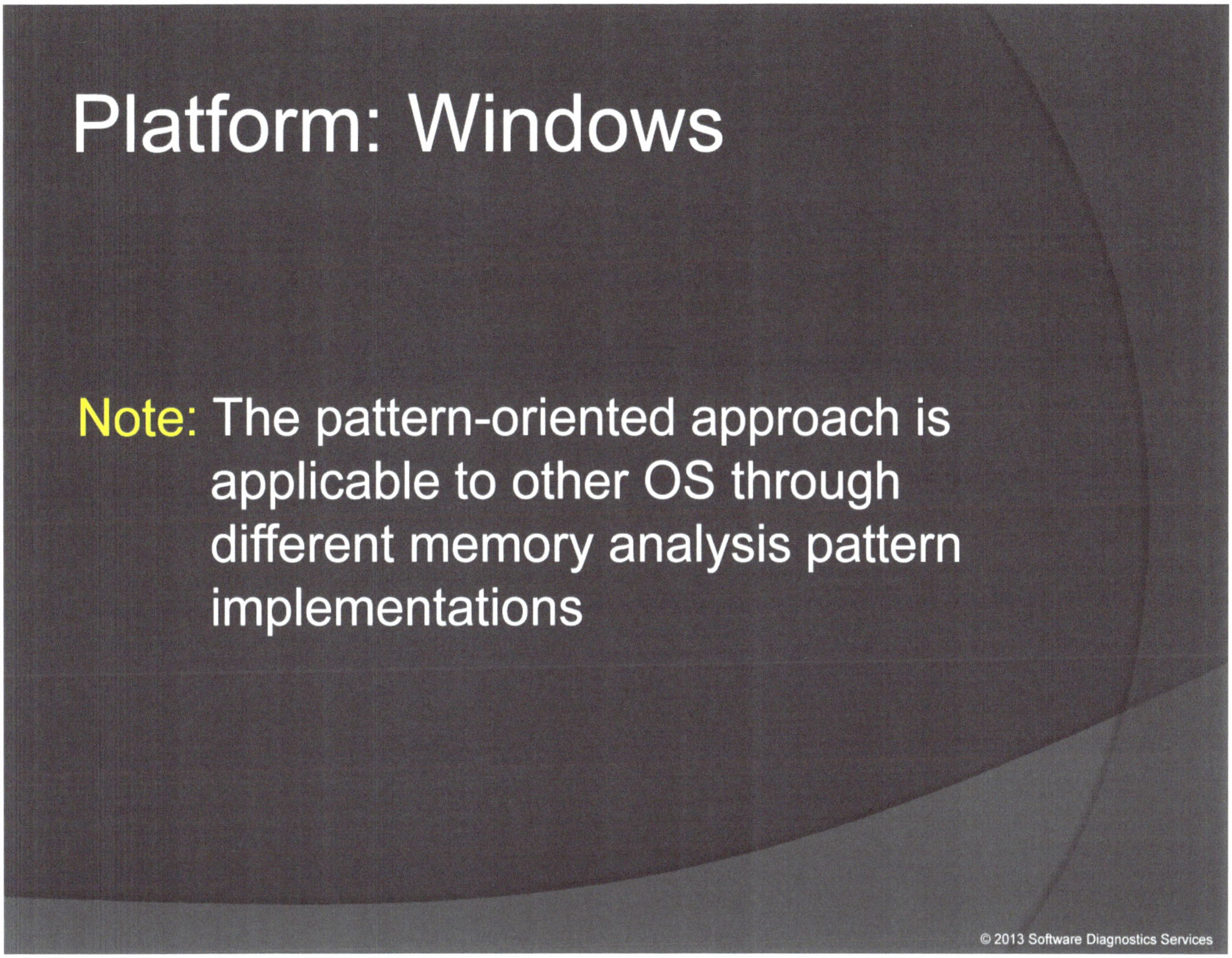

In this presentation we cover only Windows desktop and server platforms. But the pattern-oriented approach can be reused for other platforms.

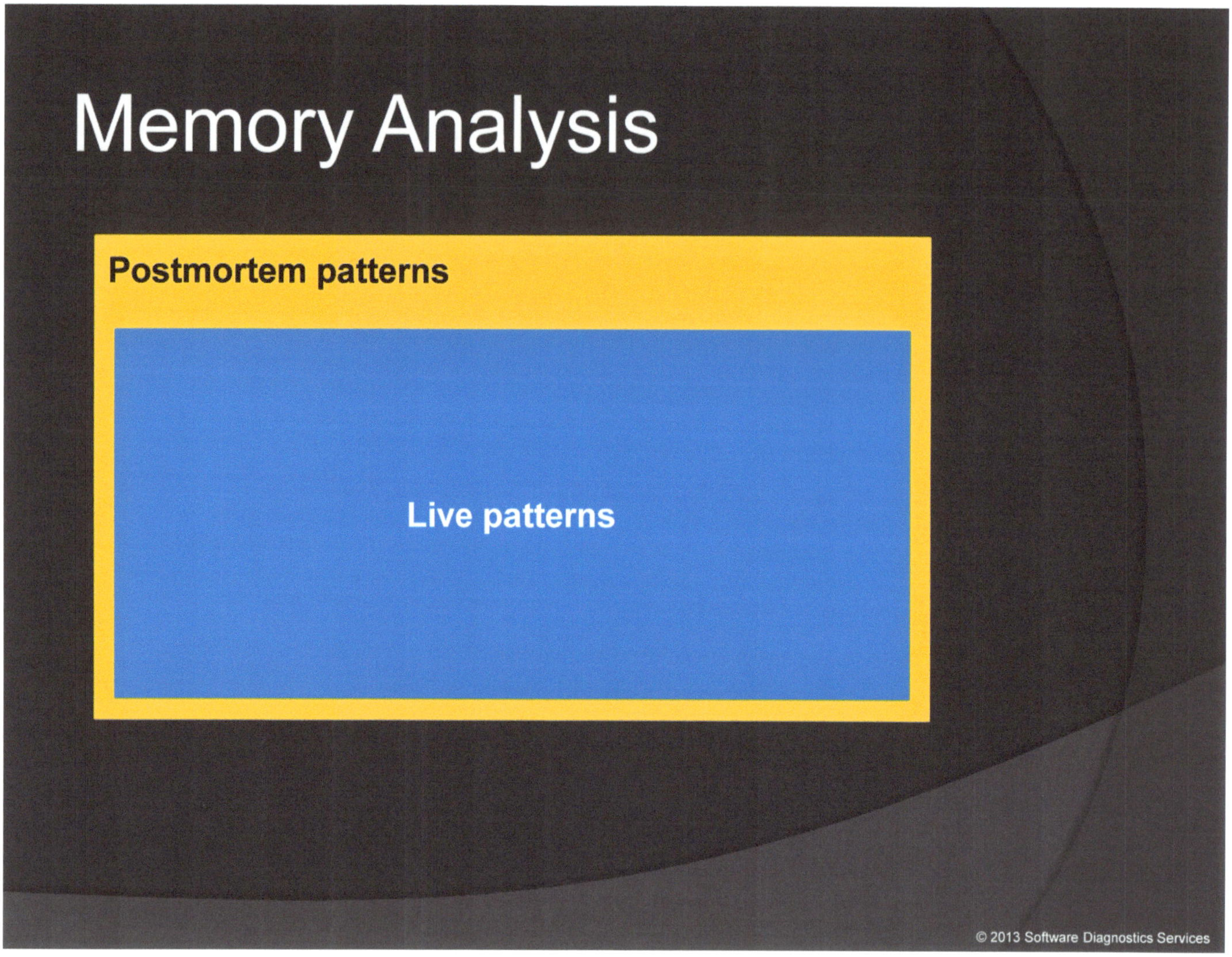

Physical memory analysis can be live, for example, during a debugging session or it can be postmortem via memory dumps. The same catalogue of memory analysis patterns is used. Fr example, a memory leak can be diagnosed on a live system by examining memory at different times and in the case of postmortem memory dump analysis we need a set of consecutive memory dumps saved after some interval. However, in the case of a live analysis some patterns may not be available such as related to memory dump specifics.

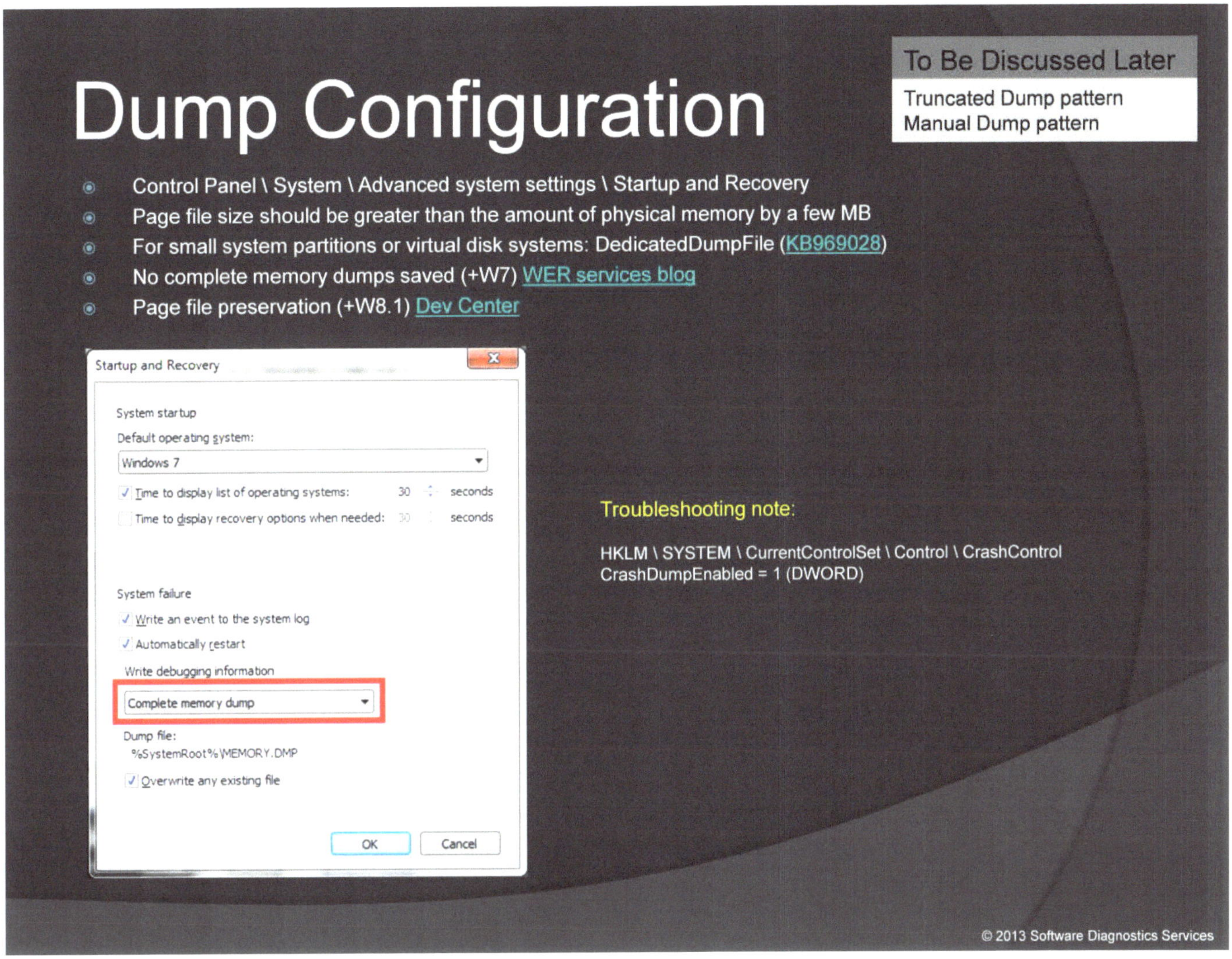

Why do we need complete memory dumps? Suppose we have an incident when a system doesn't respond to user, program or network requests (appears hang) or very sluggish for users (long delays). We can get a kernel memory dump to check for various patterns such as spikes in kernel mode, kernel pool leaks, insufficient physical memory (extensive paging), resource contention or deadlocks between executive resources (famous **!locks** command). However, we might not find all of that and would need to look at processes to find if there are any blocked GUI threads; wait chains between processes, deadlocks in user-mode synchronization mechanisms such as critical sections; process heap corruption, spikes in user mode, error message boxes. In summary, we would need to look at process spaces that are missing in kernel memory dumps. Other typical scenarios occur in terminal services environments like user session freeze or connection denied messages. Sometimes it is the only option available when we want to examine a live system offline.

KB969028:
http://support.microsoft.com/kb/969028/en-us

WER services blog:
http://blogs.msdn.com/b/wer/archive/2009/02/09/kernel-dump-storage-and-clean-up-behavior-in-windows-7.aspx

Dev Center:
http://msdn.microsoft.com/en-US/library/windows/hardware/dn265151(v=vs.85).aspx#!

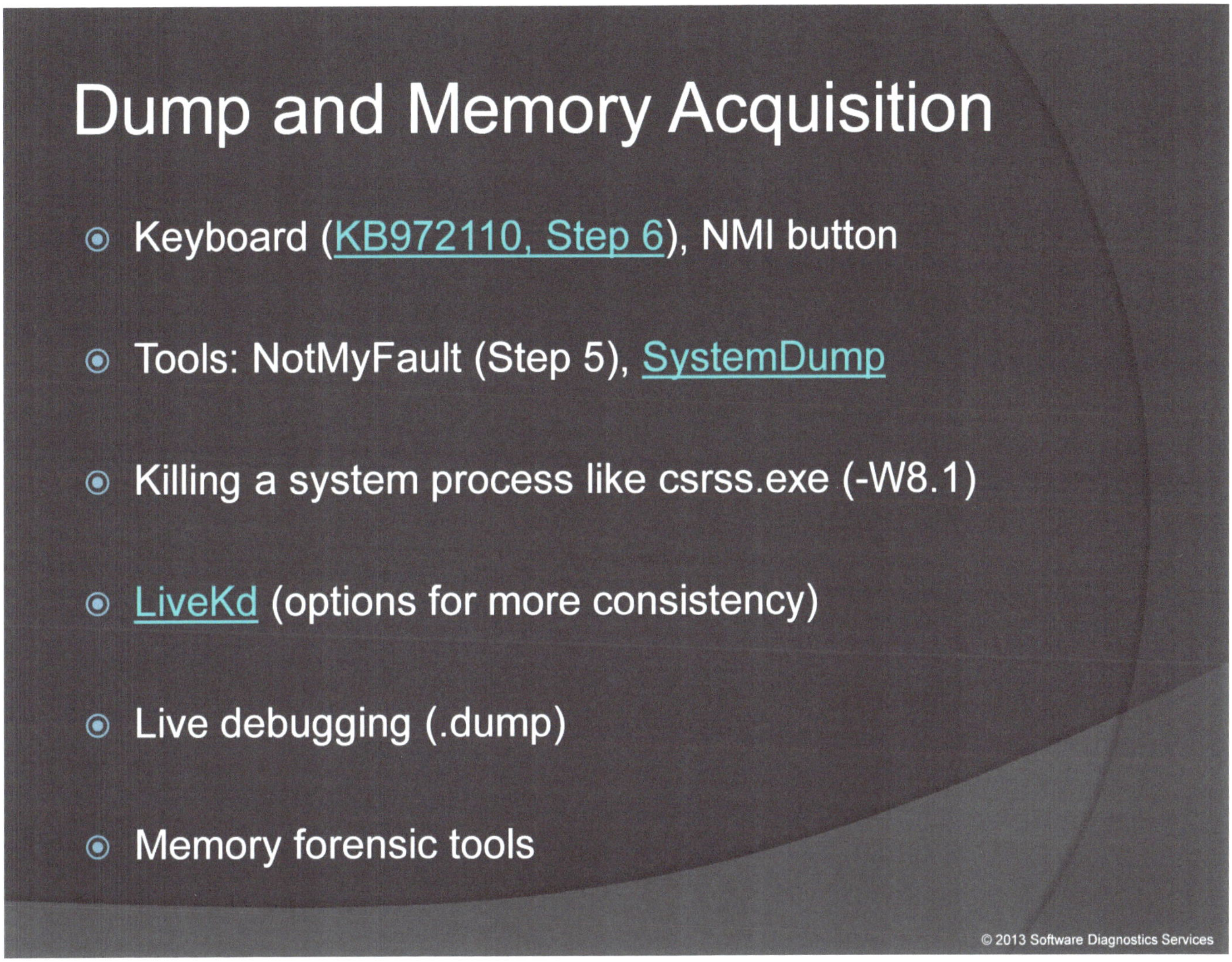

There are many methods to force a physical memory dump from a live system. Some methods freeze all CPUs except the one that is currently saving memory directly to a page file bypassing file systems. This ensures memory dump consistency. Live methods therefore may save a non-consistent memory dumps as parts to be saved may change pointers to the first parts already saved. However, the latest versions of Windows Sysinternals LiveKd tool provide options for more consistency. You can also find 3rd-party tools for memory acquisition.

KB972110:
http://support.microsoft.com/kb/972110/en-usa

SystemDump:
http://support.citrix.com/article/CTX111072

LiveKd:
http://technet.microsoft.com/en-us/sysinternals/bb897415.aspx

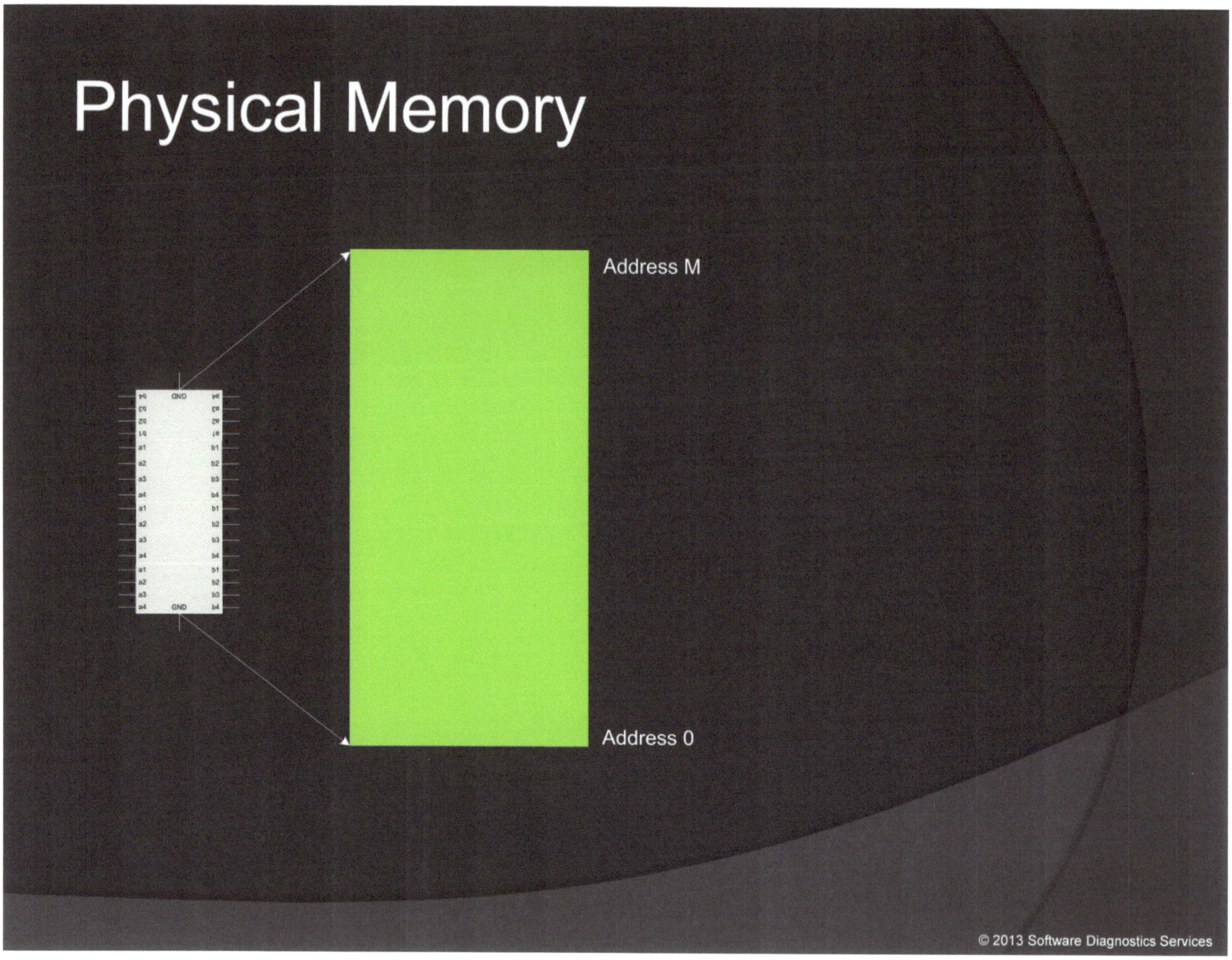

Before we look at a debugger's view of physical memory we recall a few definitions. Physical memory space is just a linear ordering of physical memory cells.

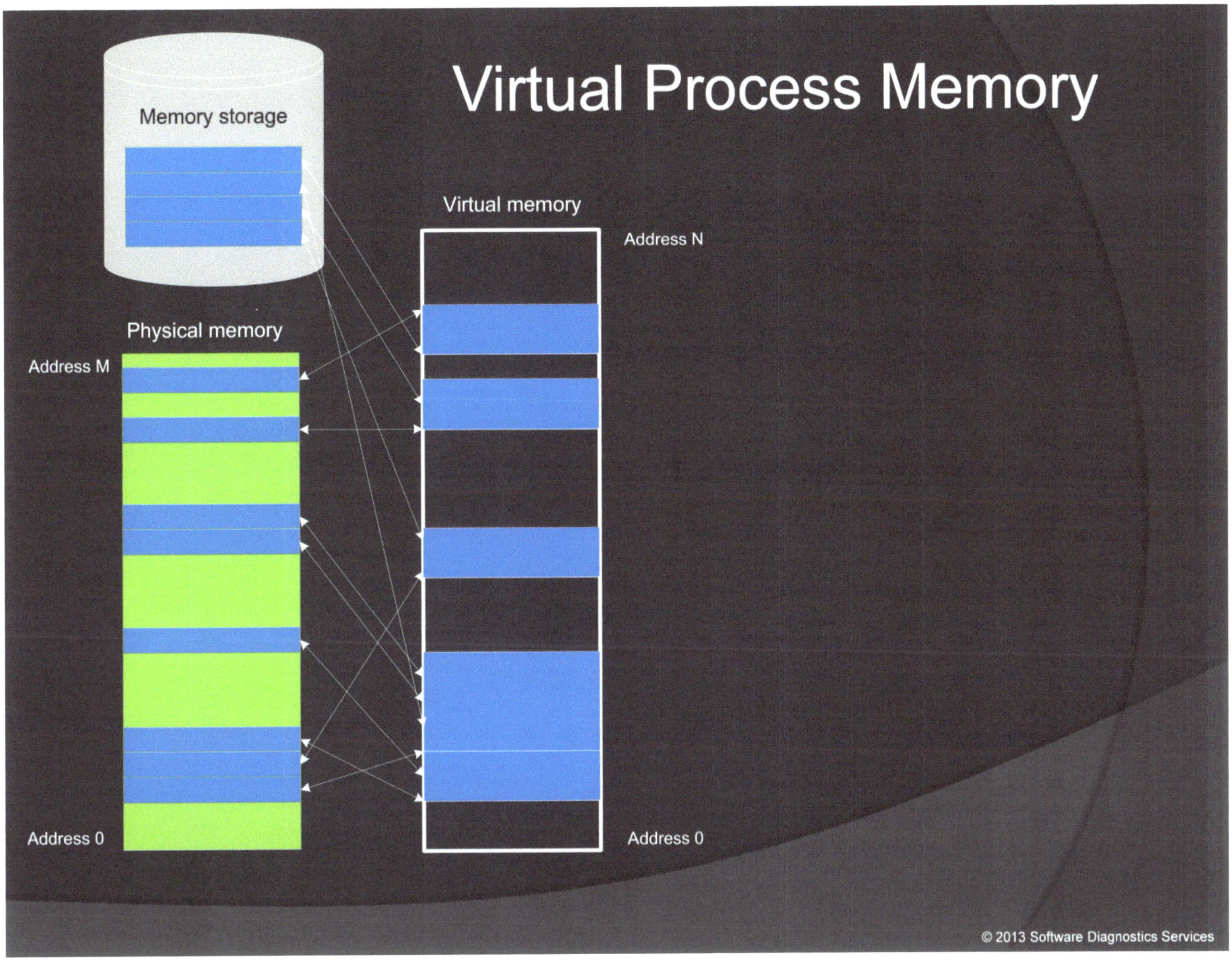

A virtual process memory is a how a process sees its memory during execution and how we see it in a debugger. Process pages can be randomly distributed in physical memory and even some can be located in a page file. However, when we break into a debugger on a live system or open a complete memory dump we see a linear ordering of memory cells that comprise a current process memory. The debugger takes care of this physical to virtual address space mapping.

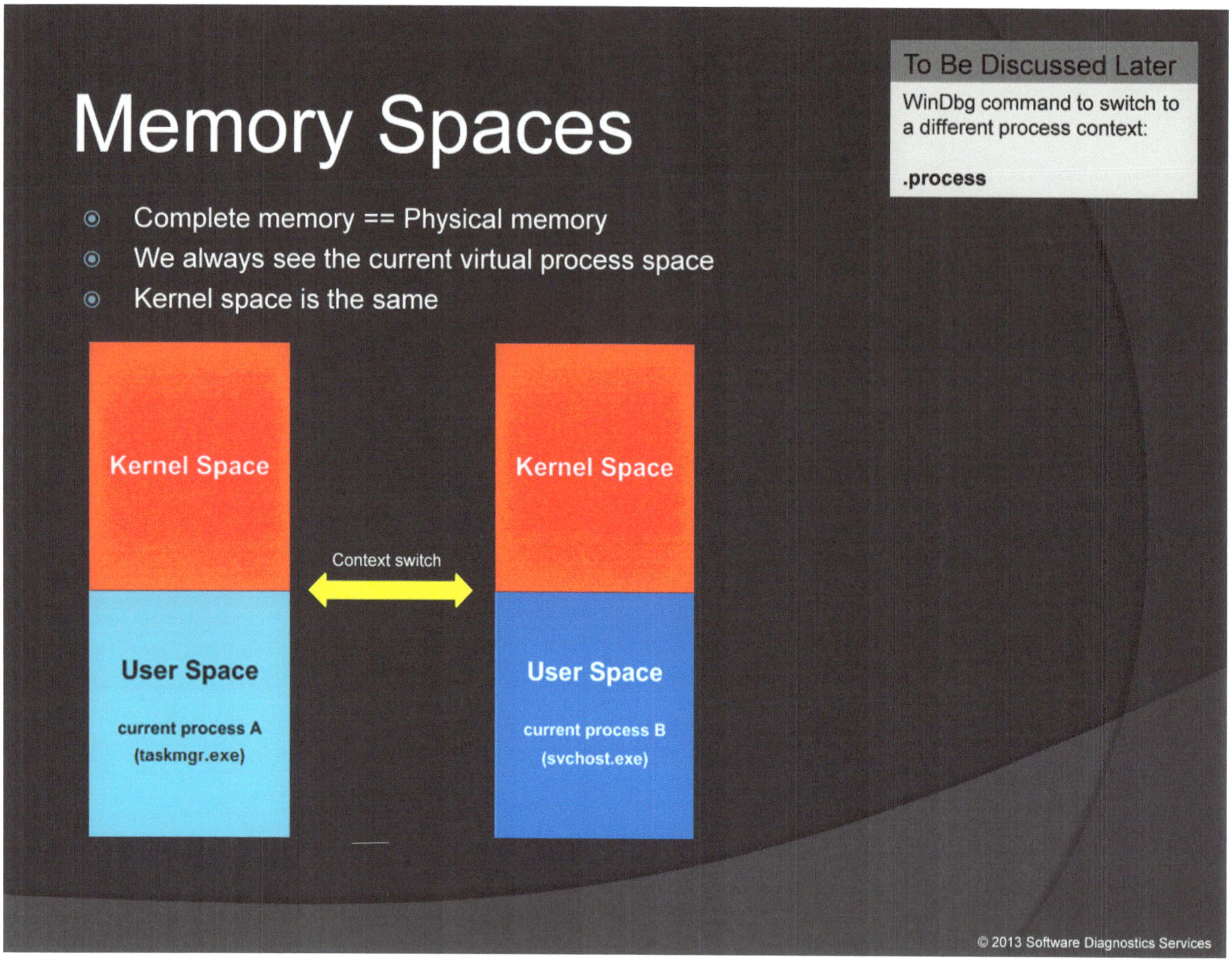

So, when we open a complete physical memory dump we see the virtual space of the current process (called the current process context). We need to be aware of the current process and when we switch to another process we need to make sure that the debugger switched to the appropriate physical to virtual space mapping and reloaded symbols for user space modules. Kernel space always stays the same.

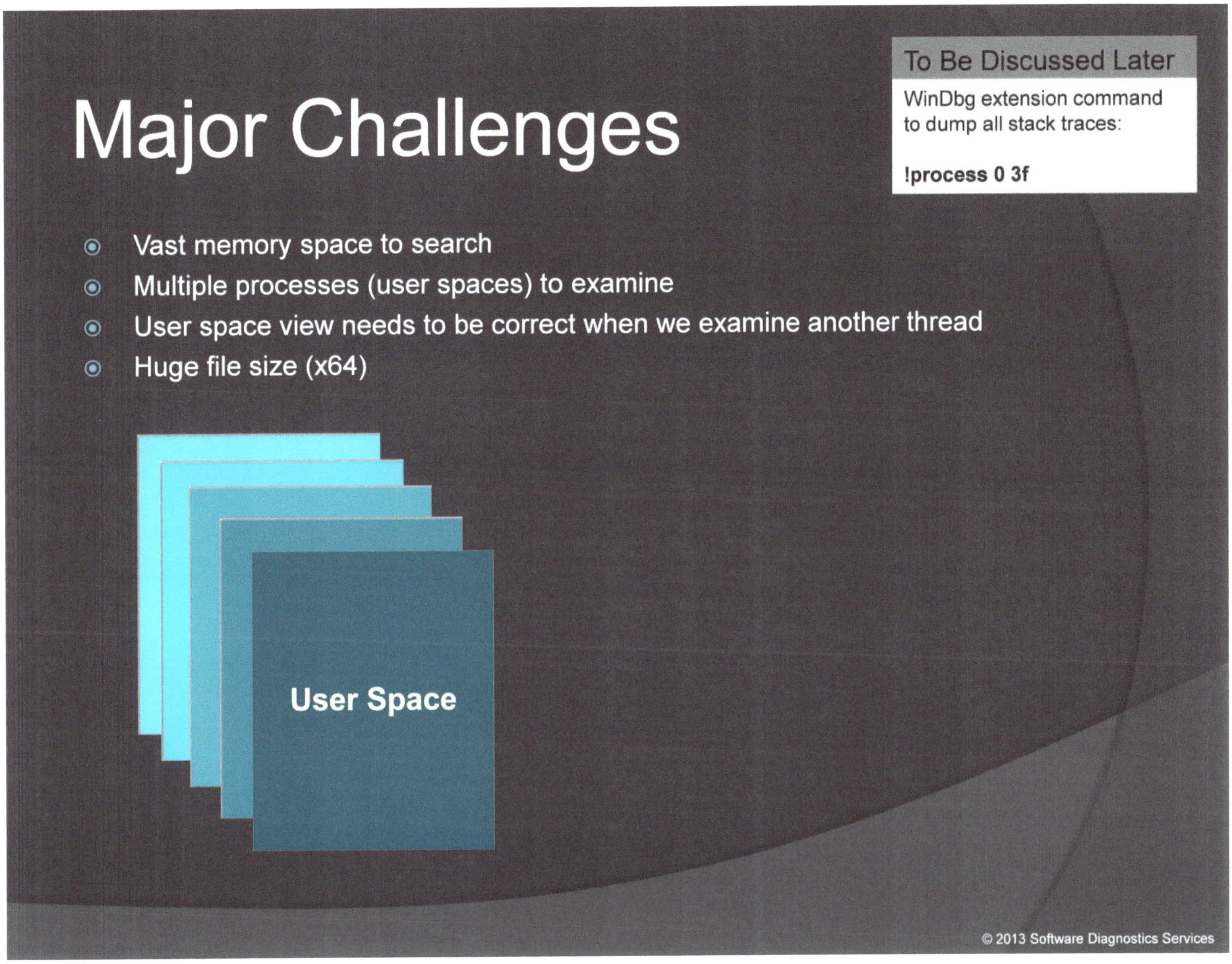

The simple approach for blue screen crash dumps to check their problem thread stack traces is no longer applicable here. Even checking a few processes of interest is not enough because we might miss something. All challenges are obvious except the 3rd one about examining threads. Because threads belong to processes when we examine them we need to make sure we also have correct process context: physical to virtual memory mapping and correct symbols for user space are loaded.

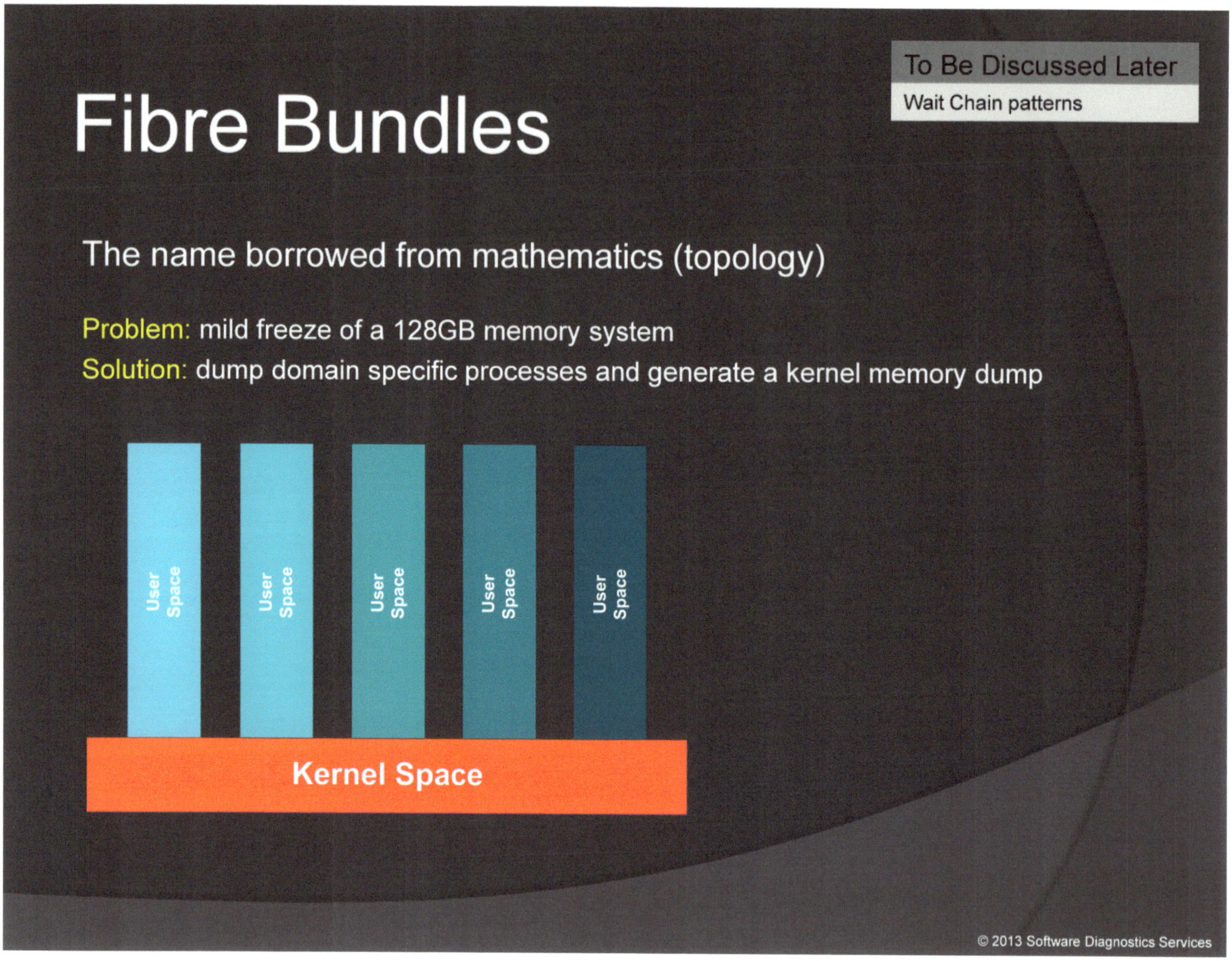

In case of huge physical memory there exists another alternative. Fiber bundle is a memory space that consists of kernel space and individual process virtual address spaces. Whereas a "complete" dump of physical memory might miss some pages residing in a page file a fiber bundle set of memory dumps is more complete because missing pages of process memory are brought from the page file when we dump individual processes. What we lose here is synchronicity that could make some memory references inconsistent because kernel and process memory dumps are generated at different times.

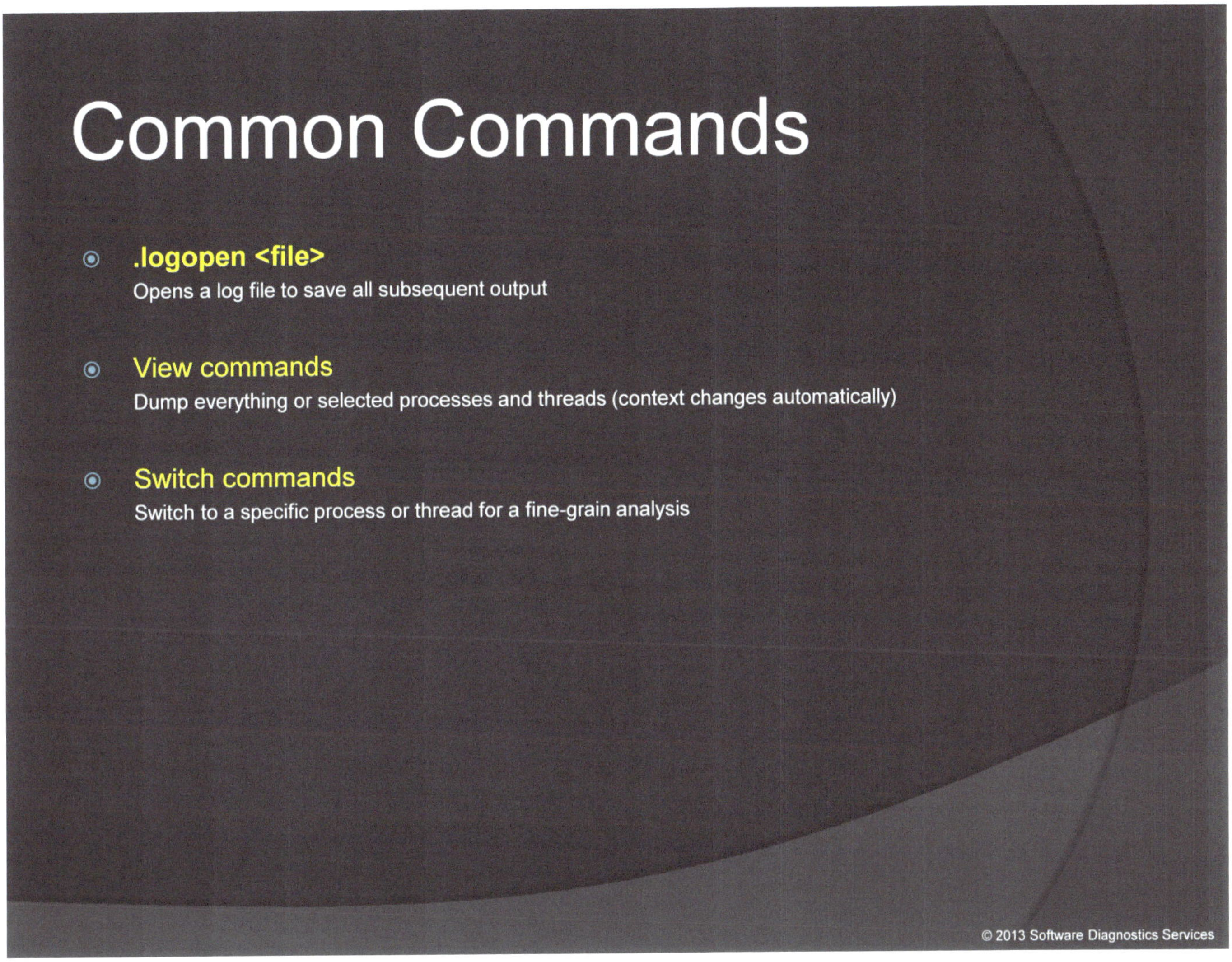

Because the output of commands is very lengthy most of the time it is useful to open a log file and later analyze its content as a text. To save time we can include many commands in a script. Such scripts are also useful for secure environments if you don't want to send a memory dump but prefer to extract textual information and send it to 3rd-party technical support.

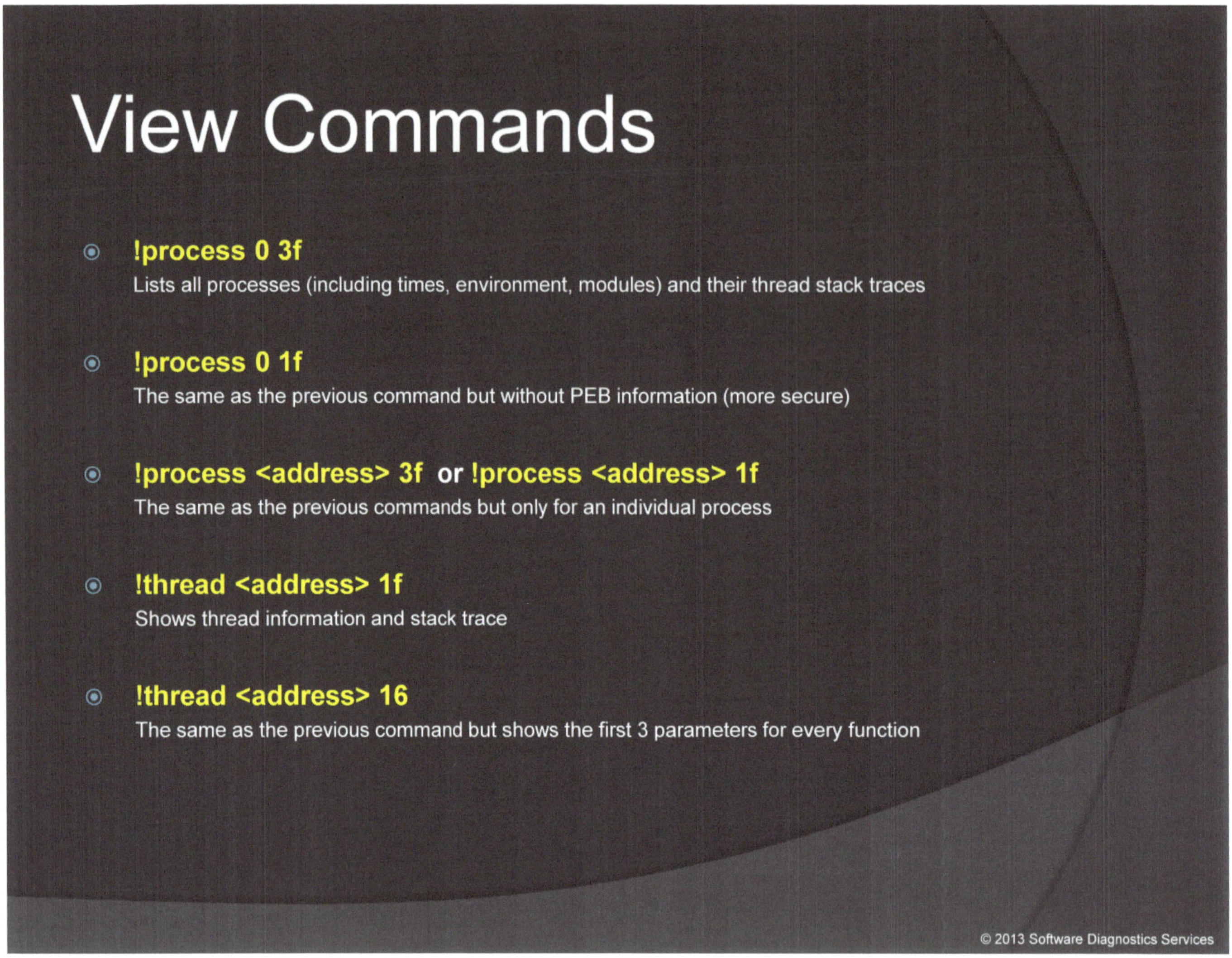

These are different commands to view an individual process and its threads and all processes and threads with automatic process context change and symbols reload.

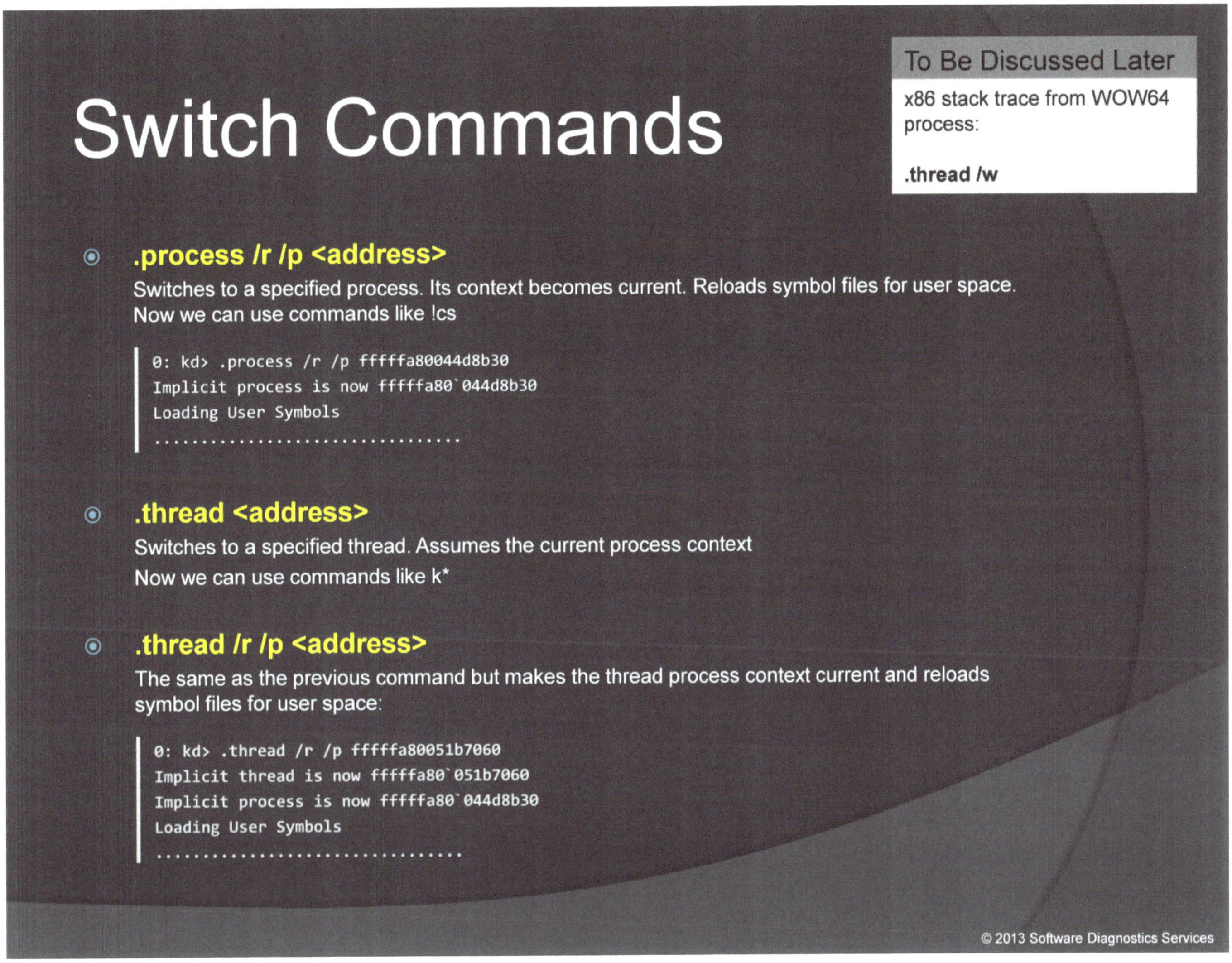

After we check the command output or the contents of a log file we might need to manually switch to a particular process context or a thread when we find something suspicious and want to investigate further.

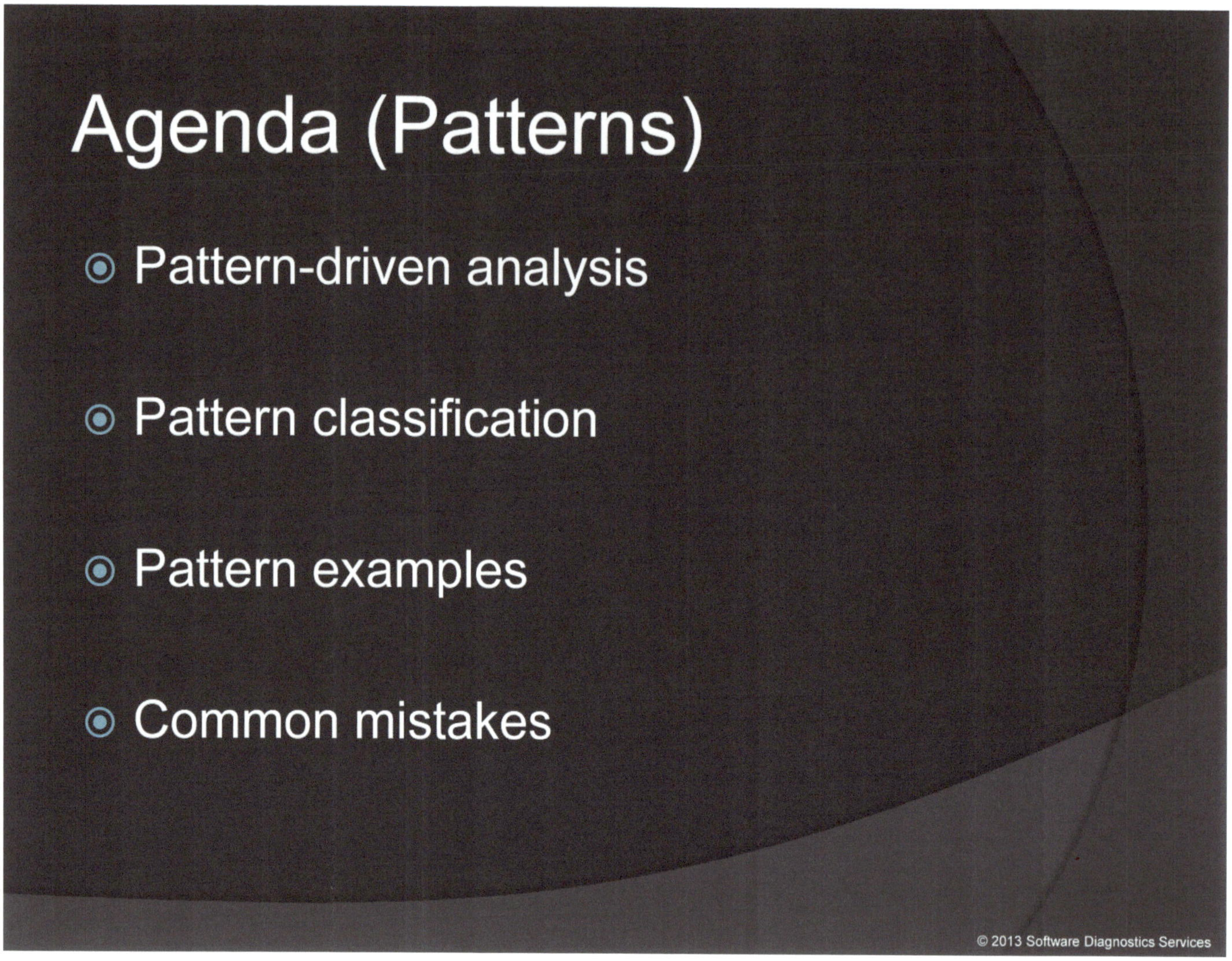

Now I briefly talk about patterns.

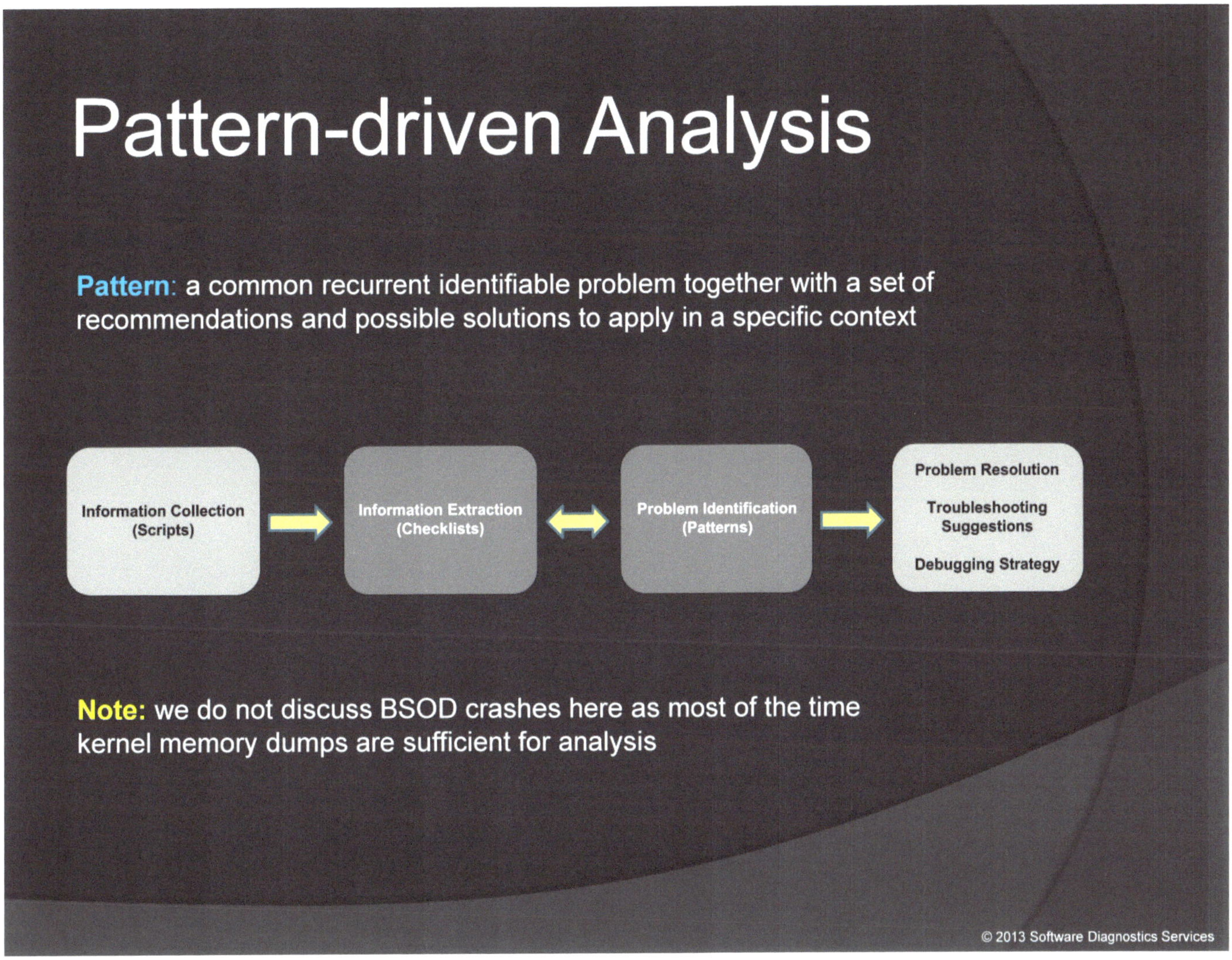

Typical pattern example: we identified process heap corruption and suggested program instrumentation to narrow down a set of suspicious modules by using either gflags.exe from Debugging Tools for Windows or Application Verifier.

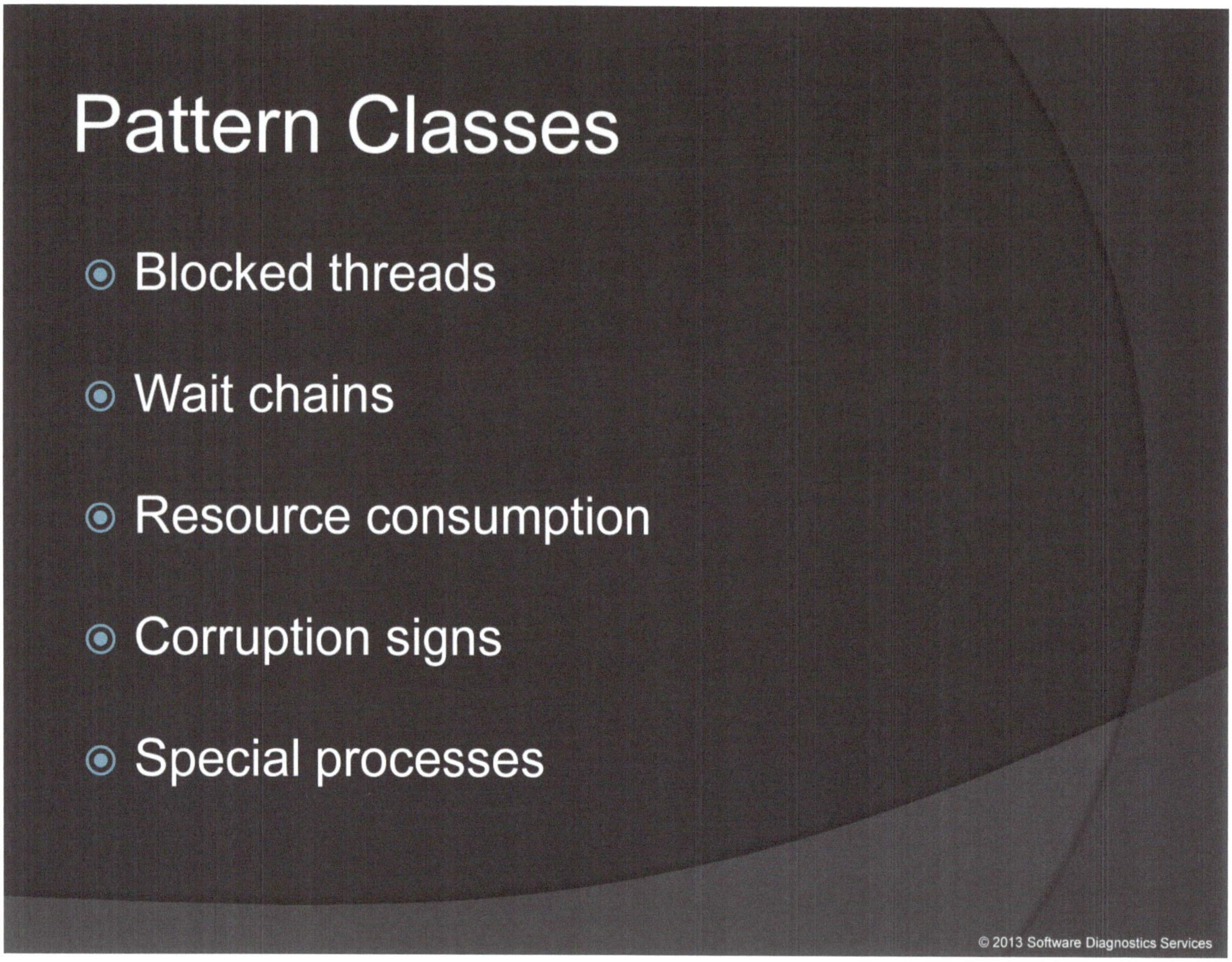

On this slide you see a few pattern classes. An example of a blocked thread could be a print spooler that attempted a print driver setup presenting a dialog box or some service loaded module showing an error message box. Wait chains can include threads waiting for critical sections, executive resources or involving interprocess communication mechanisms such as remote and local procedure calls (RPC/LPC/ALPC). Resource consumption can include kernel pool memory, CPU and handle usage. Corruption signs can include heap and pool corruption, freeing the same memory twice. Special processes can include Windows Error Reporting (WerFault.exe).

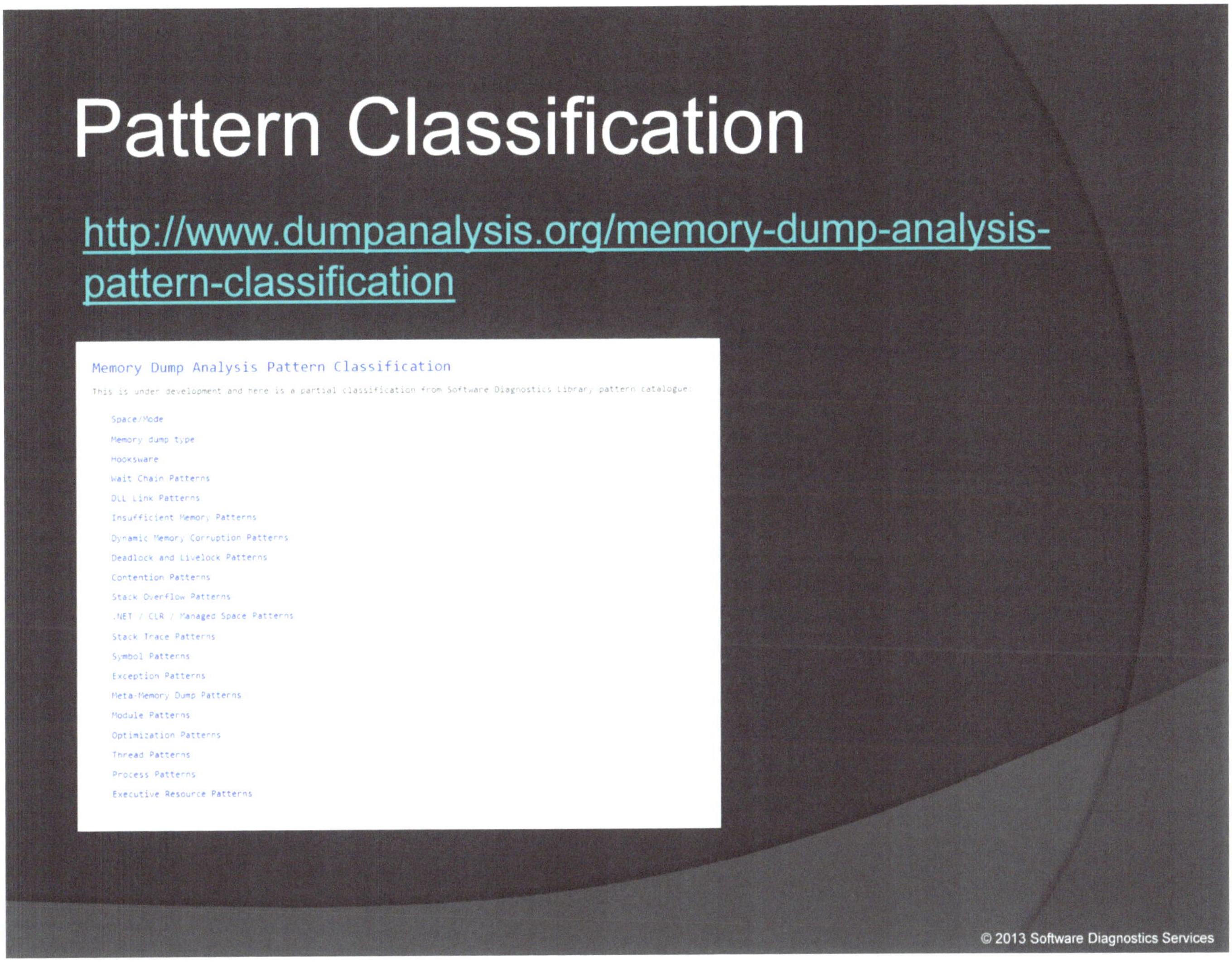

Users of Software Diagnostics Library can have access to advanced pattern classification and pattern catalogue.

http://www.dumpanalysis.org/memory-dump-analysis-pattern-classification

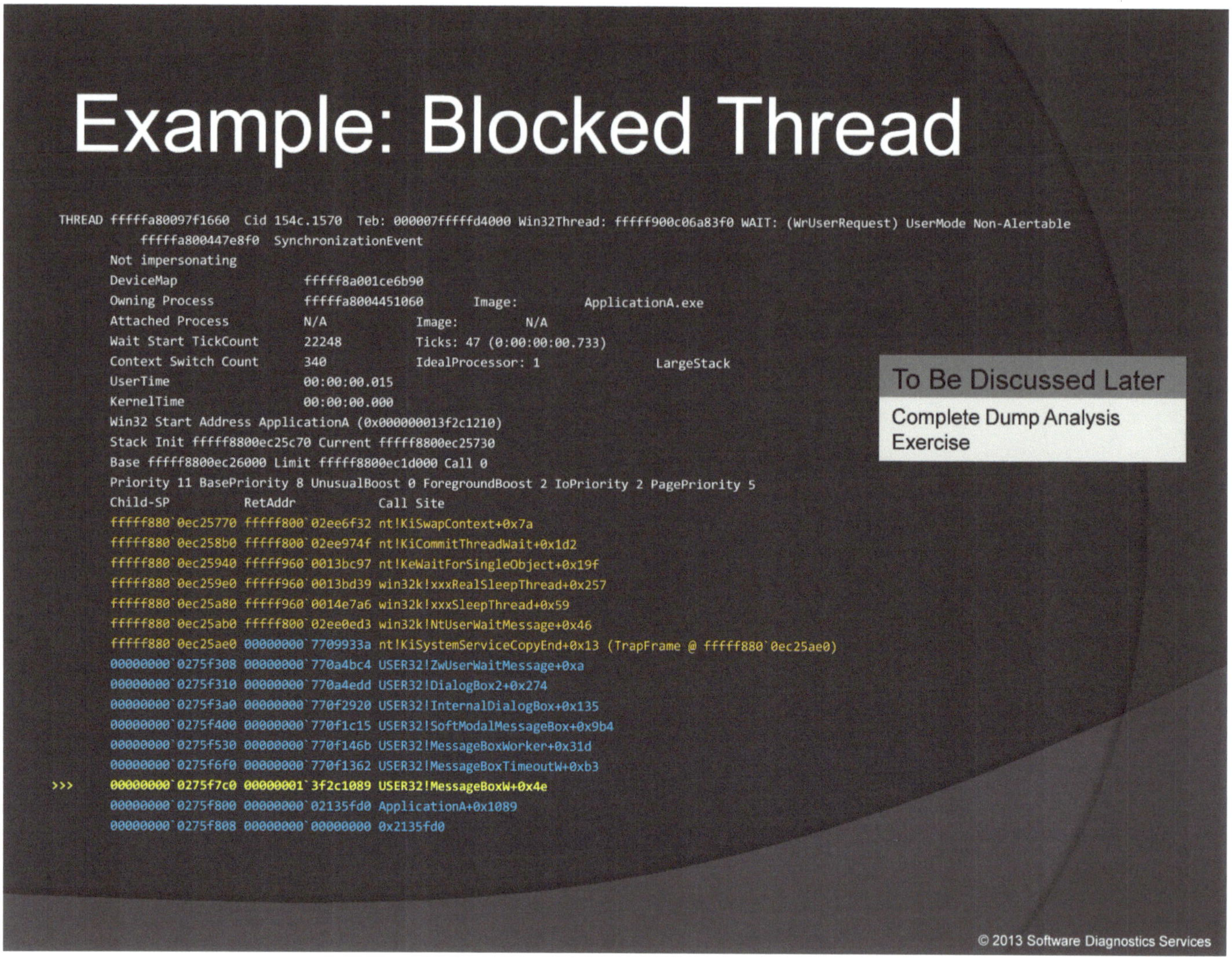

Now I show you a few fragments from the log file you can later download after you get this presentation slides.

Example: Wait Chain

To Be Discussed Later

Complete Dump Analysis Exercise

```
THREAD fffffa8004514060  Cid 07f4.1470  Teb: 000007fffffae000 Win32Thread: 0000000000000000 WAIT: (UserRequest) UserMode Non-Alertable
>>>         fffffa80044c53c0  Mutant - owning thread fffffa8004569750
        Not impersonating
        DeviceMap                 fffff8a001ce6b90
        Owning Process            fffffa8004546060       Image:         ApplicationC.exe
        Attached Process          N/A            Image:         N/A
        Wait Start TickCount      14474          Ticks: 7821 (0:00:02:02.008)
        Context Switch Count      2              IdealProcessor: 1
        UserTime                  00:00:00.000
        KernelTime                00:00:00.000
        Win32 Start Address ApplicationC (0x000000013f6c12a0)
        Stack Init fffff8800d196c70 Current fffff8800d1967c0
        Base fffff8800d197000 Limit fffff8800d191000 Call 0
        Priority 11 BasePriority 8 UnusualBoost 0 ForegroundBoost 2 IoPriority 2 PagePriority 5
        Child-SP          RetAddr           Call Site
        fffff880`0d196800 fffff800`02ee6f32 nt!KiSwapContext+0x7a
        fffff880`0d196940 fffff800`02ee974f nt!KiCommitThreadWait+0x1d2
        fffff880`0d1969d0 fffff800`031d844e nt!KeWaitForSingleObject+0x19f
        fffff880`0d196a70 fffff800`02ee0ed3 nt!NtWaitForSingleObject+0xde
        fffff880`0d196ae0 00000000`772f135a nt!KiSystemServiceCopyEnd+0x13 (TrapFrame @ fffff880`0d196ae0)
        00000000`0107f708 000007fe`fd9e10dc ntdll!NtWaitForSingleObject+0xa
        00000000`0107f710 00000001`3f6c112e KERNELBASE!WaitForSingleObjectEx+0x79
        00000000`0107f7b0 00000000`00586570 ApplicationC+0x112e
        00000000`0107f7b8 00000000`00000000 0x586570
```

Example: Consumption

To Be Discussed Later

Complete Dump Analysis Exercise

```
1: kd> !process 0 0
**** NT ACTIVE PROCESS DUMP ****
PROCESS fffffa80042d5400
    SessionId: none  Cid: 0004    Peb: 00000000  ParentCid: 0000
    DirBase: 00187000  ObjectTable: fffff8a0000017e0  HandleCount: 785.
    Image: System

PROCESS fffffa8006fa8750
    SessionId: none  Cid: 0144    Peb: 7fffffda000  ParentCid: 0004
    DirBase: 107226000  ObjectTable: fffff8a0002dcf90  HandleCount:  32.
    Image: smss.exe

PROCESS fffffa80083cdb30
    SessionId: 0  Cid: 01ec    Peb: 7fffffdc000  ParentCid: 01a8
    DirBase: 918c1000  ObjectTable: fffff8a0013b98a0  HandleCount: 679.
    Image: csrss.exe


[...]

PROCESS fffffa800442ab30
    SessionId: 1  Cid: 1418    Peb: 7fffffde000  ParentCid: 0840
>>> DirBase: 11e2c5000  ObjectTable: fffff8a004cc3b50  HandleCount: 20014.
    Image: ApplicationE.exe

[...]
```

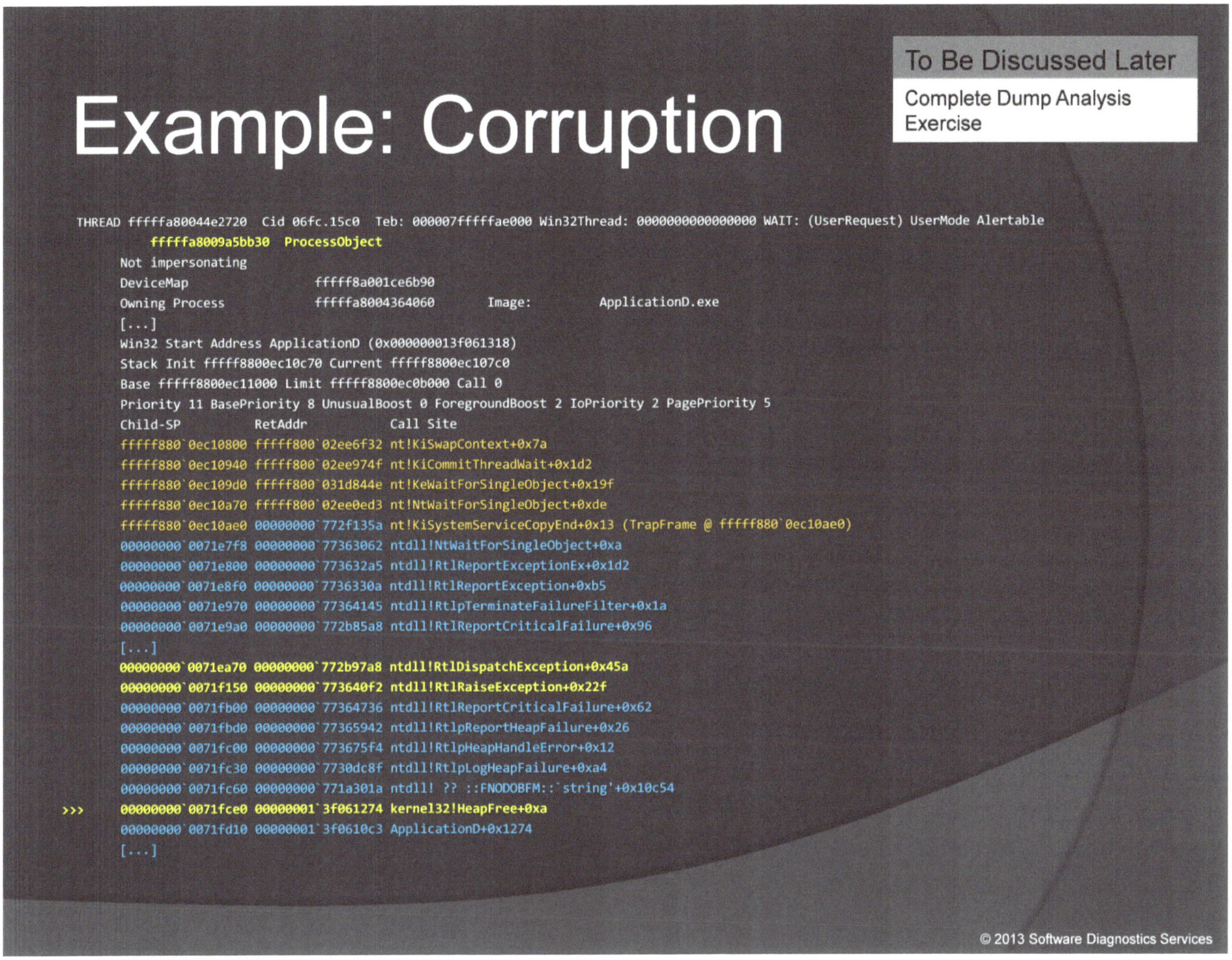
To Be Discussed Later
Complete Dump Analysis Exercise
Example: Corruption
THREAD fffffa80044e2720 Cid 06fc.15c0 Teb: 000007fffffae000 Win32Thread: 0000000000000000 WAIT: (UserRequest) UserMode Alertable
fffffa8009a5bb30 ProcessObject
Not impersonating
DeviceMap   fffff8a001ce6b90
Owning Process   fffffa8004364060   Image: ApplicationD.exe
[...]
Win32 Start Address ApplicationD (0x000000013f061318)
Stack Init fffff8800ec10c70 Current fffff8800ec107c0
Base fffff8800ec11000 Limit fffff8800ec0b000 Call 0
Priority 11 BasePriority 8 UnusualBoost 0 ForegroundBoost 2 IoPriority 2 PagePriority 5
Child-SP   RetAddr   Call Site
fffff880`0ec10800 fffff800`02ee6f32 nt!KiSwapContext+0x7a
fffff880`0ec10940 fffff800`02ee974f nt!KiCommitThreadWait+0x1d2
fffff880`0ec109d0 fffff800`031d844e nt!KeWaitForSingleObject+0x19f
fffff880`0ec10a70 fffff800`02ee0ed3 nt!NtWaitForSingleObject+0xde
fffff880`0ec10ae0 00000000`772f135a nt!KiSystemServiceCopyEnd+0x13 (TrapFrame @ fffff880`0ec10ae0)
00000000`0071e7f8 00000000`77363062 ntdll!NtWaitForSingleObject+0xa
00000000`0071e800 00000000`773632a5 ntdll!RtlReportExceptionEx+0x1d2
00000000`0071e8f0 00000000`7736330a ntdll!RtlReportException+0xb5
00000000`0071e970 00000000`77364145 ntdll!RtlpTerminateFailureFilter+0x1a
00000000`0071e9a0 00000000`772b85a8 ntdll!RtlReportCriticalFailure+0x96
[...]
00000000`0071ea70 00000000`772b97a8 ntdll!RtlDispatchException+0x45a
00000000`0071f150 00000000`773640f2 ntdll!RtlRaiseException+0x22f
00000000`0071fb00 00000000`77364736 ntdll!RtlReportCriticalFailure+0x62
00000000`0071fbd0 00000000`77365942 ntdll!RtlpReportHeapFailure+0x26
00000000`0071fc00 00000000`773675f4 ntdll!RtlpHeapHandleError+0x12
00000000`0071fc30 00000000`7730dc8f ntdll!RtlpLogHeapFailure+0xa4
00000000`0071fc60 00000000`771a301a ntdll! ?? ::FNODOBFM::`string'+0x10c54
>>> 00000000`0071fce0 00000001`3f061274 kernel32!HeapFree+0xa
00000000`0071fd10 00000001`3f0610c3 ApplicationD+0x1274
[...]
© 2013 Software Diagnostics Services

Example: Special Process

```
1: kd> !vm

[...]

         0458 svchost.exe        1922 (      7688 Kb)
         0bfc iexplore.exe       1891 (      7564 Kb)
         0bf4 msseces.exe        1863 (      7452 Kb)
         0fc8 NisSrv.exe         1845 (      7380 Kb)
         0584 StageRemoteSer     1776 (      7104 Kb)
         05dc spoolsv.exe        1729 (      6916 Kb)
         11e8 mscorsvw.exe       1620 (      6480 Kb)
         0c6c vmware-authd.e     1593 (      6372 Kb)
         02d8 services.exe       1560 (      6240 Kb)
>>>      1134 WerFault.exe       1558 (      6232 Kb)
         0c1c StageRemote.ex     1518 (      6072 Kb)
         135c taskmgr.exe        1513 (      6052 Kb)
         0ea4 WmiPrvSE.exe       1411 (      5644 Kb)
         0350 svchost.exe        1283 (      5132 Kb)
         02e0 lsass.exe          1218 (      4872 Kb)
         03b8 svchost.exe        1214 (      4856 Kb)
         09b0 SftService.exe     1171 (      4684 Kb)
         13fc daemonu.exe        1117 (      4468 Kb)
         0b5c igfxpers.exe       1080 (      4320 Kb)
         080c DTLite.exe         1051 (      4204 Kb)
         1194 DTShellHlp.exe     1008 (      4032 Kb)
         04c8 taskhost.exe        975 (      3900 Kb)
         0b34 STService.exe       933 (      3732 Kb)
         0270 csrss.exe           855 (      3420 Kb)
         029c winlogon.exe        845 (      3380 Kb)
[...]
```

To Be Discussed Later

Complete Dump Analysis Exercise

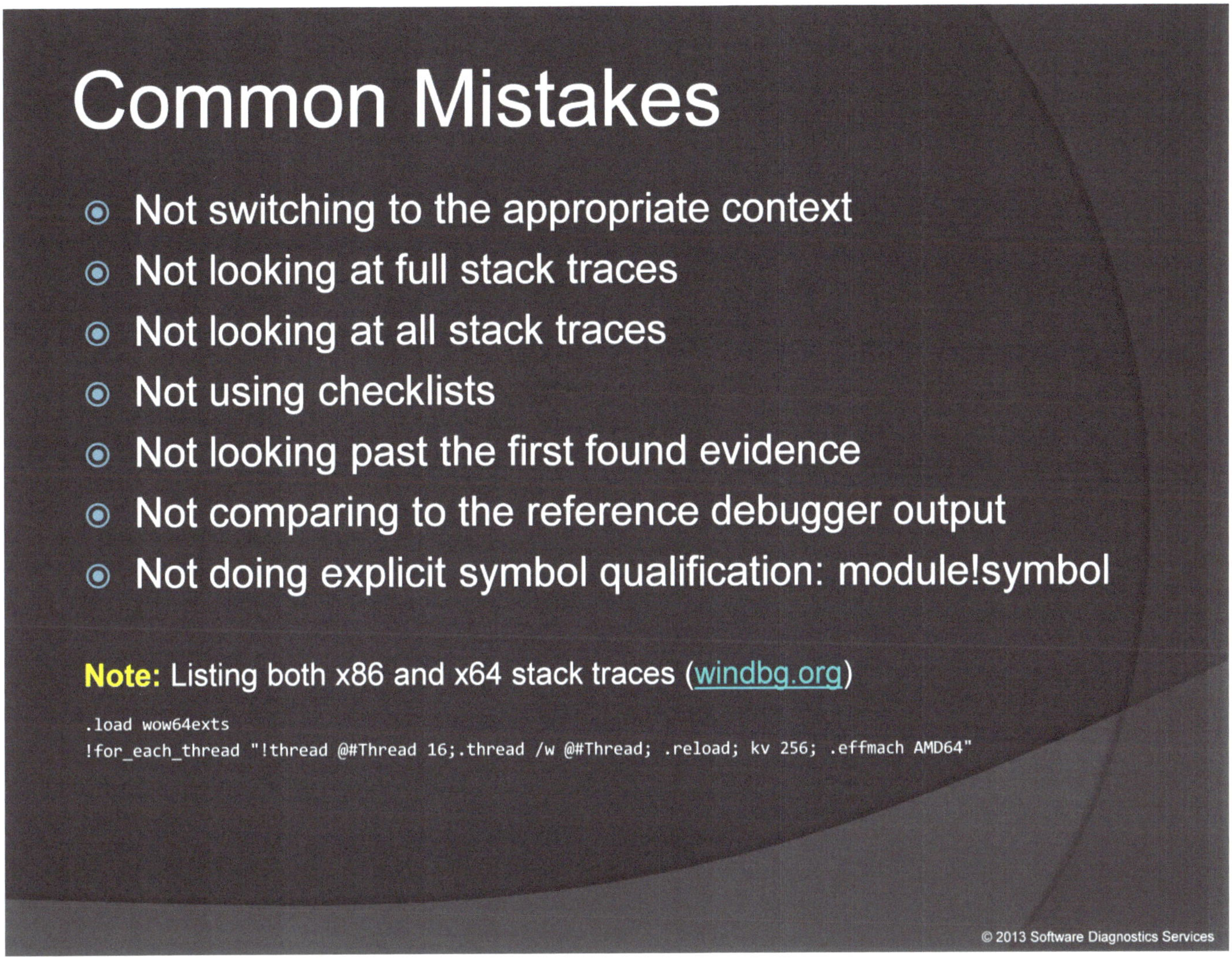

The first mistake is when we forget to apply switches or flags to WinDbg process and thread view and switch commands. The second mistake is when we forget that some commands show only partial stack traces based on the default number of stack frames to display. The third mistake is when we look only at a subset of processes. Other mistakes are obvious except the last one. Sometimes we need to explicitly qualify symbols when we have both 32-bit and 64-bit modules loaded at the same time such as **ntdll**. Also as we would see during exercise most of the time we would need to list both 32-bit and 64-bit stack traces. You can use a script that can also be found on windbg.org.

http://www.windbg.org/

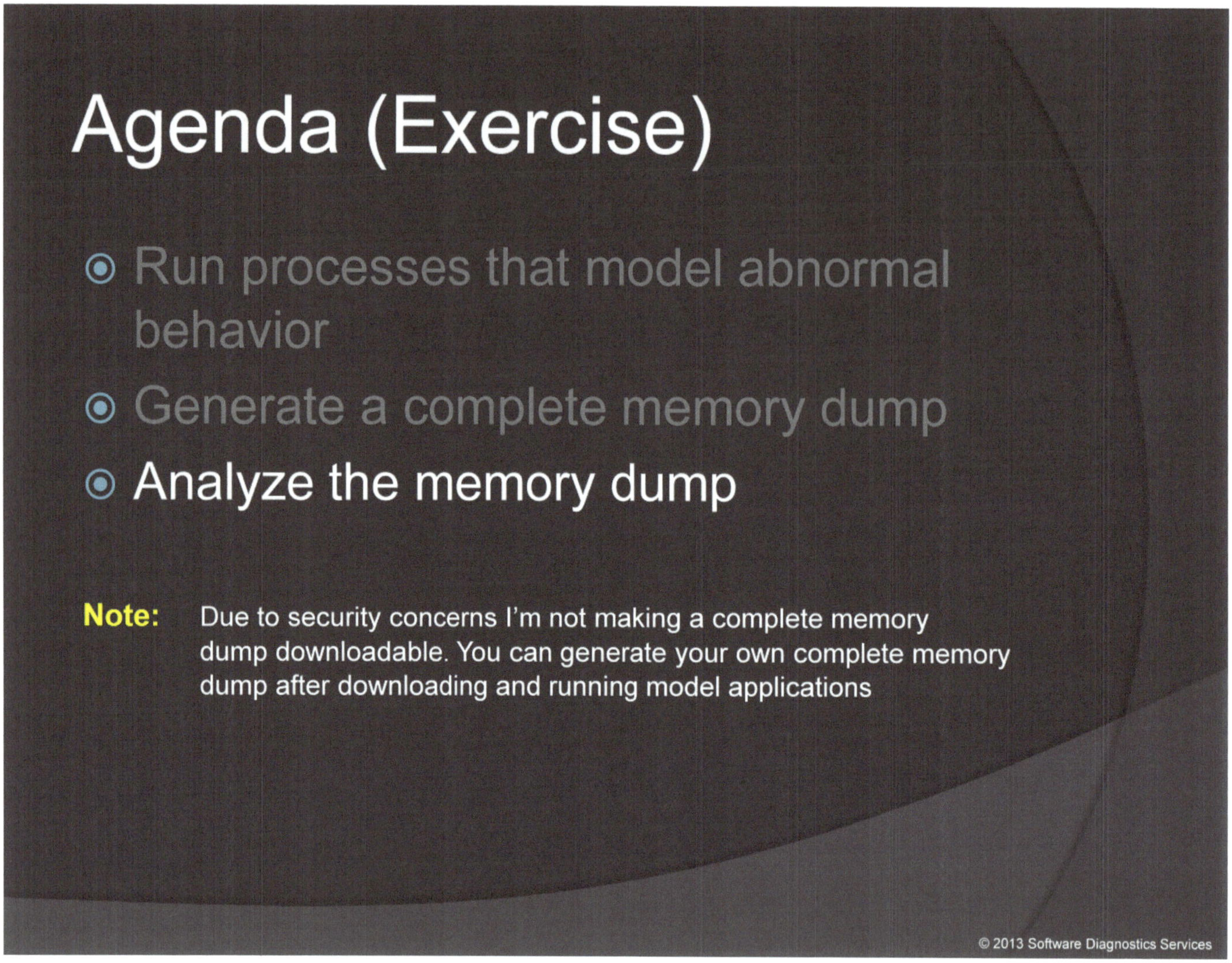

The approach I devised for this presentation is to run a few specifically constructed applications that model abnormal software behavior. The first 2 steps I did before the presentation and I also pre-analyzed a memory dump by running a few commands and saving the output in a log file I will make available for download after this presentation.

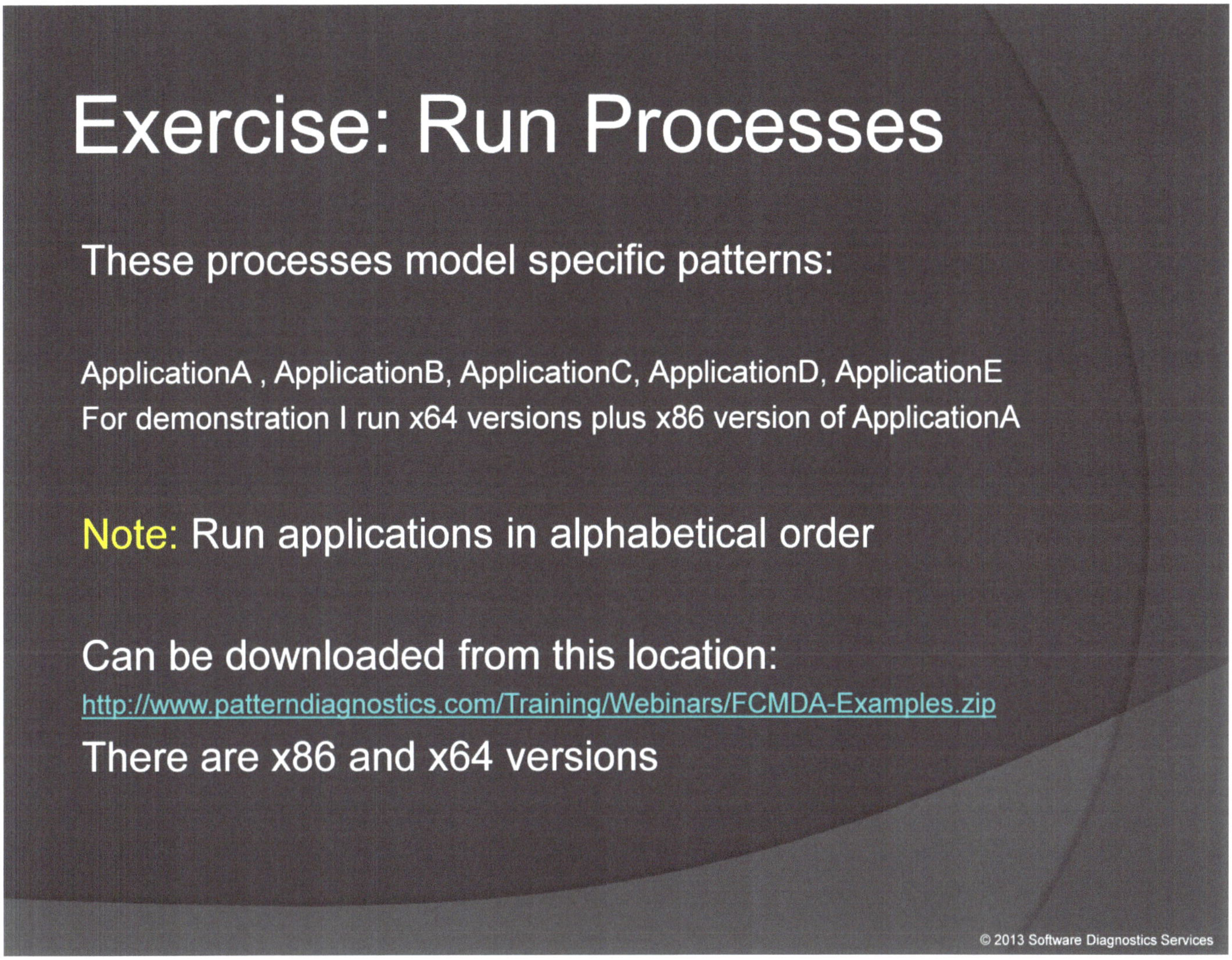

I chose generic application names to hide what these applications are doing and also make them visible to differentiate them from OS and other 3rd-party modules.

ApplicationA: Blocked Thread and Message Box
ApplicationB and **ApplicationC:** Wait Chain
ApplicationD: Dynamic Memory Corruption (Process Heap) and Special Process
ApplicationE: Insufficient Memory (Handle Leak) and Spiking Thread

http://www.patterndiagnostics.com/Training/Webinars/FCMDA-Examples.zip

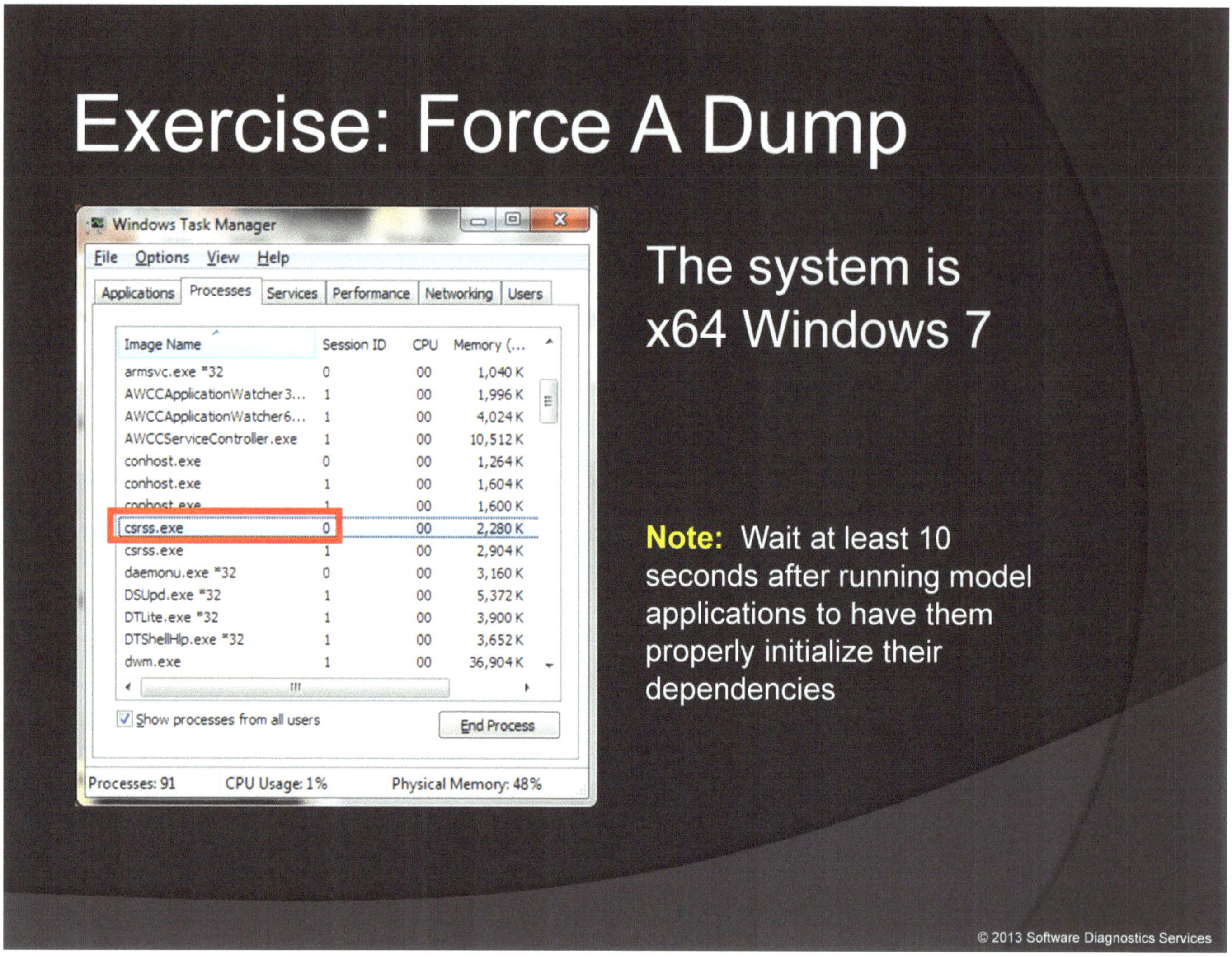

In the first version of this presentation I used NotMyFault tool. For the second version I decided to use a simpler approach by killing session 0 csrss.exe process. The previous demonstration used x64 Windows Server 2008 R2 and the second used x64 Windows 7. For this presentation I reuse the same dump file.

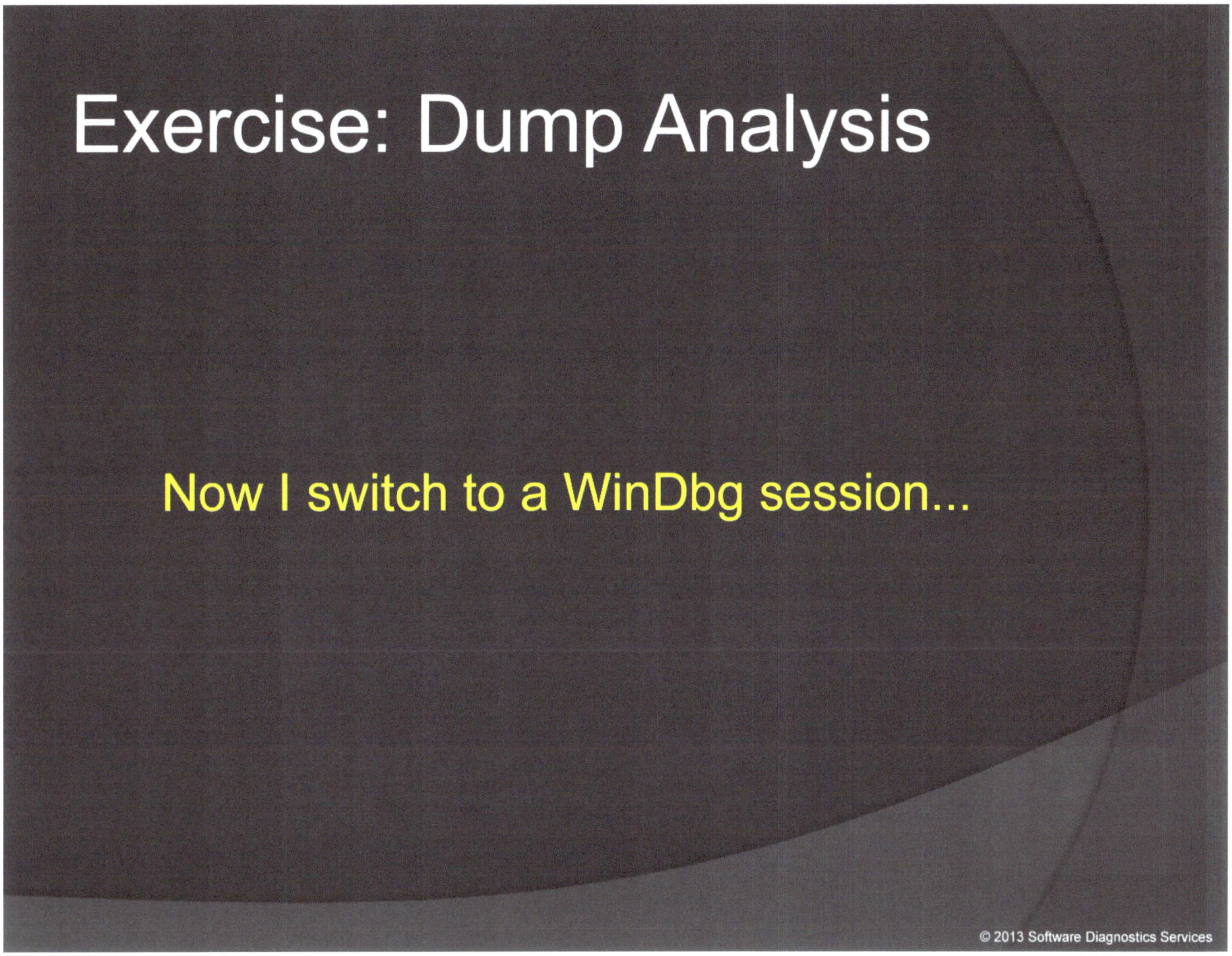

WinDbg log from a complete memory dump:
http://www.patterndiagnostics.com/files/fpma.txt

WinDbg log (scripting both 32-bit and 64-bit stack traces):
http://www.patterndiagnostics.com/files/fpma-full.txt

0. We open a dump and then apply symbols:

```
0: kd> .symfix c:\mss

0: kd> .reload
Loading Kernel Symbols
...............................................................
................................................................
............................................
Loading User Symbols
..................................................
Loading unloaded module list
....*** ERROR: Symbol file could not be found.  Defaulted to export symbols for ntdll.dll -


************* Symbol Loading Error Summary **************
Module name            Error
ntdll                  The PDB file is no longer available :
SRV*c:\mss*http://msdl.microsoft.com/download/symbols

You can troubleshoot most symbol related issues by turning on symbol loading diagnostics (!sym noisy) and
repeating the command that caused symbols to be loaded.
You should also verify that your symbol search path (.sympath) is correct.
```

1. Then we check the current process context:

```
0: kd> !process
PROCESS fffffa800434c060
    SessionId: 1  Cid: 135c    Peb: 7fffffdc000  ParentCid: 170c
    DirBase: 11100c000  ObjectTable: fffff8a000e65c70  HandleCount: 144.
    Image: taskmgr.exe
    VadRoot fffffa8004666570 Vads 174 Clone 0 Private 1303. Modified 0. Locked 0.
    DeviceMap fffff8a001bd3160
    Token                             fffff8a004769a50
    ElapsedTime                       00:00:17.209
    UserTime                          00:00:00.000
    KernelTime                        00:00:00.000
    QuotaPoolUsage[PagedPool]         173584
    QuotaPoolUsage[NonPagedPool]      20824
    Working Set Sizes (now,min,max)  (3407, 50, 345) (13628KB, 200KB, 1380KB)
    PeakWorkingSetSize                3407
    VirtualSize                       102 Mb
    PeakVirtualSize                   159 Mb
    PageFaultCount                    4420
    MemoryPriority                    BACKGROUND
    BasePriority                      13
    CommitCharge                      1513

        THREAD fffffa80045cfb60  Cid 135c.12ec  Teb: 000007fffffde000 Win32Thread: fffff900c25fc450 RUNNING on processor 0

        THREAD fffffa800455cb60  Cid 135c.0bcc  Teb: 000007fffffda000 Win32Thread: fffff900c2b90c20 WAIT: (WrUserRequest) UserMode Non-Alertable
            fffffa8009e47430  SynchronizationEvent

        THREAD fffffa80095d9790  Cid 135c.14ef8  Teb: 000007fffffd8000 Win32Thread: 0000000000000000 WAIT: (UserRequest) UserMode Alertable
            fffffa800455c9f0  SynchronizationTimer
            fffffa8004435a80  SynchronizationEvent
            fffffa8004360ce0  SynchronizationTimer
            fffffa8009e859f0  SynchronizationTimer

        THREAD fffffa8004404060  Cid 135c.14f18  Teb: 000007fffffd6000 Win32Thread: fffff900c1fb5010 WAIT: (WrQueue) UserMode Alertable
            fffffa800919cac0  QueueObject

        THREAD fffffa8009482b60  Cid 135c.14f28  Teb: 000007fffffd4000 Win32Thread: fffff900c2a30c20 WAIT: (UserRequest) UserMode Non-Alertable
            fffffa800948d3a0  SynchronizationEvent

        THREAD fffffa800454a060  Cid 135c.14f2c  Teb: 000007fffffae000 Win32Thread: fffff900c2b8a010 WAIT: (WrQueue) UserMode Alertable
            fffffa800919cac0  QueueObject

        THREAD fffffa8009d22b60  Cid 135c.14f54  Teb: 000007fffffac000 Win32Thread: fffff900c2ba3010 WAIT: (WrQueue) UserMode Alertable
            fffffa800919cac0  QueueObject

        THREAD fffffa80044c9b60  Cid 135c.14f50  Teb: 000007fffffaa000 Win32Thread: fffff900c205ec20 WAIT: (WrQueue) UserMode Alertable
            fffffa800919cac0  QueueObject

        THREAD fffffa80044a81b0  Cid 135c.0f3c  Teb: 000007fffffa8000 Win32Thread: 0000000000000000 WAIT: (WrQueue) UserMode Alertable
            fffffa800919cac0  QueueObject

        THREAD fffffa8004527b60  Cid 135c.14e88  Teb: 000007fffffa6000 Win32Thread: fffff900c2ba0010 WAIT: (WrQueue) UserMode Alertable
            fffffa800919cac0  QueueObject

        THREAD fffffa80044c9060  Cid 135c.14f48  Teb: 000007fffffa4000 Win32Thread: 0000000000000000 WAIT: (WrQueue) UserMode Alertable
            fffffa800919cac0  QueueObject

        THREAD fffffa800454ab60  Cid 135c.14f3c  Teb: 000007fffffa2000 Win32Thread: 0000000000000000 WAIT: (WrQueue) UserMode Alertable
            fffffa800919cac0  QueueObject

        THREAD fffffa8004526b60  Cid 135c.030c  Teb: 000007fffffa0000 Win32Thread: 0000000000000000 WAIT: (WrQueue) UserMode Alertable
            fffffa800919cac0  QueueObject

        THREAD fffffa80045fa660  Cid 135c.14f30  Teb: 000007fffff9e000 Win32Thread: 0000000000000000 WAIT: (WrQueue) UserMode Alertable
            fffffa800919cac0  QueueObject
```

```
THREAD fffffa800a959660  Cid 135c.1678  Teb: 000007fffff9c000 Win32Thread: 0000000000000000 WAIT: (WrQueue) UserMode Alertable
    fffffa800919cac0  QueueObject

THREAD fffffa80044deb60  Cid 135c.14f34  Teb: 000007fffff9a000 Win32Thread: 0000000000000000 WAIT: (WrQueue) UserMode Alertable
    fffffa800919cac0  QueueObject

THREAD fffffa8004404660  Cid 135c.14e64  Teb: 000007fffff98000 Win32Thread: 0000000000000000 WAIT: (WrQueue) UserMode Alertable
    fffffa800919cac0  QueueObject

THREAD fffffa80044de060  Cid 135c.14e60  Teb: 000007fffff96000 Win32Thread: 0000000000000000 WAIT: (WrQueue) UserMode Alertable
    fffffa800919cac0  QueueObject

THREAD fffffa80045cf660  Cid 135c.0aa4  Teb: 000007fffff94000 Win32Thread: 0000000000000000 WAIT: (WrQueue) UserMode Alertable
    fffffa800919cac0  QueueObject

THREAD fffffa800b074660  Cid 135c.14f38  Teb: 000007fffff92000 Win32Thread: 0000000000000000 WAIT: (WrQueue) UserMode Alertable
    fffffa800919cac0  QueueObject

THREAD fffffa800b05d060  Cid 135c.15d8  Teb: 000007fffff90000 Win32Thread: 0000000000000000 WAIT: (WrQueue) UserMode Alertable
    fffffa800919cac0  QueueObject

THREAD fffffa800b064060  Cid 135c.0740  Teb: 000007fffff8e000 Win32Thread: 0000000000000000 WAIT: (WrQueue) UserMode Alertable
    fffffa800919cac0  QueueObject

THREAD fffffa800b075060  Cid 135c.08b0  Teb: 000007fffff8c000 Win32Thread: 0000000000000000 WAIT: (WrQueue) UserMode Alertable
    fffffa800919cac0  QueueObject

THREAD fffffa800b07a060  Cid 135c.14f88  Teb: 000007fffff8a000 Win32Thread: 0000000000000000 WAIT: (WrQueue) UserMode Alertable
    fffffa800919cac0  QueueObject

THREAD fffffa800b07b720  Cid 135c.1658  Teb: 000007fffff88000 Win32Thread: 0000000000000000 WAIT: (WrQueue) UserMode Alertable
    fffffa800919cac0  QueueObject

THREAD fffffa800b068b60  Cid 135c.1128  Teb: 000007fffff86000 Win32Thread: 0000000000000000 WAIT: (WrQueue) UserMode Alertable
    fffffa800919cac0  QueueObject

THREAD fffffa800b07e720  Cid 135c.14f80  Teb: 000007fffff84000 Win32Thread: 0000000000000000 WAIT: (WrQueue) UserMode Alertable
    fffffa800919cac0  QueueObject

THREAD fffffa800b07d060  Cid 135c.14f84  Teb: 000007fffff82000 Win32Thread: 0000000000000000 WAIT: (WrQueue) UserMode Alertable
    fffffa800919cac0  QueueObject

THREAD fffffa800b080060  Cid 135c.14f78  Teb: 000007fffff80000 Win32Thread: 0000000000000000 WAIT: (WrQueue) UserMode Alertable
    fffffa800919cac0  QueueObject

THREAD fffffa800b082b60  Cid 135c.14f6c  Teb: 000007fffff7e000 Win32Thread: 0000000000000000 WAIT: (WrQueue) UserMode Alertable
    fffffa800919cac0  QueueObject

THREAD fffffa800b081760  Cid 135c.14f74  Teb: 000007fffff7c000 Win32Thread: 0000000000000000 WAIT: (WrQueue) UserMode Alertable
    fffffa800919cac0  QueueObject

THREAD fffffa800b079060  Cid 135c.14f68  Teb: 000007fffff7a000 Win32Thread: 0000000000000000 WAIT: (WrQueue) UserMode Alertable
    fffffa800919cac0  QueueObject

THREAD fffffa800b082060  Cid 135c.0e64  Teb: 000007fffff78000 Win32Thread: 0000000000000000 WAIT: (WrQueue) UserMode Alertable
    fffffa800919cac0  QueueObject

THREAD fffffa80045fa060  Cid 135c.0ef8  Teb: 000007fffff76000 Win32Thread: 0000000000000000 WAIT: (WrQueue) UserMode Alertable
    fffffa800919cac0  QueueObject

THREAD fffffa800b0b1b60  Cid 135c.171c  Teb: 000007fffff74000 Win32Thread: 0000000000000000 WAIT: (WrQueue) UserMode Alertable
    fffffa800919cac0  QueueObject

THREAD fffffa800b139720  Cid 135c.0e70  Teb: 000007fffff72000 Win32Thread: 0000000000000000 WAIT: (WrQueue) UserMode Alertable
    fffffa800919cac0  QueueObject
```

2. Then we list user space modules:

```
0: kd> lmu
start             end                 module name
00000000`0f000000 00000000`0f006000   detoured   (deferred)
00000000`77080000 00000000`7717a000   USER32     (deferred)
00000000`77180000 00000000`7729f000   kernel32   (deferred)
00000000`772a0000 00000000`77449000   ntdll      (export symbols)       ntdll.dll
00000000`ff900000 00000000`ff945000   taskmgr    (deferred)
000007fe`ea090000 000007fe`ea0a7000   UTILDLL    (deferred)
000007fe`ea0b0000 000007fe`ea0e4000   credui     (deferred)
000007fe`f6b00000 000007fe`f6b12000   BROWCLI    (deferred)
000007fe`f9ab0000 000007fe`f9af2000   nvdxgiwrapx   (deferred)
000007fe`f9b60000 000007fe`f9ba4000   nvd3d9wrapx   (deferred)
000007fe`fa940000 000007fe`fa954000   SAMCLI     (deferred)
000007fe`fa960000 000007fe`fa975000   wkscli     (deferred)
000007fe`fa9f0000 000007fe`fa9fc000   netutils   (deferred)
000007fe`faa00000 000007fe`faa16000   NETAPI32   (deferred)
000007fe`fb750000 000007fe`fb75b000   WINNSI     (deferred)
000007fe`fb760000 000007fe`fb787000   IPHLPAPI   (deferred)
000007fe`fb850000 000007fe`fb85b000   slc        (deferred)
000007fe`fba60000 000007fe`fbaa3000   DUser      (deferred)
000007fe`fbb10000 000007fe`fbb28000   dwmapi     (deferred)
000007fe`fc130000 000007fe`fc186000   UxTheme    (deferred)
000007fe`fc190000 000007fe`fc2bc000   PROPSYS    (deferred)
```

```
000007fe`fc310000 000007fe`fc504000   COMCTL32   (deferred)
000007fe`fc800000 000007fe`fc80c000   VERSION    (deferred)
000007fe`fc9b0000 000007fe`fc9bd000   pcwum      (deferred)
000007fe`fcd40000 000007fe`fcd70000   LOGONCLI   (deferred)
000007fe`fd160000 000007fe`fd1cd000   wevtapi    (deferred)
000007fe`fd1f0000 000007fe`fd213000   srvcli     (deferred)
000007fe`fd350000 000007fe`fd35b000   Secur32    (deferred)
000007fe`fd520000 000007fe`fd545000   SSPICLI    (deferred)
000007fe`fd5b0000 000007fe`fd5bf000   CRYPTBASE   (deferred)
000007fe`fd680000 000007fe`fd6bd000   WINSTA     (deferred)
000007fe`fd6c0000 000007fe`fd6fc000   nvinitx    (deferred)
000007fe`fd850000 000007fe`fd86a000   DEVOBJ     (deferred)
000007fe`fd9e0000 000007fe`fda4c000   KERNELBASE   (deferred)
000007fe`fda50000 000007fe`fda86000   CFGMGR32   (deferred)
000007fe`fdad0000 000007fe`fdb99000   USP10      (deferred)
000007fe`fddb0000 000007fe`fdfb3000   ole32      (deferred)
000007fe`fdfc0000 000007fe`fdfdf000   sechost    (deferred)
000007fe`fdfe0000 000007fe`fdfe8000   NSI        (deferred)
000007fe`fdff0000 000007fe`fe01e000   IMM32      (deferred)
000007fe`fe020000 000007fe`feda8000   SHELL32    (deferred)
000007fe`fedb0000 000007fe`feeb9000   MSCTF      (deferred)
000007fe`fef40000 000007fe`ff01b000   ADVAPI32   (deferred)
000007fe`ff020000 000007fe`ff14d000   RPCRT4     (deferred)
000007fe`ff150000 000007fe`ff1c1000   SHLWAPI    (deferred)
000007fe`ff1d0000 000007fe`ff237000   GDI32      (deferred)
000007fe`ff240000 000007fe`ff417000   SETUPAPI   (deferred)
000007fe`ff420000 000007fe`ff42e000   LPK        (deferred)
000007fe`ff430000 000007fe`ff507000   OLEAUT32   (deferred)
000007fe`ff510000 000007fe`ff5af000   msvcrt     (deferred)
```

3. And list kernel space modules:

```
0: kd> lmk
start             end                 module name
fffff800`00ba8000 fffff800`00bb2000   kdcom      (deferred)
fffff800`02e1c000 fffff800`02e65000   hal        (deferred)
fffff800`02e65000 fffff800`0344e000   nt         (pdb symbols)
c:\mss\ntkrnlmp.pdb\47F5C3BF9E0A493C9F63BB8F6413358B2\ntkrnlmp.pdb
fffff880`00c07000 fffff880`00c56000   mcupdate_GenuineIntel   (deferred)
fffff880`00c56000 fffff880`00c6a000   PSHED      (deferred)
fffff880`00c6a000 fffff880`00cc8000   CLFS       (deferred)
fffff880`00cc8000 fffff880`00d88000   CI         (deferred)
fffff880`00d88000 fffff880`00da2000   mountmgr   (deferred)
fffff880`00da2000 fffff880`00dee000   fltmgr     (deferred)
fffff880`00e00000 fffff880`00e15000   volmgr     (deferred)
fffff880`00e15000 fffff880`00e71000   volmgrx    (deferred)
fffff880`00e74000 fffff880`00f18000   Wdf01000   (deferred)
fffff880`00f18000 fffff880`00f27000   WDFLDR     (deferred)
fffff880`00f27000 fffff880`00f7e000   ACPI       (deferred)
fffff880`00f7e000 fffff880`00f87000   WMILIB     (deferred)
fffff880`00f87000 fffff880`00f91000   msisadrv   (deferred)
fffff880`00f91000 fffff880`00fc4000   pci        (deferred)
fffff880`00fc4000 fffff880`00fd1000   vdrvroot   (deferred)
fffff880`00fd1000 fffff880`00fe6000   partmgr    (deferred)
fffff880`00fe6000 fffff880`00fef000   compbatt   (deferred)
fffff880`00fef000 fffff880`00ffb000   BATTC      (deferred)
fffff880`0100b000 fffff880`0115f000   iaStor     (deferred)
fffff880`0115f000 fffff880`01168000   atapi      (deferred)
fffff880`01168000 fffff880`01192000   ataport    (deferred)
fffff880`01192000 fffff880`0119d000   msahci     (deferred)
fffff880`0119d000 fffff880`011ad000   PCIIDEX    (deferred)
fffff880`011ad000 fffff880`011b8000   amdxata    (deferred)
fffff880`011b8000 fffff880`011cc000   fileinfo   (deferred)
fffff880`01200000 fffff880`01214000   termdd     (deferred)
fffff880`01253000 fffff880`013f6000   Ntfs       (deferred)
fffff880`01400000 fffff880`01489000   afd        (deferred)
fffff880`01489000 fffff880`014af000   pacer      (deferred)
fffff880`014af000 fffff880`014c5000   vwififlt   (deferred)
fffff880`014d6000 fffff880`01534000   msrpc      (deferred)
fffff880`01534000 fffff880`0154f000   ksecdd     (deferred)
fffff880`0154f000 fffff880`015c1000   cng        (deferred)
fffff880`015c1000 fffff880`015d2000   pcw        (deferred)
fffff880`015d2000 fffff880`015dc000   Fs_Rec     (deferred)
fffff880`015dc000 fffff880`015f7000   wanarp     (deferred)
fffff880`01600000 fffff880`01622000   tdx        (deferred)
fffff880`01622000 fffff880`01667000   netbt      (deferred)
```

```
fffff880`01667000 fffff880`01676000   netbios    (deferred)
fffff880`01679000 fffff880`0176c000   ndis       (deferred)
fffff880`0176c000 fffff880`017cc000   NETIO      (deferred)
fffff880`017cc000 fffff880`017f7000   ksecpkg    (deferred)
fffff880`01800000 fffff880`0183a000   fvevol     (deferred)
fffff880`0183a000 fffff880`01844000   EMSC       (deferred)
fffff880`01844000 fffff880`0185a000   disk       (deferred)
fffff880`0185a000 fffff880`0188a000   CLASSPNP   (deferred)
fffff880`01898000 fffff880`018a1000   rdpencdd   (deferred)
fffff880`018a1000 fffff880`018aa000   rdprefmp   (deferred)
fffff880`018aa000 fffff880`018b5000   Msfs       (deferred)
fffff880`018b5000 fffff880`018c6000   Npfs       (deferred)
fffff880`018c6000 fffff880`018d3000   TDI        (deferred)
fffff880`018d3000 fffff880`018de000   ws2ifsl    (deferred)
fffff880`018e3000 fffff880`01ae7000   tcpip      (deferred)
fffff880`01ae7000 fffff880`01b31000   fwpkclnt   (deferred)
fffff880`01b31000 fffff880`01b7d000   volsnap    (deferred)
fffff880`01b7d000 fffff880`01b86000   stdcfltn   (deferred)
fffff880`01b86000 fffff880`01b8e000   spldr      (deferred)
fffff880`01b8e000 fffff880`01bc8000   rdyboost   (deferred)
fffff880`01bc8000 fffff880`01bccb00   nvpciflt   (deferred)
fffff880`01bcd000 fffff880`01bdf000   mup        (deferred)
fffff880`01bdf000 fffff880`01be9000   johci      (deferred)
fffff880`01be9000 fffff880`01bf2000   hwpolicy   (deferred)
fffff880`01bf2000 fffff880`01bfb000   wfplwf     (deferred)
fffff880`02e00000 fffff880`02e09000   Null       (deferred)
fffff880`02e09000 fffff880`02e10000   Beep       (deferred)
fffff880`02e10000 fffff880`02e1e000   vga        (deferred)
fffff880`02e1e000 fffff880`02e2e000   watchdog   (deferred)
fffff880`02e2e000 fffff880`02e37000   RDPCDD     (deferred)
fffff880`02e37000 fffff880`02f8b000   dump_iaStor   (deferred)
fffff880`02fa1000 fffff880`02fc6000   VIDEOPRT   (deferred)
fffff880`02fcb000 fffff880`02ffc000   MpFilter   (deferred)
fffff880`03c00000 fffff880`03c09000   wmiacpi    (deferred)
fffff880`03c09000 fffff880`03c19000   CompositeBus   (deferred)
fffff880`03c19000 fffff880`03c2f000   AgileVpn   (deferred)
fffff880`03c2f000 fffff880`03c53000   rasl2tp    (deferred)
fffff880`03c53000 fffff880`03c5f000   ndistapi   (deferred)
fffff880`03c5f000 fffff880`03c60480   swenum     (deferred)
fffff880`03c68000 fffff880`03dc6000   SynTP      (deferred)
fffff880`03dc6000 fffff880`03dd5000   mouclass   (deferred)
fffff880`03dd5000 fffff880`03de5000   Accelern   (deferred)
fffff880`03de5000 fffff880`03dfb000   intelppm   (deferred)
fffff880`04035000 fffff880`04086000   rdbss      (deferred)
fffff880`04086000 fffff880`04092000   nsiproxy   (deferred)
fffff880`04092000 fffff880`0409d000   mssmbios   (deferred)
fffff880`0409d000 fffff880`040ac000   discache   (deferred)
fffff880`040ac000 fffff880`040ca000   dfsc       (deferred)
fffff880`040ca000 fffff880`040db000   blbdrive   (deferred)
fffff880`040db000 fffff880`04101000   tunnel     (deferred)
fffff880`04101000 fffff880`04122000   raspptp    (deferred)
fffff880`04122000 fffff880`0413c000   rassstp    (deferred)
fffff880`0413c000 fffff880`0417f000   ks         (deferred)
fffff880`0417f000 fffff880`041c5000   dtsoftbus01   (deferred)
fffff880`041c5000 fffff880`041d5000   WDKMD      (deferred)
fffff880`041d5000 fffff880`041ee000   nusb3hub   (deferred)
fffff880`04a00000 fffff880`04a56000   USBPORT    (deferred)
fffff880`04a56000 fffff880`04a5a500   CmBatt     (deferred)
fffff880`04a5b000 fffff880`04a79000   i8042prt   (deferred)
fffff880`04a7e000 fffff880`052e9000   NETwNs64   (deferred)
fffff880`052e9000 fffff880`052f6000   vwifibus   (deferred)
fffff880`052f6000 fffff880`05307c80   ohci1394   (deferred)
fffff880`05308000 fffff880`05320000   1394BUS    (deferred)
fffff880`05320000 fffff880`0534e000   jmcr       (deferred)
fffff880`0534e000 fffff880`0537d000   SCSIPORT   (deferred)
fffff880`0537d000 fffff880`053ae000   nusb3xhc   (deferred)
fffff880`053ae000 fffff880`053aff00   USBD       (deferred)
fffff880`053b0000 fffff880`053c1000   usbehci    (deferred)
fffff880`053c1000 fffff880`053d0000   kbdclass   (deferred)
fffff880`053d0000 fffff880`053db000   VMkbd      (deferred)
fffff880`053db000 fffff880`053f6000   raspppoe   (deferred)
fffff880`053f6000 fffff880`053fe000   vmnetadapter   (deferred)
fffff880`07400000 fffff880`07424000   HDAudBus   (deferred)
fffff880`07424000 fffff880`07436000   umbus      (deferred)
fffff880`07437000 fffff880`07fe8bc0   igdkmd64   (deferred)
fffff880`07fe9000 fffff880`07ffa000   HECIx64    (deferred)
fffff880`0a200000 fffff880`0a213000   ndisuio    (deferred)
fffff880`0a213000 fffff880`0a22b000   rspndr     (deferred)
```

```
fffff880`0a22b000 fffff880`0a294000   srv2       (deferred)
fffff880`0a2b4000 fffff880`0a30e000   usbhub     (deferred)
fffff880`0a30e000 fffff880`0a323000   NDProxy    (deferred)
fffff880`0a323000 fffff880`0a34dfe0   CtClsFlt   (deferred)
fffff880`0a34e000 fffff880`0a35c000   monitor    (deferred)
fffff880`0a35c000 fffff880`0a37f000   luafv      (deferred)
fffff880`0a37f000 fffff880`0a38f000   vmnetbridge   (deferred)
fffff880`0a38f000 fffff880`0a3a4000   lltdio     (deferred)
fffff880`0a3a4000 fffff880`0a3f7000   nwifi      (deferred)
fffff880`0a400000 fffff880`0a42d280   usbvideo   (deferred)
fffff880`0a42e000 fffff880`0a43c000   hidusb     (deferred)
fffff880`0a43c000 fffff880`0a444080   HIDPARSE   (deferred)
fffff880`0a447000 fffff880`0a6e1000   RTKVHD64   (deferred)
fffff880`0a6e1000 fffff880`0a71e000   portcls    (deferred)
fffff880`0a71e000 fffff880`0a740000   drmk       (deferred)
fffff880`0a740000 fffff880`0a745200   ksthunk    (deferred)
fffff880`0a746000 fffff880`0a799000   IntcDAud   (deferred)
fffff880`0a799000 fffff880`0a7a7000   crashdmp   (deferred)
fffff880`0a7a7000 fffff880`0a7ba000   dump_dumpfve   (deferred)
fffff880`0a7ba000 fffff880`0a7c6000   Dxapi      (deferred)
fffff880`0a7c6000 fffff880`0a7e3000   usbccgp    (deferred)
fffff880`0a7e3000 fffff880`0a7fc000   HIDCLASS   (deferred)
fffff880`0c800000 fffff880`0c82d000   mrxsmb     (deferred)
fffff880`0c82d000 fffff880`0c87b000   mrxsmb10   (deferred)
fffff880`0c87b000 fffff880`0c89f000   mrxsmb20   (deferred)
fffff880`0c89f000 fffff880`0c8ab000   hcmon      (deferred)
fffff880`0c8ab000 fffff880`0c8c3000   vmci       (deferred)
fffff880`0c8ef000 fffff880`0c9b8000   HTTP       (deferred)
fffff880`0c9b8000 fffff880`0c9d6000   bowser     (deferred)
fffff880`0c9d6000 fffff880`0c9ee000   mpsdrv     (deferred)
fffff880`0c9ee000 fffff880`0c9fe000   MpNWMon    (deferred)
fffff880`0cc00000 fffff880`0cca6000   peauth     (deferred)
fffff880`0cca6000 fffff880`0ccb1000   secdrv     (deferred)
fffff880`0ccb1000 fffff880`0cce2000   srvnet     (deferred)
fffff880`0cce2000 fffff880`0ccf4000   tcpipreg   (deferred)
fffff880`0ccfb000 fffff880`0cdd1000   vmx86      (deferred)
fffff880`0cdd1000 fffff880`0cddb000   vwifimp    (deferred)
fffff880`0cddb000 fffff880`0cde5000   vmnetuserif   (deferred)
fffff880`0cde5000 fffff880`0cdf1000   vstor2_ws60   (deferred)
fffff880`0e8a8000 fffff880`0e940000   srv        (deferred)
fffff880`0e940000 fffff880`0e958000   NisDrvWFP   (deferred)
fffff880`0e958000 fffff880`0e98e000   fastfat    (deferred)
fffff880`0e98e000 fffff880`0e9ff000   spsys      (deferred)
fffff880`0f200000 fffff880`0f215000   L1C62x64   (deferred)
fffff880`0f215000 fffff880`0f244000   ndiswan    (deferred)
fffff880`0f244000 fffff880`0f24e000   VMNET      (deferred)
fffff880`0f250000 fffff880`0fec1f80   nvlddmkm   (deferred)
fffff880`0fec2000 fffff880`0fec3180   nvBridge   (deferred)
fffff880`0fec4000 fffff880`0ffb8000   dxgkrnl    (deferred)
fffff880`0ffb8000 fffff880`0fffe000   dxgmms1    (deferred)
fffff960`00070000 fffff960`00383000   win32k     (deferred)
fffff960`00590000 fffff960`0059a000   TSDDD      (deferred)
fffff960`007d0000 fffff960`007f7000   cdd        (deferred)

Unloaded modules:
fffff880`0188a000 fffff880`01898000   crashdmp.sys
fffff880`02e3a000 fffff880`02f8e000   dump_iaStor.sys
fffff880`02f8e000 fffff880`02fa1000   dump_dumpfve.sys
fffff880`02fa1000 fffff880`02fcb000   cdrom.sys
```

4. Then we list processes:

```
0: kd> !process 0 0
**** NT ACTIVE PROCESS DUMP ****
PROCESS fffffa80042d5400
    SessionId: none  Cid: 0004    Peb: 00000000  ParentCid: 0000
    DirBase: 00187000  ObjectTable: fffff8a0000017e0  HandleCount: 785.
    Image: System

PROCESS fffffa8006fa8750
    SessionId: none  Cid: 0144    Peb: 7fffffda000  ParentCid: 0004
    DirBase: 107226000  ObjectTable: fffff8a0002dcf90  HandleCount:  32.
    Image: smss.exe
```

```
PROCESS fffffa80083cdb30
    SessionId: 0  Cid: 01ec    Peb: 7fffffdc000  ParentCid: 01a8
    DirBase: 918c1000  ObjectTable: fffff8a0013b98a0  HandleCount: 679.
    Image: csrss.exe

PROCESS fffffa8008ee73d0
    SessionId: 1  Cid: 0270    Peb: 7fffffd8000  ParentCid: 0268
    DirBase: 8af20000  ObjectTable: fffff8a0016e9380  HandleCount: 742.
    Image: csrss.exe

PROCESS fffffa8008f00b30
    SessionId: 0  Cid: 0278    Peb: 7fffffdd000  ParentCid: 01a8
    DirBase: 8ab87000  ObjectTable: fffff8a0066663f0  HandleCount:  82.
    Image: wininit.exe

PROCESS fffffa8008f32b30
    SessionId: 1  Cid: 029c    Peb: 7fffffdf000  ParentCid: 0268
    DirBase: 90026000  ObjectTable: fffff8a001709a10  HandleCount: 114.
    Image: winlogon.exe

PROCESS fffffa8008fa0b30
    SessionId: 0  Cid: 02d8    Peb: 7fffffdf000  ParentCid: 0278
    DirBase: 87d59000  ObjectTable: fffff8a001094500  HandleCount: 269.
    Image: services.exe

PROCESS fffffa8009051060
    SessionId: 0  Cid: 02e0    Peb: 7fffffdd000  ParentCid: 0278
    DirBase: 8e77a000  ObjectTable: fffff8a001021560  HandleCount: 823.
    Image: lsass.exe

PROCESS fffffa8008f18b30
    SessionId: 0  Cid: 02ec    Peb: 7fffffdf000  ParentCid: 0278
    DirBase: 58d41000  ObjectTable: fffff8a00105f4e0  HandleCount: 179.
    Image: lsm.exe

PROCESS fffffa80090fe060
    SessionId: 0  Cid: 0350    Peb: 7fffffda000  ParentCid: 02d8
    DirBase: 8d677000  ObjectTable: fffff8a0010ca3e0  HandleCount: 400.
    Image: svchost.exe

PROCESS fffffa8008f1db30
    SessionId: 0  Cid: 0390    Peb: 7fffffd8000  ParentCid: 02d8
    DirBase: 81918000  ObjectTable: fffff8a001838bf0  HandleCount: 116.
    Image: nvvsvc.exe

PROCESS fffffa8008328b30
    SessionId: 0  Cid: 03b8    Peb: 7fffffdf000  ParentCid: 02d8
    DirBase: 809df000  ObjectTable: fffff8a001884210  HandleCount: 357.
    Image: svchost.exe

PROCESS fffffa800916b060
    SessionId: 0  Cid: 03f4    Peb: 7fffffde000  ParentCid: 02d8
    DirBase: 8b768000  ObjectTable: fffff8a0019070c0  HandleCount: 554.
    Image: MsMpEng.exe

PROCESS fffffa80091b7060
    SessionId: 0  Cid: 020c    Peb: 7fffffdd000  ParentCid: 02d8
    DirBase: 8a771000  ObjectTable: fffff8a0019147a0  HandleCount: 543.
    Image: svchost.exe

PROCESS fffffa80091ce780
    SessionId: 0  Cid: 0234    Peb: 7fffffd3000  ParentCid: 02d8
    DirBase: 8b1b6000  ObjectTable: fffff8a0018b6890  HandleCount: 591.
    Image: svchost.exe

PROCESS fffffa80091d5b30
    SessionId: 0  Cid: 0274    Peb: 7fffffdf000  ParentCid: 02d8
    DirBase: 7e682000  ObjectTable: fffff8a001163260  HandleCount: 1440.
    Image: svchost.exe

PROCESS fffffa80092a9b30
    SessionId: 0  Cid: 0424    Peb: 7fffffd9000  ParentCid: 020c
    DirBase: 8992b000  ObjectTable: fffff8a00118af90  HandleCount: 139.
    Image: audiodg.exe
```

```
PROCESS fffffa80092b0b30
    SessionId: 0  Cid: 0458    Peb: 7fffffdf000  ParentCid: 02d8
    DirBase: 7c608000  ObjectTable: fffff8a0019e3910  HandleCount: 320.
    Image: svchost.exe

PROCESS fffffa800903ab30
    SessionId: 0  Cid: 04a0    Peb: 7fffffdc000  ParentCid: 02d8
    DirBase: 88ab2000  ObjectTable: fffff8a0019bb760  HandleCount: 421.
    Image: svchost.exe

PROCESS fffffa800935db30
    SessionId: 0  Cid: 0564    Peb: 7fffffda000  ParentCid: 0234
    DirBase: 76707000  ObjectTable: fffff8a001a8e680  HandleCount: 411.
    Image: wlanext.exe

PROCESS fffffa800515a060
    SessionId: 0  Cid: 058c    Peb: 7fffffdb000  ParentCid: 01ec
    DirBase: 76656000  ObjectTable: fffff8a0011f0160  HandleCount:  34.
    Image: conhost.exe

PROCESS fffffa8009322b30
    SessionId: 1  Cid: 05b8    Peb: 7fffffdb000  ParentCid: 0390
    DirBase: 74e9d000  ObjectTable: fffff8a001a800d0  HandleCount: 342.
    Image: NvXDSync.exe

PROCESS fffffa8009400b30
    SessionId: 1  Cid: 05c4    Peb: 7fffffd3000  ParentCid: 0390
    DirBase: 81ca2000  ObjectTable: fffff8a00183ac60  HandleCount: 191.
    Image: nvvsvc.exe

PROCESS fffffa800941db30
    SessionId: 0  Cid: 05dc    Peb: 7fffffde000  ParentCid: 02d8
    DirBase: 8353e000  ObjectTable: fffff8a001931950  HandleCount: 289.
    Image: spoolsv.exe

PROCESS fffffa80083c6060
    SessionId: 0  Cid: 062c    Peb: 7fffffdd000  ParentCid: 02d8
    DirBase: 80868000  ObjectTable: fffff8a0019f5b10  HandleCount: 321.
    Image: svchost.exe

PROCESS fffffa80094b48e0
    SessionId: 0  Cid: 0790    Peb: 7efdf000  ParentCid: 02d8
    DirBase: 734fa000  ObjectTable: fffff8a00236a6f0  HandleCount:  75.
    Image: armsvc.exe

PROCESS fffffa8008273b30
    SessionId: 0  Cid: 07dc    Peb: 7fffffd6000  ParentCid: 02d8
    DirBase: 706a1000  ObjectTable: fffff8a001d15280  HandleCount:  42.
    Image: AERTSr64.exe

PROCESS fffffa8009508b30
    SessionId: 0  Cid: 0418    Peb: 7fffffda000  ParentCid: 02d8
    DirBase: 713a8000  ObjectTable: fffff8a00238bc60  HandleCount: 283.
    Image: EvtEng.exe

PROCESS fffffa8009562b30
    SessionId: 0  Cid: 0514    Peb: 7fffffd3000  ParentCid: 02d8
    DirBase: 6058a000  ObjectTable: fffff8a001d96b90  HandleCount: 337.
    Image: sqlservr.exe

PROCESS fffffa8009628230
    SessionId: 1  Cid: 04c8    Peb: 7fffffd5000  ParentCid: 02d8
    DirBase: 5a844000  ObjectTable: fffff8a001d23a30  HandleCount: 193.
    Image: taskhost.exe

PROCESS fffffa80096beb30
    SessionId: 1  Cid: 07bc    Peb: 7fffffdd000  ParentCid: 0234
    DirBase: 5989f000  ObjectTable: fffff8a002fc43f0  HandleCount: 148.
    Image: dwm.exe

PROCESS fffffa80096cbb30
    SessionId: 1  Cid: 0840    Peb: 7fffffde000  ParentCid: 0710
    DirBase: 66aaa000  ObjectTable: fffff8a002629ef0  HandleCount: 936.
    Image: explorer.exe
```

```
PROCESS fffffa80097a1b30
    SessionId: 0  Cid: 08f0    Peb: 7fffffdd000  ParentCid: 02d8
    DirBase: 62823000  ObjectTable: fffff8a00263d530  HandleCount:  93.
    Image: RegSrvc.exe

PROCESS fffffa800989e060
    SessionId: 0  Cid: 09b0    Peb: 7efdf000  ParentCid: 02d8
    DirBase: 5f7aa000  ObjectTable: fffff8a001d460a0  HandleCount: 156.
    Image: SftService.exe

PROCESS fffffa8009840b30
    SessionId: 0  Cid: 09c8    Peb: 7fffffdf000  ParentCid: 02d8
    DirBase: 5d830000  ObjectTable: fffff8a0027fd240  HandleCount:  83.
    Image: sqlwriter.exe

PROCESS fffffa8009838b30
    SessionId: 0  Cid: 09e0    Peb: 7efdf000  ParentCid: 02d8
    DirBase: 5d9f6000  ObjectTable: fffff8a0027905f0  HandleCount: 100.
    Image: nvSCPAPISvr.exe

PROCESS fffffa800992c060
    SessionId: 0  Cid: 0a60    Peb: 7efdf000  ParentCid: 02d8
    DirBase: 4a0c8000  ObjectTable: fffff8a001c38e00  HandleCount: 103.
    Image: vmware-usbarbitrator.exe

PROCESS fffffa80099b2060
    SessionId: 0  Cid: 0ac0    Peb: 7efdf000  ParentCid: 02d8
    DirBase: 4758e000  ObjectTable: fffff8a002748150  HandleCount:  74.
    Image: vmnat.exe

PROCESS fffffa80099ca060
    SessionId: 1  Cid: 0acc    Peb: 7efdf000  ParentCid: 09b0
    DirBase: 569b4000  ObjectTable: 00000000  HandleCount:   0.
    Image: hstart.exe

PROCESS fffffa800995cb30
    SessionId: 1  Cid: 0b14    Peb: 7efdf000  ParentCid: 09b0
    DirBase: 55bfd000  ObjectTable: fffff8a002991ad0  HandleCount: 348.
    Image: Toaster.exe

PROCESS fffffa8009969b30
    SessionId: 1  Cid: 0b2c    Peb: 7fffffdf000  ParentCid: 0840
    DirBase: 44299000  ObjectTable: fffff8a0019a4590  HandleCount: 211.
    Image: SynTPEnh.exe

PROCESS fffffa8009a38b30
    SessionId: 1  Cid: 0b44    Peb: 7fffffd3000  ParentCid: 0840
    DirBase: 43719000  ObjectTable: fffff8a001dbe730  HandleCount:  81.
    Image: igfxtray.exe

PROCESS fffffa80099d26f0
    SessionId: 1  Cid: 0b54    Peb: 7fffffde000  ParentCid: 0840
    DirBase: 5243e000  ObjectTable: fffff8a00284f890  HandleCount:  87.
    Image: hkcmd.exe

PROCESS fffffa8009a32b30
    SessionId: 1  Cid: 0b5c    Peb: 7fffffd9000  ParentCid: 0840
    DirBase: 517fa000  ObjectTable: fffff8a003005c70  HandleCount: 110.
    Image: igfxpers.exe

PROCESS fffffa8009a3cb30
    SessionId: 1  Cid: 0b70    Peb: 7fffffd4000  ParentCid: 0840
    DirBase: 43c46000  ObjectTable: fffff8a00276df00  HandleCount: 249.
    Image: RtkNGUI64.exe

PROCESS fffffa8009a50b30
    SessionId: 1  Cid: 0b90    Peb: 7fffffd4000  ParentCid: 0840
    DirBase: 515ff000  ObjectTable: fffff8a002774180  HandleCount: 196.
    Image: RAVBg64.exe

PROCESS fffffa8009a3ab30
    SessionId: 1  Cid: 0bac    Peb: 7fffffdc000  ParentCid: 0840
    DirBase: 3fc88000  ObjectTable: fffff8a0027457a0  HandleCount: 185.
    Image: iFrmewrk.exe
```

```
PROCESS fffffa8009a34060
    SessionId: 0  Cid: 08dc    Peb: 7efdf000  ParentCid: 02d8
    DirBase: 43c94000  ObjectTable: fffff8a00299b710  HandleCount:  50.
    Image: vmnetdhcp.exe

PROCESS fffffa8009af7060
    SessionId: 1  Cid: 095c    Peb: 7efdf000  ParentCid: 0840
    DirBase: 3fa91000  ObjectTable: fffff8a00311b9e0  HandleCount: 111.
    Image: FF_Protection.exe

PROCESS fffffa8009af2b30
    SessionId: 1  Cid: 0abc    Peb: 7efdf000  ParentCid: 09b0
    DirBase: 4baec000  ObjectTable: 00000000  HandleCount:   0.
    Image: RPLauncher.exe

PROCESS fffffa8009afbb30
    SessionId: 1  Cid: 0b34    Peb: 7efdf000  ParentCid: 09b0
    DirBase: 4be31000  ObjectTable: fffff8a0030f9cd0  HandleCount: 148.
    Image: STService.exe

PROCESS fffffa8009b6cb30
    SessionId: 1  Cid: 0c1c    Peb: 7efdf000  ParentCid: 0840
    DirBase: 3abd9000  ObjectTable: fffff8a003089010  HandleCount: 185.
    Image: StageRemote.exe

PROCESS fffffa8009aebb30
    SessionId: 1  Cid: 0c34    Peb: 7efdf000  ParentCid: 0acc
    DirBase: 3a59d000  ObjectTable: fffff8a0030f1b70  HandleCount: 292.
    Image: DSUpd.exe

PROCESS fffffa8009c03b30
    SessionId: 0  Cid: 0c6c    Peb: 7efdf000  ParentCid: 02d8
    DirBase: 49a7a000  ObjectTable: fffff8a0030bd2c0  HandleCount: 275.
    Image: vmware-authd.exe

PROCESS fffffa8009ae5060
    SessionId: 1  Cid: 0d50    Peb: 7fffffd8000  ParentCid: 0350
    DirBase: 476ff000  ObjectTable: fffff8a001ac35d0  HandleCount:  79.
    Image: unsecapp.exe

PROCESS fffffa8009e89b30
    SessionId: 0  Cid: 0e38    Peb: 7fffffdf000  ParentCid: 0350
    DirBase: 137801000  ObjectTable: fffff8a000966bb0  HandleCount:  68.
    Image: unsecapp.exe

PROCESS fffffa8009d8db30
    SessionId: 0  Cid: 0e50    Peb: 7fffffd3000  ParentCid: 0350
    DirBase: 31747000  ObjectTable: fffff8a0032757d0  HandleCount: 301.
    Image: WmiPrvSE.exe

PROCESS fffffa8009d18b30
    SessionId: 0  Cid: 0ea4    Peb: 7fffffdf000  ParentCid: 0350
    DirBase: 31f17000  ObjectTable: fffff8a001723db0  HandleCount: 184.
    Image: WmiPrvSE.exe

PROCESS fffffa8009aafb30
    SessionId: 1  Cid: 0d0c    Peb: 7fffffdd000  ParentCid: 096c
    DirBase: 2b9d0000  ObjectTable: fffff8a00376d9f0  HandleCount: 256.
    Image: AWCCServiceController.exe

PROCESS fffffa8009fecb30
    SessionId: 1  Cid: 0bf4    Peb: 7fffffdf000  ParentCid: 0840
    DirBase: 3bbf2000  ObjectTable: fffff8a001911cc0  HandleCount: 271.
    Image: msseces.exe

PROCESS fffffa800a011b30
    SessionId: 1  Cid: 080c    Peb: 7efdf000  ParentCid: 0840
    DirBase: 40e01000  ObjectTable: fffff8a003399dc0  HandleCount: 149.
    Image: DTLite.exe

PROCESS fffffa800a02bb30
    SessionId: 1  Cid: 0d80    Peb: 7efdf000  ParentCid: 0840
    DirBase: 282c8000  ObjectTable: fffff8a0037df730  HandleCount: 320.
    Image: sidebar.exe
```

```
PROCESS fffffa800a082060
    SessionId: 1  Cid: 0584    Peb: 7efdf000  ParentCid: 0c1c
    DirBase: 28212000  ObjectTable: fffff8a0037a96b0  HandleCount: 135.
    Image: StageRemoteService.exe

PROCESS fffffa800a09eb30
    SessionId: 0  Cid: 0d64    Peb: 7fffffdc000  ParentCid: 02d8
    DirBase: 27e5f000  ObjectTable: fffff8a003560780  HandleCount: 662.
    Image: SearchIndexer.exe

PROCESS fffffa800a06a960
    SessionId: 1  Cid: 0f0c    Peb: 7efdf000  ParentCid: 0700
    DirBase: 384f9000  ObjectTable: fffff8a003842d40  HandleCount: 357.
    Image: IAStorIcon.exe

PROCESS fffffa8007034630
    SessionId: 0  Cid: 0fc8    Peb: 7fffffdc000  ParentCid: 02d8
    DirBase: 371ed000  ObjectTable: fffff8a00366a010  HandleCount: 247.
    Image: NisSrv.exe

PROCESS fffffa800941fb30
    SessionId: 1  Cid: 112c    Peb: 7efdf000  ParentCid: 0700
    DirBase: 1f70f000  ObjectTable: fffff8a003990a10  HandleCount: 136.
    Image: AlienwareOn-ScreenDisplay.exe

PROCESS fffffa80094feb30
    SessionId: 1  Cid: 11e0    Peb: 7efdf000  ParentCid: 096c
    DirBase: 30eff000  ObjectTable: fffff8a001df4b80  HandleCount: 427.
    Image: AlienwareAlienFXController.exe

PROCESS fffffa800958db30
    SessionId: 1  Cid: 11ec    Peb: 7fffffd8000  ParentCid: 0b2c
    DirBase: 2d525000  ObjectTable: fffff8a0038a9e00  HandleCount:  35.
    Image: SynTPHelper.exe

PROCESS fffffa8006f96580
    SessionId: 1  Cid: 11f4    Peb: 7efdf000  ParentCid: 0700
    DirBase: 1d759000  ObjectTable: fffff8a0037a8970  HandleCount: 188.
    Image: WebcamInt.exe

PROCESS fffffa800914d4e0
    SessionId: 1  Cid: 121c    Peb: 7efdf000  ParentCid: 0700
    DirBase: 1cb5f000  ObjectTable: fffff8a003e20c90  HandleCount:  68.
    Image: NeroLauncher.exe

PROCESS fffffa80091c99e0
    SessionId: 1  Cid: 1288    Peb: 7efdf000  ParentCid: 0700
    DirBase: 2a3ac000  ObjectTable: fffff8a003411c70  HandleCount: 370.
    Image: accuweather.exe

PROCESS fffffa8009781b30
    SessionId: 1  Cid: 1290    Peb: 7efdf000  ParentCid: 0700
    DirBase: 2c2f5000  ObjectTable: fffff8a003fddf00  HandleCount: 171.
    Image: AdobeARM.exe

PROCESS fffffa80097fbb30
    SessionId: 1  Cid: 1298    Peb: 7efdf000  ParentCid: 0700
    DirBase: 2c87f000  ObjectTable: fffff8a003fe92d0  HandleCount:  59.
    Image: jusched.exe

PROCESS fffffa8009846b30
    SessionId: 1  Cid: 12a0    Peb: 7efdf000  ParentCid: 0700
    DirBase: 18d07000  ObjectTable: fffff8a003929620  HandleCount:  60.
    Image: vmware-tray.exe

PROCESS fffffa8009b06760
    SessionId: 0  Cid: 13b8    Peb: 7fffffdb000  ParentCid: 02d8
    DirBase: 0ee10000  ObjectTable: fffff8a003843210  HandleCount: 157.
    Image: svchost.exe

PROCESS fffffa8009b47060
    SessionId: 1  Cid: 1354    Peb: 7efdf000  ParentCid: 0d0c
    DirBase: 1883e000  ObjectTable: fffff8a004809ea0  HandleCount: 137.
    Image: AWCCApplicationWatcher32.exe
```

```
PROCESS fffffa8008fdf970
    SessionId: 1  Cid: 0694    Peb: 7fffffd5000  ParentCid: 0270
    DirBase: 1541d6000  ObjectTable: fffff8a0049825a0  HandleCount:  36.
    Image: conhost.exe

PROCESS fffffa8009eb3b30
    SessionId: 1  Cid: 05e8    Peb: 7fffffdf000  ParentCid: 0d0c
    DirBase: 18d32000  ObjectTable: fffff8a00402fac0  HandleCount: 130.
    Image: AWCCApplicationWatcher64.exe

PROCESS fffffa8009bab9e0
    SessionId: 1  Cid: 0ea0    Peb: 7fffffd4000  ParentCid: 0270
    DirBase: 15285c000  ObjectTable: fffff8a00663e990  HandleCount:  37.
    Image: conhost.exe

PROCESS fffffa800436db30
    SessionId: 1  Cid: 1194    Peb: 7efdf000  ParentCid: 0d80
    DirBase: 0bce5000  ObjectTable: fffff8a0030d2780  HandleCount: 137.
    Image: DTShellHlp.exe

PROCESS fffffa8008edeb30
    SessionId: 1  Cid: 0bfc    Peb: 7efdf000  ParentCid: 0840
    DirBase: 146c8a000  ObjectTable: fffff8a002757a50  HandleCount: 361.
    Image: iexplore.exe

PROCESS fffffa8009cbc060
    SessionId: 1  Cid: 03b0    Peb: 7efdf000  ParentCid: 0bfc
    DirBase: 14629b000  ObjectTable: fffff8a003889260  HandleCount: 352.
    Image: iexplore.exe

PROCESS fffffa80044a2b30
    SessionId: 1  Cid: 12b0    Peb: 7fffffd7000  ParentCid: 0840
    DirBase: 137213000  ObjectTable: fffff8a003aa04a0  HandleCount:  68.
    Image: notepad.exe

PROCESS fffffa8009d2f060
    SessionId: 0  Cid: 0de0    Peb: 7fffffdf000  ParentCid: 02d8
    DirBase: 133f16000  ObjectTable: fffff8a004843610  HandleCount: 201.
    Image: AlienFusionService.exe

PROCESS fffffa80044627e0
    SessionId: 0  Cid: 03c8    Peb: fffdf000  ParentCid: 02d8
    DirBase: 13189c000  ObjectTable: fffff8a003370ea0  HandleCount:  91.
    Image: mscorsvw.exe

PROCESS fffffa800444a630
    SessionId: 0  Cid: 11e8    Peb: 7fffffdf000  ParentCid: 02d8
    DirBase: 143fa9000  ObjectTable: fffff8a003b37650  HandleCount:  84.
    Image: mscorsvw.exe

PROCESS fffffa8009c1c420
    SessionId: 1  Cid: 0c9c    Peb: 7efdf000  ParentCid: 0de0
    DirBase: 14d542000  ObjectTable: fffff8a003a2bb10  HandleCount: 175.
    Image: AlienFusionController.exe

PROCESS fffffa80044abb30
    SessionId: 0  Cid: 0f90    Peb: 7efdf000  ParentCid: 02d8
    DirBase: 142873000  ObjectTable: fffff8a003a1aca0  HandleCount: 269.
    Image: IAStorDataMgrSvc.exe

PROCESS fffffa8004392b30
    SessionId: 0  Cid: 05ec    Peb: 7efdf000  ParentCid: 02d8
    DirBase: 9b6c2000  ObjectTable: fffff8a002890b60  HandleCount: 119.
    Image: NASvc.exe

PROCESS fffffa80044a1060
    SessionId: 0  Cid: 13fc    Peb: 7efdf000  ParentCid: 02d8
    DirBase: 13018f000  ObjectTable: fffff8a003a00a20  HandleCount: 202.
    Image: daemonu.exe

PROCESS fffffa8004583b30
    SessionId: 0  Cid: 143c    Peb: 7fffffd4000  ParentCid: 02d8
    DirBase: 12de17000  ObjectTable: fffff8a004beb4b0  HandleCount: 149.
    Image: sppsvc.exe
```

```
PROCESS fffffa8004451060
    SessionId: 1  Cid: 154c    Peb: 7fffffda000  ParentCid: 0840
    DirBase: 129f5a000  ObjectTable: fffff8a004725c10  HandleCount:  56.
    Image: ApplicationA.exe

PROCESS fffffa800447e060
    SessionId: 1  Cid: 1554    Peb: 7fffffd8000  ParentCid: 0270
    DirBase: 138be4000  ObjectTable: fffff8a004c02f90  HandleCount:  55.
    Image: conhost.exe

PROCESS fffffa80044da060
    SessionId: 1  Cid: 16d0    Peb: 7fffffd9000  ParentCid: 0840
    DirBase: 8b439000  ObjectTable: fffff8a0045775f0  HandleCount:  15.
    Image: ApplicationB.exe

PROCESS fffffa8009adf060
    SessionId: 1  Cid: 16d8    Peb: 7fffffdb000  ParentCid: 0270
    DirBase: 128315000  ObjectTable: fffff8a0045ac520  HandleCount:  55.
    Image: conhost.exe

PROCESS fffffa8004546060
    SessionId: 1  Cid: 07f4    Peb: 7fffffdf000  ParentCid: 0840
    DirBase: 124e1c000  ObjectTable: fffff8a0046ad510  HandleCount:  17.
    Image: ApplicationC.exe

PROCESS fffffa80044ff060
    SessionId: 1  Cid: 0374    Peb: 7fffffdd000  ParentCid: 0270
    DirBase: 138df0000  ObjectTable: fffff8a003672a50  HandleCount:  55.
    Image: conhost.exe

PROCESS fffffa8004364060
    SessionId: 1  Cid: 06fc    Peb: 7fffffd4000  ParentCid: 0840
    DirBase: 5fbc2000  ObjectTable: fffff8a004c8e930  HandleCount:  16.
    Image: ApplicationD.exe

PROCESS fffffa800454eb30
    SessionId: 1  Cid: 14b4    Peb: 7fffffda000  ParentCid: 0270
    DirBase: 137ebf000  ObjectTable: fffff8a004bedc40  HandleCount:  55.
    Image: conhost.exe

PROCESS fffffa8008ef96e0
    SessionId: 0  Cid: 15d4    Peb: 7fffffdf000  ParentCid: 02d8
    DirBase: 135473000  ObjectTable: fffff8a0044695b0  HandleCount:  75.
    Image: svchost.exe

PROCESS fffffa8009a5bb30
    SessionId: 1  Cid: 1134    Peb: 7fffffd3000  ParentCid: 15d4
    DirBase: 124cc6000  ObjectTable: fffff8a004bf68f0  HandleCount: 138.
    Image: WerFault.exe
```

PROCESS fffffa800442ab30
SessionId: 1 Cid: 1418   Peb: 7fffffde000 ParentCid: 0840
DirBase: 11e2c5000 ObjectTable: fffff8a004cc3b50 HandleCount: 20014.
Image: ApplicationE.exe

```
PROCESS fffffa800441c6f0
    SessionId: 1  Cid: 17f8    Peb: 7fffffd6000  ParentCid: 0270
    DirBase: 11e5d1000  ObjectTable: fffff8a00447d010  HandleCount:  55.
    Image: conhost.exe

PROCESS fffffa8009fe0060
    SessionId: 1  Cid: 14fb0    Peb: 7efdf000  ParentCid: 0840
    DirBase: 125476000  ObjectTable: fffff8a004d45d10  HandleCount:  64.
    Image: ApplicationA.exe

PROCESS fffffa800a01a630
    SessionId: 1  Cid: 14fb8    Peb: 7fffffd8000  ParentCid: 0270
    DirBase: 112705000  ObjectTable: fffff8a004beaf90  HandleCount:  56.
    Image: conhost.exe

PROCESS fffffa80044fc060
    SessionId: 0  Cid: 04cc    Peb: 7fffffdf000  ParentCid: 0274
    DirBase: 110885000  ObjectTable: fffff8a004c7e6c0  HandleCount:  91.
    Image: WMIADAP.exe
```

```
PROCESS fffffa800434c060
    SessionId: 1  Cid: 135c    Peb: 7fffffdc000  ParentCid: 170c
    DirBase: 11100c000  ObjectTable: fffff8a000e65c70  HandleCount: 144.
    Image: taskmgr.exe
```

4. We notice *ApplicationE* process has an abnormally high number of handles. We thus identified **Handle Leak** pattern. We then look at the output of **!process 0 3f** command[1] and search for **Message Box** pattern (from a 64-bit process):

```
        THREAD fffffa80097f1660  Cid 154c.1570  Teb: 000007fffffd4000 Win32Thread: fffff900c06a83f0 WAIT:
(WrUserRequest) UserMode Non-Alertable
            fffffa800447e8f0  SynchronizationEvent
        Not impersonating
        DeviceMap                 fffff8a001ce6b90
        Owning Process            fffffa8004451060       Image:         ApplicationA.exe
        Attached Process          N/A            Image:         N/A
        Wait Start TickCount      22248          Ticks: 47 (0:00:00:00.733)
        Context Switch Count      340            IdealProcessor: 1                 LargeStack
        UserTime                  00:00:00.015
        KernelTime                00:00:00.000
        Win32 Start Address ApplicationA (0x000000013f2c1210)
        Stack Init fffff8800ec25c70 Current fffff8800ec25730
        Base fffff8800ec26000 Limit fffff8800ec1d000 Call 0
        Priority 11 BasePriority 8 UnusualBoost 0 ForegroundBoost 2 IoPriority 2 PagePriority 5

        Child-SP          RetAddr           Call Site
        fffff880`0ec25770 fffff800`02ee6f32 nt!KiSwapContext+0x7a
        fffff880`0ec258b0 fffff800`02ee974f nt!KiCommitThreadWait+0x1d2
        fffff880`0ec25940 fffff960`0013bc97 nt!KeWaitForSingleObject+0x19f
        fffff880`0ec259e0 fffff960`0013bd39 win32k!memset+0x7ac7
        fffff880`0ec25a80 fffff960`0014e7a6 win32k!memset+0x7b69
        fffff880`0ec25ab0 fffff800`02ee0ed3 win32k!W32pArgumentTable+0xa68a
        fffff880`0ec25ae0 00000000`7709933a nt!KiSystemServiceCopyEnd+0x13 (TrapFrame @ fffff880`0ec25ae0)
        00000000`0275f308 00000000`770a4bc4 USER32!NtUserWaitMessage+0xa
        00000000`0275f310 00000000`770a4edd USER32!DialogBox2+0x274
        00000000`0275f3a0 00000000`770f2920 USER32!InternalDialogBox+0x135
        00000000`0275f400 00000000`770f1c15 USER32!SoftModalMessageBox+0x9b4
        00000000`0275f530 00000000`770f146b USER32!MessageBoxWorker+0x31d
        00000000`0275f6f0 00000000`770f1362 USER32!MessageBoxTimeoutW+0xb3
        00000000`0275f7c0 00000001`3f2c1089 USER32!MessageBoxW+0x4e
        00000000`0275f800 00000000`02135fd0 ApplicationA+0x1089
        00000000`0275f808 00000000`00000000 0x2135fd0
```

5. We then look at the fpma.txt log again and search for one of **Wait Chain** pattern variants – for kernel synchronization object Mutant (Mutex):

```
        THREAD fffffa8004514060  Cid 07f4.1470  Teb: 000007fffffae000 Win32Thread: 0000000000000000 WAIT:
(UserRequest) UserMode Non-Alertable
            fffffa80044c53c0  Mutant - owning thread fffffa8004569750
        Not impersonating
        DeviceMap                 fffff8a001ce6b90
        Owning Process            fffffa8004546060       Image:         ApplicationC.exe
        Attached Process          N/A            Image:         N/A
        Wait Start TickCount      14474          Ticks: 7821 (0:00:02:02.008)
        Context Switch Count      2              IdealProcessor: 1
        UserTime                  00:00:00.000
        KernelTime                00:00:00.000
        Win32 Start Address ApplicationC (0x000000013f6c12a0)
        Stack Init fffff8800d196c70 Current fffff8800d1967c0
        Base fffff8800d197000 Limit fffff8800d191000 Call 0
        Priority 11 BasePriority 8 UnusualBoost 0 ForegroundBoost 2 IoPriority 2 PagePriority 5
        Child-SP          RetAddr           Call Site
        fffff880`0d196800 fffff800`02ee6f32 nt!KiSwapContext+0x7a
        fffff880`0d196940 fffff800`02ee974f nt!KiCommitThreadWait+0x1d2
        fffff880`0d1969d0 fffff800`031d844e nt!KeWaitForSingleObject+0x19f
        fffff880`0d196a70 fffff800`02ee0ed3 nt!NtWaitForSingleObject+0xde
        fffff880`0d196ae0 00000000`772f135a nt!KiSystemServiceCopyEnd+0x13 (TrapFrame @ fffff880`0d196ae0)
        00000000`0107f708 00000000`00000000 ntdll!NtWaitForSingleObject+0xa
```

[1] http://www.patterndiagnostics.com/files/fpma.txt

6. We see it is owned by a different thread so we search for it in the fpma.txt log:

```
        THREAD fffffa8004569750  Cid 16d0.16ec  Teb: 000007fffffda000 Win32Thread: 0000000000000000 WAIT:
(DelayExecution) UserMode Non-Alertable
            fffffa8004569b10  Semaphore Limit 0x1
        Not impersonating
        DeviceMap                 fffff8a001ce6b90
        Owning Process            fffffa80044da060       Image:         ApplicationB.exe
        Attached Process          N/A            Image:         N/A
        Wait Start TickCount      18147          Ticks: 4148 (0:00:01:04.709)
        Context Switch Count      4              IdealProcessor: 3
        UserTime                  00:00:00.000
        KernelTime                00:00:00.000
        Win32 Start Address ApplicationB (0x000000013f161200)
        Stack Init fffff8800e3c3c70 Current fffff8800e3c3830
        Base fffff8800e3c4000 Limit fffff8800e3be000 Call 0
        Priority 11 BasePriority 8 UnusualBoost 0 ForegroundBoost 2 IoPriority 2 PagePriority 5
        Child-SP          RetAddr           Call Site
        fffff880`0e3c3870 fffff800`02ee6f32 nt!KiSwapContext+0x7a
        fffff880`0e3c39b0 fffff800`02ee8742 nt!KiCommitThreadWait+0x1d2
        fffff880`0e3c3a40 fffff800`031d84de nt!KeDelayExecutionThread+0x186
        fffff880`0e3c3ab0 fffff800`02ee0ed3 nt!NtDelayExecution+0x59
        fffff880`0e3c3ae0 00000000`772f165a nt!KiSystemServiceCopyEnd+0x13 (TrapFrame @ fffff880`0e3c3ae0)
        00000000`007af858 00000000`00000000 ntdll!NtDelayExecution+0xa
```

7. What we found is a wait chain from *ApplicationC* process thread to *ApplicationB* process thread. Alternatively we could list the latter thread stack trace with appropriate flags to set its process context during the command execution:

```
0: kd> !thread fffffa8004569750 1f
Setting context for owner process...
.process /p /r fffffa80044da060

THREAD fffffa8004569750  Cid 16d0.16ec  Teb: 000007fffffda000 Win32Thread: 0000000000000000 WAIT:
(DelayExecution) UserMode Non-Alertable
    fffffa8004569b10  Semaphore Limit 0x1
Not impersonating
DeviceMap                 fffff8a001ce6b90
Owning Process            fffffa80044da060       Image:         ApplicationB.exe
Attached Process          N/A            Image:         N/A
Wait Start TickCount      18147          Ticks: 4148 (0:00:01:04.709)
Context Switch Count      4              IdealProcessor: 3
UserTime                  00:00:00.000
KernelTime                00:00:00.000
*** ERROR: Module load completed but symbols could not be loaded for ApplicationB.exe
Win32 Start Address ApplicationB (0x000000013f161200)
Stack Init fffff8800e3c3c70 Current fffff8800e3c3830
Base fffff8800e3c4000 Limit fffff8800e3be000 Call 0
Priority 11 BasePriority 8 UnusualBoost 0 ForegroundBoost 2 IoPriority 2 PagePriority 5
*** ERROR: Symbol file could not be found.  Defaulted to export symbols for ntdll.dll -
Child-SP          RetAddr           Call Site
fffff880`0e3c3870 fffff800`02ee6f32 nt!KiSwapContext+0x7a
fffff880`0e3c39b0 fffff800`02ee8742 nt!KiCommitThreadWait+0x1d2
fffff880`0e3c3a40 fffff800`031d84de nt!KeDelayExecutionThread+0x186
fffff880`0e3c3ab0 fffff800`02ee0ed3 nt!NtDelayExecution+0x59
fffff880`0e3c3ae0 00000000`772f165a nt!KiSystemServiceCopyEnd+0x13 (TrapFrame @ fffff880`0e3c3ae0)
00000000`007af858 00000000`00000000 ntdll!NtDelayExecution+0xa
```

8. We now check for **Spiking Thread** pattern (the thread running on CPU 0 is a Task Manager thread we saw at step #1 above):

```
0: kd> !running

System Processors:  (000000000000000f)
  Idle Processors:  (000000000000000a) (0000000000000000) (0000000000000000) (0000000000000000)

       Prcbs             Current         (pri) Next            (pri) Idle
  0    fffff80003057e80  fffffa80045cfb60 (15)                       fffff80003065cc0  ................
  2    fffff88003165180  fffffa800451d720 ( 8)                       fffff8800316ffc0  ................
```

```
0: kd> !thread fffffa800451d720 1f
Setting context for owner process...
.process /p /r fffffa800442ab30

THREAD fffffa800451d720  Cid 1418.17fc  Teb: 000007fffffdc000 Win32Thread: 0000000000000000 RUNNING on
processor 2
Not impersonating
DeviceMap                 fffff8a001ce6b90
Owning Process            fffffa800442ab30       Image:         ApplicationE.exe
Attached Process          N/A            Image:         N/A
Wait Start TickCount      22295          Ticks: 0
Context Switch Count      27960          IdealProcessor: 2
UserTime                  00:01:25.332
KernelTime                00:00:00.015
*** ERROR: Module load completed but symbols could not be loaded for ApplicationE.exe
Win32 Start Address ApplicationE (0x000000013f0f1578)
Stack Init fffff8800723cc70 Current fffff8800723c960
Base fffff8800723d000 Limit fffff88007237000 Call 0
Priority 8 BasePriority 8 UnusualBoost 0 ForegroundBoost 0 IoPriority 2 PagePriority 5
Child-SP          RetAddr           Call Site
00000000`0021f9e0 00000000`00000000 ApplicationE+0x6cd3
```

8. We see that the thread running on CPU 2 consumed some time in user mode and space. Then we also check for patterns in the combined x86 and x64 script output log[2] and find another instance of **Message Box** pattern (now from a 32-bit process):

```
THREAD fffffa8004438b60  Cid 14fb0.14fd8  Teb: 000000007efaa000 Win32Thread: fffff900c2a20010 WAIT: (WrUserRequest) UserMode Non-Alertable
    fffffa8004543a60  SynchronizationEvent
Not impersonating
DeviceMap                 fffff8a001ce6b90
Owning Process            fffffa8009fe0060       Image:         ApplicationA.exe
Attached Process          N/A            Image:         N/A
Wait Start TickCount      22248          Ticks: 47 (0:00:00:00.733)
Context Switch Count      319            IdealProcessor: 2                 LargeStack
UserTime                  00:00:00.000
KernelTime                00:00:00.000
*** ERROR: Module load completed but symbols could not be loaded for ApplicationA.exe
Win32 Start Address ApplicationA (0x000000000011d117f)
Stack Init fffff8800ca12c70 Current fffff8800ca12730
Base fffff8800ca13000 Limit fffff8800ca0a000 Call 0
Priority 10 BasePriority 8 UnusualBoost 0 ForegroundBoost 2 IoPriority 2 PagePriority 5
*** ERROR: Symbol file could not be found.  Defaulted to export symbols for win32k.sys -
*** ERROR: Symbol file could not be found.  Defaulted to export symbols for ntdll.dll -
Child-SP          RetAddr           : Args to Child                                                           : Call Site
fffff880`0ca12770 fffff800`02ee6f32 : fffff900`c2a20010 fffffa80`04438b60 fffff900`c2a20010 00000000`00000008 : nt!KiSwapContext+0x7a
fffff880`0ca128b0 fffff800`02ee974f : fffffa80`08f16790 fffff800`02ee423f fffffa80`00000000 fffff880`03165180 : nt!KiCommitThreadWait+0x1d2
fffff880`0ca12940 fffff960`0013bc97 : fffff900`c2a20000 fffffa80`0000000d fffff880`03165101 00000000`00000000 : nt!KeWaitForSingleObject+0x19f
fffff880`0ca129e0 fffff960`0013bd39 : 00000000`00000000 00000000`00000000 00000000`00000001 00000000`00000000 : win32k!memset+0x7ac7
fffff880`0ca12a80 fffff960`0014e7a6 : fffffa80`04438b60 fffff880`0ca12b60 00000000`0125cf60 00000000`0053fd18 : win32k!memset+0x7b69
fffff880`0ca12ab0 fffff800`02ee0ed3 : fffffa80`04438b60 00000000`0053aee0 00000000`00540178 00000000`00000020 : win32k!W32pArgumentTable+0xa68a
fffff880`0ca12ae0 00000000`73042e09 : 00000000`73042dbf 00000000`74c80735 00000000`00000023 00000000`00000246 : nt!KiSystemServiceCopyEnd+0x13
(TrapFrame @ fffff880`0ca12ae0)
00000000`0049edb8 00000000`73042dbf : 00000000`74c80735 00000000`00000023 00000000`00000246 00000000`0274f830 : wow64cpu!CpupSyscallStub+0x9
00000000`0049edc0 00000000`730bd07e : 00000000`00000000 00000000`73041920 00000000`00000000 00000000`00000000 : wow64cpu!Thunk0Arg+0x5
00000000`0049ee80 00000000`730bc549 : 00000000`00000000 00000000`00000000 00000000`00000000 00000000`00000000 : wow64!RunCpuSimulation+0xa
00000000`0049eed0 00000000`7731e707 : 00000000`00000000 00000000`7efdf000 00000000`7efaa000 00000000`00000000 : wow64!Wow64LdrpInitialize+0x429
00000000`0049f420 00000000`00000000 : 00000000`7efdf000 00000000`7efaa000 00000000`00000000 00000000`00000000 :
ntdll!RtlIsDosDeviceName_U+0x24c87

.process /p /r 0
Implicit thread is now fffffa80`04438b60
WARNING: WOW context retrieval requires
switching to the thread's process context.
Use .process /p fffffa80`0434c060 to switch back.
Implicit process is now fffffa80`09fe0060
*** ERROR: Symbol file could not be found.  Defaulted to export symbols for ntdll.dll -
x86 context set
Loading Kernel Symbols
...............................................................
................................................................
............................................
Loading User Symbols
.....
Loading unloaded module list
....*** ERROR: Symbol file could not be found.  Defaulted to export symbols for ntdll.dll -

Loading Wow64 Symbols
...........................

************* Symbol Loading Error Summary **************
Module name            Error
ntdll                  The PDB file is no longer available : SRV*c:\mss*http://msdl.microsoft.com/download/symbols

You can troubleshoot most symbol related issues by turning on symbol loading diagnostics (!sym noisy) and repeating the command that caused
symbols to be loaded.
You should also verify that your symbol search path (.sympath) is correct.
```

---

2 http://www.patterndiagnostics.com/files/fpma-full.txt

```
ChildEBP          RetAddr           Args to Child
0274f898 74c9cd46 00000000 00000000 00000000 USER32!NtUserWaitMessage+0x15 (FPO: [0,0,0])
0274f8d4 74c9cf5c 00040554 00000000 00000000 USER32!DialogBox2+0x222 (FPO: [Non-Fpo])
0274f900 74ccf73c 74c60000 00531888 00000000 USER32!InternalDialogBox+0xe5 (FPO: [Non-Fpo])
0274f9b4 74ccfa18 00000000 758410ff 74ccfd3f USER32!SoftModalMessageBox+0x757 (FPO: [Non-Fpo])
0274fb0c 74ccfb1f 0274fb18 00000028 00000000 USER32!MessageBoxWorker+0x269 (FPO: [Non-Fpo])
0274fb78 74ccfd15 00000000 011d929c 011d9290 USER32!MessageBoxTimeoutW+0x52 (FPO: [Non-Fpo])
0274fb98 74ccfd57 00000000 011d929c 011d9290 USER32!MessageBoxExW+0x1b (FPO: [Non-Fpo])
*** ERROR: Module load completed but symbols could not be loaded for ApplicationA.exe
0274fbb4 011d1050 00000000 011d929c 011d9290 USER32!MessageBoxW+0x18 (FPO: [Non-Fpo])
WARNING: Stack unwind information not available. Following frames may be wrong.
0274fc08 011d11f5 0274fc1c 7584339a 001f1b08 ApplicationA+0x1050
0274fc10 7584339a 001f1b08 0274fc5c 774b9ed2 ApplicationA+0x11f5
0274fc1c 774b9ed2 001f1b08 752897e6 00000000 kernel32!BaseThreadInitThunk+0xe (FPO: [Non-Fpo])
0274fc5c 774b9ea5 011d117f 001f1b08 00000000 ntdll_77480000!__RtlUserThreadStart+0x70 (FPO: [Non-Fpo])
0274fc74 00000000 011d117f 001f1b08 00000000 ntdll_77480000!_RtlUserThreadStart+0x1b (FPO: [Non-Fpo])
```

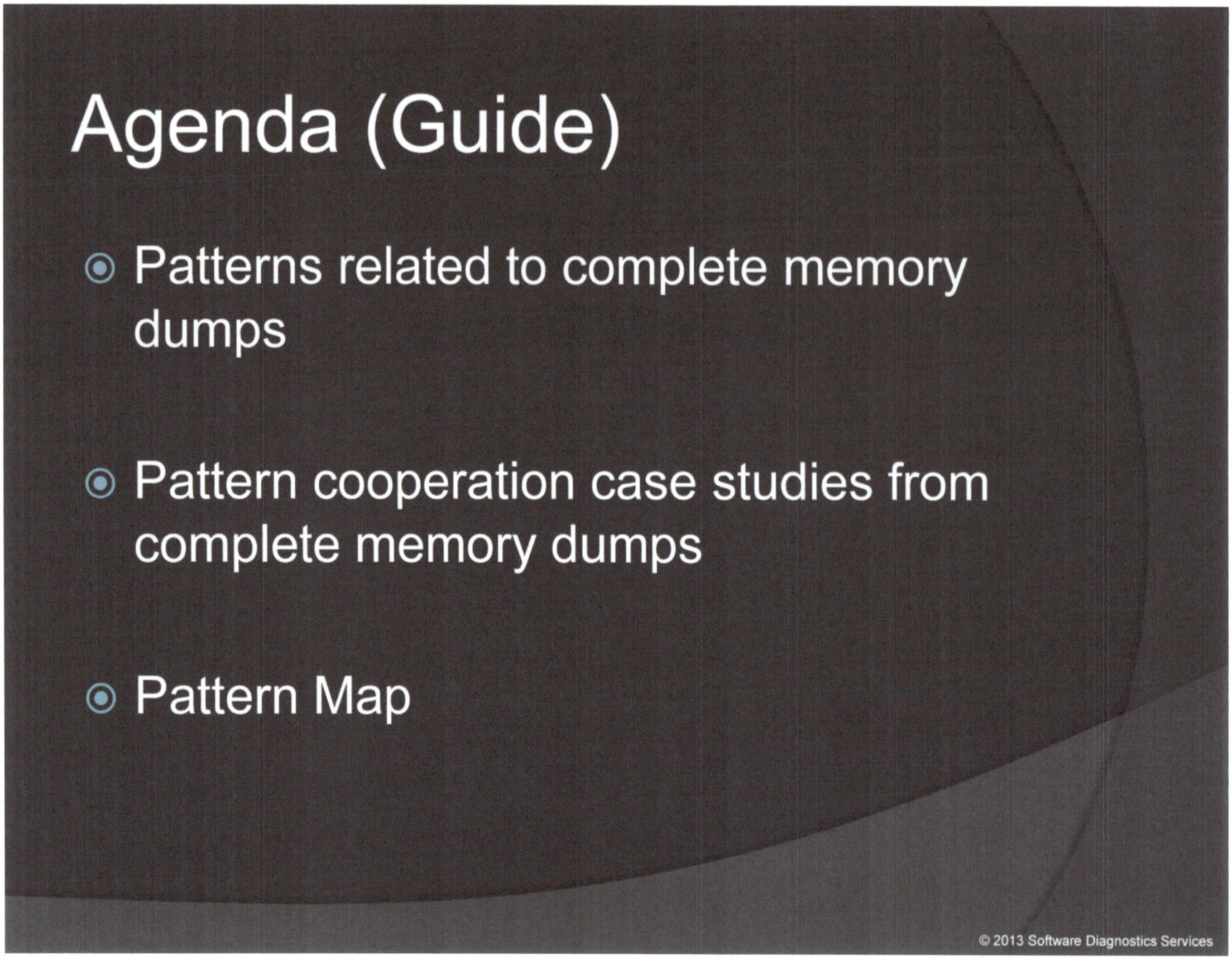

Now I show you a few pattern names and their description links. Since the second version the pattern descriptions and case studies are only available for users of Software Diagnostics Library or in Memory Dump Analysis Anthology volumes.

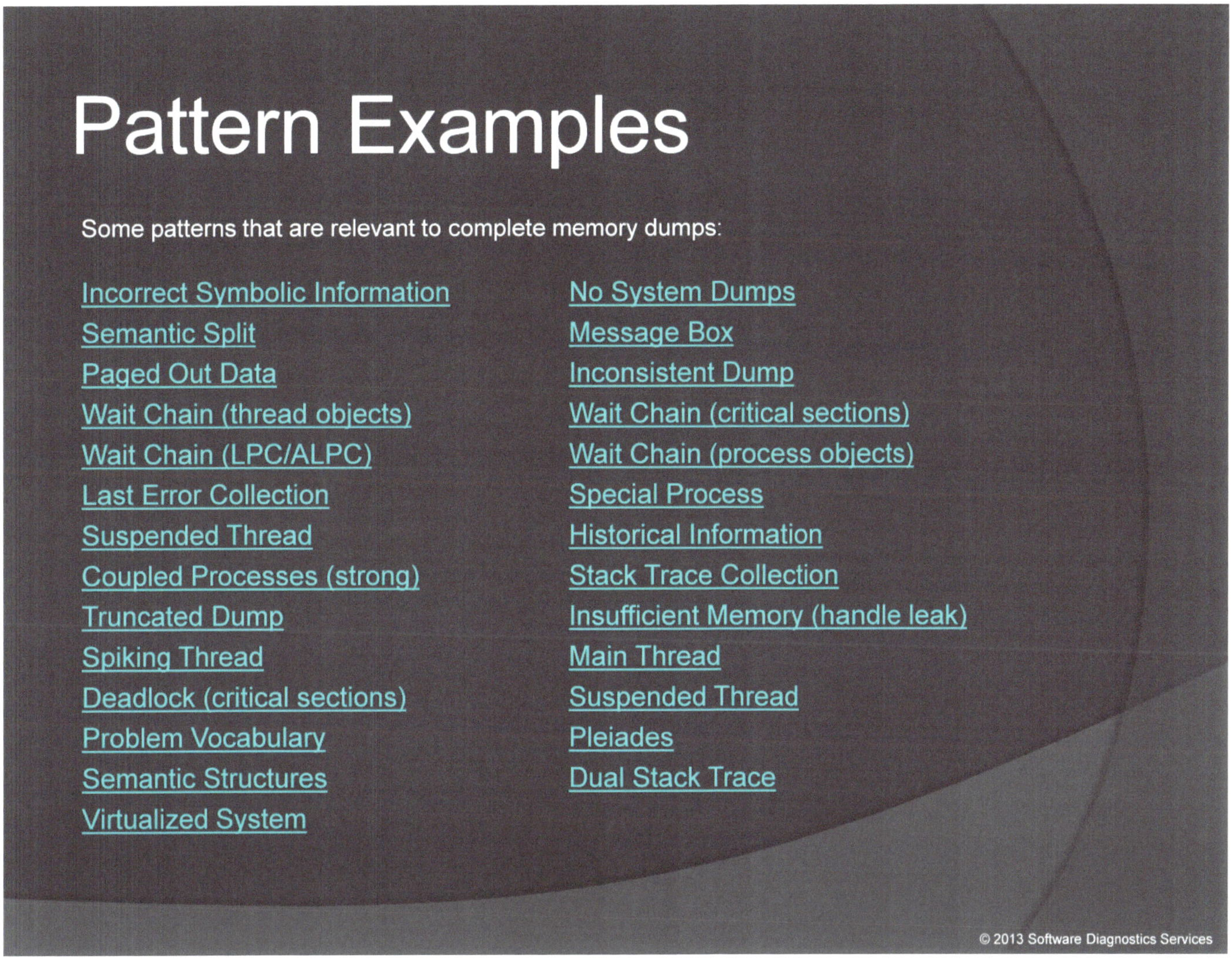

There are many more patterns in fact. Here I only list a few. All of them can be found at Software Diagnostics Institute and its Software Diagnostics Library: www.DumpAnalysis.org

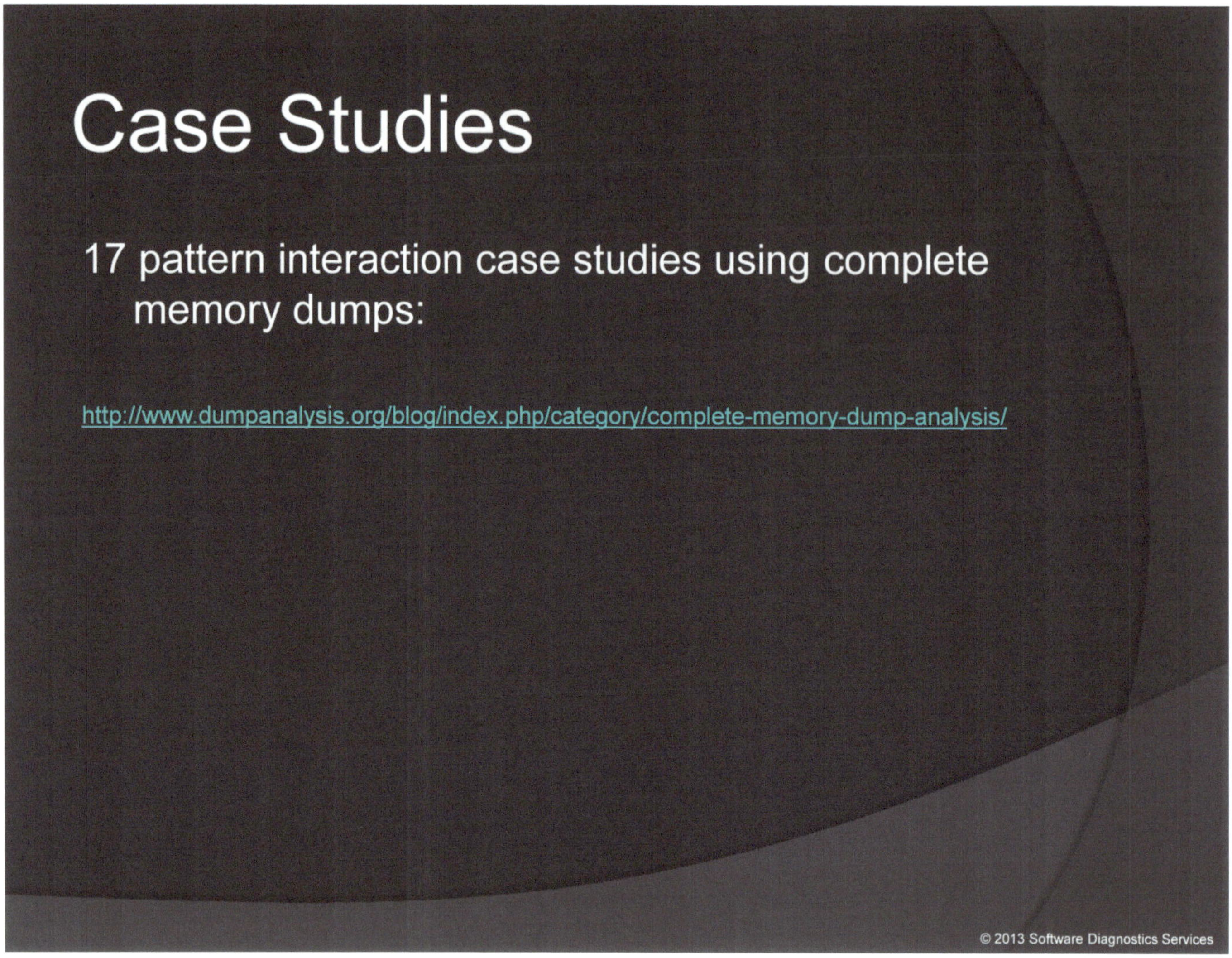

Each case study includes several patterns and is useful to see how patterns are diagnosed in context. The content is available for users of Software Diagnostics Library and from Memory Dump Analysis Anthology volumes:

http://www.dumpanalysis.org/blog/index.php/category/complete-memory-dump-analysis/

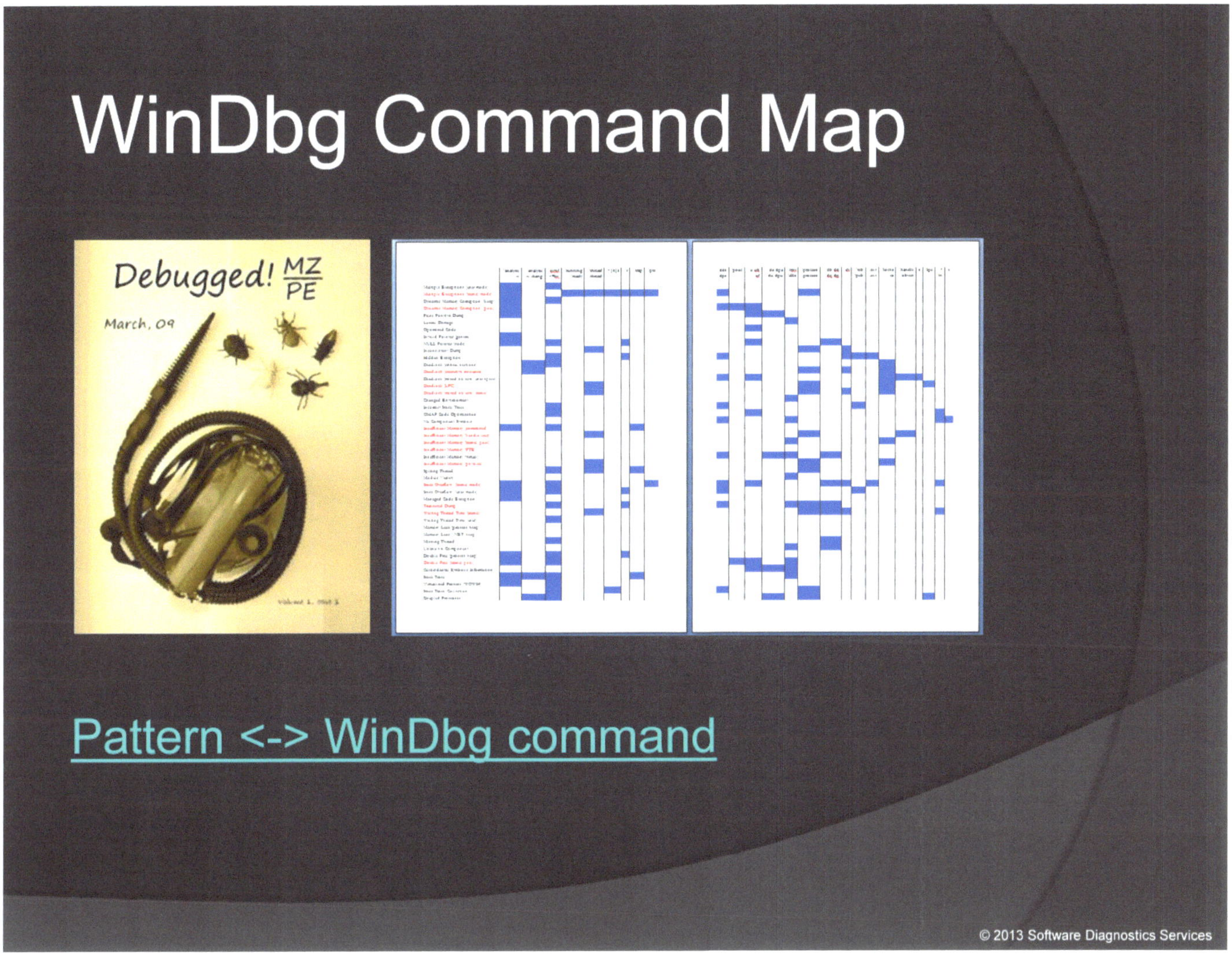

This is a very useful table and map compiled from pattern examples that shows what WinDbg commands can be used for memory dump inspection if you suspect a certain pattern. Unfortunately, more than a hundred patterns have been added since the publication of this map so it needs a revision in 2014.

Pattern <-> WinDbg command:
http://www.amazon.com/Debugged-MZ-PE-Practicing-Engineers/dp/1906717389/

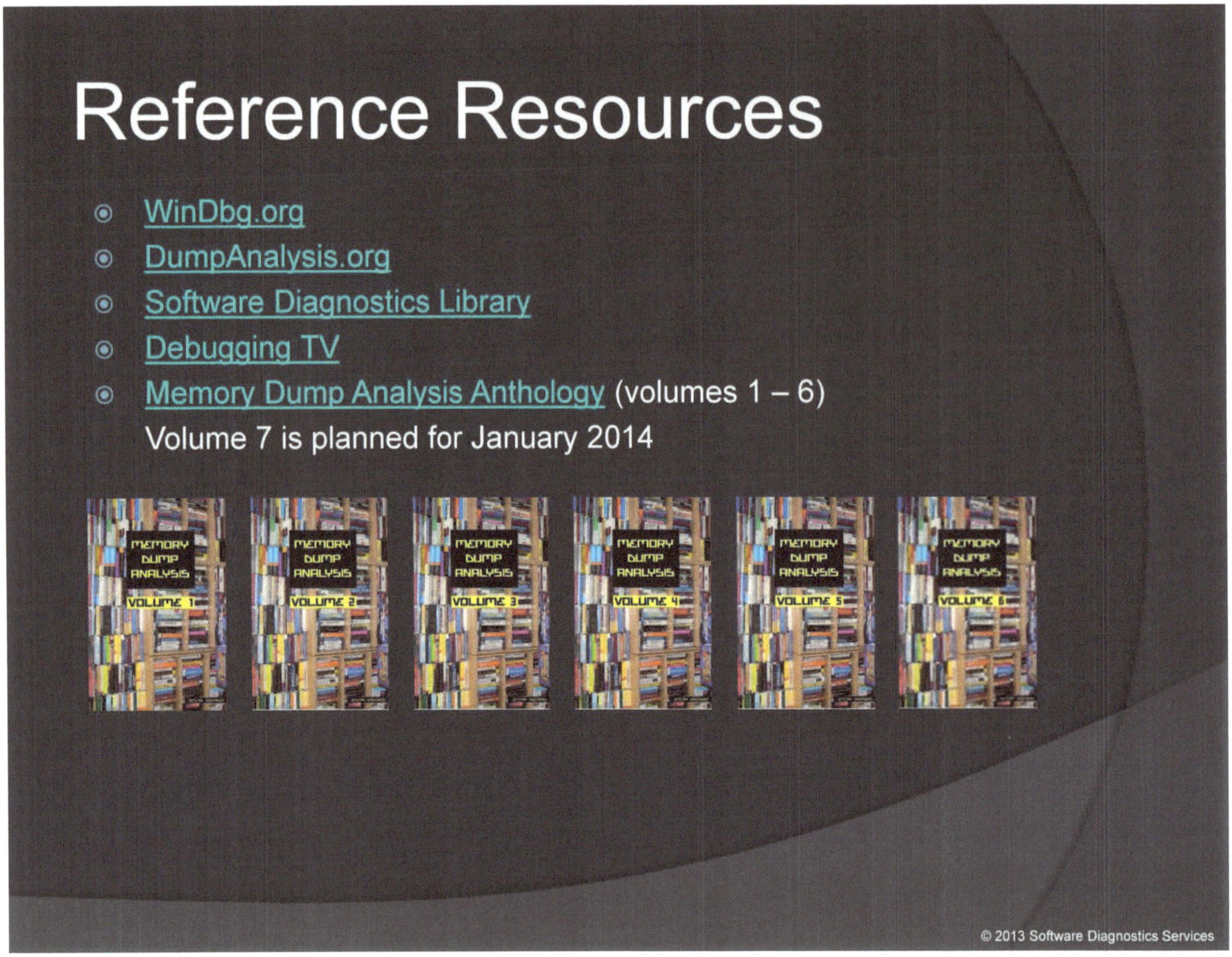

Some useful resources. WinDbg.org also contains links to various WinDbg-related books written by me and other authors.

Software Diagnostics Institute:
http://www.dumpanalysis.org

Debugging TV:
http://www.debugging.tv/

Memory Dump Analysis Anthology: Volumes 1 – 6:
http://www.patterndiagnostics.com/ultimate-memory-analysis-reference

Software Diagnostics Library:
http://www.dumpanalysis.org/blog/

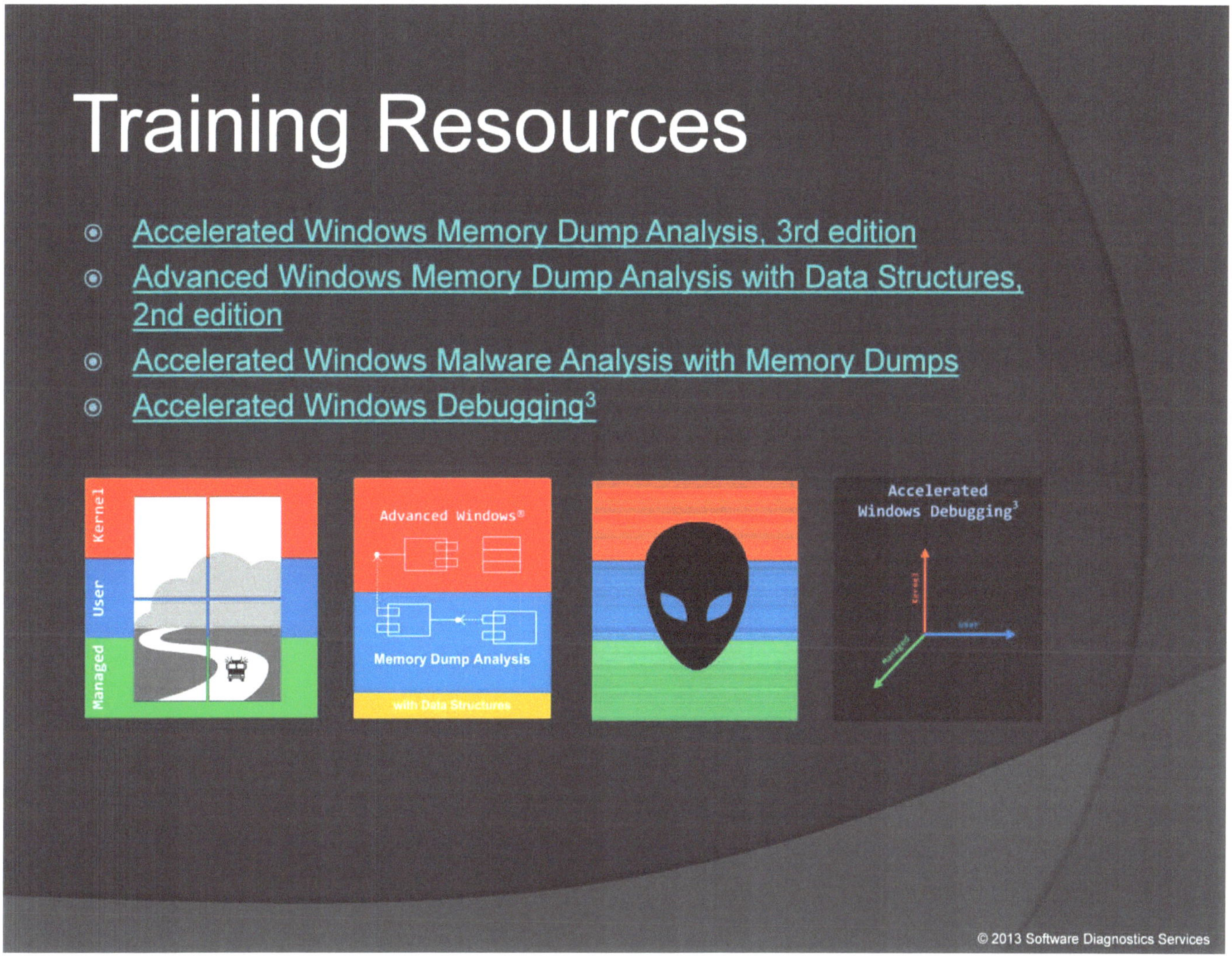

There were 2 new courses added since the second version of this training and the old ones are now having new editions.

Accelerated Windows Memory Dump Analysis, 3rd edition:
http://www.patterndiagnostics.com/accelerated-windows-memory-dump-analysis

Advanced Windows Memory Dump Analysis with Data Structures, 2nd edition:
http://www.patterndiagnostics.com/advanced-windows-memory-dump-analysis

Accelerated Windows Malware Analysis with Memory Dumps:
http://www.patterndiagnostics.com/accelerated-malware-analysis

Accelerated Windows Debugging[3]:
http://www.patterndiagnostics.com/accelerated-windows-debugging-3

The Old New Crash
Cloud Memory Dump Analysis
Dmitry Vostokov
Software Diagnostics Services

Published by OpenTask, Republic of Ireland

OpenTask books and magazines are available through booksellers and distributors worldwide. For further information or comments send requests to press@opentask.com.

A CIP catalogue record for this book is available from the British Library.

ISBN-l3: 978-1-908043-28-3 (Paperback)

First printing, 2013

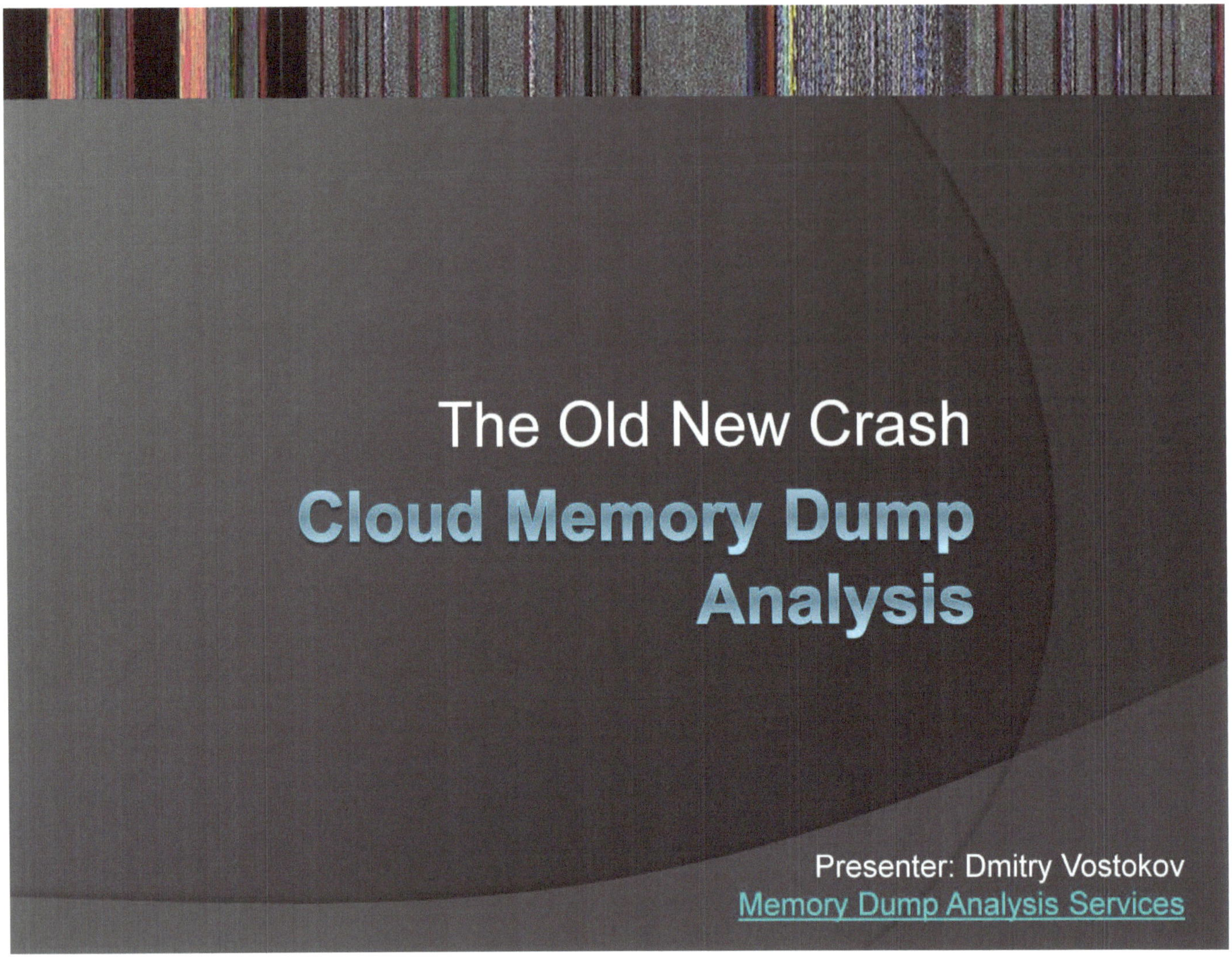

Hello Everyone! My name is Dmitry Vostokov and I'm a founder of Memory Dump Analysis Services which specializes in crash dump analysis and debugging. The topic of today's presentation is cloud memory dump analysis. While preparing for it I learnt a great deal about clouds but this is just a beginning. First a few words about memory dump analysis services.

Memory Dump Analysis Services[1]:
www.dumpanalysis.com

[1] Now **Software Diagnostics Services**: www.patterndiagnostics.com

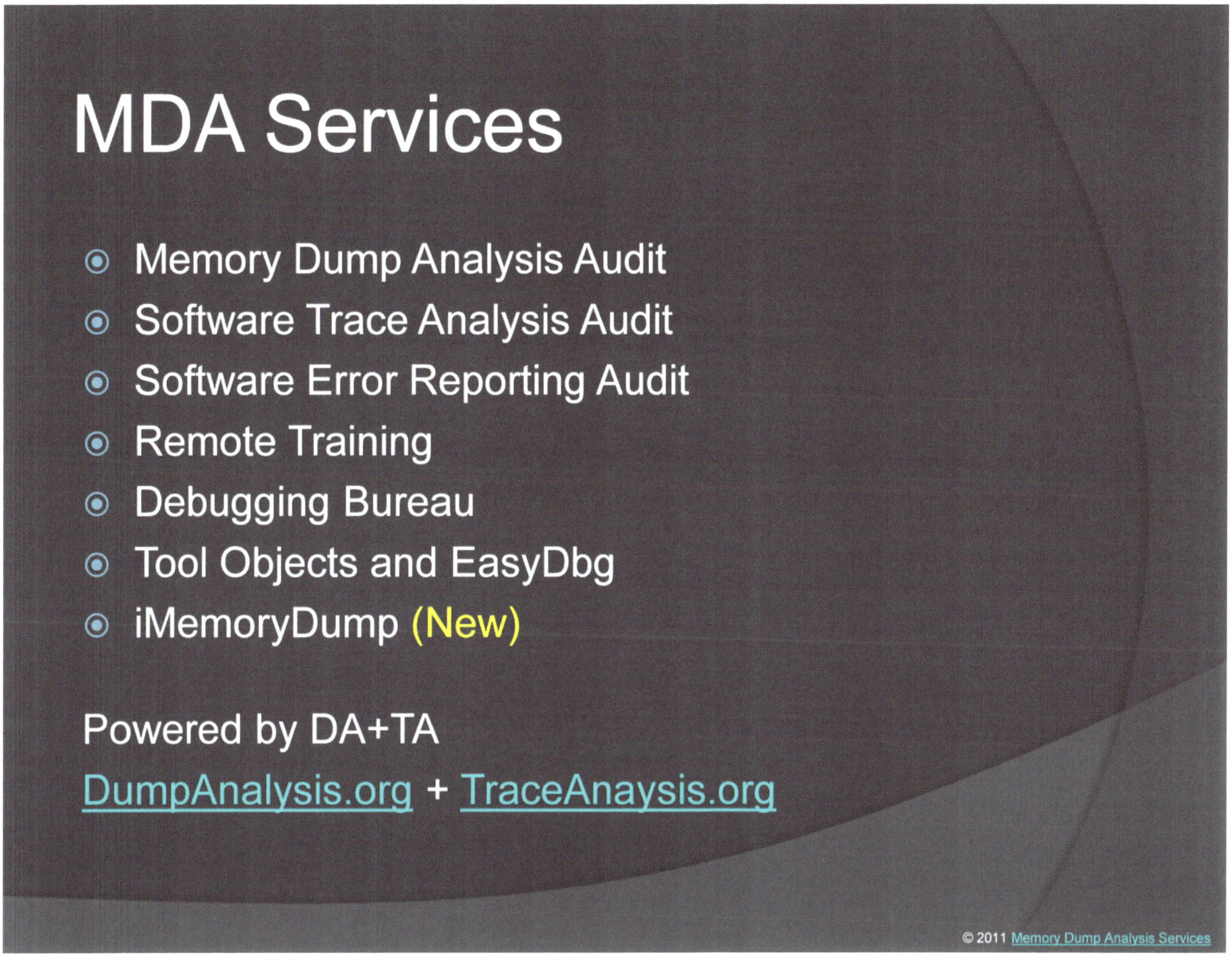

Memory Dump Analysis (MDA) Services was established last summer to provide state of the art training and support to enterprise customers especially in the area of high profile software incidents that require substantial expertise in memory analysis. Later on some other services were added such as software error reporting audit for companies that need to review their software incident reporting and artifact collection and processing. Debugging Bureau of Investigations was modeled on FBI. Memory Dump Analysis Services also owns Tool Objects and Easy Debugger – a powerful platform for integration of troubleshooting and debugging tools (forthcoming later this summer). And, of course, the substantial part of our services is training and seminars. We are fortunate to be powered by DumpAnalysis.org portal – a repository of pattern-driven software problem solving. Some services like iMemoryDump cloud memory dump analysis platform are in development at this time.

I assume that you already have some experience in software troubleshooting and debugging on non-cloud platforms. There is something for everyone in this presentation even if you have used other cloud platforms than Microsoft Windows Azure ('æʒə).

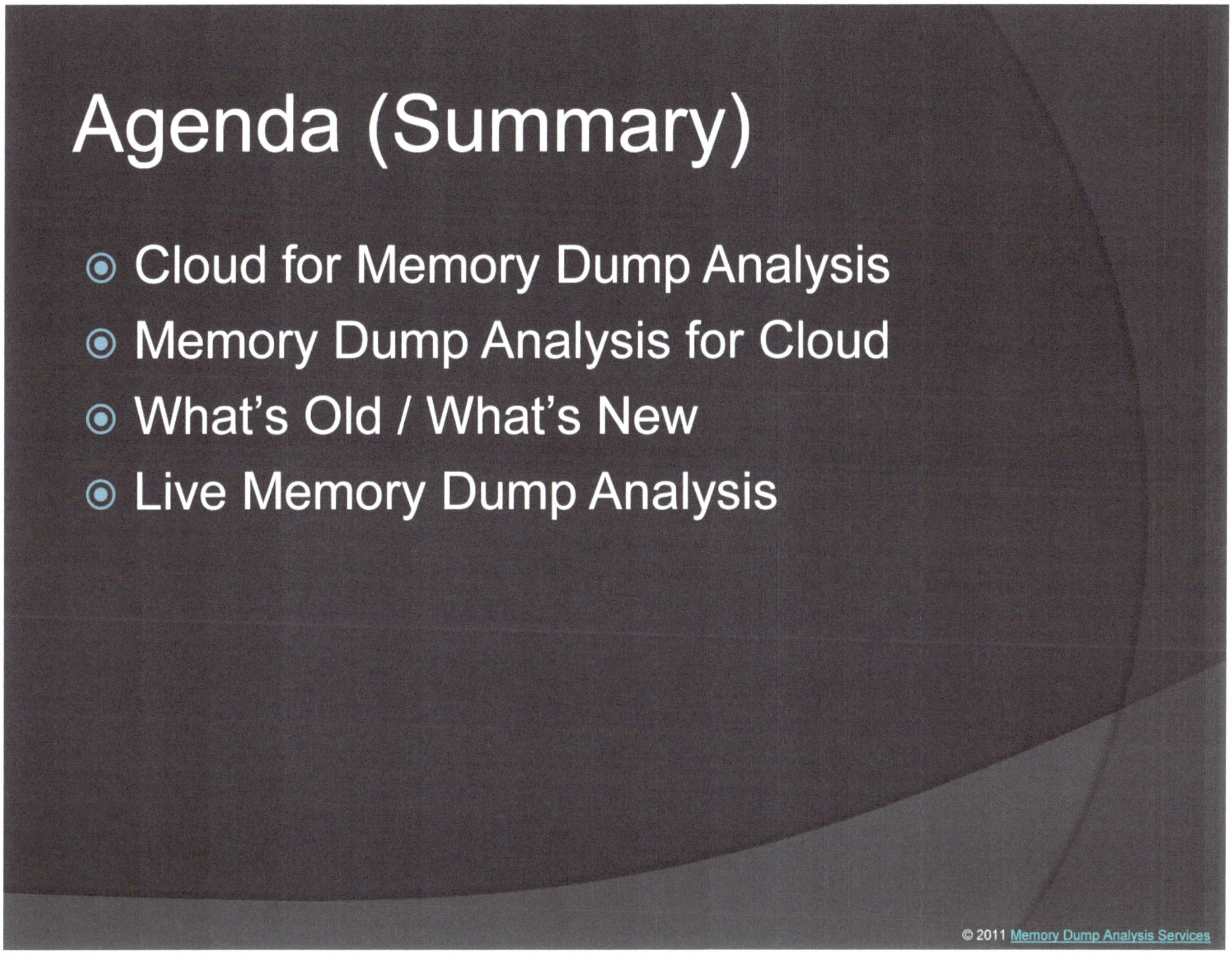

This is a short presentation with 2 hands on live analysis sessions. Instead of trying to cover everything about cloud memory I only provide brief overview, hints and links where to find further information. First, cloud platforns can be used as an infrastructure for doing memory dump analysis. Second, cloud platforms obviously run software and we need to analyse its abnormal behaviour. So, we cover an example of cloud memory dump analysis and see what remains old from non-cloud and what's new.

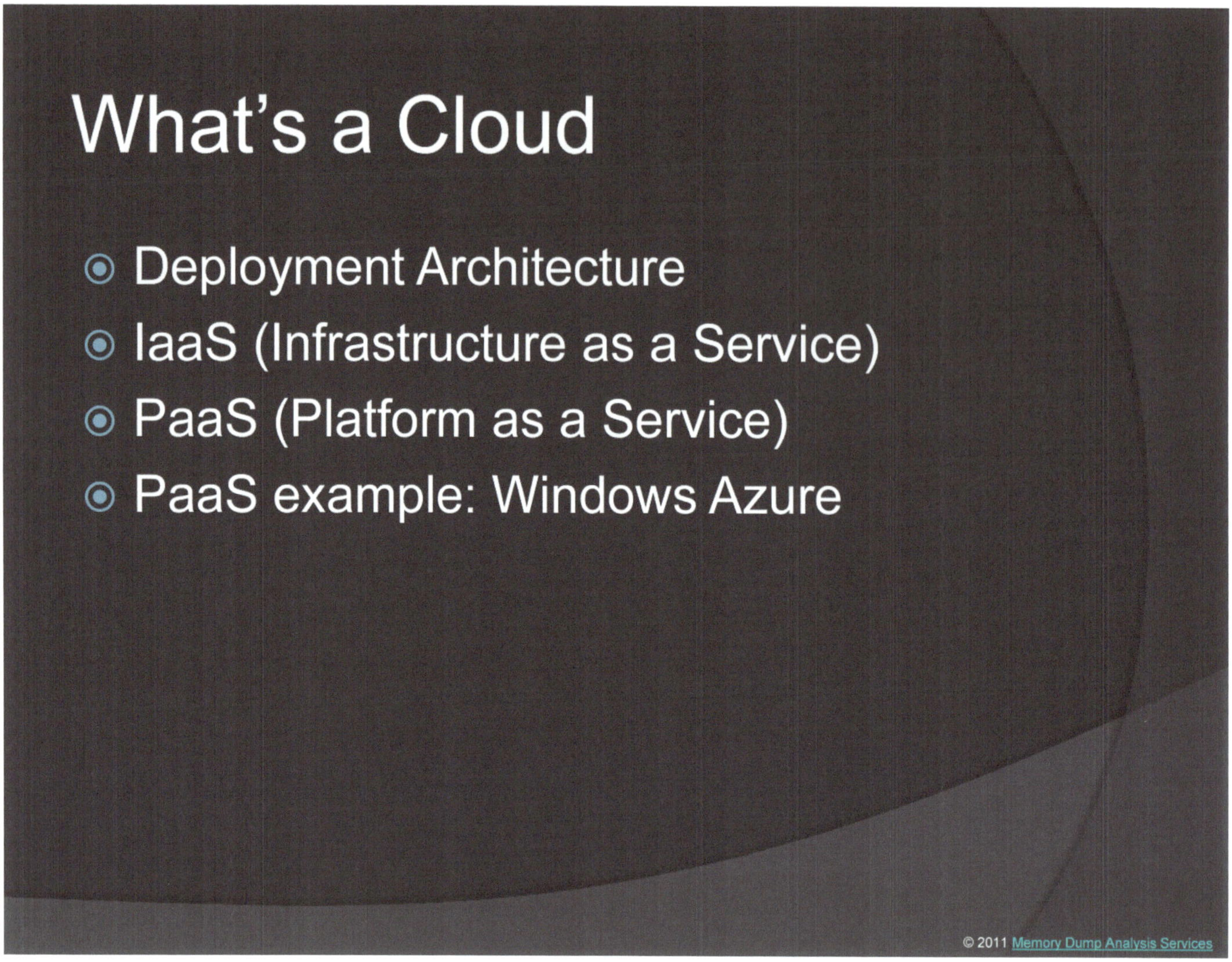

This slide is for you if you only heard about cloud (memory dump analysts are a bit conservative for new technology). So, what's a cloud actually? This is just a deployment platform for your services, in short. Where as in the past you had your own deployment infrastructure or application and virtual/dedicated machine service providers (that are basically like your own) now you use virtual machines / cores located in the centralized huge cloud and assigned to you on demand. We need to understand a few acronims: IaaS (Infrastructure as a Service) and PaaS (Platform as a Service). For the former you use hardware / virtualization infrastructure provided by a cloud provider and supply your own virtual machine templates to provision VMs on demand. For the latter you already use standard VMs with builtin platform for developing your own applications (for example, Microsoft Windows Azure is Windows Server 2008 kernel VM and NET platform for development, although you can always run your own native applications).

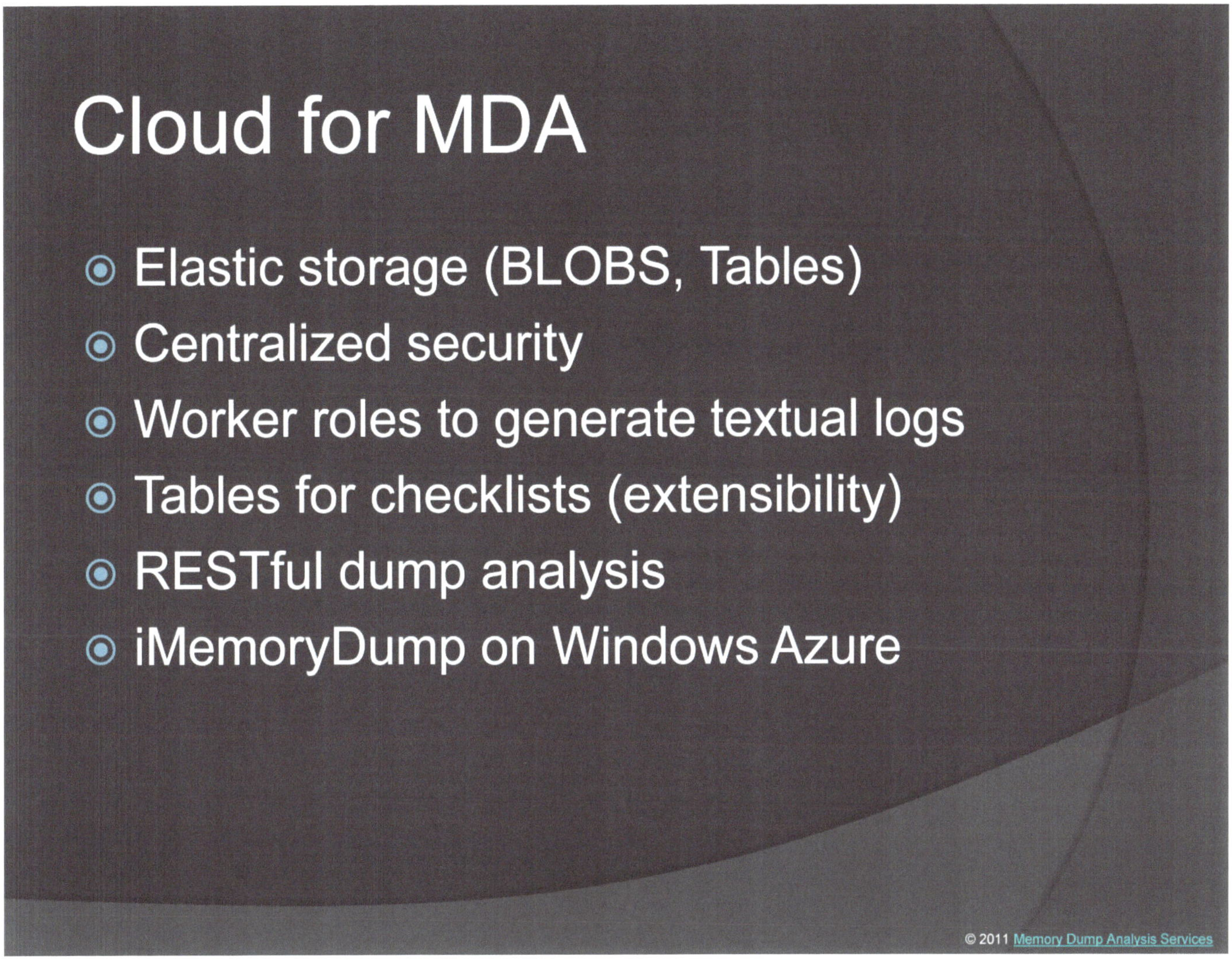

As I mentioned before, cloud platforns can be used as an infrastructure for doing memory dump analysis. What are the advantages then? First, is the elastic BLOB storage for terabytes of memory dumps. You can also use table services for minidumps. There is also a centralized security with fences and guards for your and your customers' memory dumps. Worker roles (Windows Azue terminology) or background services are here to process memory dumps on demand to generate textual logs and other useful information for comparative analysis. You can utilize cloud tables for dynamic checklists to extend your uninterrupted 24x7 memory dump analysis on the fly. Your can also use REST API to peek and poke you memory dumps (in short, use HTTP to query your memory dumps or execute commands). Finally, even Memory Dump Analysis Servivces is jumping into a cloud with a future iMemoryDump service (do you know that to memory dump is a verb?).

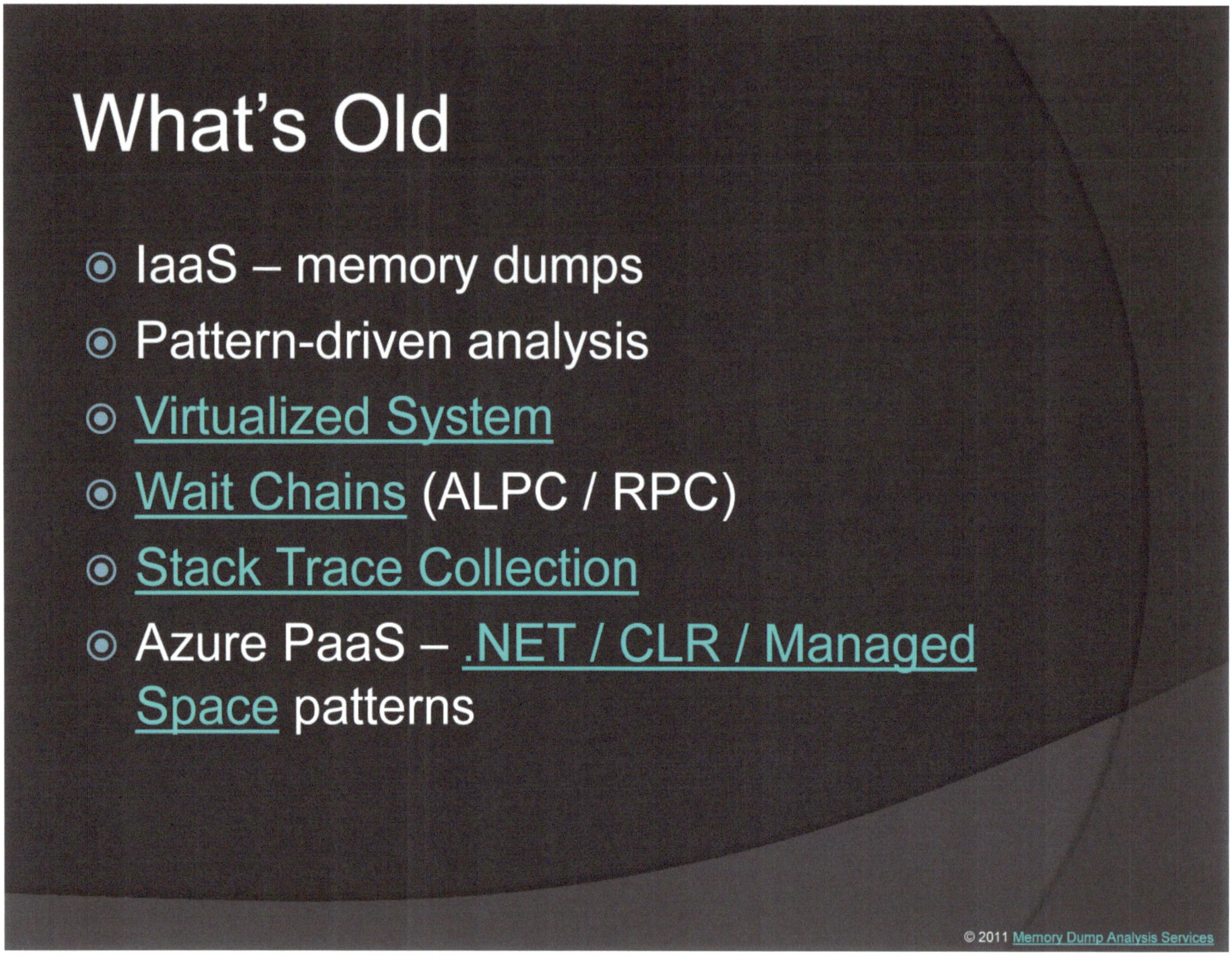

So when we move into cloud realm what does remain the same from old non-cloud times? First of all, if you use IaaS then everything remains the same and most remains the same if you use PaaS. So pattern-driven memory analysis remains the same and simplifies software problem solving in a cloud. Some patterns I would like to highlight are Virtualized System, Wait Chains for PaaS because the cloud platform needs to kown the health of your cloud applications and services. Because of the mass of uniform cloud virtual machines you need to have reference stack traces to compare your traces against. For Windows Azure PaaS you also have traditional .NET managed space memory analysis patterns as well.

Virtualized System:
http://www.dumpanalysis.org/blog/index.php/2009/07/10/crash-dump-analysis-patterns-part-87/

Wait Chains:
http://www.dumpanalysis.org/blog/index.php/2009/02/17/wait-chain-patterns/

Stack Trace Collection:
http://www.dumpanalysis.org/blog/index.php/2007/09/14/crash-dump-analysis-patterns-part-27/

.NET / CLR / Managed Space:
http://www.dumpanalysis.org/blog/index.php/2011/04/22/net-clr-managed-space-patterns/

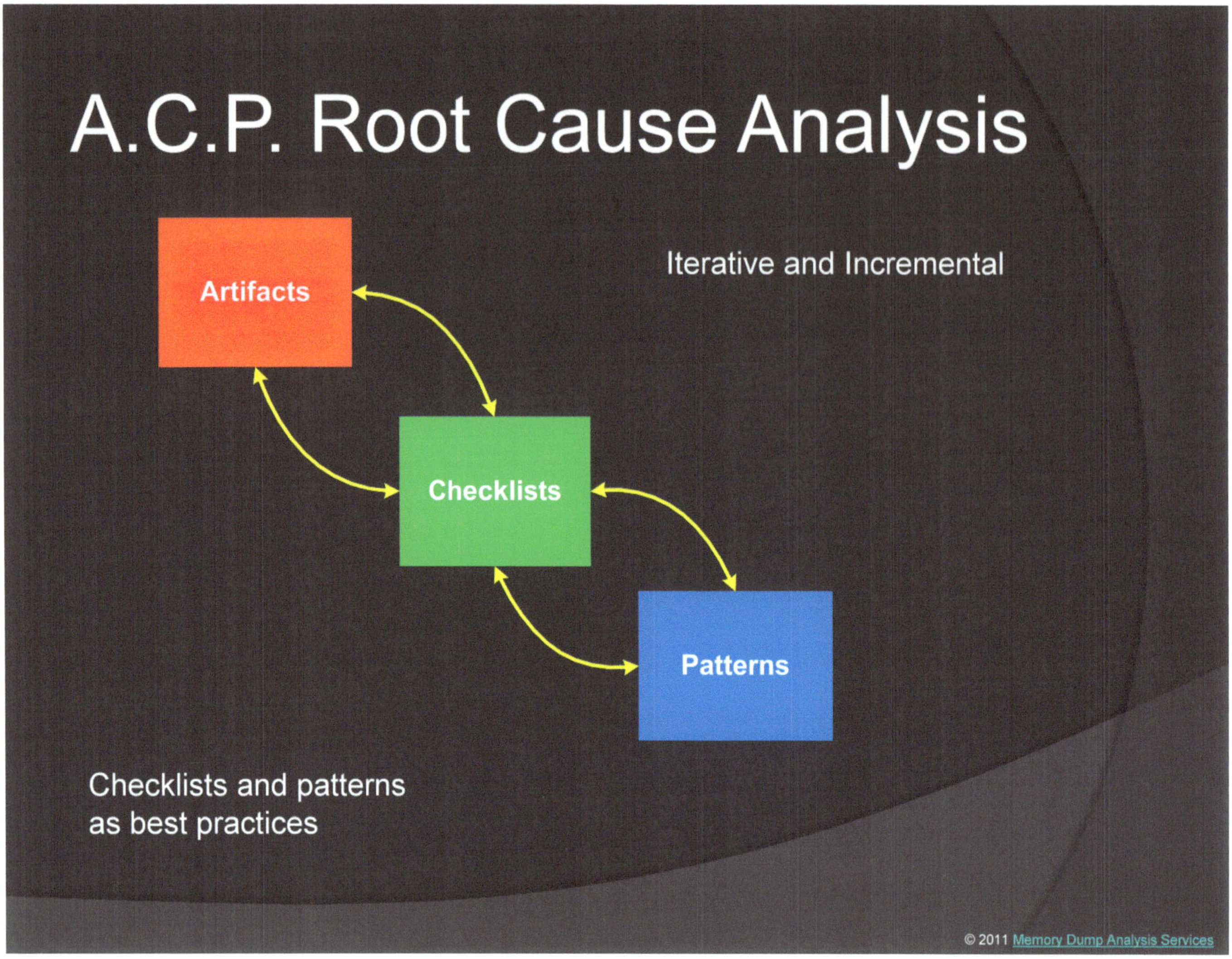

This slide reminds you of a pattern-driven approach to analysis of memory dump artifacts. We are evangelists of A.C.P. iterative and incremental root cause analysis methodology that includes artifacts such as software traces and memory dumps, checklists, and patterns.

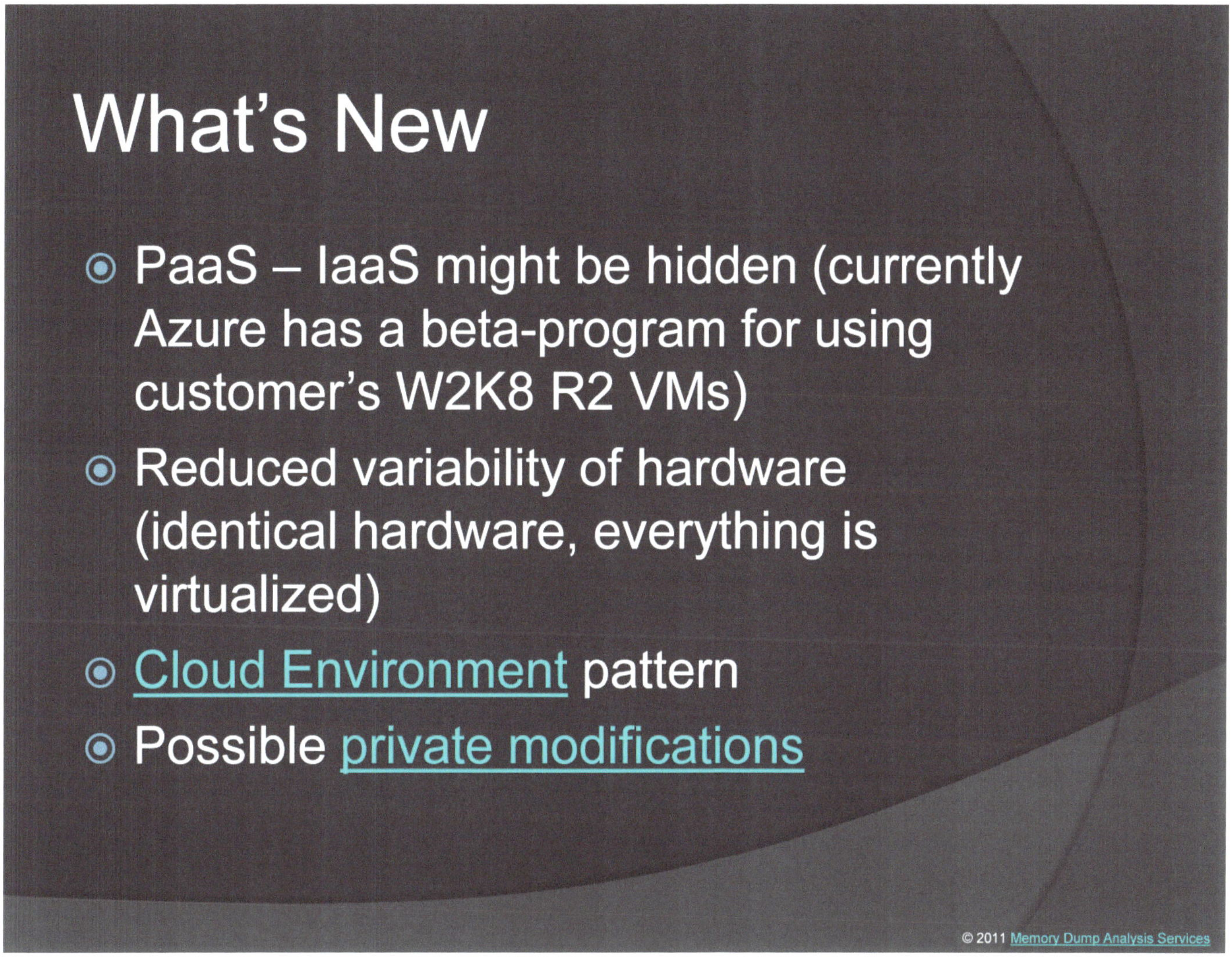

Now, what's new. We have discovered that in using PaaS platform the underlying infrastructure including VM internals might be hidden. The closed private infrastructure might reduce the amout of information available for troubleshooting and debugging. For cloud platforms (especially PaaS) uniform deployment environment greatly reduces some classes of abnormal software behaviour and some patterns will be less frequent. There is one new Cloud Environment pattern and a few are forthcoming soon.

Cloud Environment:
http://www.dumpanalysis.org/blog/index.php/2011/06/12/crash-dump-analysis-patterns-part-137/

Private modifications:
http://www.dumpanalysis.org/blog/index.php/2011/06/12/crash-dump-analysis-patterns-part-138/

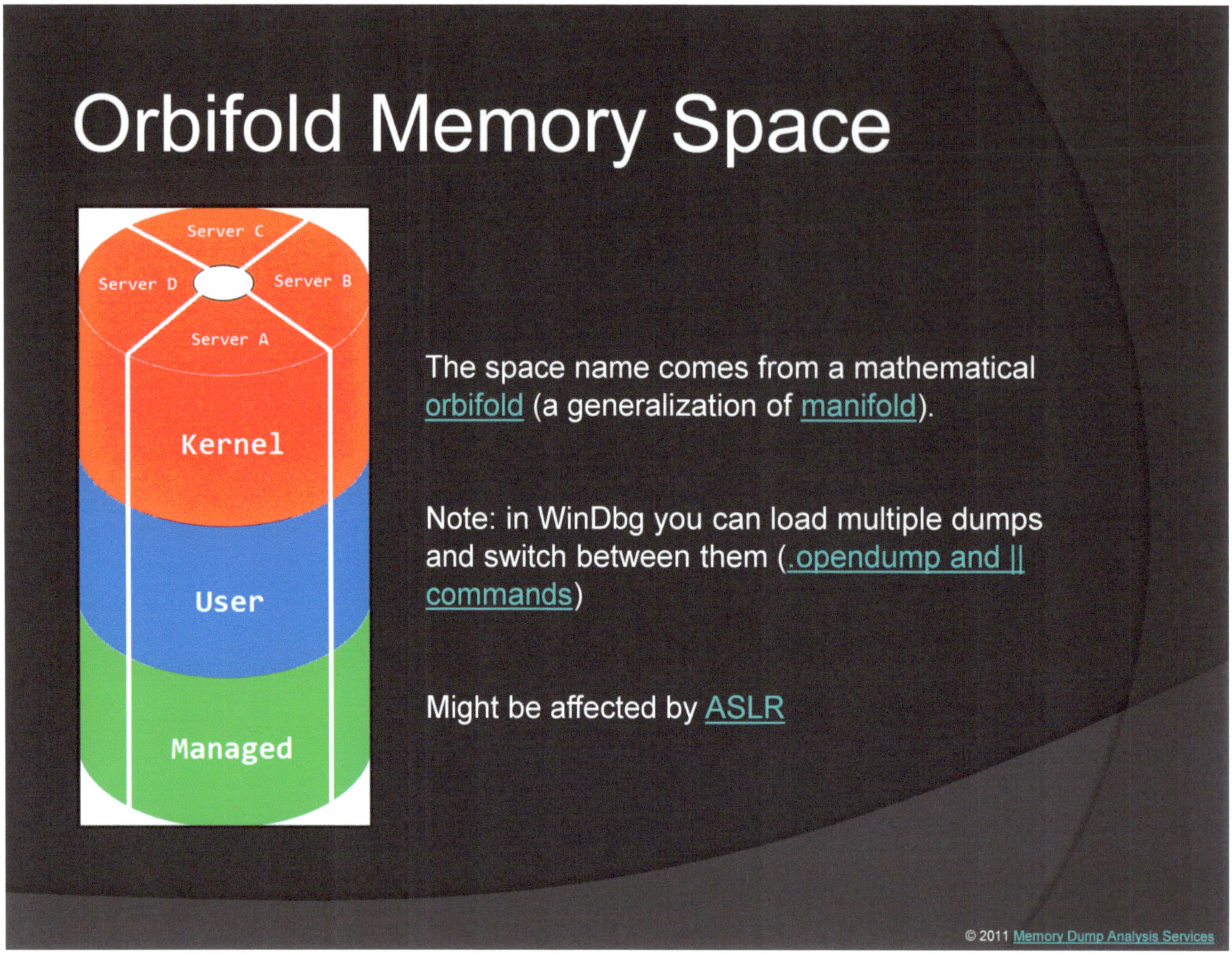

Because of so many similar standardized memory spaces they can be combined into one giant memory space that we call an orbifold memory space.

Orbifold:
http://en.wikipedia.org/wiki/Orbifold

Manifold:
http://en.wikipedia.org/wiki/Manifold

.opendump and || commands:
http://www.dumpanalysis.org/blog/index.php/2010/01/06/windbg-shortcuts-opendump/

ASLR:
http://www.dumpanalysis.org/blog/index.php/2007/05/22/aslr-address-space-layout-randomization/

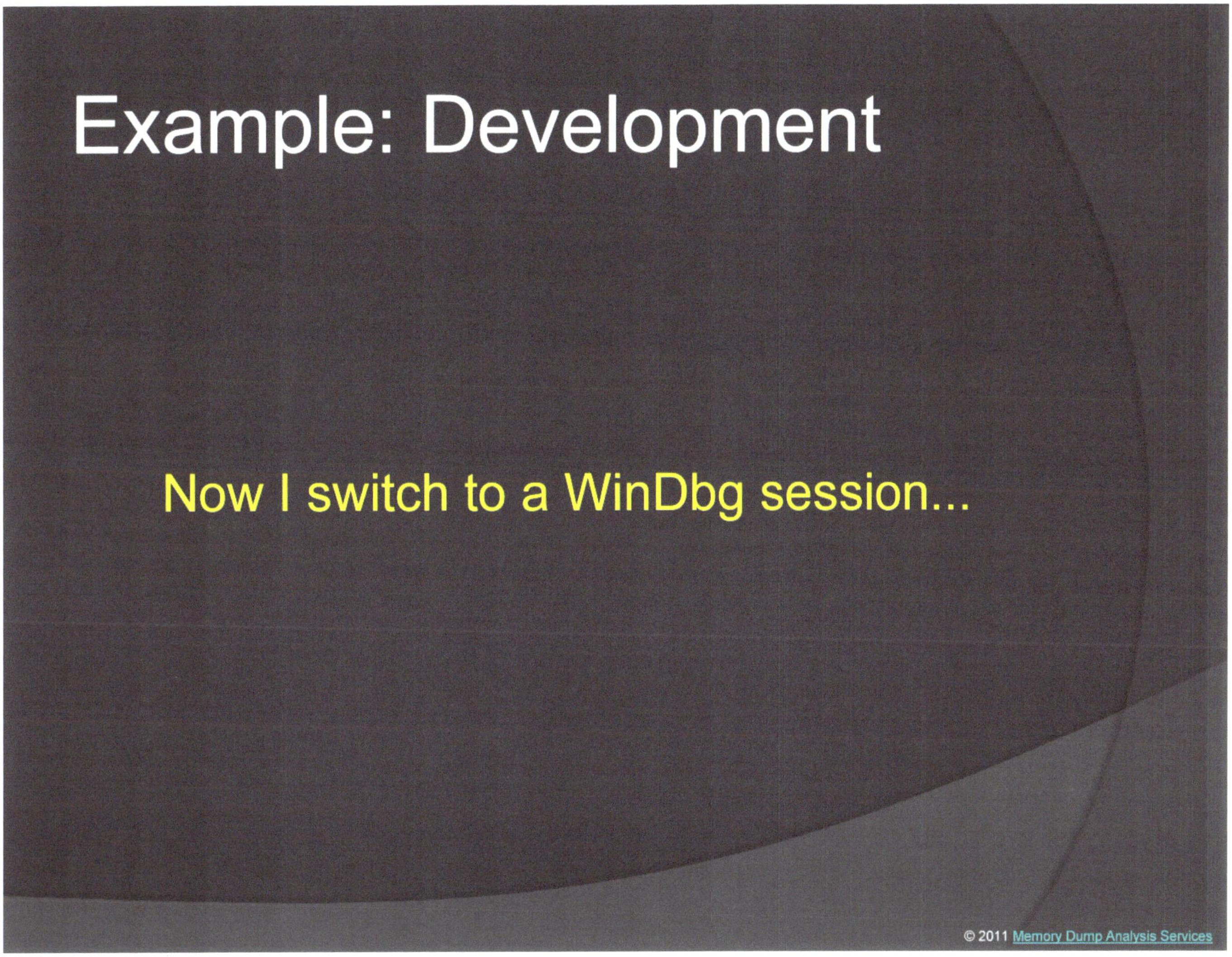

I chose Microsoft Windows Azure because most pattern examples are for Windows platforms.

Before you deploy to a stage or production Azure cloud you typically debug in your development Azure environment.

To generate crash dumps I created a .NET worker service role for Windows Azure that does a NULL pointer dereference. Here is a source code from WorkerRole.cs:

```
using System;
using System.Collections.Generic;
using System.Diagnostics;
using System.Linq;
using System.Net;
using System.Threading;
using Microsoft.WindowsAzure;
using Microsoft.WindowsAzure.Diagnostics;
using Microsoft.WindowsAzure.ServiceRuntime;
using Microsoft.WindowsAzure.StorageClient;
using Microsoft.WindowsAzure.Diagnostics.Management;

namespace TestWERWorker
{
    public class WorkerRole : RoleEntryPoint
    {
        public override void Run()
        {
            Trace.WriteLine("TestWAERWorker entry point called", "Information");

            Thread.Sleep(60000);

            unsafe
            {
                int* p = null;
                *p = 1;
            };

            while (true)
            {
                Thread.Sleep(10000);
                Trace.WriteLine("Working", "Information");
            }
        }

        public override bool OnStart()
        {
            // Set the maximum number of concurrent connections
            ServicePointManager.DefaultConnectionLimit = 12;

            CrashDumps.EnableCollection(true);

            DiagnosticMonitorConfiguration config = DiagnosticMonitor.GetDefaultInitialConfiguration();
            string conn_str =
RoleEnvironment.GetConfigurationSettingValue("Microsoft.WindowsAzure.Plugins.Diagnostics.ConnectionString");
            CloudStorageAccount account = CloudStorageAccount.Parse(conn_str);
            config.Directories.ScheduledTransferPeriod = TimeSpan.FromMinutes(1);
            DiagnosticMonitor diagnosticMonitor = DiagnosticMonitor.Start(account, config);

            CrashDumps.EnableCollection(true);

            return base.OnStart();
        }
    }
}
```

The following forum discussion really helped me to get things right:
http://stackoverflow.com/questions/5727692/azure-crash-dumps-not-appearing.
So I'd like to thank Oliver Bock here.

If you want to deploy it to Windows Azure then don't forget to add your storage account name and its key in the service configuration file. For your development environment you will need to replace the whole value with "UseDevelopmentStorage=true".

Here is the output of some WinDbg commands from the log file:

```
Opened log file 'c:\training\wasession2.log'
0:016> !analyze -v
*******************************************************************************
*                                                                             *
*                        Exception Analysis                                   *
*                                                                             *
*******************************************************************************

!pe
Exception object: 0000000002ff6c58
Exception type:   System.NullReferenceException
Message:          Object reference not set to an instance of an object.
InnerException:   <none>
StackTrace (generated):
    SP               IP               Function
    0000000024ADE600 000007FF00803D1E TestWER!TestWER.WorkerRole.Run()+0x5e
    0000000024ADE640 000007FF00803AB7 Microsoft_WindowsAzure_ServiceRuntime!Microsoft.WindowsAzure.ServiceRuntime.RoleEnvironment.StartRoleInternal()+0x137
    0000000024ADE6E0 000007FF00803956 Microsoft_WindowsAzure_ServiceRuntime!Microsoft.WindowsAzure.ServiceRuntime.RoleEnvironment.StartRole()+0x96
    0000000024ADE730 000007FF00803898
Microsoft_WindowsAzure_ServiceRuntime!Microsoft.WindowsAzure.ServiceRuntime.Implementation.Loader.RoleRuntimeBridge.<StartRole>b__1()+0x38
    0000000024ADE770 000007FEEA4E181C mscorlib_ni!System.Threading.ExecutionContext.Run(System.Threading.ExecutionContext, System.Threading.ContextCallback,
System.Object, Boolean)+0xdc
    0000000024ADE7D0 000007FEEA4E172B mscorlib_ni!System.Threading.ExecutionContext.Run(System.Threading.ExecutionContext, System.Threading.ContextCallback,
System.Object)+0x3b
    0000000024ADE820 000007FEEA576F2D mscorlib_ni!System.Threading.ThreadHelper.ThreadStart()+0x4d

StackTraceString: <none>
HResult: 80004003
!pe 2ff6c58

Exception object: 0000000002ff6c58
Exception type:   System.NullReferenceException
Message:          Object reference not set to an instance of an object.
InnerException:   <none>
StackTrace (generated):
    SP               IP               Function
    0000000024ADE600 000007FF00803D1E TestWER!TestWER.WorkerRole.Run()+0x5e
    0000000024ADE640 000007FF00803AB7 Microsoft_WindowsAzure_ServiceRuntime!Microsoft.WindowsAzure.ServiceRuntime.RoleEnvironment.StartRoleInternal()+0x137
    0000000024ADE6E0 000007FF00803956 Microsoft_WindowsAzure_ServiceRuntime!Microsoft.WindowsAzure.ServiceRuntime.RoleEnvironment.StartRole()+0x96
    0000000024ADE730 000007FF00803898
Microsoft_WindowsAzure_ServiceRuntime!Microsoft.WindowsAzure.ServiceRuntime.Implementation.Loader.RoleRuntimeBridge.<StartRole>b__1()+0x38
    0000000024ADE770 000007FEEA4E181C mscorlib_ni!System.Threading.ExecutionContext.Run(System.Threading.ExecutionContext, System.Threading.ContextCallback,
System.Object, Boolean)+0xdc
    0000000024ADE7D0 000007FEEA4E172B mscorlib_ni!System.Threading.ExecutionContext.Run(System.Threading.ExecutionContext, System.Threading.ContextCallback,
System.Object)+0x3b
    0000000024ADE820 000007FEEA576F2D mscorlib_ni!System.Threading.ThreadHelper.ThreadStart()+0x4d

StackTraceString: <none>
HResult: 80004003
GetPageUrlData failed, server returned HTTP status 404
URL requested: http://watson.microsoft.com/StageOne/WaWorkerHost_exe/6_0_6002_18009/4d6ac6d0/unknown/0_0_0_0/bbbbbbb4/c0000005/00803d1e.htm?Retriage=1

FAULTING_IP:
+6d38af0
000007ff`00803d1e c70001000000    mov     dword ptr [rax],1

EXCEPTION_RECORD:  ffffffffffffffff -- (.exr 0xffffffffffffffff)
.exr 0xffffffffffffffff
ExceptionAddress: 000007ff00803d1e
   ExceptionCode: c0000005 (Access violation)
  ExceptionFlags: 00000000
NumberParameters: 2
   Parameter[0]: 0000000000000001
   Parameter[1]: 0000000000000000
Attempt to write to address 0000000000000000

PROCESS_NAME:  WaWorkerHost.exe

ERROR_CODE: (NTSTATUS) 0xc0000005 - The instruction at 0x%08lx referenced memory at 0x%08lx. The memory could not be %s.

EXCEPTION_CODE: (NTSTATUS) 0xc0000005 - The instruction at 0x%08lx referenced memory at 0x%08lx. The memory could not be %s.

EXCEPTION_PARAMETER1:  0000000000000001

EXCEPTION_PARAMETER2:  0000000000000000

WRITE_ADDRESS:  0000000000000000

FOLLOWUP_IP:
+6d38af0
000007ff`00803d1e c70001000000    mov     dword ptr [rax],1

FAILED_INSTRUCTION_ADDRESS:
+6d38af0
000007ff`00803d1e c70001000000    mov     dword ptr [rax],1

MOD_LIST: <ANALYSIS/>

NTGLOBALFLAG:  0

APPLICATION_VERIFIER_FLAGS:  0

MANAGED_STACK:
SP               IP               Function
    0000000024ADE600 000007FF00803D1E TestWER!TestWER.WorkerRole.Run()+0x5e
    0000000024ADE640 000007FF00803AB7 Microsoft_WindowsAzure_ServiceRuntime!Microsoft.WindowsAzure.ServiceRuntime.RoleEnvironment.StartRoleInternal()+0x137
    0000000024ADE6E0 000007FF00803956 Microsoft_WindowsAzure_ServiceRuntime!Microsoft.WindowsAzure.ServiceRuntime.RoleEnvironment.StartRole()+0x96
```

```
    0000000024ADE730 000007FF00803898
Microsoft_WindowsAzure_ServiceRuntime!Microsoft.WindowsAzure.ServiceRuntime.Implementation.Loader.RoleRuntimeBridge.<StartRole>b__1()+0x38
    0000000024ADE770 000007FEEA4E181C mscorlib_ni!System.Threading.ExecutionContext.Run(System.Threading.ExecutionContext, System.Threading.ContextCallback,
System.Object, Boolean)+0xdc
    0000000024ADE7D0 000007FEEA4E172B mscorlib_ni!System.Threading.ExecutionContext.Run(System.Threading.ExecutionContext, System.Threading.ContextCallback,
System.Object)+0x3b
    0000000024ADE820 000007FEEA576F2D mscorlib_ni!System.Threading.ThreadHelper.ThreadStart()+0x4d

StackTraceString: <none>
HResult: 80004003

EXCEPTION_OBJECT: !pe 2ff6c58
!pe 2ff6c58

Exception object: 0000000002ff6c58
Exception type:   System.NullReferenceException
Message:          Object reference not set to an instance of an object.
InnerException:   <none>
StackTrace (generated):
    SP               IP               Function
    0000000024ADE600 000007FF00803D1E TestWER!TestWER.WorkerRole.Run()+0x5e
    0000000024ADE640 000007FF00803AB7 Microsoft_WindowsAzure_ServiceRuntime!Microsoft.WindowsAzure.ServiceRuntime.RoleEnvironment.StartRoleInternal()+0x137
    0000000024ADE6E0 000007FF00803956 Microsoft_WindowsAzure_ServiceRuntime!Microsoft.WindowsAzure.ServiceRuntime.RoleEnvironment.StartRole()+0x96
    0000000024ADE730 000007FF00803898
Microsoft_WindowsAzure_ServiceRuntime!Microsoft.WindowsAzure.ServiceRuntime.Implementation.Loader.RoleRuntimeBridge.<StartRole>b__1()+0x38
    0000000024ADE770 000007FEEA4E181C mscorlib_ni!System.Threading.ExecutionContext.Run(System.Threading.ExecutionContext, System.Threading.ContextCallback,
System.Object, Boolean)+0xdc
    0000000024ADE7D0 000007FEEA4E172B mscorlib_ni!System.Threading.ExecutionContext.Run(System.Threading.ExecutionContext, System.Threading.ContextCallback,
System.Object)+0x3b
    0000000024ADE820 000007FEEA576F2D mscorlib_ni!System.Threading.ThreadHelper.ThreadStart()+0x4d

StackTraceString: <none>
HResult: 80004003

MANAGED_OBJECT: !dumpobj 2f4e3c8
!dumpobj 2f4e3c8

Name:        System.String
MethodTable: 000007feea636960
EEClass:     000007feea1beec8
Size:        132(0x84) bytes
File:        C:\Windows\Microsoft.Net\assembly\GAC_64\mscorlib\v4.0_4.0.0.0__b77a5c561934e089\mscorlib.dll
String:      Object reference not set to an instance of an object.
Fields:
              MT    Field   Offset                 Type VT     Attr            Value Name
000007feea63c848  40000ed        8         System.Int32  1 instance               53 m_stringLength
000007feea63b388  40000ee        c          System.Char  1 instance               4f m_firstChar
000007feea636960  40000ef       10        System.String  0   shared           static Empty
                                 >> Domain:Value  00000000006f7f10:0000000002eb1420 00000000007a3b00:0000000002eb1420 <<

EXCEPTION_MESSAGE:  Object reference not set to an instance of an object.

MANAGED_OBJECT_NAME:  System.NullReferenceException

MANAGED_STACK_COMMAND:  !pe 2ff6c58


LAST_CONTROL_TRANSFER:  from 000007feeb70507c to 000007fefd72aa7d

ADDITIONAL_DEBUG_TEXT:  Followup set based on attribute [Is_ChosenCrashFollowupThread] from Frame:[0] on thread:[PSEUDO_THREAD]

FAULTING_THREAD:  ffffffffffffffff

DEFAULT_BUCKET_ID:  NULL_INSTRUCTION_PTR_CALL

PRIMARY_PROBLEM_CLASS:  NULL_INSTRUCTION_PTR_CALL

BUGCHECK_STR:  APPLICATION_FAULT_NULL_INSTRUCTION_PTR_NULL_POINTER_WRITE_WRONG_SYMBOLS_CALL__SYSTEM.NULLREFERENCEEXCEPTION

STACK_TEXT:
00000000`24ade600 00000000`ffffffff testwer!TestWER.WorkerRole.Run+0x5e
00000000`24ade640 00000000`ffffffff microsoft_windowsazure_serviceruntime!Microsoft.WindowsAzure.ServiceRuntime.RoleEnvironment.StartRoleInternal+0x137
00000000`24ade6e0 00000000`ffffffff microsoft_windowsazure_serviceruntime!Microsoft.WindowsAzure.ServiceRuntime.RoleEnvironment.StartRole+0x96
00000000`24ade730 00000000`ffffffff
microsoft_windowsazure_serviceruntime!Microsoft.WindowsAzure.ServiceRuntime.Implementation.Loader.RoleRuntimeBridge._StartRole_b__1+0x38
00000000`24ade770 00000000`ffffffff mscorlib_ni!System.Threading.ExecutionContext.Run+0xdc
00000000`24ade7d0 00000000`ffffffff mscorlib_ni!System.Threading.ExecutionContext.Run+0x3b
00000000`24ade820 00000000`ffffffff mscorlib_ni!System.Threading.ThreadHelper.ThreadStart+0x4d


SYMBOL_NAME:  testwer!TestWER.WorkerRole.Run

FOLLOWUP_NAME:  MachineOwner

MODULE_NAME: testwer

IMAGE_NAME:  TestWER.dll

DEBUG_FLR_IMAGE_TIMESTAMP:  4df49fd7

STACK_COMMAND:  !pe 2ff6c58
 ; ** Pseudo Context ** ; kb

FAILURE_BUCKET_ID:  NULL_INSTRUCTION_PTR_CALL_c0000005_TestWER.dll!TestWER.WorkerRole.Run

BUCKET_ID:
X64_APPLICATION_FAULT_NULL_INSTRUCTION_PTR_NULL_POINTER_WRITE_WRONG_SYMBOLS_CALL__SYSTEM.NULLREFERENCEEXCEPTION_BAD_IP_testwer!TestWER.WorkerRole.Run

WATSON_STAGEONE_URL:  http://watson.microsoft.com/StageOne/WaWorkerHost_exe/6_0_6002_18009/4d6ac6d0/unknown/0_0_0_0/bbbbbbb4/c0000005/00803d1e.htm?Retriage=1

Followup: MachineOwner
```

```
0:016> lmt m Wa*
start             end                 module name
00000000`00da0000 00000000`00dac000   WaWorkerHost  Sun Feb 27 21:49:04 2011 (4D6AC6D0)
00000000`5db40000 00000000`5db4d000   WaRuntimeProxy  Sun Feb 27 21:51:42 2011 (4D6AC76E)
0:016> lmt m *Azure*
start             end                 module name
00000000`57cd0000 00000000`57d26000   Microsoft_WindowsAzure_StorageClient  Fri Jan 28 23:40:44 2011 (4D4353FC)
00000000`58820000 00000000`5886c000   Microsoft_WindowsAzure_Diagnostics  Sun Feb 27 21:48:08 2011 (4D6AC698)
00000000`5c750000 00000000`5c764000   Microsoft_WindowsAzure_ServiceRuntime  Sun Feb 27 21:48:41 2011 (4D6AC6B9)

0:016> lmv m ntdll
start             end                 module name
00000000`775a0000 00000000`7774b000   ntdll      (pdb symbols)
c:\mss\ntdll.pdb\CFF40300FD804691B73E12CF2A150EE02\ntdll.pdb
    Loaded symbol image file: ntdll.dll
    Image path: C:\Windows\System32\ntdll.dll
    Image name: ntdll.dll
    Timestamp:        Tue Jul 14 02:32:27 2009 (4A5BE02B)
    CheckSum:         001B1CB5
    ImageSize:        001AB000
    File version:     6.1.7600.16385
    Product version:  6.1.7600.16385
    File flags:       0 (Mask 3F)
    File OS:          40004 NT Win32
    File type:        2.0 Dll
    File date:        00000000.00000000
    Translations:     0409.04b0
    CompanyName:      Microsoft Corporation
    ProductName:      Microsoft® Windows® Operating System
    InternalName:     ntdll.dll
    OriginalFilename: ntdll.dll
    ProductVersion:   6.1.7600.16385
    FileVersion:      6.1.7600.16385 (win7_rtm.090713-1255)
    FileDescription:  NT Layer DLL
    LegalCopyright:   © Microsoft Corporation. All rights reserved.

0:016> lmt
start             end                 module name
00000000`00da0000 00000000`00dac000   WaWorkerHost  Sun Feb 27 21:49:04 2011 (4D6AC6D0)
00000000`57990000 00000000`57a00000   System_Data_Services_Client  Thu Mar 18 08:24:26 2010 (4BA1E33A)
00000000`57cd0000 00000000`57d26000   Microsoft_WindowsAzure_StorageClient  Fri Jan 28 23:40:44 2011 (4D4353FC)
00000000`57ec0000 00000000`583ac000   System_Web  Thu Mar 18 13:01:44 2010 (4BA22438)
00000000`583b0000 00000000`585ce000   System_Xml  Thu Mar 18 08:10:20 2010 (4BA1DFEC)
00000000`58820000 00000000`5886c000   Microsoft_WindowsAzure_Diagnostics  Sun Feb 27 21:48:08 2011 (4D6AC698)
00000000`58870000 00000000`589bc000   System_Core  Thu Mar 18 08:10:22 2010 (4BA1DFEE)
00000000`589c0000 00000000`58d16000   System    Thu Mar 18 08:10:28 2010 (4BA1DFF4)
00000000`599c0000 00000000`59a28000   System_Configuration  Thu Mar 18 08:11:55 2010 (4BA1E04B)
00000000`59a90000 00000000`59a98000   TestWER   Sun Jun 12 12:15:35 2011 (4DF49FD7)
00000000`59aa0000 00000000`59aac000   Diagnostics  Sun Feb 27 21:51:23 2011 (4D6AC75B)
00000000`59ac0000 00000000`59ae6000   System_Xml_Linq  Thu Mar 18 08:26:06 2010 (4BA1E39E)
00000000`5a4e0000 00000000`5a4e8000   Microsoft_ServiceHosting_Tools_DevelopmentFabric_Runtime  Sun Feb 27 21:48:24
2011 (4D6AC6A8)
00000000`5c640000 00000000`5c687000   msshrtmi  Sun Feb 27 21:51:39 2011 (4D6AC76B)
00000000`5c750000 00000000`5c764000   Microsoft_WindowsAzure_ServiceRuntime  Sun Feb 27 21:48:41 2011 (4D6AC6B9)
00000000`5c880000 00000000`5c8af000   mswasri   Sun Feb 27 21:51:32 2011 (4D6AC764)
00000000`5db40000 00000000`5db4d000   WaRuntimeProxy  Sun Feb 27 21:51:42 2011 (4D6AC76E)
00000000`77380000 00000000`7749f000   kernel32  Tue Jul 14 02:31:11 2009 (4A5BDFDF)
00000000`774a0000 00000000`7759a000   user32    Tue Jul 14 02:34:00 2009 (4A5BE088)
00000000`775a0000 00000000`7774b000   ntdll     Tue Jul 14 02:32:27 2009 (4A5BE02B)
00000000`77760000 00000000`77767000   psapi     Tue Jul 14 00:26:21 2009 (4A5BC29D)
000007fe`e20d0000 000007fe`e2f9b000   System_Web_ni  Thu Mar 18 13:01:44 2010 (4BA22438)
000007fe`e4bd0000 000007fe`e4c81000   webengine4  Thu Mar 18 13:03:12 2010 (4BA22490)
000007fe`e4c90000 000007fe`e4e3d000   System_Data_Services_Client_ni  Thu Mar 18 08:24:26 2010 (4BA1E33A)
000007fe`e50d0000 000007fe`e51f5000   dbghelp   Tue Jul 14 02:26:28 2009 (4A5BDEC4)
000007fe`e5470000 000007fe`e555a000   diasymreader  Thu Mar 18 14:26:21 2010 (4BA2380D)
000007fe`e5d00000 000007fe`e5e33000   System_Configuration_ni  Thu Mar 18 08:11:55 2010 (4BA1E04B)
000007fe`e6190000 000007fe`e6213000   System_Xml_Linq_ni  Thu Mar 18 08:26:06 2010 (4BA1E39E)
000007fe`e6220000 000007fe`e68ca000   System_Xml_ni  Thu Mar 18 08:10:20 2010 (4BA1DFEC)
000007fe`e8130000 000007fe`e8aed000   System_Core_ni  Thu Mar 18 08:10:22 2010 (4BA1DFEE)
000007fe`e94c0000 000007fe`e9ff0000   System_ni  Thu Mar 18 08:10:28 2010 (4BA1DFF4)
000007fe`e9ff0000 000007fe`ea167000   clrjit    Thu Mar 18 12:42:46 2010 (4BA21FC6)
000007fe`ea170000 000007fe`eb3e7000   mscorlib_ni  Thu Mar 18 12:43:45 2010 (4BA22001)
000007fe`eb3f0000 000007fe`eb4c1000   MSVCR100_CLR0400  Thu Mar 18 12:48:28 2010 (4BA2211C)
000007fe`eb4d0000 000007fe`ebe35000   clr       Thu Mar 18 12:39:07 2010 (4BA21EEB)
000007fe`ec940000 000007fe`ec954000   nlssorting  Thu Mar 18 12:27:27 2010 (4BA21C2F)
000007fe`f73e0000 000007fe`f73e7000   shfolder  Tue Jul 14 02:33:09 2009 (4A5BE055)
```

```
000007fe`fa130000 000007fe`fa194000   webio     Sat Oct 16 06:10:24 2010 (4CB933C0)
000007fe`fa1e0000 000007fe`fa24e000   winhttp   Tue Jul 14 02:34:34 2009 (4A5BE0AA)
000007fe`fa2e0000 000007fe`fa370000   mscoreei  Thu Mar 18 12:27:36 2010 (4BA21C38)
000007fe`fa370000 000007fe`fa3df000   mscoree   Fri Nov 06 05:09:26 2009 (4AF3AF86)
000007fe`faf10000 000007fe`faf21000   rtutils   Sat Jun 19 07:46:38 2010 (4C1C67CE)
000007fe`faf30000 000007fe`faf4c000   rasman    Tue Jul 14 02:32:38 2009 (4A5BE036)
000007fe`faf50000 000007fe`fafb2000   rasapi32  Tue Jul 14 02:32:30 2009 (4A5BE02E)
000007fe`fb040000 000007fe`fb06c000   powrprof  Tue Jul 14 02:33:22 2009 (4A5BE062)
000007fe`fb520000 000007fe`fb538000   dhcpcsvc  Tue Jul 14 02:26:30 2009 (4A5BDEC6)
000007fe`fb540000 000007fe`fb575000   xmllite   Tue Jul 14 02:34:16 2009 (4A5BE098)
000007fe`fb5e0000 000007fe`fb5f1000   dhcpcsvc6  Tue Jul 14 02:26:31 2009 (4A5BDEC7)
000007fe`fb870000 000007fe`fb87b000   winnsi    Tue Jul 14 02:34:41 2009 (4A5BE0B1)
000007fe`fb910000 000007fe`fb937000   IPHLPAPI  Tue Jul 14 02:28:55 2009 (4A5BDF57)
000007fe`fc630000 000007fe`fc65d000   ntmarta   Tue Jul 14 02:32:45 2009 (4A5BE03D)
000007fe`fc660000 000007fe`fc66c000   version   Tue Jul 14 02:33:54 2009 (4A5BE082)
000007fe`fc730000 000007fe`fc737000   WSHTCPIP  Tue Jul 14 02:34:47 2009 (4A5BE0B7)
000007fe`fc840000 000007fe`fc85e000   userenv   Tue Jul 14 02:34:03 2009 (4A5BE08B)
000007fe`fc990000 000007fe`fc999000   credssp   Tue Jul 14 02:29:49 2009 (4A5BDF8D)
000007fe`fca90000 000007fe`fcad7000   rsaenh    Tue Jul 14 02:32:41 2009 (4A5BE039)
000007fe`fcd20000 000007fe`fcd27000   wship6    Tue Jul 14 02:34:41 2009 (4A5BE0B1)
000007fe`fcd30000 000007fe`fcd84000   mswsock   Tue Jul 14 02:30:44 2009 (4A5BDFC4)
000007fe`fcd90000 000007fe`fcda7000   cryptsp   Tue Jul 14 02:29:58 2009 (4A5BDF96)
000007fe`fcee0000 000007fe`fcf02000   bcrypt    Tue Jul 14 02:25:13 2009 (4A5BDE79)
000007fe`fd360000 000007fe`fd385000   sspicli   Tue Jul 14 02:34:13 2009 (4A5BE095)
000007fe`fd390000 000007fe`fd3e7000   apphelp   Tue Jul 14 02:26:04 2009 (4A5BDEAC)
000007fe`fd3f0000 000007fe`fd3ff000   CRYPTBASE  Tue Jul 14 02:29:53 2009 (4A5BDF91)
000007fe`fd4e0000 000007fe`fd4f4000   RpcRtRemote  Tue Jul 14 02:32:38 2009 (4A5BE036)
000007fe`fd500000 000007fe`fd50f000   profapi   Tue Jul 14 02:32:15 2009 (4A5BE01F)
000007fe`fd5a0000 000007fe`fd5af000   msasn1    Sat Aug 29 08:40:40 2009 (4A98DB78)
000007fe`fd5b0000 000007fe`fd716000   crypt32   Tue Jul 14 02:29:52 2009 (4A5BDF90)
000007fe`fd720000 000007fe`fd78b000   KERNELBASE  Tue Jul 14 02:31:12 2009 (4A5BDFE0)
000007fe`fd790000 000007fe`fd7c6000   cfgmgr32  Tue Jul 14 02:26:02 2009 (4A5BDEAA)
000007fe`fd870000 000007fe`fd88a000   devobj    Tue Jul 14 02:26:57 2009 (4A5BDEE1)
000007fe`fd8d0000 000007fe`fdb29000   iertutil  Thu Nov 04 06:22:41 2010 (4CD25131)
000007fe`fdbd0000 000007fe`fdc41000   shlwapi   Tue Jul 14 02:33:13 2009 (4A5BE059)
000007fe`fde20000 000007fe`fde4e000   imm32     Tue Jul 14 02:28:32 2009 (4A5BDF40)
000007fe`fde50000 000007fe`fdf7e000   rpcrt4    Tue Jul 14 02:32:37 2009 (4A5BE035)
000007fe`fdf80000 000007fe`fe057000   oleaut32  Tue Jul 14 02:32:14 2009 (4A5BE01E)
000007fe`fe060000 000007fe`fe262000   ole32     Tue Jun 29 06:30:11 2010 (4C2984E3)
000007fe`fe270000 000007fe`fe447000   setupapi  Tue Jul 14 02:33:06 2009 (4A5BE052)
000007fe`fe470000 000007fe`fe50f000   msvcrt    Tue Jul 14 02:30:38 2009 (4A5BDFBE)
000007fe`fe510000 000007fe`fe5da000   usp10     Tue Jul 14 02:34:04 2009 (4A5BE08C)
000007fe`fe5e0000 000007fe`fe5ff000   sechost   Tue Jul 14 02:33:18 2009 (4A5BE05E)
000007fe`fe600000 000007fe`fe6db000   advapi32  Tue Jul 14 02:24:59 2009 (4A5BDE6B)
000007fe`fe6e0000 000007fe`fe730000   Wldap32   Tue Jul 14 02:35:25 2009 (4A5BE0DD)
000007fe`fe730000 000007fe`fe839000   msctf     Tue Jul 14 02:30:18 2009 (4A5BDFAA)
000007fe`fe840000 000007fe`fe84e000   lpk       Tue Jul 14 02:29:03 2009 (4A5BDF5F)
000007fe`fe850000 000007fe`fe8b7000   gdi32     Tue Jul 14 02:27:29 2009 (4A5BDF01)
000007fe`fe940000 000007fe`ff6c6000   shell32   Tue Jul 27 15:51:09 2010 (4C4EF25D)
000007fe`ff6d0000 000007fe`ff71d000   ws2_32    Tue Jul 14 02:34:13 2009 (4A5BE095)
000007fe`ff720000 000007fe`ff898000   urlmon    Thu Nov 04 06:27:12 2010 (4CD25240)
000007fe`ff8a0000 000007fe`ff8a8000   nsi       Tue Jul 14 02:32:25 2009 (4A5BE029)

Unloaded modules:
00000000`59830000 00000000`599ab000   mscordacwks.dll
    Timestamp: Thu Mar 18 12:42:15 2010 (4BA21FA7)
    Checksum:  0017AF00
    ImageSize:  0017B000
00000000`59830000 00000000`599ab000   mscordacwks.dll
    Timestamp: Thu Mar 18 12:42:15 2010 (4BA21FA7)
    Checksum:  0017AF00
    ImageSize:  0017B000
00000000`59830000 00000000`599ab000   mscordacwks.dll
    Timestamp: Thu Mar 18 12:42:15 2010 (4BA21FA7)
    Checksum:  0017AF00
    ImageSize:  0017B000
00000000`59830000 00000000`599ab000   mscordacwks.dll
    Timestamp: Thu Mar 18 12:42:15 2010 (4BA21FA7)
    Checksum:  0017AF00
    ImageSize:  0017B000
00000000`59830000 00000000`599ab000   mscordacwks.dll
    Timestamp: Thu Mar 18 12:42:15 2010 (4BA21FA7)
    Checksum:  0017AF00
    ImageSize:  0017B000
00000000`59830000 00000000`599ab000   mscordacwks.dll
    Timestamp: Thu Mar 18 12:42:15 2010 (4BA21FA7)
```

```
    Checksum:  0017AF00
    ImageSize:  0017B000
00000000`59830000 00000000`599ab000   mscordacwks.dll
    Timestamp: Thu Mar 18 12:42:15 2010 (4BA21FA7)
    Checksum:  0017AF00
    ImageSize:  0017B000
00000000`59830000 00000000`599ab000   mscordacwks.dll
    Timestamp: Thu Mar 18 12:42:15 2010 (4BA21FA7)
    Checksum:  0017AF00
    ImageSize:  0017B000
00000000`59830000 00000000`599ab000   mscordacwks.dll
    Timestamp: Thu Mar 18 12:42:15 2010 (4BA21FA7)
    Checksum:  0017AF00
    ImageSize:  0017B000
00000000`59830000 00000000`599ab000   mscordacwks.dll
    Timestamp: Thu Mar 18 12:42:15 2010 (4BA21FA7)
    Checksum:  0017AF00
    ImageSize:  0017B000
00000000`59830000 00000000`599ab000   mscordacwks.dll
    Timestamp: Thu Mar 18 12:42:15 2010 (4BA21FA7)
    Checksum:  0017AF00
    ImageSize:  0017B000
00000000`59830000 00000000`599ab000   mscordacwks.dll
    Timestamp: Thu Mar 18 12:42:15 2010 (4BA21FA7)
    Checksum:  0017AF00
    ImageSize:  0017B000
00000000`59830000 00000000`599ab000   mscordacwks.dll
    Timestamp: Thu Mar 18 12:42:15 2010 (4BA21FA7)
    Checksum:  0017AF00
    ImageSize:  0017B000
00000000`59830000 00000000`599ab000   mscordacwks.dll
    Timestamp: Thu Mar 18 12:42:15 2010 (4BA21FA7)
    Checksum:  0017AF00
    ImageSize:  0017B000
00000000`59830000 00000000`599ab000   mscordacwks.dll
    Timestamp: Thu Mar 18 12:42:15 2010 (4BA21FA7)
    Checksum:  0017AF00
    ImageSize:  0017B000
0:016> q
quit:
```

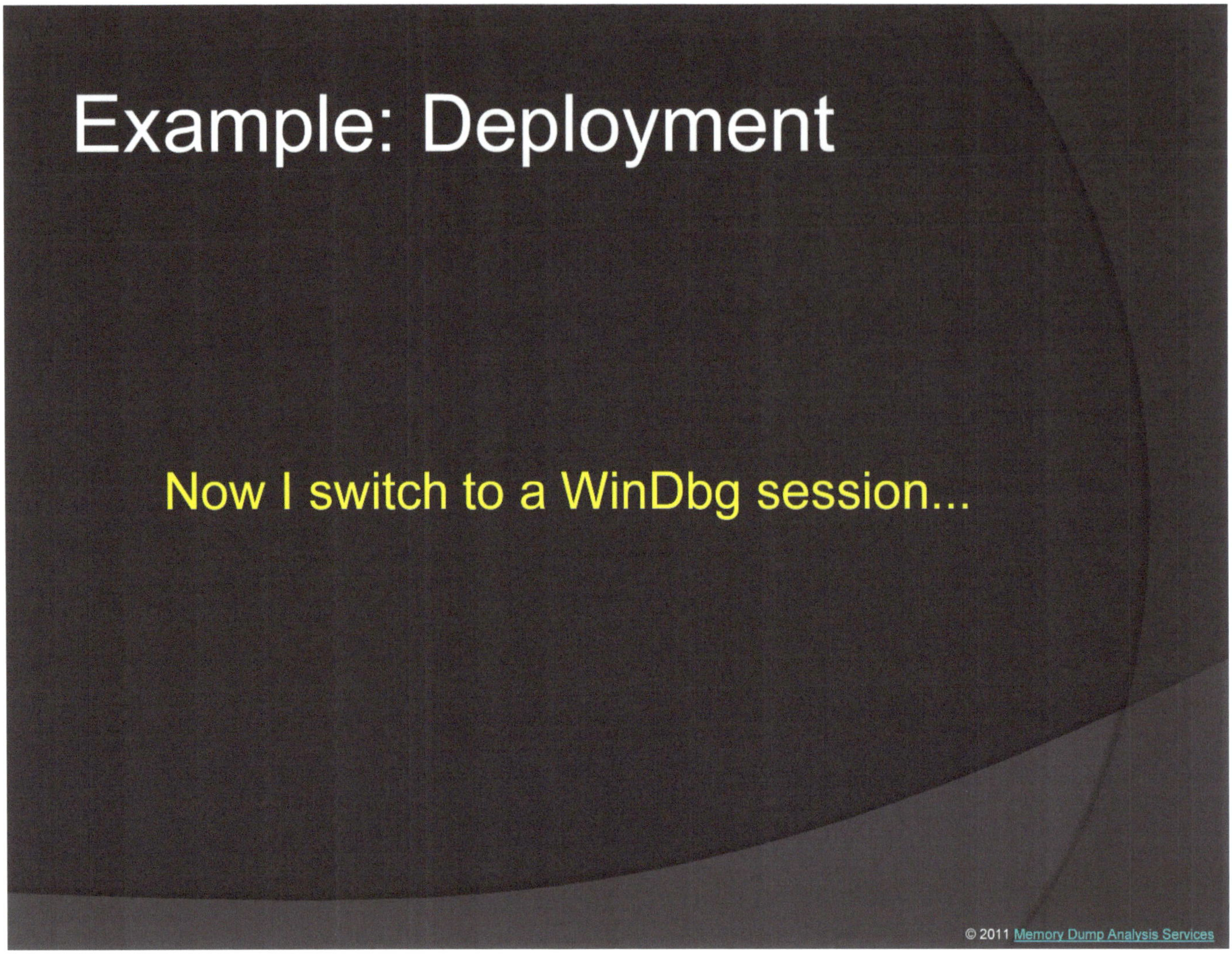

Now I show you an output of some WinDbg commands from a process dump file coming from a stage deployment VM. We don't have the appropriate SOS extension and associated DLLs so the output is only limited to unmanaged code.

```
Opened log file 'c:\training\wasession3.log'

0:015> !analyze -v
*******************************************************************************
*                                                                             *
*                        Exception Analysis                                   *
*                                                                             *
*******************************************************************************

FAULTING_IP:
kernel32!RaiseException+39
00000000`76b776fd 4881c4c8000000  add     rsp,0C8h

EXCEPTION_RECORD:  ffffffffffffffff -- (.exr 0xffffffffffffffff)
.exr 0xffffffffffffffff
ExceptionAddress: 0000000076b776fd (kernel32!RaiseException+0x0000000000000039)
   ExceptionCode: e0434352 (CLR exception)
  ExceptionFlags: 00000001
NumberParameters: 5
   Parameter[0]: ffffffff80004003
   Parameter[1]: 0000000000000000
   Parameter[2]: 0000000000000000
   Parameter[3]: 0000000000000000
   Parameter[4]: 000007fef7df0000

PROCESS_NAME:  WaWorkerHost.exe

ERROR_CODE: (NTSTATUS) 0xe0434352 - <Unable to get error code text>

EXCEPTION_CODE: (NTSTATUS) 0xe0434352 - <Unable to get error code text>

EXCEPTION_PARAMETER1:  ffffffff80004003

EXCEPTION_PARAMETER2:  0000000000000000

EXCEPTION_PARAMETER3:  0000000000000000

EXCEPTION_PARAMETER4: 0

MOD_LIST: <ANALYSIS/>

ADDITIONAL_DEBUG_TEXT:  Followup set based on attribute [Is_ChosenCrashFollowupThread] from Frame:[0] on thread:[PSEUDO_THREAD]

LAST_CONTROL_TRANSFER:  from 000007fef7f2f8ed to 0000000076b776fd

FAULTING_THREAD:  ffffffffffffffff

DEFAULT_BUCKET_ID:  STACKIMMUNE

PRIMARY_PROBLEM_CLASS:  STACKIMMUNE

BUGCHECK_STR:  APPLICATION_FAULT_STACKIMMUNE_NOSOS_CLR_EXCEPTION

STACK_TEXT:
00000000`00000000 00000000`00000000 waworkerhost.exe+0x0

SYMBOL_NAME:  waworkerhost.exe

FOLLOWUP_NAME:  MachineOwner

MODULE_NAME: waworkerhost

IMAGE_NAME:  WaWorkerHost.exe

DEBUG_FLR_IMAGE_TIMESTAMP:  4d6ac6d0

STACK_COMMAND:  ** Pseudo Context ** ; kb

FAILURE_BUCKET_ID:  STACKIMMUNE_e0434352_WaWorkerHost.exe!Unknown

BUCKET_ID:  X64_APPLICATION_FAULT_STACKIMMUNE_NOSOS_CLR_EXCEPTION_waworkerhost.exe

FOLLOWUP_IP:
WaWorkerHost!COM+_Entry_Point <PERF> (WaWorkerHost+0x0)+0
00000000`00040000 4d5a            pop     r10

WATSON_STAGEONE_URL:
http://watson.microsoft.com/StageOne/WaWorkerHost_exe/6_0_6002_18009/4d6ac6d0/kernel32_dll/6_0_6002_18005/49e041d1/e0434352/000176fd.ht
m?Retriage=1

Followup: MachineOwner
---------
```

```
0:015> lmv m ntdll
start             end                 module name
00000000`76de0000 00000000`76f5f000   ntdll      (pdb symbols)
c:\mss\ntdll.pdb\05A648A7625D42E7B7367816F0CA1E0C2\ntdll.pdb
    Loaded symbol image file: ntdll.dll
    Image path: D:\Windows\System32\ntdll.dll
    Image name: ntdll.dll
    Timestamp:        Fri May 13 21:45:21 2011 (4DCD9861)
    CheckSum:         00188814
    ImageSize:        0017F000
    File version:     6.0.6002.18446
    Product version:  6.0.6002.18446
    File flags:       0 (Mask 3F)
    File OS:          40004 NT Win32
    File type:        2.0 Dll
    File date:        00000000.00000000
    Translations:     0409.04b0
    CompanyName:      Microsoft Corporation
    ProductName:      Microsoft® Windows® Operating System
    InternalName:     ntdll.dll
    OriginalFilename: ntdll.dll
    ProductVersion:   6.0.6002.18446
    FileVersion:      6.0.6002.18446 (rd_os_v1.110513-1321)
    FileDescription:  NT Layer DLL
    LegalCopyright:   © Microsoft Corporation. All rights reserved.

0:015> !teb  ; Stack trace is incomplete / truncated and we attempt to dump raw stack data
TEB at 000007ffffefc000
*************************************************************************
***                                                                   ***
***                                                                   ***
***    Your debugger is not using the correct symbols                 ***
***                                                                   ***
***    In order for this command to work properly, your symbol path   ***
***    must point to .pdb files that have full type information.      ***
***                                                                   ***
***    Certain .pdb files (such as the public OS symbols) do not      ***
***    contain the required information.  Contact the group that     ***
***    provided you with these symbols if you need this command to    ***
***    work.                                                          ***
***                                                                   ***
***    Type referenced: nt!_TEB                                       ***
***                                                                   ***
*************************************************************************
error InitTypeRead( TEB )...

0:015> dq 000007ffffefc000
000007ff`ffefc000  00000000`00000000 00000000`1d0e0000
000007ff`ffefc010  00000000`1d0d8000 00000000`00000000
000007ff`ffefc020  00000000`00001e00 00000000`00000000
000007ff`ffefc030  000007ff`ffefc000 00000000`00000000
000007ff`ffefc040  00000000`00000aa0 00000000`00000994
000007ff`ffefc050  00000000`00000000 000007ff`ffefc058
000007ff`ffefc060  000007ff`fffd6000 00000000`00000057
000007ff`ffefc070  00000000`00000000 fffff900`c1e01a90

0:015> dqs 00000000`1d0d8000 00000000`1d0e0000
00000000`1d0d8000  00000000`00000000
00000000`1d0d8008  00000000`00000000
00000000`1d0d8010  00000000`00000000
00000000`1d0d8018  00000000`00000000
00000000`1d0d8020  00000000`00000000
00000000`1d0d8028  00000000`00000000
00000000`1d0d8030  00000000`00000000
00000000`1d0d8038  00000000`00000000
00000000`1d0d8040  00000000`00000000
00000000`1d0d8048  00000000`00000000
00000000`1d0d8050  00000000`00000000
00000000`1d0d8058  00000000`00000000

[… Parts of raw stack skipped …]

00000000`1d0de928  00000000`00000080
00000000`1d0de930  00000000`020d80a0
00000000`1d0de938  00000000`020a3d60
00000000`1d0de940  00000000`0000000c
```

```
00000000`1d0de948  00000000`76b776c0 kernel32!RaiseException
00000000`1d0de950  000007fe`f8362dd7 clr!Thread::RaiseCrossContextException+0x2a8
00000000`1d0de958  00000000`76b60000 kernel32!SetThreadPreferredUILanguages <PERF> (kernel32+0x0)
00000000`1d0de960  00000000`76c7c4a8 kernel32!__PchSym_ <PERF> (kernel32+0x11c4a8)
00000000`1d0de968  000007fe`f7df0000
clr!StateHolder<&MarkOSAlertableWait,&UnMarkOSAlertableWait,2>::~StateHolder<&MarkOSAlertableWait,&UnMarkOSAlertableWa
it,2> <PERF> (clr+0x0)
00000000`1d0de970  000007fe`f86e383c clr!_dyn_tls_init_callback <PERF> (clr+0x8f383c)
00000000`1d0de978  000007fe`f7df0000
clr!StateHolder<&MarkOSAlertableWait,&UnMarkOSAlertableWait,2>::~StateHolder<&MarkOSAlertableWait,&UnMarkOSAlertableWa
it,2> <PERF> (clr+0x0)
00000000`1d0de980  000007fe`f8731af4 clr!_dyn_tls_init_callback <PERF> (clr+0x941af4)
00000000`1d0de988  000007fe`f7df0000
clr!StateHolder<&MarkOSAlertableWait,&UnMarkOSAlertableWait,2>::~StateHolder<&MarkOSAlertableWait,&UnMarkOSAlertableWa
it,2> <PERF> (clr+0x0)
00000000`1d0de990  000007fe`f8731c14 clr!_dyn_tls_init_callback <PERF> (clr+0x941c14)
00000000`1d0de998  000007fe`f7df0000
clr!StateHolder<&MarkOSAlertableWait,&UnMarkOSAlertableWait,2>::~StateHolder<&MarkOSAlertableWait,&UnMarkOSAlertableWa
it,2> <PERF> (clr+0x0)
00000000`1d0de9a0  000007fe`f8739570 clr!_dyn_tls_init_callback <PERF> (clr+0x949570)
00000000`1d0de9a8  000007fe`f7df0000
clr!StateHolder<&MarkOSAlertableWait,&UnMarkOSAlertableWait,2>::~StateHolder<&MarkOSAlertableWait,&UnMarkOSAlertableWa
it,2> <PERF> (clr+0x0)
00000000`1d0de9b0  000007fe`f873957c clr!_dyn_tls_init_callback <PERF> (clr+0x94957c)
00000000`1d0de9b8  000007fe`f7df0000
clr!StateHolder<&MarkOSAlertableWait,&UnMarkOSAlertableWait,2>::~StateHolder<&MarkOSAlertableWait,&UnMarkOSAlertableWa
it,2> <PERF> (clr+0x0)
00000000`1d0de9c0  000007fe`f873d698 clr!_dyn_tls_init_callback <PERF> (clr+0x94d698)
00000000`1d0de9c8  000007fe`f7df0000
clr!StateHolder<&MarkOSAlertableWait,&UnMarkOSAlertableWait,2>::~StateHolder<&MarkOSAlertableWait,&UnMarkOSAlertableWa
it,2> <PERF> (clr+0x0)
00000000`1d0de9d0  000007fe`f8725128 clr!_dyn_tls_init_callback <PERF> (clr+0x935128)
00000000`1d0de9d8  000007fe`f7df0000
clr!StateHolder<&MarkOSAlertableWait,&UnMarkOSAlertableWait,2>::~StateHolder<&MarkOSAlertableWait,&UnMarkOSAlertableWa
it,2> <PERF> (clr+0x0)
00000000`1d0de9e0  000007fe`f86d63b4 clr!_dyn_tls_init_callback <PERF> (clr+0x8e63b4)
00000000`1d0de9e8  000007fe`f7df0000
clr!StateHolder<&MarkOSAlertableWait,&UnMarkOSAlertableWait,2>::~StateHolder<&MarkOSAlertableWait,&UnMarkOSAlertableWa
it,2> <PERF> (clr+0x0)
00000000`1d0de9f0  000007fe`f86d6324 clr!_dyn_tls_init_callback <PERF> (clr+0x8e6324)
00000000`1d0de9f8  000007fe`f7df0000
clr!StateHolder<&MarkOSAlertableWait,&UnMarkOSAlertableWait,2>::~StateHolder<&MarkOSAlertableWait,&UnMarkOSAlertableWa
it,2> <PERF> (clr+0x0)
00000000`1d0dea00  000007fe`f86d6318 clr!_dyn_tls_init_callback <PERF> (clr+0x8e6318)
00000000`1d0dea08  000007fe`f7df0000
clr!StateHolder<&MarkOSAlertableWait,&UnMarkOSAlertableWait,2>::~StateHolder<&MarkOSAlertableWait,&UnMarkOSAlertableWa
it,2> <PERF> (clr+0x0)
00000000`1d0dea10  000007fe`f86d633c clr!_dyn_tls_init_callback <PERF> (clr+0x8e633c)
00000000`1d0dea18  00000000`00000000
00000000`1d0dea20  00000000`6be7e65d
00000000`1d0dea28  00000005`00010001
00000000`1d0dea30  00000000`1d0df6d8
00000000`1d0dea38  00000000`e0434352
00000000`1d0dea40  00000000`1d0df238
00000000`1d0dea48  00000000`00000005
00000000`1d0dea50  00000000`76df3496 ntdll!RtlRaiseException+0x36
00000000`1d0dea58  00000000`00000001
00000000`1d0dea60  00000000`00000000
00000000`1d0dea68  00000000`76df3549 ntdll!RtlRaiseException+0xe9
00000000`1d0dea70  00000000`00000000
00000000`1d0dea78  00000000`00000000
00000000`1d0dea80  00000000`1d0df0c0
00000000`1d0dea88  00000000`00000000
00000000`1d0dea90  00000000`1d0dea00
00000000`1d0dea98  00000000`1d0deab8
00000000`1d0deaa0  00000000`1d0deac0
00000000`1d0deaa8  00000000`00000000
00000000`1d0deab0  00000000`76de0000 ntdll!NtDllUserStubs <PERF> (ntdll+0x0)
00000000`1d0deab8  00000000`020c26d8
00000000`1d0deac0  00000000`1d0dea70
00000000`1d0deac8  00000000`1d0deb00
00000000`1d0dead0  00000000`00000000
00000000`1d0dead8  00000000`00000000
00000000`1d0deae0  00000000`00000000
00000000`1d0deae8  00000000`76b6de0a kernel32!FlushInstructionCache+0xa
00000000`1d0deaf0  00000000`00000000
```

```
00000000`1d0deaf8  00000000`1d0deb50
00000000`1d0deb00  00001fa0`0010000f
00000000`1d0deb08  0053002b`002b0033
00000000`1d0deb10  00000206`002b002b
00000000`1d0deb18  000007fe`f7e84c12 clr!Precode::SetTargetInterlocked+0x1d2
00000000`1d0deb20  00000000`00000000
00000000`1d0deb28  000007fe`ef4b6d28 mscorlib_ni+0x4c6d28
00000000`1d0deb30  ffffffff`fffffffe
00000000`1d0deb38  000007fe`ef4b6d28 mscorlib_ni+0x4c6d28
00000000`1d0deb40  000007fe`ef06c320 mscorlib_ni+0x7c320
00000000`1d0deb48  00000000`6be7ef8d
00000000`1d0deb50  00000000`1d0dead0
00000000`1d0deb58  00000000`00000158
00000000`1d0deb60  00000000`1c12d2c0
00000000`1d0deb68  00000000`1d0df0a0
00000000`1d0deb70  00000000`1d0dff30
00000000`1d0deb78  00000000`00000001
00000000`1d0deb80  00000000`00000001
00000000`1d0deb88  00000000`00000000
00000000`1d0deb90  00000000`00000000
00000000`1d0deb98  00000000`00000059
00000000`1d0deba0  00000000`1d0df0e0
00000000`1d0deba8  00000000`00000005
00000000`1d0debb0  00000000`1d0df238
00000000`1d0debb8  00000000`e0434352
00000000`1d0debc0  00000000`1d0df6d8
00000000`1d0debc8  00000000`76b776fd kernel32!RaiseException+0x39
00000000`1d0debd0  00000000`0000027f
00000000`1d0debd8  000007fe`ef4b3679 mscorlib_ni+0x4c3679
00000000`1d0debe0  ffffffff`ffffffff
00000000`1d0debe8  0002ffff`00001fa0
00000000`1d0debf0  00000000`00000000
00000000`1d0debf8  00000000`00000000
00000000`1d0dec00  00000000`00000000
00000000`1d0dec08  00000000`00000000
00000000`1d0dec10  00000000`00000000
00000000`1d0dec18  00000000`00000000
00000000`1d0dec20  00000000`00000000
00000000`1d0dec28  00000000`00000000
00000000`1d0dec30  00000000`00000000
00000000`1d0dec38  00000000`00000000
00000000`1d0dec40  00000000`00000000
00000000`1d0dec48  00000000`00000000
00000000`1d0dec50  00000000`00000000
00000000`1d0dec58  00000000`00000000
00000000`1d0dec60  00000000`00000000
00000000`1d0dec68  00000000`00000000
00000000`1d0dec70  00000000`020c26d8
00000000`1d0dec78  00000000`00000000
00000000`1d0dec80  00000000`f7e83534
00000000`1d0dec88  00000000`00000000
00000000`1d0dec90  00000000`020a3438
00000000`1d0dec98  00000000`00000000
00000000`1d0deca0  00000000`1d0df110
00000000`1d0deca8  00000000`00000000
00000000`1d0decb0  00000000`00000000
00000000`1d0decb8  00000000`00000000
00000000`1d0decc0  00000000`00000000
00000000`1d0decc8  00000000`00000000
00000000`1d0decd0  00000000`00000000
00000000`1d0decd8  00000000`00000000
00000000`1d0dece0  00000000`00000000
00000000`1d0dece8  00000000`00000000
00000000`1d0decf0  00000000`00000000
00000000`1d0decf8  00000000`00000000
00000000`1d0ded00  00000000`00000000
00000000`1d0ded08  00000000`00000000
00000000`1d0ded10  00000000`00000000
00000000`1d0ded18  00000000`00000000
00000000`1d0ded20  00000000`00000000
00000000`1d0ded28  00000000`00000000
00000000`1d0ded30  00000000`00000000
00000000`1d0ded38  00000000`00000000
00000000`1d0ded40  00000000`00000000
00000000`1d0ded48  00000000`00000000
00000000`1d0ded50  00000000`00000000
```

```
00000000`1d0ded58  00000000`00000000
00000000`1d0ded60  00000000`00000000
00000000`1d0ded68  00000000`00000000
00000000`1d0ded70  00000000`020c26d8
00000000`1d0ded78  00000000`00000248
00000000`1d0ded80  00000000`020d8348
00000000`1d0ded88  000007fe`ef383684 mscorlib_ni+0x393684
00000000`1d0ded90  00000000`020a3438
00000000`1d0ded98  00000000`00000000
00000000`1d0deda0  00000000`1d0df110
00000000`1d0deda8  00000000`00000000
00000000`1d0dedb0  00000000`00000000
00000000`1d0dedb8  00000000`00000000
00000000`1d0dedc0  00000000`020d8348
00000000`1d0dedc8  000007fe`ef9ceaa0 mscorlib_ni+0x9deaa0
00000000`1d0dedd0  00000000`1d0dee28
00000000`1d0dedd8  00000000`1d0def90
00000000`1d0dede0  00000000`00000000
00000000`1d0dede8  00000000`1d0dee50
00000000`1d0dedf0  00000000`00000000
00000000`1d0dedf8  00000000`1d0dee28
00000000`1d0dee00  00000000`1d0def90
00000000`1d0dee08  00000000`1d0dee50
00000000`1d0dee10  00000000`00000000
00000000`1d0dee18  000007fe`f7e83534 clr!CallDescrWorker+0x84
00000000`1d0dee20  00000000`020c26d8
00000000`1d0dee28  000007fe`f7e83534 clr!CallDescrWorker+0x84
00000000`1d0dee30  00000000`020a3438
00000000`1d0dee38  00000000`1d0df110
00000000`1d0dee40  000007fe`ef2f4818 mscorlib_ni+0x304818
00000000`1d0dee48  00000000`00000000
00000000`1d0dee50  00000000`1d0df080
00000000`1d0dee58  00000000`00000001
00000000`1d0dee60  00000000`1c12d2c0
00000000`1d0dee68  000007fe`f7e83649 clr!CallDescrWorkerWithHandler+0xa9
00000000`1d0dee70  00000000`1c12d2c0
00000000`1d0dee78  000007fe`f7e83649 clr!CallDescrWorkerWithHandler+0xa9
00000000`1d0dee80  00000000`1d0deec0
00000000`1d0dee88  00000000`00000000
00000000`1d0dee90  000007fe`ef315850 mscorlib_ni+0x325850
00000000`1d0dee98  00000000`00000000
00000000`1d0deea0  00000000`00000001
00000000`1d0deea8  00000000`1d0df1a8
00000000`1d0deeb0  00000000`00000000
00000000`1d0deeb8  00000000`1c12d2c0
00000000`1d0deec0  00000000`00000001
00000000`1d0deec8  00000000`00000001
00000000`1d0deed0  00000000`00000068
00000000`1d0deed8  00000000`00000001
00000000`1d0deee0  00000000`00000000
00000000`1d0deee8  000007fe`f7e836d1 clr!MethodDesc::CallDescr+0x2ad
00000000`1d0deef0  00000000`1d0def88
00000000`1d0deef8  00000000`00000001
00000000`1d0def00  00000000`1d0def90
00000000`1d0def08  00000000`1d0df1a0
00000000`1d0def10  000007fe`ef315850 mscorlib_ni+0x325850
00000000`1d0def18  00000000`00000000
00000000`1d0def20  000007fe`ef9b9510 mscorlib_ni+0x9c9510
00000000`1d0def28  000007fe`f7e895bb clr!MetaSig::MetaSig+0x4b
00000000`1d0def30  000007fe`f84ad7e8 clr!gsige_SM_Obj_RetArrByte+0x4
00000000`1d0def38  000007fe`f7e895bb clr!MetaSig::MetaSig+0x4b
00000000`1d0def40  00000000`00000003
00000000`1d0def48  00000000`1d0df408
00000000`1d0def50  00000000`1d0def90
00000000`1d0def58  000007fe`f7e896c6 clr!MethodDesc::CallDescr+0xed
00000000`1d0def60  00000000`1d0def90
00000000`1d0def68  000007fe`f7dff2ac clr!HardCodedMetaSig::GetBinarySig+0x59
00000000`1d0def70  00000000`020bf2d0
00000000`1d0def78  00000000`00000000
00000000`1d0def80  00000000`1d0df228
00000000`1d0def88  00000000`020c26d8
00000000`1d0def90  000007fe`eeff1000 mscorlib_ni+0x1000
00000000`1d0def98  000007fe`f847e334 clr!gsige_IM_RetInt
00000000`1d0defa0  00000000`00000000
00000000`1d0defa8  ffffffff`ffffffff
00000000`1d0defb0  00000000`00000000
```

```
00000000`1d0defb8  00000000`00000000
00000000`1d0defc0  0000861b`00000000
00000000`1d0defc8  000007fe`f847e333 clr!gsige_IM_RetVoid+0x3
00000000`1d0defd0  00000000`00000001
00000000`1d0defd8  000007fe`f847e331 clr!gsige_IM_RetVoid+0x1
00000000`1d0defe0  00000000`00000000
00000000`1d0defe8  00000008`00000003
00000000`1d0deff0  00000001`00000000
00000000`1d0deff8  000007fe`f7e83a4c clr!HndCreateHandle+0xcd
00000000`1d0df000  00000000`00000000
00000000`1d0df008  00000000`00000000
00000000`1d0df010  00000000`00000000
00000000`1d0df018  00000000`00000000
00000000`1d0df020  000007fe`f866da00 clr!g_StubLinkerUnwindInfoListInitializer
00000000`1d0df028  000007fe`00000000
00000000`1d0df030  ffffffff`fffffffe
00000000`1d0df038  000007fe`f7dff499 clr!Binder::GetMethod+0x3e
00000000`1d0df040  000007fe`f847e331 clr!gsige_IM_RetVoid+0x1
00000000`1d0df048  0000861b`00000003
00000000`1d0df050  ffffffff`00000008
00000000`1d0df058  000007fe`f7f2f6af clr!Thread::SetLastThrownObject+0xf8
00000000`1d0df060  00000000`1c12d2c0
00000000`1d0df068  00000000`020c26d8
00000000`1d0df070  00002026`00000001
00000000`1d0df078  000007fe`f847e331 clr!gsige_IM_RetVoid+0x1
00000000`1d0df080  00000000`6be7ef8d
00000000`1d0df088  00000000`1d0df198
00000000`1d0df090  00000000`00000001
00000000`1d0df098  00000000`76b776fd kernel32!RaiseException+0x39
00000000`1d0df0a0  ffffffff`00000008
00000000`1d0df0a8  00000000`1c12d2c0
00000000`1d0df0b0  00000000`1d0dff30
00000000`1d0df0b8  00000000`00000001
00000000`1d0df0c0  00000001`e0434352
00000000`1d0df0c8  00000000`00000000
00000000`1d0df0d0  00000000`76b776fd kernel32!RaiseException+0x39
00000000`1d0df0d8  00000000`00000005
00000000`1d0df0e0  ffffffff`80004003
00000000`1d0df0e8  00000000`00000000
00000000`1d0df0f0  00000000`00000000
00000000`1d0df0f8  00000000`00000000
00000000`1d0df100  000007fe`f7df0000
clr!StateHolder<&MarkOSAlertableWait,&UnMarkOSAlertableWait,2>::~StateHolder<&MarkOSAlertableWait,&UnMarkOSAlertableWa
it,2> <PERF> (clr+0x0)
00000000`1d0df108  00000000`1c12d2c0
00000000`1d0df110  00000000`1d0df328
00000000`1d0df118  000007fe`00000001
00000000`1d0df120  00000000`00000000
00000000`1d0df128  000007fe`f7dfcc1a clr!Binder::IsClass+0x9a
00000000`1d0df130  00000000`1d0df1f0
00000000`1d0df138  000007fe`f7e0aa80 clr!GCHolderBase<0,0,0,0>::EnterInternal+0x3c
00000000`1d0df140  ffffffff`fffffffe
00000000`1d0df148  000007fe`00000000
00000000`1d0df150  000007fe`eeff1000 mscorlib_ni+0x1000
00000000`1d0df158  000007fe`02000059
00000000`1d0df160  00000000`00000001
00000000`1d0df168  000007fe`f7f2f8ed clr!RaiseTheExceptionInternalOnly+0x363
00000000`1d0df170  00000000`1c12d2c0
00000000`1d0df178  00000000`00000001
00000000`1d0df180  00000000`1d0dff30
00000000`1d0df188  00000000`020c26d8
00000000`1d0df190  00000000`020c26d8
00000000`1d0df198  00000000`020c26d8
00000000`1d0df1a0  0000861b`0c02ec95
00000000`1d0df1a8  000007fe`f84718b0 clr!GCFrame::`vftable'
00000000`1d0df1b0  00000000`1d0df328
00000000`1d0df1b8  00000000`1d0df190
00000000`1d0df1c0  00000000`00000001
00000000`1d0df1c8  00000000`1d0de330
00000000`1d0df1d0  00000000`1d0df220
00000000`1d0df1d8  000007fe`80004003
00000000`1d0df1e0  00000000`1c12d2c0
00000000`1d0df1e8  000007fe`ef315850 mscorlib_ni+0x325850
00000000`1d0df1f0  000007fe`eeff1000 mscorlib_ni+0x1000
00000000`1d0df1f8  00000000`1d0de330
00000000`1d0df200  00000000`00000000
```

```
00000000`1d0df208  000007fe`f7df0000
clr!StateHolder<&MarkOSAlertableWait,&UnMarkOSAlertableWait,2>::~StateHolder<&MarkOSAlertableWait,&UnMarkOSAlertableWa
it,2> <PERF> (clr+0x0)
00000000`1d0df210  00000000`1c12d2c0
00000000`1d0df218  00000000`00000001
00000000`1d0df220  0000861b`00000000
00000000`1d0df228  00000000`020c26d8
00000000`1d0df230  00000000`00000000
00000000`1d0df238  ffffffff`80004003
00000000`1d0df240  00000000`00000000
00000000`1d0df248  00000000`00000000
00000000`1d0df250  00000000`00000000
00000000`1d0df258  000007fe`f7df0000
clr!StateHolder<&MarkOSAlertableWait,&UnMarkOSAlertableWait,2>::~StateHolder<&MarkOSAlertableWait,&UnMarkOSAlertableWa
it,2> <PERF> (clr+0x0)
00000000`1d0df260  00000000`1c12d2c0
00000000`1d0df268  00000000`1c12d520
00000000`1d0df270  00000000`1c12d2c0
00000000`1d0df278  00000000`020bf2d0
00000000`1d0df280  00000000`00000000
00000000`1d0df288  00000000`00000000
00000000`1d0df290  00000000`00000002
00000000`1d0df298  000007fe`f828bd64 clr!RaiseTheException+0xa4
00000000`1d0df2a0  000007fe`f847e331 clr!gsige_IM_RetVoid+0x1
00000000`1d0df2a8  0000861b`00000003
00000000`1d0df2b0  00000000`00000053
00000000`1d0df2b8  00000000`020c26d8
00000000`1d0df2c0  00000000`00000000
00000000`1d0df2c8  000007fe`f828c6b6 clr!BStrFromString+0x66
00000000`1d0df2d0  00000000`00000002
00000000`1d0df2d8  00000000`00000000
00000000`1d0df2e0  0000861b`110a4a68
00000000`1d0df2e8  00000000`00000000
00000000`1d0df2f0  00000000`1d0dff30
00000000`1d0df2f8  000007fe`f830b63b clr!RealCOMPlusThrow+0x3b
00000000`1d0df300  00000000`00000002
00000000`1d0df308  00000000`1d0dff30
00000000`1d0df310  00000000`00000000
00000000`1d0df318  00000000`00000000
00000000`1d0df320  0000861b`0c02ec95
00000000`1d0df328  000007fe`f84718b0 clr!GCFrame::`vftable'
00000000`1d0df330  00000000`1d0df508
00000000`1d0df338  00000000`1d0df370
00000000`1d0df340  ffffffff`00000001
00000000`1d0df348  00000000`1c12d2c0
00000000`1d0df350  00010026`00000000
00000000`1d0df358  00000000`00000000
00000000`1d0df360  00000000`00000057
00000000`1d0df368  000007fe`f830b649 clr!RealCOMPlusThrow+0x9
00000000`1d0df370  00000000`020c26d8
00000000`1d0df378  00000000`00000000
00000000`1d0df380  00000000`00000000
00000000`1d0df388  00000000`00000000
00000000`1d0df390  00000000`00000057
00000000`1d0df398  000007fe`f8362dd6 clr!Thread::RaiseCrossContextException+0x2a7
00000000`1d0df3a0  00000000`00000057
00000000`1d0df3a8  00000000`1d0dff30
00000000`1d0df3b0  00000000`00000000
00000000`1d0df3b8  00000000`00000000
00000000`1d0df3c0  00000000`1d0df418
00000000`1d0df3c8  00000000`1d0df420
00000000`1d0df3d0  00000057`01070008
00000000`1d0df3d8  00000000`00000000
00000000`1d0df3e0  00000000`00000002
00000000`1d0df3e8  000007fe`f7e91b2f clr!FullSegmentIterator+0x194
00000000`1d0df3f0  00000000`00000000
00000000`1d0df3f8  00000000`00000000
00000000`1d0df400  00000000`020c26d8
00000000`1d0df408  00000000`020bf2d0
00000000`1d0df410  006d005c`00340036
00000000`1d0df418  00000000`020a3438
00000000`1d0df420  00000000`020bf2d0
00000000`1d0df428  000007fe`f8484630 clr!Exception::`vftable'
00000000`1d0df430  00000000`00000000
00000000`1d0df438  00000000`00000000
00000000`1d0df440  00000000`019679c0
```

```
00000000`1d0df448  000007fe`00000000
00000000`1d0df450  00000000`1d0df540
00000000`1d0df458  00000000`1c12d2c0
00000000`1d0df460  00000000`1c12d2c0
00000000`1d0df468  00000000`1d0df540
00000000`1d0df470  00000000`00000001
00000000`1d0df478  00000000`00000000
00000000`1d0df480  00000000`00798190
00000000`1d0df488  000007fe`f7e1c874 clr!Thread::SafeSetLastThrownObject+0x74
00000000`1d0df490  00000004`ffffffff
00000000`1d0df498  00000000`00000000
00000000`1d0df4a0  00000000`1d0df6d8
00000000`1d0df4a8  000007fe`f97c2113 MSVCR100_CLR0400!getptd+0xb
00000000`1d0df4b0  00000000`1d0df540
00000000`1d0df4b8  00000000`1c12d2c0
00000000`1d0df4c0  00000000`00000001
00000000`1d0df4c8  0000861b`0c02ec95
00000000`1d0df4d0  000007fe`f84718b0 clr!GCFrame::`vftable'
00000000`1d0df4d8  00000000`1d0df6d8
00000000`1d0df4e0  00000000`1d0df418
00000000`1d0df4e8  000007fe`00000002
00000000`1d0df4f0  00000000`1c12d2c0
00000000`1d0df4f8  000007fe`00000000
00000000`1d0df500  0000861b`0c02ec95
00000000`1d0df508  000007fe`f84718b0 clr!GCFrame::`vftable'
00000000`1d0df510  00000000`1d0df900
00000000`1d0df518  00000000`1d0df3f8
00000000`1d0df520  00000000`00000003
00000000`1d0df528  00000000`1c12d2c0
00000000`1d0df530  00000000`00000000
00000000`1d0df538  0000861b`0c02ec95
00000000`1d0df540  000007fe`f8482a30 clr!DebuggerU2MCatchHandlerFrame::`vftable'
00000000`1d0df548  00000000`1d0df6d8
00000000`1d0df550  00000000`1d0df528
00000000`1d0df558  00000000`1c12d2c0
00000000`1d0df560  00000000`1d0df6d8
00000000`1d0df568  00000000`00000000
00000000`1d0df570  00000000`0070fb01
00000000`1d0df578  00000000`1c12d2c0
00000000`1d0df580  00000000`00000000
00000000`1d0df588  000007fe`f7e91d88 clr!MetaData::HotHeap::GetData+0xa4
00000000`1d0df590  00000000`1d0df970
00000000`1d0df598  00000000`1c12d2c0
00000000`1d0df5a0  00000000`0070fb01
00000000`1d0df5a8  00000000`1c12d2c0
00000000`1d0df5b0  00000000`00798190
00000000`1d0df5b8  000007fe`f81f3973 clr! ?? ::FNODOBFM::`string'+0xaeeb3
00000000`1d0df5c0  00000000`00000000
00000000`1d0df5c8  00000000`0070fb20
00000000`1d0df5d0  00000000`00798190
00000000`1d0df5d8  00000000`006e0000
00000000`1d0df5e0  00000000`76ef5870 ntdll!RtlpInterceptorRoutines
00000000`1d0df5e8  00000000`00000000
00000000`1d0df5f0  00000000`00000100
00000000`1d0df5f8  00000000`1c12d2c0
00000000`1d0df600  00000000`00000000
00000000`1d0df608  00000000`00000000
00000000`1d0df610  00000000`00000002
00000000`1d0df618  00000000`00000001
00000000`1d0df620  00000000`00000000
00000000`1d0df628  00000000`00000000
00000000`1d0df630  00000000`6be7f0ad
00000000`1d0df638  00000000`22197dfe
00000000`1d0df640  000007fe`fdbe8780 ole32!gTlsLock
00000000`1d0df648  000007fe`fda64d08 ole32!COleStaticMutexSem::Request+0x28
00000000`1d0df650  00000000`00000000
00000000`1d0df658  00000000`00000000
00000000`1d0df660  00000000`00000001
00000000`1d0df668  000007fe`fda501f5 ole32!InitThreadCtx+0x41
00000000`1d0df670  00000000`1c12d2c0
00000000`1d0df678  00000000`1d0df6d8
00000000`1d0df680  00000000`00000001
00000000`1d0df688  ffffffff`fffffffe
00000000`1d0df690  00000000`1d0df670
00000000`1d0df698  000007fe`f8484630 clr!Exception::`vftable'
00000000`1d0df6a0  00000000`00000000
```

```
00000000`1d0df6a8  00000000`00000000
00000000`1d0df6b0  00000000`1c12d2c0
00000000`1d0df6b8  00000000`00000001
00000000`1d0df6c0  00000000`ffffffff
00000000`1d0df6c8  00000000`00000000
00000000`1d0df6d0  0000861b`0c02ec95
00000000`1d0df6d8  000007fe`f8482980 clr!ContextTransitionFrame::`vftable'
00000000`1d0df6e0  00000000`1d0df900
00000000`1d0df6e8  00000000`00710bf0
00000000`1d0df6f0  00000000`00000000
00000000`1d0df6f8  00000000`00000000
00000000`1d0df700  00000000`00000000
00000000`1d0df708  00000000`00000000
00000000`1d0df710  00000000`00000000
00000000`1d0df718  00000000`00000018
00000000`1d0df720  00000000`1d0dff30
00000000`1d0df728  000007fe`f7df3f1e clr!CrstBase::Enter+0xc7
00000000`1d0df730  00000000`00000000
00000000`1d0df738  000007fe`f7df3b89 clr!ClrFlsGetValue+0xe
00000000`1d0df740  00000000`006f9a50
00000000`1d0df748  00000000`00000000
00000000`1d0df750  00000000`00000000
00000000`1d0df758  00000000`00000000
00000000`1d0df760  00000000`00000000
00000000`1d0df768  000007fe`f7e91dd0 clr!VirtualCallStubManager::GenerateResolveCacheElem+0xdf
00000000`1d0df770  00000000`00000002
00000000`1d0df778  00000000`1d0df970
00000000`1d0df780  00000000`1d0df970
00000000`1d0df788  00000000`1c12d2c0
00000000`1d0df790  00000000`00000000
00000000`1d0df798  000007fe`f7f0b8f0 clr!ThreadStore::TransferStartedThread+0x84
00000000`1d0df7a0  00000000`1c12d2c0
00000000`1d0df7a8  000007fe`f7e91b2f clr!FullSegmentIterator+0x194
00000000`1d0df7b0  00000000`00000000
00000000`1d0df7b8  00000000`1c12d2c0
00000000`1d0df7c0  ffffffff`fffffffe
00000000`1d0df7c8  00000000`1c12d2c0
00000000`1d0df7d0  00000000`1c12d2c0
00000000`1d0df7d8  000007fe`f7f0b846 clr!Thread::HasStarted+0x29a
00000000`1d0df7e0  00000000`00000000
00000000`1d0df7e8  00000000`00000001
00000000`1d0df7f0  00000000`00000001
00000000`1d0df7f8  00000000`00000000
00000000`1d0df800  00000000`76eeb880 ntdll!PebLdr+0x20
00000000`1d0df808  00000000`1c23c160
00000000`1d0df810  00000000`1d0df900
00000000`1d0df818  00000000`1c12d2c0
00000000`1d0df820  00000000`1c12d2c0
00000000`1d0df828  00000000`1d0df900
00000000`1d0df830  00000001`00000001
00000000`1d0df838  00000000`00000000
00000000`1d0df840  00000000`00000001
00000000`1d0df848  00000000`76e15a95 ntdll!RtlAllocateHeap+0x111
00000000`1d0df850  00000004`00000004
00000000`1d0df858  00000000`000000a8
00000000`1d0df860  00000000`00000000
00000000`1d0df868  ffffffff`ffffffff
00000000`1d0df870  ffffffff`ffffffff
00000000`1d0df878  00000000`1d0df820
00000000`1d0df880  ffffffff`ffffffff
00000000`1d0df888  00000000`0000b420
00000000`1d0df890  00000000`1c12d2c0
00000000`1d0df898  00000000`1d0df970
00000000`1d0df8a0  ffffffff`ffffffff
00000000`1d0df8a8  000007fe`f7e91a9c clr!ClrSafeInt<unsigned int>::ClrSafeInt<unsigned int><unsigned __int64>+0xb5
00000000`1d0df8b0  00000000`00000000
00000000`1d0df8b8  00000000`00000000
00000000`1d0df8c0  00000000`00000000
00000000`1d0df8c8  00000000`00000000
00000000`1d0df8d0  00000000`1d0de330
00000000`1d0df8d8  00000000`1d0df8e8
00000000`1d0df8e0  00000000`1d0de330
00000000`1d0df8e8  00000000`1d0df900
00000000`1d0df8f0  00000000`1d0df970
00000000`1d0df8f8  0000861b`0c02ec95
00000000`1d0df900  000007fe`f8482a30 clr!DebuggerU2MCatchHandlerFrame::`vftable'
```

```
00000000`1d0df908  ffffffff`ffffffff
00000000`1d0df910  00000000`1d0df8e8
00000000`1d0df918  00000000`1c12d2c0
00000000`1d0df920  ffffffff`ffffffff
00000000`1d0df928  00000000`00000000
00000000`1d0df930  00000000`1c12d2c0
00000000`1d0df938  00000000`00000000
00000000`1d0df940  00000000`00000000
00000000`1d0df948  000007fe`f7e91bf3 clr!HndCountAllHandles+0xef
00000000`1d0df950  ffffffff`ffffffff
00000000`1d0df958  00000000`1c12d2c0
00000000`1d0df960  00000000`00000000
00000000`1d0df968  00000000`00000000
00000000`1d0df970  00000000`00000002
00000000`1d0df978  00000000`00000000
00000000`1d0df980  00000000`00000001
00000000`1d0df988  000007fe`f8018a20 clr!ThreadNative::KickOffThread_Worker
00000000`1d0df990  00000000`1d0dfa10
00000000`1d0df998  00000002`00000002
00000000`1d0df9a0  00000000`00000000
00000000`1d0df9a8  000007fe`f80189b8 clr!ThreadNative::KickOffThread+0xc0
00000000`1d0df9b0  00000000`1c12d2c0
00000000`1d0df9b8  00000000`1d0dff30
00000000`1d0df9c0  00000000`00000001
00000000`1d0df9c8  00000000`00000000
00000000`1d0df9d0  00000000`00000000
00000000`1d0df9d8  00000000`00000000
00000000`1d0df9e0  00000000`1d0dff00
00000000`1d0df9e8  00000000`76b8c4ca kernel32!HeapFree+0xa
00000000`1d0df9f0  00000000`00000000
00000000`1d0df9f8  00000000`00000000
00000000`1d0dfa00  00000000`00000000
00000000`1d0dfa08  00000000`00000000
00000000`1d0dfa10  00000000`1c12d2c0
00000000`1d0dfa18  00000000`00000000
00000000`1d0dfa20  00000000`00000000
00000000`1d0dfa28  00000000`00000000
00000000`1d0dfa30  00000000`00000000
00000000`1d0dfa38  00000000`00000000
00000000`1d0dfa40  00000000`00000000
00000000`1d0dfa48  000007fe`f7df6994 clr!operator delete+0x45
00000000`1d0dfa50  00000000`0000054f
00000000`1d0dfa58  00000000`00000000
00000000`1d0dfa60  00000000`76de0000 ntdll!NtDllUserStubs <PERF> (ntdll+0x0)
00000000`1d0dfa68  00000000`76e16046 ntdll!LdrpInitialize+0x36
00000000`1d0dfa70  ffffffff`fffffffe
00000000`1d0dfa78  00000000`00000000
00000000`1d0dfa80  000007fe`f80188f8 clr!ThreadNative::KickOffThread
00000000`1d0dfa88  000007fe`f7f0a236 clr!Thread::intermediateThreadProc+0x7d
00000000`1d0dfa90  00000000`1d321970
00000000`1d0dfa98  00000000`1d0dfa28
00000000`1d0dfaa0  00000000`1c12d2c0
00000000`1d0dfaa8  00000000`00000000
00000000`1d0dfab0  00000000`00000000
00000000`1d0dfab8  00000000`00000000
00000000`1d0dfac0  00000000`00000000
00000000`1d0dfac8  00000000`00000000
00000000`1d0dfad0  00000000`00000000
00000000`1d0dfad8  00000000`00000000
00000000`1d0dfae0  00000000`00000000
00000000`1d0dfae8  00000000`00000000
00000000`1d0dfaf0  00000000`00000000
00000000`1d0dfaf8  00000000`00000000
00000000`1d0dfb00  00000000`00000000
00000000`1d0dfb08  00000000`00000000
00000000`1d0dfb10  00000000`00000000
00000000`1d0dfb18  00000000`00000000
00000000`1d0dfb20  00001f80`0010001b
00000000`1d0dfb28  00000000`00000033
00000000`1d0dfb30  00000200`002b0000
00000000`1d0dfb38  00000000`00000000
00000000`1d0dfb40  00000000`00000000
00000000`1d0dfb48  00000000`00000000
00000000`1d0dfb50  00000000`00000000
00000000`1d0dfb58  00000000`00000000
00000000`1d0dfb60  00000000`00000000
```

```
00000000`1d0dfb68  00000000`00000000
00000000`1d0dfb70  000007fe`f7f0a1c0 clr!Thread::intermediateThreadProc
00000000`1d0dfb78  00000000`019679c0
00000000`1d0dfb80  00000000`00000000
00000000`1d0dfb88  00000000`1d0dffc8
00000000`1d0dfb90  00000000`00000000
00000000`1d0dfb98  00000000`00000000
00000000`1d0dfba0  00000000`00000000
00000000`1d0dfba8  00000000`00000000
00000000`1d0dfbb0  00000000`00000000
00000000`1d0dfbb8  00000000`00000000
00000000`1d0dfbc0  00000000`00000000
00000000`1d0dfbc8  00000000`00000000
00000000`1d0dfbd0  00000000`00000000
00000000`1d0dfbd8  00000000`00000000
00000000`1d0dfbe0  00000000`00000000
00000000`1d0dfbe8  00000000`76e16160 ntdll!RtlUserThreadStart
00000000`1d0dfbf0  00000000`0000027f
00000000`1d0dfbf8  00000000`00000000
00000000`1d0dfc00  00000000`00000000
00000000`1d0dfc08  0002ffff`00001f80
00000000`1d0dfc10  00000000`00000000
00000000`1d0dfc18  00000000`00000000
00000000`1d0dfc20  00000000`00000000
00000000`1d0dfc28  00000000`00000000
00000000`1d0dfc30  00000000`00000000
00000000`1d0dfc38  00000000`00000000
00000000`1d0dfc40  00000000`00000000
00000000`1d0dfc48  00000000`00000000
00000000`1d0dfc50  00000000`00000000
00000000`1d0dfc58  00000000`00000000
00000000`1d0dfc60  00000000`00000000
00000000`1d0dfc68  00000000`00000000
00000000`1d0dfc70  00000000`00000000
00000000`1d0dfc78  00000000`00000000
00000000`1d0dfc80  00000000`00000000
00000000`1d0dfc88  00000000`00000000
00000000`1d0dfc90  00000000`00000000
00000000`1d0dfc98  00000000`00000000
00000000`1d0dfca0  00000000`00000000
00000000`1d0dfca8  00000000`00000000
00000000`1d0dfcb0  00000000`00000000
00000000`1d0dfcb8  00000000`00000000
00000000`1d0dfcc0  00000000`00000000
00000000`1d0dfcc8  00000000`00000000
00000000`1d0dfcd0  00000000`00000000
00000000`1d0dfcd8  00000000`00000000
00000000`1d0dfce0  00000000`00000000
00000000`1d0dfce8  00000000`00000000
00000000`1d0dfcf0  00000000`00000000
00000000`1d0dfcf8  00000000`00000000
00000000`1d0dfd00  00000000`00000000
00000000`1d0dfd08  00000000`00000000
00000000`1d0dfd10  00000000`00000000
00000000`1d0dfd18  00000000`00000000
00000000`1d0dfd20  00000000`00000000
00000000`1d0dfd28  00000000`00000000
00000000`1d0dfd30  00000000`00000000
00000000`1d0dfd38  00000000`00000000
00000000`1d0dfd40  00000000`00000000
00000000`1d0dfd48  00000000`00000000
00000000`1d0dfd50  00000000`00000000
00000000`1d0dfd58  00000000`00000000
00000000`1d0dfd60  00000000`00000000
00000000`1d0dfd68  00000000`00000000
00000000`1d0dfd70  00000000`00000000
00000000`1d0dfd78  00000000`00000000
00000000`1d0dfd80  00000000`00000000
00000000`1d0dfd88  00000000`00000000
00000000`1d0dfd90  00000000`00000000
00000000`1d0dfd98  00000000`00000000
00000000`1d0dfda0  00000000`00000000
00000000`1d0dfda8  00000000`00000000
00000000`1d0dfdb0  00000000`00000000
00000000`1d0dfdb8  00000000`00000000
00000000`1d0dfdc0  00000000`00000000
```

```
00000000`1d0dfdc8  00000000`00000000
00000000`1d0dfdd0  00000000`00000000
00000000`1d0dfdd8  00000000`00000000
00000000`1d0dfde0  00000000`00000000
00000000`1d0dfde8  00000000`00000000
00000000`1d0dfdf0  00000000`00000000
00000000`1d0dfdf8  00000000`00000000
00000000`1d0dfe00  00000000`00000000
00000000`1d0dfe08  00000000`00000000
00000000`1d0dfe10  00000000`00000000
00000000`1d0dfe18  00000000`00000000
00000000`1d0dfe20  00000000`00000000
00000000`1d0dfe28  00000000`00000000
00000000`1d0dfe30  00000000`00000000
00000000`1d0dfe38  00000000`00000000
00000000`1d0dfe40  00000000`00000000
00000000`1d0dfe48  00000000`00000000
00000000`1d0dfe50  00000000`00000000
00000000`1d0dfe58  00000000`00000000
00000000`1d0dfe60  00000000`00000000
00000000`1d0dfe68  00000000`00000000
00000000`1d0dfe70  00000000`00000000
00000000`1d0dfe78  00000000`00000000
00000000`1d0dfe80  00000000`00000000
00000000`1d0dfe88  00000000`00000000
00000000`1d0dfe90  00000000`00000000
00000000`1d0dfe98  00000000`00000000
00000000`1d0dfea0  00000000`00000000
00000000`1d0dfea8  00000000`00000000
00000000`1d0dfeb0  00000000`00000000
00000000`1d0dfeb8  00000000`00000000
00000000`1d0dfec0  00000000`00000000
00000000`1d0dfec8  00000000`00000000
00000000`1d0dfed0  00000000`00000000
00000000`1d0dfed8  00000000`00000000
00000000`1d0dfee0  00000000`00000000
00000000`1d0dfee8  00000000`00000000
00000000`1d0dfef0  00000000`00000000
00000000`1d0dfef8  00000000`00000000
00000000`1d0dff00  00000000`00000000
00000000`1d0dff08  000007fe`f7f0a21f clr!Thread::intermediateThreadProc+0x66
00000000`1d0dff10  00000000`00000000
00000000`1d0dff18  00000000`00000000
00000000`1d0dff20  00000000`00000000
00000000`1d0dff28  00000000`00000000
00000000`1d0dff30  0000861b`110a4438
00000000`1d0dff38  00000000`00000000
00000000`1d0dff40  00000000`00000000
00000000`1d0dff48  00000000`76b7be3d kernel32!BaseThreadInitThunk+0xd
00000000`1d0dff50  00000000`00000000
00000000`1d0dff58  00000000`00000000
00000000`1d0dff60  00000000`00000000
00000000`1d0dff68  00000000`00000000
00000000`1d0dff70  00000000`00000000
00000000`1d0dff78  00000000`76e16181 ntdll!RtlUserThreadStart+0x1d
00000000`1d0dff80  00000000`00000000
00000000`1d0dff88  00000000`00000000
00000000`1d0dff90  00000000`00000000
00000000`1d0dff98  00000000`00000000
00000000`1d0dffa0  00000000`76c1c870 kernel32!UnhandledExceptionFilter
00000000`1d0dffa8  00000000`76c1c870 kernel32!UnhandledExceptionFilter
00000000`1d0dffb0  00000000`1d0de320
00000000`1d0dffb8  00000000`00000000
00000000`1d0dffc0  00000000`00000000
00000000`1d0dffc8  00000000`00000000
00000000`1d0dffd0  00000000`00000000
00000000`1d0dffd8  00000000`00000000
00000000`1d0dffe0  00000000`00000000
00000000`1d0dffe8  00000000`00000000
00000000`1d0dfff0  00000000`00000000
00000000`1d0dfff8  00000000`00000000
00000000`1d0e0000  00000000`00000000
```

```
0:015> lmt m Wa*
start             end                 module name
00000000`00040000 00000000`0004c000   WaWorkerHost  Sun Feb 27 21:49:04 2011 (4D6AC6D0)
00000000`74fb0000 00000000`74fbd000   WaRuntimeProxy  Sun Feb 27 21:51:42 2011 (4D6AC76E)

0:015> lmt m *Azure*
start             end                 module name
00000000`73410000 00000000`73466000   Microsoft_WindowsAzure_StorageClient  Fri Jan 28 23:40:44 2011 (4D4353FC)
00000000`73ec0000 00000000`73f0c000   Microsoft_WindowsAzure_Diagnostics  Sun Feb 27 21:48:08 2011 (4D6AC698)
00000000`74cb0000 00000000`74cc4000   Microsoft_WindowsAzure_ServiceRuntime  Sun Feb 27 21:48:41 2011 (4D6AC6B9)

0:015> ~*k

   0  Id: aa0.914 Suspend: 0 Teb: 000007ff`fffde000 Unfrozen
Child-SP          RetAddr           Call Site
00000000`0054e558 00000000`76b8c1b8 ntdll!ZwDelayExecution+0xa
00000000`0054e560 000007fe`f7e08e15 kernel32!SleepEx+0x84
00000000`0054e5e0 000007fe`f80218e2 clr!EESleepEx+0x22
00000000`0054e610 000007fe`f8021a40 clr!Thread::UserSleep+0x97
00000000`0054e660 000007ff`00183cf2 clr!ThreadNative::Sleep+0x100
00000000`0054e7f0 000007ff`00182416 0x7ff`00183cf2
00000000`0054e860 000007fe`f7e83534 0x7ff`00182416
00000000`0054e8c0 000007fe`f7e83649 clr!CallDescrWorker+0x84
00000000`0054e910 000007fe`f7e836c5 clr!CallDescrWorkerWithHandler+0xa9
00000000`0054e990 000007fe`f801da99 clr!MethodDesc::CallDescr+0x2a1
00000000`0054ebc0 000007fe`f801dbd0 clr!ClassLoader::RunMain+0x228
00000000`0054ee10 000007fe`f801d986 clr!Assembly::ExecuteMainMethod+0xac
00000000`0054f0c0 000007fe`f801fd46 clr!SystemDomain::ExecuteMainMethod+0x452
00000000`0054f670 000007fe`f801fc63 clr!ExecuteEXE+0x43
00000000`0054f6d0 000007fe`f7ffba85 clr!CorExeMainInternal+0xc4
00000000`0054f740 000007fe`f95f3309 clr!CorExeMain+0x15
00000000`0054f780 000007fe`f9a85b21 mscoreei!CorExeMain+0x41
00000000`0054f7b0 00000000`76b7be3d mscoree!CorExeMain_Exported+0x57
00000000`0054f7e0 00000000`76e16181 kernel32!BaseThreadInitThunk+0xd
00000000`0054f810 00000000`00000000 ntdll!RtlUserThreadStart+0x1d

   1  Id: aa0.9cc Suspend: 0 Teb: 000007ff`fffdc000 Unfrozen
Child-SP          RetAddr           Call Site
00000000`01dbf9e8 00000000`76b7bc03 ntdll!ZwWaitForMultipleObjects+0xa
00000000`01dbf9f0 00000000`76b71aa1 kernel32!WaitForMultipleObjectsEx+0x10b
00000000`01dbfb00 000007fe`f7ff5716 kernel32!WaitForMultipleObjects+0x11
00000000`01dbfb40 000007fe`f7ff564b clr!DebuggerRCThread::MainLoop+0xba
00000000`01dbfbf0 000007fe`f7ff5551 clr!DebuggerRCThread::ThreadProc+0xe4
00000000`01dbfc50 00000000`76b7be3d clr!DebuggerRCThread::ThreadProcStatic+0x4d
00000000`01dbfcb0 00000000`76e16181 kernel32!BaseThreadInitThunk+0xd
00000000`01dbfce0 00000000`00000000 ntdll!RtlUserThreadStart+0x1d

   2  Id: aa0.990 Suspend: 0 Teb: 000007ff`fffda000 Unfrozen
Child-SP          RetAddr           Call Site
00000000`1a96f938 00000000`76b7bc03 ntdll!ZwWaitForMultipleObjects+0xa
00000000`1a96f940 00000000`76b71aa1 kernel32!WaitForMultipleObjectsEx+0x10b
00000000`1a96fa50 000007fe`f7f7f15f kernel32!WaitForMultipleObjects+0x11
00000000`1a96fa90 000007fe`f7f802d3 clr!WKS::WaitForFinalizerEvent+0xcb
00000000`1a96fac0 000007fe`f7e91b9a clr!WKS::GCHeap::FinalizerThreadWorker+0x33
00000000`1a96faf0 000007fe`f7e91b2f clr!VirtualCallStubManager::GenerateResolveCacheElem+0xaa
00000000`1a96fb30 000007fe`f7e91a9c clr!FullSegmentIterator+0x194
00000000`1a96fc30 000007fe`f801fafe clr!ClrSafeInt<unsigned int>::ClrSafeInt<unsigned int><unsigned __int64>+0xb5
00000000`1a96fcd0 000007fe`f801ff6f clr!ManagedThreadBase_NoADTransition+0x3f
00000000`1a96fd30 000007fe`f7f0a236 clr!WKS::GCHeap::FinalizerThreadStart+0x93
00000000`1a96fd70 00000000`76b7be3d clr!Thread::intermediateThreadProc+0x7d
00000000`1a96fe30 00000000`76e16181 kernel32!BaseThreadInitThunk+0xd
00000000`1a96fe60 00000000`00000000 ntdll!RtlUserThreadStart+0x1d

   3  Id: aa0.980 Suspend: 0 Teb: 000007ff`fffd8000 Unfrozen
Child-SP          RetAddr           Call Site
00000000`1b31f808 00000000`76b7f65c ntdll!ZwRemoveIoCompletion+0xa
00000000`1b31f810 00000000`76cd7d2d kernel32!GetQueuedCompletionStatus+0x48
00000000`1b31f870 00000000`76cd7c33 rpcrt4!COMMON_ProcessCalls+0x7d
00000000`1b31f900 00000000`76cda0e9 rpcrt4!LOADABLE_TRANSPORT::ProcessIOEvents+0x133
00000000`1b31f9b0 00000000`76cda0a4 rpcrt4!ProcessIOEventsWrapper+0x9
00000000`1b31f9e0 00000000`76cda174 rpcrt4!BaseCachedThreadRoutine+0x94
00000000`1b31fa20 00000000`76b7be3d rpcrt4!ThreadStartRoutine+0x24
00000000`1b31fa50 00000000`76e16181 kernel32!BaseThreadInitThunk+0xd
00000000`1b31fa80 00000000`00000000 ntdll!RtlUserThreadStart+0x1d
```

```
   4  Id: aa0.9ac Suspend: 0 Teb: 000007ff`fffd4000 Unfrozen
Child-SP          RetAddr           Call Site
00000000`1b8cf7d8 00000000`76b8c0b0 ntdll!ZwWaitForSingleObject+0xa
00000000`1b8cf7e0 000007fe`f7e0d5c7 kernel32!WaitForSingleObjectEx+0x9c
00000000`1b8cf8a0 000007fe`f7e0d574 clr!Thread::LeaveRuntimeNoThrow+0x7c
00000000`1b8cf8e0 000007fe`f7e0d437 clr!Thread::LeaveRuntimeNoThrow+0xec
00000000`1b8cf940 000007fe`f7f565e4 clr!CLREvent::WaitEx+0x5e
00000000`1b8cf9e0 000007fe`f7f0a236 clr!AppDomain::ADUnloadThreadStart+0x144
00000000`1b8cfb20 00000000`76b7be3d clr!Thread::intermediateThreadProc+0x7d
00000000`1b8cfc60 00000000`76e16181 kernel32!BaseThreadInitThunk+0xd
00000000`1b8cfc90 00000000`00000000 ntdll!RtlUserThreadStart+0x1d

   5  Id: aa0.9b0 Suspend: 0 Teb: 000007ff`ffefe000 Unfrozen
Child-SP          RetAddr           Call Site
00000000`1bd8fc68 00000000`76b8c0b0 ntdll!ZwWaitForSingleObject+0xa
00000000`1bd8fc70 000007fe`fda57740 kernel32!WaitForSingleObjectEx+0x9c
00000000`1bd8fd30 000007fe`fda57a36 ole32!CRpcThread::WorkerLoop+0x60
00000000`1bd8fd70 00000000`76b7be3d ole32!CRpcThreadCache::RpcWorkerThreadEntry+0x1a
00000000`1bd8fda0 00000000`76e16181 kernel32!BaseThreadInitThunk+0xd
00000000`1bd8fdd0 00000000`00000000 ntdll!RtlUserThreadStart+0x1d

   6  Id: aa0.99c Suspend: 0 Teb: 000007ff`ffefa000 Unfrozen
Child-SP          RetAddr           Call Site
00000000`1dcae198 00000000`76b7bc03 ntdll!ZwWaitForMultipleObjects+0xa
00000000`1dcae1a0 000007fe`f7e26db5 kernel32!WaitForMultipleObjectsEx+0x10b
00000000`1dcae2b0 000007fe`f7e26b92 clr!WaitForMultipleObjectsEx_SO_TOLERANT+0x91
00000000`1dcae340 000007fe`f7e26a19 clr!Thread::DoAppropriateAptStateWait+0x56
00000000`1dcae380 000007fe`f7e26b13 clr!Thread::DoAppropriateWaitWorker+0x1b1
00000000`1dcae480 000007fe`f845b1dd clr!Thread::DoAppropriateWait+0x73
00000000`1dcae500 000007fe`efa7a936 clr!WaitHandleNative::CorWaitMultipleNative+0x2ad
00000000`1dcae780 000007ff`005d14e5 mscorlib_ni+0xa8a936
00000000`1dcae7e0 000007fe`ef36181c 0x7ff`005d14e5
00000000`1dcae8a0 000007fe`ef36172b mscorlib_ni+0x37181c
00000000`1dcae900 000007fe`ef3f6f2d mscorlib_ni+0x37172b
00000000`1dcae950 000007fe`f7e83534 mscorlib_ni+0x406f2d
00000000`1dcae9a0 000007fe`f7e83649 clr!CallDescrWorker+0x84
00000000`1dcae9f0 000007fe`f7e836c5 clr!CallDescrWorkerWithHandler+0xa9
00000000`1dcaea70 000007fe`f7e88cd4 clr!MethodDesc::CallDescr+0x2a1
00000000`1dcaeca0 000007fe`f8018b68 clr!MethodDesc::CallTargetWorker+0x44
00000000`1dcaece0 000007fe`f7e91b9a clr!ThreadNative::KickOffThread_Worker+0x148
00000000`1dcaf000 000007fe`f7e91b2f clr!VirtualCallStubManager::GenerateResolveCacheElem+0xaa
00000000`1dcaf040 000007fe`f7e91a9c clr!FullSegmentIterator+0x194
00000000`1dcaf140 000007fe`f7e91d9c clr!ClrSafeInt<unsigned int>::ClrSafeInt<unsigned int><unsigned __int64>+0xb5
00000000`1dcaf1e0 000007fe`f7e4c45b clr!MetaData::HotHeap::GetData+0xb9
00000000`1dcaf210 000007fe`f7e91dd0 clr!Thread::DoADCallBack+0x127
00000000`1dcaf3c0 000007fe`f7e91b2f clr!VirtualCallStubManager::GenerateResolveCacheElem+0xdf
00000000`1dcaf400 000007fe`f7e91a9c clr!FullSegmentIterator+0x194
00000000`1dcaf500 000007fe`f7e91bf3 clr!ClrSafeInt<unsigned int>::ClrSafeInt<unsigned int><unsigned __int64>+0xb5
00000000`1dcaf5a0 000007fe`f80189b8 clr!HndCountAllHandles+0xef
00000000`1dcaf600 000007fe`f7f0a236 clr!ThreadNative::KickOffThread+0xc0
00000000`1dcaf6e0 00000000`76b7be3d clr!Thread::intermediateThreadProc+0x7d
00000000`1dcaf920 00000000`76e16181 kernel32!BaseThreadInitThunk+0xd
00000000`1dcaf950 00000000`00000000 ntdll!RtlUserThreadStart+0x1d

   7  Id: aa0.9c8 Suspend: 0 Teb: 000007ff`ffef8000 Unfrozen
Child-SP          RetAddr           Call Site
00000000`1e31f7a8 00000000`76b8c1b8 ntdll!ZwDelayExecution+0xa
00000000`1e31f7b0 000007fe`f7e08e15 kernel32!SleepEx+0x84
00000000`1e31f830 000007fe`f7e08e30 clr!EESleepEx+0x22
00000000`1e31f860 000007fe`f7ea18f5 clr!__DangerousSwitchToThread+0x6a
00000000`1e31f890 00000000`76b7be3d clr!ThreadpoolMgr::GateThreadStart+0xdc
00000000`1e31f990 00000000`76e16181 kernel32!BaseThreadInitThunk+0xd
00000000`1e31f9c0 00000000`00000000 ntdll!RtlUserThreadStart+0x1d

   8  Id: aa0.9d0 Suspend: 0 Teb: 000007ff`ffef6000 Unfrozen
Child-SP          RetAddr           Call Site
00000000`1e78f4c8 00000000`76b7f65c ntdll!ZwRemoveIoCompletion+0xa
00000000`1e78f4d0 000007fe`f7e1bcf7 kernel32!GetQueuedCompletionStatus+0x48
00000000`1e78f530 000007fe`f7f0a236 clr!ThreadpoolMgr::CompletionPortThreadStart+0x113
00000000`1e78f5e0 00000000`76b7be3d clr!Thread::intermediateThreadProc+0x7d
00000000`1e78f8a0 00000000`76e16181 kernel32!BaseThreadInitThunk+0xd
00000000`1e78f8d0 00000000`00000000 ntdll!RtlUserThreadStart+0x1d
```

```
   9  Id: aa0.988 Suspend: 0 Teb: 000007ff`ffef4000 Unfrozen
Child-SP          RetAddr           Call Site
00000000`1ecaf758 00000000`76b8c1b8 ntdll!ZwDelayExecution+0xa
00000000`1ecaf760 000007fe`f7ed851c kernel32!SleepEx+0x84
00000000`1ecaf7e0 000007fe`f7ed84d6 clr!ThreadpoolMgr::TimerThreadFire+0x44
00000000`1ecaf880 00000000`76b7be3d clr!ThreadpoolMgr::TimerThreadStart+0x6e
00000000`1ecaf8b0 00000000`76e16181 kernel32!BaseThreadInitThunk+0xd
00000000`1ecaf8e0 00000000`00000000 ntdll!RtlUserThreadStart+0x1d

  10  Id: aa0.9d4 Suspend: 0 Teb: 000007ff`ffef2000 Unfrozen
Child-SP          RetAddr           Call Site
00000000`1f22f6c8 00000000`76b8c1b8 ntdll!ZwDelayExecution+0xa
00000000`1f22f6d0 000007fe`f8424f5c kernel32!SleepEx+0x84
00000000`1f22f750 00000000`76b7be3d clr!ThreadpoolMgr::WaitThreadStart+0x9c
00000000`1f22f7c0 00000000`76e16181 kernel32!BaseThreadInitThunk+0xd
00000000`1f22f7f0 00000000`00000000 ntdll!RtlUserThreadStart+0x1d

  11  Id: aa0.9c0 Suspend: 0 Teb: 000007ff`ffef0000 Unfrozen
Child-SP          RetAddr           Call Site
00000000`1f7ffb88 000007fe`fca4539d ntdll!ZwRemoveIoCompletion+0xa
00000000`1f7ffb90 00000000`76b7be3d mswsock!SockAsyncThread+0x77
00000000`1f7ffbf0 00000000`76e16181 kernel32!BaseThreadInitThunk+0xd
00000000`1f7ffc20 00000000`00000000 ntdll!RtlUserThreadStart+0x1d

  12  Id: aa0.8e8 Suspend: 0 Teb: 000007ff`ffeee000 Unfrozen
Child-SP          RetAddr           Call Site
00000000`1fc4f5a8 00000000`76e01d0d ntdll!ZwWaitForWorkViaWorkerFactory+0xa
00000000`1fc4f5b0 00000000`76b7be3d ntdll!TppWorkerThread+0x23e
00000000`1fc4f830 00000000`76e16181 kernel32!BaseThreadInitThunk+0xd
00000000`1fc4f860 00000000`00000000 ntdll!RtlUserThreadStart+0x1d

  13  Id: aa0.984 Suspend: 0 Teb: 000007ff`ffeec000 Unfrozen
Child-SP          RetAddr           Call Site
00000000`201ff788 00000000`76e02468 ntdll!ZwWaitForMultipleObjects+0xa
00000000`201ff790 00000000`76b7be3d ntdll!TppWaiterpThread+0x3b2
00000000`201ffa40 00000000`76e16181 kernel32!BaseThreadInitThunk+0xd
00000000`201ffa70 00000000`00000000 ntdll!RtlUserThreadStart+0x1d

  14  Id: aa0.90c Suspend: 0 Teb: 000007ff`ffee8000 Unfrozen
Child-SP          RetAddr           Call Site
00000000`20b3f3d8 00000000`76b8c0b0 ntdll!ZwWaitForSingleObject+0xa
00000000`20b3f3e0 000007fe`f7e46d0e kernel32!WaitForSingleObjectEx+0x9c
00000000`20b3f4a0 000007fe`f7e470e7 clr!CLRSemaphore::Wait+0xaa
00000000`20b3f560 000007fe`f7e47280 clr!ThreadpoolMgr::UnfairSemaphore::Wait+0x140
00000000`20b3f5a0 000007fe`f7f0beab clr!ThreadpoolMgr::NewWorkerThreadStart+0x2a7
00000000`20b3f640 000007fe`f7f0a236 clr!ThreadpoolMgr::WorkerThreadStart+0x3b
00000000`20b3f6e0 00000000`76b7be3d clr!Thread::intermediateThreadProc+0x7d
00000000`20b3faa0 00000000`76e16181 kernel32!BaseThreadInitThunk+0xd
00000000`20b3fad0 00000000`00000000 ntdll!RtlUserThreadStart+0x1d

# 15  Id: aa0.994 Suspend: 0 Teb: 000007ff`ffefc000 Unfrozen
Child-SP          RetAddr           Call Site
00000000`1d0dc728 00000000`006eb1a0 ntdll!ZwGetContextThread+0xa
00000000`1d0dc730 00000000`00000000 0x6eb1a0

  16  Id: aa0.23c Suspend: 0 Teb: 000007ff`ffee4000 Unfrozen
Child-SP          RetAddr           Call Site
00000000`2160f908 00000000`76df1d2e ntdll!ZwTraceControl+0xa
00000000`2160f910 00000000`76b7be3d ntdll!EtwpNotificationThread+0x5e
00000000`2160f950 00000000`76e16181 kernel32!BaseThreadInitThunk+0xd
00000000`2160f980 00000000`00000000 ntdll!RtlUserThreadStart+0x1d

  17  Id: aa0.53c Suspend: 0 Teb: 000007ff`ffee2000 Unfrozen
Child-SP          RetAddr           Call Site
00000000`21befb18 00000000`76b7f65c ntdll!ZwRemoveIoCompletion+0xa
00000000`21befb20 00000000`76cd7d2d kernel32!GetQueuedCompletionStatus+0x48
00000000`21befb80 00000000`76cd7c33 rpcrt4!COMMON_ProcessCalls+0x7d
00000000`21befc10 00000000`76cda0e9 rpcrt4!LOADABLE_TRANSPORT::ProcessIOEvents+0x133
00000000`21befcc0 00000000`76cda0a4 rpcrt4!ProcessIOEventsWrapper+0x9
00000000`21befcf0 00000000`76cda174 rpcrt4!BaseCachedThreadRoutine+0x94
00000000`21befd30 00000000`76b7be3d rpcrt4!ThreadStartRoutine+0x24
00000000`21befd60 00000000`76e16181 kernel32!BaseThreadInitThunk+0xd
00000000`21befd90 00000000`00000000 ntdll!RtlUserThreadStart+0x1d
```

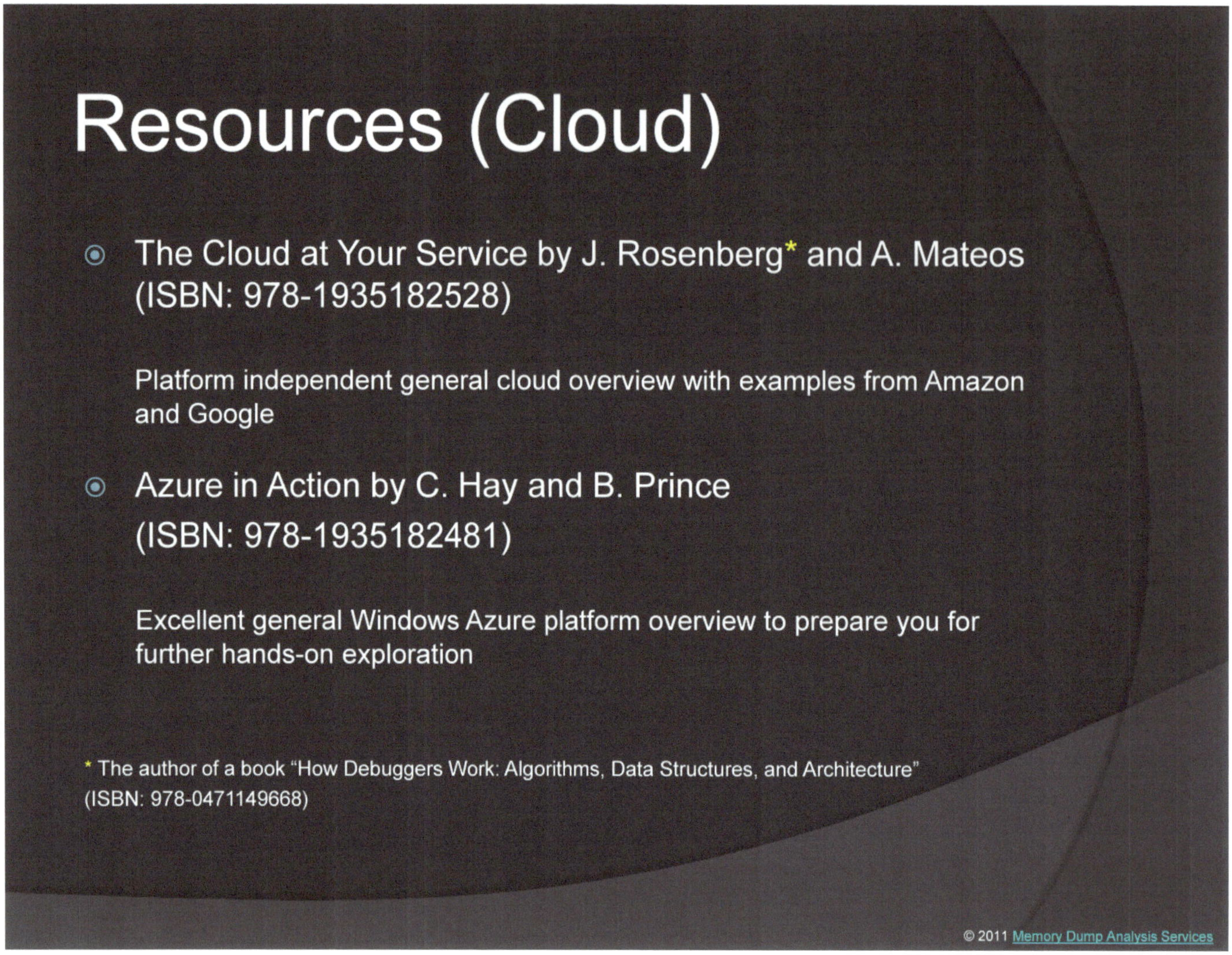

The two books I read before into a cloud are on this slide and I highly recommend them for a structured overview and brush up on some WEB technologies, .NET, and database concepts if you have been deep in traditional desktop development.

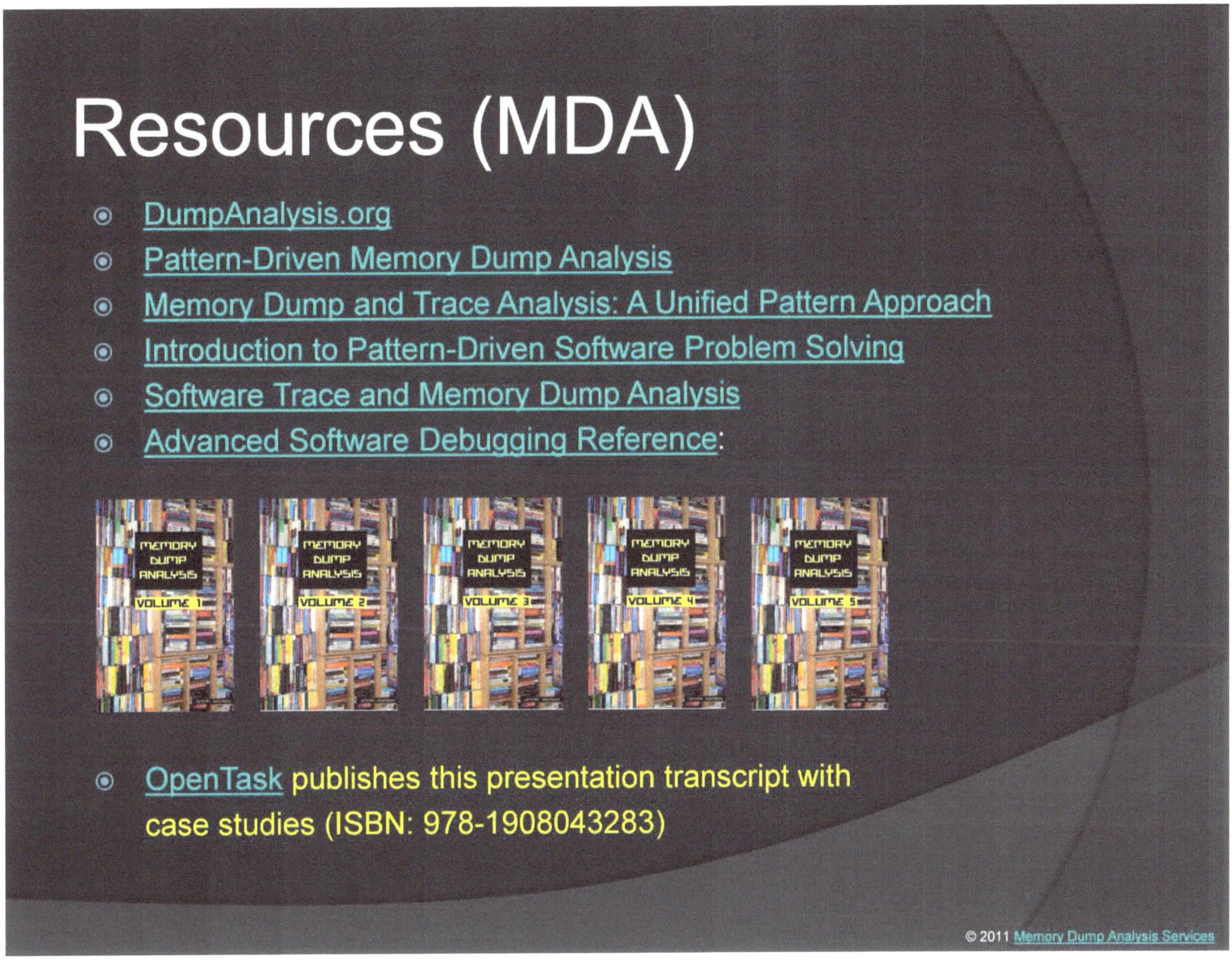

This slide has links for further study including a presentation with full transcript comments about pattern-driven memory dump analysis I delivered 2 years ago and a full case study from Debugging Experts Magazine. I also recently organized two free Webinars on pattern-driven software problem solving which also cover troubleshooting and debugging tools patterns (Debugware), software trace analysis, workaround patterns, structural memory patterns and unified debugging patterns.

Pattern-Driven Memory Dump Analysis:
http://blogs.citrix.com/author/dmitryv/

Memory Dump and Trace Analysis: A Unified Pattern Approach:
http://www.debuggingexperts.com/memory-dump-trace-analysis-unified-pattern-approach

Introduction to Pattern-Driven Software Problem Solving:
http://www.patterndiagnostics.com/PDSPSI-materials

Software Trace and Memory Dump Analysis:
http://www.patterndiagnostics.com/STMDA-materials

Advanced Software Debugging Reference:
http://www.dumpanalysis.org/advanced-software-debugging-reference

OpenTask:
http://www.opentask.com

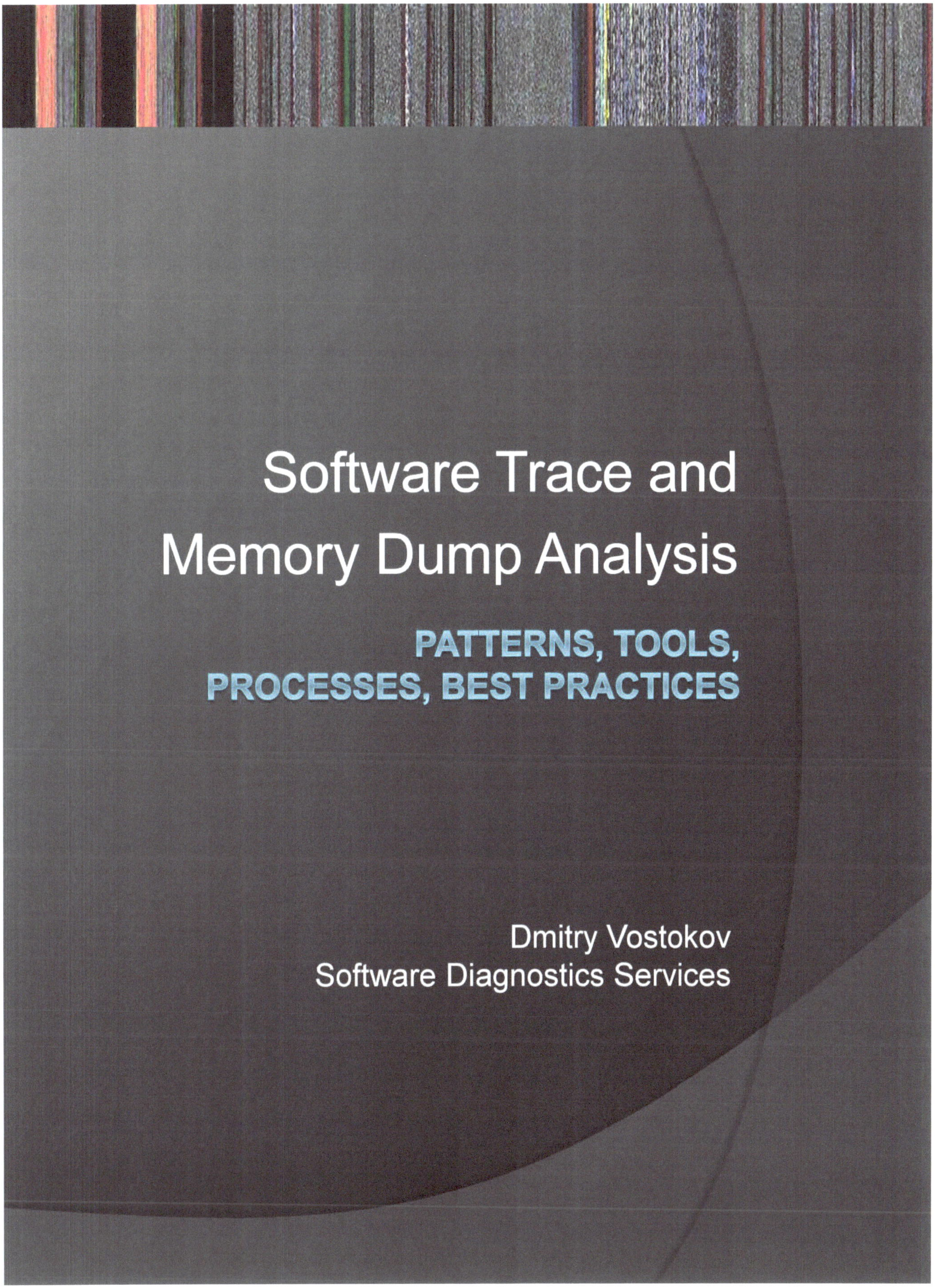
Software Trace and
Memory Dump Analysis
PATTERNS, TOOLS,
PROCESSES, BEST PRACTICES
Dmitry Vostokov
Software Diagnostics Services

Published by OpenTask, Republic of Ireland

OpenTask books and magazines are available through booksellers and distributors worldwide. Please send requests to press@opentask.com for further information or comments.

A CIP catalogue record for this book is available from the British Library.

ISBN-l3: 978-1-908043-23-8 (Paperback)

First printing, 2014

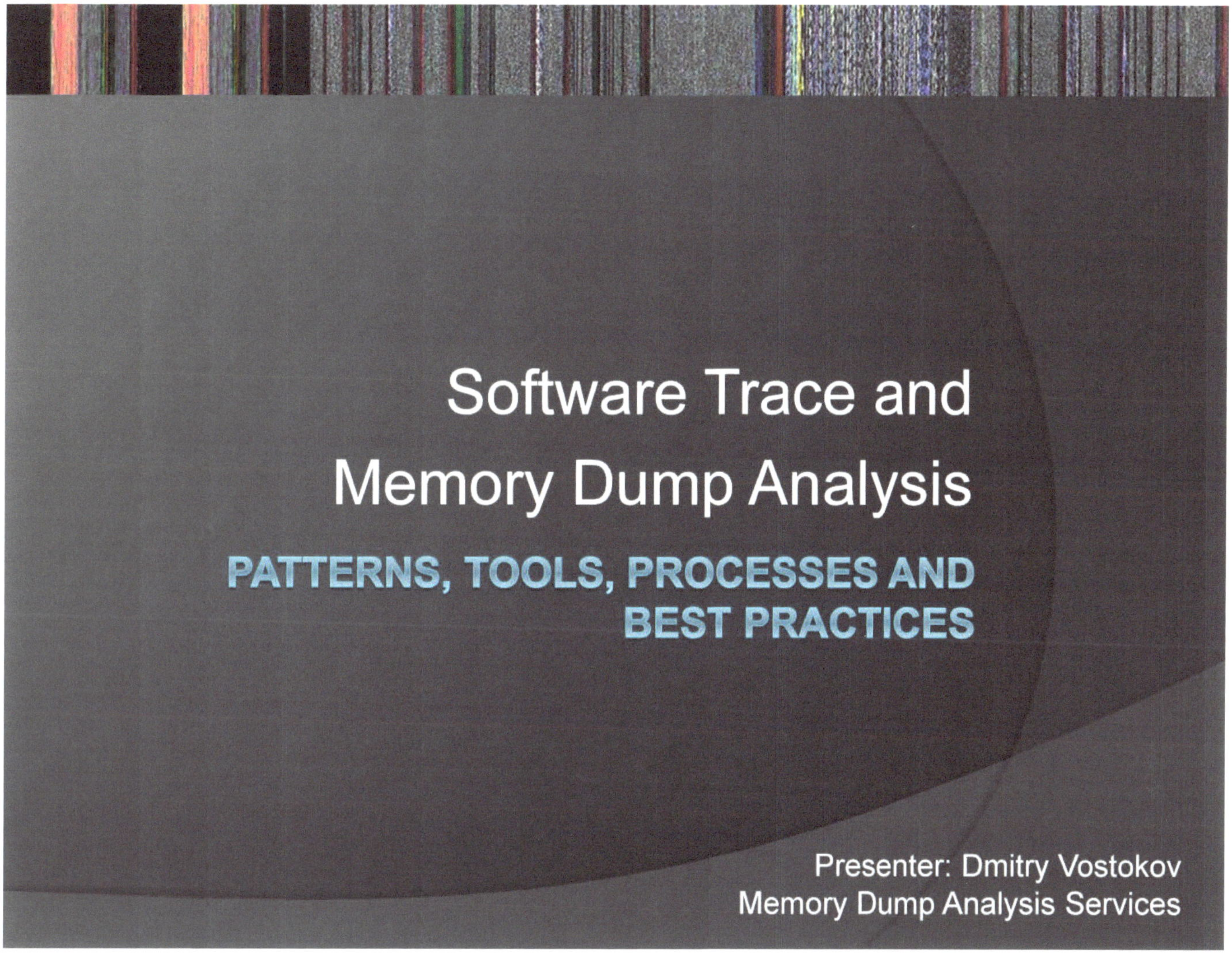

Hello Everyone! My name is Dmitry Vostokov, and I'm the founder of Memory Dump Analysis Services[1] which specializes in crash dump analysis, software trace analysis and debugging in general, not tied to a particular vendor. The topic of today's presentation is patterns, tools, processes and best practices for software trace and memory dump analysis. The topic is so big that I devised this particular presentation as just an introduction. I also put more emphasis on software trace analysis here and speak about memory dump analysis as continuity from previous research or as a part of case studies that include software traces.

[1] Now **Software Diagnostics Services**: www.patterndiagnostics.com

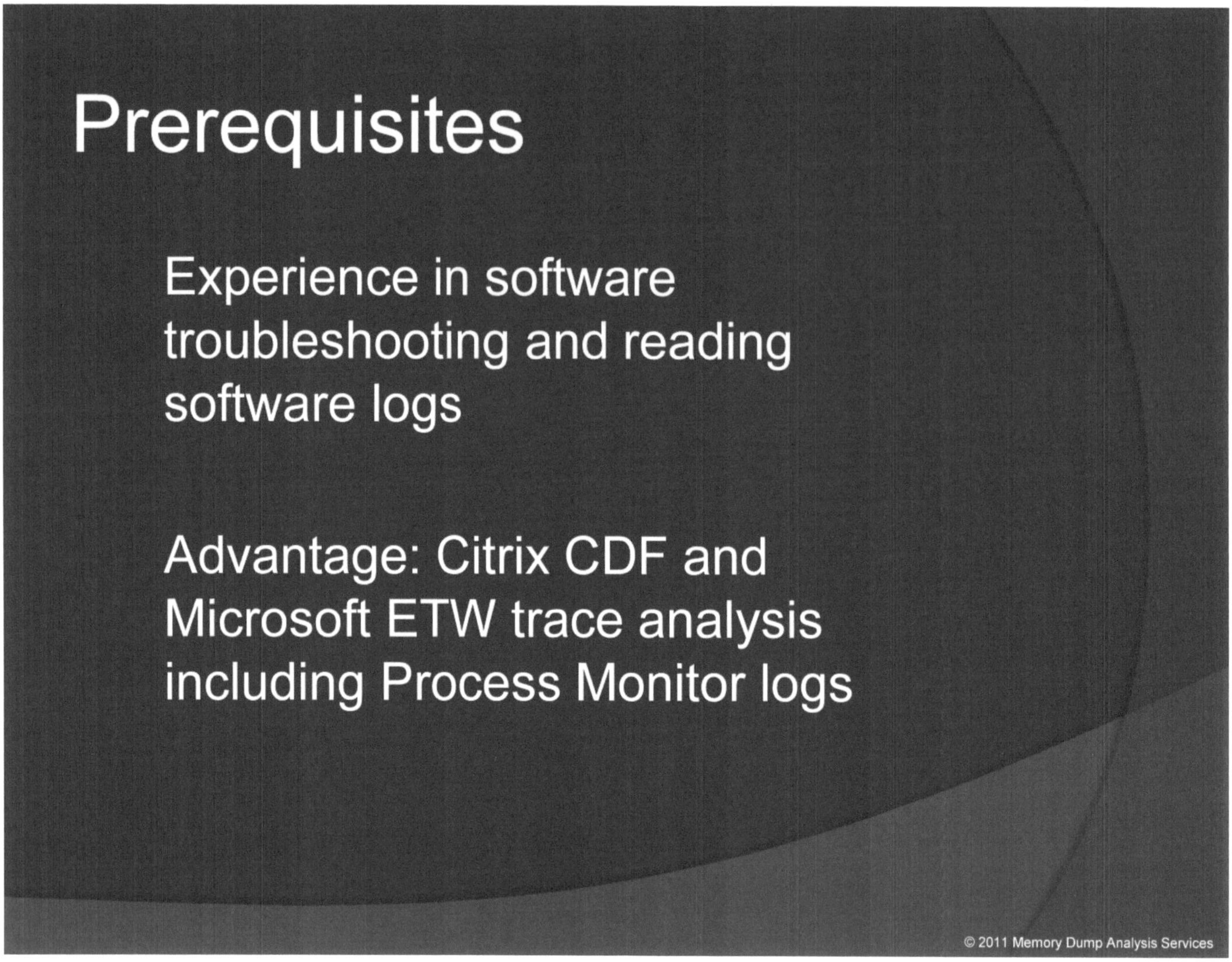

I assume that you already have some experience in software troubleshooting or debugging. There is something for everyone in this presentation. Because almost every computer program generates software traces and considering the variety of trace formats and tools, I had to restrict myself to vendors and tools you are most familiar with: Citrix and Microsoft. As you already may know, Citrix Common Diagnostic Format (CDF) is based on Microsoft Event Tracing for Windows (ETW). So everything we discuss here is applicable to pure Microsoft troubleshooting and debugging too.

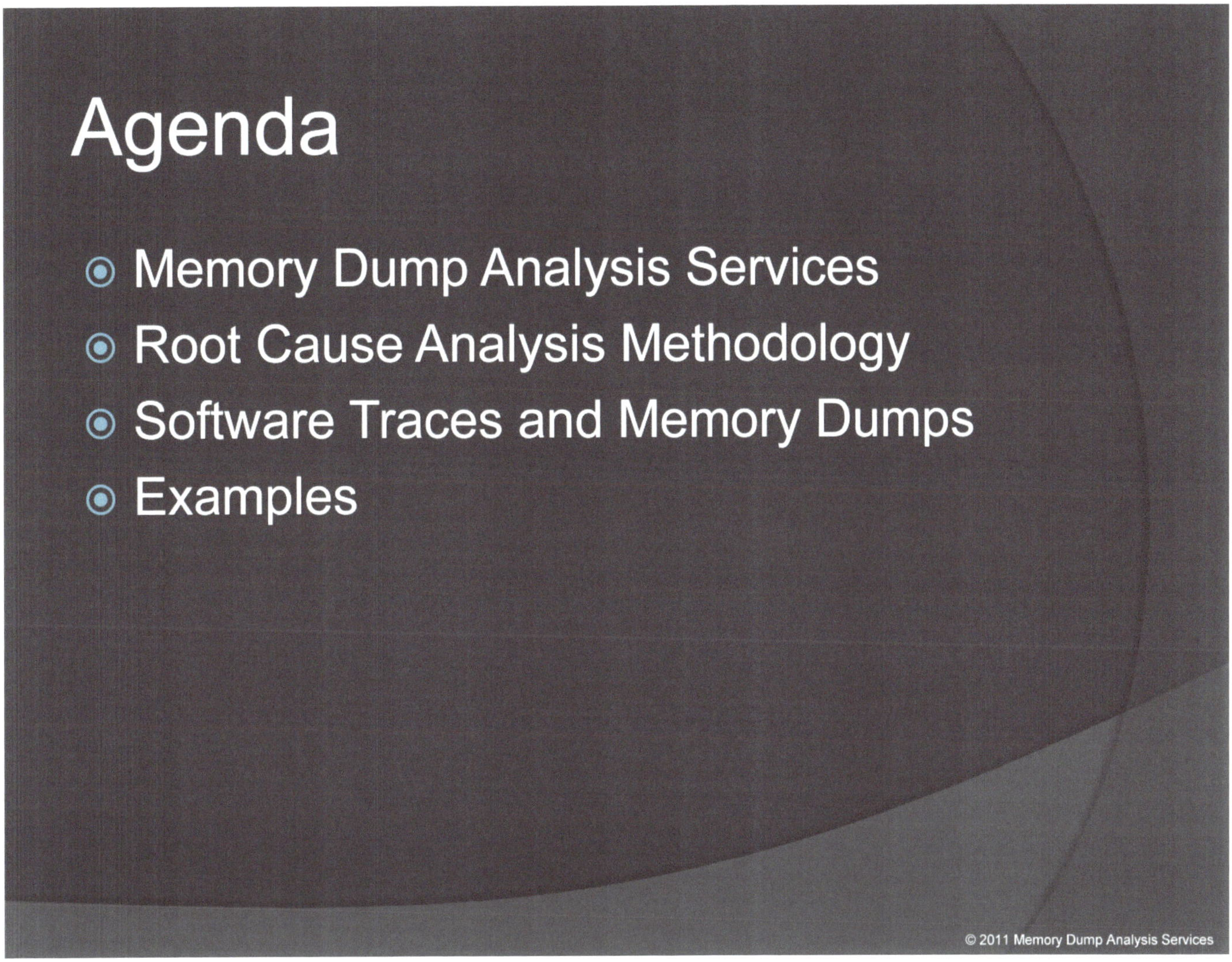

This presentation is short. Instead of trying to cover everything about software trace analysis I sometimes only provide hints and links where to find further information. First, I briefly talk about Memory Dump Analysis Services, and then we discuss the root cause analysis methodology which, as a generic framework, includes tools, processes, and best practices. Then we spend most of the time talking about software traces and pattern examples.

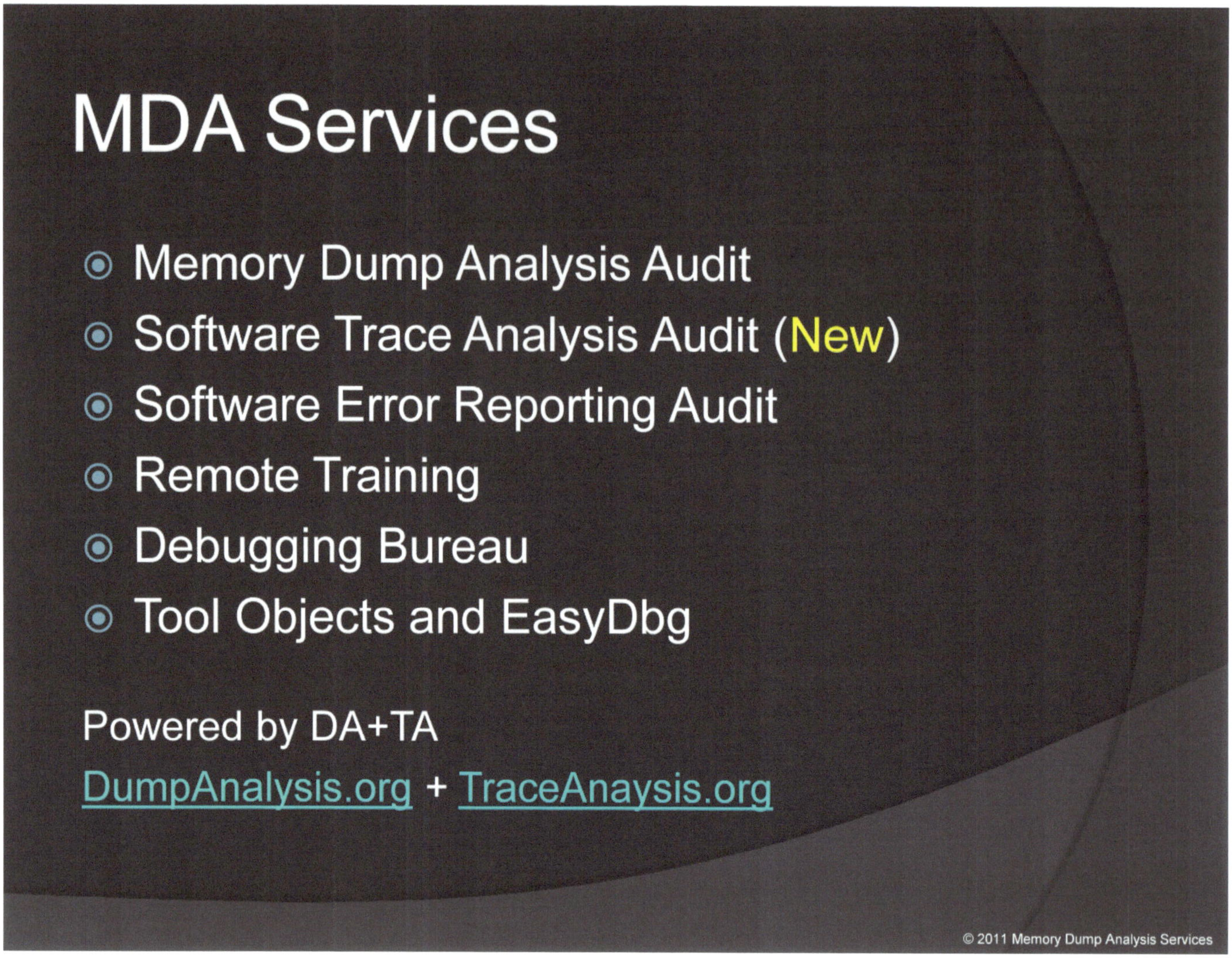

Memory Dump Analysis (MDA) Services was established in summer 2010 to provide state of the art training and support to enterprise customers especially in the area of high profile software incidents that require substantial expertise in memory analysis. Later on some other services were added such as software error reporting audit for companies that need to review their software incident reporting, artifact collection and processing. We modeled "Debugging Bureau of Investigations" on FBI. Memory Dump Analysis Services also owns Tool Objects and Easy Debugger – a powerful platform for integration of troubleshooting and debugging tools. And, of course, the substantial part of our services is training and seminars. We are powered by DumpAnalysis.org portal – a repository of software problem solving patterns.

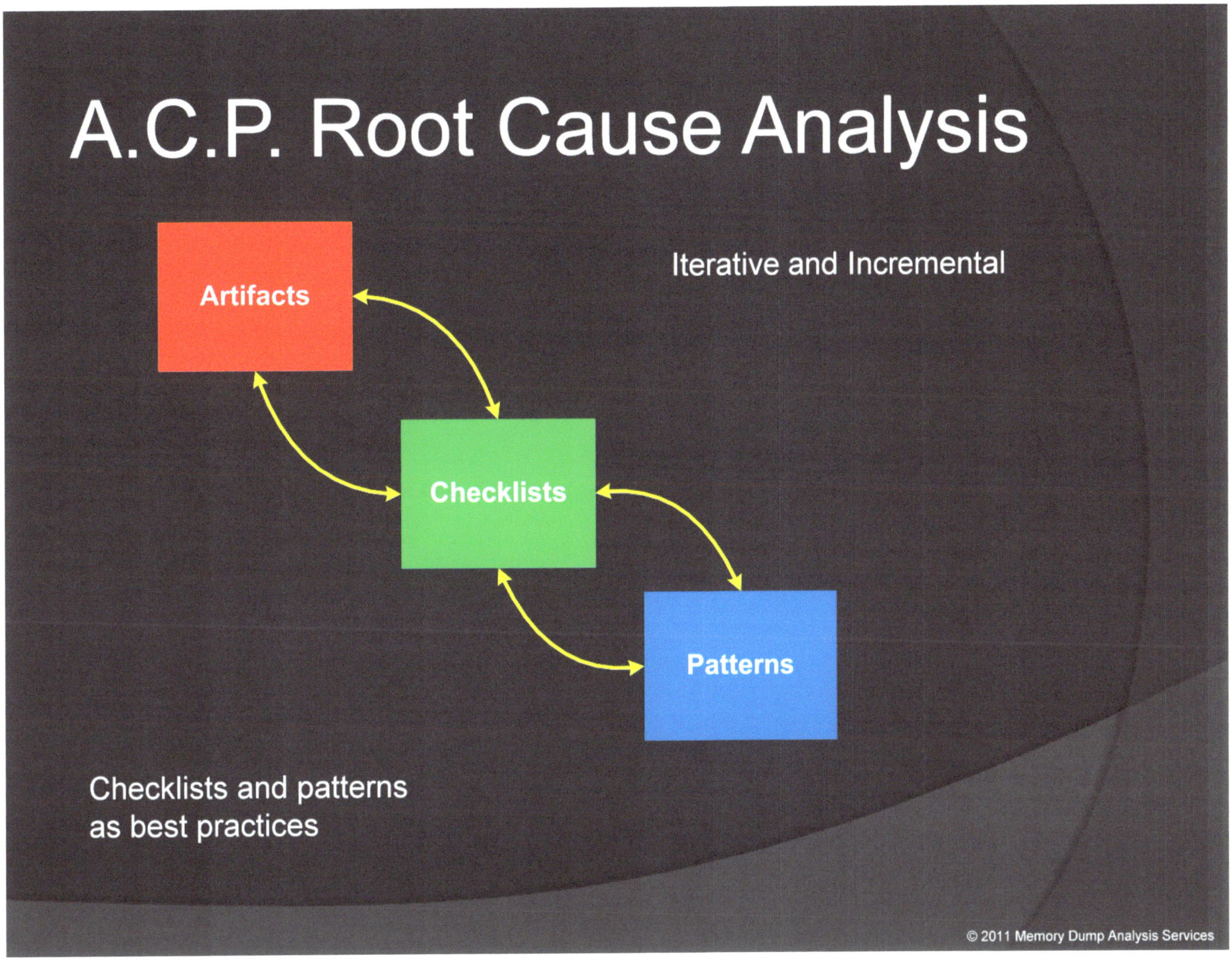

We are evangelists of A.C.P. iterative and incremental root cause analysis process that includes artifacts such as software traces and memory dumps, checklists, and patterns. The latter we consider as best practices.

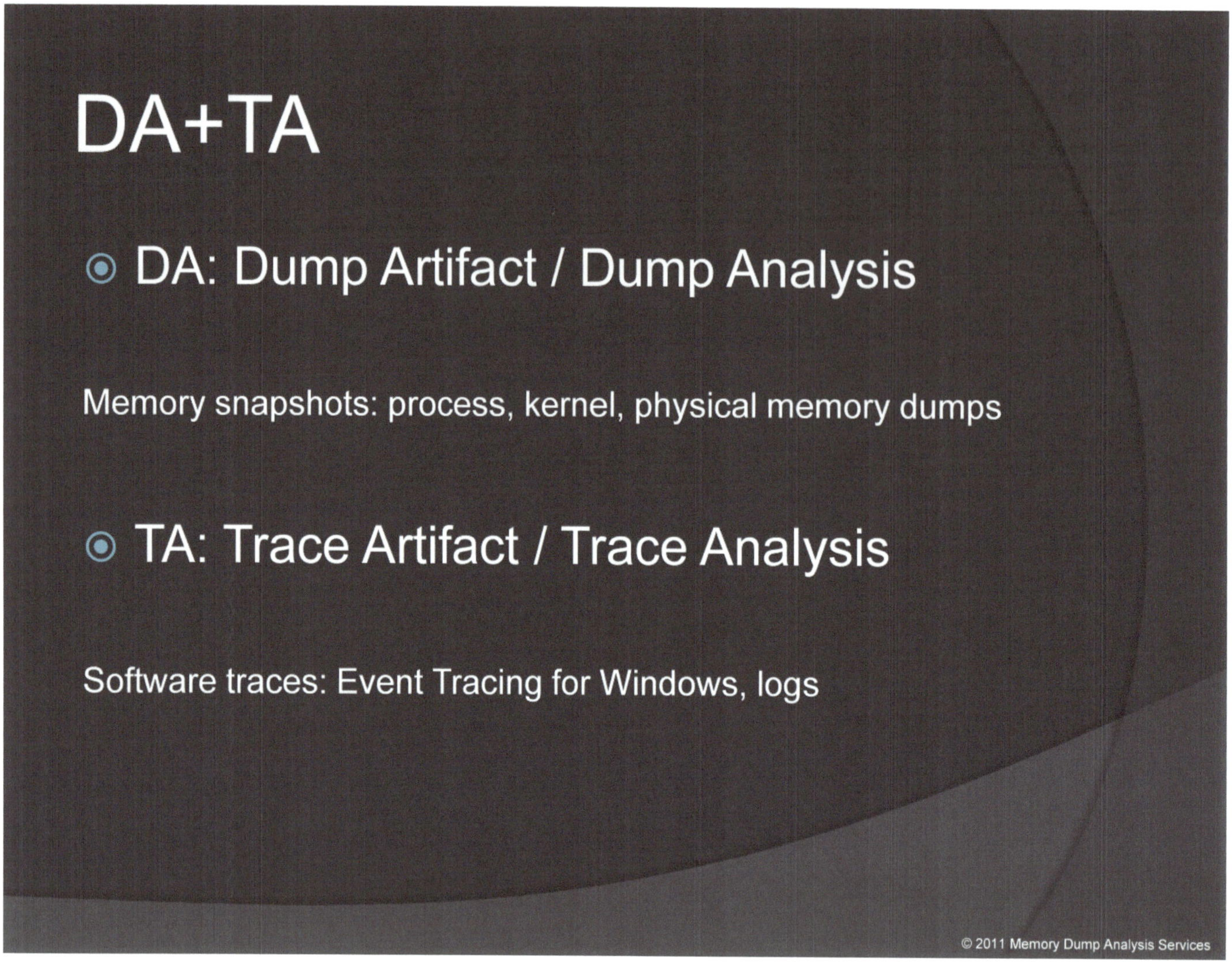

By chance, DATA looks like a good abbreviation for Dump (Artifact) Analysis and Trace (Artifact) Analysis. By a dump we mean a memory snapshot, usually called a memory dump, crash dump, or core dump. By a trace, we mean a log, for example, Process Monitor logs or Citrix CDF traces which are based on Microsoft Event Tracing for Windows. Network traces are also examples of software traces, but we won't cover them in this presentation.

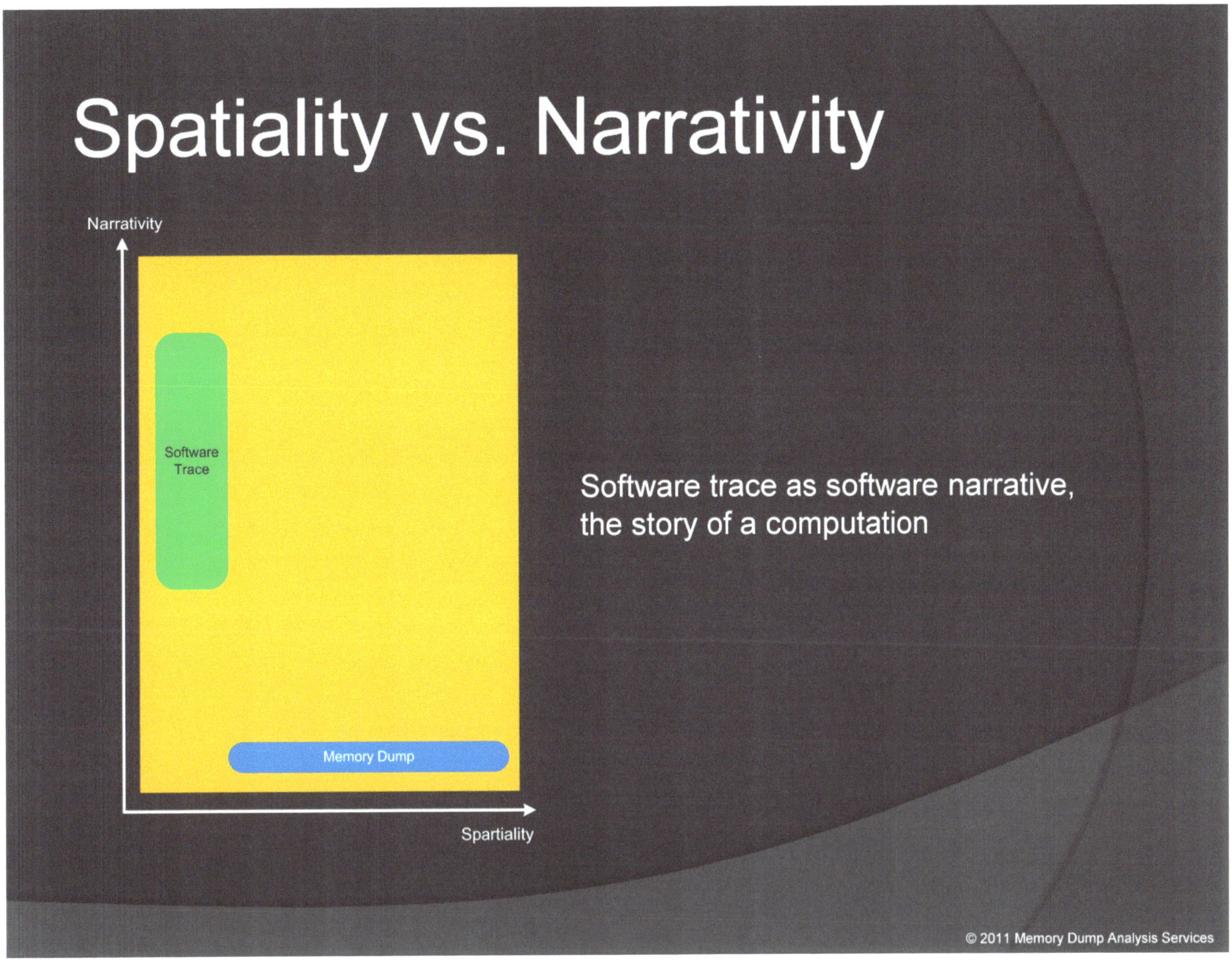

Once I was asked how to explain the essence of software traces to an end-user, and I came up with an idea to treat them as software narratives, stories of computation. They belong more to a temporal story-telling perspective where many details are omitted like in real stories. In contrast memory dumps (especially dumps of physical memory) have everything for a specific moment but lack temporal perspective. Fortunately, memory dumps have lots of traces inside too. Software traces consist of trace messages, and these can be considered as "pico" or "femto" memory dumps. On the other hand, a sequence of process memory dumps consecutively saved can be considered as a huge software trace. So we see that software traces and logs are special cases of memory dumps and the other way around. But enough generalizations here: we move to more practical things and talk about best practices: tools, checklists and patterns.

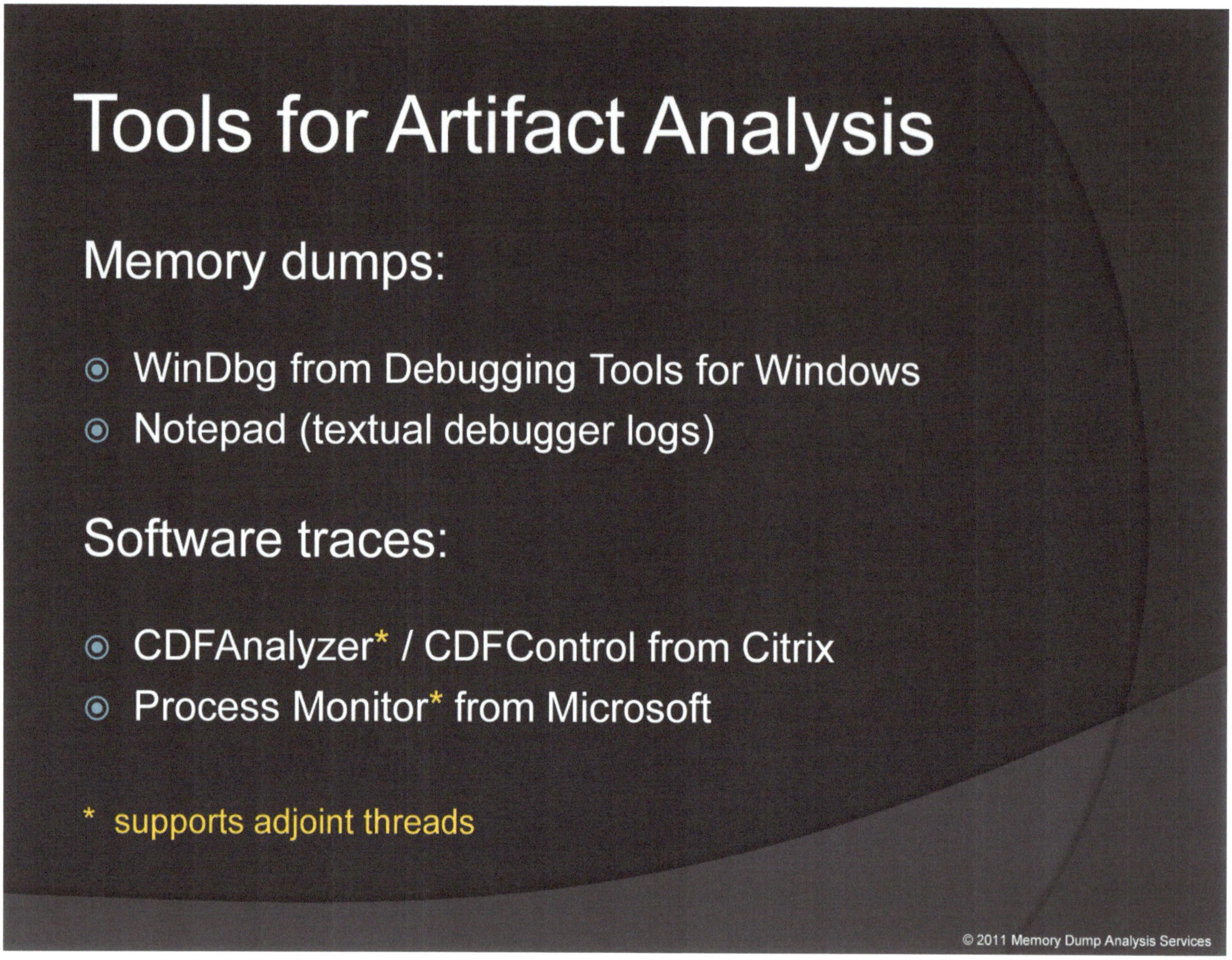

My favorite tools for artifact analysis include Debugging Tools for Windows and Notepad for memory dumps and debugger logs. For CDF trace analysis, I recommend CDFAnalyzer from Citrix because it supports adjoint threads we would talk about later.

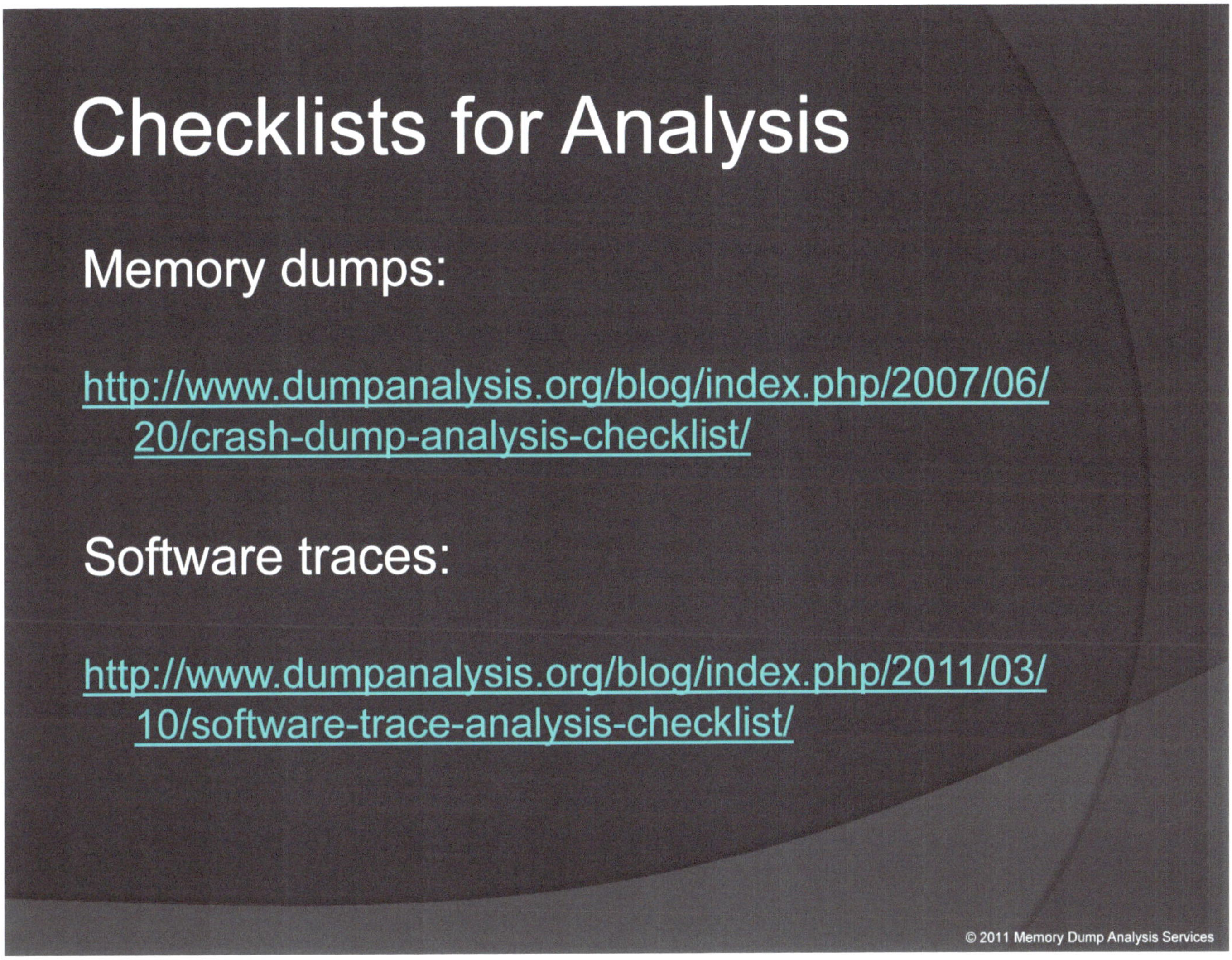

Here I put two links for checklists to use when analyzing memory dumps and software traces. Please bear in mind that these checklists are constantly developing and improving especially the recent one about software traces.

Memory dumps:
http://www.dumpanalysis.org/windows-memory-analysis-checklist

Software traces:
http://www.dumpanalysis.org/blog/index.php/2011/03/10/software-trace-analysis-checklist/

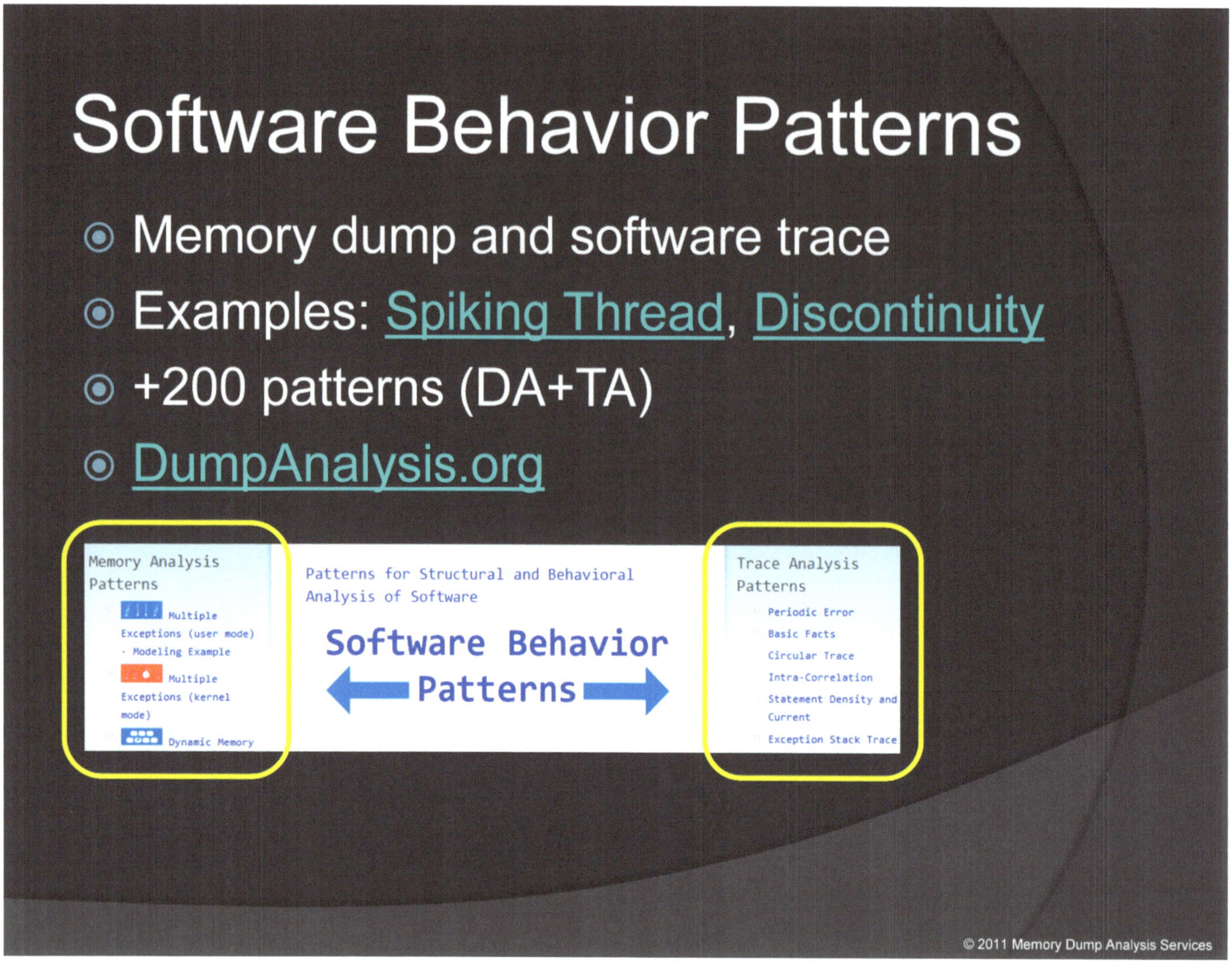

The main part of best practices is software behavior patterns that are visible and discernible signs in memory dump and software trace artifacts. Some of them result from software defects and some result from unanticipated and unexpected software interaction. There are lots of patterns on DumpAnalysis.org portal[2]. The picture shows that when you go there on the left-hand side you will see memory dump analysis patterns and on the right-hand side you would see software trace analysis patterns. You may notice some pictures or icons on the left: this is a not yet completed project to give each pattern a corresponding pattern icon.

Spiking Thread:
http://www.dumpanalysis.org/blog/index.php/2007/05/11/crash-dump-analysis-patterns-part-14/

Discontinuity:
http://www.dumpanalysis.org/blog/index.php/2009/08/04/trace-analysis-patterns-part-8/

[2] +400 in 2014.

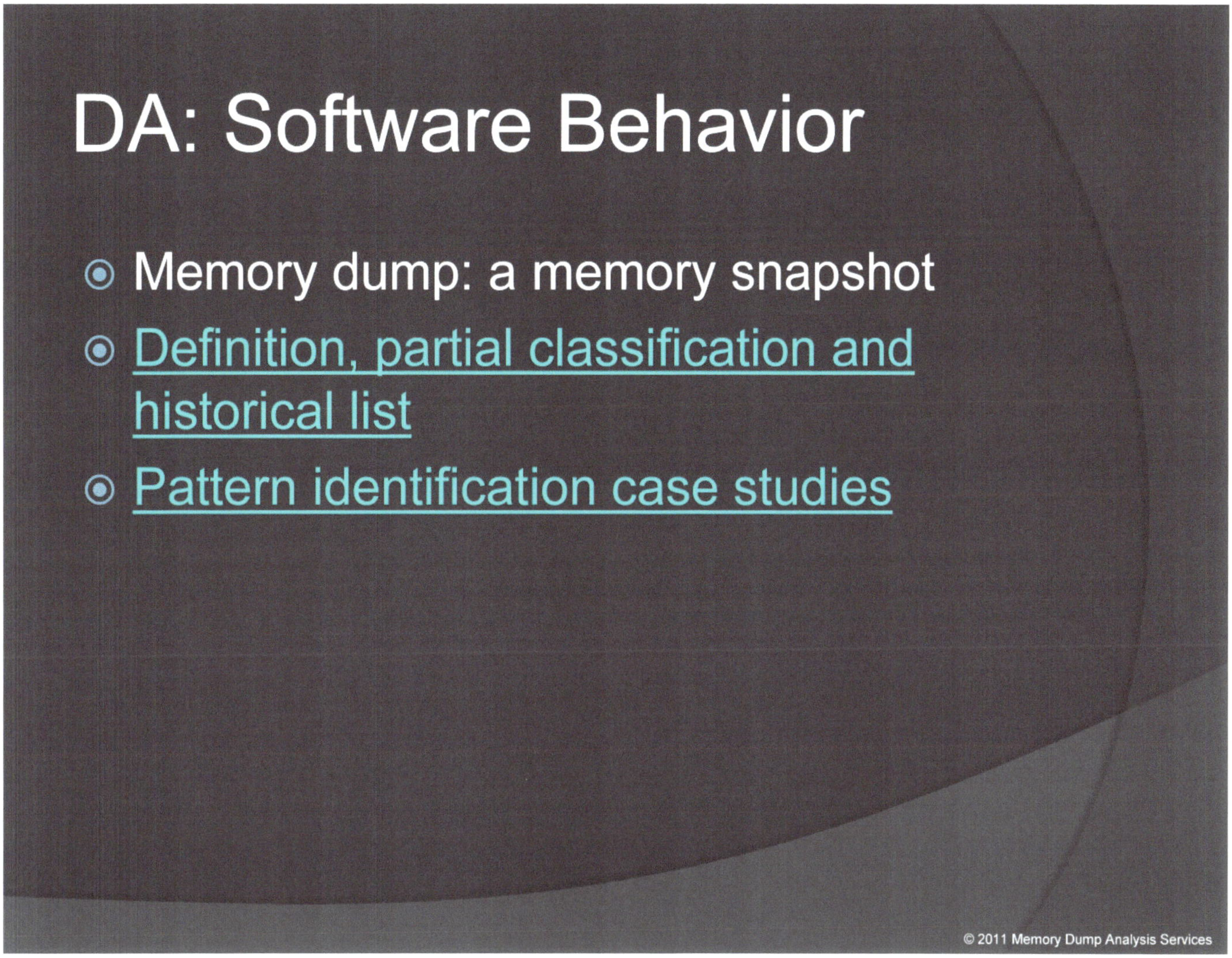

This slide provides various links to memory dump analysis patterns and their case studies.

Definition, a partial classification, and historical list:
http://www.dumpanalysis.org/blog/index.php/crash-dump-analysis-patterns/

Pattern identification case studies:
http://www.dumpanalysis.org/blog/index.php/pattern-cooperation/

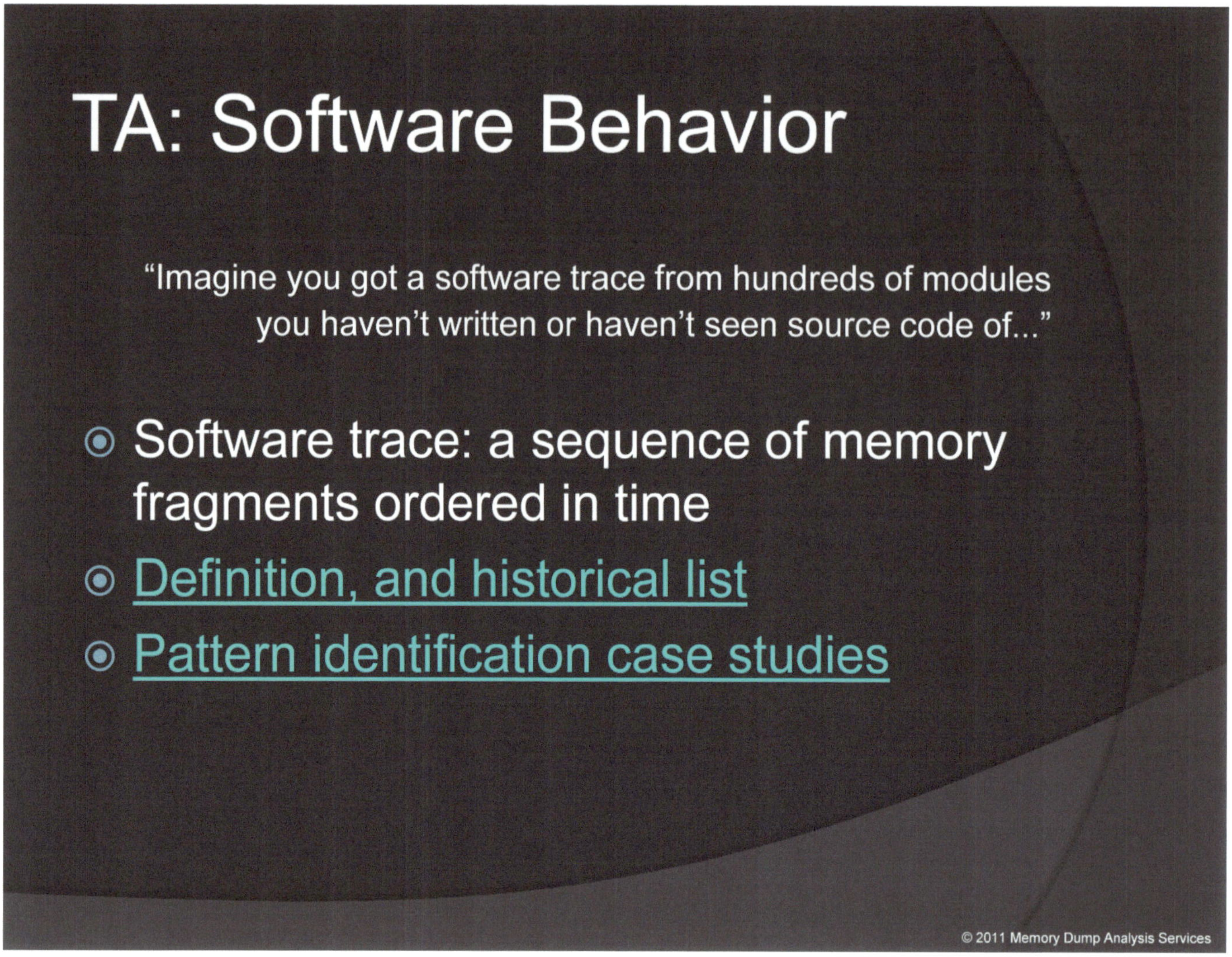

Similar links are available for software trace analysis patterns and their case studies. There are parallels between some software trace patterns and memory dump patterns. For example, stack traces can be analyzed using some trace analysis patterns. These patterns are general and not tied to a specific product. In the past, I used to analyze software traces with millions of lines and messages from hundreds of components. Most of the traces were completely unfamiliar for me, and I have never seen their underlying source code. Because of that I proposed the very general patterns that can be used even for network traces. Now we come to even more practical examples, and I show you a typical CDFAnalyzer tool screenshot.

Definition and historical list:
http://www.dumpanalysis.org/blog/index.php/trace-analysis-patterns/

Pattern identification case studies:
http://www.dumpanalysis.org/blog/index.php/pattern-cooperation/

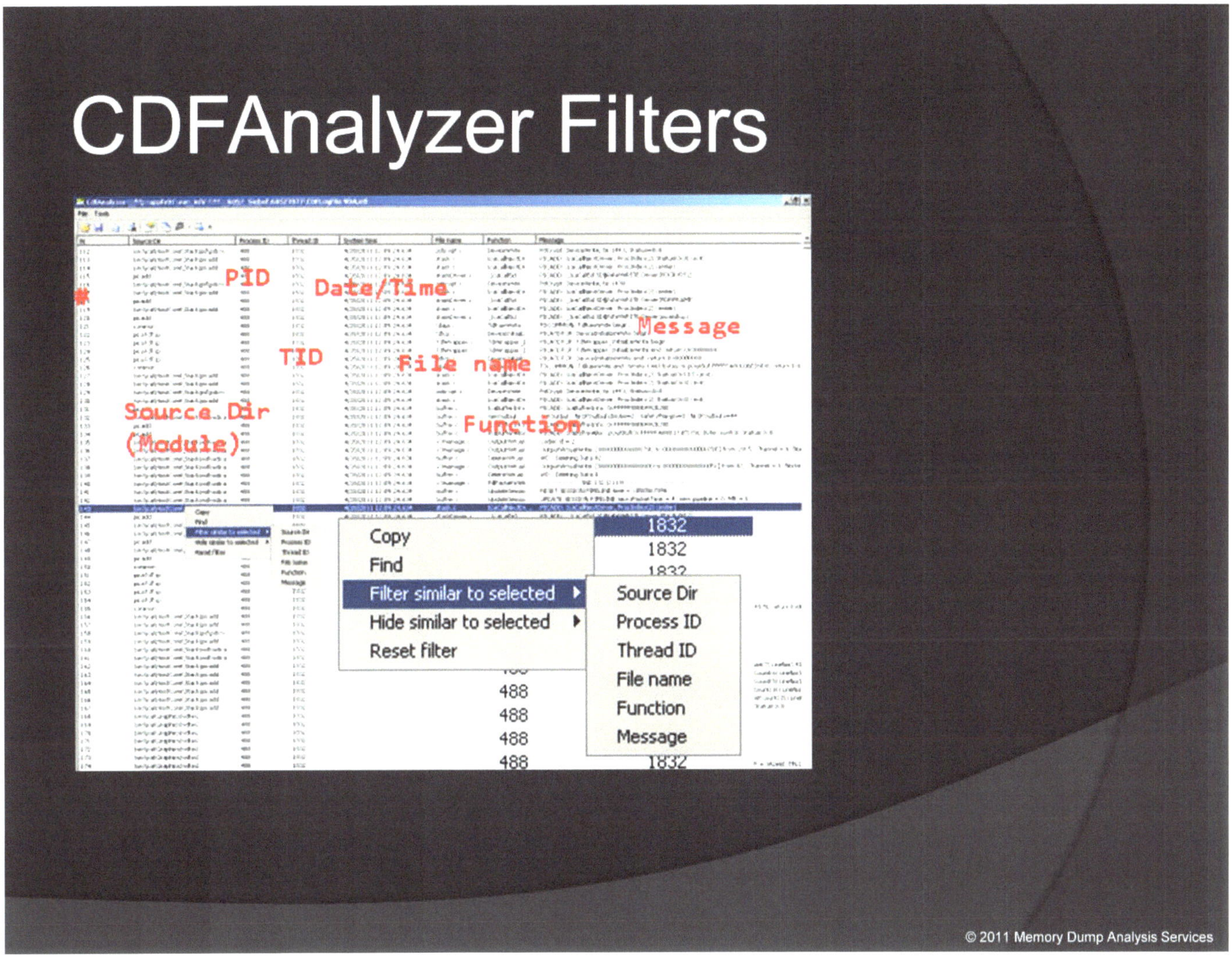

If you are not familiar with this tool, you can download it from Citrix Support[3]. You see various columns such as process and thread IDs. The main feature of CDFAnalyzer is its support of adjoint threading. The latter is a fancy computer science term I invented to describe filtering by similarity. We see that we can filter text messages by process or thread ID, file name, function or even message text. We can find the same filtering in Process Monitor, for example. Let me now explain why I called the filtering results adjoint threads. Let's first recall ordinary threads.

[3] http://support.citrix.com/article/ctx122741

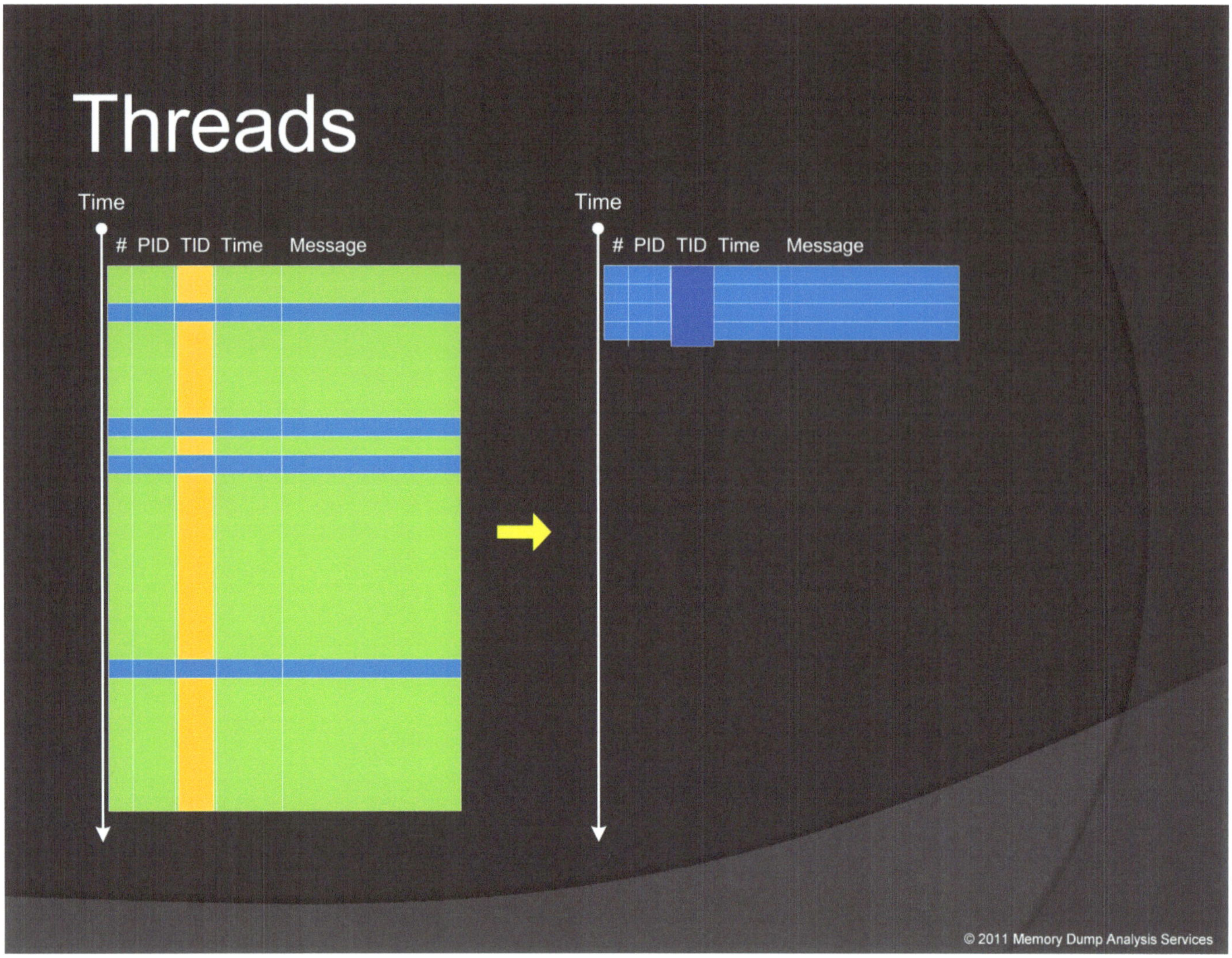

From a software trace perspective, threads are just messages with a particular thread ID (TID) invariant. When we select such messages or apply filtering, we get the temporal sequence of thread execution narrative story.

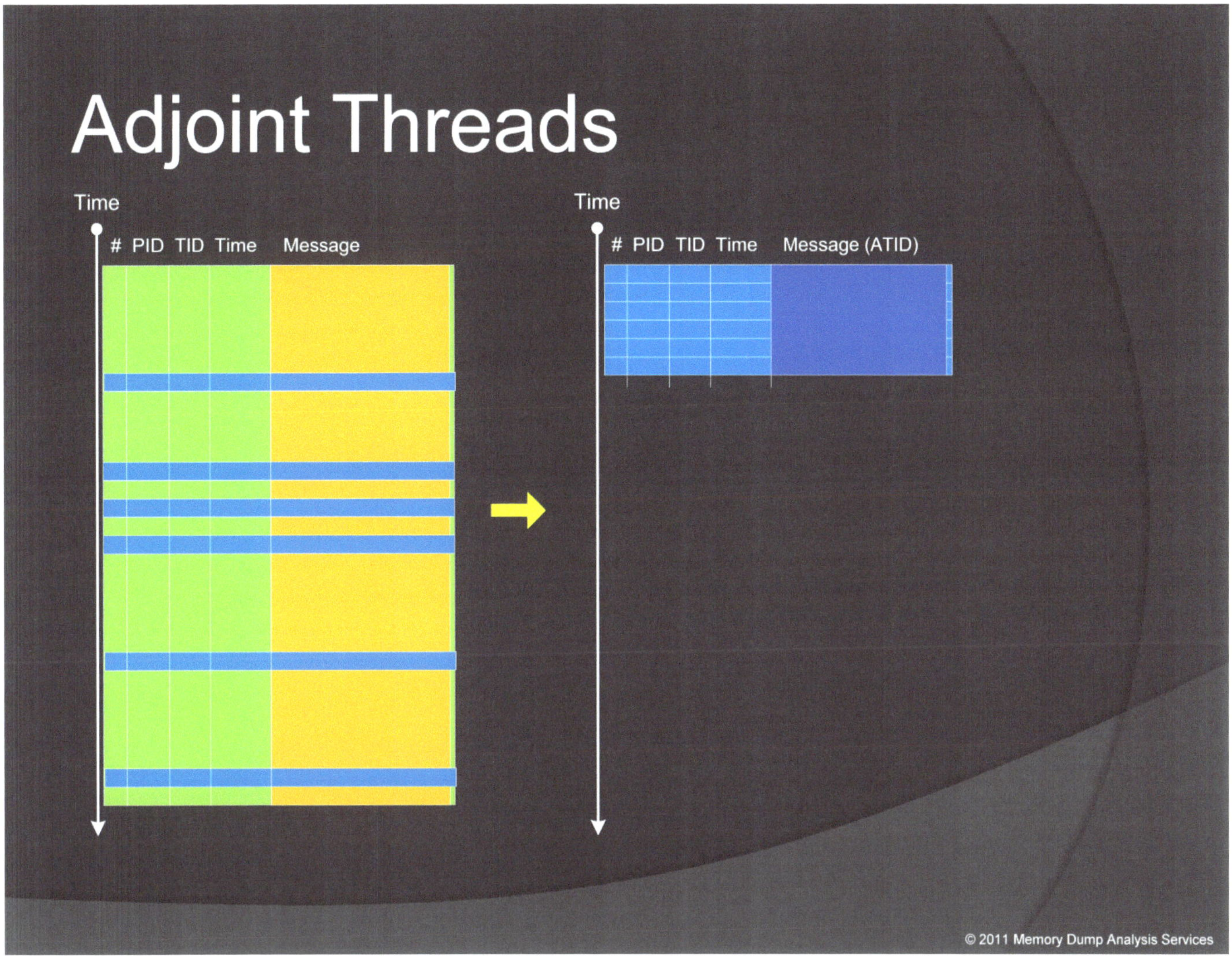

By a similar way, we can generalize for other columns and consider their column invariant as a type of a more general thread concept that I call adjoint thread with the corresponding adjoint thread ID (ATID). It could be, for example, all messages generated by a particular function or module, etc. On this picture, we show an adjoint thread consisting of all messages such as "Process xxx has been launched". Every such message is an example of a **Significant Event** pattern in many troubleshooting scenarios.

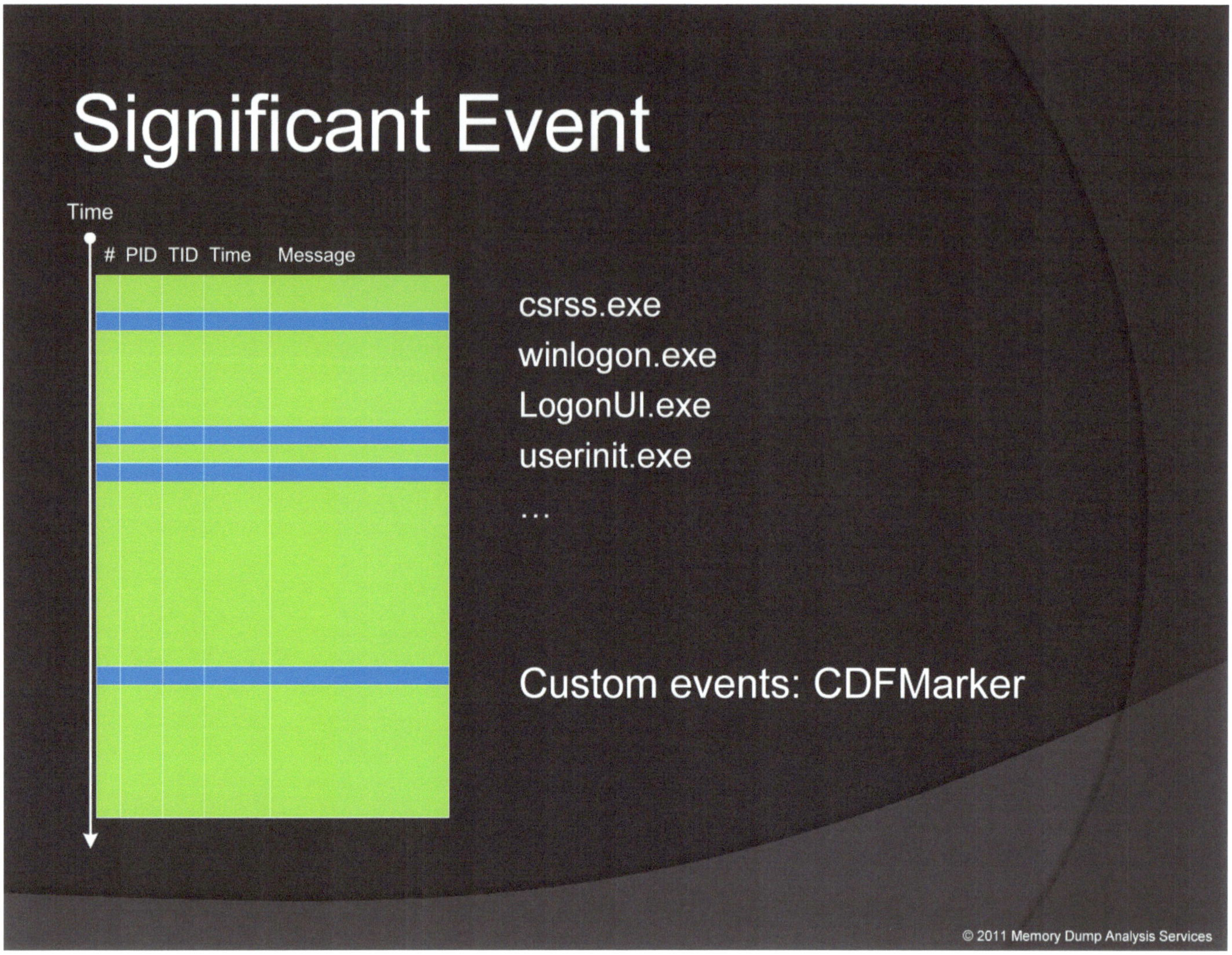

Useful for the analysis of process startup sequences, for example, how much time it took each session process to launch.

CDFMarker:
http://support.citrix.com/article/CTX125347

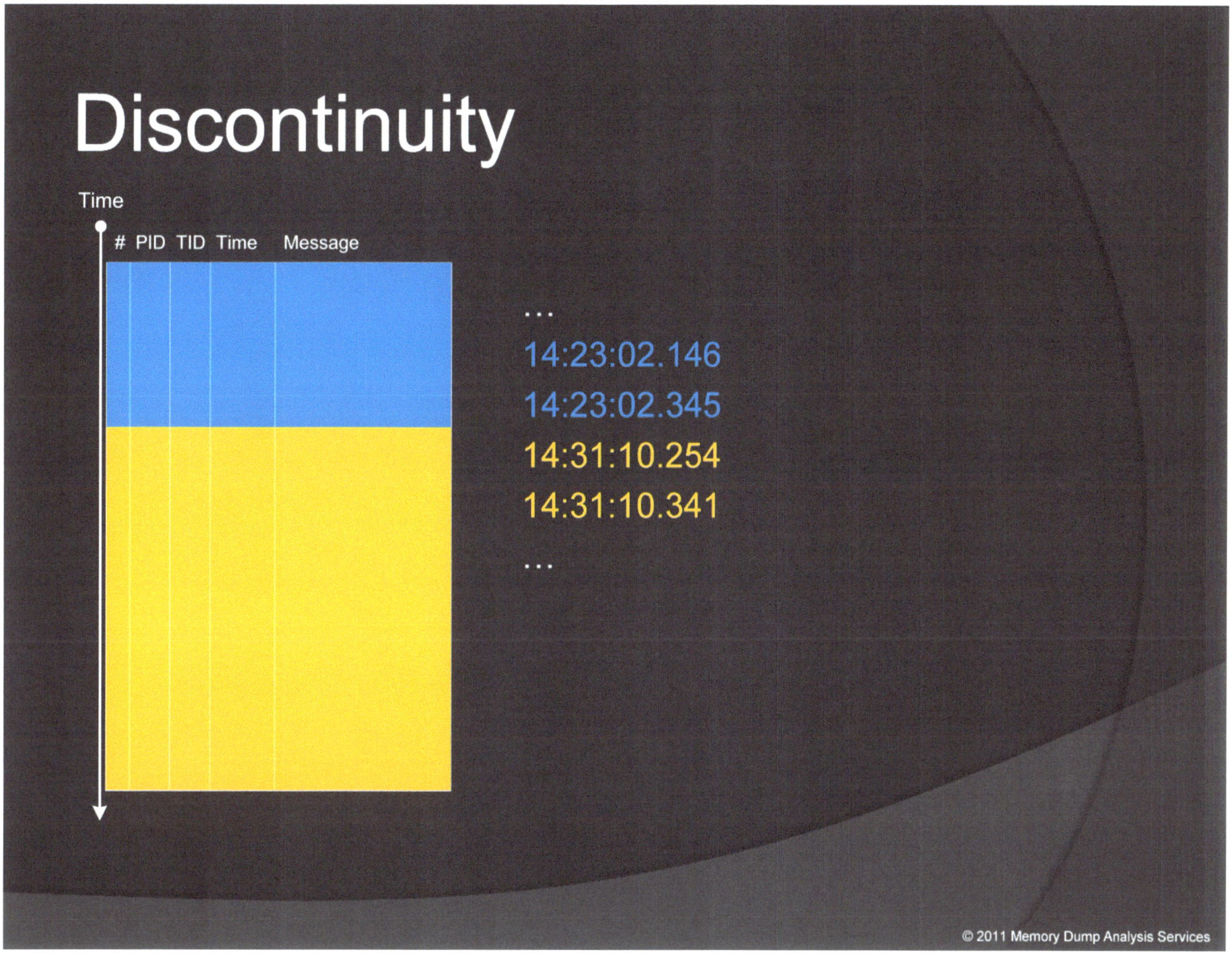

Useful for the analysis of delays, for example, again for analysis of process startup sequences, blocked threads, etc.

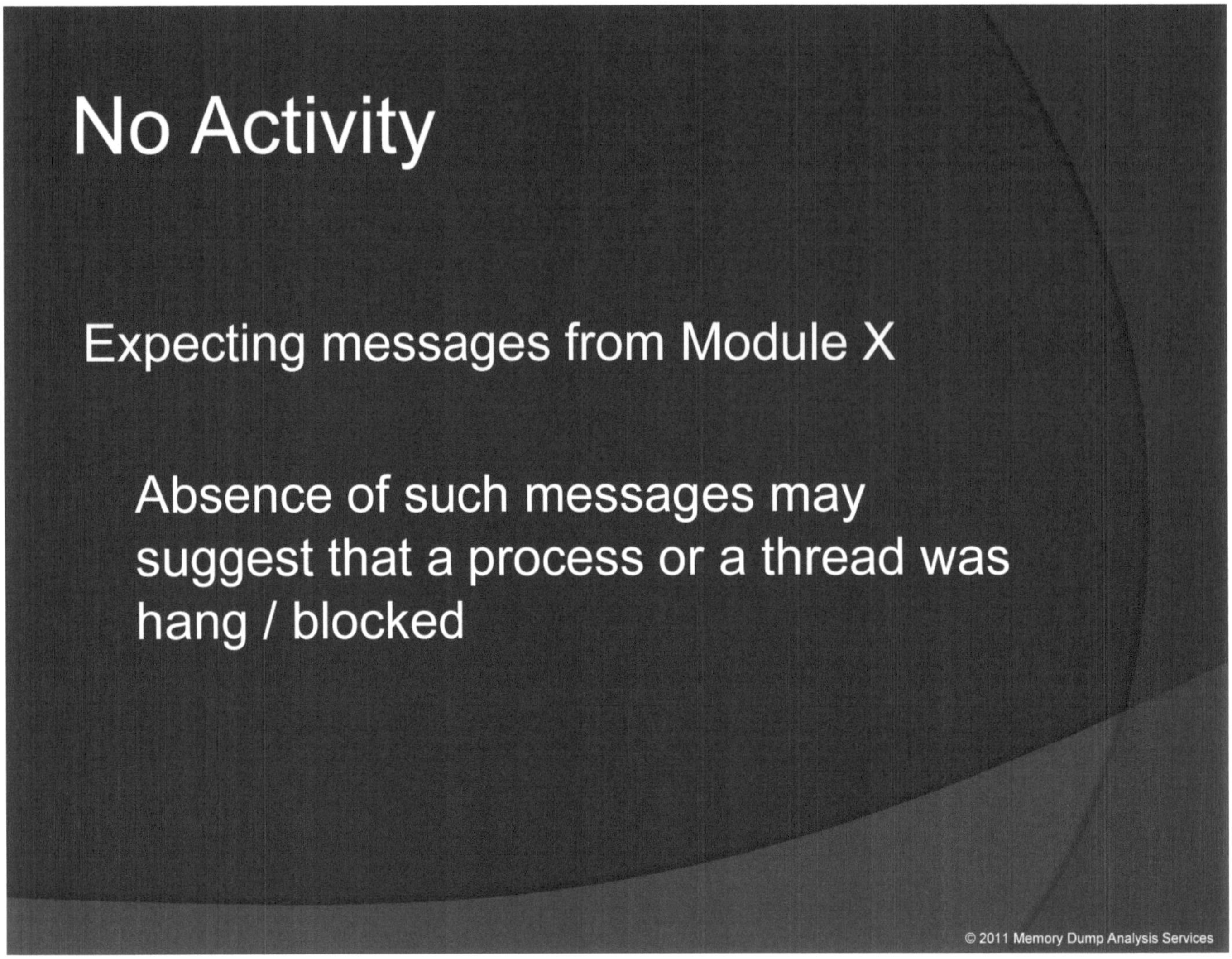

If we expect messages from some component and don't see them, it may point to a blocked thread.

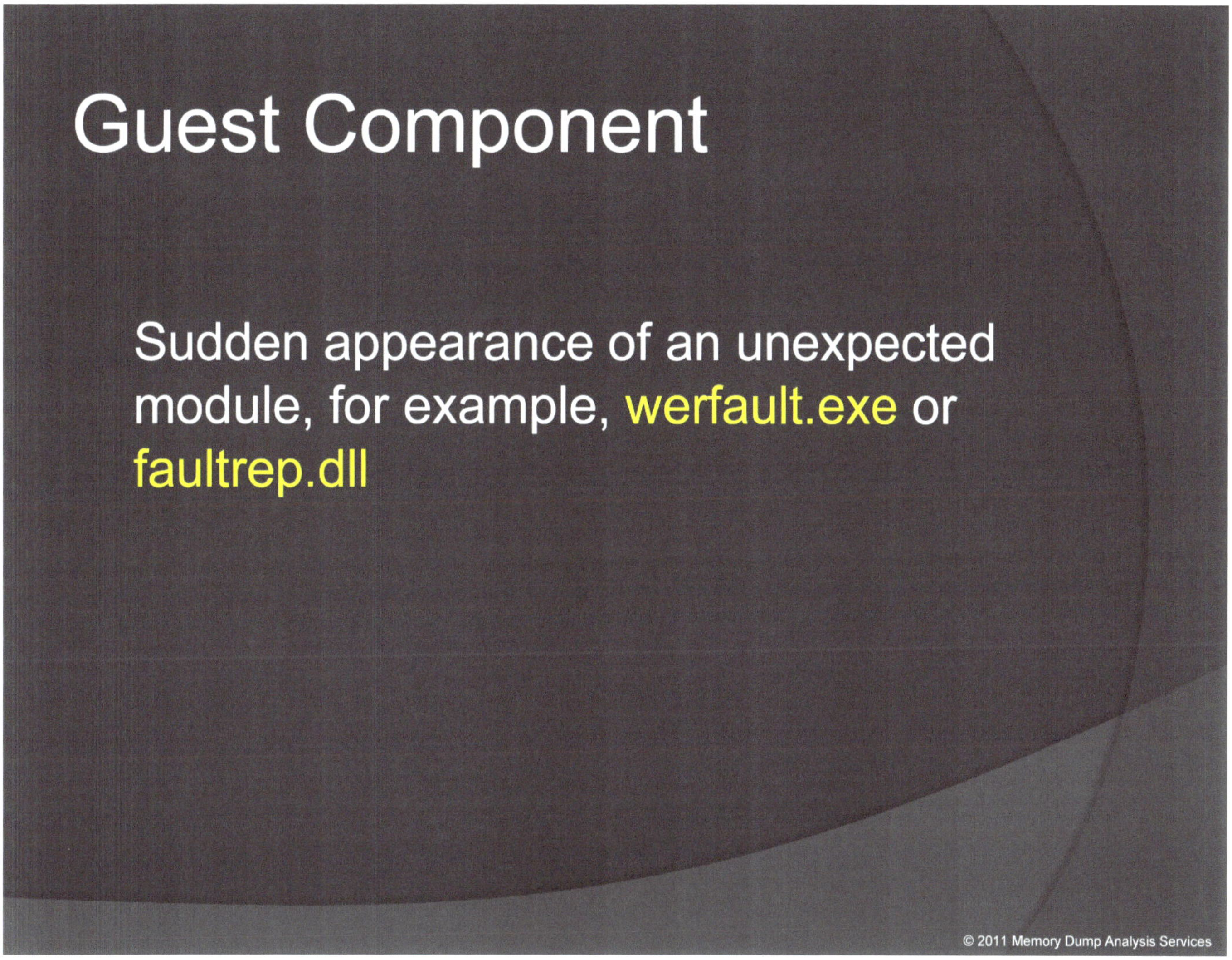

Some components may appear in logs when we don't expect them.

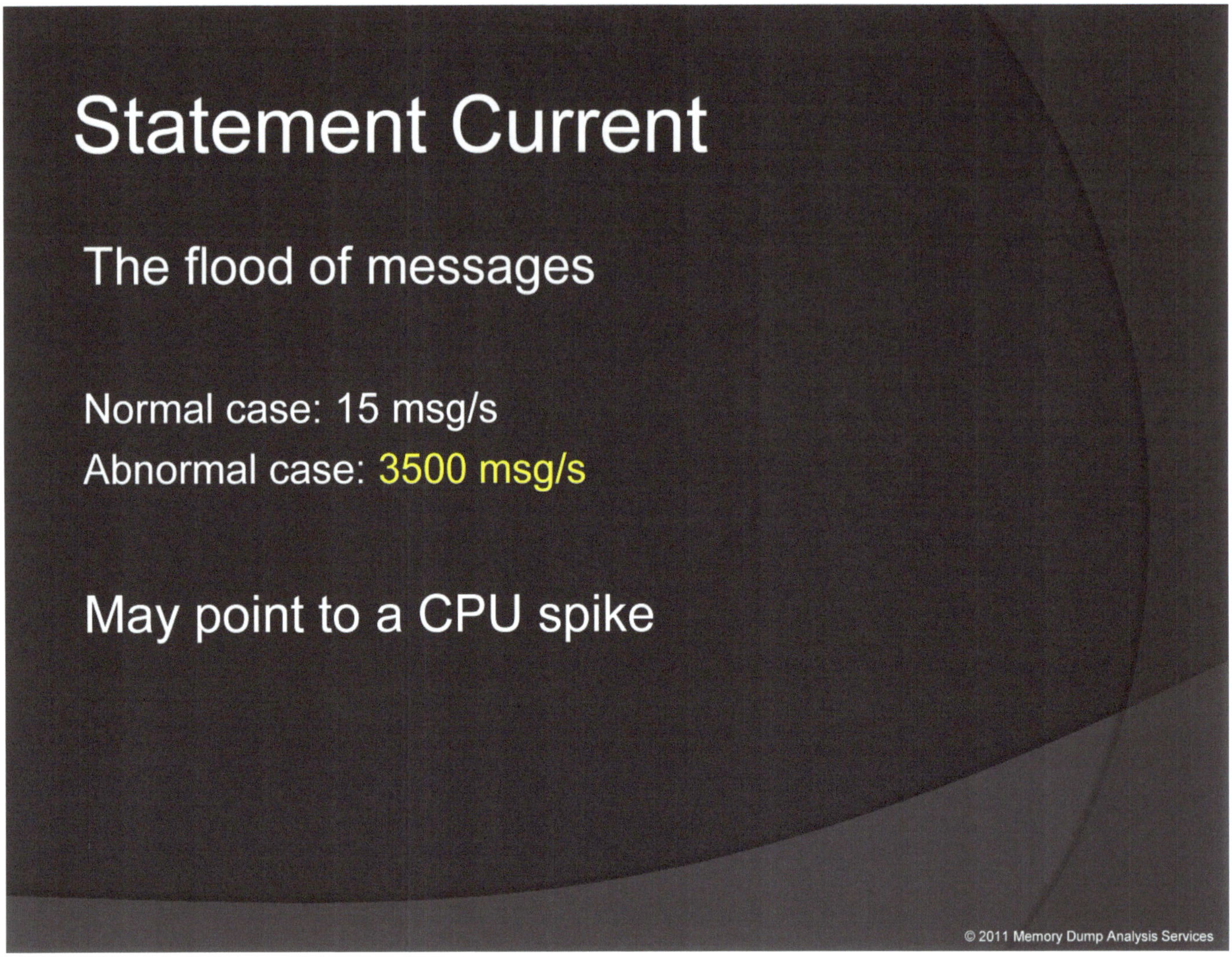

The abnormal number of some messages per second of tracing may point to components consuming CPU if they loop in the code with trace statements or call traced API.

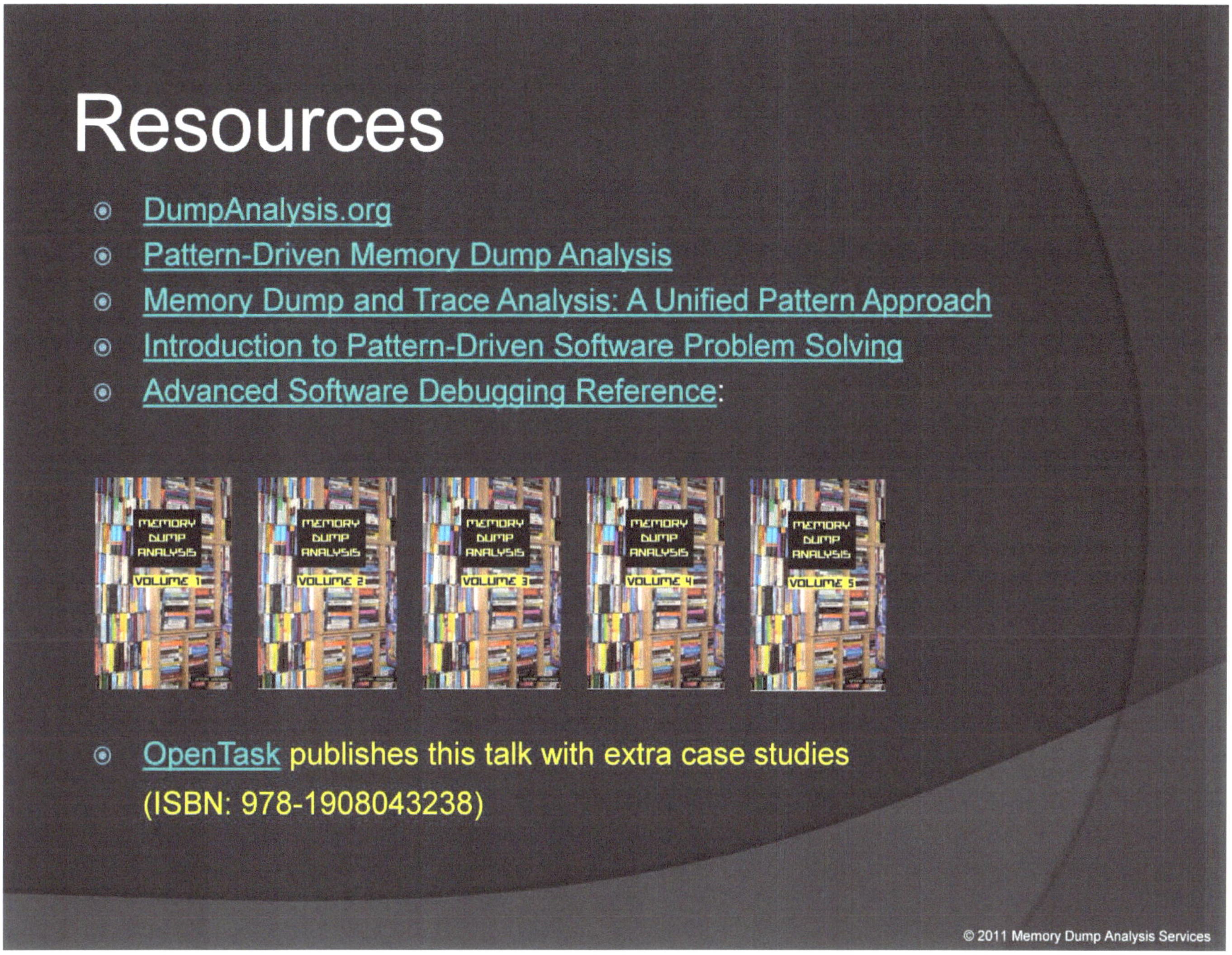

This slide has links for further study including a presentation with full transcript comments about pattern-driven memory dump analysis I delivered two years ago and a full case study from Debugging Experts Magazine. I also recently organized a free Webinar on pattern-driven software problem solving which also covers troubleshooting and debugging tools patterns (Debugware), workaround patterns, structural memory patterns and unified debugging patterns.

Pattern-Driven Memory Dump Analysis:
http://blogs.citrix.com/author/dmitryv/

Memory Dump and Trace Analysis: A Unified Pattern Approach:
http://www.debuggingexperts.com/memory-dump-trace-analysis-unified-pattern-approach

Introduction to Pattern-Driven Software Problem Solving:
http://www.patterndiagnostics.com/PDSPSI-materials

Advanced Software Debugging Reference:
http://www.dumpanalysis.org/advanced-software-debugging-reference

OpenTask:
http://www.opentask.com

Trace Analysis Case Study

We add a case study to this lecture transcript to illustrate software trace and log analysis patterns from Software Diagnostics Institute[4] pattern catalogue. Real application names were replaced to make this example more general.

A particular application feature was not available on the first launch of ***App A*** and was only available after another application from the same package was launched (***App B***). After that, every launch of ***App A*** had that feature available. 3 Windows Process Monitor logs were collected one for each scenario:

1. ***App A*** launched – feature is not available. ***App A*** closed.
2. ***App B*** launched and closed.
3. ***App A*** launched - feature is available.

We opened these logs and checked that ***App A*** and ***B*** were launched indeed (**Basic Facts** pattern[5]). The problem feature had a particular name, and we searched for it in logs and found its first occurrence as a part of Windows registry access in each log (**Vocabulary Index** pattern[6]). However, such first read access was successful only in the log #3 (**Bifurcation Point** pattern[7]). Moreover, in the log #2 after we filtered all registry access for that feature name (**Data Flow** pattern[8]) we saw that a different process started after unsuccessful read (**Guest Component** pattern[9]). That process (***App C***) created the necessary registry entry. Therefore, the following workaround was advised: to create a command file *AppA.cmd* where ***App C*** starts first (in command line mode) and then ***App A*** starts with the necessary registry key already available on the first launch.

---

4 www.DumpAnalysis.org or www.TraceAnalysis.org
5 http://www.dumpanalysis.org/blog/index.php/2009/05/07/trace-analysis-patterns-part-2/
6 http://www.dumpanalysis.org/blog/index.php/2009/12/31/trace-analysis-patterns-part-13/
7 http://www.dumpanalysis.org/blog/index.php/2009/09/01/trace-analysis-patterns-part-10/
8 http://www.dumpanalysis.org/blog/index.php/2012/10/26/trace-analysis-patterns-part-56/
9 http://www.dumpanalysis.org/blog/index.php/2010/09/20/trace-analysis-patterns-part-29/

Software Forensics

Pattern-Oriented

Version 1.0

Dmitry Vostokov
Software Diagnostics Services

Published by OpenTask, Republic of Ireland

OpenTask books and magazines are available through booksellers and distributors worldwide. For further information or comments send requests to press@opentask.com.

A CIP catalogue record for this book is available from the British Library.

ISBN-13: 978-1-908043-69-6 (Paperback)

First printing, 2014

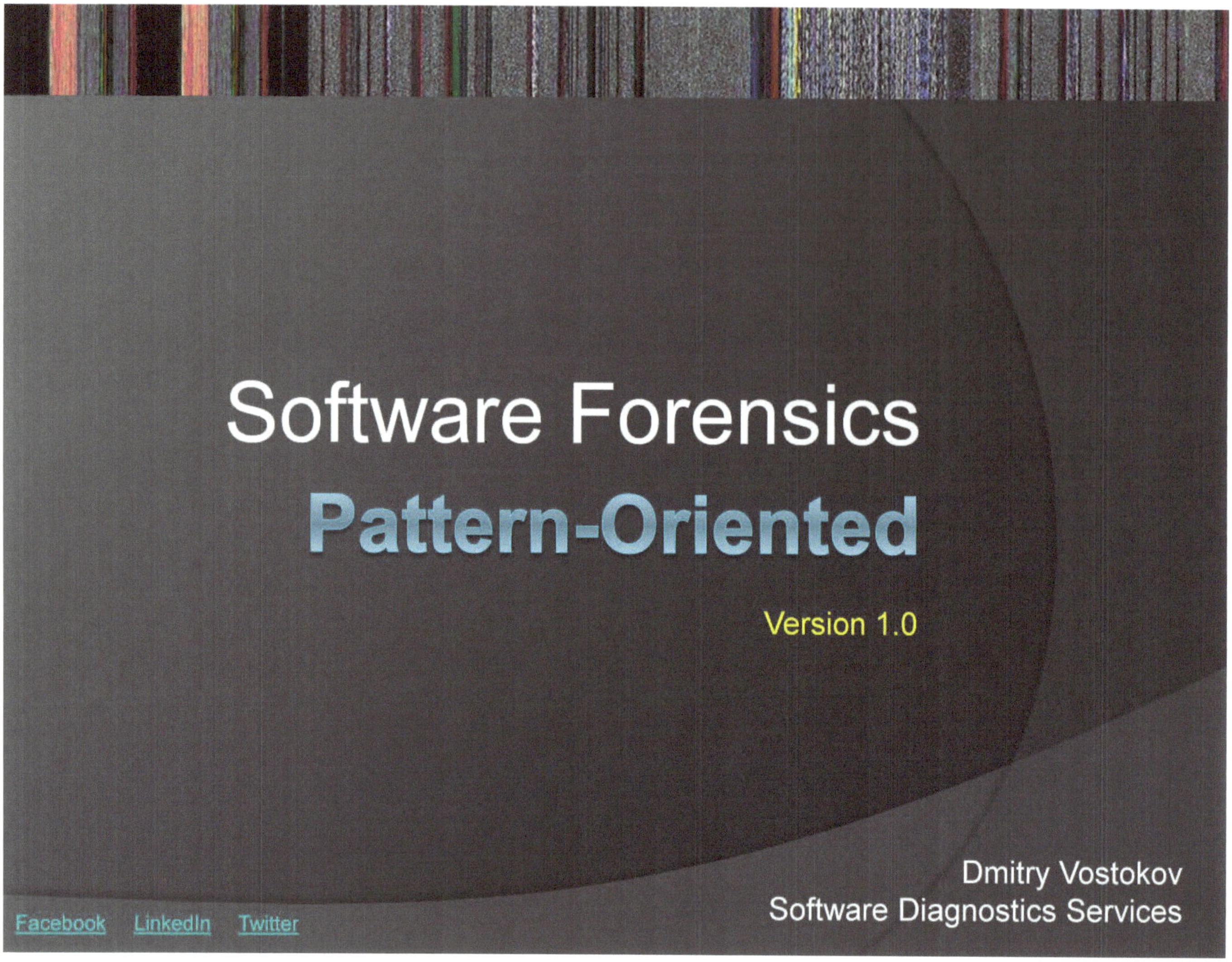

Hello everyone, my name is Dmitry Vostokov and I introduce today a pattern-oriented approach to software forensics. I decided to keep this presentation short and as simple as possible. If anything needs to be added or modified in the future I create another version of it.

Facebook:
http://www.facebook.com/SoftwareDiagnosticsServices

LinkedIn:
http://www.linkedin.com/company/software-diagnostics-services

Twitter:
http://twitter.com/DumpAnalysis

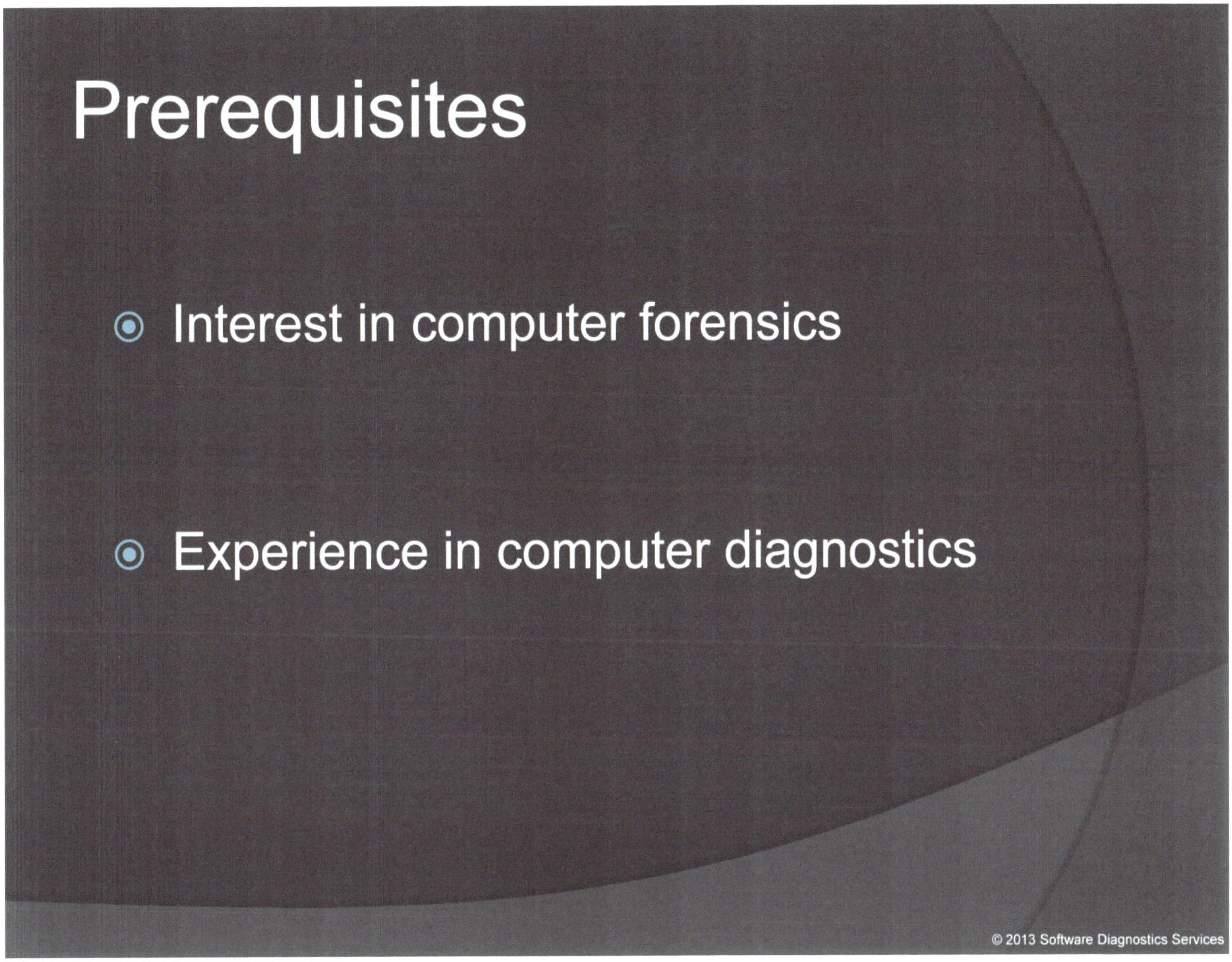

Prerequisites for this presentation are very simple and I suppose you all like me enjoy computer diagnostics, especially memory and log analysis. If you don't have an experience in computer forensics or at least have only a familiarity with it I hope this webinar outlines a unified big picture. If you have such an experience this webinar proposes a pattern-oriented foundational approach.

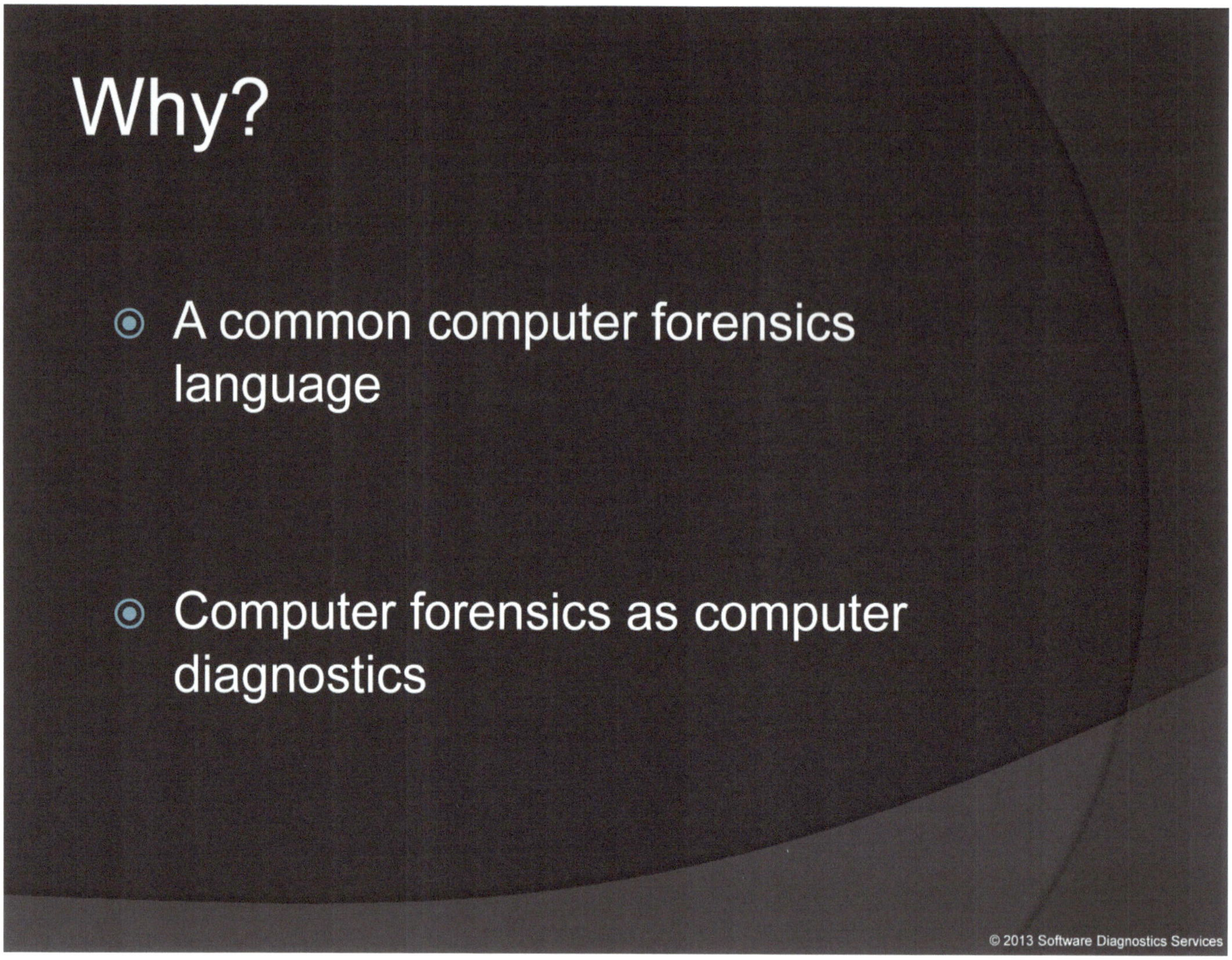

Why we advocate a general pattern approach to traditional computer forensics? Because we need a unified common language and computer forensics is largely a part of computer diagnostics. As we would see later computer forensic artifacts structure and dynamics are the same as traditional diagnostic artifacts such as memory dumps, software logs and network traces.

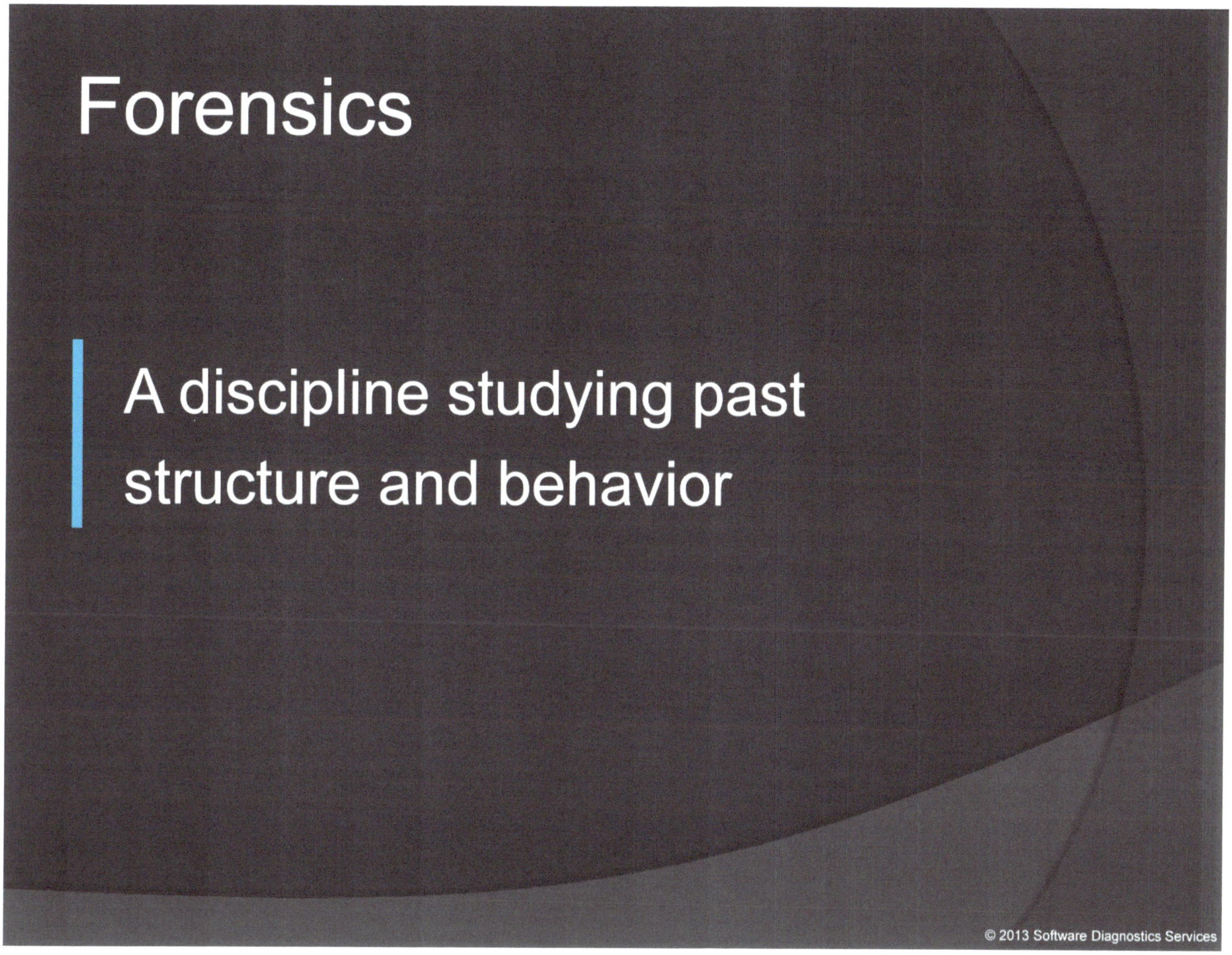

Now we look at some definitions. The first one is about forensic science or forensics.

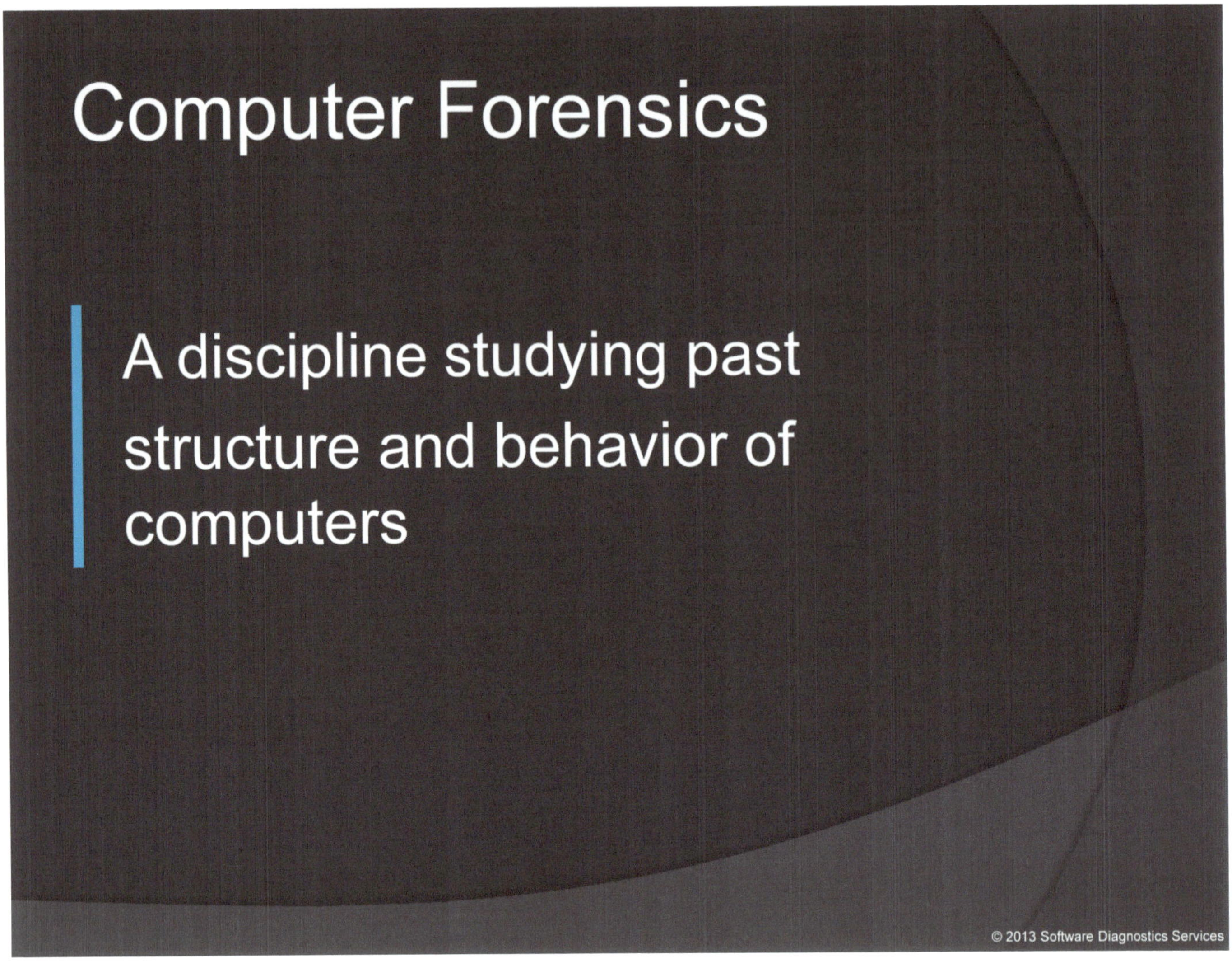

There are many specialized forensics. Our concern is with digital computers.

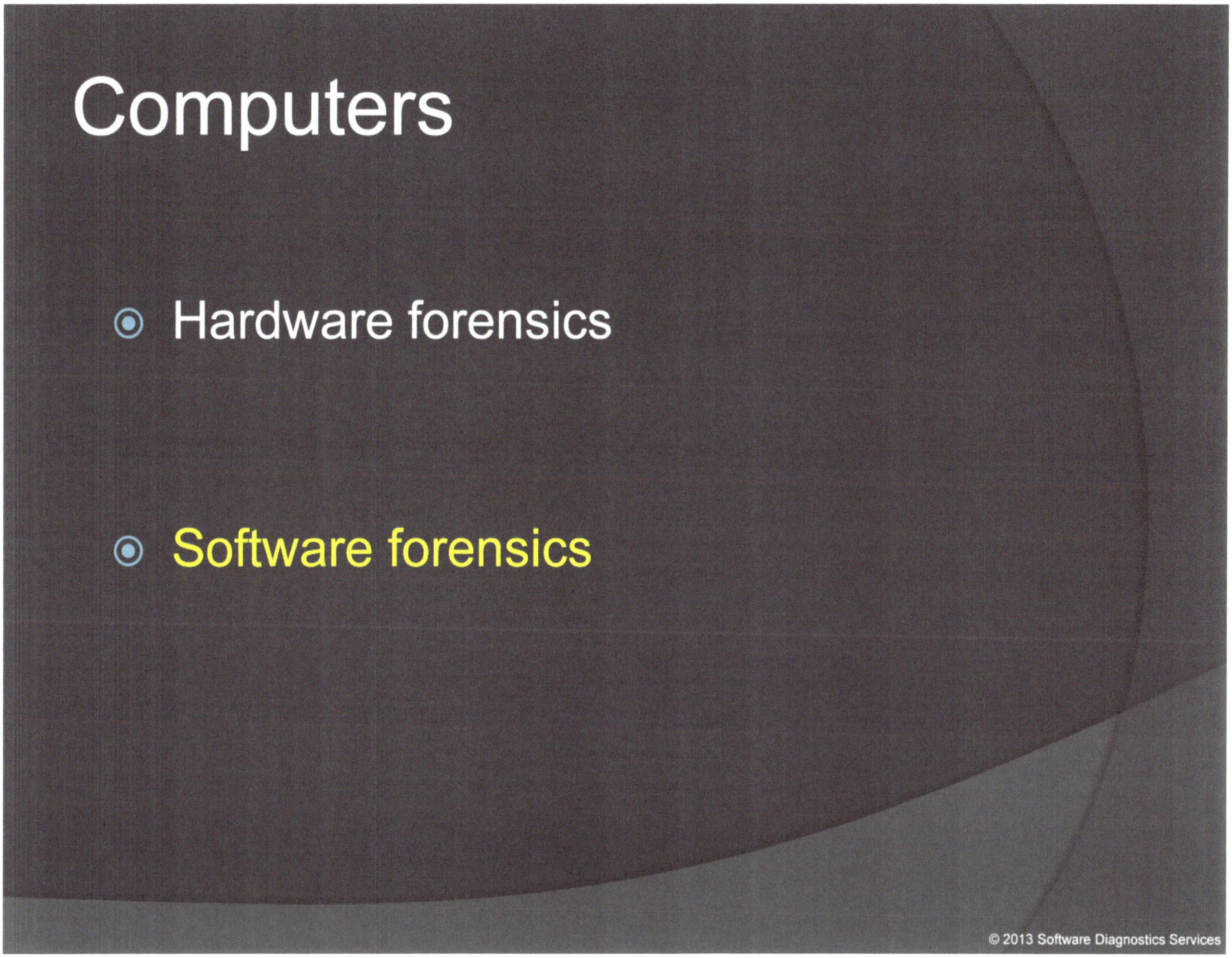

In computer forensics our main concern is a software part although we provide a direction for hardware later.

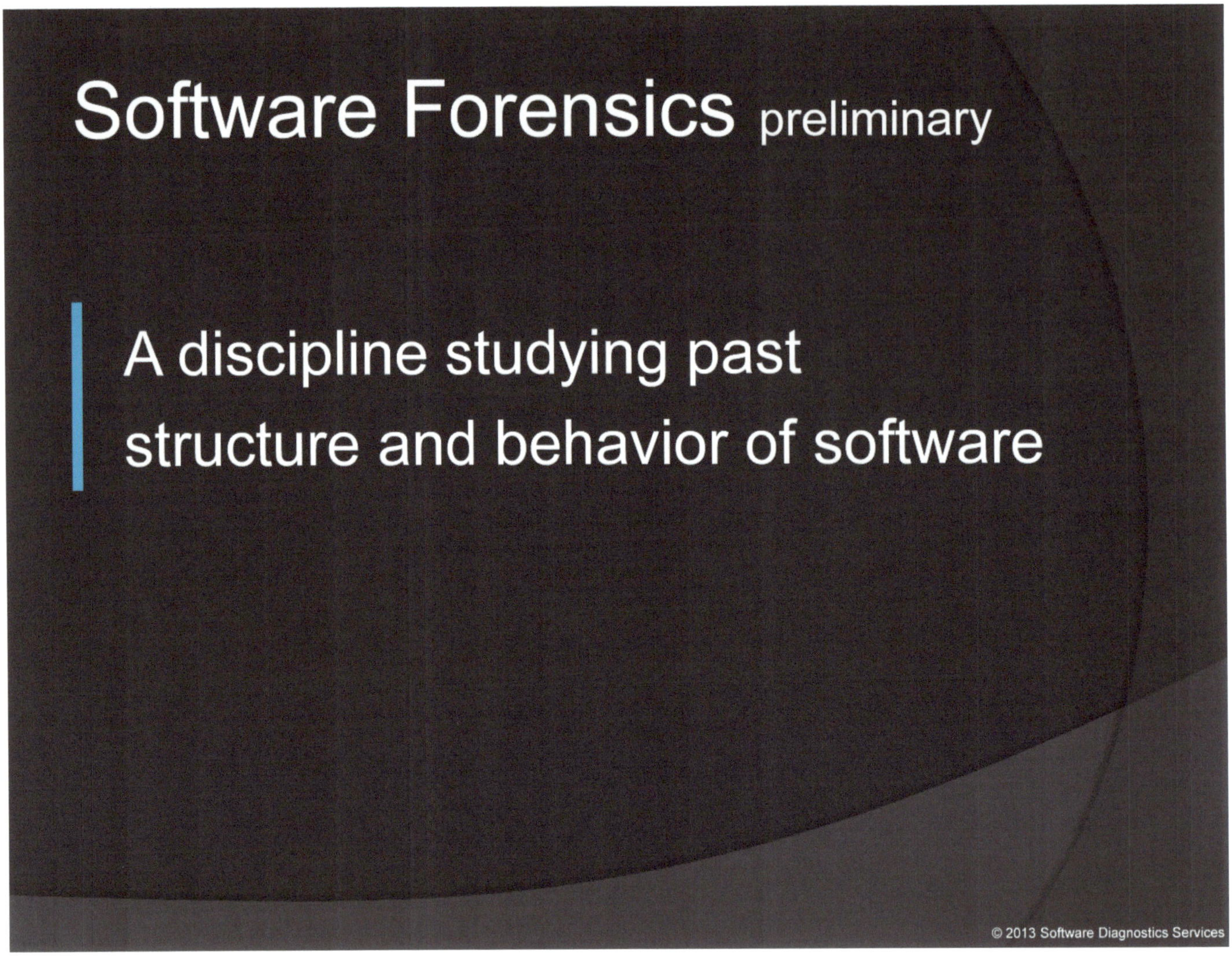

So we come to a preliminary definition of software forensics.

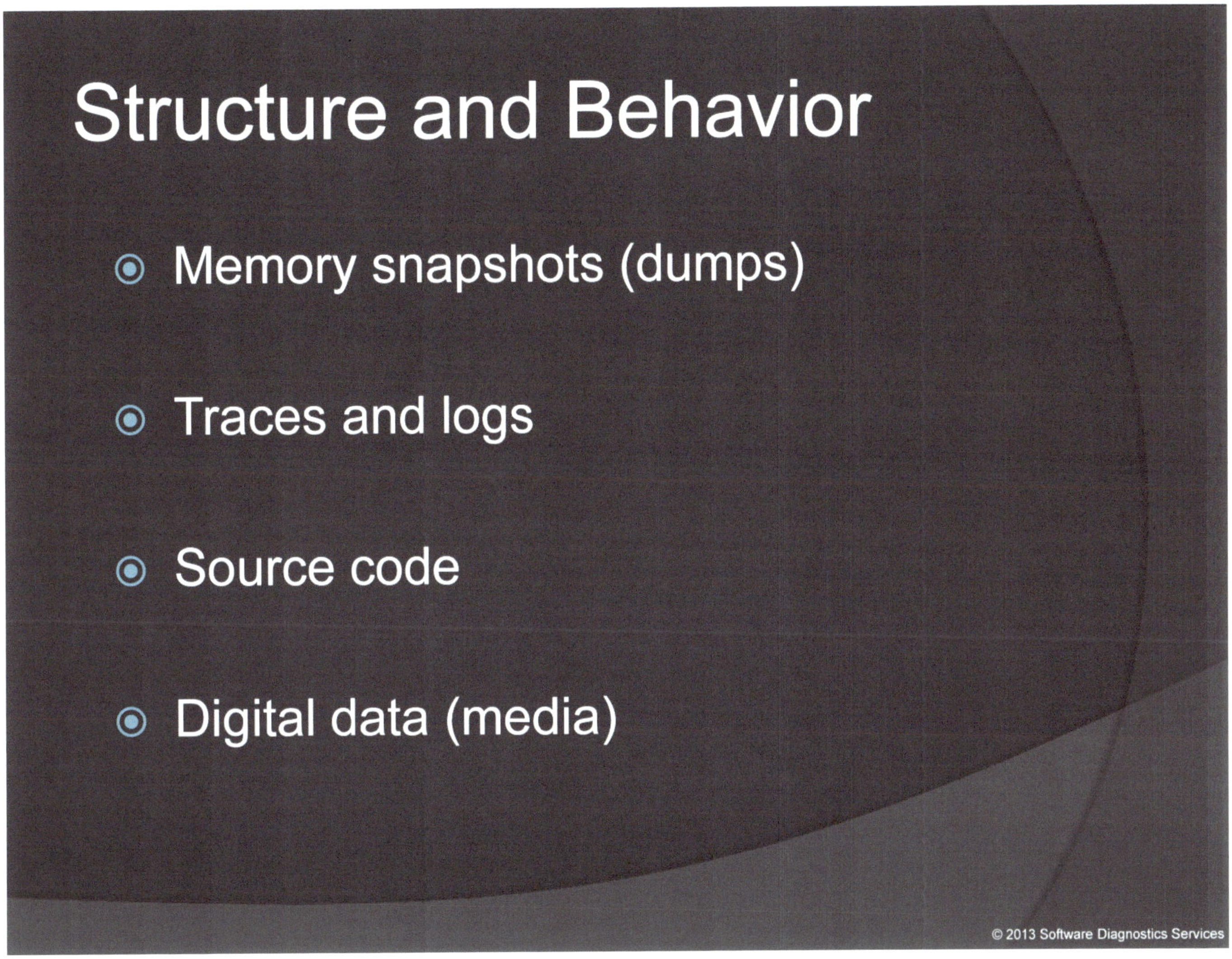

Past structure and behavior can be seen and analyzed in various software execution artefacts.

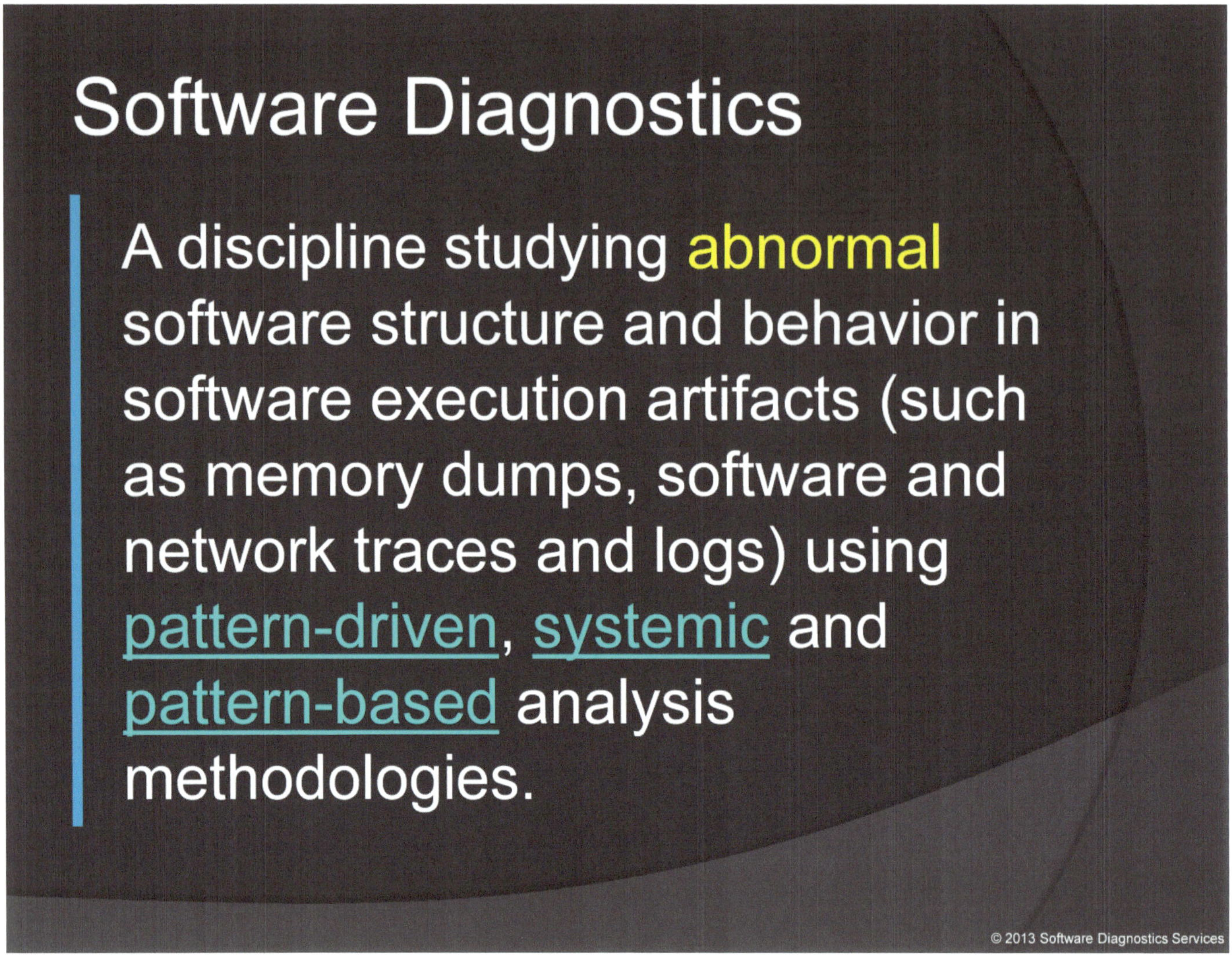

Now I take a detour and remind you a definition of software diagnostics we put forward in our previous webinars.

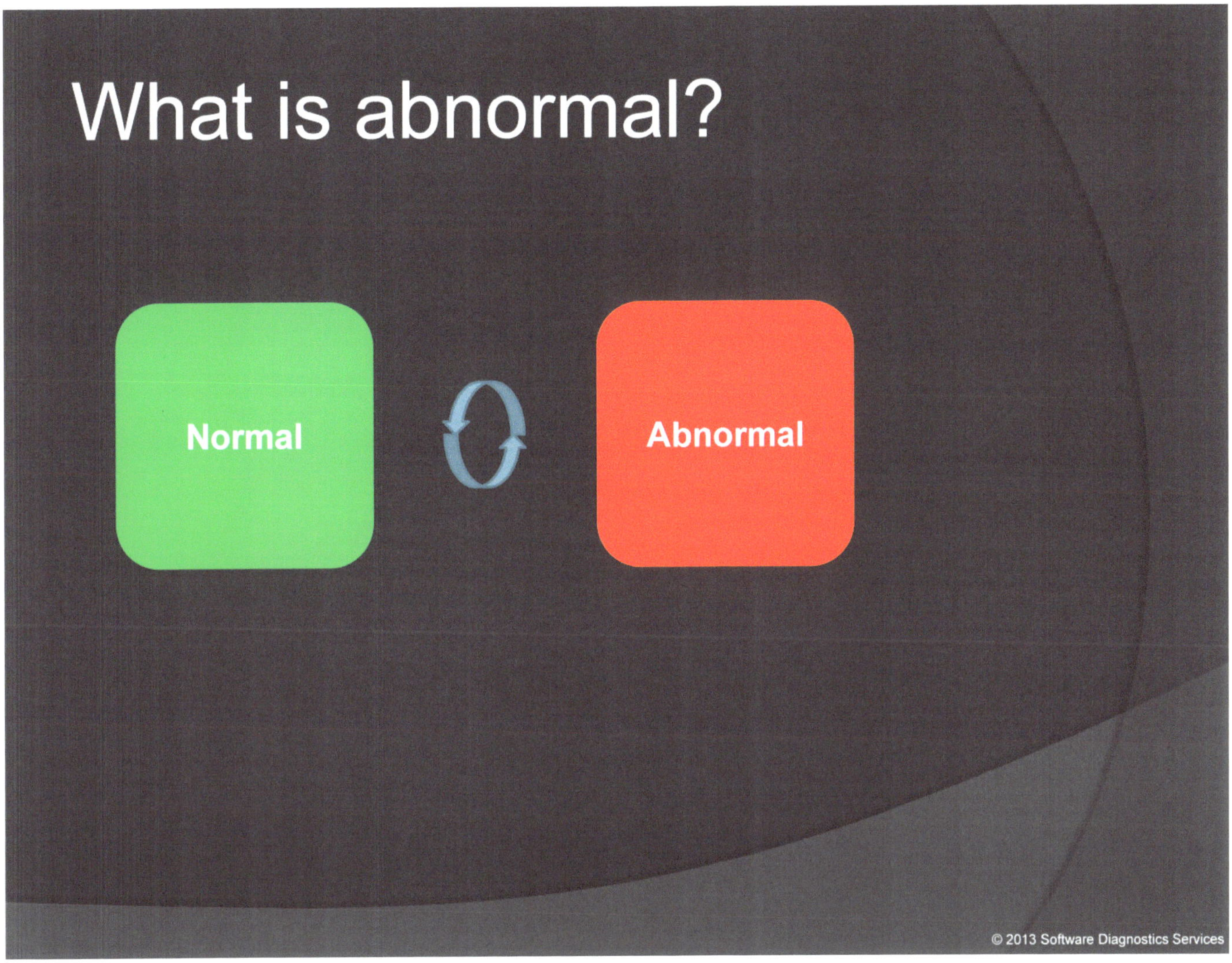

What is considered abnormal is dependent upon specific requirements: functional such as use cases and non-functional such as resource usage. Requirements can change: what was abnormal becomes normal and vice versa.

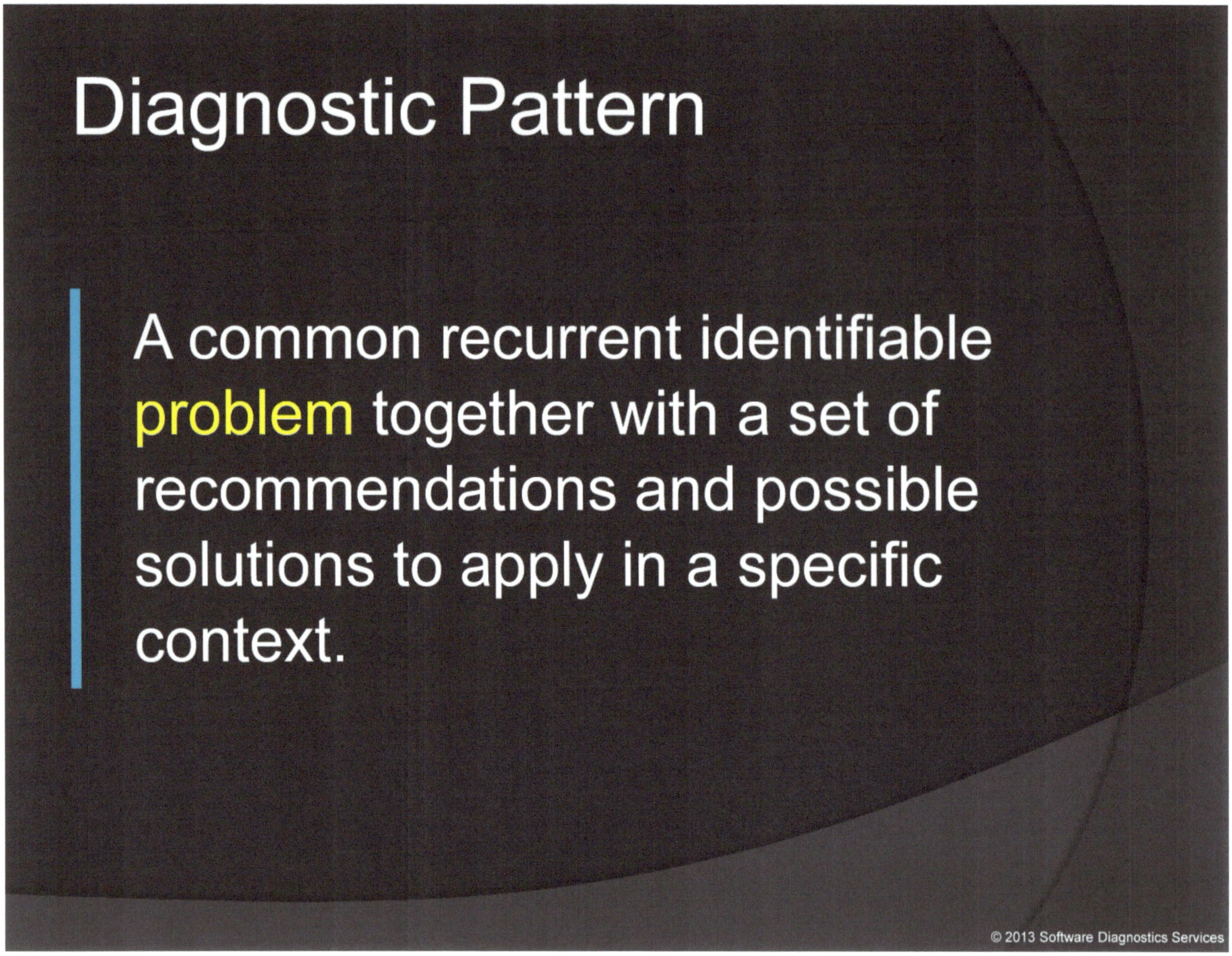

Next we would like to remind you a definition of a software diagnostic pattern.

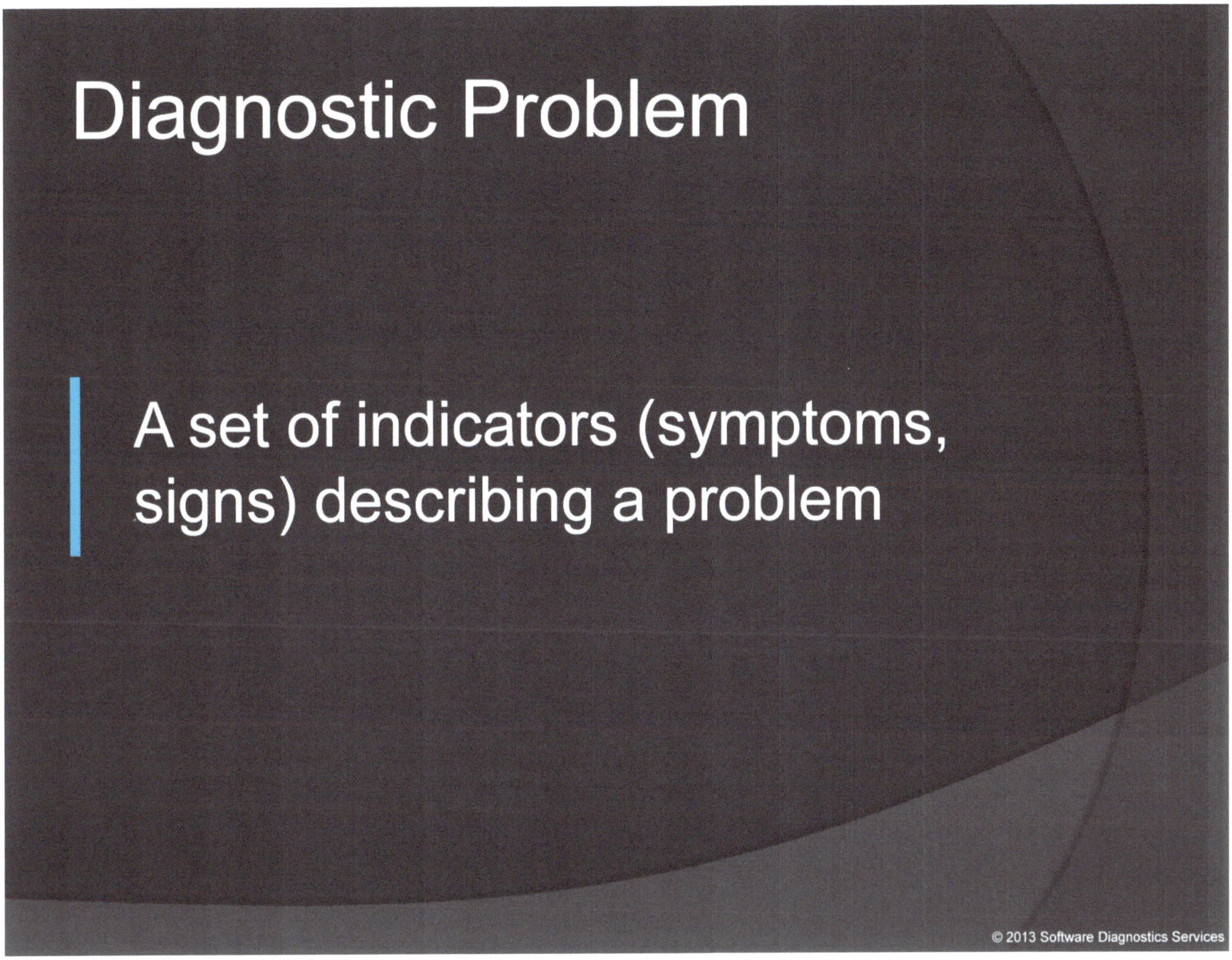

Here a problem is described by a set of signs or symptoms or simply by a set of various indicators. Please note that a problem may not even be reported but be hidden and only can be seen though health monitoring and analysis.

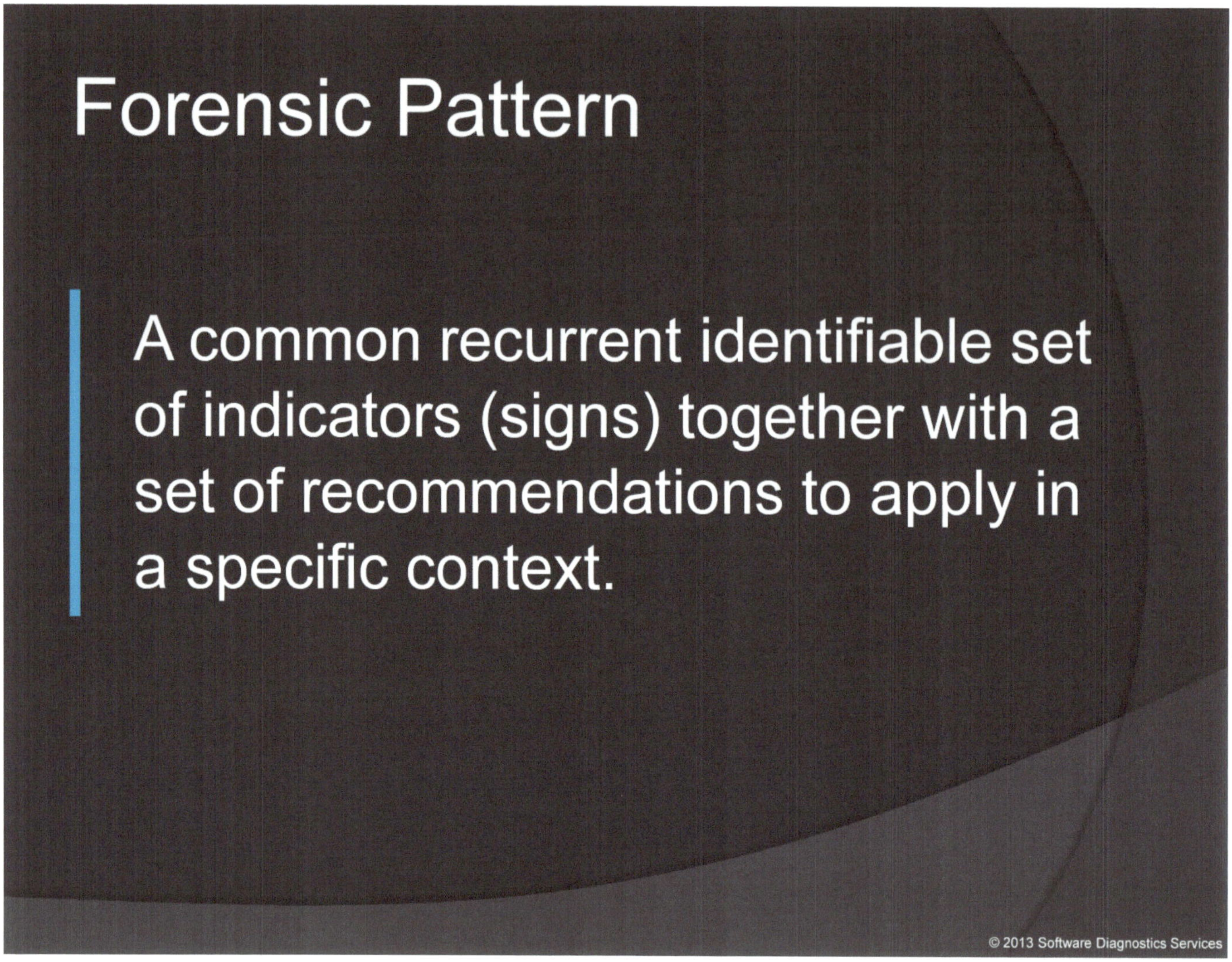

We therefore derive a definition of a forensic pattern. Here instead of a problem (or a set of problem indicators or signs) we have just a set of indicators.

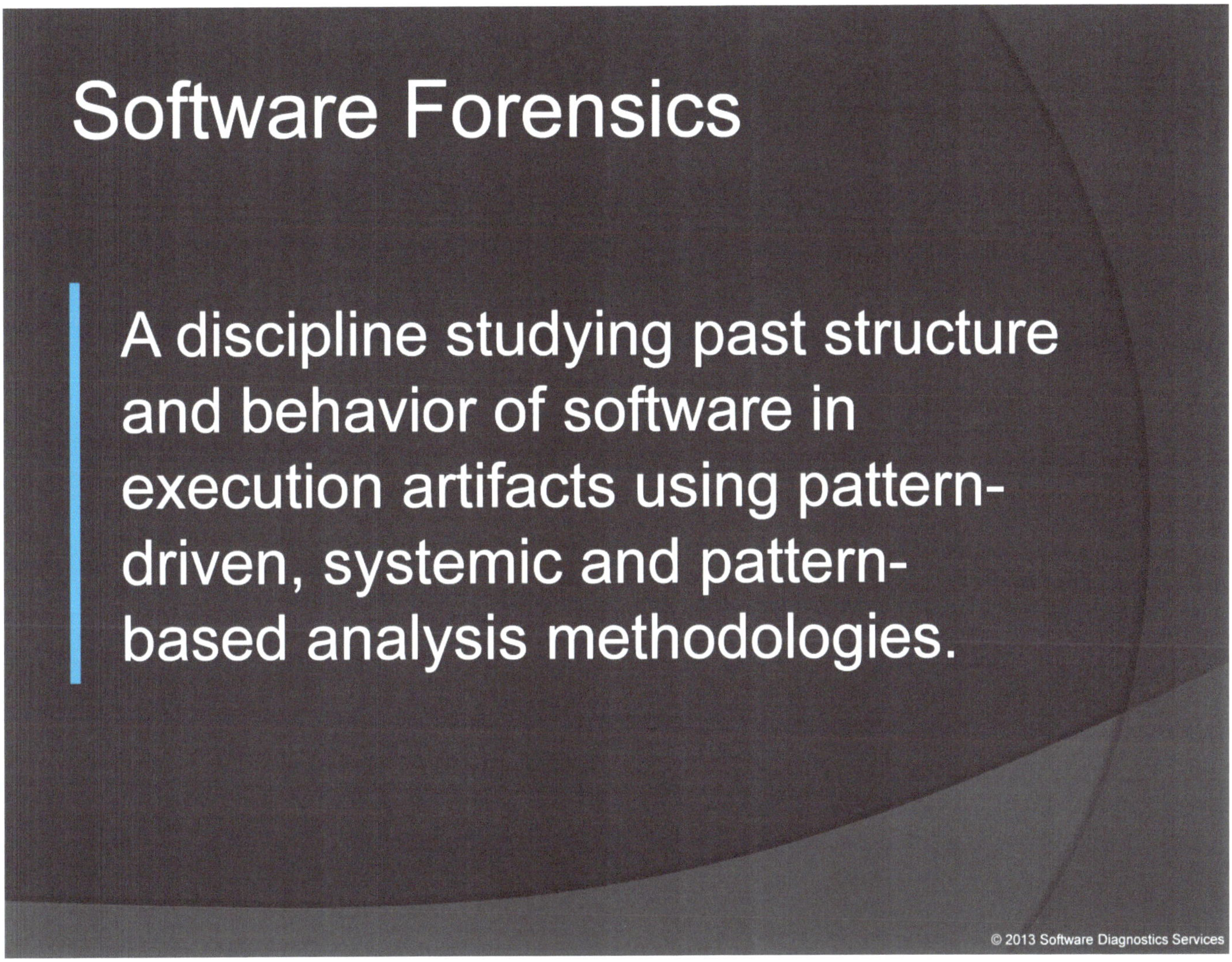

And therefore we come to a fuller definition of software forensics.

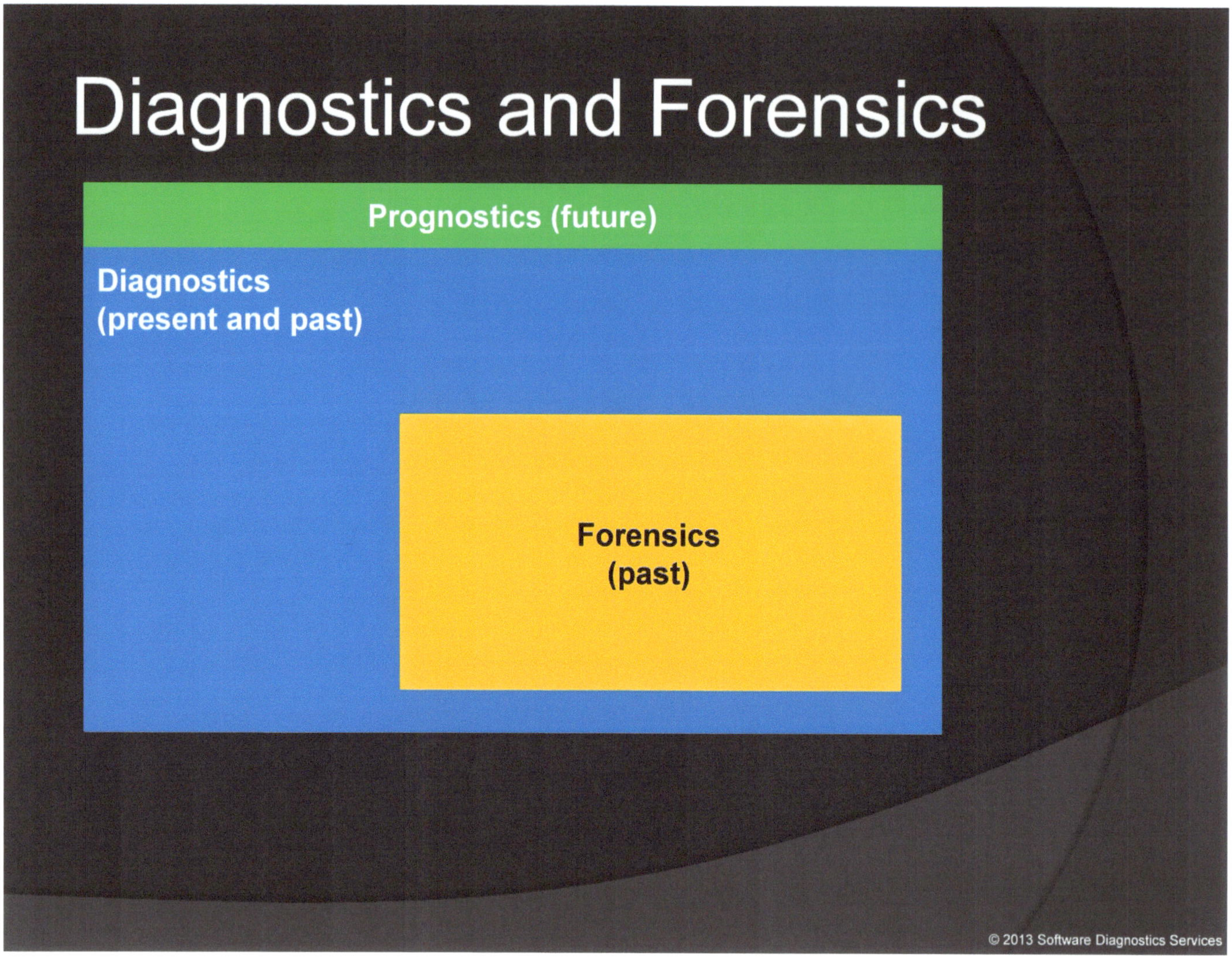

Here we visualized a relationship between diagnostics and forensics. Just as a side note, diagnostics and its forensics part can be used for prognosis of software behavior (the so called software prognostics).

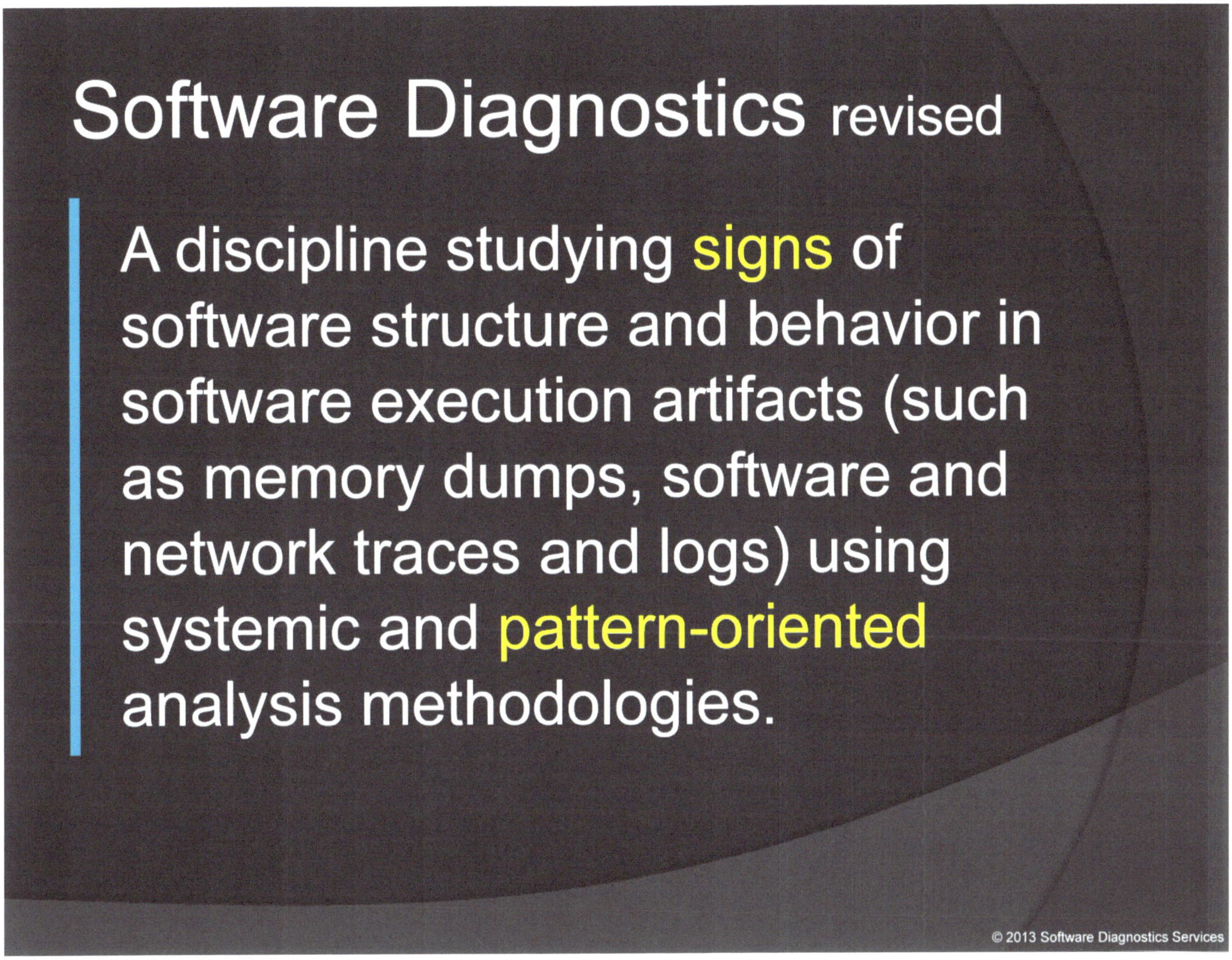

And as a consequence we revise our definition of software diagnostics where we replace abnormal with a set of indicators we call signs and combine pattern-driven and pattern-based methodologies into pattern-oriented one. In the following slides we would use software forensics but keep in mind that it is a part of software diagnostics.

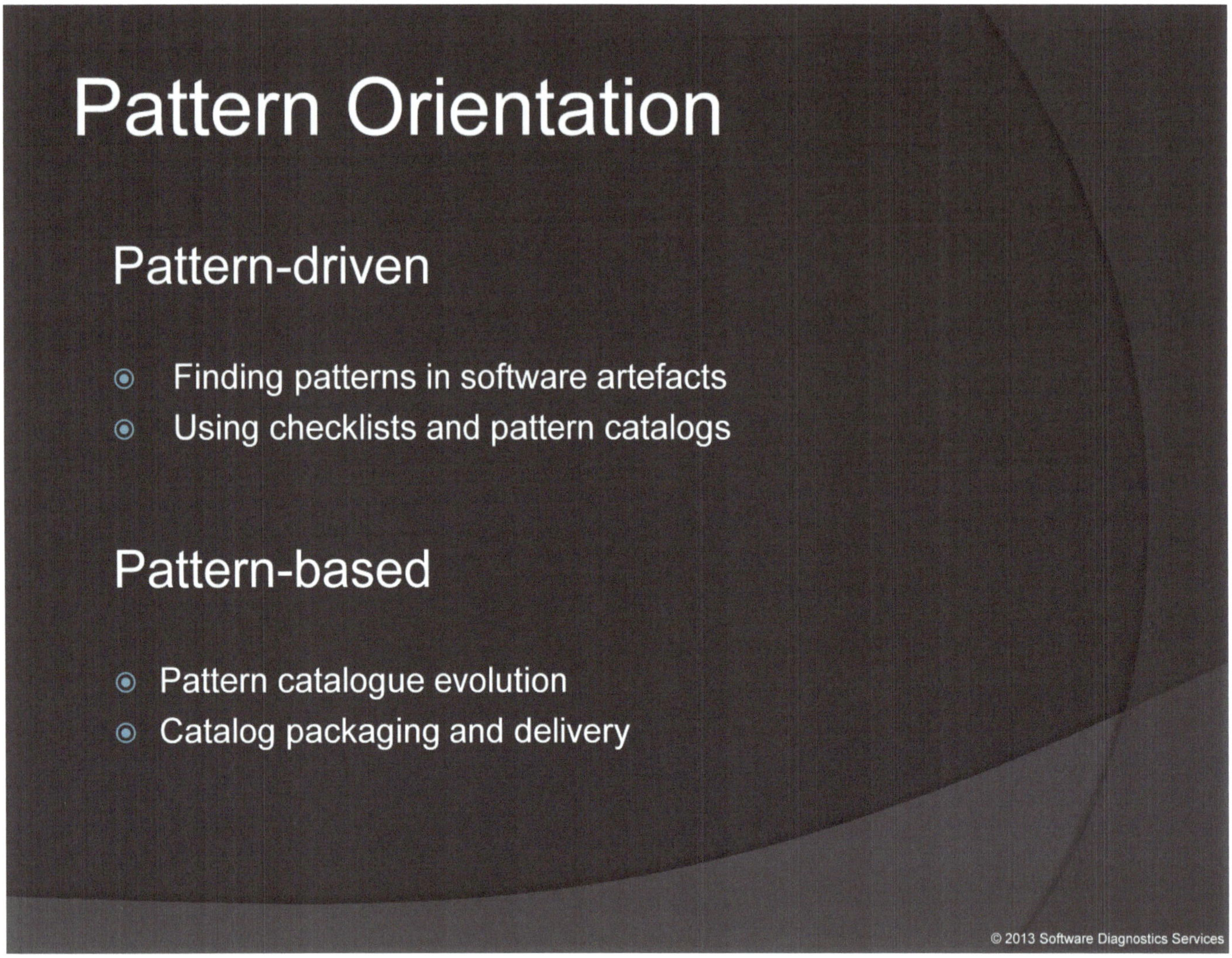

So we see that software forensics is about patterns and pattern recognition. We say it is pattern-driven when we talk about a forensic process and pattern-based when we talk about pattern life cycle. We start with the pattern-driven part first.

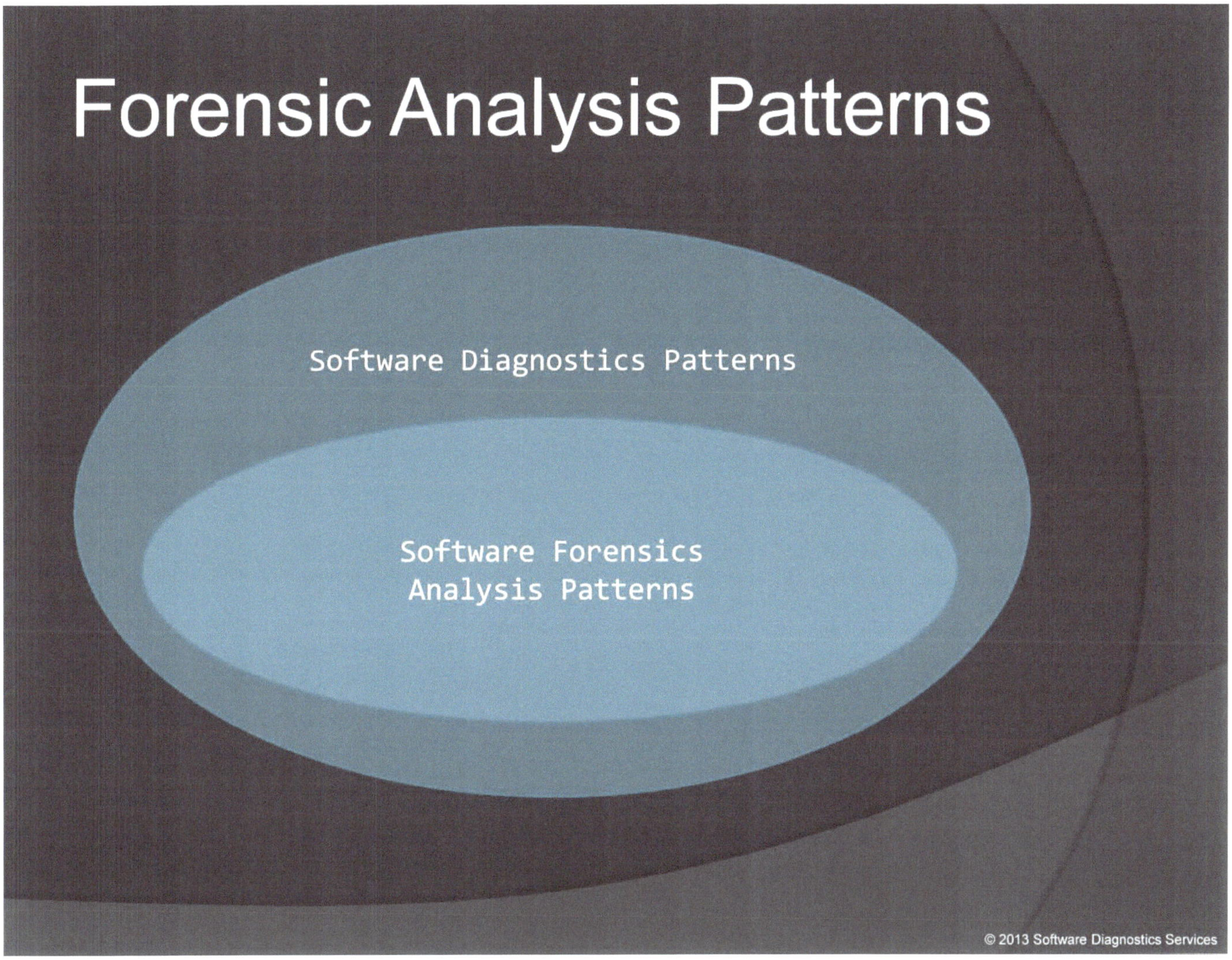

By software forensic analysis patterns we consider a subset of software diagnostics patterns because they all have the same underlying sign structure and interpretation.

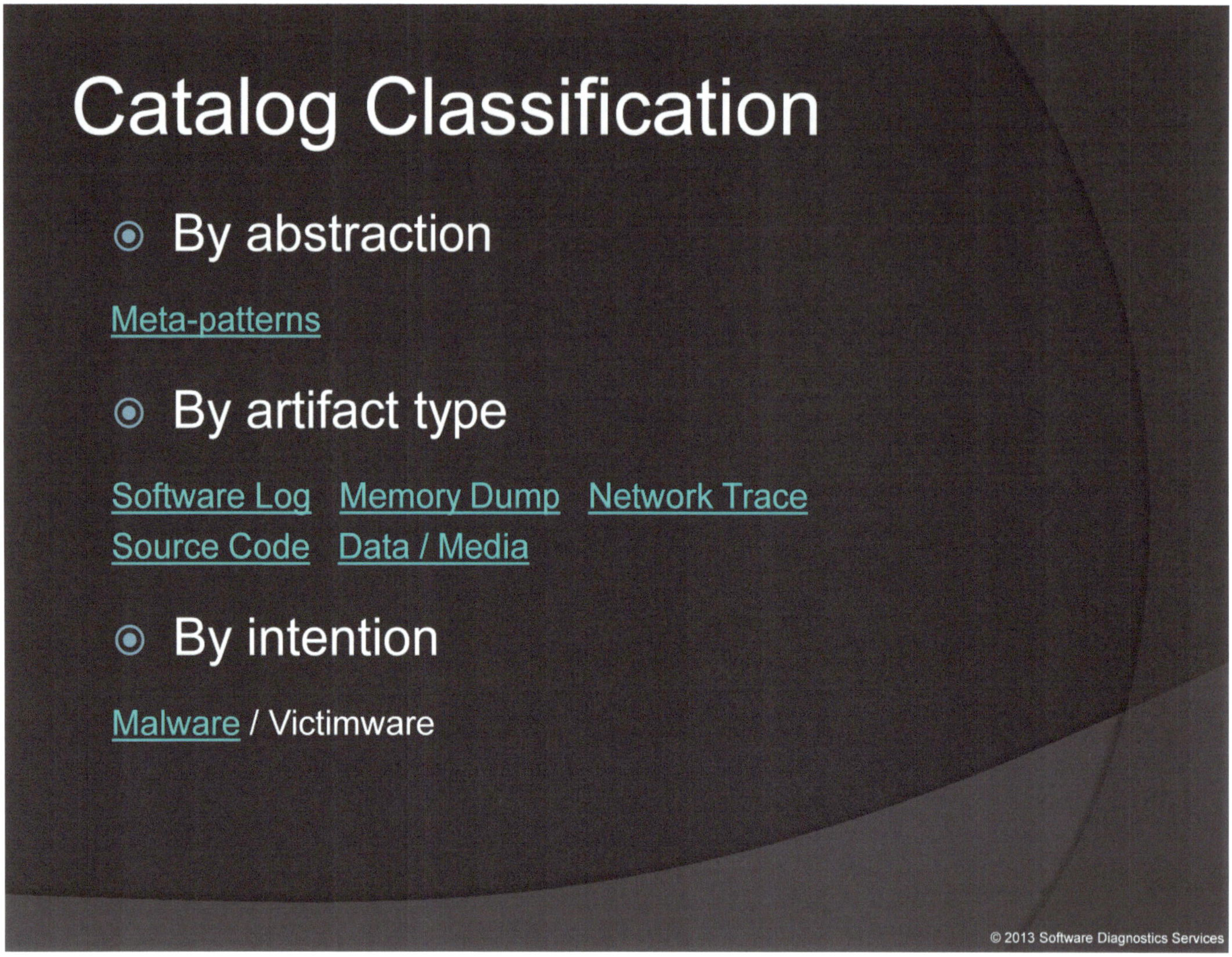

In a pattern-driven analysis we use pattern catalogs of pattern descriptions. Catalogs can be classified by abstraction, for example, as software forensic meta-patterns which are patterns of software forensics itself, by the type of software artifacts, such as source code, media data, software traces and logs, memory dumps and network traces. Also we can separate patterns by intention such as malware (with unintentional patterns, the rest, all grouped as Victimware).

Meta-patterns:
http://www.dumpanalysis.org/blog/index.php/2012/06/09/patterns-of-software-diagnostics-part-1/

Software Log:
http://www.dumpanalysis.org/blog/index.php/trace-analysis-patterns/

Memory Dump:
http://www.dumpanalysis.org/blog/index.php/crash-dump-analysis-patterns/

Network Trace:
http://www.dumpanalysis.org/blog/index.php/2012/07/19/network-trace-analysis-patterns-part-1/

Source Code:
http://www.dumpanalysis.org/blog/index.php/category/static-code-analysis-patterns/

Data / Media:
http://www.dumpanalysis.org/blog/index.php/2013/03/25/generalized-software-narrative-and-trace/

Malware:
http://www.dumpanalysis.org/blog/index.php/malware-analysis-patterns/

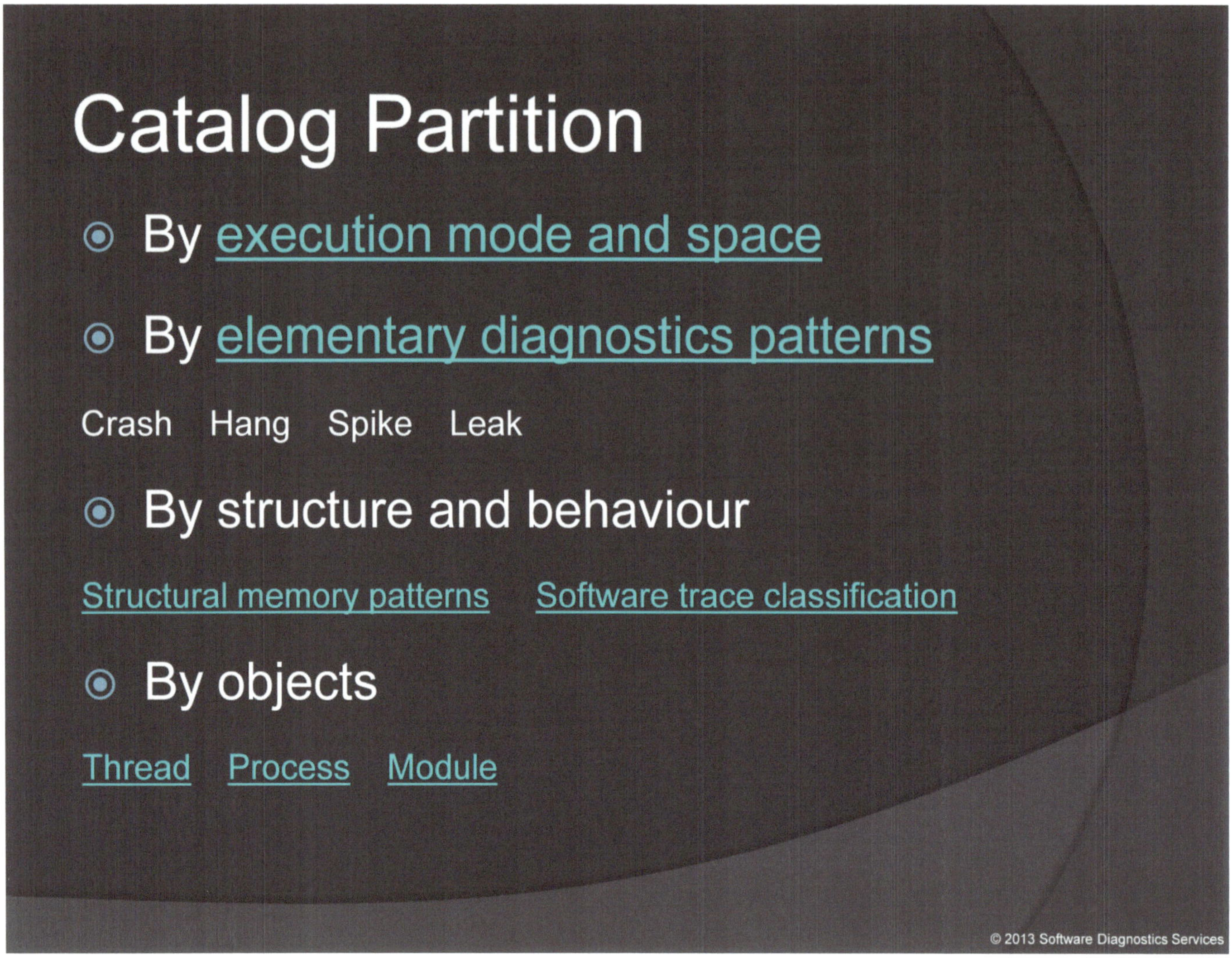

Some catalogs become large and need partitioning. Memory analysis pattern catalog, for example, consists of more than 250 patterns; software log analysis pattern catalog consists of almost 80 patterns at the time of this writing. For example, we can partition memory analysis patterns by execution space or problem type, such as crash, hang, spike or leak. We can also partition them by structure and behavior, for example, to create a smaller catalog for structural memory patterns. Another fruitful partition is by object types such as threads, processes and modules.

Execution mode and space:
http://www.dumpanalysis.org/blog/index.php/2008/07/21/cda-pattern-classification-spacemode/

Elementary diagnostics patterns:
http://www.dumpanalysis.org/elementary-diagnostics-patterns

Structural memory patterns:
http://www.dumpanalysis.org/blog/index.php/structural-memory-analysis-patterns/

Software traces classification:
http://www.dumpanalysis.com/Training/Accelerated-Windows-Software-Trace-Analysis-Public.pdf

Thread:
http://www.dumpanalysis.org/blog/index.php/2013/01/05/thread-patterns

Process:
http://www.dumpanalysis.org/blog/index.php/2013/01/05/process-patterns/

Module:
http://www.dumpanalysis.org/blog/index.php/2012/07/15/module-patterns/

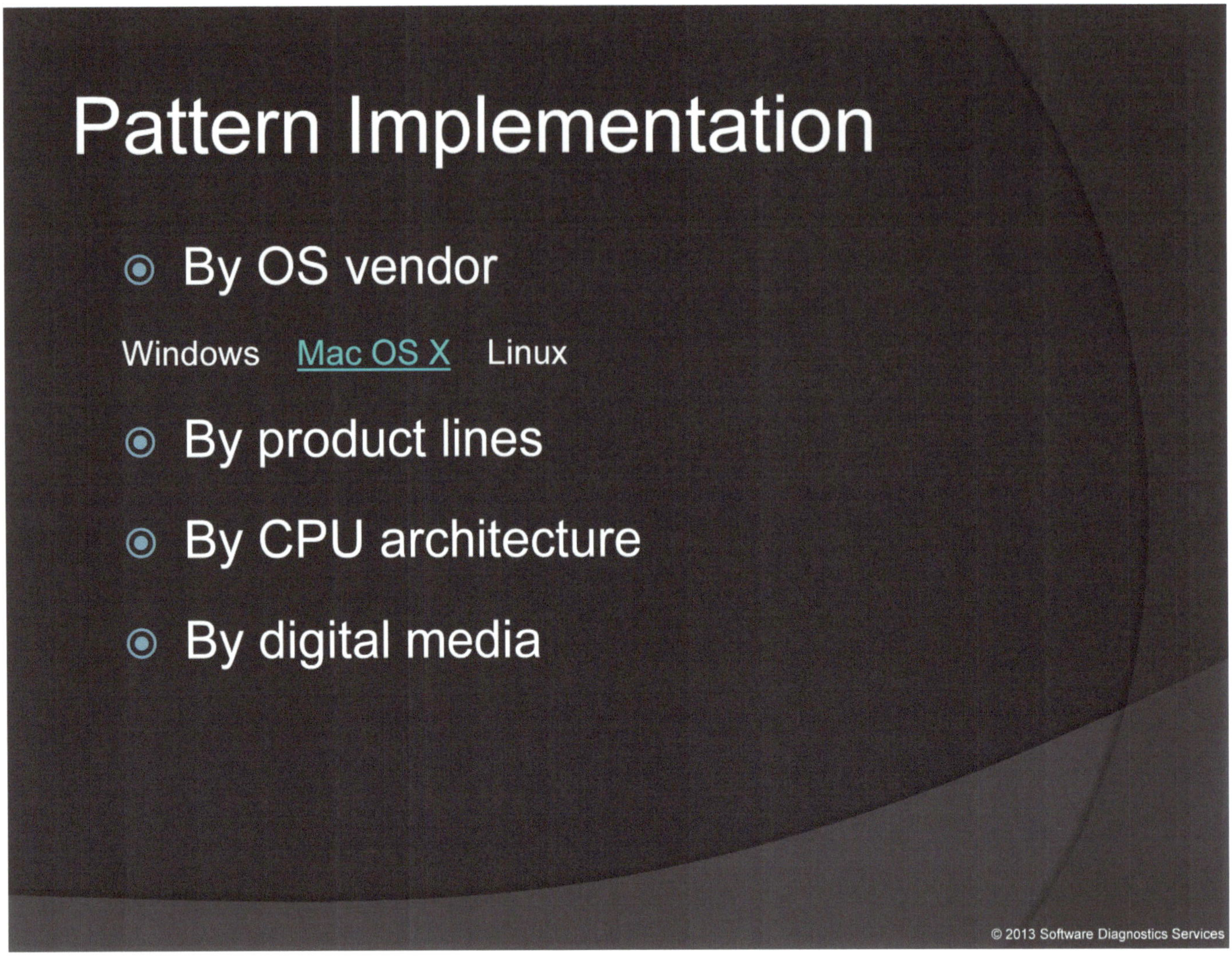

Ultimately patterns are found on specific platforms. By pattern implementation we mean differences in operating systems, product lines, media types, CPU, and hardware architectures.

Mac OS X:
http://www.dumpanalysis.org/blog/index.php/category/mac-os-x/

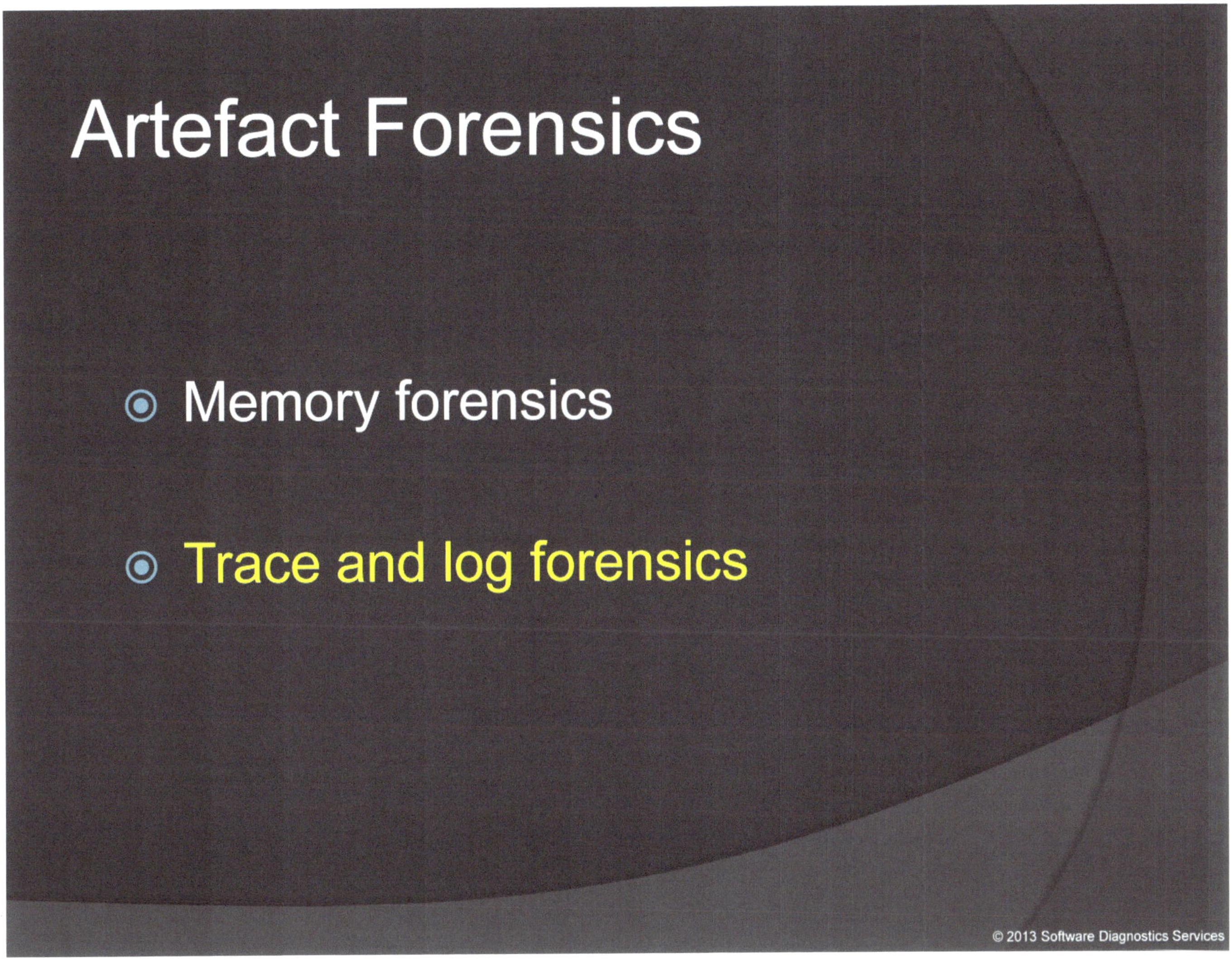

Considering classification by artefact type there are two main types – memory forensics and trace and log forensics. Although traces and logs are derived from memory and are memory based nevertheless we advocate a different structural and behavioral analysis approach based on software narratology.

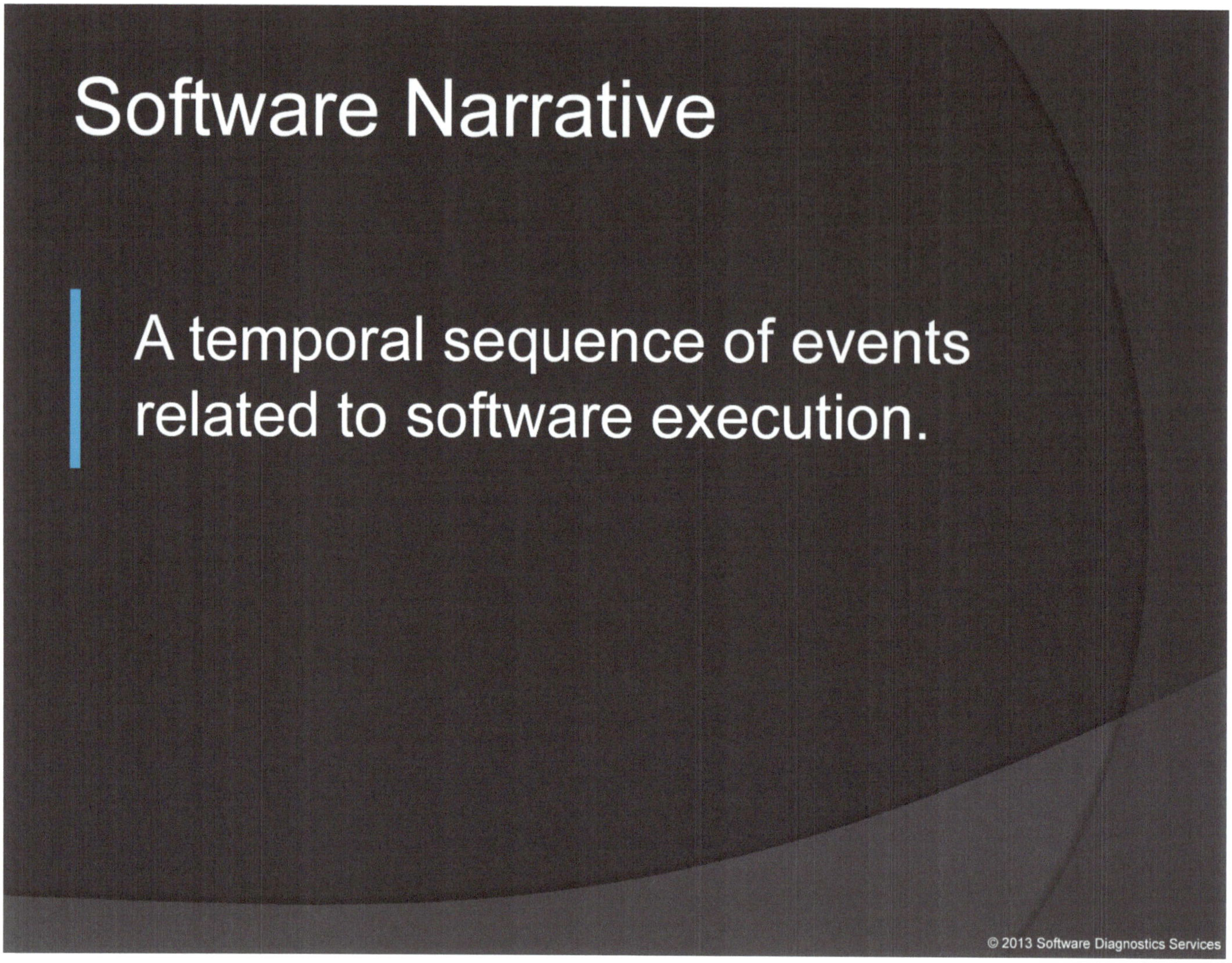

The analysis of traces and logs uses narratology, the discipline that studies various narrative forms such as stories, novels, chronicles, dialogues. All these narratives have the same unified structure such as events ordered by time.

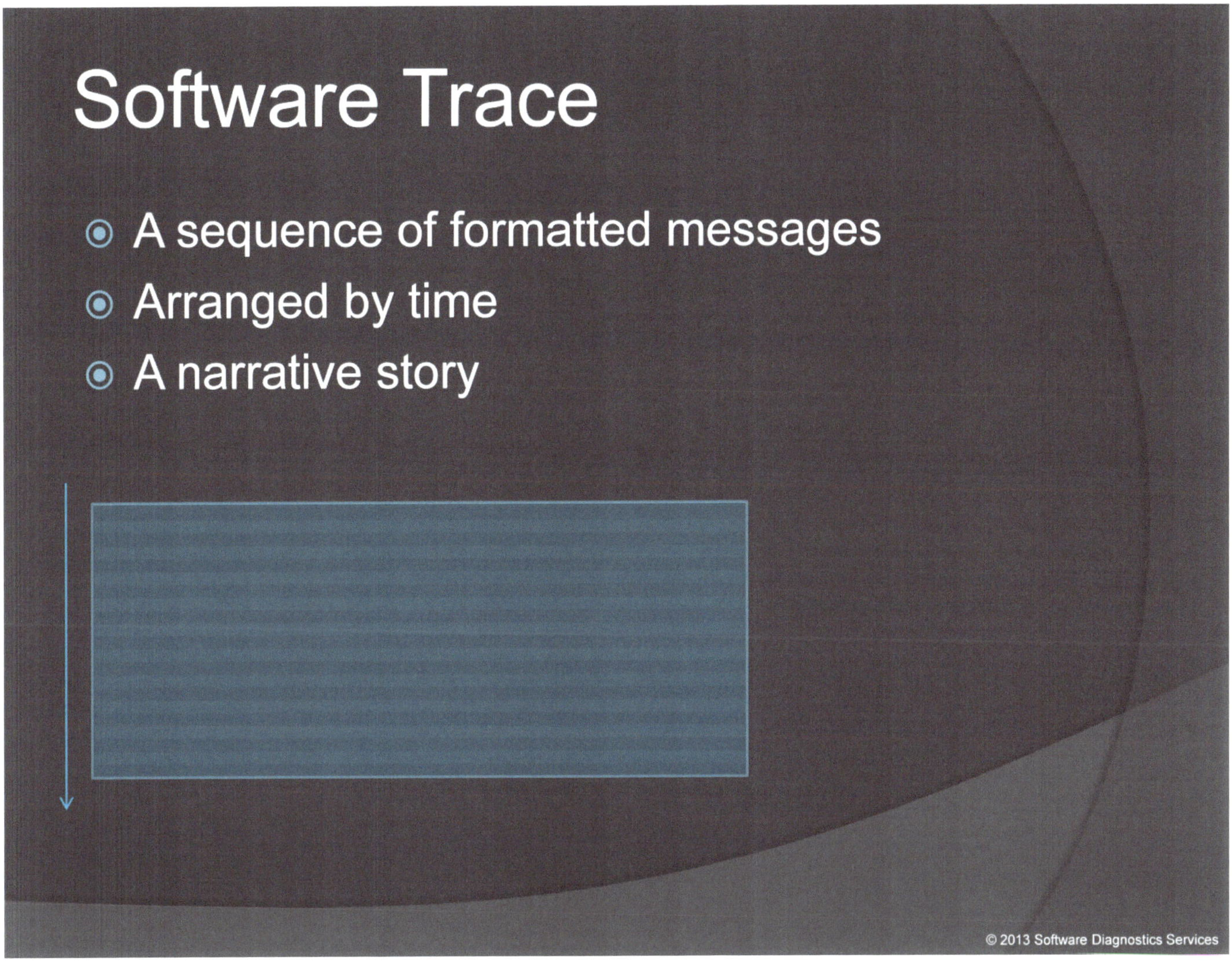

For our purposes a software trace or log is just a sequence of formatted messages sent from running software, for example, an event log or intercepted and formatted API requests such as a log from Process Monitor tool or a network trace. They are usually arranged by time and can be considered as a software narrative story.

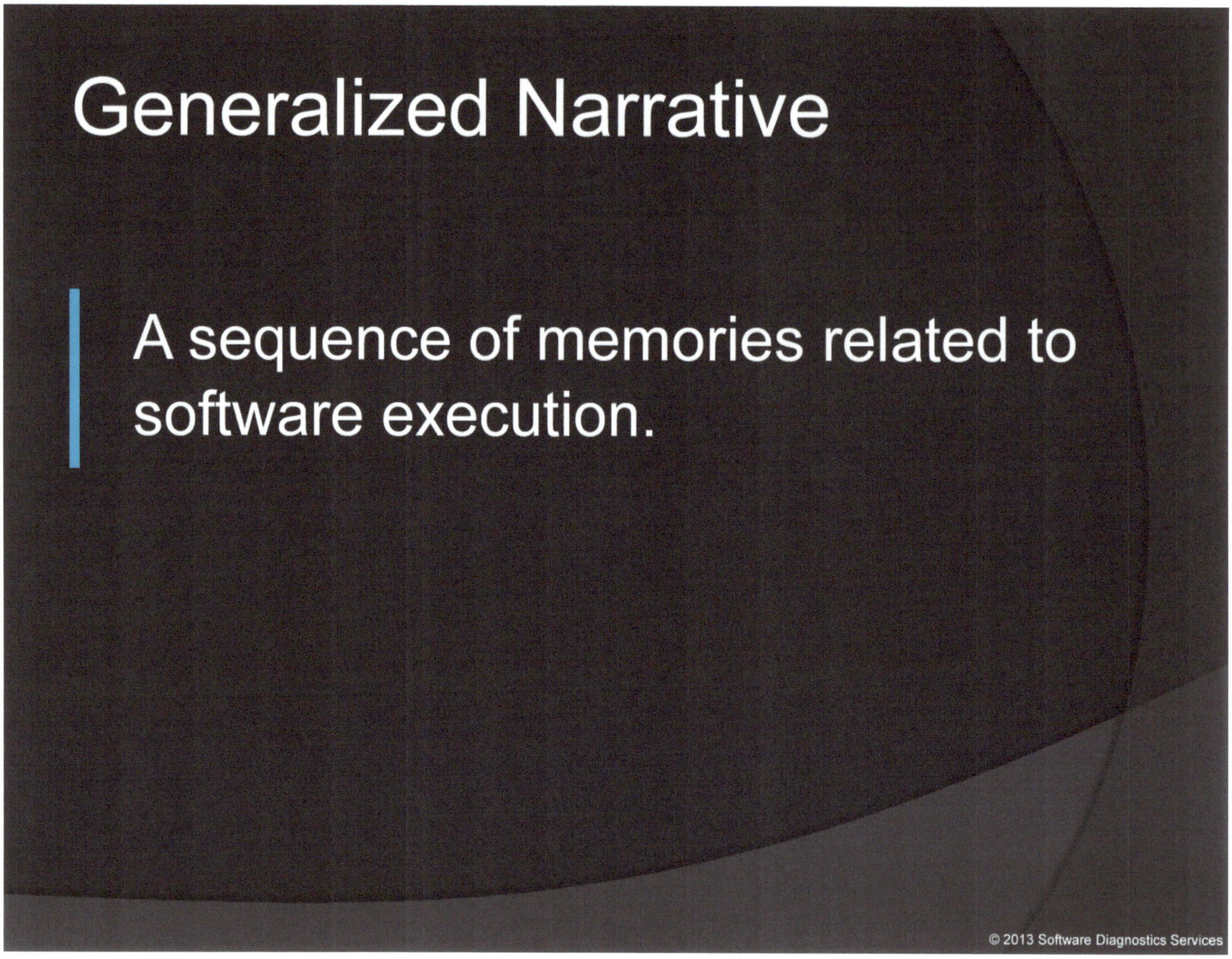

We can extend the notion of a temporal order and consider arbitrarily ordered memories. For example, memory ordered by memory.

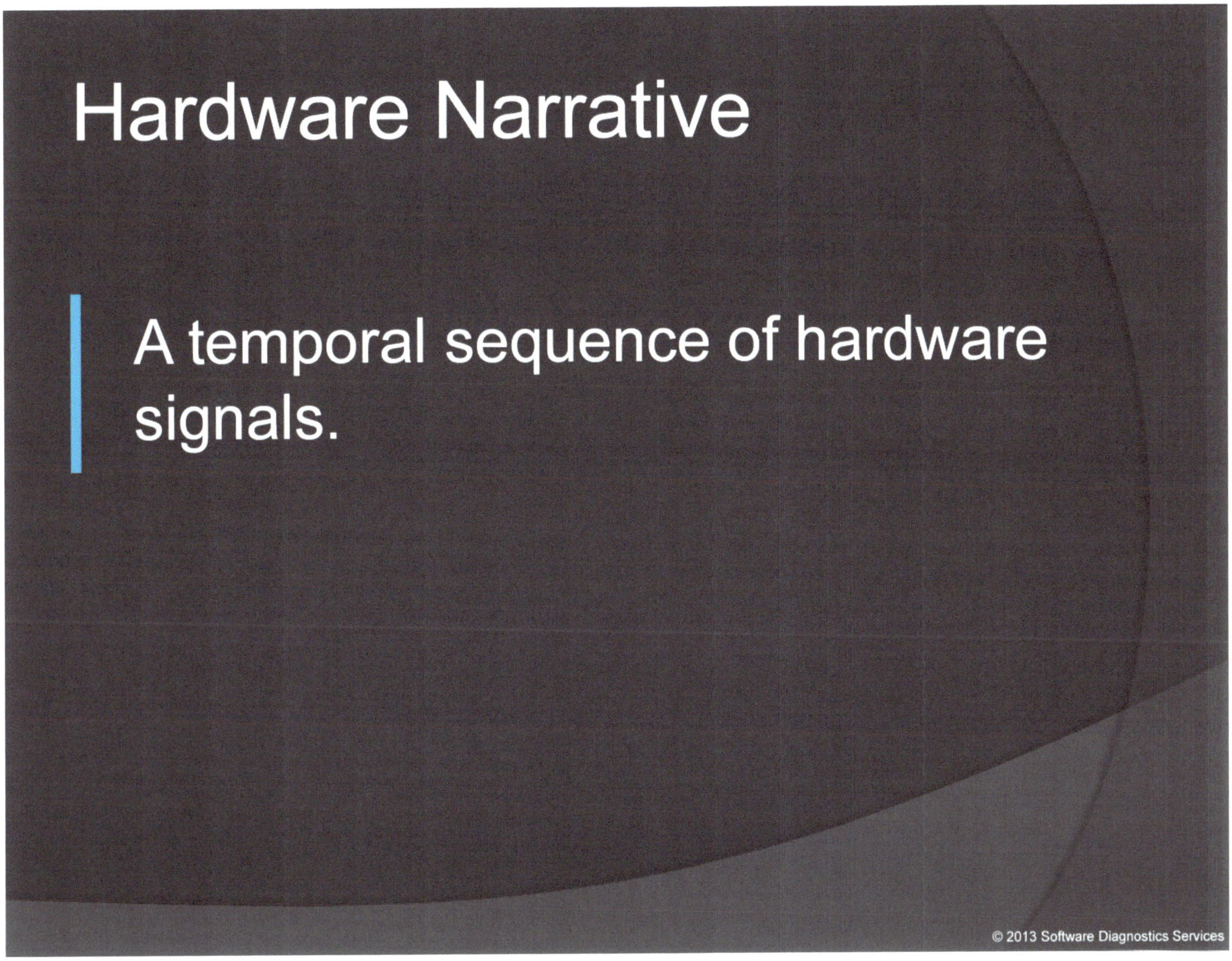

Finally this narrative approach can also be extended to real hardware and we can reuse patterns from software trace analysis catalogue.

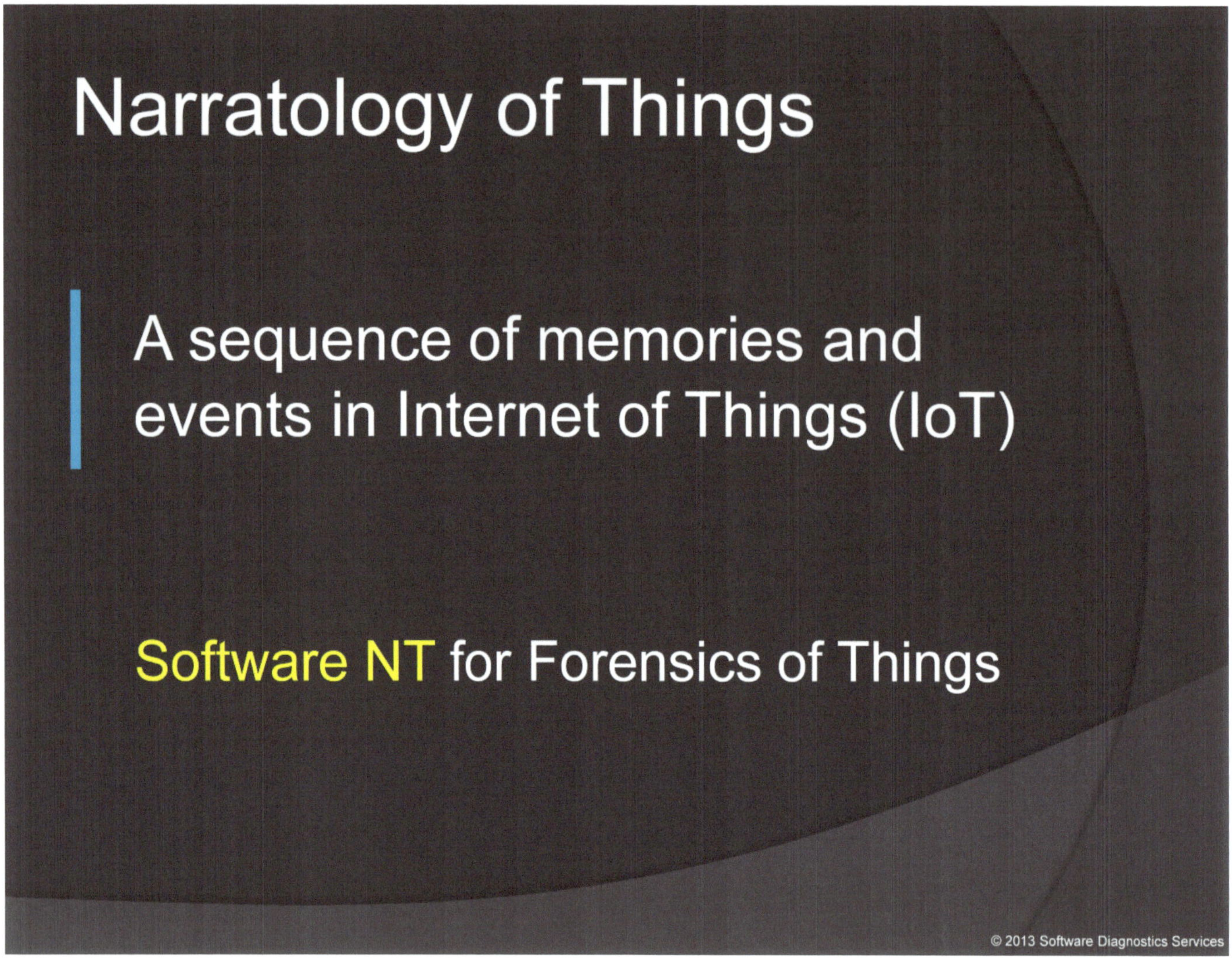

Ultimately we can also talk about things as hardware / software devices and their internetworking.

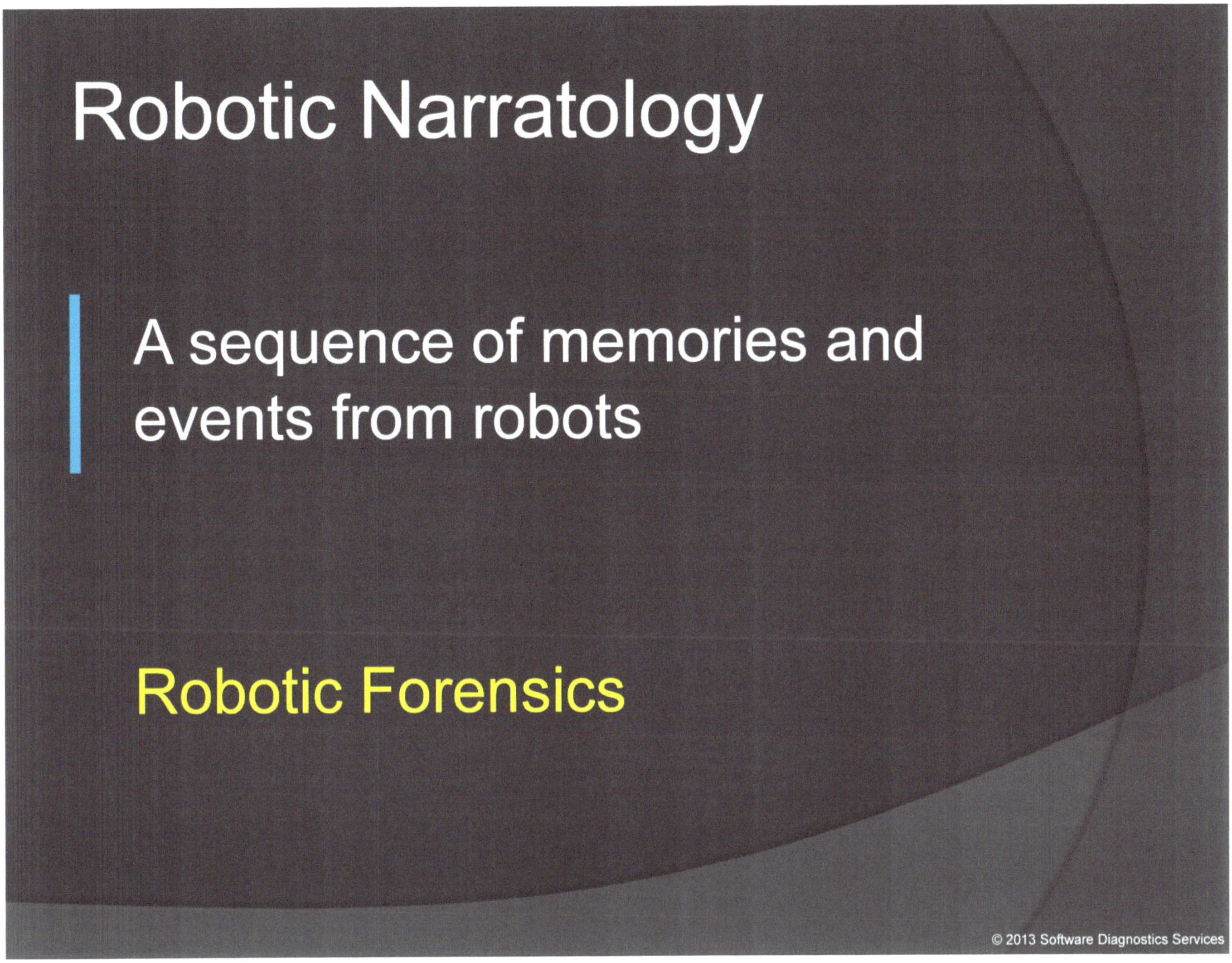

And we project this into the future as narratology of robots. The analysis of their communication between themselves and with humans is based on computer narratology. Here robotic forensics is a part.

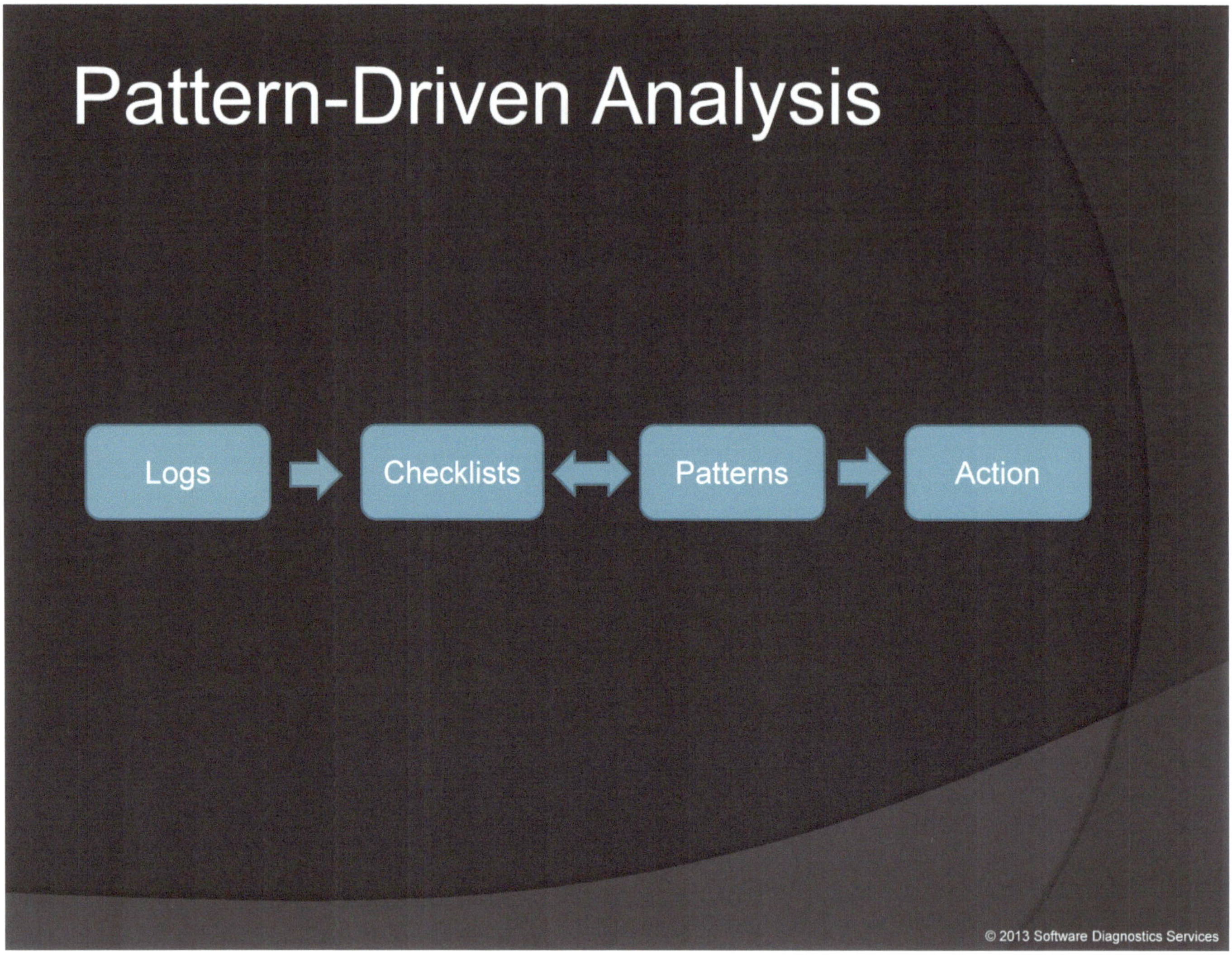

At the end a few words about logs, checklists, and patterns. You probably have seen the same diagram in previous seminars. This is an essential feature of pattern-driven software diagnostics and therefore software forensics.

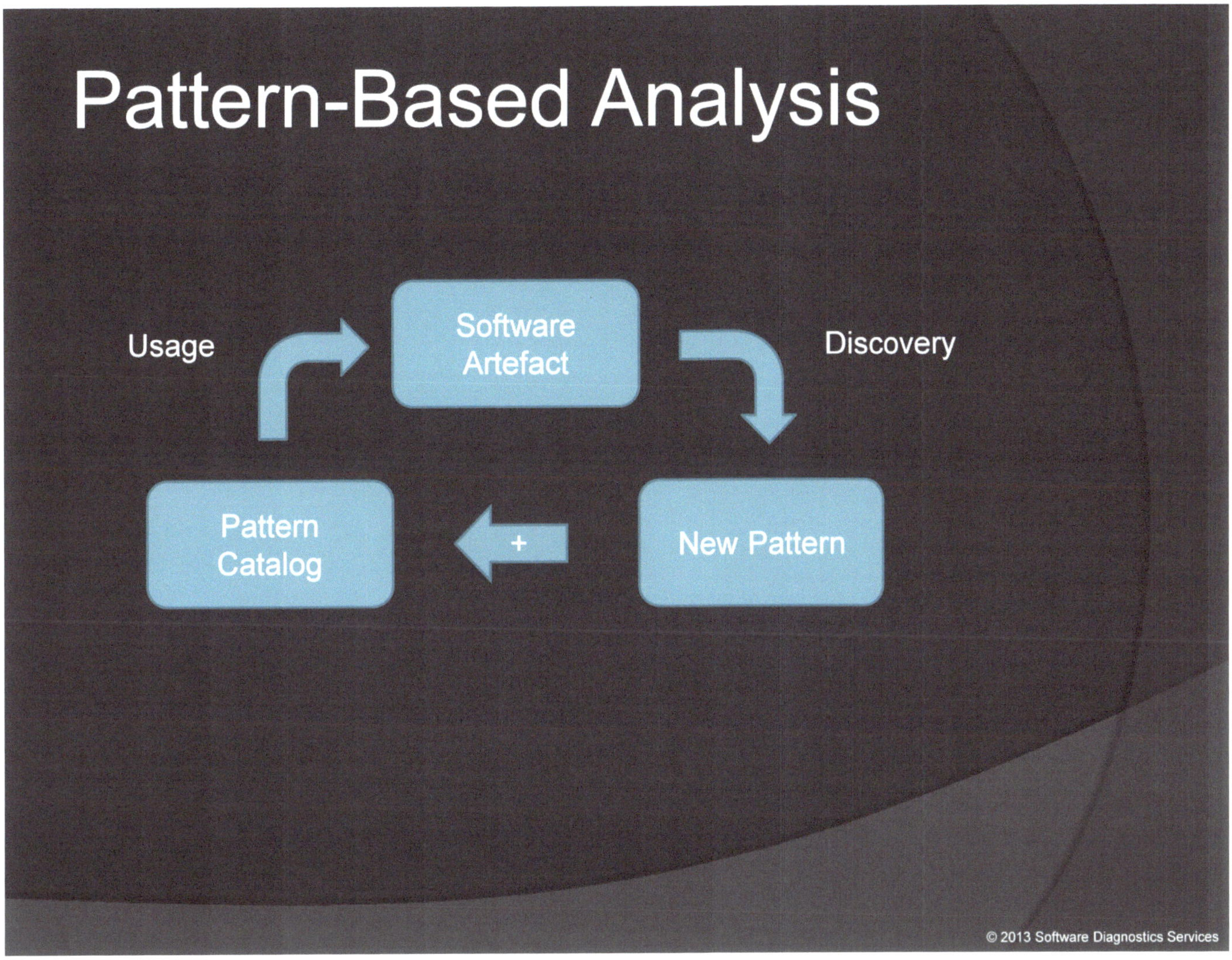

Pattern catalogs are rarely fixed. New patterns are constantly discerned or refined. This is the essence of pattern-based part of pattern orientation.

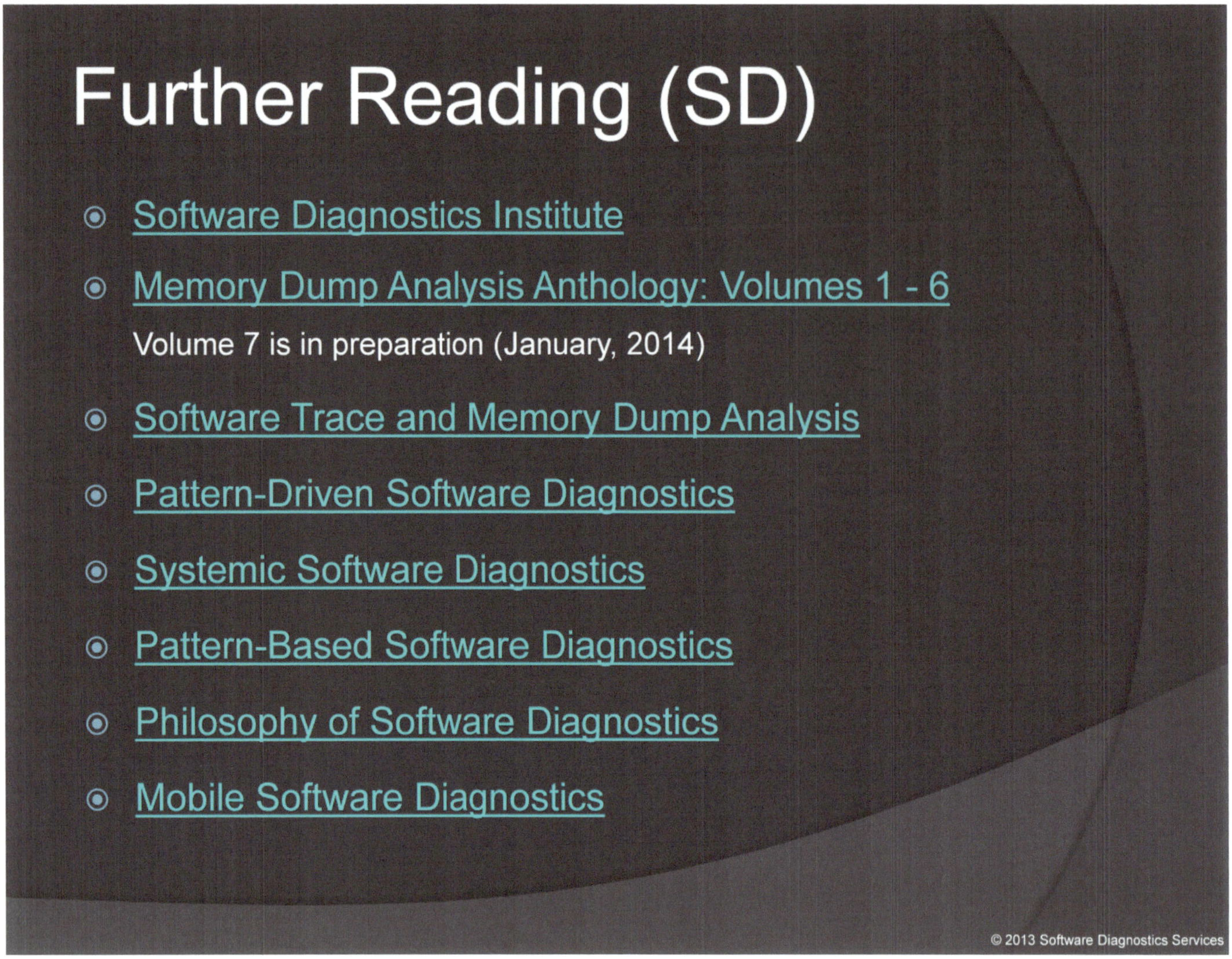

Here are some links for further reading about pattern-oriented software diagnostics which can serve as a foundation for pattern-oriented forensics. Most of them are presentations with recordings with transcripts published as books.

Software Diagnostics Institute:
http://www.dumpanalysis.org

Memory Dump Analysis Anthology: Volumes 1 – 6:
http://www.patterndiagnostics.com/ultimate-memory-analysis-reference

Software Trace and Memory Dump Analysis:
http://www.patterndiagnostics.com/STMDA-materials

Pattern-Driven Software Diagnostics:
http://www.patterndiagnostics.com/Introduction-Software-Diagnostics-materials

Systemic Software Diagnostics:
http://www.patterndiagnostics.com/systemic-diagnostics-materials

Pattern-Based Software Diagnostics:
http://www.patterndiagnostics.com/pattern-based-diagnostics-materials

Philosophy of Software Diagnostics:
http://www.patterndiagnostics.com/philosophy-diagnostics-materials

Mobile Software Diagnostics:
http://www.patterndiagnostics.com/mobile-software-diagnostics-materials

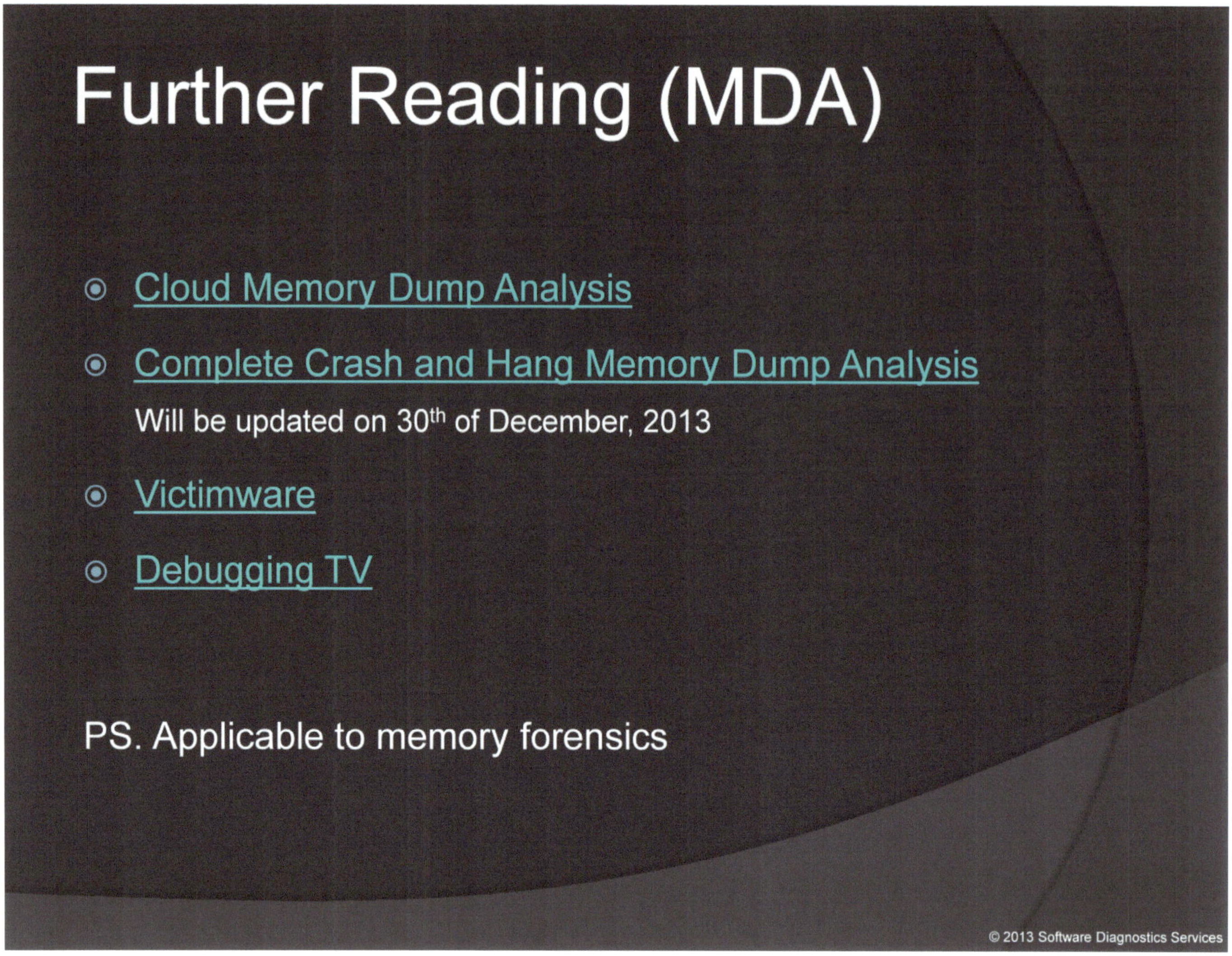

Here are links to memory dump analysis presentations which are also applicable to memory forensics. Many Debugging TV episodes also cover memory analysis and tools such as WinDbg from debugging Tools for Windows.

Cloud Memory Dump Analysis:
http://www.patterndiagnostics.com/CMDA-materials

Complete Crash and Hang Memory Dump Analysis:
http://www.patterndiagnostics.com/FCMDA-materials-Rev2

Victimware:
http://www.patterndiagnostics.com/Victimware-materials

Debugging TV:
http://www.debugging.tv/

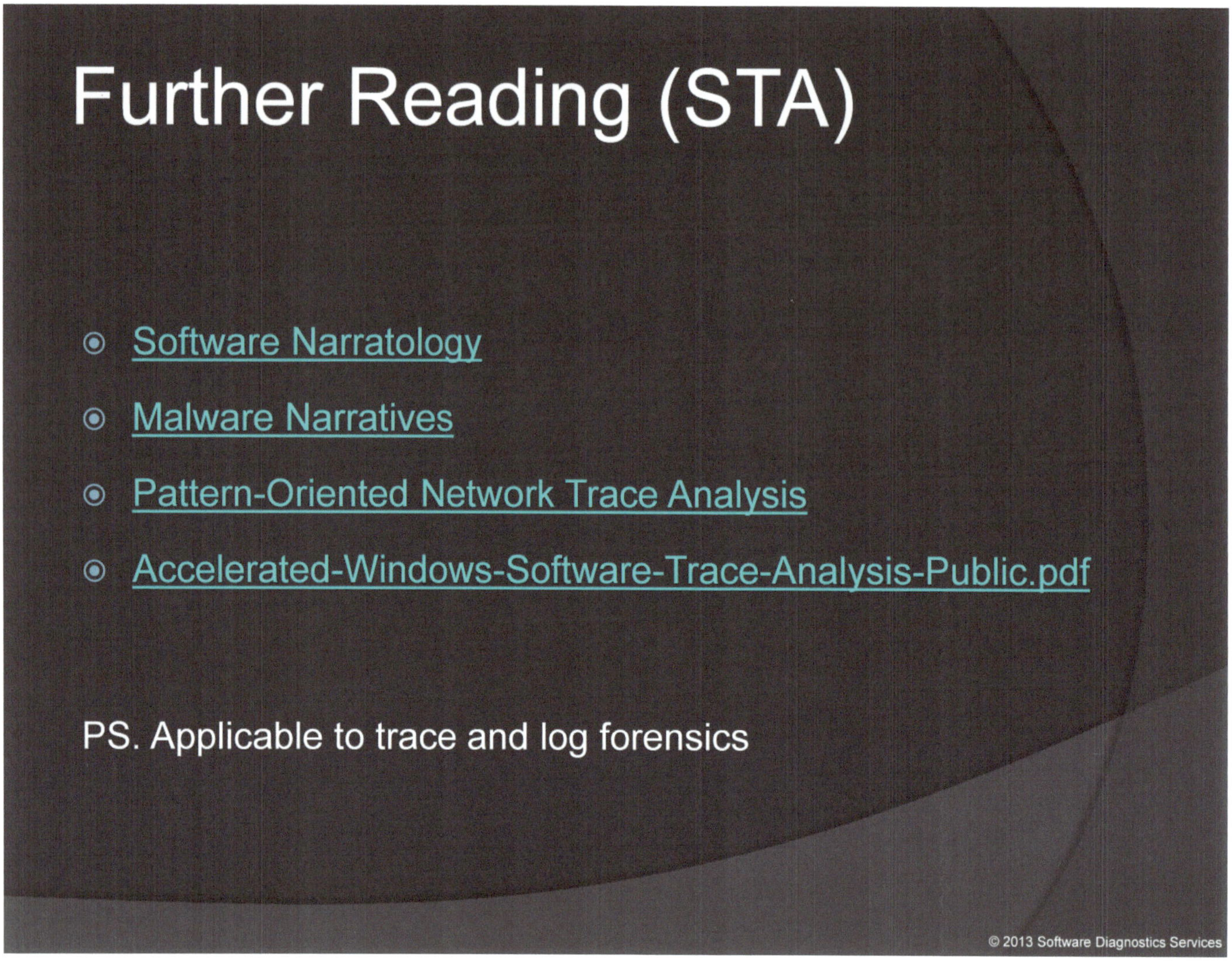

Here are links related to software trace and log analysis. Most of it is applicable to trace and log forensics.

Software Narratology:
http://www.patterndiagnostics.com/Introduction-Software-Narratology-materials

Malware Narratives:
http://www.patterndiagnostics.com/malware-narratives-materials

Pattern-Oriented Network Trace Analysis:
http://www.patterndiagnostics.com/pattern-oriented-network-trace-analysis-materials

Reference:
http://www.patterndiagnostics.com/Training/Accelerated-Windows-Software-Trace-Analysis-Public.pdf

Software Diagnostics Services has also published a few courses related to Windows memory forensics. There are great discounts till the end of January, 2014. Please have a look later on when we publish a presentation link.

Windows Memory Forensics Training Pack:
http://www.patterndiagnostics.com/memory-forensics-pack

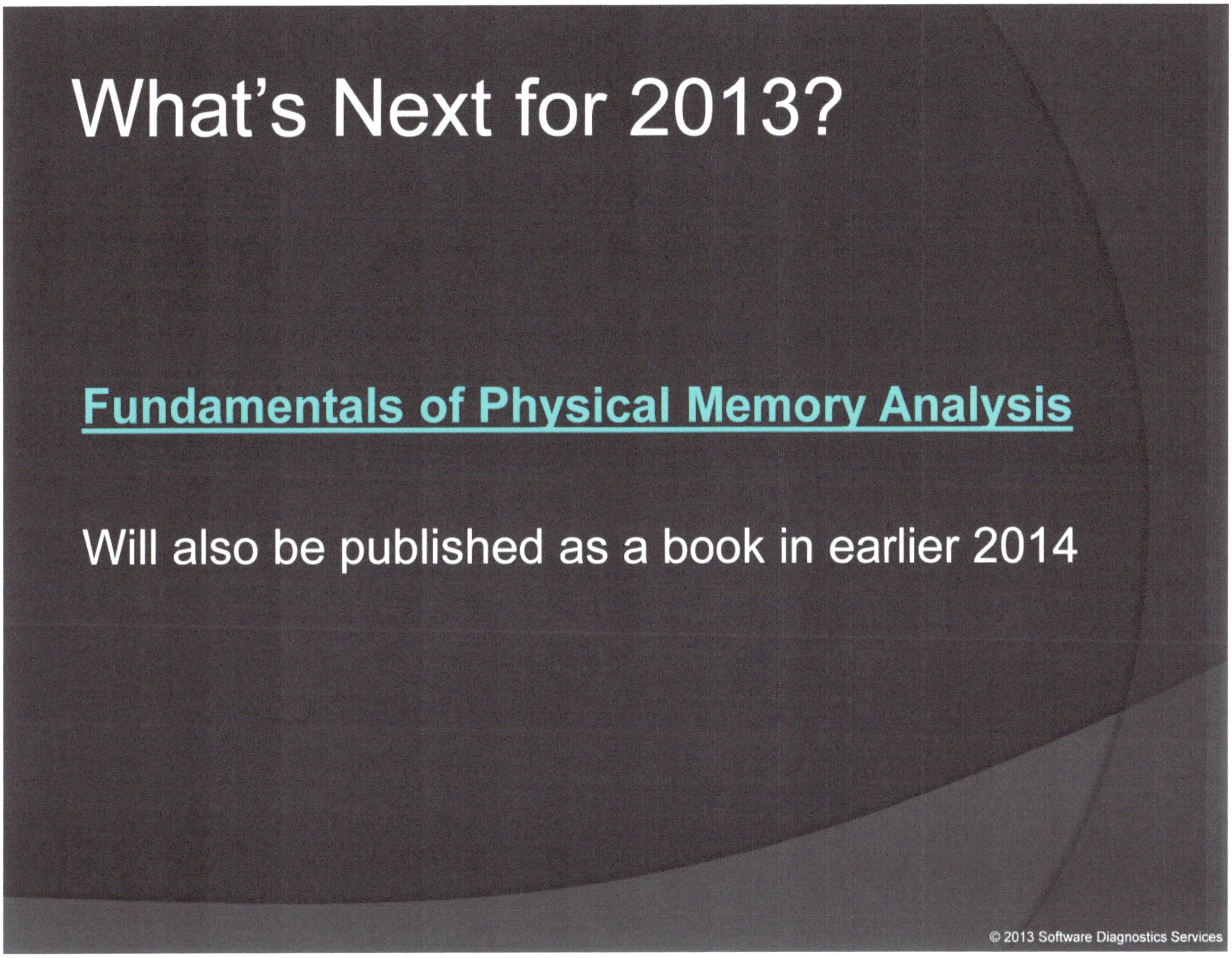

Although this year is about to end soon we still have the last seminar on the 30th of December. It will cover the theory behind the physical memory analysis. It is an extension and correction of two previous seminars on complete memory dump analysis delivered in 2010 and 2011.

Fundamentals of Physical Memory Analysis:
http://www.patterndiagnostics.com/physical-memory-analysis

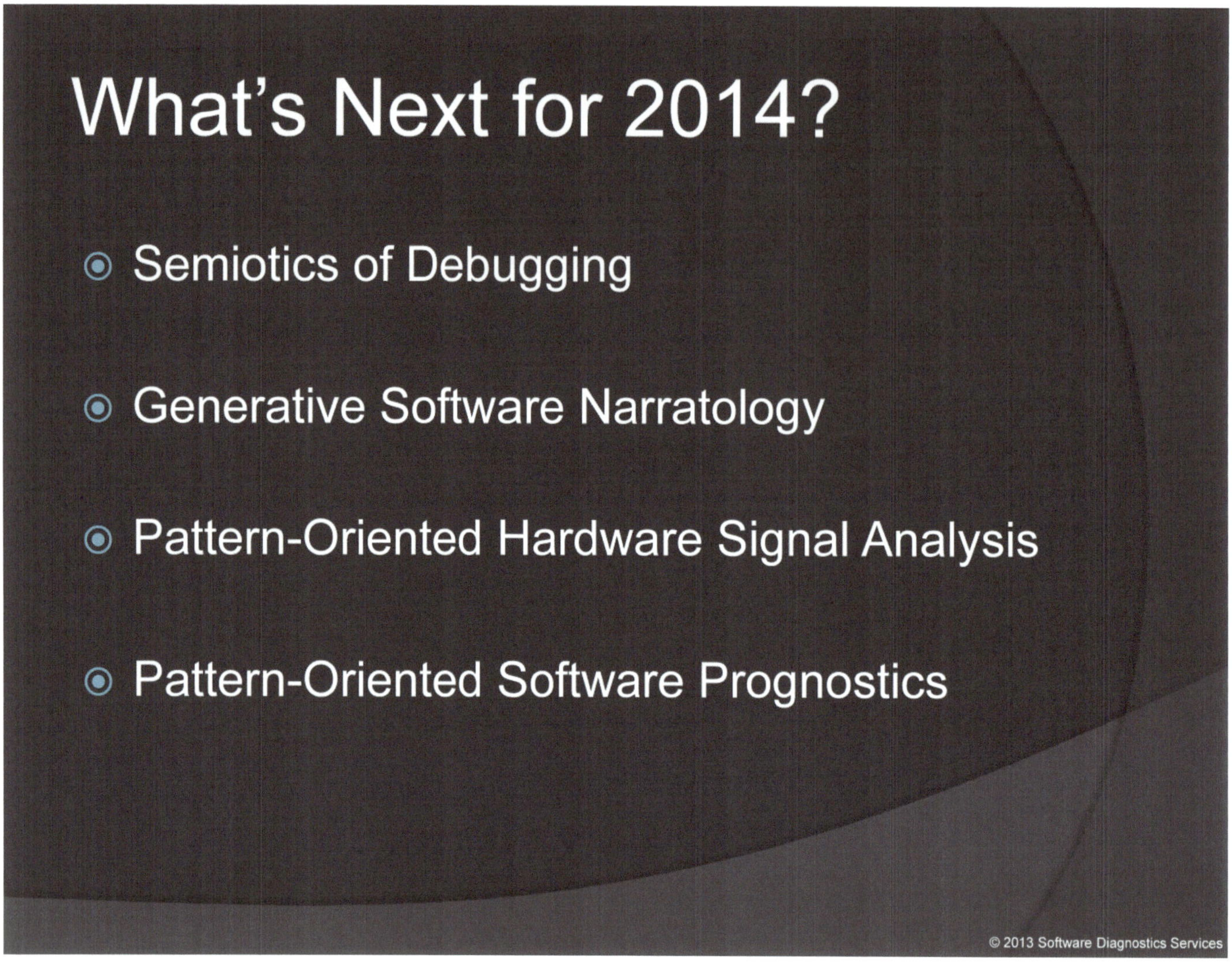

This is a selection of seminars planned for 2014. They will also be published as books. You may have already familiar with this partial list. To it we only added a seminar about pattern-oriented software prognostics that covers prognosis of software structure and behavior based on diagnosis.

Pattern-Oriented
Memory Forensics

Dmitry Vostokov
Software Diagnostics Institute

Published by OpenTask, Republic of Ireland

OpenTask books and magazines are available through booksellers and distributors worldwide. For further information or comments send requests to press@opentask.com.

A CIP catalogue record for this book is available from the British Library.

ISBN-13: 978-1-908043-76-4 (Paperback)

First printing, 2014

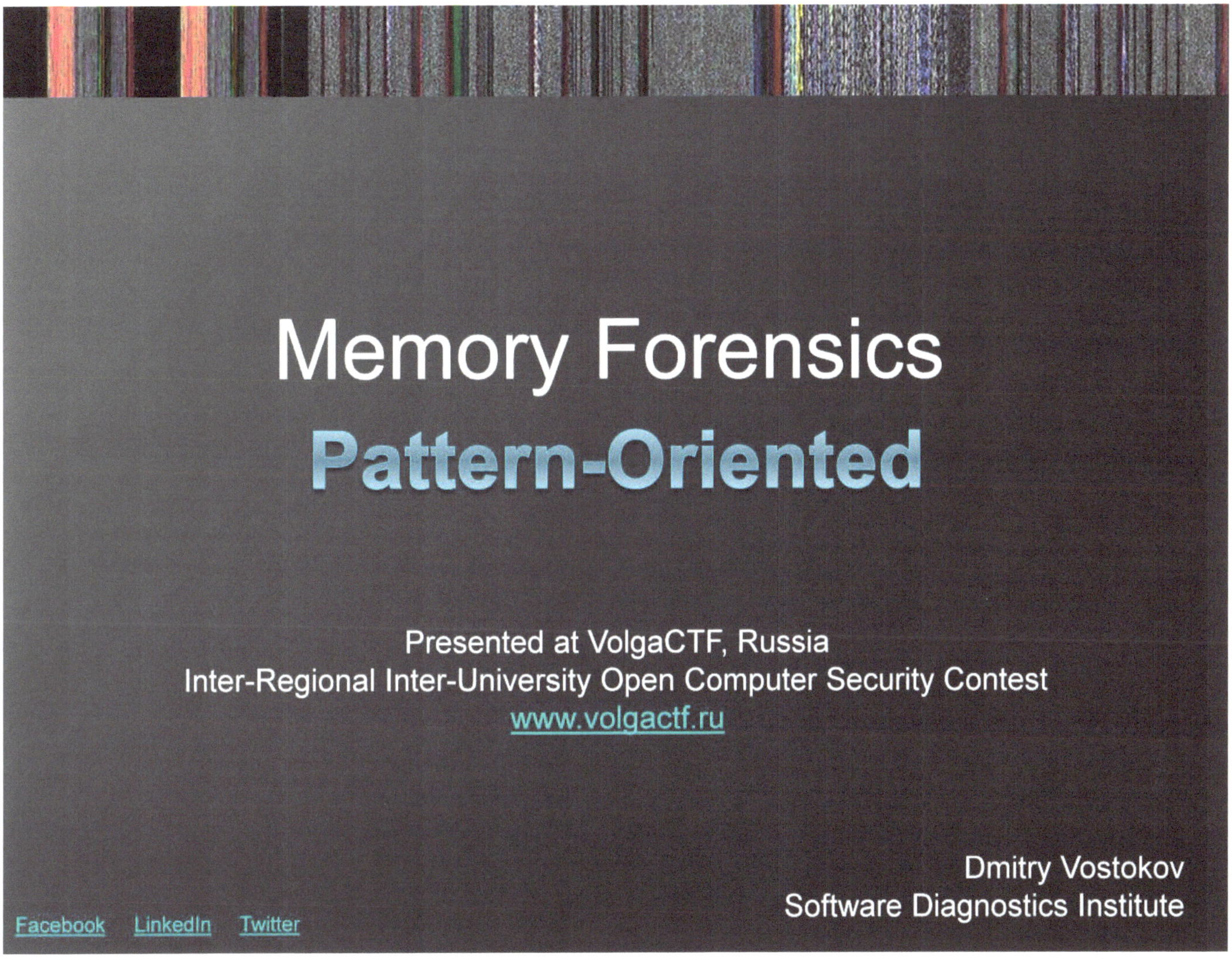

Hello Everyone, my name is Dmitry Vostokov and I introduce today a pattern language for memory forensics. First we start with a short theoretical part, provide a few definitions, and then we illustrate the pattern-oriented approach with a few crash dump analysis examples by using WinDbg debugger from Microsoft Debugging Tools for Windows.

Facebook:
http://www.facebook.com/DumpAnalysis

LinkedIn:
http://www.linkedin.com/in/vostokov

Twitter:
http://twitter.com/DumpAnalysis

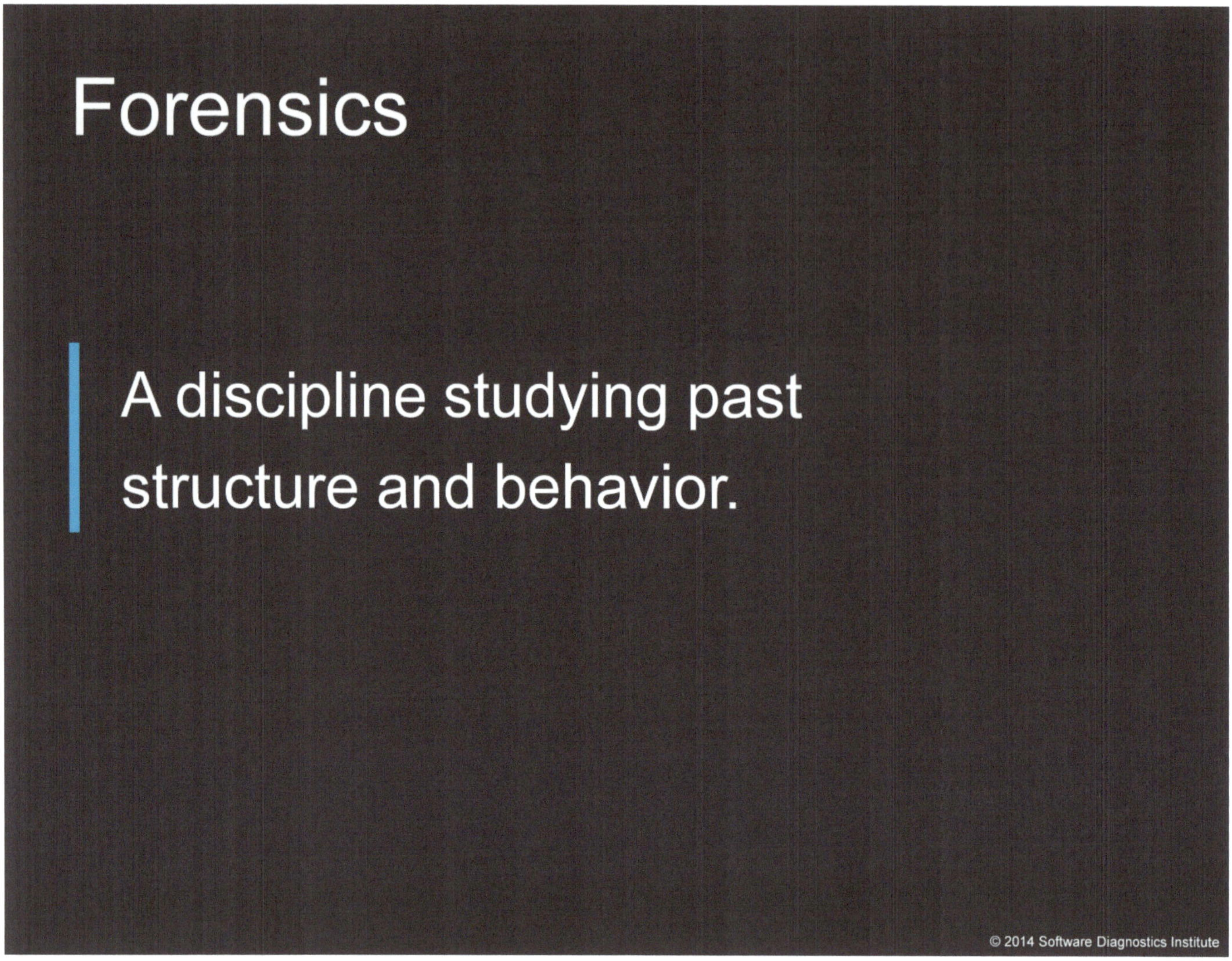

This is a typical definition of forensic science or forensics: a discipline studying past structure and behavior.

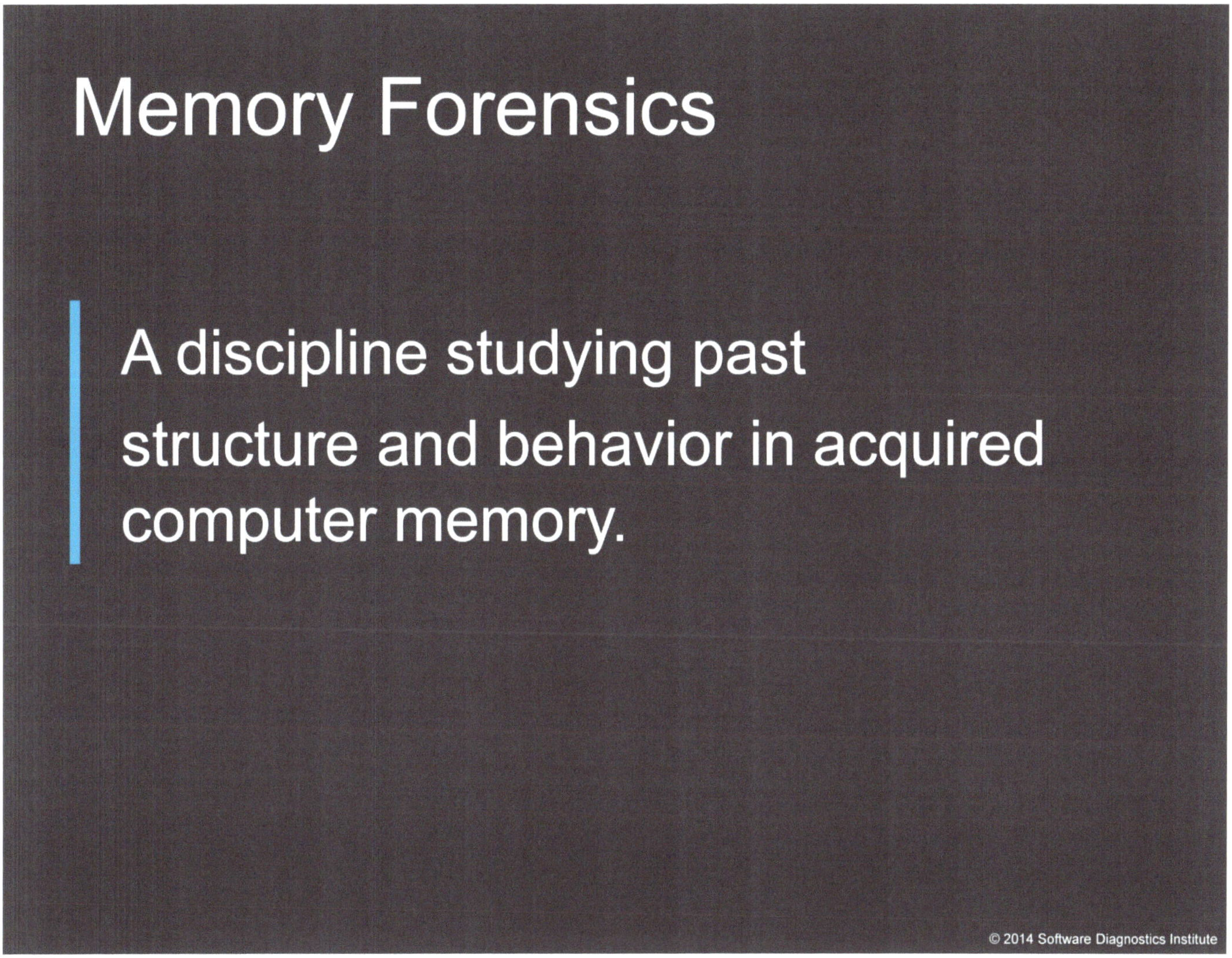

There are many specialized forensics. Our concern is with memory forensics - investigation of past software structure behaviour in memory snapshots.

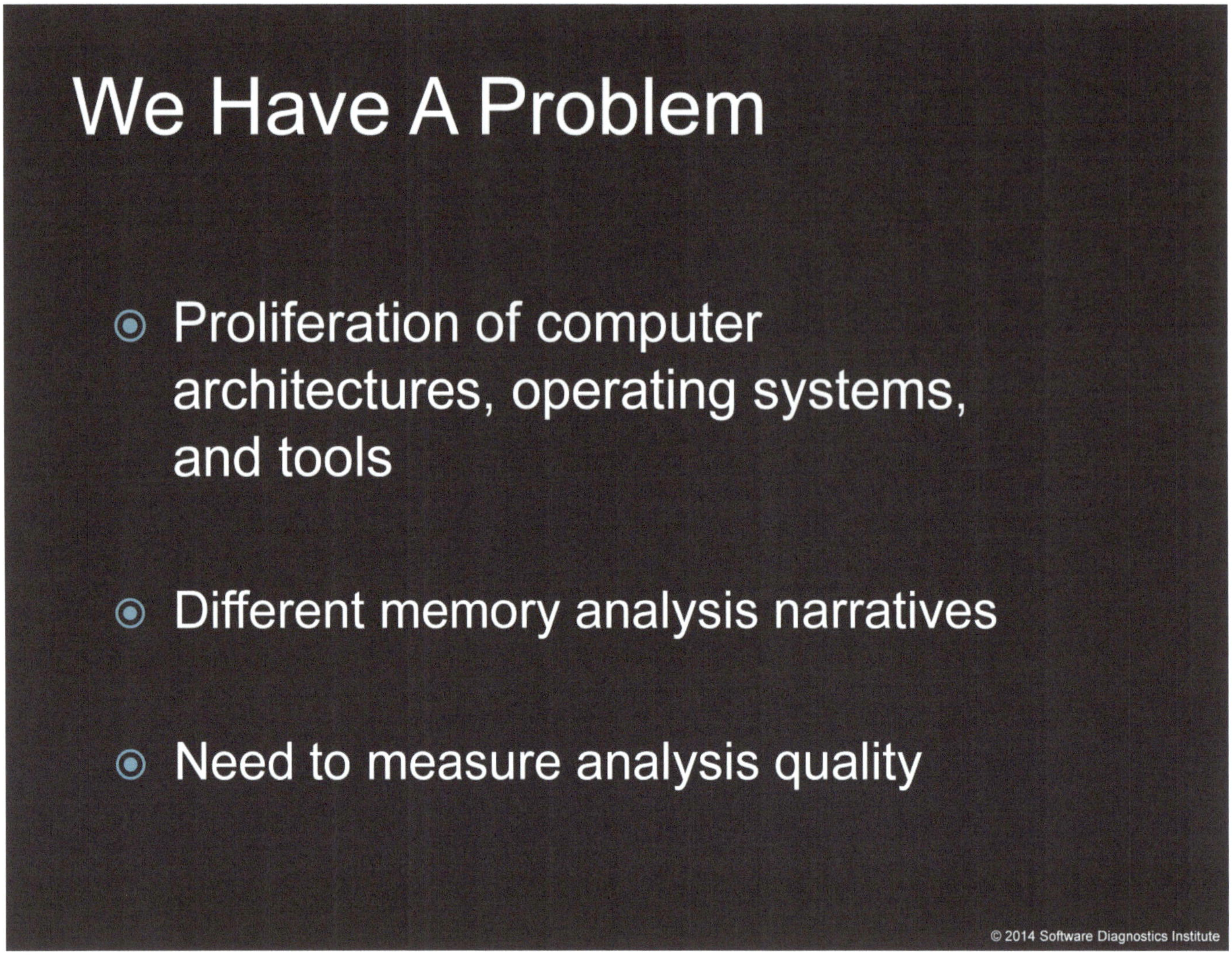

However, we have a problem. There are so many different hardware and CPU architectures, operating systems, and even memory acquisition and analysis tools for the same hardware and software. If the same tool is used by different people we get different memory analysis reports where the same problems and incidents are retold differently. There is also the absence of quality measurements or if there are some measurements they are subjective at most.

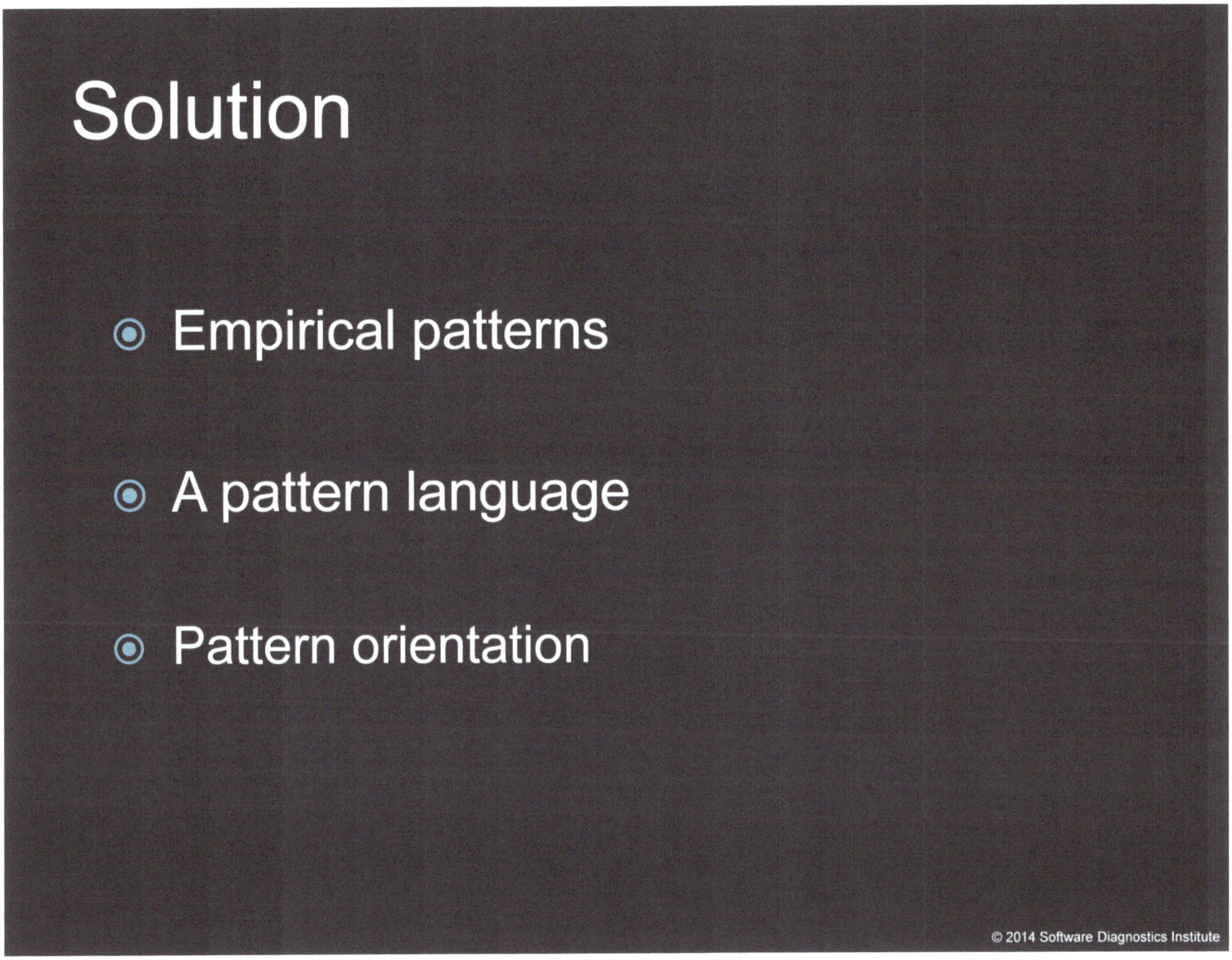

The solution to this problem is a unified language for discussing and communicating detection and analysis results. Such a language is usually called a pattern language. Empirically encountered patterns of detection and analysis are discerned and organized into pattern catalogues. This approach is very similar to software design patterns and was originally devised for town and building architecture by Christopher Alexander. We can paraphrase his book *"The Timeless Way of Building"* as *"The Timeless Way of Memory Forensics"*. By pattern orientation we mean the whole system of such patterns, their discovery, systematic usage, and life cycle.

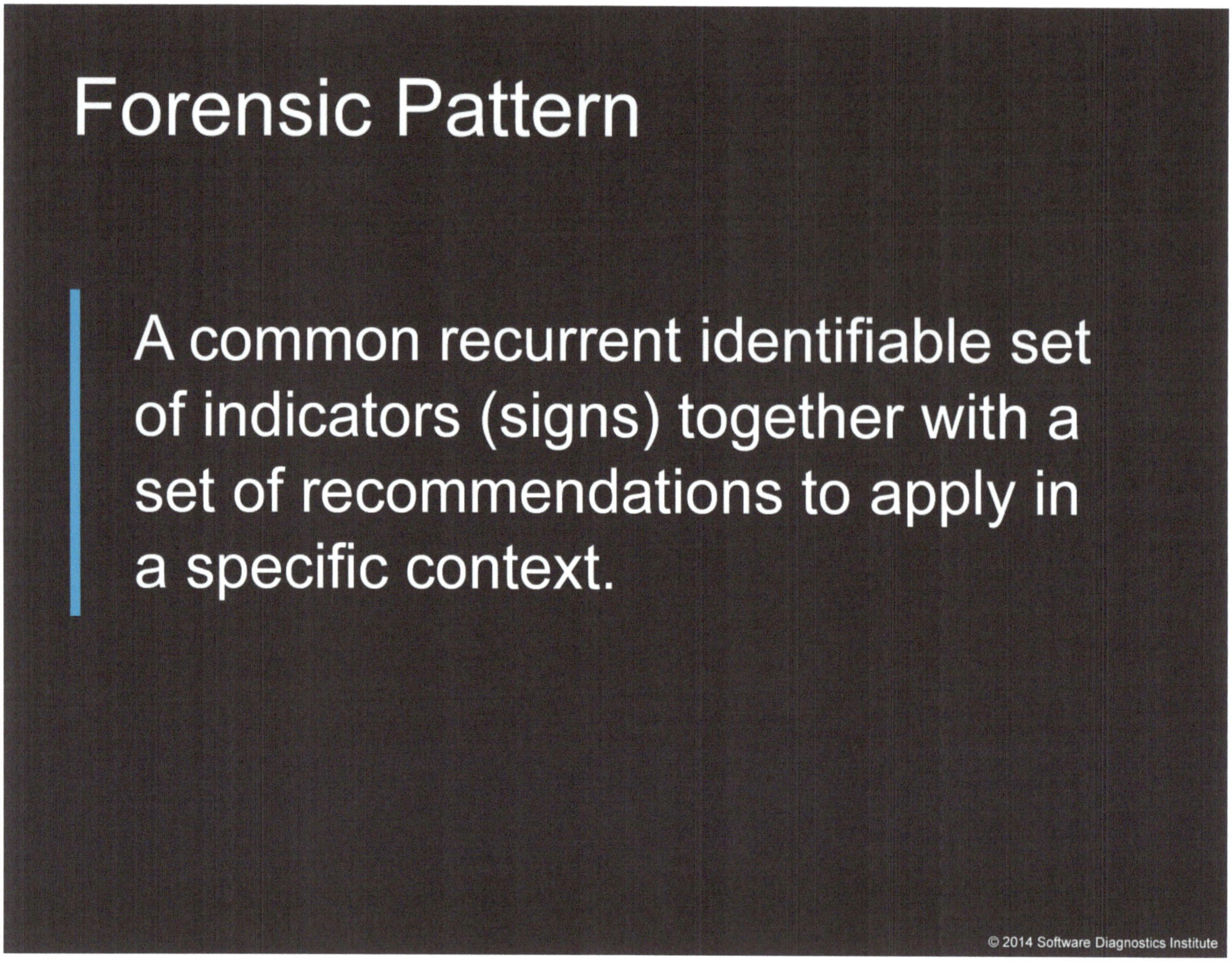

Here we provide a definition of a general forensic pattern already put forward in our previous presentations: a common recurrent identifiable set of indicators (signs) together with a set of recommendations to apply in a specific context.

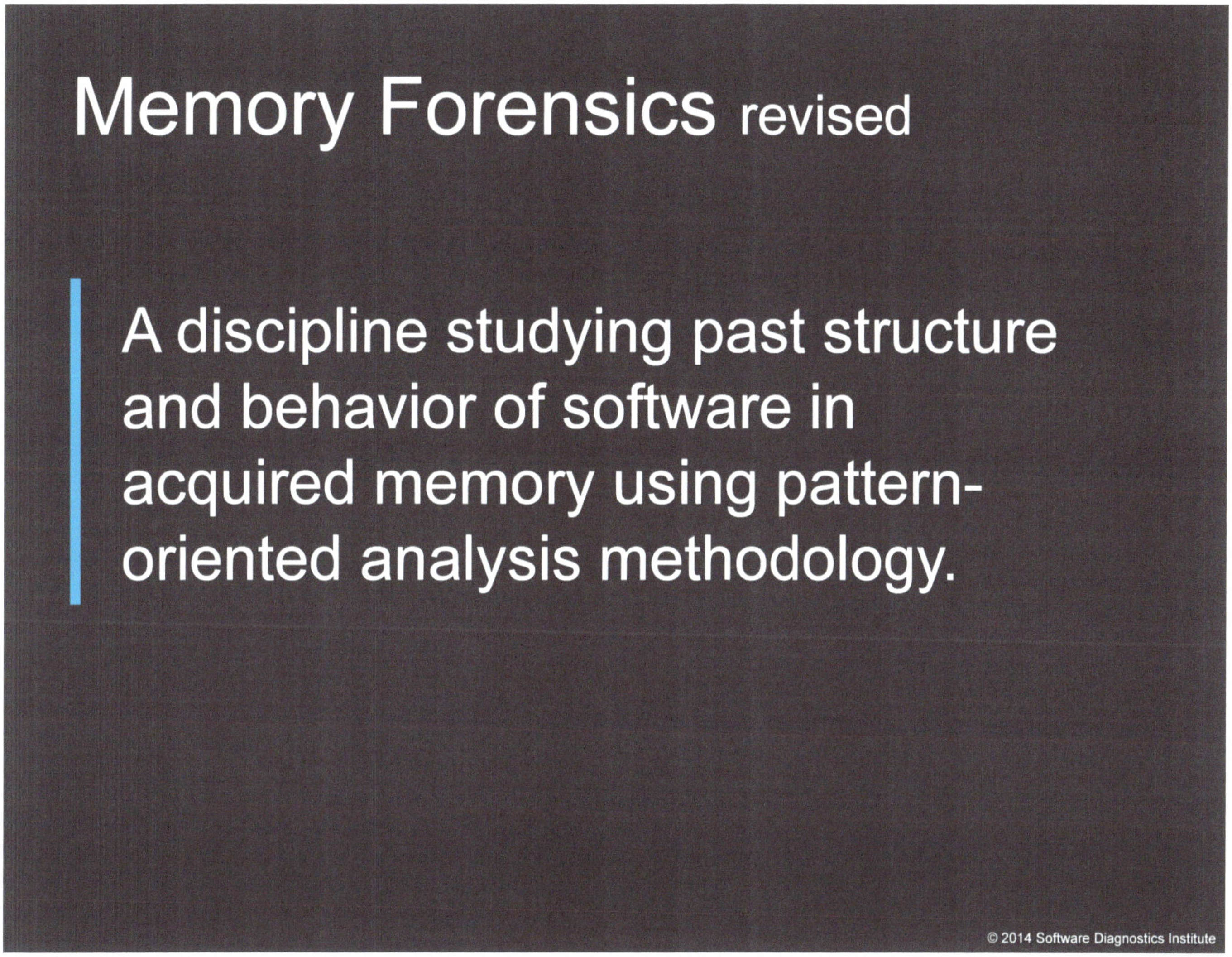

Now, we revise memory forensics definition taking into account the proposed pattern orientation.

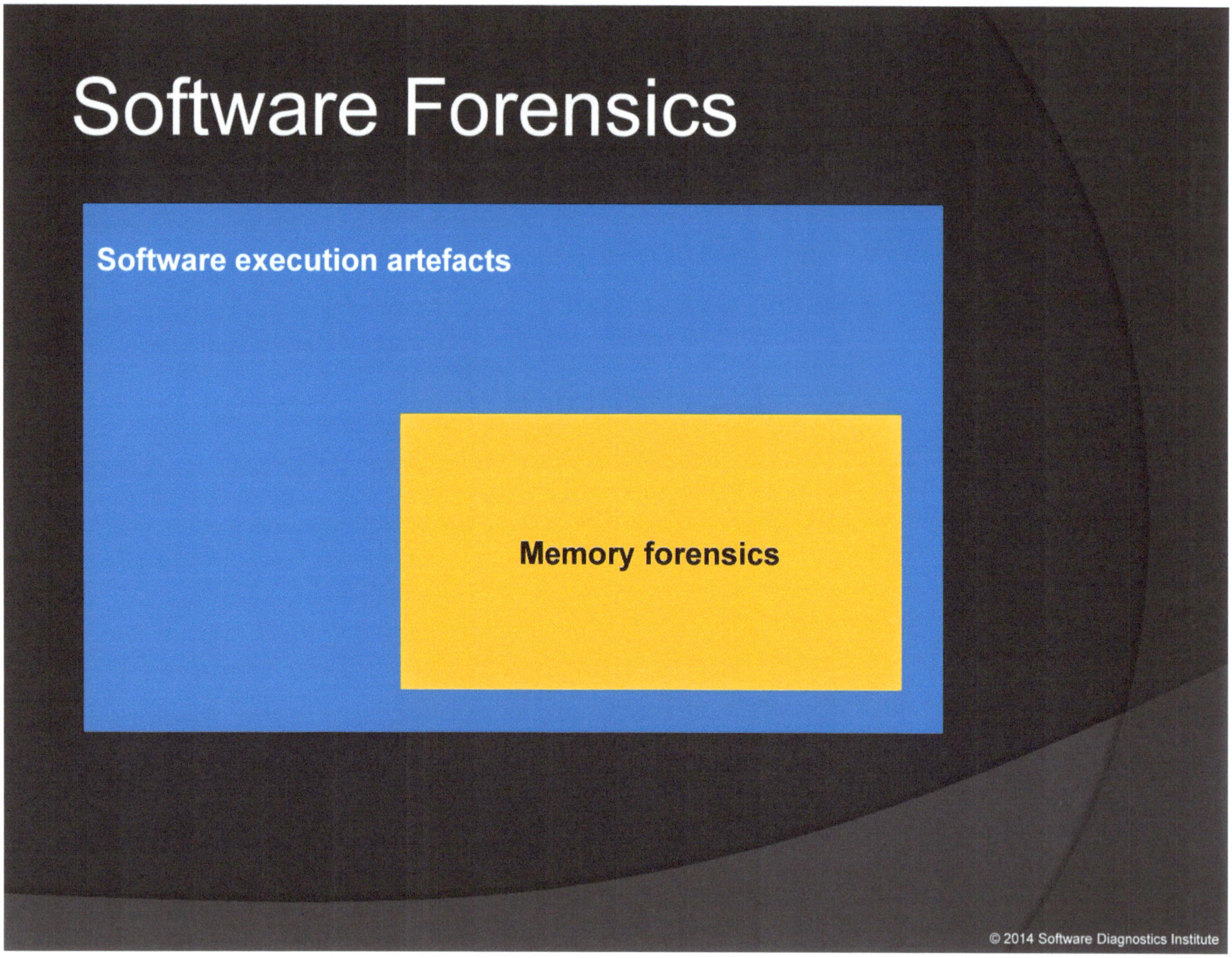

Memory forensics is a part of software forensics which considers many types of software execution artefacts and not only memory snapshots.

Software Forensics

A discipline studying past structure and behavior of software in execution artifacts using systemic and pattern-oriented analysis methodologies.

This is a definition of software forensics we put forward in one of our previous presentations: a discipline studying past structure and behavior of software in execution artifacts using systemic and pattern-oriented analysis methodologies. Please notice the addition of the so called "systemic" approach. Although this is beyond the scope of this lecture we devoted one slide for it later on.

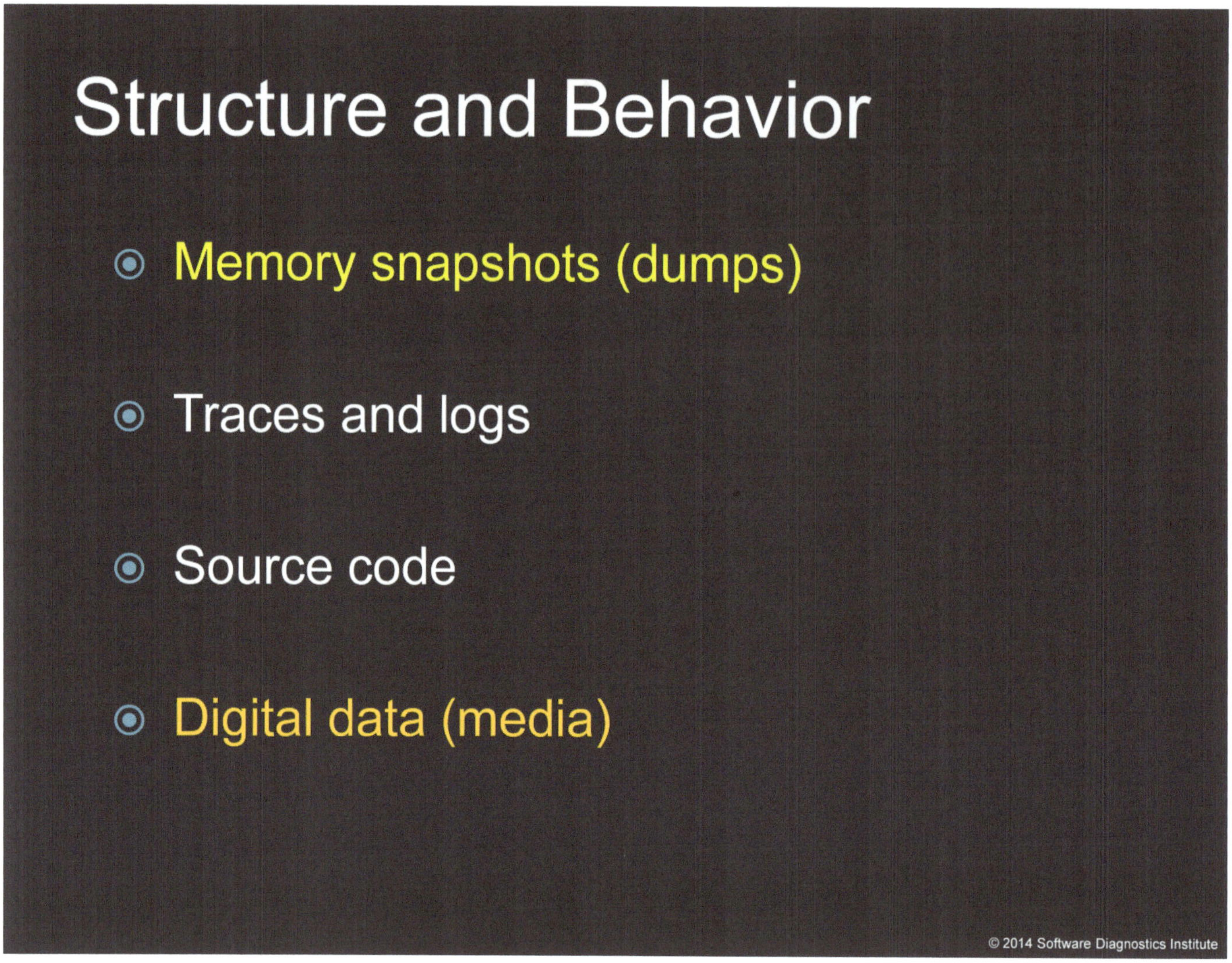

Here we provide the list of various software execution artefacts studied by software forensics. In memory forensics we are concerned mostly with memory dumps but the same approach and language can be applied to other digital data.

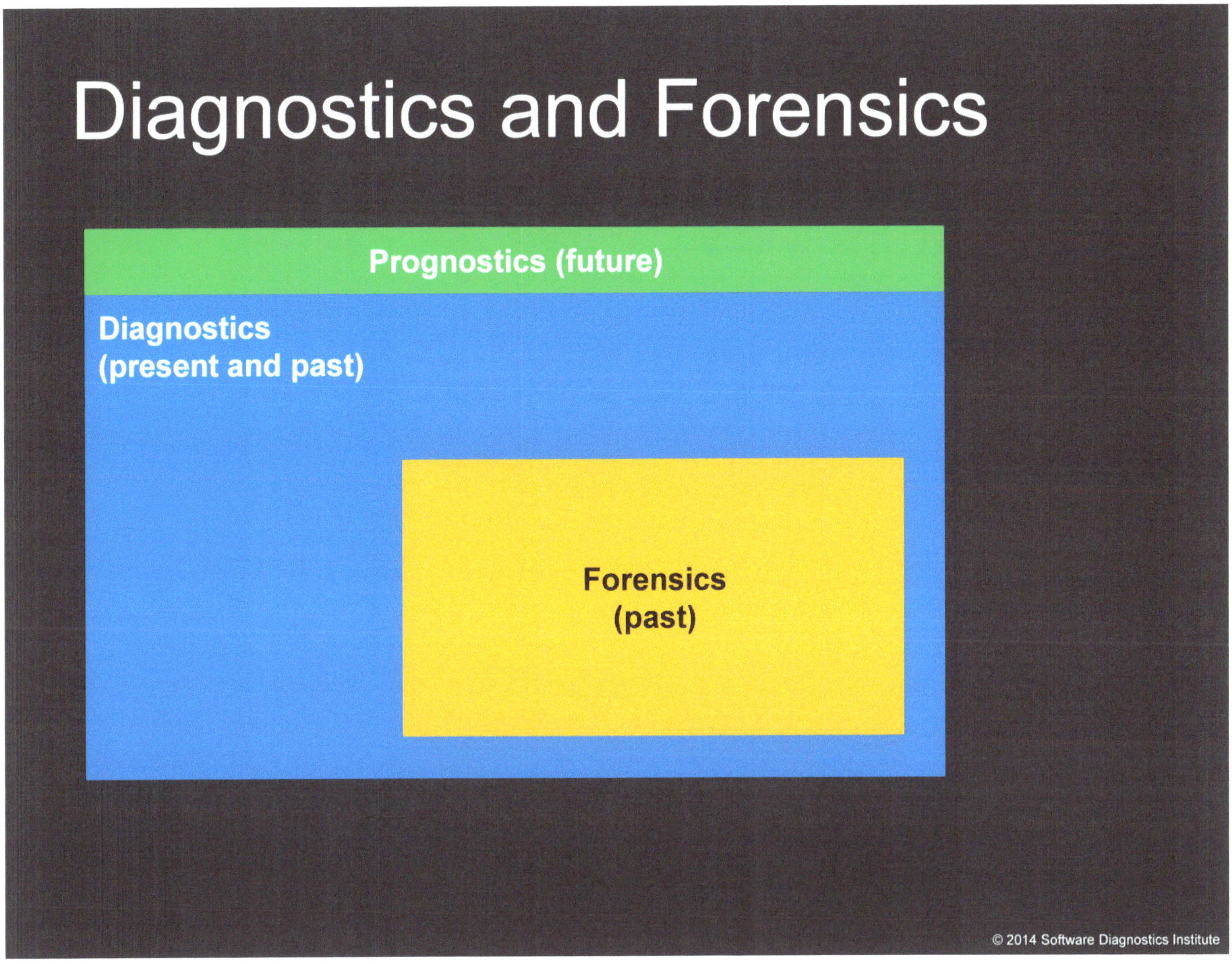

We also put software forensics and therefore memory forensics as a part of software diagnostics which analyses present and past of software execution.

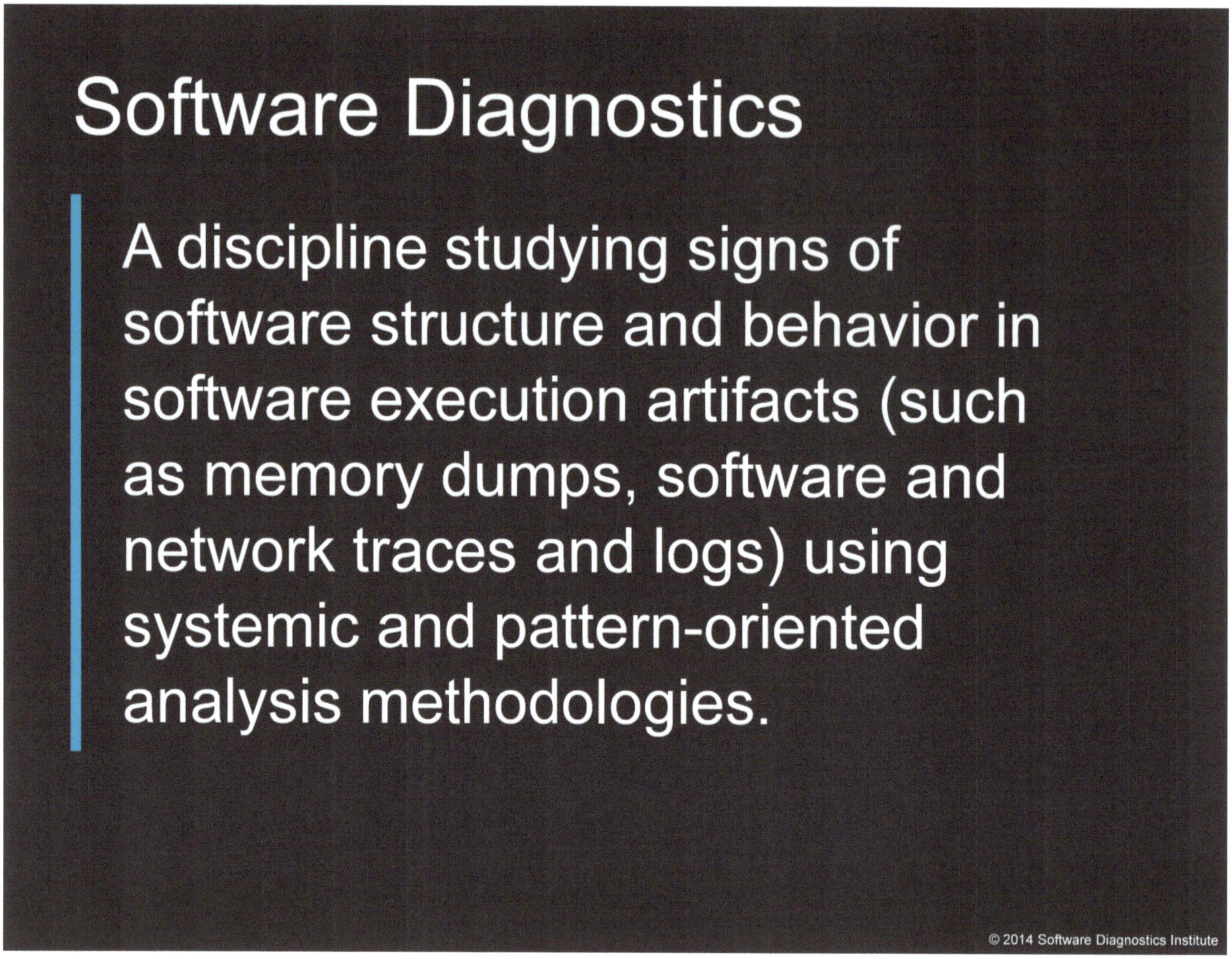

Here we provide a encompassing definition of software diagnostics: a discipline studying signs of software structure and behavior in software execution artifacts (such as memory dumps, software and network traces and logs) using systemic and pattern-oriented analysis methodologies.

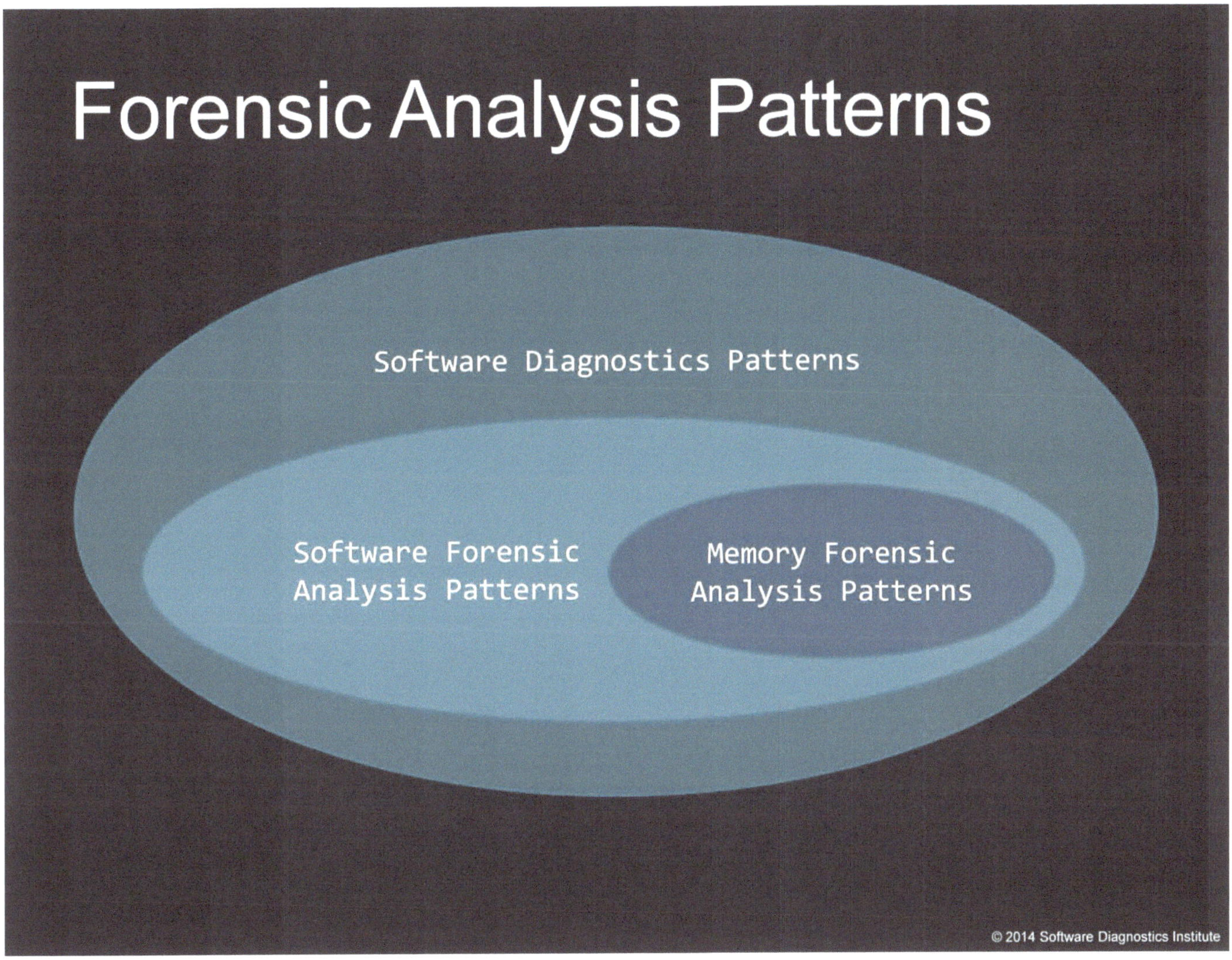

Naturally, because of that inclusion relationship, a set of memory forensic analysis patterns is a subset of software diagnostics patterns.

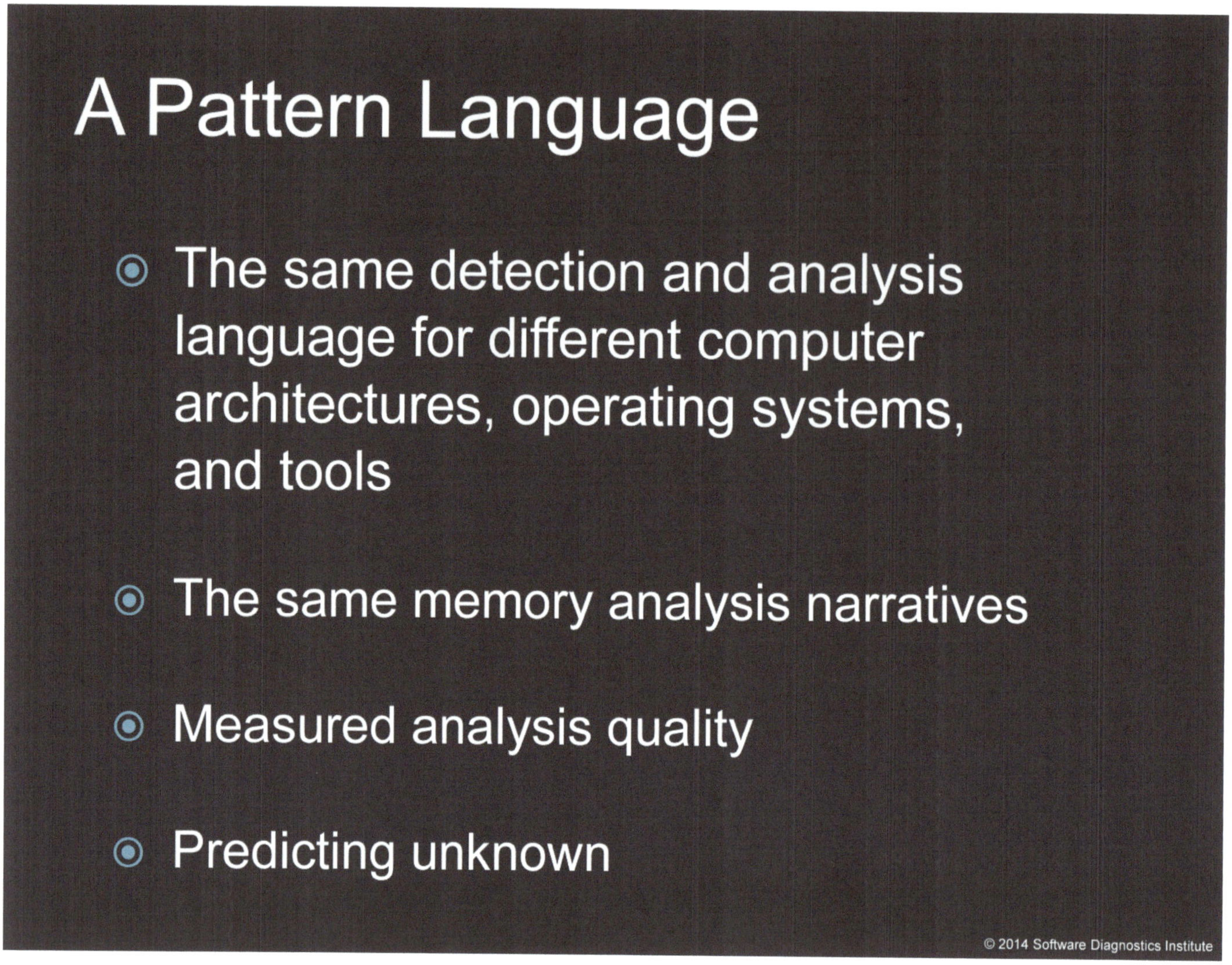

Now having a pattern language we can state its benefits. Moreover, we can predict unknown software structure and behavior for a new computer platform by using the same pattern language from a more *"developed"* system. Here, by a more *developed* system we mean a system where the most patterns were discovered and elaborated. For example, we were able to do it for Mac OS X by reusing the same patterns from Windows, for ARM by reusing from x86/x64, and for GDB and LLDB by reusing WinDbg. We are now working on applying the same pattern language to Volatility.

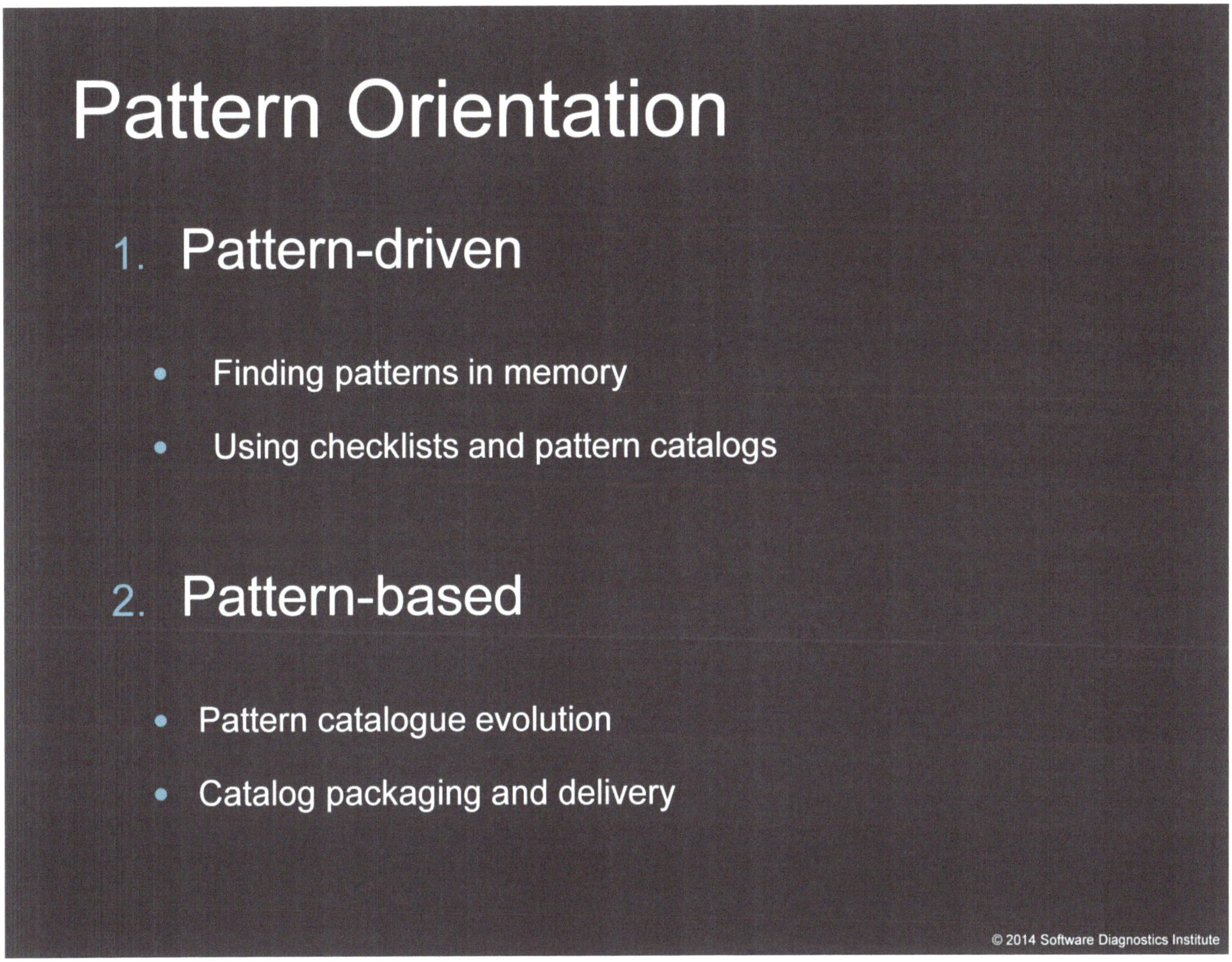

Now we'd like to say a few words about pattern orientation. We say it is pattern-driven when we talk about a forensic process and pattern recognition and a pattern-based when we talk about pattern life cycle. We start with the pattern-driven part first.

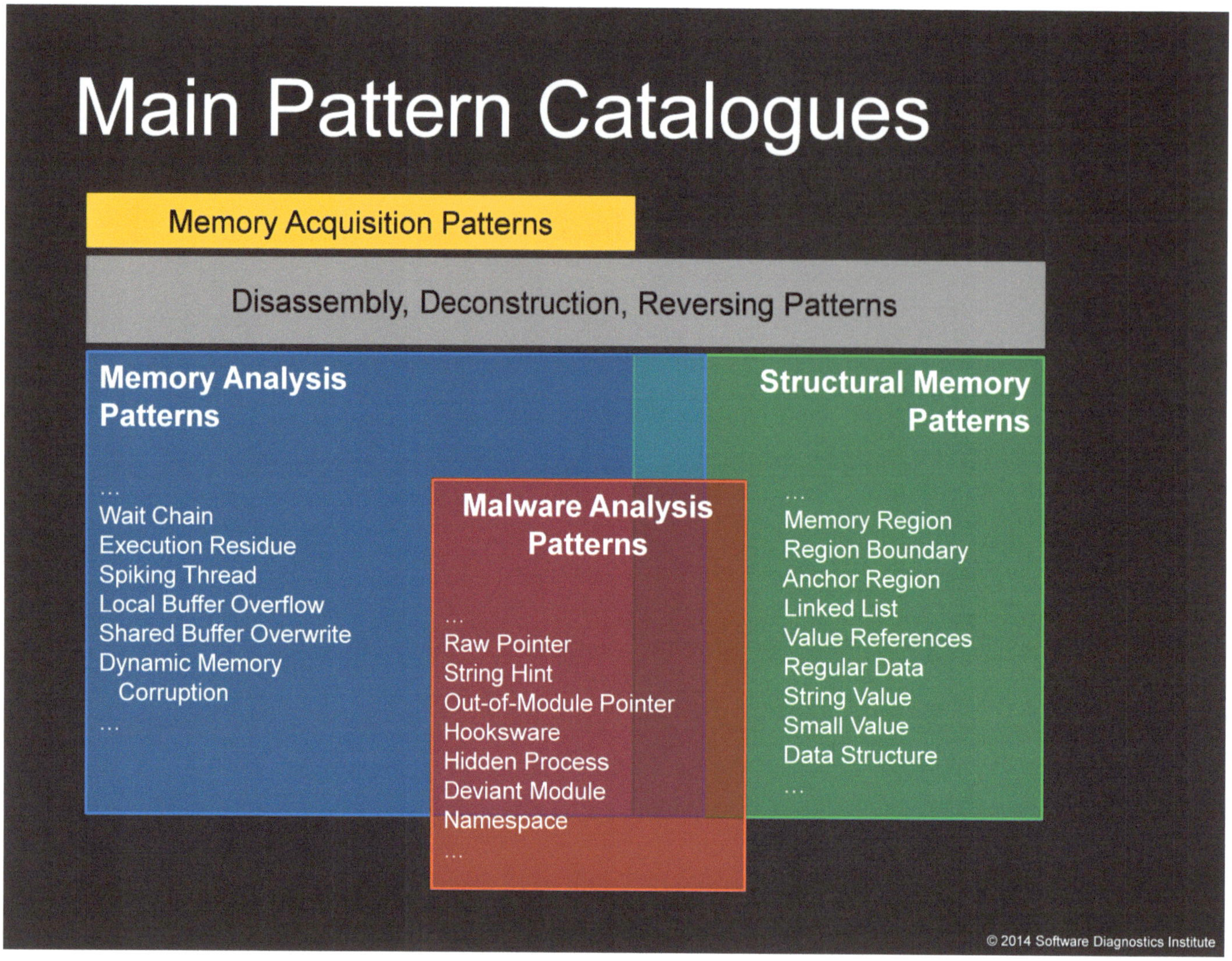

Patterns are organized into pattern catalogues. For memory forensics we are interested in 3 main ones such as memory analysis patterns, structural memory patterns and malware analysis patterns. These catalogues overlap because it is not easy sometimes to classify patterns rigidly. The basic motivation behind malware patterns is intentional abnormal software structure and behaviour whereas historically memory analysis patterns were collected for unintentional software behaviour arising from software defects with structural patterns added later but before the malware catalogue. In case of malware, rootkits, viruses, and in some complex cases of unintentional incidents a bit of disassembly and reversing may be required and we recently added a special pattern catalogue. Obviously, the timeless way of memory acquisition can be analysed and systematized in a pattern language terminology too. For the first 3 overlapping catalogues we provided a few pattern name examples and some of them will be shown in the practical part.

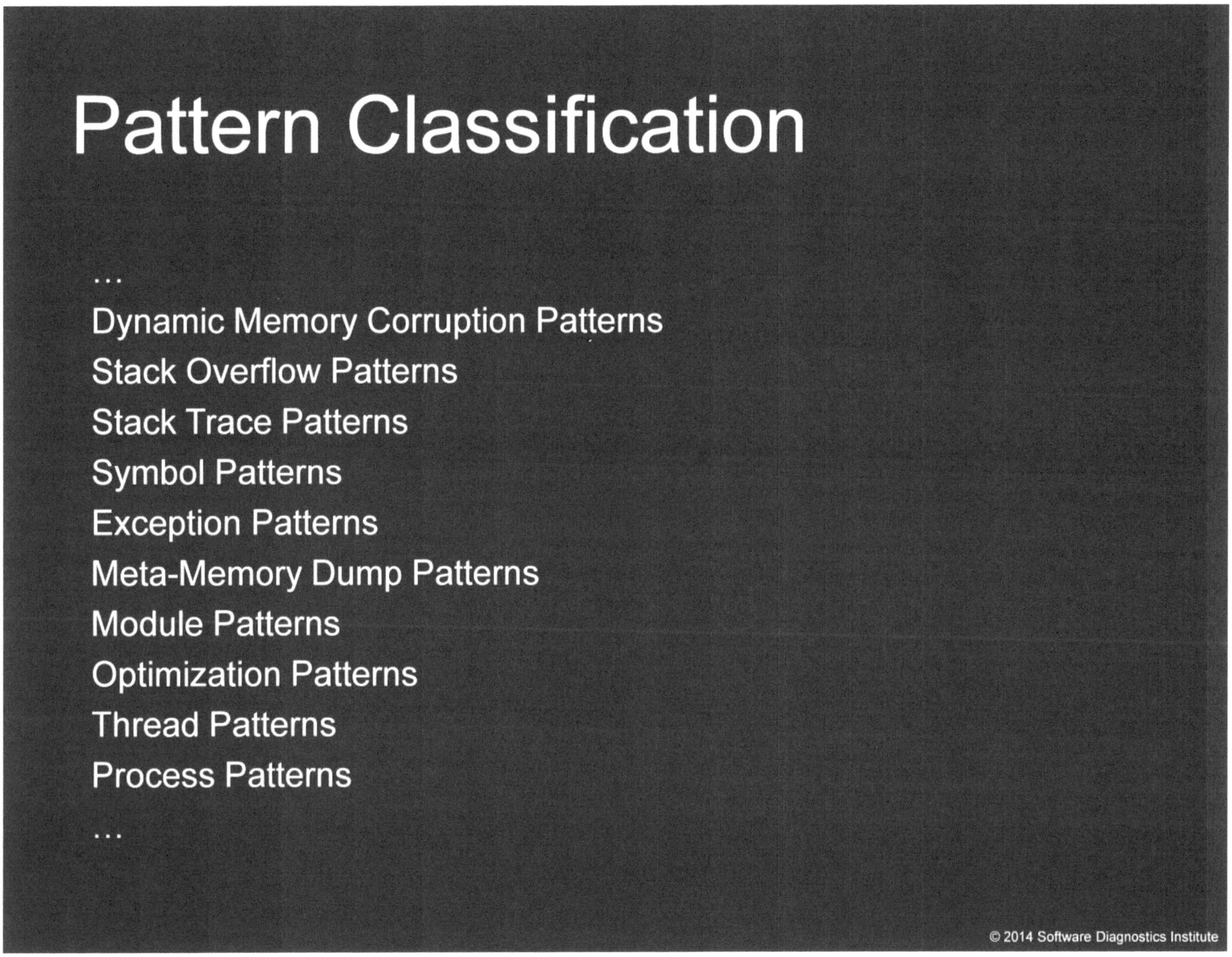

If a catalogue is too big it can be split into subcatalogues. For example, memory analysis catalogue contains almost 300 patterns and it was classified further. It is an ongoing process.

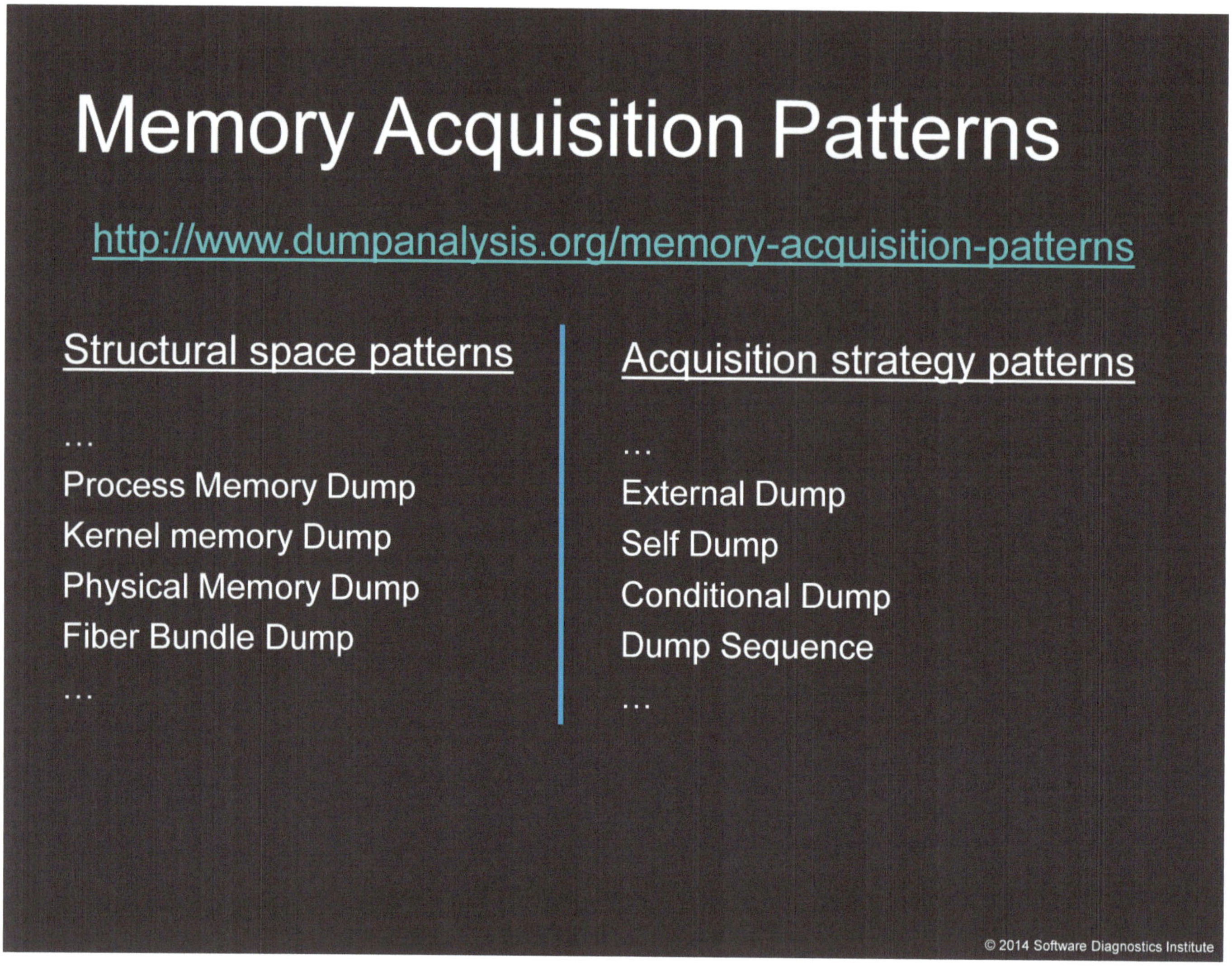

We also proposed a set of memory acquisition patterns and even split them into two groups based on what we dump, and why, how, and when we dump. Here we provide a few self-evident pattern name examples.

The current list of memory acquisition patterns:
http://www.dumpanalysis.org/memory-acquisition-patterns

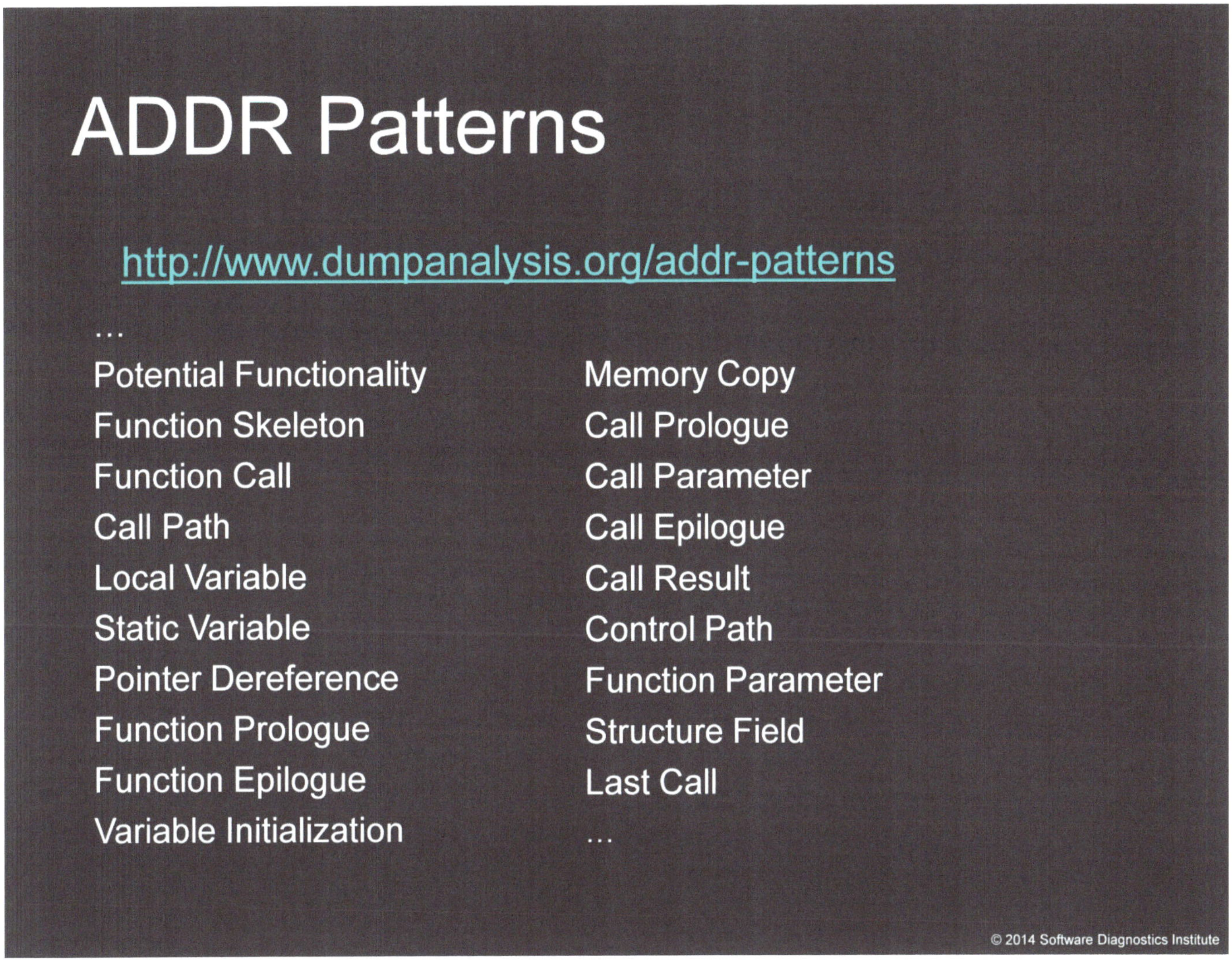

These are typical patterns we call ADDR. The complete description will be available in the forthcoming volume 8 of Memory Dump Analysis Anthology. The name ADDR is based on the name if the course Accelerated Disassembly, Deconstruction, and Reversing where they were first introduced.

The current list of ADDR patterns:
http://www.dumpanalysis.org/addr-patterns

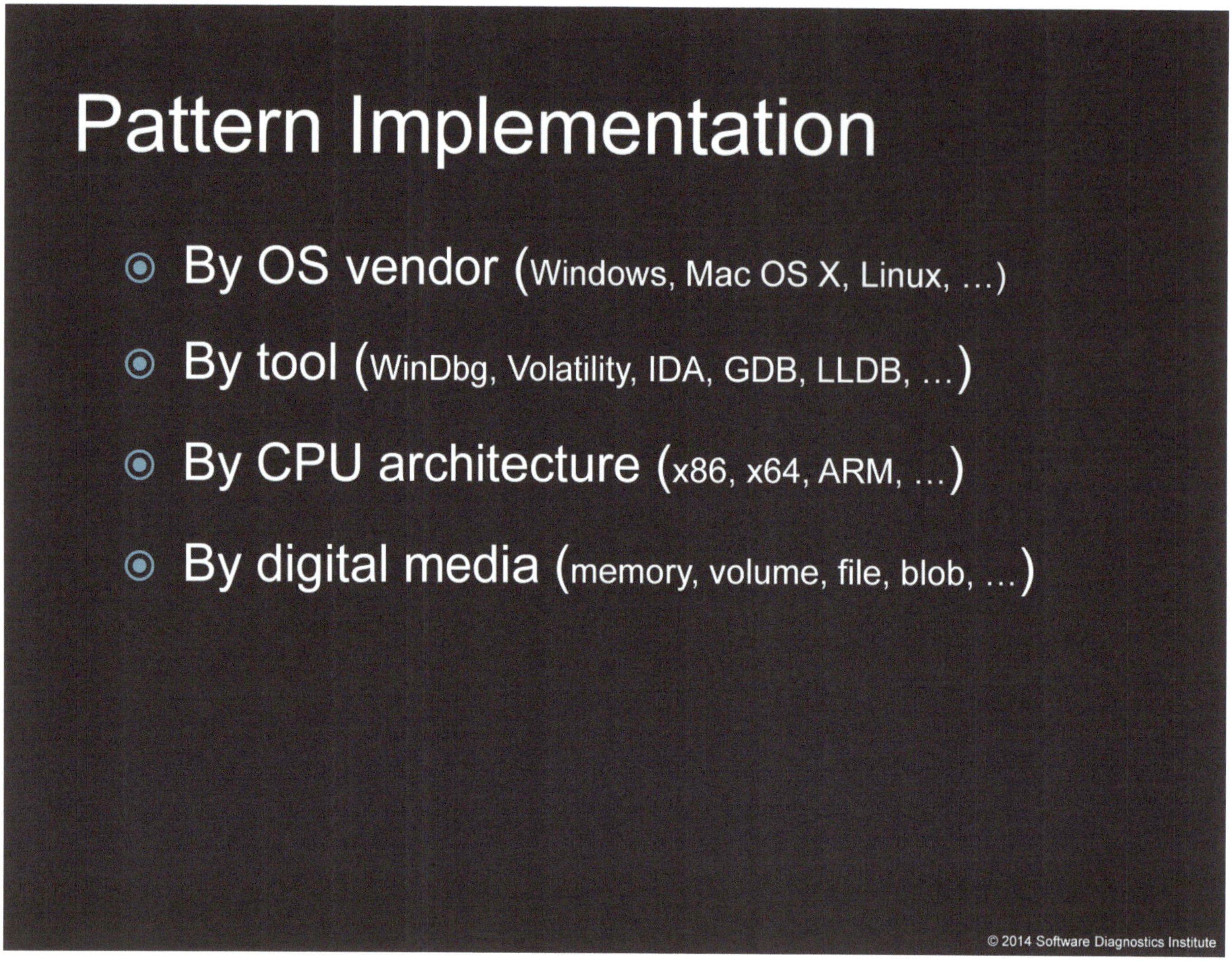

Ultimately patterns are found on specific platforms. By pattern implementation we mean differences in operating systems, product lines, media types, CPU and hardware architectures. The same name may share different implementations.

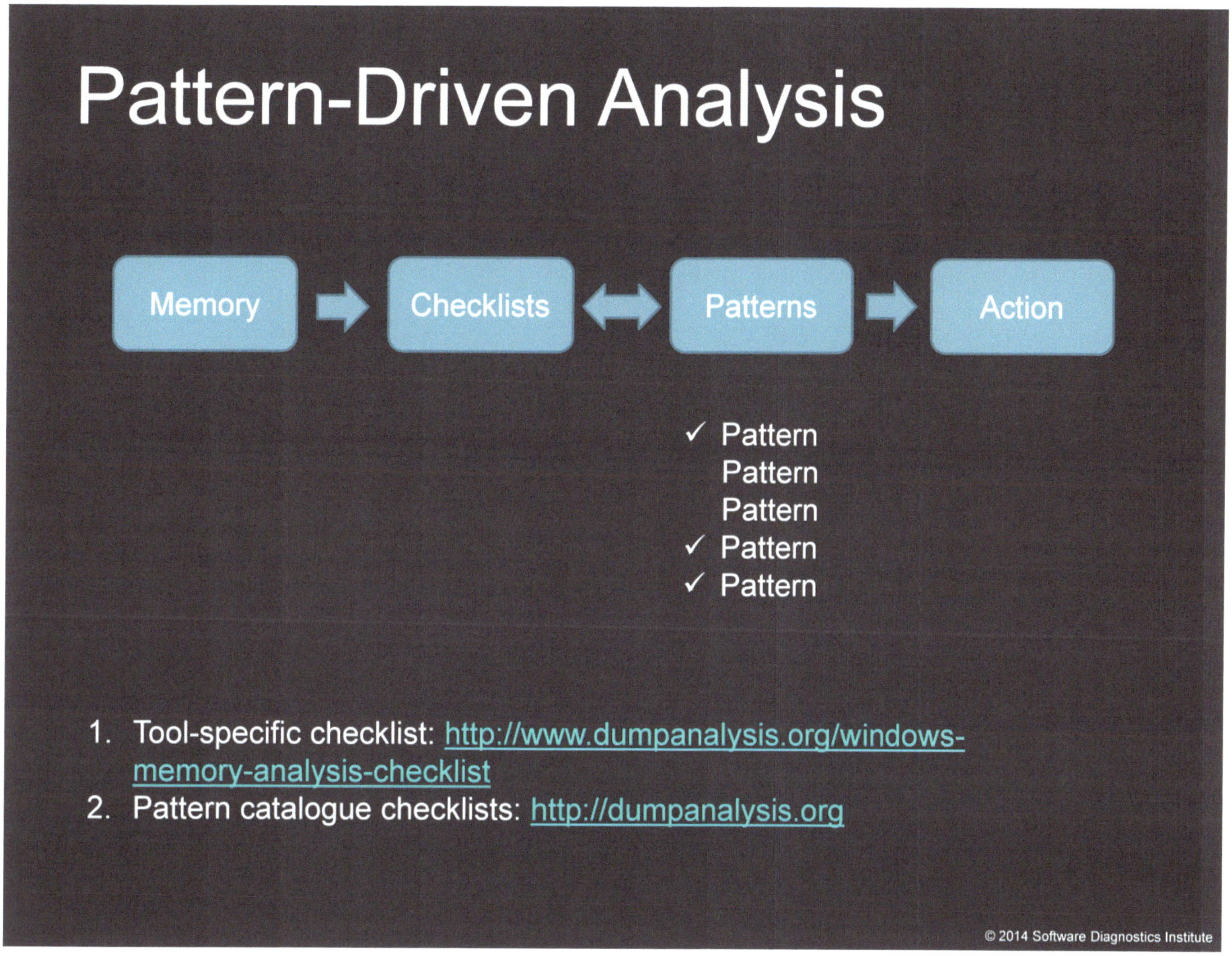

Now we'd like to say a few words about checklists. This is an essential feature of pattern-driven software diagnostics and therefore memory forensics. There are 2 types of checklists. A tool specific checklist may be the list of commands and recommendations. More general pattern catalogue checklist provides the list of patterns to check for.

Tool-specific checklist:
http://www.dumpanalysis.org/windows-memory-analysis-checklist

Pattern catalogue checklists:
http://dumpanalysis.org

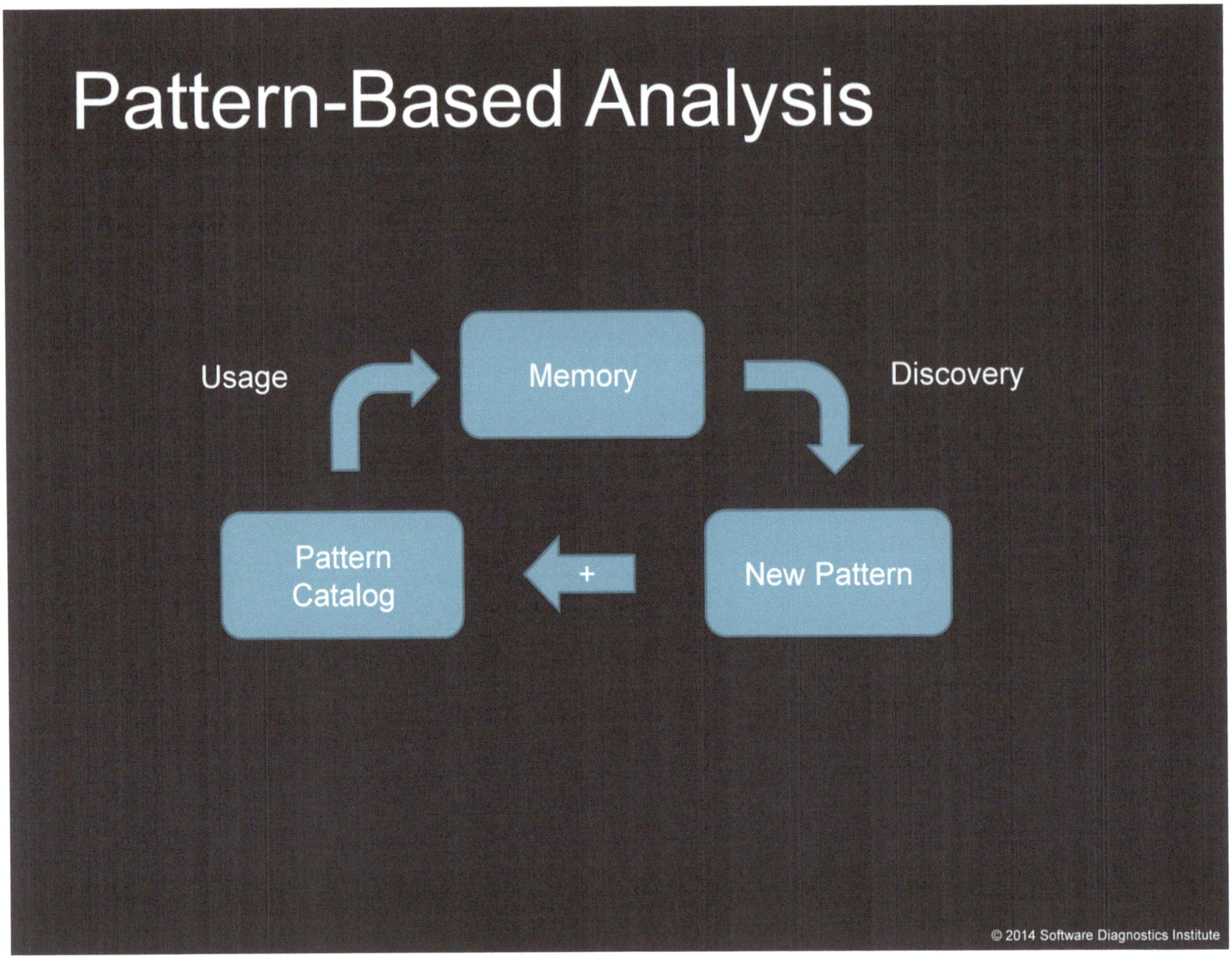

Pattern catalogs are rarely fixed. New patterns are constantly discerned, refined, and reclassified. This is the essence of the pattern-based part of pattern orientation.

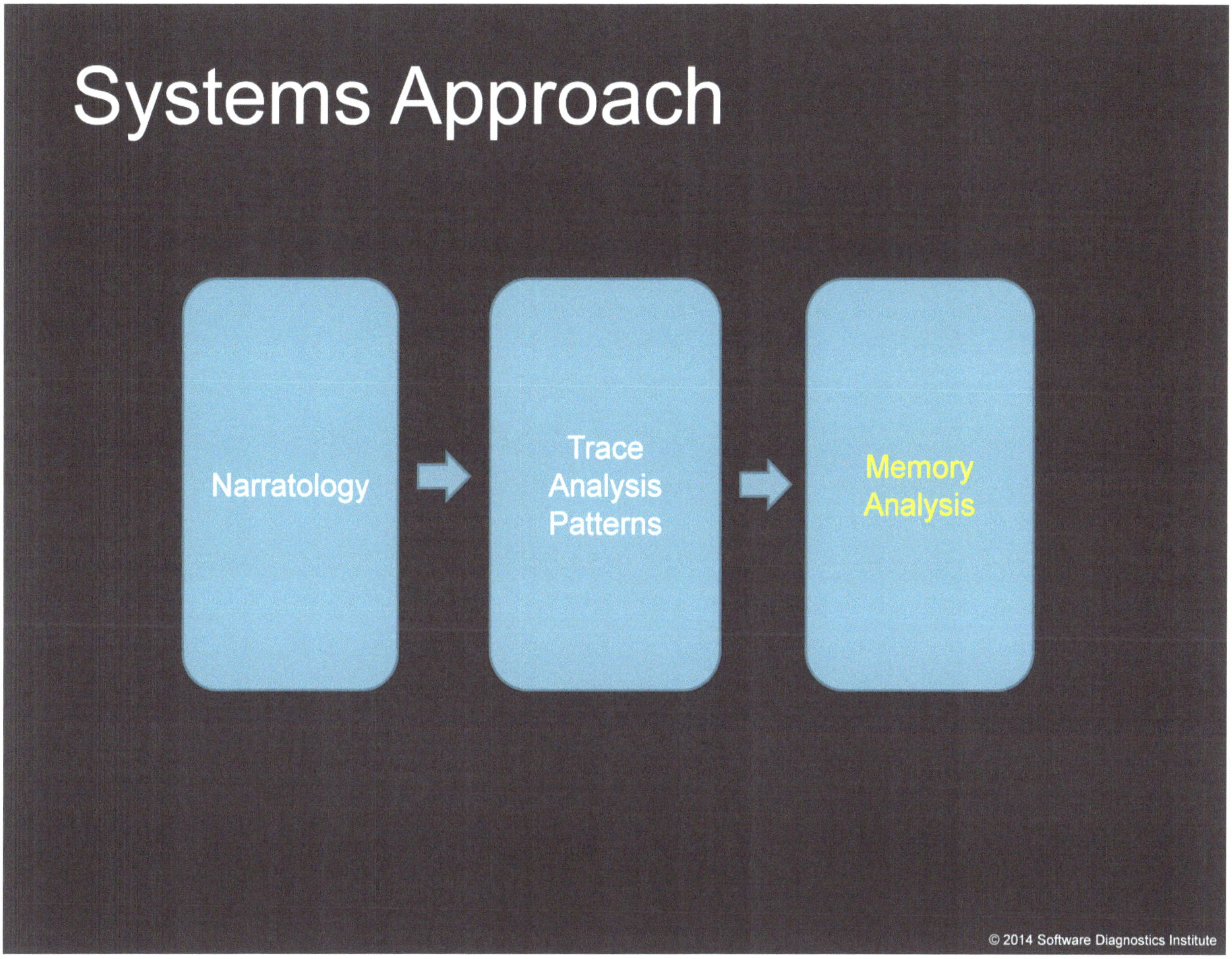

At the end of this theoretical part we provide a few words about the systems approach mentioned earlier. This is an application of ideas and methods from different disciplines. For example, narratology, a study of narratives such as novels and stories, was applied to trace and log analysis. The result was a trace analysis pattern catalogue which can also be applied to memory analysis and even to analysis process itself. We list a reference to Systemic Software Diagnostics at the end of this presentation.

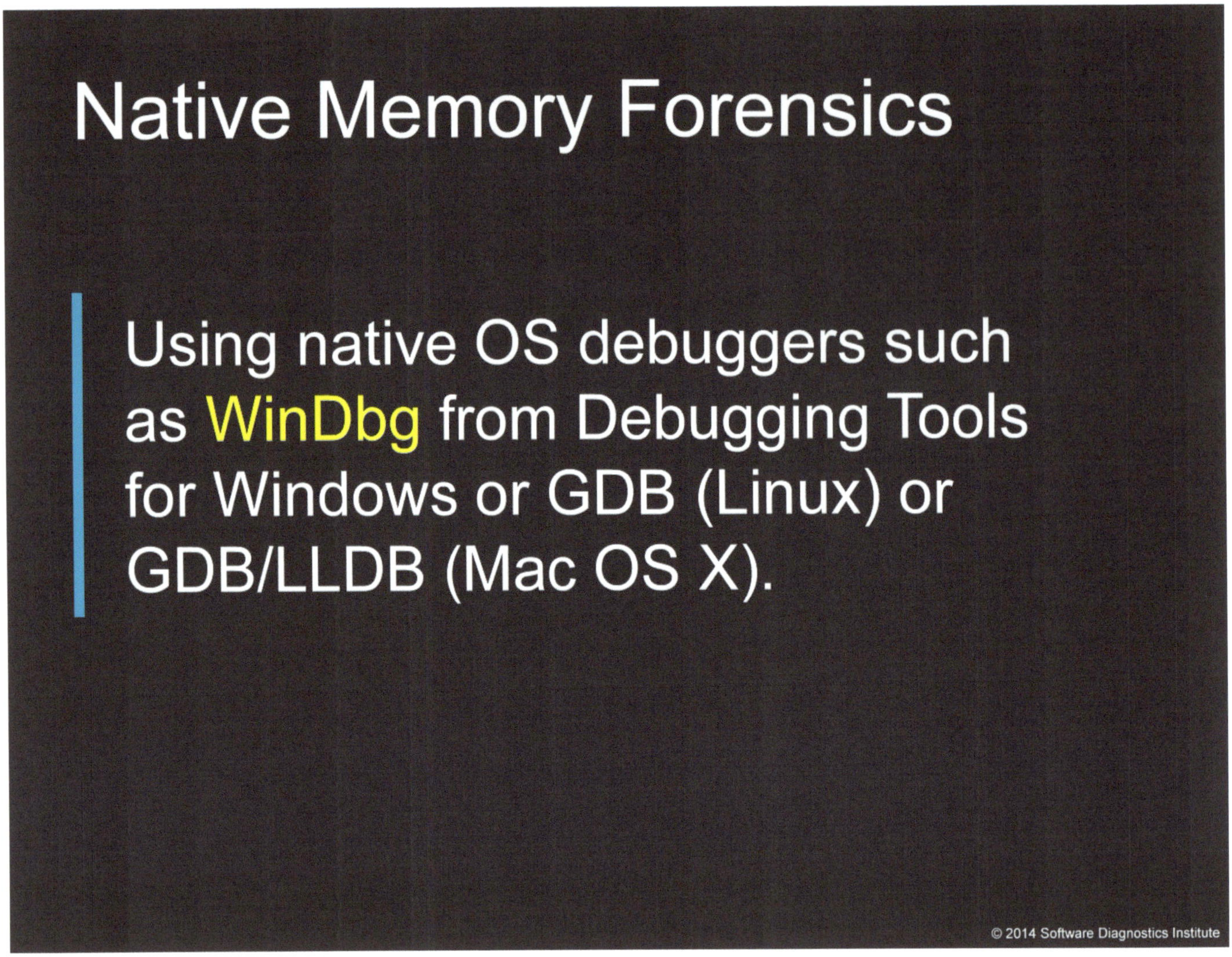

We'd like to make a note before the practical part. Among different tools for memory forensic analysis native OS debuggers can be used. We use one of them here to illustrate the pattern language.

Practical Examples

WinDbg session…

Patterns for Example A

- Tampered Dump
- Exception Stack Trace
- Stored Exception
- Lateral Damage
- Execution Residue
- Hidden Exception
- NULL Data Pointer

*This example is adapted with some modifications from **Tampered Dump** pattern description published in Software Diagnostics Library.*

The availability of direct dump modification raises the possibility of **Tampered Dumps**. These are memory dumps specifically modified to alter structural and behavioral diagnostic patterns, for example, to suppress certain module involvement or introduce fictitious past objects and interaction traces. There can be 2 types of such artefacts: strong tampering with new or altered information completely integrated into memory fabric and weak tampering to confuse inexperienced software support engineers and memory forensics analysts.

In this exercise we look at one such experimental process memory dump made from the previously crashed Windows Calculator, calc.exe.

After we open the dump we fix symbols, set up a log file to record all command output, and list loaded modules:

```
0:003> .symfix c:\mss

0:003> .reload

0:003> .logopen C:\MemoryDumps\tampered.log
Opened log file ' C:\MemoryDumps\tampered.log'

0:003> lm
start             end                 module name
00000000`76ea0000 00000000`76fbf000   kernel32   (deferred)
00000000`76fc0000 00000000`770ba000   user32     (deferred)
00000000`770c0000 00000000`77269000   ntdll      (pdb symbols)
c:\mss\ntdll.pdb\9D04EB0AA387494FBD81ED062072B99C2\ntdll.pdb
00000000`ffd90000 00000000`ffe73000   calc       (deferred)
000007fe`f5c00000 000007fe`f5c54000   oleacc     (deferred)
000007fe`f6850000 000007fe`f6a66000   GdiPlus    (deferred)
000007fe`f9c10000 000007fe`f9c4b000   winmm      (deferred)
000007fe`fae80000 000007fe`fafe1000   WindowsCodecs   (deferred)
000007fe`fb1d0000 000007fe`fb1e8000   dwmapi     (deferred)
000007fe`fb600000 000007fe`fb656000   uxtheme    (deferred)
000007fe`fb7e0000 000007fe`fb9d4000   comctl32   (deferred)
000007fe`fbf90000 000007fe`fbf9c000   version    (deferred)
000007fe`fcdb0000 000007fe`fcdbf000   CRYPTBASE   (deferred)
000007fe`fd060000 000007fe`fd0cb000   KERNELBASE   (pdb symbols)
c:\mss\kernelbase.pdb\88D04DC8E39B4CBB9CB12366C2AE475F2\kernelbase.pdb
000007fe`fd2b0000 000007fe`fd34f000   msvcrt     (deferred)
000007fe`fd350000 000007fe`fd42b000   advapi32   (deferred)
000007fe`fd430000 000007fe`fd45e000   imm32      (deferred)
000007fe`fd460000 000007fe`fd47f000   sechost    (deferred)
000007fe`fd480000 000007fe`fd683000   ole32      (deferred)
000007fe`fd690000 000007fe`fd729000   clbcatq    (deferred)
000007fe`fd7b0000 000007fe`fd7be000   lpk        (deferred)
000007fe`fdc00000 000007fe`fdcc9000   usp10      (deferred)
000007fe`fdcd0000 000007fe`fea58000   shell32    (deferred)
000007fe`fef60000 000007fe`fefc7000   gdi32      (deferred)
000007fe`fefd0000 000007fe`ff0a7000   oleaut32   (deferred)
000007fe`ff0b0000 000007fe`ff1dd000   rpcrt4     (deferred)
000007fe`ff240000 000007fe`ff2b1000   shlwapi    (deferred)
000007fe`ff2c0000 000007fe`ff3c9000   msctf      (deferred)
```

We see **Exception Stack Trace** pointing to a problem in *calc* module:

```
0:003> k
Child-SP RetAddr Call Site
00000000`0244e858 000007fe`fd061430 ntdll!NtWaitForMultipleObjects+0xa
00000000`0244e860 00000000`76ec1723 KERNELBASE!WaitForMultipleObjectsEx+0xe8
00000000`0244e960 00000000`76f3b5e5 kernel32!WaitForMultipleObjectsExImplementation+0xb3
00000000`0244e9f0 00000000`76f3b767 kernel32!WerpReportFaultInternal+0x215
00000000`0244ea90 00000000`76f3b7bf kernel32!WerpReportFault+0x77
00000000`0244eac0 00000000`76f3b9dc kernel32!BasepReportFault+0x1f
00000000`0244eaf0 00000000`77153398 kernel32!UnhandledExceptionFilter+0x1fc
00000000`0244ebd0 00000000`770d85c8 ntdll! ?? ::FNODOBFM::`string'+0x2365
00000000`0244ec00 00000000`770e9d2d ntdll!_C_specific_handler+0x8c
00000000`0244ec70 00000000`770d91cf ntdll!RtlpExecuteHandlerForException+0xd
00000000`0244eca0 00000000`77111248 ntdll!RtlDispatchException+0x45a
00000000`0244f380 00000000`ffdbdb27 ntdll!KiUserExceptionDispatch+0x2e
00000000`0244fab0 00000000`76eb59ed calc!CTimedCalc::WatchDogThread+0xb2
00000000`0244faf0 00000000`770ec541 kernel32!BaseThreadInitThunk+0xd
00000000`0244fb20 00000000`00000000 ntdll!RtlUserThreadStart+0x1d
```

The default analysis command (**!analyse -v**) diagnoses *"stack corruption"*:

```
FAULTING_IP:
kernel32!UnhandledExceptionFilter+1fc
00000000`76f3b9dc 448bf0 mov r14d,eax

EXCEPTION_RECORD: ffffffffffffffff -- (.exr 0xffffffffffffffff)
ExceptionAddress: 0000000076f3b9dc (kernel32!UnhandledExceptionFilter+0x00000000000001fc)
ExceptionCode: 0244e9f0
ExceptionFlags: 00000000
NumberParameters: 0

DEFAULT_BUCKET_ID: STACK_CORRUPTION

PRIMARY_PROBLEM_CLASS: STACK_CORRUPTION

BUGCHECK_STR: APPLICATION_FAULT_STACK_CORRUPTION

IP_ON_HEAP: 8d483674c33bfffa
The fault address in not in any loaded module, please check your build's rebase
log at <releasedir>\bin\build_logs\timebuild\ntrebase.log for module which may
contain the address if it were loaded.

UNALIGNED_STACK_POINTER: 0000000076f3b767

STACK_TEXT:
00000000`00000000 00000000`00000000 calc!CTimedCalc::WatchDogThread+0x0

FOLLOWUP_IP:
calc!CTimedCalc::WatchDogThread+0
00000000`ffd92254 48895c2408 mov qword ptr [rsp+8],rbx
```

Stored Exception resembles signs of **Local Buffer Overflow** (but segment register values and CPU flags have suspiciously invalid values, possibly **Lateral Damage**):

```
0:003> .ecxr
rax=0000000000000000 rbx=0000000000000001 rcx=000000000244ec30
rdx=000000000244ec30 rsi=0100000000000080 rdi=0000000000000158
rip=0000000076f3b9dc rsp=0000000076f3b767 rbp=0000000000000000
r8=0000000000000000 r9=ffffffffffffffff r10=0000000076f3b7bf
r11=000000000244ec30 r12=0000000000000001 r13=0000000000000000
r14=0000000000000000 r15=0000000000000000
iopl=0 nv up di pl nz na pe nc
cs=0000 ss=0000 ds=0266 es=0000 fs=0000 gs=0154 efl=00000000
kernel32!UnhandledExceptionFilter+0x1fc:
00000000`76f3b9dc 448bf0 mov r14d,eax

0:003> k
*** Stack trace for last set context - .thread/.cxr resets it
Child-SP RetAddr Call Site
00000000`76f3b767 8d483674`c33bfffa kernel32!UnhandledExceptionFilter+0x1fc
00000000`76f3b847 5aa3e800`05bfac0d 0x8d483674`c33bfffa
00000000`76f3b84f ebffcf83`48ccfff9 0x5aa3e800`05bfac0d
00000000`76f3b857 8348c000`0409ba27 0xebffcf83`48ccfff9
00000000`76f3b85f 54dfe8cf`8b48ffcf 0x8348c000`0409ba27
00000000`76f3b867 4c02778d`db33fff9 0x54dfe8cf`8b48ffcf
00000000`76f3b86f 4c000000`e024a48b 0x4c02778d`db33fff9
00000000`76f3b877 ffcf8348`04ebeb8b 0x4c000000`e024a48b
00000000`76f3b87f fffc59e9`e8cc8b49 0xffcf8348`04ebeb8b
00000000`76f3b887 42e9c78b`0775c73b 0xfffc59e9`e8cc8b49
00000000`76f3b88f fffa6fa9`e8000003 0x42e9c78b`0775c73b
00000000`76f3b897 32e9c033`0774c33b 0xfffa6fa9`e8000003
00000000`76f3b89f fa7f3d8d`4c000003 0x32e9c033`0774c33b
00000000`76f3b8a7 de15ffcf`8b490006 0xfa7f3d8d`4c000003
00000000`76f3b8af f9370d8b`4800000e 0xde15ffcf`8b490006
00000000`76f3b8b7 000014a1`15ff0006 0xf9370d8b`4800000e
00000000`76f3b8bf 840fc33b`48f08b4c 0x000014a1`15ff0006
00000000`76f3b8c7 f6158b48`00000099 0x840fc33b`48f08b4c
00000000`76f3b8cf 0238c281`480006f3 0xf6158b48`00000099
00000000`76f3b8d7 48cfe8c8`8b480000 0x0238c281`480006f3
00000000`76f3b8df 8b4c7f74`c33bfff9 0x48cfe8c8`8b480000
00000000`76f3b8e7 888b4900`06f3dc05 0x8b4c7f74`c33bfff9
00000000`76f3b8ef 75083949`00000238 0x888b4900`06f3dc05
00000000`76f3b8f7 00000240`808b496c 0x75083949`00000238
00000000`76f3b8ff 8b415f75`08403949 0x00000240`808b496c
00000000`76f3b907 00024880`3b411040 0x8b415f75`08403949
00000000`76f3b90f 01040000`a9527500 0x00024880`3b411040
00000000`76f3b917 00025090`8d491874 0x01040000`a9527500
00000000`76f3b91f c68a4418`488d4900 0x00025090`8d491874
00000000`76f3b927 c33a0000`117315ff 0xc68a4418`488d4900
00000000`76f3b92f 4e15ffcf`8b493374 0xc33a0000`117315ff
00000000`76f3b937 ff41cc8b`4900000e 0x4e15ffcf`8b493374
00000000`76f3b93f 00028c84`0fc63bd6 0xff41cc8b`4900000e
00000000`76f3b947 00028484`0fc73b00 0x00028c84`0fc63bd6
00000000`76f3b94f 6ee7e819`75c33b00 0x00028484`0fc73b00
00000000`76f3b957 c0331074`c33bfffa 0x6ee7e819`75c33b00
00000000`76f3b95f cf8b4900`000270e9 0xc0331074`c33bfffa
00000000`76f3b967 8b490000`0e1b15ff 0xcf8b4900`000270e9
00000000`76f3b96f 3b000013`e215ffcc 0x8b490000`0e1b15ff
00000000`76f3b977 0253e9c7`8b0775c7 0x3b000013`e215ffcc
00000000`76f3b97f 41fff959`4ae80000 0x0253e9c7`8b0775c7
00000000`76f3b987 c6844100`000002be 0x41fff959`4ae80000
```

```
00000000`76f3b98f 15ff0000`023d850f 0xc6844100`000002be
00000000`76f3b997 850f20a8`00000f65 0x15ff0000`023d850f
00000000`76f3b99f 245c8948`0000022f 0x850f20a8`00000f65
00000000`76f3b9a7 448d4c3e`4e8d4520 0x245c8948`0000022f
00000000`76f3b9af ffc933d6`8b416024 0x448d4c3e`4e8d4520
00000000`76f3b9b7 7cc33b00`0009f415 0xffc933d6`8b416024
00000000`76f3b9bf 730a7024`64ba0f0f 0x7cc33b00`0009f415
00000000`76f3b9c7 00000205`e9c68b07 0x730a7024`64ba0f0f
00000000`76f3b9cf cc8b49d6`8bfb8b44 0x00000205`e9c68b07
00000000`76f3b9d7 f08b44ff`fffdc4e8 0xcc8b49d6`8bfb8b44
00000000`76f3b9df e9c03307`7508f883 0xf08b44ff`fffdc4e8
00000000`76f3b9e7 7506f883`000001e9 0xe9c03307`7508f883
00000000`76f3b9ef c33bfffa`6e4be810 0x7506f883`000001e9
00000000`76f3b9f7 0001d4e9`c0330774 0xc33bfffa`6e4be810
00000000`76f3b9ff 86850f04`fe834100 0x0001d4e9`c0330774
00000000`76f3ba07 0000024a`ba000001 0x86850f04`fe834100
00000000`76f3ba0f 00b841ce`8b45c933 0x0000024a`ba000001
00000000`76f3ba17 fff7a249`e8000010 0x00b841ce`8b45c933
00000000`76f3ba1f 0775c33b`48e88b4c 0xfff7a249`e8000010
00000000`76f3ba27 48000001`a6e9c033 0x0775c33b`48e88b4c
00000000`76f3ba2f 24448948`3024448d 0x48000001`a6e9c033
00000000`76f3ba37 0000f024`8c8d4c20 0x24448948`3024448d
00000000`76f3ba3f 49000001`25b84100 0x0000f024`8c8d4c20
00000000`76f3ba47 8a0fe8cf`8b48d58b 0x49000001`25b84100
00000000`76f3ba4f 4166097c`c33bfffe 0x8a0fe8cf`8b48d58b
00000000`76f3ba57 39fe450f`44005d39 0x4166097c`c33bfffe
00000000`76f3ba5f 850f0000`00f0249c 0x39fe450f`44005d39
00000000`76f3ba67 240c8b49`000000bc 0x850f0000`00f0249c
00000000`76f3ba6f 40244489`48016348 0x240c8b49`000000bc
00000000`76f3ba77 24448948`10418b48 0x40244489`48016348
00000000`76f3ba7f 75c00000`06398148 0x24448948`10418b48
00000000`76f3ba87 480b7203`18798318 0x75c00000`06398148
00000000`76f3ba8f 50244489`4830418b 0x480b7203`18798318
00000000`76f3ba97 eb50245c`89481ceb 0x50244489`4830418b
00000000`76f3ba9f 8b480b72`18713915 0xeb50245c`89481ceb
00000000`76f3baa7 eb502444`89482041 0x8b480b72`18713915
00000000`76f3baaf 02ba5024`5c894805 0xeb502444`89482041
00000000`76f3bab7 0b721851`39000000 0x02ba5024`5c894805
00000000`76f3babf 24448948`28418b48 0x0b721851`39000000
00000000`76f3bac7 58245c89`4805eb58 0x24448948`28418b48
00000000`76f3bacf ba1d3808`74fb3b44 0x58245c89`4805eb58
00000000`76f3bad7 48d68b02`740006fd 0xba1d3808`74fb3b44
00000000`76f3badf 48000000`e824848d 0x48d68b02`740006fd
00000000`76f3bae7 20245489`28244489 0x48000000`e824848d
00000000`76f3baef c0334540`244c8d4c 0x20245489`28244489
00000000`76f3baf7 000144b9`04508d41 0xc0334540`244c8d4c
00000000`76f3baff ba00000d`7215ffd0 0x000144b9`04508d41
00000000`76f3bb07 8c8bc223`c0000000 0xba00000d`7215ffd0
00000000`76f3bb0f b8c23b00`0000e824 0x8c8bc223`c0000000
00000000`76f3bb17 89c8440f`00000006 0xb8c23b00`0000e824
00000000`76f3bb1f 07eb0000`00e8248c 0x89c8440f`00000006
00000000`76f3bb27 44000000`e8248c8b 0x07eb0000`00e8248c
00000000`76f3bb2f 7403f983`5d74fb3b 0x44000000`e8248c8b
00000000`76f3bb37 000000f0`249c3909 0x7403f983`5d74fb3b
00000000`76f3bb3f 0006fd4d`058a4f74 0x000000f0`249c3909
00000000`76f3bb47 f85f5ce8`4b75c33a 0x0006fd4d`058a4f74
00000000`76f3bb4f 448b3b75`5c5838ff 0xf85f5ce8`4b75c33a
00000000`76f3bb57 894c2824`44893024 0x448b3b75`5c5838ff
00000000`76f3bb5f 08244c8b`4d20246c 0x894c2824`44893024
00000000`76f3bb67 fec2c748`24048b4d 0x08244c8b`4d20246c
```

```
00000000`76f3bb6f b6e8cf8b`48ffffff 0xfec2c748`24048b4d
00000000`76f3bb77 fd130db6`0fffffea 0xb6e8cf8b`48ffffff
00000000`76f3bb7f 88ce4c0f`c33b0006 0xfd130db6`0fffffea
00000000`76f3bb87 ebfb8b00`06fd080d 0x88ce4c0f`c33b0006
00000000`76f3bb8f 3a0006fc`fe058a29 0xebfb8b00`06fd080d
00000000`76f3bb97 8b240c8b`491874c3 0x3a0006fc`fe058a29
00000000`76f3bb9f 060f15ff`cf8b4811 0x8b240c8b`491874c3
00000000`76f3bba7 0000f824`bc8b0000 0x060f15ff`cf8b4811
00000000`76f3bbaf 00f824bc`8b07eb00 0x0000f824`bc8b0000
00000000`76f3bbb7 331074eb`3b4c0000 0x00f824bc`8b07eb00
00000000`76f3bbbf 49000080`00b841d2 0x331074eb`3b4c0000
00000000`76f3bbc7 8bfff74b`5ae8cd8b 0x49000080`00b841d2
00000000`76f3bbcf c48148c6`8b02ebc7 0x8bfff74b`5ae8cd8b
00000000`76f3bbd7 5e415f41`000000a0 0xc48148c6`8b02ebc7
00000000`76f3bbdf c35b5e5f`5c415d41 0x5e415f41`000000a0
00000000`76f3bbe7 158ead00`00000090 0xc35b5e5f`5c415d41
00000000`76f3bbef 00000200`00000053 0x158ead00`00000090
00000000`76f3bbf7 09bc2400`00002500 0x00000200`00000053
00000000`76f3bbff 00000000`09b42400 0x09bc2400`00002500
00000000`76f3bc07 7e023553`158ead00 0x9b42400
00000000`76f3bc0f 00000400`00000a19 0x7e023553`158ead00
00000000`76f3bc17 09b42000`09bc2000 0x00000400`00000a19
00000000`76f3bc1f 445352bb`03197e00 0x09b42000`09bc2000
00000000`76f3bc27 4c886225`48e28953 0x445352bb`03197e00
00000000`76f3bc2f 4fb29af4`dfbb8344 0x4c886225`48e28953
00000000`76f3bc37 72656b00`0000020e 0x4fb29af4`dfbb8344
00000000`76f3bc3f 64702e32`336c656e 0x72656b00`0000020e
00000000`76f3bc47 00000000`00000062 0x64702e32`336c656e
```

We check for any **Hidden Exceptions** among **Execution Residue** and find it was **NULL Data Pointer**:

```
0:003> .cxr
Resetting default scope

0:003> k
Child-SP RetAddr Call Site
00000000`0244e858 000007fe`fd061430 ntdll!NtWaitForMultipleObjects+0xa
00000000`0244e860 00000000`76ec1723 KERNELBASE!WaitForMultipleObjectsEx+0xe8
00000000`0244e960 00000000`76f3b5e5 kernel32!WaitForMultipleObjectsExImplementation+0xb3
00000000`0244e9f0 00000000`76f3b767 kernel32!WerpReportFaultInternal+0x215
00000000`0244ea90 00000000`76f3b7bf kernel32!WerpReportFault+0x77
00000000`0244eac0 00000000`76f3b9dc kernel32!BasepReportFault+0x1f
00000000`0244eaf0 00000000`77153398 kernel32!UnhandledExceptionFilter+0x1fc
00000000`0244ebd0 00000000`770d85c8 ntdll! ?? ::FNODOBFM::`string'+0x2365
00000000`0244ec00 00000000`770e9d2d ntdll!_C_specific_handler+0x8c
00000000`0244ec70 00000000`770d91cf ntdll!RtlpExecuteHandlerForException+0xd
00000000`0244eca0 00000000`77111248 ntdll!RtlDispatchException+0x45a
00000000`0244f380 00000000`ffdbdb27 ntdll!KiUserExceptionDispatch+0x2e
00000000`0244fab0 00000000`76eb59ed calc!CTimedCalc::WatchDogThread+0xb2
00000000`0244faf0 00000000`770ec541 kernel32!BaseThreadInitThunk+0xd
00000000`0244fb20 00000000`00000000 ntdll!RtlUserThreadStart+0x1d
```

```
0:003> dps 00000000`0244eca0 00000000`0244fab0
00000000`0244eca0 00000000`02450000
00000000`0244eca8 00000000`76fadda0 kernel32!__PchSym_ <PERF> (kernel32+0x10dda0)
00000000`0244ecb0 00000000`00012f00
00000000`0244ecb8 00000000`7711920a ntdll!RtlDosApplyFileIsolationRedirection_Ustr+0x3da
00000000`0244ecc0 00000000`00000005
00000000`0244ecc8 00000000`00000000
00000000`0244ecd0 00000000`00000000
00000000`0244ecd8 00000000`00000000
00000000`0244ece0 00000000`0244fb20
00000000`0244ece8 00000000`00000000
00000000`0244ecf0 00000000`77202dd0 ntdll!CsrPortMemoryRemoteDelta <PERF> (ntdll+0x142dd0)
00000000`0244ecf8 00000000`00000000
00000000`0244ed00 00000000`00000000
00000000`0244ed08 00000000`02450000
00000000`0244ed10 00000000`771e8180 ntdll!`string'+0xc040
00000000`0244ed18 00000000`0244b000
00000000`0244ed20 00000000`0244f250
00000000`0244ed28 00000000`770c0000 ntdll!RtlDeactivateActivationContext <PERF> (ntdll+0x0)
00000000`0244ed30 00000000`770ec541 ntdll!RtlUserThreadStart+0x1d
00000000`0244ed38 00000000`770c0000 ntdll!RtlDeactivateActivationContext <PERF> (ntdll+0x0)
00000000`0244ed40 00000000`77202dd0 ntdll!CsrPortMemoryRemoteDelta <PERF> (ntdll+0x142dd0)
00000000`0244ed48 00000000`0244fb20
00000000`0244ed50 00000000`771d7718 ntdll!LdrpDefaultExtension
00000000`0244ed58 00000000`0244ed80
00000000`0244ed60 00000000`770d852c ntdll!_C_specific_handler
00000000`0244ed68 00000000`771e8180 ntdll!`string'+0xc040
00000000`0244ed70 00000000`0244f250
00000000`0244ed78 00000000`00000000
00000000`0244ed80 00000000`00000000
00000000`0244ed88 00000000`00000000
00000000`0244ed90 00000000`00000000
00000000`0244ed98 00000000`00000000
00000000`0244eda0 00000000`00000000
00000000`0244eda8 00000000`00000000
00000000`0244edb0 00001f80`00000000
00000000`0244edb8 00000000`00000033
00000000`0244edc0 00010246`002b0000
00000000`0244edc8 00000000`00000000
00000000`0244edd0 00000000`00000000
00000000`0244edd8 00000000`00000000
00000000`0244ede0 00000000`00000000
00000000`0244ede8 000007fe`ff3625c0 msctf!s_szCompClassName
00000000`0244edf0 00000000`00200000
00000000`0244edf8 00000000`0244ee40
00000000`0244ee00 00000000`0244ee40
00000000`0244ee08 00000000`0244ee40
00000000`0244ee10 00000000`00000000
00000000`0244ee18 00000000`0244fb70
00000000`0244ee20 00000000`00000000
00000000`0244ee28 00000000`00000000
00000000`0244ee30 00000000`00000000
00000000`0244ee38 000007fe`fd602790 ole32!`string'
00000000`0244ee40 00000000`00292170
00000000`0244ee48 00000000`770e7a33 ntdll!LdrpFindOrMapDll+0x138
00000000`0244ee50 00000000`0244ef68
00000000`0244ee58 00000000`00000000
00000000`0244ee60 00000000`00000000
00000000`0244ee68 00000000`00000000
00000000`0244ee70 00000000`00000000
```

```
00000000`0244ee78 00000000`00000000
00000000`0244ee80 00000000`0000027f
00000000`0244ee88 00000000`00000000
00000000`0244ee90 00000000`00000000
00000000`0244ee98 0000ffff`00001f80
00000000`0244eea0 00000000`00000000
00000000`0244eea8 00000000`00000000
00000000`0244eeb0 00000000`00000000
00000000`0244eeb8 00000000`00000000
00000000`0244eec0 00000000`00000000
00000000`0244eec8 00000000`00000000
00000000`0244eed0 00000000`00000000
00000000`0244eed8 00000000`00000000
00000000`0244eee0 00000000`00000000
00000000`0244eee8 00000000`00000000
00000000`0244eef0 00000000`00000000
00000000`0244eef8 00000000`00000000
00000000`0244ef00 00000000`00000000
00000000`0244ef08 00000000`00000000
00000000`0244ef10 00000000`00000000
00000000`0244ef18 00000000`00000000
00000000`0244ef20 00000000`00000000
00000000`0244ef28 00000000`771192a8 ntdll!LdrpApplyFileNameRedirection+0x2d3
00000000`0244ef30 00000000`00000000
00000000`0244ef38 00000000`00000000
00000000`0244ef40 00000000`00000000
00000000`0244ef48 00000000`02080000
00000000`0244ef50 00000000`0244f028
00000000`0244ef58 00000000`0244f020
00000000`0244ef60 00000000`00000000
00000000`0244ef68 00000000`00000000
00000000`0244ef70 00000000`00000000
00000000`0244ef78 000007fe`fd602848 ole32!`string'
00000000`0244ef80 00000000`00000000
00000000`0244ef88 00000000`00000000
00000000`0244ef90 00000000`00000000
00000000`0244ef98 00000000`00000000
00000000`0244efa0 00000000`00000000
00000000`0244efa8 00000000`00000000
00000000`0244efb0 00000000`00000000
00000000`0244efb8 00000000`00000000
00000000`0244efc0 00000000`00000000
00000000`0244efc8 00000000`00000000
00000000`0244efd0 00000000`00000000
00000000`0244efd8 00000000`00000000
00000000`0244efe0 00000000`00000000
00000000`0244efe8 00000000`00000000
00000000`0244eff0 00000000`00000000
00000000`0244eff8 00000000`00000000
00000000`0244f000 00000000`00000000
00000000`0244f008 00000000`00000000
00000000`0244f010 00000000`00000000
00000000`0244f018 00000000`00000000
00000000`0244f020 00000000`0244f038
00000000`0244f028 00000000`0000011b
00000000`0244f030 00000000`024d0000
00000000`0244f038 00000080`001a024d
00000000`0244f040 00000000`01c0c8a0
00000000`0244f048 00000000`002f0101
00000000`0244f050 00000000`00000000
```

```
00000000`0244f058 00000000`00000022
00000000`0244f060 00000000`002f9b00
00000000`0244f068 00000000`01bd5390
00000000`0244f070 00000000`002f7c00
00000000`0244f078 00000000`01bd5580
00000000`0244f080 00000000`01bd57b0
00000000`0244f088 00000000`002f9b00
00000000`0244f090 00000000`00000000
00000000`0244f098 00000024`00000003
00000000`0244f0a0 00000000`002e91b0
00000000`0244f0a8 00000000`00000022
00000000`0244f0b0 00000000`771d5430 ntdll!RtlpInterceptorRoutines
00000000`0244f0b8 00000000`00000000
00000000`0244f0c0 00000000`00000010
00000000`0244f0c8 00000000`01bd0000
00000000`0244f0d0 00000000`00000008
00000000`0244f0d8 00000000`00000001
00000000`0244f0e0 00000000`01bd0288
00000000`0244f0e8 00000000`77113448 ntdll!RtlAllocateHeap+0xe4
00000000`0244f0f0 00000000`00000000
00000000`0244f0f8 00000000`00000001
00000000`0244f100 000002b2`000f002f
00000000`0244f108 00000000`01bd5780
00000000`0244f110 00000000`00250230
00000000`0244f118 00000000`000000df
00000000`0244f120 00000000`002551a0
00000000`0244f128 00000000`00255210
00000000`0244f130 00000000`002f9b00
00000000`0244f138 00000000`002551a0
00000000`0244f140 00000000`000000df
00000000`0244f148 00000000`10000010
00000000`0244f150 00000000`00250230
00000000`0244f158 00000000`00000000
00000000`0244f160 00000000`00250498
00000000`0244f168 00000000`0025026c
00000000`0244f170 00000000`002f9b00
00000000`0244f178 00000000`002551a0
00000000`0244f180 00000000`00000022
00000000`0244f188 00000000`76fd88b8 user32!GetPropW+0x4d
00000000`0244f190 00000000`00002974
00000000`0244f198 00000000`76fd88b8 user32!GetPropW+0x4d
00000000`0244f1a0 00000000`00250230
00000000`0244f1a8 00000000`76fd7931 user32!IsWindow+0x9
00000000`0244f1b0 00000000`002ed6d0
00000000`0244f1b8 00000000`76fd7931 user32!IsWindow+0x9
00000000`0244f1c0 00000000`00000000
00000000`0244f1c8 00000000`01c0c8d0
00000000`0244f1d0 00000000`01c0c8a0
00000000`0244f1d8 00000000`00000000
00000000`0244f1e0 00000000`00000008
00000000`0244f1e8 00000000`01bd0000
00000000`0244f1f0 00000000`00000000
00000000`0244f1f8 00000000`770f41c8 ntdll!RtlpReAllocateHeap+0x178
00000000`0244f200 00000000`00000002
00000000`0244f208 00000000`00000002
00000000`0244f210 00000000`00000000
00000000`0244f218 000007fe`4f00024d
00000000`0244f220 00000000`00000000
00000000`0244f228 000007fe`fb601381 uxtheme!CThemeWnd::_PreDefWindowProc+0x31
00000000`0244f230 00000000`00000082
```

```
00000000`0244f238 00000000`00000000
00000000`0244f240 00000000`7a337100
00000000`0244f248 00000000`01c0c8c0
00000000`0244f250 00000000`00000003
00000000`0244f258 00000000`76eb59e0 kernel32!BaseThreadInitThunk
00000000`0244f260 00000000`ffdbdb32 calc!CTimedCalc::Start+0xa9
00000000`0244f268 00000000`ffd90000 calc!CCalculatorController::CCalculatorController <PERF>
(calc+0x0)
00000000`0244f270 00000000`ffe0ac64 calc!_dyn_tls_init_callback <PERF> (calc+0x7ac64)
00000000`0244f278 00000000`76ea0000 kernel32!TestResourceDataMatchEntry <PERF> (kernel32+0x0)
00000000`0244f280 00000000`76fadda0 kernel32!__PchSym_ <PERF> (kernel32+0x10dda0)
00000000`0244f288 00000000`770c0000 ntdll!RtlDeactivateActivationContext <PERF> (ntdll+0x0)
00000000`0244f290 00000000`77202dd0 ntdll!CsrPortMemoryRemoteDelta <PERF> (ntdll+0x142dd0)
00000000`0244f298 00000000`76fd760e user32!RealDefWindowProcW+0x5a
00000000`0244f2a0 00000000`00000001
00000000`0244f2a8 000007fe`fb600037 uxtheme!operator delete <PERF> (uxtheme+0x37)
00000000`0244f2b0 00000000`01bd0158
00000000`0244f2b8 00000000`00000082
00000000`0244f2c0 00000000`00000000
00000000`0244f2c8 00000000`00000003
00000000`0244f2d0 00000000`000111f2
00000000`0244f2d8 00000000`00000054
00000000`0244f2e0 00000000`00000000
00000000`0244f2e8 00000000`00000000
00000000`0244f2f0 00000000`00000001
00000000`0244f2f8 00000000`01c11c60
00000000`0244f300 00000000`0244f462
00000000`0244f308 00000000`01bd0230
00000000`0244f310 00000000`00000000
00000000`0244f318 00000000`00000000
00000000`0244f320 00000000`00000000
00000000`0244f328 00000000`14010015
00000000`0244f330 00000000`01c11570
00000000`0244f338 00000000`00000000
00000000`0244f340 00000000`00000000
00000000`0244f348 00000000`00000000
00000000`0244f350 00000000`00009c40
00000000`0244f358 00000000`00000000
00000000`0244f360 00000000`00000000
00000000`0244f368 00000000`00000000
00000000`0244f370 00000000`00002710
00000000`0244f378 00000000`77111248 ntdll!KiUserExceptionDispatch+0x2e
00000000`0244f380 00000000`0244f870
00000000`0244f388 00000000`0244f380
00000000`0244f390 00000000`00000000
00000000`0244f398 00000000`00000000
00000000`0244f3a0 000007fe`fb63fb40 uxtheme!$$VProc_ImageExportDirectory
00000000`0244f3a8 00000000`00000ad5
00000000`0244f3b0 00001f80`0010005f
00000000`0244f3b8 0053002b`002b0033
00000000`0244f3c0 00010246`002b002b
00000000`0244f3c8 00000000`00000000
00000000`0244f3d0 00000000`00000000
00000000`0244f3d8 00000000`00000000
00000000`0244f3e0 00000000`00000000
00000000`0244f3e8 00000000`00000000
00000000`0244f3f0 00000000`00000000
00000000`0244f3f8 00000000`0012c770
00000000`0244f400 00000000`00000000
00000000`0244f408 00000000`00000000
```

```
00000000`0244f410 00000000`00002710
00000000`0244f418 00000000`0244fab0
00000000`0244f420 00000000`00000000
00000000`0244f428 00000000`00000000
00000000`0244f430 00000000`00000000
00000000`0244f438 00000000`0244f938
00000000`0244f440 00000000`00962210
00000000`0244f448 00000000`00000000
00000000`0244f450 00000000`0244f9a0
00000000`0244f458 00000000`00009c40
00000000`0244f460 00000000`00000000
00000000`0244f468 00000000`00000000
00000000`0244f470 00000000`00000000
00000000`0244f478 00000000`ffdbdb27 calc!CTimedCalc::WatchDogThread+0xb2
00000000`0244f480 00000000`0000027f
00000000`0244f488 00000000`00000000
00000000`0244f490 00000000`00000000
00000000`0244f498 0000ffff`00001f80
00000000`0244f4a0 00000000`00000000
00000000`0244f4a8 00000000`00000000
00000000`0244f4b0 00000000`00000000
00000000`0244f4b8 00000000`00000000
00000000`0244f4c0 00000000`00000000
00000000`0244f4c8 00000000`00000000
00000000`0244f4d0 00000000`00000000
00000000`0244f4d8 00000000`00000000
00000000`0244f4e0 00000000`00000000
00000000`0244f4e8 00000000`00000000
00000000`0244f4f0 00000000`00000000
00000000`0244f4f8 00000000`00000000
00000000`0244f500 00000000`00000000
00000000`0244f508 00000000`00000000
00000000`0244f510 00000000`00000000
00000000`0244f518 00000000`00000000
00000000`0244f520 00000000`00000000
00000000`0244f528 00000000`00000000
00000000`0244f530 00000000`00000000
00000000`0244f538 00000000`00000000
00000000`0244f540 00000000`00000000
00000000`0244f548 00000000`00000000
00000000`0244f550 00000000`00000000
00000000`0244f558 00000000`00000000
00000000`0244f560 00000000`00000000
00000000`0244f568 00000000`00000000
00000000`0244f570 00000000`00000000
00000000`0244f578 00000000`00000000
00000000`0244f580 00000000`00000000
00000000`0244f588 00000000`00000000
00000000`0244f590 00000000`00000000
00000000`0244f598 00000000`00000000
00000000`0244f5a0 00000000`00000000
00000000`0244f5a8 00000000`00000000
00000000`0244f5b0 00000000`00000000
00000000`0244f5b8 00000000`00000000
00000000`0244f5c0 00000000`00000000
00000000`0244f5c8 00000000`00000000
00000000`0244f5d0 00000000`00000000
00000000`0244f5d8 00000000`00000000
00000000`0244f5e0 00000000`00000000
00000000`0244f5e8 00000000`00000000
```

```
00000000`0244f5f0 00000000`00000000
00000000`0244f5f8 00000000`00000000
00000000`0244f600 00000000`00000000
00000000`0244f608 00000000`00000000
00000000`0244f610 00000000`00000000
00000000`0244f618 00000000`00000000
00000000`0244f620 00000000`00000000
00000000`0244f628 00000000`00000000
00000000`0244f630 00000000`00000000
00000000`0244f638 00000000`00000000
00000000`0244f640 00000000`00000000
00000000`0244f648 00000000`00000000
00000000`0244f650 00000000`00000000
00000000`0244f658 00000000`00000000
00000000`0244f660 00000000`00000000
00000000`0244f668 fffff800`032d5e53
00000000`0244f670 00000000`00000002
00000000`0244f678 00000000`00000000
00000000`0244f680 00000000`01c11580
00000000`0244f688 00000000`00000082
00000000`0244f690 00000000`00000082
00000000`0244f698 00000000`000111e4
00000000`0244f6a0 00000000`00000002
00000000`0244f6a8 00000000`0244f6f0
00000000`0244f6b0 00000000`00000002
00000000`0244f6b8 00000000`00000000
00000000`0244f6c0 00000000`000111e4
00000000`0244f6c8 00000000`00000000
00000000`0244f6d0 00000000`00000082
00000000`0244f6d8 00000000`00000000
00000000`0244f6e0 00000000`00000000
00000000`0244f6e8 00000000`76fe76c2 user32!DefDlgProcW+0x36
00000000`0244f6f0 00000000`00000000
00000000`0244f6f8 00000000`00000000
00000000`0244f700 00000000`000111e4
00000000`0244f708 00000000`00000000
00000000`0244f710 00000000`00000082
00000000`0244f718 00000000`00000000
00000000`0244f720 00000000`0244f908
00000000`0244f728 00000000`76fd9bef user32!UserCallWinProcCheckWow+0x1cb
00000000`0244f730 00000000`00962210
00000000`0244f738 00000000`00000001
00000000`0244f740 00000000`00000000
00000000`0244f748 00000000`00000000
00000000`0244f750 00000000`0244f768
00000000`0244f758 00000000`0244f778
00000000`0244f760 00000000`00000001
00000000`0244f768 00000000`00000000
00000000`0244f770 00000000`00000000
00000000`0244f778 00000000`00000000
00000000`0244f780 00000000`00000048
00000000`0244f788 00000000`00000001
00000000`0244f790 00000000`00000000
00000000`0244f798 00000000`00000000
00000000`0244f7a0 00000000`00000070
00000000`0244f7a8 ffffffff`ffffffff
00000000`0244f7b0 ffffffff`ffffffff
00000000`0244f7b8 00000000`76fd9b43 user32!UserCallWinProcCheckWow+0x99
00000000`0244f7c0 00000000`76fd9bef user32!UserCallWinProcCheckWow+0x1cb
00000000`0244f7c8 00000000`00000000
```

```
00000000`0244f7d0 00000000`00000000
00000000`0244f7d8 00000000`00000000
00000000`0244f7e0 00000000`00000000
00000000`0244f7e8 00000000`76fd72cb user32!DispatchClientMessage+0xc3
00000000`0244f7f0 00000000`00000000
00000000`0244f7f8 00000000`770e46b4 ntdll!NtdllDialogWndProc_W
00000000`0244f800 00000000`00000000
00000000`0244f808 00000000`00000000
00000000`0244f810 00000000`00000000
00000000`0244f818 00000000`00000000
00000000`0244f820 00000000`00962238
00000000`0244f828 00000000`00000001
00000000`0244f830 00000000`00000000
00000000`0244f838 00000000`00000000
00000000`0244f840 00000000`00000000
00000000`0244f848 00000000`00000000
00000000`0244f850 00000730`fffffb30
00000000`0244f858 000004d0`fffffb30
00000000`0244f860 00000170`000000f0
00000000`0244f868 0000002c`00000001
00000000`0244f870 00000000`c0000005
00000000`0244f878 00000000`00000000
00000000`0244f880 00000000`ffdbdb27 calc!CTimedCalc::WatchDogThread+0xb2
00000000`0244f888 00000000`00000002
00000000`0244f890 00000000`00000000
00000000`0244f898 00000000`00000000
00000000`0244f8a0 00000000`00000000
00000000`0244f8a8 00000000`00000000
00000000`0244f8b0 00000000`00000000
00000000`0244f8b8 00000000`00000000
00000000`0244f8c0 00000000`00000000
00000000`0244f8c8 00000000`00000000
00000000`0244f8d0 00000000`00000000
00000000`0244f8d8 00000000`00000000
00000000`0244f8e0 00000000`00000000
00000000`0244f8e8 00000000`00000000
00000000`0244f8f0 00000000`00000000
00000000`0244f8f8 00000000`00000000
00000000`0244f900 00000000`00000000
00000000`0244f908 00000000`00962210
00000000`0244f910 00000000`ffdbdb27 calc!CTimedCalc::WatchDogThread+0xb2
00000000`0244f918 00000000`00000000
00000000`0244f920 00000000`00000000
00000000`0244f928 00000000`0244fab0
00000000`0244f930 00000000`77101530 ntdll!NtdllDispatchMessage_W
00000000`0244f938 00000000`76fe505b user32!DialogBox2+0x2ec
00000000`0244f940 00000000`00000000
00000000`0244f948 00000000`00000000
00000000`0244f950 00000000`00000000
00000000`0244f958 00000000`00000000
00000000`0244f960 00000000`00000000
00000000`0244f968 00000000`00000000
00000000`0244f970 00000000`00000000
00000000`0244f978 00000000`00000000
00000000`0244f980 00000000`00000002
00000000`0244f988 00000000`000111f0
00000000`0244f990 00000271`0f689359
00000000`0244f998 00000000`00000030
00000000`0244f9a0 00000000`00000000
00000000`0244f9a8 00000000`00000000
```

```
00000000`0244f9b0 00000000`ffd90000 calc!CCalculatorController::CCalculatorController <PERF>
(calc+0x0)
00000000`0244f9b8 00000000`001a17e0
00000000`0244f9c0 00000000`00000000
00000000`0244f9c8 00000000`76fe4edd user32!InternalDialogBox+0x135
00000000`0244f9d0 00000000`00000000
00000000`0244f9d8 00000000`ffdcedb0 calc!CTimedCalc::TimeOutDlgProc
00000000`0244f9e0 00000000`00000000
00000000`0244f9e8 00000000`00000000
00000000`0244f9f0 00000000`ffdcedb0 calc!CTimedCalc::TimeOutDlgProc
00000000`0244f9f8 00000000`00000000
00000000`0244fa00 00000000`00000001
00000000`0244fa08 00000000`00000000
00000000`0244fa10 00000000`00000000
00000000`0244fa18 00000000`00009c40
00000000`0244fa20 00000000`ffd90000 calc!CCalculatorController::CCalculatorController <PERF>
(calc+0x0)
00000000`0244fa28 00000000`76fe4f52 user32!DialogBoxIndirectParamAorW+0x58
00000000`0244fa30 00000000`001a17e0
00000000`0244fa38 00000000`00000000
00000000`0244fa40 00000000`ffdcedb0 calc!CTimedCalc::TimeOutDlgProc
00000000`0244fa48 00000000`ffdcedb0 calc!CTimedCalc::TimeOutDlgProc
00000000`0244fa50 00000000`00000000
00000000`0244fa58 00000000`00000001
00000000`0244fa60 00000000`ffd90000 calc!CCalculatorController::CCalculatorController <PERF>
(calc+0x0)
00000000`0244fa68 00000000`76fdd476 user32!DialogBoxParamW+0x66
00000000`0244fa70 ffffffff`ffffffff
00000000`0244fa78 00000000`00000000
00000000`0244fa80 00000000`ffdcedb0 calc!CTimedCalc::TimeOutDlgProc
00000000`0244fa88 00000000`00000000
00000000`0244fa90 00000000`00000000
00000000`0244fa98 00000000`00000000
00000000`0244faa0 00000000`00000000
00000000`0244faa8 00000000`ffdbdafa calc!CTimedCalc::WatchDogThread+0x72
00000000`0244fab0 00000000`00002710
```

Segment registers and flags now look normal:

```
0:003> .cxr 00000000`0244f380
rax=000000000012c770 rbx=0000000000002710 rcx=0000000000000000
rdx=0000000000000000 rsi=0000000000000000 rdi=0000000000000000
rip=00000000ffdbdb27 rsp=000000000244fab0 rbp=0000000000000000
r8=000000000244f938 r9=0000000000962210 r10=0000000000000000
r11=000000000244f9a0 r12=0000000000009c40 r13=0000000000000000
r14=0000000000000000 r15=0000000000000000
iopl=0 nv up ei pl zr na po nc
cs=0033 ss=002b ds=002b es=002b fs=0053 gs=002b efl=00010246
calc!CTimedCalc::WatchDogThread+0xb2:
00000000`ffdbdb27 488b01 mov rax,qword ptr [rcx] ds:00000000`00000000=????????????????

0:003> k
*** Stack trace for last set context - .thread/.cxr resets it
Child-SP RetAddr Call Site
00000000`0244fab0 00000000`76eb59ed calc!CTimedCalc::WatchDogThread+0xb2
00000000`0244faf0 00000000`770ec541 kernel32!BaseThreadInitThunk+0xd
00000000`0244fb20 00000000`00000000 ntdll!RtlUserThreadStart+0x1d
```

Patterns for Example B

- Heap Corruption
- Stack Trace Collection
- RIP Stack Trace
- Hooksware
- Patched Code
- Hidden Module
- Deviant Module
- String Hint
- Fake Module
- No Component Symbols
- Namespace

This example is adapted with modifications from Accelerated Windows Malware Analysis training course for a different process memory dump.

We load a process memory dump:

```
Microsoft (R) Windows Debugger Version 6.3.9600.16384 AMD64
Copyright (c) Microsoft Corporation. All rights reserved.


Loading Dump File [C:\MemoryDumps\iexplore.exe.5152.dmp]
User Mini Dump File with Full Memory: Only application data is available

Symbol search path is: *** Invalid ***
****************************************************************************
* Symbol loading may be unreliable without a symbol search path.           *
* Use .symfix to have the debugger choose a symbol path.                   *
* After setting your symbol path, use .reload to refresh symbol locations. *
****************************************************************************
Executable search path is:
Windows Server 2008/Windows Vista Version 6002 (Service Pack 2) MP (2 procs) Free x86
compatible
Product: WinNt, suite: SingleUserTS Personal
Machine Name:
Debug session time: Tue Sep 28 21:18:39.000 2010 (UTC + 1:00)
System Uptime: 1 days 8:45:34.374
Process Uptime: 0 days 0:19:42.000
................................................................
................................................................
.........
Loading unloaded module list
......
This dump file has an exception of interest stored in it.
The stored exception information can be accessed via .ecxr.
(1420.cf0): Unknown exception - code c0000374 (first/second chance not available)
*** ERROR: Symbol file could not be found.  Defaulted to export symbols for ntdll.dll -
eax=00000000 ebx=00000000 ecx=00000400 edx=00000000 esi=09a20000 edi=00001420
eip=77005e74 esp=06d2f37c ebp=06d2f400 iopl=0         nv up ei pl nz na pe nc
cs=001b  ss=0023  ds=0023  es=0023  fs=003b  gs=0000             efl=00000206
ntdll!KiFastSystemCallRet:
77005e74 c3              ret
```

Note the message about **Stored Exception**.

We set up a link to Microsoft symbol server and reload symbols:

```
0:012> .symfix c:\mss

0:012> .reload
................................................................
................................................................
.........
Loading unloaded module list
......
```

We first check the current stack trace:

```
0:012> k
ChildEBP RetAddr
06d2f378 77005620 ntdll!KiFastSystemCallRet
06d2f37c 77033c62 ntdll!ZwWaitForSingleObject+0xc
06d2f400 77033d4b ntdll!RtlReportExceptionEx+0x14b
06d2f440 7704fa87 ntdll!RtlReportException+0x3c
06d2f454 7704fb0d ntdll!RtlpTerminateFailureFilter+0x14
06d2f460 76fa9bdc ntdll!RtlReportCriticalFailure+0x6b
06d2f474 76fa4067 ntdll!_EH4_CallFilterFunc+0x12
06d2f49c 77005f79 ntdll!_except_handler4+0x8e
06d2f4c0 77005f4b ntdll!ExecuteHandler2+0x26
06d2f570 77005dd7 ntdll!ExecuteHandler+0x24
06d2f570 7704faf8 ntdll!KiUserExceptionDispatcher+0xf
06d2f8e4 77050704 ntdll!RtlReportCriticalFailure+0x5b
06d2f8f4 770507f2 ntdll!RtlpReportHeapFailure+0x21
06d2f928 77050a64 ntdll!RtlpLogHeapFailure+0xa1
06d2f980 7701bafe ntdll!RtlpAnalyzeHeapFailure+0x25a
06d2fa6c 77006e0c ntdll!RtlpAllocateHeap+0x62f
06d2fae4 76fc4b2a ntdll!RtlAllocateHeap+0x1e3
06d2fbfc 76fddd4a ntdll!RtlpReAllocateHeap+0x864
06d2fc70 77115aac ntdll!RtlReAllocateHeap+0x2bf
06d2fcc4 73cb1d28 kernel32!GlobalReAlloc+0x2ba
06d2fcf0 73cb138b msacm32!mapWaveOpen+0x22f
06d2fd14 738e4d20 msacm32!wodMessage+0x79
06d2fd64 738e5215 winmm!waveOutOpen+0x280
06d2fdb4 738e4fe4 winmm!soundOpen+0xb1
06d2fdc4 738e5093 winmm!soundPlay+0x22
06d2fe00 738e14fc winmm!sndMessage+0x199
06d2fe34 7566fd72 winmm!mmWndProc+0x1a3
06d2fe60 7566fe4a user32!InternalCallWinProc+0x23
06d2fed8 7567018d user32!UserCallWinProcCheckWow+0x14b
06d2ff3c 75668b7c user32!DispatchMessageWorker+0x322
06d2ff4c 738e148c user32!DispatchMessageA+0xf
06d2ff78 7715d0e9 winmm!mciwindow+0xf9
06d2ff84 76fe19bb kernel32!BaseThreadInitThunk+0xe
06d2ffc4 76fe198e ntdll!__RtlUserThreadStart+0x23
06d2ffdc 00000000 ntdll!_RtlUserThreadStart+0x1b
```

We see **Heap Corruption** (or process **Dynamic Memory Corruption**) diagnostics. The usual impulse here is to enable full page heap and collect a new dump. But now analyze the memory dump a bit further.

Let's check **Stack Trace Collection** from all process threads:

```
0:012> ~*k

   0  Id: 1420.113c Suspend: 1 Teb: 7ffdf000 Unfrozen
ChildEBP RetAddr
001ef764 77005610 ntdll!KiFastSystemCallRet
001ef768 7715a5d7 ntdll!ZwWaitForMultipleObjects+0xc
001ef804 75670f8d kernel32!WaitForMultipleObjectsEx+0x11d
001ef858 7649334a user32!RealMsgWaitForMultipleObjectsEx+0x13c
001ef8a8 76494942 iertutil!IsoDispatchMessageToArtifacts+0x22c
001ef8c8 7016416a iertutil!IsoManagerThreadZero_WindowsPump+0x52
001ef918 008512e3 ieframe!LCIEStartAsTabProcess+0x25f
001efa64 0085147a iexplore!wWinMain+0x368
```

```
001efaf8 7715d0e9 iexplore!_initterm_e+0x1b1
001efb04 76fe19bb kernel32!BaseThreadInitThunk+0xe
001efb44 76fe198e ntdll!__RtlUserThreadStart+0x23
001efb5c 00000000 ntdll!_RtlUserThreadStart+0x1b

   1  Id: 1420.a54 Suspend: 1 Teb: 7ffde000 Unfrozen
ChildEBP RetAddr
01f6fb80 77005610 ntdll!KiFastSystemCallRet
01f6fb84 76fe2934 ntdll!ZwWaitForMultipleObjects+0xc
01f6fd18 7715d0e9 ntdll!TppWaiterpThread+0x328
01f6fd24 76fe19bb kernel32!BaseThreadInitThunk+0xe
01f6fd64 76fe198e ntdll!__RtlUserThreadStart+0x23
01f6fd7c 00000000 ntdll!_RtlUserThreadStart+0x1b

   2  Id: 1420.1544 Suspend: 1 Teb: 7ffdc000 Unfrozen
ChildEBP RetAddr
0234eb6c 77005610 ntdll!KiFastSystemCallRet
0234eb70 7715a5d7 ntdll!ZwWaitForMultipleObjects+0xc
0234ec0c 7715a6f0 kernel32!WaitForMultipleObjectsEx+0x11d
0234ec28 7648f08c kernel32!WaitForMultipleObjects+0x18
0234fc54 76494819 iertutil!CForeignProcessToCurrentProcessMessaging::_vThreadProc+0xa1
0234fc5c 7715d0e9 iertutil!CForeignProcessToCurrentProcessMessaging::_sThreadProc+0xd
0234fc68 76fe19bb kernel32!BaseThreadInitThunk+0xe
0234fca8 76fe198e ntdll!__RtlUserThreadStart+0x23
0234fcc0 00000000 ntdll!_RtlUserThreadStart+0x1b

   3  Id: 1420.bb8 Suspend: 1 Teb: 7ffdb000 Unfrozen
ChildEBP RetAddr
0250fdb4 77005610 ntdll!KiFastSystemCallRet
0250fdb8 7715a5d7 ntdll!ZwWaitForMultipleObjects+0xc
0250fe54 75670f8d kernel32!WaitForMultipleObjectsEx+0x11d
0250fea8 7649334a user32!RealMsgWaitForMultipleObjectsEx+0x13c
0250fef8 764948b6 iertutil!IsoDispatchMessageToArtifacts+0x22c
0250ff18 7715d0e9 iertutil!IsoManagerThreadNonzero_WindowsPump+0x59
0250ff24 76fe19bb kernel32!BaseThreadInitThunk+0xe
0250ff64 76fe198e ntdll!__RtlUserThreadStart+0x23
0250ff7c 00000000 ntdll!_RtlUserThreadStart+0x1b

   4  Id: 1420.16c8 Suspend: 1 Teb: 7ffda000 Unfrozen
ChildEBP RetAddr
028bd934 7567073f ntdll!KiFastSystemCallRet
028bd938 701ec23a user32!NtUserWaitMessage+0xc
028bfa3c 7019337e ieframe!CTabWindow::_TabWindowThreadProc+0x633
028bfaf4 7649426d ieframe!LCIETab_ThreadProc+0x2c1
028bfb04 7715d0e9 iertutil!CIsoScope::RegisterThread+0xab
028bfb10 76fe19bb kernel32!BaseThreadInitThunk+0xe
028bfb50 76fe198e ntdll!__RtlUserThreadStart+0x23
028bfb68 00000000 ntdll!_RtlUserThreadStart+0x1b

   5  Id: 1420.17d8 Suspend: 1 Teb: 7ffd9000 Unfrozen
ChildEBP RetAddr
029cf41c 77005610 ntdll!KiFastSystemCallRet
029cf420 7715a5d7 ntdll!ZwWaitForMultipleObjects+0xc
029cf4bc 7715a6f0 kernel32!WaitForMultipleObjectsEx+0x11d
*** ERROR: Symbol file could not be found.  Defaulted to export symbols for msidcrl40.dll -
029cf4d8 275c55c0 kernel32!WaitForMultipleObjects+0x18
WARNING: Stack unwind information not available. Following frames may be wrong.
029cf620 76fe4123 msidcrl40!CreatePassportAuthUIContext+0x2ab30
029cf65c 76fe3e23 ntdll!RtlpTpTimerCallback+0x62
029cf680 76fe2fcf ntdll!TppTimerpExecuteCallback+0x14d
```

```
029cf7b0 7715d0e9 ntdll!TppWorkerThread+0x545
029cf7bc 76fe19bb kernel32!BaseThreadInitThunk+0xe
029cf7fc 76fe198e ntdll!__RtlUserThreadStart+0x23
029cf814 00000000 ntdll!_RtlUserThreadStart+0x1b

   6  Id: 1420.60c Suspend: 1 Teb: 7ffd4000 Unfrozen
ChildEBP RetAddr
03d0f830 770057b0 ntdll!KiFastSystemCallRet
03d0f834 76fe2eb0 ntdll!NtWaitForWorkViaWorkerFactory+0xc
03d0f964 7715d0e9 ntdll!TppWorkerThread+0x1f6
03d0f970 76fe19bb kernel32!BaseThreadInitThunk+0xe
03d0f9b0 76fe198e ntdll!__RtlUserThreadStart+0x23
03d0f9c8 00000000 ntdll!_RtlUserThreadStart+0x1b

   7  Id: 1420.a74 Suspend: 1 Teb: 7ffaf000 Unfrozen
ChildEBP RetAddr
03fffbf0 77005620 ntdll!KiFastSystemCallRet
03fffbf4 77159884 ntdll!ZwWaitForSingleObject+0xc
03fffc64 771597f2 kernel32!WaitForSingleObjectEx+0xbe
03fffc78 6c8da731 kernel32!WaitForSingleObject+0x12
03fffc98 6c840778 mshtml!CDwnTaskExec::ThreadExec+0x23c
03fffca0 6c84083b mshtml!CExecFT::ThreadProc+0x39
03fffcac 7715d0e9 mshtml!CExecFT::StaticThreadProc+0xe
03fffcb8 76fe19bb kernel32!BaseThreadInitThunk+0xe
03fffcf8 76fe198e ntdll!__RtlUserThreadStart+0x23
03fffd10 00000000 ntdll!_RtlUserThreadStart+0x1b

   8  Id: 1420.151c Suspend: 1 Teb: 7ffad000 Unfrozen
ChildEBP RetAddr
05adf750 77005620 ntdll!KiFastSystemCallRet
05adf754 77159884 ntdll!ZwWaitForSingleObject+0xc
05adf7c4 771597f2 kernel32!WaitForSingleObjectEx+0xbe
05adf7d8 6c8da731 kernel32!WaitForSingleObject+0x12
05adf7f8 6c840778 mshtml!CDwnTaskExec::ThreadExec+0x23c
05adf800 6c84083b mshtml!CExecFT::ThreadProc+0x39
05adf80c 7715d0e9 mshtml!CExecFT::StaticThreadProc+0xe
05adf818 76fe19bb kernel32!BaseThreadInitThunk+0xe
05adf858 76fe198e ntdll!__RtlUserThreadStart+0x23
05adf870 00000000 ntdll!_RtlUserThreadStart+0x1b

   9  Id: 1420.f64 Suspend: 1 Teb: 7ffac000 Unfrozen
ChildEBP RetAddr
05fbf878 77005620 ntdll!KiFastSystemCallRet
05fbf87c 77159884 ntdll!ZwWaitForSingleObject+0xc
05fbf8ec 771597f2 kernel32!WaitForSingleObjectEx+0xbe
05fbf900 6c8da731 kernel32!WaitForSingleObject+0x12
05fbf920 6c840778 mshtml!CDwnTaskExec::ThreadExec+0x23c
05fbf928 6c84083b mshtml!CExecFT::ThreadProc+0x39
05fbf934 7715d0e9 mshtml!CExecFT::StaticThreadProc+0xe
05fbf940 76fe19bb kernel32!BaseThreadInitThunk+0xe
05fbf980 76fe198e ntdll!__RtlUserThreadStart+0x23
05fbf998 00000000 ntdll!_RtlUserThreadStart+0x1b

  10  Id: 1420.680 Suspend: 1 Teb: 7ffab000 Unfrozen
ChildEBP RetAddr
0640f958 77005610 ntdll!KiFastSystemCallRet
0640f95c 7715a5d7 ntdll!ZwWaitForMultipleObjects+0xc
0640f9f8 7715a6f0 kernel32!WaitForMultipleObjectsEx+0x11d
0640fa14 275b4879 kernel32!WaitForMultipleObjects+0x18
WARNING: Stack unwind information not available. Following frames may be wrong.
```

```
0640fd38 275b4a58 msidcrl40!CreatePassportAuthUIContext+0x19de9
0640fd60 275c9655 msidcrl40!CreatePassportAuthUIContext+0x19fc8
0640fd98 275c96fa msidcrl40!CreatePassportAuthUIContext+0x2ebc5
0640fdac 76fe19bb msidcrl40!CreatePassportAuthUIContext+0x2ec6a
0640fdec 76fe198e ntdll!__RtlUserThreadStart+0x23
0640fe04 00000000 ntdll!_RtlUserThreadStart+0x1b

  11  Id: 1420.12a4 Suspend: 1 Teb: 7ffaa000 Unfrozen
ChildEBP RetAddr
0615f6fc 77005610 ntdll!KiFastSystemCallRet
0615f700 7715a5d7 ntdll!ZwWaitForMultipleObjects+0xc
0615f79c 7715a6f0 kernel32!WaitForMultipleObjectsEx+0x11d
0615f7b8 275b4879 kernel32!WaitForMultipleObjects+0x18
WARNING: Stack unwind information not available. Following frames may be wrong.
0615fadc 275b4a58 msidcrl40!CreatePassportAuthUIContext+0x19de9
0615fb04 275c9655 msidcrl40!CreatePassportAuthUIContext+0x19fc8
0615fb3c 275c96fa msidcrl40!CreatePassportAuthUIContext+0x2ebc5
0615fb50 76fe19bb msidcrl40!CreatePassportAuthUIContext+0x2ec6a
0615fb90 76fe198e ntdll!__RtlUserThreadStart+0x23
0615fba8 00000000 ntdll!_RtlUserThreadStart+0x1b

# 12  Id: 1420.cf0 Suspend: 0 Teb: 7ffa9000 Unfrozen
ChildEBP RetAddr
06d2f378 77005620 ntdll!KiFastSystemCallRet
06d2f37c 77033c62 ntdll!ZwWaitForSingleObject+0xc
06d2f400 77033d4b ntdll!RtlReportExceptionEx+0x14b
06d2f440 7704fa87 ntdll!RtlReportException+0x3c
06d2f454 7704fb0d ntdll!RtlpTerminateFailureFilter+0x14
06d2f460 76fa9bdc ntdll!RtlReportCriticalFailure+0x6b
06d2f474 76fa4067 ntdll!_EH4_CallFilterFunc+0x12
06d2f49c 77005f79 ntdll!_except_handler4+0x8e
06d2f4c0 77005f4b ntdll!ExecuteHandler2+0x26
06d2f570 77005dd7 ntdll!ExecuteHandler+0x24
06d2f570 7704faf8 ntdll!KiUserExceptionDispatcher+0xf
06d2f8e4 77050704 ntdll!RtlReportCriticalFailure+0x5b
06d2f8f4 770507f2 ntdll!RtlpReportHeapFailure+0x21
06d2f928 77050a64 ntdll!RtlpLogHeapFailure+0xa1
06d2f980 7701bafe ntdll!RtlpAnalyzeHeapFailure+0x25a
06d2fa6c 77006e0c ntdll!RtlpAllocateHeap+0x62f
06d2fae4 76fc4b2a ntdll!RtlAllocateHeap+0x1e3
06d2fbfc 76fddd4a ntdll!RtlpReAllocateHeap+0x864
06d2fc70 77115aac ntdll!RtlReAllocateHeap+0x2bf
06d2fcc4 73cb1d28 kernel32!GlobalReAlloc+0x2ba
06d2fcf0 73cb138b msacm32!mapWaveOpen+0x22f
06d2fd14 738e4d20 msacm32!wodMessage+0x79
06d2fd64 738e5215 winmm!waveOutOpen+0x280
06d2fdb4 738e4fe4 winmm!soundOpen+0xb1
06d2fdc4 738e5093 winmm!soundPlay+0x22
06d2fe00 738e14fc winmm!sndMessage+0x199
06d2fe34 7566fd72 winmm!mmWndProc+0x1a3
06d2fe60 7566fe4a user32!InternalCallWinProc+0x23
06d2fed8 7567018d user32!UserCallWinProcCheckWow+0x14b
06d2ff3c 75668b7c user32!DispatchMessageWorker+0x322
06d2ff4c 738e148c user32!DispatchMessageA+0xf
06d2ff78 7715d0e9 winmm!mciwindow+0xf9
06d2ff84 76fe19bb kernel32!BaseThreadInitThunk+0xe
06d2ffc4 76fe198e ntdll!__RtlUserThreadStart+0x23
06d2ffdc 00000000 ntdll!_RtlUserThreadStart+0x1b
```

```
  13  Id: 1420.12f8 Suspend: 1 Teb: 7ffa8000 Unfrozen
ChildEBP RetAddr
06f2fa5c 77005610 ntdll!KiFastSystemCallRet
06f2fa60 7715a5d7 ntdll!ZwWaitForMultipleObjects+0xc
06f2fafc 73804f1d kernel32!WaitForMultipleObjectsEx+0x11d
06f2fb34 73807e96 wdmaud!CWorker::_ThreadProc+0x5e
06f2fb40 7715d0e9 wdmaud!CWorker::_StaticThreadProc+0x18
06f2fb4c 76fe19bb kernel32!BaseThreadInitThunk+0xe
06f2fb8c 76fe198e ntdll!__RtlUserThreadStart+0x23
06f2fba4 00000000 ntdll!_RtlUserThreadStart+0x1b

  14  Id: 1420.162c Suspend: 1 Teb: 7ffa7000 Unfrozen
ChildEBP RetAddr
06e2f95c 77005620 ntdll!KiFastSystemCallRet
06e2f960 74c716c7 ntdll!ZwWaitForSingleObject+0xc
06e2f9a0 74c7179d mswsock!SockWaitForSingleObject+0x3a
06e2fa8c 76521693 mswsock!WSPSelect+0x38c
06e2fb0c 7670e9a9 ws2_32!select+0x494
06e2fe64 7672deab wininet!ICAsyncThread::SelectThread+0x242
06e2fe6c 7715d0e9 wininet!ICAsyncThread::SelectThreadWrapper+0xd
06e2fe78 76fe19bb kernel32!BaseThreadInitThunk+0xe
06e2feb8 76fe198e ntdll!__RtlUserThreadStart+0x23
06e2fed0 00000000 ntdll!_RtlUserThreadStart+0x1b

  15  Id: 1420.bd0 Suspend: 1 Teb: 7ffa6000 Unfrozen
ChildEBP RetAddr
0748fb18 770050b0 ntdll!KiFastSystemCallRet
0748fb1c 74c764f1 ntdll!NtRemoveIoCompletion+0xc
0748fb54 7715d0e9 mswsock!SockAsyncThread+0x69
0748fb60 76fe19bb kernel32!BaseThreadInitThunk+0xe
0748fba0 76fe198e ntdll!__RtlUserThreadStart+0x23
0748fbb8 00000000 ntdll!_RtlUserThreadStart+0x1b

  16  Id: 1420.10a4 Suspend: 1 Teb: 7ffd6000 Unfrozen
ChildEBP RetAddr
02b2fdd8 77004780 ntdll!KiFastSystemCallRet
02b2fddc 77159990 ntdll!NtDelayExecution+0xc
02b2fe44 77111c6c kernel32!SleepEx+0x62
02b2fe54 76e93f1d kernel32!Sleep+0xf
02b2fe60 76eaeb46 ole32!CROIDTable::WorkerThreadLoop+0x14
[d:\longhorn\com\ole32\com\dcomrem\refcache.cxx @ 1345]
02b2fe7c 76e957ab ole32!CRpcThread::WorkerLoop+0x26
[d:\longhorn\com\ole32\com\dcomrem\threads.cxx @ 257]
02b2fe8c 7715d0e9 ole32!CRpcThreadCache::RpcWorkerThreadEntry+0x16
[d:\longhorn\com\ole32\com\dcomrem\threads.cxx @ 63]
02b2fe98 76fe19bb kernel32!BaseThreadInitThunk+0xe
02b2fed8 76fe198e ntdll!__RtlUserThreadStart+0x23
02b2fef0 00000000 ntdll!_RtlUserThreadStart+0x1b

  17  Id: 1420.8f0 Suspend: 1 Teb: 7ff9f000 Unfrozen
ChildEBP RetAddr
093efb78 7567073f ntdll!KiFastSystemCallRet
093efb7c 70278291 user32!NtUserWaitMessage+0xc
093efbb8 7025f3e0 ieframe!IEDownload_ThreadProc+0x17a
093efc28 7715d0e9 ieframe!WrapperThreadProc+0x9b
093efc34 76fe19bb kernel32!BaseThreadInitThunk+0xe
093efc74 76fe198e ntdll!__RtlUserThreadStart+0x23
093efc8c 00000000 ntdll!_RtlUserThreadStart+0x1b
```

```
  18  Id: 1420.1640 Suspend: 1 Teb: 7ffa5000 Unfrozen
ChildEBP RetAddr
0b52f934 7567073f ntdll!KiFastSystemCallRet
0b52f938 70278291 user32!NtUserWaitMessage+0xc
0b52f974 7025f3e0 ieframe!IEDownload_ThreadProc+0x17a
0b52f9e4 7715d0e9 ieframe!WrapperThreadProc+0x9b
0b52f9f0 76fe19bb kernel32!BaseThreadInitThunk+0xe
0b52fa30 76fe198e ntdll!__RtlUserThreadStart+0x23
0b52fa48 00000000 ntdll!_RtlUserThreadStart+0x1b

  19  Id: 1420.1270 Suspend: 1 Teb: 7ffd8000 Unfrozen
ChildEBP RetAddr
0765fb8c 770057b0 ntdll!KiFastSystemCallRet
0765fb90 76fe2eb0 ntdll!NtWaitForWorkViaWorkerFactory+0xc
0765fcc0 7715d0e9 ntdll!TppWorkerThread+0x1f6
0765fccc 76fe19bb kernel32!BaseThreadInitThunk+0xe
0765fd0c 76fe198e ntdll!__RtlUserThreadStart+0x23
0765fd24 00000000 ntdll!_RtlUserThreadStart+0x1b

  20  Id: 1420.11b0 Suspend: 1 Teb: 7ffd7000 Unfrozen
ChildEBP RetAddr
091ffe58 770050b0 ntdll!KiFastSystemCallRet
091ffe5c 7715d11e ntdll!NtRemoveIoCompletion+0xc
091ffe88 76bb03c8 kernel32!GetQueuedCompletionStatus+0x29
091ffec4 76bb04fd rpcrt4!COMMON_ProcessCalls+0xb5
091fff34 76bb011c rpcrt4!LOADABLE_TRANSPORT::ProcessIOEvents+0x138
091fff3c 76bb00e3 rpcrt4!ProcessIOEventsWrapper+0xd
091fff60 76bb0166 rpcrt4!BaseCachedThreadRoutine+0x5c
091fff6c 7715d0e9 rpcrt4!ThreadStartRoutine+0x1e
091fff78 76fe19bb kernel32!BaseThreadInitThunk+0xe
091fffb8 76fe198e ntdll!__RtlUserThreadStart+0x23
091fffd0 00000000 ntdll!_RtlUserThreadStart+0x1b

  21  Id: 1420.163c Suspend: 1 Teb: 7ffdd000 Unfrozen
ChildEBP RetAddr
095efcb8 770057b0 ntdll!KiFastSystemCallRet
095efcbc 76fe2eb0 ntdll!NtWaitForWorkViaWorkerFactory+0xc
095efdec 7715d0e9 ntdll!TppWorkerThread+0x1f6
095efdf8 76fe19bb kernel32!BaseThreadInitThunk+0xe
095efe38 76fe198e ntdll!__RtlUserThreadStart+0x23
095efe50 00000000 ntdll!_RtlUserThreadStart+0x1b

  22  Id: 1420.12ec Suspend: 1 Teb: 7ffd3000 Unfrozen
ChildEBP RetAddr
08f789a8 77005620 ntdll!KiFastSystemCallRet
08f789ac 76fde16a ntdll!ZwWaitForSingleObject+0xc
08f78a10 76fde04d ntdll!RtlpWaitOnCriticalSection+0x155
08f78a38 76fde6d8 ntdll!RtlEnterCriticalSection+0x152
08f78a6c 7712c119 ntdll!RtlLockHeap+0x3d
08f78aac 76af27bc kernel32!LocalReAlloc+0x51
08f78acc 76af28a2 advapi32!UnicodeToMultiByte+0x56
08f78c00 0005180f advapi32!GetCurrentHwProfileA+0x5d
WARNING: Frame IP not in any known module. Following frames may be wrong.
08f78c10 00050e8b 0x5180f
08f78dec 771d006c 0x50e8b
08f78ee8 00049e68 kernel32!WerpGetFlags+0x24
08f78fa4 76d3b7b1 0x49e68
08f78fe4 76d3b32b urlmon!CINetHttp::INetAsyncSendRequest+0x347
08f79804 76d3b4c8 urlmon!CINetHttp::INetAsyncOpenRequest+0x2cf
08f79818 76d3ac97 urlmon!CINet::INetAsyncConnect+0x24b
```

```
08f79830 76d26af9 urlmon!CINet::INetAsyncOpen+0x11b
08f79840 76d26aaa urlmon!CINet::INetAsyncStart+0x1a
08f7985c 76d2693f urlmon!CINet::StartCommon+0x198
08f79878 76d26b5e urlmon!CINet::StartEx+0x1c
08f798ac 76d18e84 urlmon!COInetProt::StartEx+0xc2
08f798fc 76d19411 urlmon!CTransaction::StartEx+0x3e1
08f79984 76d19022 urlmon!CBinding::StartBinding+0x602
08f799c8 76d19fc0 urlmon!CUrlMon::StartBinding+0x169
08f799f0 6c8deac6 urlmon!CUrlMon::BindToStorage+0x90
08f79a1c 6c8de9cb mshtml!CStreamProxy::Bind+0xce
08f79cbc 6c8db277 mshtml!CDwnBindData::Bind+0x74b
08f79ce4 6c8db118 mshtml!NewDwnBindData+0x15f
08f79d34 6c85f0aa mshtml!CDwnLoad::Init+0x121
08f79d88 6c8daa61 mshtml!CHtmLoad::Init+0x1fe
08f79dac 6c8da967 mshtml!CDwnInfo::SetLoad+0x119
08f79dcc 6c85e021 mshtml!CDwnCtx::SetLoad+0x7a
08f79de4 6c85ec7b mshtml!CHtmCtx::SetLoad+0x13
08f79e04 6c8525c9 mshtml!CMarkup::Load+0x167
08f7a008 6c9ff395 mshtml!CMarkup::LoadFromInfo+0xb5a
08f7a1e0 6c9ff532 mshtml!CDoc::DoNavigate+0x1508
08f7a300 6cc7557e mshtml!CDoc::FollowHyperlink2+0xda7
08f7a3c8 6cc75170 mshtml!CFormElement::DoSubmit+0x405
08f7a3dc 6c891bc5 mshtml!CFormElement::submit+0x11
08f7a3f8 6c91adc3 mshtml!Method_void_void+0x75
08f7a46c 6c926e11 mshtml!CBase::ContextInvokeEx+0x5d1
08f7a4bc 6ca19057 mshtml!CElement::ContextInvokeEx+0x9d
08f7a4f8 6c91a7c1 mshtml!CFormElement::VersionedInvokeEx+0xf0
08f7a548 6c25392a mshtml!PlainInvokeEx+0xea
08f7a588 6c253876 jscript!IDispatchExInvokeEx2+0xf8
08f7a5c4 6c254db6 jscript!IDispatchExInvokeEx+0x6a
08f7a684 6c254d10 jscript!InvokeDispatchEx+0x98
08f7a6b8 6c252bfd jscript!VAR::InvokeByName+0x135
08f7a704 6c2540c5 jscript!VAR::InvokeDispName+0x7a
08f7a734 6c254e23 jscript!VAR::InvokeByDispID+0xce
08f7a8d0 6c25123b jscript!CScriptRuntime::Run+0x2abe
08f7a9b8 6c251175 jscript!ScrFncObj::CallWithFrameOnStack+0xff
08f7aa04 6c25493c jscript!ScrFncObj::Call+0x8f
08f7aa88 6c252755 jscript!NameTbl::InvokeInternal+0x137
08f7aabc 6c252fa4 jscript!VAR::InvokeByDispID+0x17c
08f7ac58 6c25123b jscript!CScriptRuntime::Run+0x29e0
08f7ad40 6c251175 jscript!ScrFncObj::CallWithFrameOnStack+0xff
08f7ad8c 6c250fa3 jscript!ScrFncObj::Call+0x8f
08f7ae08 6c233ea3 jscript!CSession::Execute+0x175
08f7ae54 6c23552f jscript!COleScript::ExecutePendingScripts+0x1c0
08f7aeb8 6c235345 jscript!COleScript::ParseScriptTextCore+0x29a
08f7aee0 6c85a304 jscript!COleScript::ParseScriptText+0x30
08f7af38 6ca254c2 mshtml!CScriptCollection::ParseScriptText+0x219
08f7cfd0 6ca0a568 mshtml!CWindow::ExecuteScriptUri+0x19f
08f7d018 6ca25810 mshtml!CWindow::NavigateEx+0x5a
08f7d084 6ca256b5 mshtml!CDoc::ExecuteScriptUri+0x262
08f7d0c0 6caf6b68 mshtml!CDoc::ExecuteScriptURL+0x4e
08f7d114 6c9641a7 mshtml!CHyperlink::ClickAction+0x269
08f7d124 6cc3c96f mshtml!CAnchorElement::ClickAction+0x10
08f7d14c 6c96416e mshtml!CImgElement::ClickAction+0x6c
08f7d180 6c9601ff mshtml!CElement::DoClick+0x155
08f7d21c 6ca3e941 mshtml!CDoc::PumpMessage+0xf63
08f7d394 6c964408 mshtml!CDoc::OnMouseMessage+0x55d
08f7d4c0 6c939241 mshtml!CDoc::OnWindowMessage+0x9d9
08f7d4ec 7566fd72 mshtml!CServer::WndProc+0x78
08f7d518 7566fe4a user32!InternalCallWinProc+0x23
```

```
08f7d590 756709d3 user32!UserCallWinProcCheckWow+0x14b
08f7d5c0 75670979 user32!CallWindowProcAorW+0x97
*** ERROR: Symbol file could not be found.  Defaulted to export symbols for
rpbrowserrecordplugin.dll -
08f7d5e0 633da439 user32!CallWindowProcW+0x1b
08f7d600 633d6ee9 rpbrowserrecordplugin+0xa439
08f7d628 7566fd72 rpbrowserrecordplugin+0x6ee9
08f7d654 7566fe4a user32!InternalCallWinProc+0x23
08f7d6cc 7567018d user32!UserCallWinProcCheckWow+0x14b
08f7d730 7567022b user32!DispatchMessageWorker+0x322
08f7d740 701ec1d5 user32!DispatchMessageW+0xf
08f7f848 7019337e ieframe!CTabWindow::_TabWindowThreadProc+0x54c
08f7f900 7649426d ieframe!LCIETab_ThreadProc+0x2c1
08f7f910 7715d0e9 iertutil!CIsoScope::RegisterThread+0xab
08f7f91c 76fe19bb kernel32!BaseThreadInitThunk+0xe
08f7f95c 76fe198e ntdll!__RtlUserThreadStart+0x23
08f7f974 00000000 ntdll!_RtlUserThreadStart+0x1b

  23  Id: 1420.1670 Suspend: 1 Teb: 7ffae000 Unfrozen
ChildEBP RetAddr
0997f940 770050b0 ntdll!KiFastSystemCallRet
0997f944 7715d11e ntdll!NtRemoveIoCompletion+0xc
0997f970 76bb03c8 kernel32!GetQueuedCompletionStatus+0x29
0997f9ac 76bb04fd rpcrt4!COMMON_ProcessCalls+0xb5
0997fa1c 76bb011c rpcrt4!LOADABLE_TRANSPORT::ProcessIOEvents+0x138
0997fa24 76bb00e3 rpcrt4!ProcessIOEventsWrapper+0xd
0997fa48 76bb0166 rpcrt4!BaseCachedThreadRoutine+0x5c
0997fa54 7715d0e9 rpcrt4!ThreadStartRoutine+0x1e
0997fa60 76fe19bb kernel32!BaseThreadInitThunk+0xe
0997faa0 76fe198e ntdll!__RtlUserThreadStart+0x23
0997fab8 00000000 ntdll!_RtlUserThreadStart+0x1b

  24  Id: 1420.15e0 Suspend: 1 Teb: 7ffa4000 Unfrozen
ChildEBP RetAddr
09b5f7b8 770050b0 ntdll!KiFastSystemCallRet
09b5f7bc 7715d11e ntdll!NtRemoveIoCompletion+0xc
09b5f7e8 76bb03c8 kernel32!GetQueuedCompletionStatus+0x29
09b5f824 76bb04fd rpcrt4!COMMON_ProcessCalls+0xb5
09b5f894 76bb011c rpcrt4!LOADABLE_TRANSPORT::ProcessIOEvents+0x138
09b5f89c 76bb00e3 rpcrt4!ProcessIOEventsWrapper+0xd
09b5f8c0 76bb0166 rpcrt4!BaseCachedThreadRoutine+0x5c
09b5f8cc 7715d0e9 rpcrt4!ThreadStartRoutine+0x1e
09b5f8d8 76fe19bb kernel32!BaseThreadInitThunk+0xe
09b5f918 76fe198e ntdll!__RtlUserThreadStart+0x23
09b5f930 00000000 ntdll!_RtlUserThreadStart+0x1b

  25  Id: 1420.16f4 Suspend: 1 Teb: 7ffa3000 Unfrozen
ChildEBP RetAddr
090ef72c 770057b0 ntdll!KiFastSystemCallRet
090ef730 76fe2eb0 ntdll!NtWaitForWorkViaWorkerFactory+0xc
090ef860 7715d0e9 ntdll!TppWorkerThread+0x1f6
090ef86c 76fe19bb kernel32!BaseThreadInitThunk+0xe
090ef8ac 76fe198e ntdll!__RtlUserThreadStart+0x23
090ef8c4 00000000 ntdll!_RtlUserThreadStart+0x1b
```

```
  26  Id: 1420.13e8 Suspend: 1 Teb: 7ffa2000 Unfrozen
ChildEBP RetAddr
09ccf814 770057b0 ntdll!KiFastSystemCallRet
09ccf818 76fe2eb0 ntdll!NtWaitForWorkViaWorkerFactory+0xc
09ccf948 7715d0e9 ntdll!TppWorkerThread+0x1f6
09ccf954 76fe19bb kernel32!BaseThreadInitThunk+0xe
09ccf994 76fe198e ntdll!__RtlUserThreadStart+0x23
09ccf9ac 00000000 ntdll!_RtlUserThreadStart+0x1b

  27  Id: 1420.d9c Suspend: 1 Teb: 7ffa1000 Unfrozen
ChildEBP RetAddr
0cd3fe60 77005620 ntdll!KiFastSystemCallRet
0cd3fe64 77159884 ntdll!ZwWaitForSingleObject+0xc
0cd3fed4 771597f2 kernel32!WaitForSingleObjectEx+0xbe
*** ERROR: Symbol file could not be found.  Defaulted to export symbols for Flash10k.ocx -
0cd3fee8 674cd4d8 kernel32!WaitForSingleObject+0x12
WARNING: Stack unwind information not available. Following frames may be wrong.
0cd3ff70 674cd5ec Flash10k!DllUnregisterServer+0x3db6a
0cd3ff90 76fe19bb Flash10k!DllUnregisterServer+0x3dc7e
0cd3ffd0 76fe198e ntdll!__RtlUserThreadStart+0x23
0cd3ffe8 00000000 ntdll!_RtlUserThreadStart+0x1b

  28  Id: 1420.12d4 Suspend: 1 Teb: 7ffa0000 Unfrozen
ChildEBP RetAddr
0ca4fb5c 77005620 ntdll!KiFastSystemCallRet
0ca4fb60 77159884 ntdll!ZwWaitForSingleObject+0xc
0ca4fbd0 771597f2 kernel32!WaitForSingleObjectEx+0xbe
0ca4fbe4 674cd4d8 kernel32!WaitForSingleObject+0x12
WARNING: Stack unwind information not available. Following frames may be wrong.
0ca4fc6c 674cd5ec Flash10k!DllUnregisterServer+0x3db6a
0ca4fc8c 76fe19bb Flash10k!DllUnregisterServer+0x3dc7e
0ca4fccc 76fe198e ntdll!__RtlUserThreadStart+0x23
0ca4fce4 00000000 ntdll!_RtlUserThreadStart+0x1b

  29  Id: 1420.10d8 Suspend: 1 Teb: 7ff9e000 Unfrozen
ChildEBP RetAddr
0d16f738 77005620 ntdll!KiFastSystemCallRet
0d16f73c 77159884 ntdll!ZwWaitForSingleObject+0xc
0d16f7ac 771597f2 kernel32!WaitForSingleObjectEx+0xbe
0d16f7c0 674cd4d8 kernel32!WaitForSingleObject+0x12
WARNING: Stack unwind information not available. Following frames may be wrong.
0d16f848 674cd5ec Flash10k!DllUnregisterServer+0x3db6a
0d16f868 76fe19bb Flash10k!DllUnregisterServer+0x3dc7e
0d16f8a8 76fe198e ntdll!__RtlUserThreadStart+0x23
0d16f8c0 00000000 ntdll!_RtlUserThreadStart+0x1b

  30  Id: 1420.1560 Suspend: 1 Teb: 7ff9d000 Unfrozen
ChildEBP RetAddr
0d4ff6c4 770057b0 ntdll!KiFastSystemCallRet
0d4ff6c8 76fe2eb0 ntdll!NtWaitForWorkViaWorkerFactory+0xc
0d4ff7f8 7715d0e9 ntdll!TppWorkerThread+0x1f6
0d4ff804 76fe19bb kernel32!BaseThreadInitThunk+0xe
0d4ff844 76fe198e ntdll!__RtlUserThreadStart+0x23
0d4ff85c 00000000 ntdll!_RtlUserThreadStart+0x1b
```

```
  31  Id: 1420.fd0 Suspend: 1 Teb: 7ff9c000 Unfrozen
ChildEBP RetAddr
0d65fae4 77005620 ntdll!KiFastSystemCallRet
0d65fae8 77159884 ntdll!ZwWaitForSingleObject+0xc
0d65fb58 771597f2 kernel32!WaitForSingleObjectEx+0xbe
0d65fb6c 6ca78fed kernel32!WaitForSingleObject+0x12
0d65fb90 6c840778 mshtml!CTimerMan::ThreadExec+0x90
0d65fb98 6c84083b mshtml!CExecFT::ThreadProc+0x39
0d65fba4 7715d0e9 mshtml!CExecFT::StaticThreadProc+0xe
0d65fbb0 76fe19bb kernel32!BaseThreadInitThunk+0xe
0d65fbf0 76fe198e ntdll!__RtlUserThreadStart+0x23
0d65fc08 00000000 ntdll!_RtlUserThreadStart+0x1b

  32  Id: 1420.1048 Suspend: 1 Teb: 7ff9b000 Unfrozen
ChildEBP RetAddr
0db5fda0 77005610 ntdll!KiFastSystemCallRet
0db5fda4 7715a5d7 ntdll!ZwWaitForMultipleObjects+0xc
0db5fe40 75670f8d kernel32!WaitForMultipleObjectsEx+0x11d
0db5fe94 75667f5a user32!RealMsgWaitForMultipleObjectsEx+0x13c
0db5feb0 73d674b2 user32!MsgWaitForMultipleObjects+0x1f
0db5fefc 7715d0e9 GdiPlus!BackgroundThreadProc+0x59
0db5ff08 76fe19bb kernel32!BaseThreadInitThunk+0xe
0db5ff48 76fe198e ntdll!__RtlUserThreadStart+0x23
0db5ff60 00000000 ntdll!_RtlUserThreadStart+0x1b
```

We see another thread #22 trying to enter a critical section when acessing process heap. What we also see are raw instruction pointers on the stack trace (**RIP Stack Trace**). This can often be seen in managed .NET execution environment with its JIT compiled .NET code. However there is no presence of .NET CLR modules such as mscorwks.dll or clr.dll on the stack trace.

Let's look at this RIP address closely by doing backwards disassembly:

```
0:012> ub 0x49e68
00049e50 52              push    edx
00049e51 e87a5a0000      call    0004f8d0
00049e56 6a01            push    1
00049e58 6a01            push    1
00049e5a 6898aa0500      push    5AA98h
00049e5f 8b45b8          mov     eax,dword ptr [ebp-48h]
00049e62 50              push    eax
00049e63 e848280000      call    0004c6b0

0:012> u 0004c6b0
0004c6b0 55              push    ebp
0004c6b1 8bec            mov     ebp,esp
0004c6b3 81ec78010000    sub     esp,178h
0004c6b9 56              push    esi
0004c6ba 57              push    edi
0004c6bb e8e07fffff      call    000446a0
0004c6c0 8945d8          mov     dword ptr [ebp-28h],eax
0004c6c3 837dd800        cmp     dword ptr [ebp-28h],0
```

Let's check the address attribute:

```
0:012> !address 0x49e68


Mapping file section regions...
Mapping module regions...
Mapping PEB regions...
Mapping TEB and stack regions...
Mapping heap regions...
Mapping page heap regions...
Mapping other regions...
Mapping stack trace database regions...
Mapping activation context regions...


Usage:                  <unknown>
Base Address:           00040000
End Address:            0005d000
Region Size:            0001d000
State:                  00001000 MEM_COMMIT
Protect:                00000040 PAGE_EXECUTE_READWRITE
Type:                   00020000 MEM_PRIVATE
Allocation Base:        00040000
Allocation Protect:     00000040 PAGE_EXECUTE_READWRITE
```

We see that the region is also writable compared to normal code:

```
0:012> !address 73d674b2


Usage:                  Image
Base Address:           73d51000
End Address:            73ed7000
Region Size:            00186000
State:                  00001000 MEM_COMMIT
Protect:                00000020 PAGE_EXECUTE_READ
Type:                   01000000 MEM_IMAGE
Allocation Base:        73d50000
Allocation Protect:     00000080 PAGE_EXECUTE_WRITECOPY
Image Path:
C:\Windows\winsxs\x86_microsoft.windows.gdiplus_6595b64144ccf1df_1.0.6002.18005_none_9e50b396ca
17ae07\GdiPlus.dll
Module Name:            GdiPlus
Loaded Image Name:      GdiPlus.dll
Mapped Image Name:
More info:              lmv m GdiPlus
More info:              !lmi GdiPlus
More info:              ln 0x73d674b2
More info:              !dh 0x73d50000
```

Now we check if the base address contains any module information:

```
0:012> dc 00040000
00040000  00905a4d 00000003 00000004 0000ffff  MZ..............
00040010  000000b8 00000000 00000040 00000000  ........@.......
00040020  00000000 00000000 00000000 00000000  ................
00040030  00000000 00000000 00000000 000000d8  ................
00040040  0eba1f0e cd09b400 4c01b821 685421cd  ........!..L.!Th
00040050  70207369 72676f72 63206d61 6f6e6e61  is program canno
00040060  65622074 6e757220 206e6920 20534f44  t be run in DOS
00040070  65646f6d 0a0d0d2e 00000024 00000000  mode....$.......

0:012> !dh 00040000

File Type: EXECUTABLE IMAGE
FILE HEADER VALUES
     14C machine (i386)
       4 number of sections
4C9E36D3 time date stamp Sat Sep 25 18:52:19 2010

       0 file pointer to symbol table
       0 number of symbols
      E0 size of optional header
     102 characteristics
            Executable
            32 bit word machine

OPTIONAL HEADER VALUES
     10B magic #
    9.00 linker version
   12200 size of code
    7000 size of initialized data
       0 size of uninitialized data
    D5F0 address of entry point
    1000 base of code
         ----- new -----
00400000 image base
    1000 section alignment
     200 file alignment
       2 subsystem (Windows GUI)
    5.00 operating system version
    0.00 image version
    5.00 subsystem version
   1D000 size of image
     400 size of headers
       0 checksum
00100000 size of stack reserve
00001000 size of stack commit
00100000 size of heap reserve
00001000 size of heap commit
    8540  DLL characteristics
            Dynamic base
            NX compatible
            No structured exception handler
            Terminal server aware
       0 [       0] address [size] of Export Directory
       0 [       0] address [size] of Import Directory
       0 [       0] address [size] of Resource Directory
       0 [       0] address [size] of Exception Directory
```

```
       0 [       0] address [size] of Security Directory
   1C000 [     3F0] address [size] of Base Relocation Directory
       0 [       0] address [size] of Debug Directory
       0 [       0] address [size] of Description Directory
       0 [       0] address [size] of Special Directory
       0 [       0] address [size] of Thread Storage Directory
       0 [       0] address [size] of Load Configuration Directory
       0 [       0] address [size] of Bound Import Directory
       0 [       0] address [size] of Import Address Table Directory
       0 [       0] address [size] of Delay Import Directory
       0 [       0] address [size] of COR20 Header Directory
       0 [       0] address [size] of Reserved Directory


SECTION HEADER #1
   .text name
   1203B virtual size
    1000 virtual address
   12200 size of raw data
     400 file pointer to raw data
       0 file pointer to relocation table
       0 file pointer to line numbers
       0 number of relocations
       0 number of line numbers
60000020 flags
         Code
         (no align specified)
         Execute Read

SECTION HEADER #2
  .rdata name
     7D0 virtual size
   14000 virtual address
     800 size of raw data
   12600 file pointer to raw data
       0 file pointer to relocation table
       0 file pointer to line numbers
       0 number of relocations
       0 number of line numbers
40000040 flags
         Initialized Data
         (no align specified)
         Read Only

SECTION HEADER #3
   .data name
    6008 virtual size
   15000 virtual address
    4000 size of raw data
   12E00 file pointer to raw data
       0 file pointer to relocation table
       0 file pointer to line numbers
       0 number of relocations
       0 number of line numbers
C0000040 flags
         Initialized Data
         (no align specified)
         Read Write
```

```
SECTION HEADER #4
  .reloc name
     5F0 virtual size
   1C000 virtual address
     600 size of raw data
   16E00 file pointer to raw data
       0 file pointer to relocation table
       0 file pointer to line numbers
       0 number of relocations
       0 number of line numbers
42000040 flags
         Initialized Data
         Discardable
         (no align specified)
         Read Only
```

We see this **Deviant Module** doesn't have any import tables.

We now check the module range for any **String Hints**:

```
0:012> s-sa 00040000 0005d000
0004004d  "!This program cannot be run in D"
0004006d  "OS mode."
00040081  "3y@"
000400b8  "Rich"
000401d0  ".text"
000401f7  "`.rdata"
0004021f  "@.data"
00040248  ".reloc"
[...]
00054000  "HELLO"
00054008  "%s:%s"
00054010  "READY"
00054018  "GET /stat?uptime=%d&downlink=%d&"
00054038  "uplink=%d&id=%s&statpass=%s&comm"
00054058  "ent=%s HTTP/1.0"
000540ac  "%s%s%s"
000540d8  "ftp://%s:%s@%s:%d"
000540fc  "Accept-Encoding:"
00054118  "Accept-Encoding:"
00054130  "0123456789ABCDEF"
00054144  "://"
00054160  "POST %s HTTP/1.0"
00054172  "Host: %s"
0005417c  "User-Agent: %s"
0005418c  "Accept: text/html"
0005419f  "Connection: Close"
000541b2  "Content-Type: application/x-www-"
000541d2  "form-urlencoded"
000541e3  "Content-Length: %d"
000541fc  "id="
00054208  "POST %s HTTP/1.1"
0005421a  "Host: %s"
00054224  "User-Agent: %s"
00054234  "Accept: text/html"
00054247  "Connection: Close"
0005425a  "Content-Type: application/x-www-"
0005427a  "form-urlencoded"
0005428b  "Content-Length: %d"
```

```
000542a4  "id=%s&base="
000542b8  "id=%s&brw=%d&type=%d&data="
000542d8  "POST %s HTTP/1.1"
000542ea  "Host: %s"
000542f4  "User-Agent: %s"
00054304  "Accept: text/html"
00054317  "Connection: Close"
0005432a  "Content-Type: application/x-www-"
0005434a  "form-urlencoded"
0005435b  "Content-Length: %d"
00054378  "id=%s&os=%s&plist="
00054390  "POST %s HTTP/1.1"
000543a2  "Host: %s"
000543ac  "User-Agent: %s"
000543bc  "Accept: text/html"
000543cf  "Connection: Close"
000543e2  "Content-Type: application/x-www-"
00054402  "form-urlencoded"
00054413  "Content-Length: %d"
00054430  "id=%s&data=%s"
00054440  "POST %s HTTP/1.1"
00054452  "Host: %s"
0005445c  "User-Agent: %s"
0005446c  "Accept: text/html"
0005447f  "Connection: Close"
00054492  "Content-Type: application/x-www-"
000544b2  "form-urlencoded"
000544c3  "Content-Length: %d"
000544e0  "GET %s HTTP/1.0"
000544f1  "Host: %s"
000544fb  "User-Agent: %s"
0005450b  "Connection: close"
00054528  "POST /get/scr.html HTTP/1.0"
00054545  "Host: %s"
0005454f  "User-Agent: %s"
0005455f  "Connection: close"
00054572  "Content-Length: %d"
00054586  "Content-Type: multipart/form-dat"
000545a6  "a; boundary=--------------------"
000545c6  "-------%d"
000545d4  "-----------------------------%d"
000545f8  "%sContent-Disposition: form-data"
00054618  "; name="id""
00054630  "%sContent-Disposition: form-data"
00054650  "; name="screen"; filename="%d""
00054670  "Content-Type: application/octet-"
00054690  "stream"
000546a0  "%s(%d) : %s"
000546ac  "%s failed with error %d: %s"
000546c8  "%02X"
000546d8  "BlackwoodPRO"
000546e8  "FinamDirect"
000546f4  "GrayBox"
000546fc  "MbtPRO"
00054704  "Laser"
0005470c  "LightSpeed"
00054718  "LTGroup"
00054720  "Mbt"
00054724  "ScotTrader"
00054730  "SaxoTrader"
```

```
00054740  "Program:   %s"
0005474f  "Username:  %s"
0005475e  "Password:  %s"
0005476d  "AccountNO: %s"
0005477c  "Server:    %s"
00054790  "%s %s"
0005479c  "PROCESSOR_IDENTIFIER"
[...]
0005a8e0  "mintrayway.com"
0005aa98  "Mozilla/4.0 (compatible; MSIE 8."
0005aab8  "0; Windows NT 6.0; Trident/4.0; "
0005aad8  "MathPlayer 2.10d; SLCC1; .NET CL"
0005aaf8  "R 2.0.50727; Media Center PC 5.0"
0005ab18  "; .NET CLR 3.5.30729; .NET CLR 3"
0005ab38  ".0.30729)"
[...]

0:012> s-su 00040000 0005d000
[...]
00055004  "\chkntfs.exe"
00055020  "\chkntfs.dat"
[...]
00058e20  "kernel32.dll"
00058e3c  "user32.dll"
00058e54  "ws2_32.dll"
00058e6c  "ntdll.dll"
00058e80  "wininet.dll"
00058e98  "nspr4.dll"
00058eac  "ssl3.dll"
0005a4e0  "C:\Users\dima\AppData\Roaming\ch"
0005a520  "kntfs.dat"
[...]
```

We find some references to **Fake Module** chkntfs.exe here and the list of modules needed for this malware. Such modules such as wininet.dll may be checked for any **Patched Code**.

Let's now check if there are any **Hidden Modules** not shown in loaded module list by using **.imgscan** command that searches for MZ/PE signatures:

```
0:012> .imgscan
MZ at 00040000, prot 00000040, type 00020000 - size 1d000
MZ at 00060000, prot 00000008, type 00040000 - size 3000
MZ at 00850000, prot 00000002, type 01000000 - size 9c000
  Name: iexplore.exe
MZ at 01d40000, prot 00000008, type 00040000 - size b000
MZ at 01d70000, prot 00000008, type 00040000 - size a000
MZ at 01f70000, prot 00000008, type 00040000 - size 12f000
MZ at 021b0000, prot 00000002, type 00040000 - size 2000
MZ at 02200000, prot 00000008, type 00040000 - size a000
MZ at 023e0000, prot 00000008, type 00040000 - size 6000
MZ at 02530000, prot 00000002, type 00040000 - size 2000
MZ at 025a0000, prot 00000002, type 00040000 - size 5000
MZ at 028c0000, prot 00000008, type 00040000 - size 3000
MZ at 02a10000, prot 00000008, type 00040000 - size 3000
MZ at 02b90000, prot 00000008, type 00040000 - size 3000
MZ at 02ba0000, prot 00000008, type 00040000 - size 3000
MZ at 02bc0000, prot 00000008, type 00040000 - size 8000
MZ at 02d10000, prot 00000008, type 00040000 - size 4000
MZ at 038d0000, prot 00000002, type 00040000 - size 191000
```

```
MZ at 03b70000, prot 00000008, type 00040000 - size 3000
MZ at 03b80000, prot 00000008, type 00040000 - size 3000
MZ at 03bd0000, prot 00000008, type 00040000 - size 3000
MZ at 03bf0000, prot 00000008, type 00040000 - size 3000
MZ at 03c00000, prot 00000008, type 00040000 - size 3000
MZ at 04000000, prot 00000008, type 00040000 - size d000
MZ at 044f0000, prot 00000008, type 00040000 - size 5000
MZ at 04870000, prot 00000008, type 00040000 - size 3000
MZ at 04910000, prot 00000008, type 00040000 - size 4000
MZ at 04f00000, prot 00000002, type 01000000 - size 335000
  Name: igdumd32.dll
MZ at 053d0000, prot 00000008, type 00040000 - size b0000
MZ at 05b20000, prot 00000008, type 00040000 - size 7000
MZ at 05fc0000, prot 00000008, type 00040000 - size 89000
MZ at 06050000, prot 00000008, type 00040000 - size 5000
MZ at 096e0000, prot 00000002, type 01000000 - size 21000
  Name: MathMLMimer.dll
MZ at 10000000, prot 00000004, type 00020000 - size 5000
  Name: screens_dll.dll
MZ at 16080000, prot 00000002, type 01000000 - size 25000
  Name: mdnsNSP.dll
MZ at 27500000, prot 00000002, type 01000000 - size 11a000
  Name: msidcrl40.dll
MZ at 29500000, prot 00000002, type 01000000 - size 67000
  Name: IDBHO.DLL
MZ at 633d0000, prot 00000002, type 01000000 - size 4f000
  Name: rpbrowserrecordplugin.dll
MZ at 634b0000, prot 00000002, type 01000000 - size 1d000
  Name: rpchromebrowserrecordhelper.dll
MZ at 63f00000, prot 00000002, type 01000000 - size c000
  Name: mscorie.dll
MZ at 67320000, prot 00000002, type 01000000 - size 5e3000
  Name: Flash.ocx
MZ at 6c170000, prot 00000002, type 01000000 - size 57000
  Name: dxtmsft.dll
MZ at 6c230000, prot 00000002, type 01000000 - size b4000
  Name: JSCRIPT.dll
MZ at 6c460000, prot 00000002, type 01000000 - size cc000
  Name: d3dim700.dll
MZ at 6c640000, prot 00000002, type 01000000 - size 6a000
  Name: VBSCRIPT.dll
MZ at 6c6e0000, prot 00000002, type 01000000 - size 39000
  Name: dxtrans.dll
MZ at 6c830000, prot 00000002, type 01000000 - size 5b0000
  Name: MSHTML.dll
MZ at 6cde0000, prot 00000002, type 01000000 - size a000
  Name: DDRAWEX.DLL
MZ at 6cdf0000, prot 00000002, type 01000000 - size e000
  Name: PNGFILTER.DLL
MZ at 6cfe0000, prot 00000002, type 01000000 - size 29000
  Name: msls31.dll
MZ at 6d230000, prot 00000002, type 01000000 - size b000
  Name: msimtf.dll
MZ at 6d260000, prot 00000002, type 01000000 - size c000
  Name: ImgUtil.dll
MZ at 6d440000, prot 00000002, type 01000000 - size c000
  Name: jp2ssv.dll
MZ at 6dbb0000, prot 00000002, type 01000000 - size 30000
  Name: MLANG.dll
MZ at 6df80000, prot 00000002, type 01000000 - size 1b000
```

```
  Name: CRYPTNET.dll
MZ at 6ec60000, prot 00000002, type 01000000 - size 4a000
  Name: RASAPI32.dll
MZ at 6f040000, prot 00000002, type 01000000 - size 31000
  Name: TAPI32.dll
MZ at 6f0c0000, prot 00000002, type 01000000 - size 136000
  Name: MSXML3.dll
MZ at 6f310000, prot 00000002, type 01000000 - size 6000
  Name: SensApi.dll
MZ at 6f350000, prot 00000002, type 01000000 - size 14000
  Name: rasman.dll
MZ at 6f3b0000, prot 00000002, type 01000000 - size c000
  Name: rtutils.dll
MZ at 6f5a0000, prot 00000002, type 01000000 - size 6000
  Name: rasadhlp.dll
MZ at 6f620000, prot 00000002, type 01000000 - size 70000
  Name: DSOUND.dll
MZ at 6fa10000, prot 00000002, type 01000000 - size 12000
  Name: PNRPNSP.dll
MZ at 6fd00000, prot 00000002, type 01000000 - size 9b000
  Name: MSVCR80.dll
MZ at 6fec0000, prot 00000002, type 01000000 - size e5000
  Name: DDRAW.dll
MZ at 700c0000, prot 00000002, type 01000000 - size a94000
  Name: IEFRAME.dll
MZ at 712a0000, prot 00000002, type 01000000 - size 8000
  Name: WINRNR.dll
MZ at 71300000, prot 00000002, type 01000000 - size 62000
  Name: mscms.dll
MZ at 71390000, prot 00000002, type 01000000 - size 42000
  Name: WINSPOOL.DRV
MZ at 718f0000, prot 00000002, type 01000000 - size 53000
  Name: SWEEPRX.dll
MZ at 72130000, prot 00000002, type 01000000 - size 6000
  Name: DCIMAN32.dll
MZ at 721a0000, prot 00000002, type 01000000 - size 1f000
  Name: EhStorAPI.DLL
MZ at 725d0000, prot 00000002, type 01000000 - size 96000
  Name: fwpuclnt.dll
MZ at 72a30000, prot 00000002, type 01000000 - size c000
  Name: dwmapi.dll
MZ at 73090000, prot 00000002, type 01000000 - size 60000
  Name: tiptsf.dll
MZ at 73100000, prot 00000002, type 01000000 - size 4c000
  Name: Wpc.DLL
MZ at 73150000, prot 00000002, type 01000000 - size 12000
  Name: mp3acm.dll
MZ at 73240000, prot 00000002, type 01000000 - size 4a000
  Name: mscoree.dll
MZ at 73330000, prot 00000002, type 01000000 - size 8000
  Name: MSADP32.dll
MZ at 734e0000, prot 00000002, type 01000000 - size 33000
  Name: IEShims.dll
MZ at 73520000, prot 00000002, type 01000000 - size 9000
  Name: MSGSM32.dll
MZ at 73540000, prot 00000002, type 01000000 - size 8000
  Name: DispEx.dll
MZ at 73600000, prot 00000002, type 01000000 - size 40000
  Name: SWEEPRX.dll
MZ at 73650000, prot 00000002, type 01000000 - size 7000
```

```
  Name: MIDIMAP.dll
MZ at 73660000, prot 00000002, type 01000000 - size 66000
  Name: audioeng.dll
MZ at 736d0000, prot 00000002, type 01000000 - size 21000
  Name: AudioSes.DLL
MZ at 73700000, prot 00000002, type 01000000 - size f4000
  Name: WindowsCodecs.dll
MZ at 73800000, prot 00000002, type 01000000 - size 2f000
  Name: WINMMDRV.dll
MZ at 73880000, prot 00000002, type 01000000 - size 14000
  Name: MSACM32.dll
MZ at 738a0000, prot 00000002, type 01000000 - size 3d000
  Name: OLEACC.dll
MZ at 738e0000, prot 00000002, type 01000000 - size 32000
  Name: WINMM.dll
MZ at 73a10000, prot 00000002, type 01000000 - size bb000
  Name: PROPSYS.dll
MZ at 73b40000, prot 00000002, type 01000000 - size c000
  Name: wshbth.dll
MZ at 73b60000, prot 00000002, type 01000000 - size f000
  Name: NAPINSP.dll
MZ at 73b70000, prot 00000002, type 01000000 - size 8000
  Name: IMAADP32.dll
MZ at 73b90000, prot 00000002, type 01000000 - size 7000
  Name: MSG711.dll
MZ at 73ba0000, prot 00000002, type 01000000 - size 2f000
  Name: iepeers.DLL
MZ at 73cb0000, prot 00000002, type 01000000 - size 9000
  Name: MSACM32.DRV
MZ at 73d50000, prot 00000002, type 01000000 - size 1ab000
  Name: gdiplus.dll
MZ at 73f00000, prot 00000002, type 01000000 - size 4000
  Name: ksuser.dll
MZ at 743a0000, prot 00000002, type 01000000 - size 19e000
  Name: COMCTL32.dll
MZ at 74550000, prot 00000002, type 01000000 - size 2f000
  Name: XmlLite.dll
MZ at 74580000, prot 00000002, type 01000000 - size 14000
  Name: ATL.DLL
MZ at 74610000, prot 00000002, type 01000000 - size f000
  Name: nlaapi.dll
MZ at 74620000, prot 00000002, type 01000000 - size 15000
  Name: Cabinet.dll
MZ at 74640000, prot 00000002, type 01000000 - size 28000
  Name: MMDevAPI.DLL
MZ at 746a0000, prot 00000002, type 01000000 - size 3f000
  Name: UxTheme.dll
MZ at 747a0000, prot 00000002, type 01000000 - size 2d000
  Name: WINTRUST.dll
MZ at 74860000, prot 00000002, type 01000000 - size a000
  Name: WTSAPI32.dll
MZ at 74870000, prot 00000002, type 01000000 - size 7000
  Name: AVRT.dll
MZ at 74930000, prot 00000002, type 01000000 - size 5000
  Name: WSHTCPIP.dll
MZ at 74940000, prot 00000002, type 01000000 - size 5000
  Name: MSIMG32.dll
MZ at 74950000, prot 00000002, type 01000000 - size 1a000
  Name: POWRPROF.dll
MZ at 74970000, prot 00000002, type 01000000 - size 21000
```

```
  Name: NTMARTA.dll
MZ at 749d0000, prot 00000002, type 01000000 - size 15000
  Name: GPAPI.dll
MZ at 749f0000, prot 00000002, type 01000000 - size 3b000
  Name: RSAENH.dll
MZ at 74a60000, prot 00000002, type 01000000 - size 46000
  Name: SCHANNEL.dll
MZ at 74c70000, prot 00000002, type 01000000 - size 3b000
  Name: MSWSOCK.dll
MZ at 74cd0000, prot 00000002, type 01000000 - size 5000
  Name: WSHIP6.dll
MZ at 74ce0000, prot 00000002, type 01000000 - size 8000
  Name: VERSION.dll
MZ at 74db0000, prot 00000002, type 01000000 - size 45000
  Name: bcrypt.dll
MZ at 74e00000, prot 00000002, type 01000000 - size 7000
  Name: CREDSSP.dll
MZ at 74e10000, prot 00000002, type 01000000 - size 35000
  Name: ncrypt.dll
MZ at 74e60000, prot 00000002, type 01000000 - size 22000
  Name: dhcpcsvc6.DLL
MZ at 74e90000, prot 00000002, type 01000000 - size 7000
  Name: WINNSI.DLL
MZ at 74ea0000, prot 00000002, type 01000000 - size 35000
  Name: dhcpcsvc.DLL
MZ at 74ee0000, prot 00000002, type 01000000 - size 19000
  Name: IPHLPAPI.DLL
MZ at 74f00000, prot 00000002, type 01000000 - size 40000
  Name: wevtapi.dll
MZ at 74f40000, prot 00000002, type 01000000 - size 3a000
  Name: slc.dll
MZ at 74f80000, prot 00000002, type 01000000 - size f2000
  Name: CRYPT32.dll
MZ at 750e0000, prot 00000002, type 01000000 - size 12000
  Name: MSASN1.dll
MZ at 75120000, prot 00000002, type 01000000 - size 11000
  Name: SAMLIB.dll
MZ at 75140000, prot 00000002, type 01000000 - size 76000
  Name: NETAPI32.dll
MZ at 751c0000, prot 00000002, type 01000000 - size 2c000
  Name: DNSAPI.dll
MZ at 75420000, prot 00000002, type 01000000 - size 5f000
  Name: sxs.dll
MZ at 75480000, prot 00000002, type 01000000 - size 2c000
  Name: apphelp.dll
MZ at 754e0000, prot 00000002, type 01000000 - size 14000
  Name: Secur32.dll
MZ at 75500000, prot 00000002, type 01000000 - size 1e000
  Name: USERENV.dll
MZ at 75640000, prot 00000002, type 01000000 - size 7000
  Name: PSAPI.DLL
MZ at 75650000, prot 00000002, type 01000000 - size 9d000
  Name: USER32.dll
MZ at 756f0000, prot 00000002, type 01000000 - size c8000
  Name: MSCTF.dll
MZ at 757c0000, prot 00000002, type 01000000 - size 59000
  Name: SHLWAPI.dll
MZ at 75820000, prot 00000002, type 01000000 - size b10000
  Name: SHELL32.dll
MZ at 76330000, prot 00000002, type 01000000 - size 1e8000
```

```
  Name: iertutil.dll
MZ at 76520000, prot 00000002, type 01000000 - size 2d000
  Name: WS2_32.dll
MZ at 76550000, prot 00000002, type 01000000 - size 73000
  Name: COMDLG32.dll
MZ at 765d0000, prot 00000002, type 01000000 - size aa000
  Name: msvcrt.dll
MZ at 76680000, prot 00000002, type 01000000 - size 7d000
  Name: USP10.dll
MZ at 76700000, prot 00000002, type 01000000 - size e6000
  Name: WININET.dll
MZ at 767f0000, prot 00000002, type 01000000 - size 84000
  Name: CLBCatQ.DLL
MZ at 76880000, prot 00000002, type 01000000 - size 29000
  Name: imagehlp.dll
MZ at 768b0000, prot 00000002, type 01000000 - size 18a000
  Name: SETUPAPI.dll
MZ at 76a40000, prot 00000002, type 01000000 - size 4b000
  Name: GDI32.dll
MZ at 76a90000, prot 00000002, type 01000000 - size c6000
  Name: ADVAPI32.dll
MZ at 76b60000, prot 00000002, type 01000000 - size c3000
  Name: RPCRT4.dll
MZ at 76c30000, prot 00000002, type 01000000 - size 8d000
  Name: OLEAUT32.dll
MZ at 76cc0000, prot 00000002, type 01000000 - size 49000
  Name: WLDAP32.dll
MZ at 76d10000, prot 00000002, type 01000000 - size 133000
  Name: urlmon.dll
MZ at 76e50000, prot 00000002, type 01000000 - size 145000
  Name: ole32.dll
MZ at 76fa0000, prot 00000002, type 01000000 - size 127000
  Name: ntdll.dll
MZ at 770d0000, prot 00000002, type 01000000 - size 6000
  Name: NSI.dll
MZ at 770e0000, prot 00000002, type 01000000 - size 9000
  Name: LPK.dll
MZ at 770f0000, prot 00000002, type 01000000 - size 1e000
  Name: IMM32.dll
MZ at 77110000, prot 00000002, type 01000000 - size dc000
  Name: KERNEL32.dll
MZ at 771f0000, prot 00000002, type 01000000 - size 3000
  Name: Normaliz.dll
MZ at 7c340000, prot 00000002, type 01000000 - size 56000
  Name: MSVCR71.dll
MZ at 7c3a0000, prot 00000002, type 01000000 - size 7b000
  Name: MSVCP71.dll
```

We see *screens_dll.dll* module with read/write protection attribute different from all other found modules:

```
0:012> !address 10000000


Usage:                  <unknown>
Base Address:           10000000
End Address:            10001000
Region Size:            00001000
State:                  00001000 MEM_COMMIT
Protect:                00000004 PAGE_READWRITE
Type:                   00020000 MEM_PRIVATE
Allocation Base:        10000000
Allocation Protect:     00000004 PAGE_READWRITE
```

We now check module headers for this DLL:

```
0:012> !dh 10000000

File Type: DLL
FILE HEADER VALUES
     14C machine (i386)
       4 number of sections
4C8FEE9E time date stamp Tue Sep 14 22:52:30 2010

       0 file pointer to symbol table
       0 number of symbols
      E0 size of optional header
    2102 characteristics
            Executable
            32 bit word machine
            DLL

OPTIONAL HEADER VALUES
     10B magic #
    9.00 linker version
     400 size of code
     800 size of initialized data
       0 size of uninitialized data
    12F3 address of entry point
    1000 base of code
         ----- new -----
10000000 image base
    1000 section alignment
     200 file alignment
       2 subsystem (Windows GUI)
    5.00 operating system version
    0.00 image version
    5.00 subsystem version
    5000 size of image
     400 size of headers
       0 checksum
00100000 size of stack reserve
00001000 size of stack commit
00100000 size of heap reserve
00001000 size of heap commit
     140  DLL characteristics
            Dynamic base
            NX compatible
```

```
    2330 [      50] address [size] of Export Directory
    20E0 [      78] address [size] of Import Directory
       0 [       0] address [size] of Resource Directory
       0 [       0] address [size] of Exception Directory
       0 [       0] address [size] of Security Directory
    4000 [      34] address [size] of Base Relocation Directory
    2060 [      1C] address [size] of Debug Directory
       0 [       0] address [size] of Description Directory
       0 [       0] address [size] of Special Directory
       0 [       0] address [size] of Thread Storage Directory
       0 [       0] address [size] of Load Configuration Directory
       0 [       0] address [size] of Bound Import Directory
    2000 [      58] address [size] of Import Address Table Directory
       0 [       0] address [size] of Delay Import Directory
       0 [       0] address [size] of COR20 Header Directory
       0 [       0] address [size] of Reserved Directory


SECTION HEADER #1
   .text name
10001000 virtual size
    1000 virtual address
     400 size of raw data
     400 file pointer to raw data
       0 file pointer to relocation table
       0 file pointer to line numbers
       0 number of relocations
       0 number of line numbers
60000020 flags
         Code
         (no align specified)
         Execute Read

SECTION HEADER #2
  .rdata name
10002000 virtual size
    2000 virtual address
     400 size of raw data
     800 file pointer to raw data
       0 file pointer to relocation table
       0 file pointer to line numbers
       0 number of relocations
       0 number of line numbers
40000040 flags
         Initialized Data
         (no align specified)
         Read Only


Debug Directories(1)
       Type       Size      Address  Pointer
       cv           46         2094      894    Format: RSDS, guid, 1,
C:\MyWork\screens_dll\Release\screens_dll.pdb

SECTION HEADER #3
   .data name
10003000 virtual size
    3000 virtual address
       0 size of raw data
       0 file pointer to raw data
```

```
       0 file pointer to relocation table
       0 file pointer to line numbers
       0 number of relocations
       0 number of line numbers
C0000040 flags
         Initialized Data
         (no align specified)
         Read Write

SECTION HEADER #4
  .reloc name
10004000 virtual size
    4000 virtual address
     200 size of raw data
     C00 file pointer to raw data
       0 file pointer to relocation table
       0 file pointer to line numbers
       0 number of relocations
       0 number of line numbers
42000040 flags
         Initialized Data
         Discardable
         (no align specified)
         Read Only
```

It looks like a normal DLL but its import address table reveals its purpose (**Namespace**) - screen capture:

```
0:012> dps 10000000+2000 L58/4
10002000  773b6101 gdi32!CreateCompatibleDC
10002004  773b93d6 gdi32!StretchBlt
10002008  773b7461 gdi32!CreateDIBSection
1000200c  773b62a0 gdi32!SelectObject
10002010  00000000
10002014  7627a411 kernel32!lstrcmpW
10002018  762740aa kernel32!VirtualFree
1000201c  7627ad55 kernel32!VirtualAlloc
10002020  00000000
10002024  77419ced user32!ReleaseDC
10002028  77413ba7 user32!NtUserGetWindowDC
1000202c  77420e21 user32!GetWindowRect
10002030  00000000
10002034  745975e9 GdiPlus!GdiplusStartup
10002038  745876dd GdiPlus!GdipSaveImageToStream
1000203c  745bdd38 GdiPlus!GdipGetImageEncodersSize
10002040  745871cf GdiPlus!GdipDisposeImage
10002044  74598591 GdiPlus!GdipCreateBitmapFromHBITMAP
10002048  745bdbae GdiPlus!GdipGetImageEncoders
1000204c  00000000
10002050  7613d51b ole32!CreateStreamOnHGlobal
10002054  00000000
```

We should also check for any patched module code in all modules to which we have matching file binary access:

```
0:012> !for_each_module "!chkimg -d @#ModuleName"

[...]

    77004dba-77004dbd  4 bytes - ntdll!ZwQueryDirectoryFile+6
      [ 00 03 fe 7f:e8 af 05 00 ]
    770051ba-770051bd  4 bytes - ntdll!ZwResumeThread+6 (+0x400)
      [ 00 03 fe 7f:d8 af 05 00 ]
8 errors : ntdll (77004dba-770051bd)

[...]
```

The two reported NTDLL addresses are suspicious as they do not belong to IE (**Out-of-Module Pointer**) and show "garbage":

```
0:012> u 77814dba
ntdll!ZwQueryDirectoryFile+0x6:
77814dba e8af0500ff      call    shell32!MetadataLayout::UpdateDesiredSize+0x218 (7681536e)
77814dbf 12c2            adc     al,dl
77814dc1 2c00            sub     al,0
77814dc3 90              nop
ntdll!NtQueryDirectoryObject:
77814dc4 b8db000000      mov     eax,0DBh
77814dc9 ba0003fe7f      mov     edx,offset SharedUserData!SystemCallStub (7ffe0300)
77814dce ff12            call    dword ptr [edx]
77814dd0 c21c00          ret     1Ch

0:012> u 7681536e
shell32!MetadataLayout::UpdateDesiredSize+0x218:
7681536e 46              inc     esi
7681536f 18894df80f82    sbb     byte ptr [ecx-7DF007B3h],cl
76815375 51              push    ecx
76815376 ff              ???
76815377 ff              ???
76815378 ff8b46288b55    dec     dword ptr [ebx+558B2846h]
7681537e 108d04988b08    adc     byte ptr [ebp+88B9804h],cl
76815384 014df0          add     dword ptr [ebp-10h],ecx

0:004> ub 77814dba
                 ^ Unable to find valid previous instruction for 'ub 77814dba'
```

Here we needed to check the beginning of the function because the patching may be done for the part of an instruction such as changing its address or offset:

```
0:012> u ntdll!ZwQueryDirectoryFile
ntdll!ZwQueryDirectoryFile:
77814db4 b8da000000      mov     eax,0DAh
77814db9 bae8af0500      mov     edx,5AFE8h
77814dbe ff12            call    dword ptr [edx]
77814dc0 c22c00          ret     2Ch
77814dc3 90              nop
ntdll!NtQueryDirectoryObject:
77814dc4 b8db000000      mov     eax,0DBh
77814dc9 ba0003fe7f      mov     edx,offset SharedUserData!SystemCallStub (7ffe0300)
77814dce ff12            call    dword ptr [edx]
```

Note that a pointer to an indirect call has changed. In the normal case we see this:

```
0:012> dps 7ffe0300 L1
7ffe0300  77815e70 ntdll!KiFastSystemCall
```

In the abnormal case we have execution diversion to already discovered malware module:

```
0:012> dps 5AFE8h L1
0005afe8  0004efe0

0:012> u 0004efe0
0004efe0 58                pop     eax
0004efe1 8d0510ec0400      lea     eax,ds:[4EC10h]
0004efe7 ffe0              jmp     eax
0004efe9 c3                ret
0004efea cc                int     3
0004efeb cc                int     3
0004efec cc                int     3
0004efed cc                int     3

0:012> u 4EC10h
0004ec10 55                push    ebp
0004ec11 8bec              mov     ebp,esp
0004ec13 83ec38            sub     esp,38h
0004ec16 0fb64530          movzx   eax,byte ptr [ebp+30h]
0004ec1a 50                push    eax
0004ec1b 8b4d2c            mov     ecx,dword ptr [ebp+2Ch]
0004ec1e 51                push    ecx
0004ec1f 0fb65528          movzx   edx,byte ptr [ebp+28h]

0:012> !address 4EC10h

Usage:                  <unknown>
Base Address:           00040000
End Address:            0005d000
Region Size:            0001d000
State:                  00001000 MEM_COMMIT
Protect:                00000040 PAGE_EXECUTE_READWRITE
Type:                   00020000 MEM_PRIVATE
Allocation Base:        00040000
Allocation Protect:     00000040 PAGE_EXECUTE_READWRITE
```

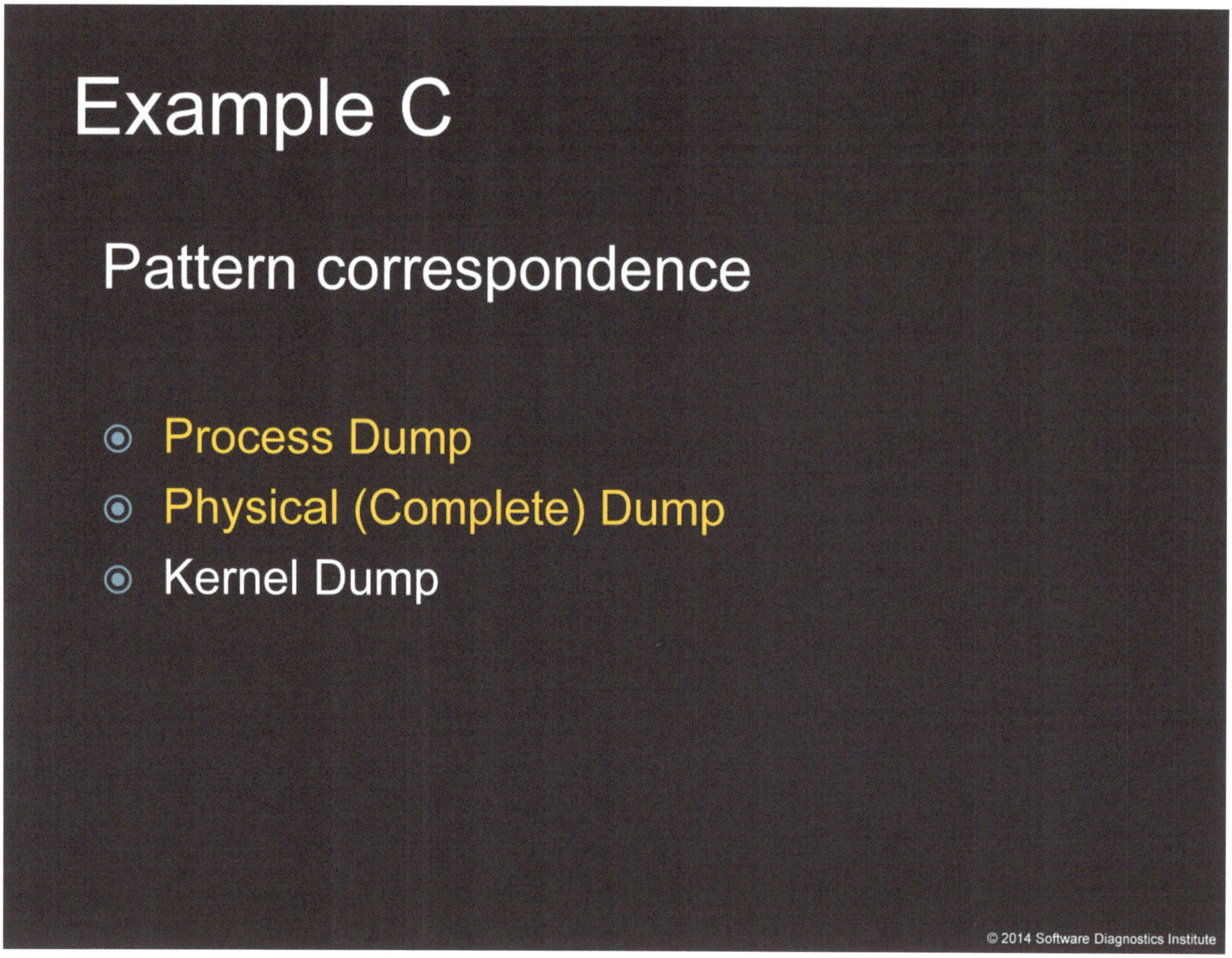

Many patterns from the two previous examples are applicable for complete memory dumps too. But we need to switch to the appropriate process context. Some patterns are applicable to kernel only memory dumps but will need different commands.

Imagine that instead of IE process memory dump a complete memory dump was generated. We could have been able to use the same commands to detect patterns. In this example we show how to find IE process to check similar information. The complete memory dump is taken from Advanced Windows Memory Dump Analysis training course.

We load a complete memory dump. It has lots of warnings due to the absence of symbols.

```
Microsoft (R) Windows Debugger Version 6.3.9600.16384 AMD64
Copyright (c) Microsoft Corporation. All rights reserved.


Loading Dump File [E:\AdvWMDA-Dumps\64-bit\Complete\MEMORY-Normal.DMP]
Kernel Complete Dump File: Full address space is available

Symbol search path is: *** Invalid ***
****************************************************************************
* Symbol loading may be unreliable without a symbol search path.           *
* Use .symfix to have the debugger choose a symbol path.                   *
* After setting your symbol path, use .reload to refresh symbol locations. *
****************************************************************************
Executable search path is:
*********************************************************************
* Symbols can not be loaded because symbol path is not initialized. *
*                                                                   *
* The Symbol Path can be set by:                                    *
*   using the _NT_SYMBOL_PATH environment variable.                 *
*   using the -y <symbol_path> argument when starting the debugger. *
*   using .sympath and .sympath+                                    *
*********************************************************************
*** ERROR: Symbol file could not be found.  Defaulted to export symbols for ntkrnlmp.exe -
Windows Vista Kernel Version 6000 MP (2 procs) Free x64
Product: WinNt, suite: TerminalServer SingleUserTS Personal
Built by: 6000.16386.amd64fre.vista_rtm.061101-2205
Machine Name:
Kernel base = 0xfffff800`01800000 PsLoadedModuleList = 0xfffff800`01999e90
Debug session time: Tue Jul 12 17:18:12.325 2011 (UTC + 1:00)
System Uptime: 0 days 0:11:03.409
*********************************************************************
* Symbols can not be loaded because symbol path is not initialized. *
*                                                                   *
* The Symbol Path can be set by:                                    *
*   using the _NT_SYMBOL_PATH environment variable.                 *
*   using the -y <symbol_path> argument when starting the debugger. *
*   using .sympath and .sympath+                                    *
*********************************************************************
*** ERROR: Symbol file could not be found.  Defaulted to export symbols for ntkrnlmp.exe -
Loading Kernel Symbols
...............................................................
................................................................
.........
Loading User Symbols
.................
Loading unloaded module list
.........*** ERROR: Symbol file could not be found.  Defaulted to export symbols for ntdll.dll
-
```

```
************* Symbol Loading Error Summary **************
Module name            Error
ntkrnlmp               The system cannot find the file specified
ntdll                  The system cannot find the file specified

You can troubleshoot most symbol related issues by turning on symbol loading diagnostics (!sym
noisy) and repeating the command that caused symbols to be loaded.
You should also verify that your symbol search path (.sympath) is correct.
*******************************************************************************
*                                                                             *
*                        Bugcheck Analysis                                    *
*                                                                             *
*******************************************************************************

Use !analyze -v to get detailed debugging information.

BugCheck D1, {fffff88002c04800, 2, 0, fffff9800e6e117a}

*** ERROR: Module load completed but symbols could not be loaded for myfault.sys
*** ERROR: Symbol file could not be found.  Defaulted to export symbols for kernel32.dll -
*** ERROR: Symbol file could not be found.  Defaulted to export symbols for USER32.dll -
***** Kernel symbols are WRONG. Please fix symbols to do analysis.

*************************************************************************
***                                                                   ***
***                                                                   ***
***    Either you specified an unqualified symbol, or your debugger   ***
***    doesn't have full symbol information.  Unqualified symbol      ***
***    resolution is turned off by default. Please either specify a   ***
***    fully qualified symbol module!symbolname, or enable resolution ***
***    of unqualified symbols by typing ".symopt- 100". Note that   ***
***    enabling unqualified symbol resolution with network symbol     ***
***    server shares in the symbol path may cause the debugger to     ***
***    appear to hang for long periods of time when an incorrect      ***
***    symbol name is typed or the network symbol server is down.     ***
***                                                                   ***
***    For some commands to work properly, your symbol path           ***
***    must point to .pdb files that have full type information.      ***
***                                                                   ***
***    Certain .pdb files (such as the public OS symbols) do not      ***
***    contain the required information.  Contact the group that      ***
***    provided you with these symbols if you need this command to    ***
***    work.                                                          ***
***                                                                   ***
***    Type referenced: nt!_KPRCB                                     ***
***                                                                   ***
*************************************************************************
*************************************************************************
***                                                                   ***
***                                                                   ***
***    Either you specified an unqualified symbol, or your debugger   ***
***    doesn't have full symbol information.  Unqualified symbol      ***
***    resolution is turned off by default. Please either specify a   ***
***    fully qualified symbol module!symbolname, or enable resolution ***
***    of unqualified symbols by typing ".symopt- 100". Note that   ***
***    enabling unqualified symbol resolution with network symbol     ***
***    server shares in the symbol path may cause the debugger to     ***
***    appear to hang for long periods of time when an incorrect      ***
***    symbol name is typed or the network symbol server is down.     ***
***                                                                   ***
```

```
***    For some commands to work properly, your symbol path           ***
***    must point to .pdb files that have full type information.      ***
***                                                                   ***
***    Certain .pdb files (such as the public OS symbols) do not      ***
***    contain the required information.  Contact the group that     ***
***    provided you with these symbols if you need this command to    ***
***    work.                                                          ***
***                                                                   ***
***    Type referenced: nt!KPRCB                                      ***
***                                                                   ***
*************************************************************************
*************************************************************************
***                                                                   ***
***                                                                   ***
***    Either you specified an unqualified symbol, or your debugger   ***
***    doesn't have full symbol information.  Unqualified symbol      ***
***    resolution is turned off by default. Please either specify a   ***
***    fully qualified symbol module!symbolname, or enable resolution ***
***    of unqualified symbols by typing ".symopt- 100". Note that   ***
***    enabling unqualified symbol resolution with network symbol     ***
***    server shares in the symbol path may cause the debugger to     ***
***    appear to hang for long periods of time when an incorrect      ***
***    symbol name is typed or the network symbol server is down.     ***
***                                                                   ***
***    For some commands to work properly, your symbol path           ***
***    must point to .pdb files that have full type information.      ***
***                                                                   ***
***    Certain .pdb files (such as the public OS symbols) do not      ***
***    contain the required information.  Contact the group that     ***
***    provided you with these symbols if you need this command to    ***
***    work.                                                          ***
***                                                                   ***
***    Type referenced: nt!_KPRCB                                     ***
***                                                                   ***
*************************************************************************
*************************************************************************
***                                                                   ***
***                                                                   ***
***    Either you specified an unqualified symbol, or your debugger   ***
***    doesn't have full symbol information.  Unqualified symbol      ***
***    resolution is turned off by default. Please either specify a   ***
***    fully qualified symbol module!symbolname, or enable resolution ***
***    of unqualified symbols by typing ".symopt- 100". Note that   ***
***    enabling unqualified symbol resolution with network symbol     ***
***    server shares in the symbol path may cause the debugger to     ***
***    appear to hang for long periods of time when an incorrect      ***
***    symbol name is typed or the network symbol server is down.     ***
***                                                                   ***
***    For some commands to work properly, your symbol path           ***
***    must point to .pdb files that have full type information.      ***
***                                                                   ***
***    Certain .pdb files (such as the public OS symbols) do not      ***
***    contain the required information.  Contact the group that     ***
***    provided you with these symbols if you need this command to    ***
***    work.                                                          ***
***                                                                   ***
***    Type referenced: nt!KPRCB                                      ***
***                                                                   ***
*************************************************************************
*************************************************************************
```

```
***                                                                     ***
***                                                                     ***
***    Either you specified an unqualified symbol, or your debugger     ***
***    doesn't have full symbol information.  Unqualified symbol        ***
***    resolution is turned off by default. Please either specify a    ***
***    fully qualified symbol module!symbolname, or enable resolution   ***
***    of unqualified symbols by typing ".symopt- 100". Note that      ***
***    enabling unqualified symbol resolution with network symbol       ***
***    server shares in the symbol path may cause the debugger to       ***
***    appear to hang for long periods of time when an incorrect        ***
***    symbol name is typed or the network symbol server is down.       ***
***                                                                     ***
***    For some commands to work properly, your symbol path             ***
***    must point to .pdb files that have full type information.        ***
***                                                                     ***
***    Certain .pdb files (such as the public OS symbols) do not        ***
***    contain the required information.  Contact the group that        ***
***    provided you with these symbols if you need this command to      ***
***    work.                                                            ***
***                                                                     ***
***    Type referenced: nt!_KPRCB                                       ***
***                                                                     ***
***************************************************************************
***************************************************************************
***                                                                     ***
***                                                                     ***
***    Either you specified an unqualified symbol, or your debugger     ***
***    doesn't have full symbol information.  Unqualified symbol        ***
***    resolution is turned off by default. Please either specify a    ***
***    fully qualified symbol module!symbolname, or enable resolution   ***
***    of unqualified symbols by typing ".symopt- 100". Note that      ***
***    enabling unqualified symbol resolution with network symbol       ***
***    server shares in the symbol path may cause the debugger to       ***
***    appear to hang for long periods of time when an incorrect        ***
***    symbol name is typed or the network symbol server is down.       ***
***                                                                     ***
***    For some commands to work properly, your symbol path             ***
***    must point to .pdb files that have full type information.        ***
***                                                                     ***
***    Certain .pdb files (such as the public OS symbols) do not        ***
***    contain the required information.  Contact the group that        ***
***    provided you with these symbols if you need this command to      ***
***    work.                                                            ***
***                                                                     ***
***    Type referenced: nt!_KPRCB                                       ***
***                                                                     ***
***************************************************************************
***************************************************************************
***                                                                     ***
***                                                                     ***
***    Either you specified an unqualified symbol, or your debugger     ***
***    doesn't have full symbol information.  Unqualified symbol        ***
***    resolution is turned off by default. Please either specify a    ***
***    fully qualified symbol module!symbolname, or enable resolution   ***
***    of unqualified symbols by typing ".symopt- 100". Note that      ***
***    enabling unqualified symbol resolution with network symbol       ***
***    server shares in the symbol path may cause the debugger to       ***
***    appear to hang for long periods of time when an incorrect        ***
***    symbol name is typed or the network symbol server is down.       ***
***                                                                     ***
```

```
***     For some commands to work properly, your symbol path            ***
***     must point to .pdb files that have full type information.       ***
***                                                                     ***
***     Certain .pdb files (such as the public OS symbols) do not       ***
***     contain the required information.  Contact the group that      ***
***     provided you with these symbols if you need this command to     ***
***     work.                                                           ***
***                                                                     ***
***     Type referenced: nt!_KPRCB                                      ***
***                                                                     ***
***************************************************************************
***************************************************************************
***                                                                     ***
***                                                                     ***
***     Either you specified an unqualified symbol, or your debugger    ***
***     doesn't have full symbol information.  Unqualified symbol       ***
***     resolution is turned off by default. Please either specify a    ***
***     fully qualified symbol module!symbolname, or enable resolution ***
***     of unqualified symbols by typing ".symopt- 100". Note that   ***
***     enabling unqualified symbol resolution with network symbol      ***
***     server shares in the symbol path may cause the debugger to      ***
***     appear to hang for long periods of time when an incorrect       ***
***     symbol name is typed or the network symbol server is down.      ***
***                                                                     ***
***     For some commands to work properly, your symbol path            ***
***     must point to .pdb files that have full type information.       ***
***                                                                     ***
***     Certain .pdb files (such as the public OS symbols) do not       ***
***     contain the required information.  Contact the group that      ***
***     provided you with these symbols if you need this command to     ***
***     work.                                                           ***
***                                                                     ***
***     Type referenced: nt!_KPRCB                                      ***
***                                                                     ***
***************************************************************************
Probably caused by : myfault.sys ( myfault+117a )

Followup: MachineOwner
---------
```

We fix symbols:

```
1: kd> .symfix c:\mss

1: kd> .reload
Loading Kernel Symbols
...............................................................
................................................................
.........
Loading User Symbols
.................
Loading unloaded module list
.........Unable to enumerate user-mode unloaded modules, NTSTATUS 0xC0000147
```

We check running processes and find IE process:

```
1: kd> !process 0 0
**** NT ACTIVE PROCESS DUMP ****
PROCESS fffffa8000c360b0
    SessionId: none  Cid: 0004    Peb: 00000000  ParentCid: 0000
    DirBase: 00124000  ObjectTable: fffff88000002010  HandleCount: 357.
    Image: System

PROCESS fffffa8002366c10
    SessionId: none  Cid: 0160    Peb: 7fffffdf000  ParentCid: 0004
    DirBase: 2e85c000  ObjectTable: fffff880001310a0  HandleCount:  28.
    Image: smss.exe

PROCESS fffffa80023cba80
    SessionId: 0  Cid: 01a4    Peb: 7fffffd6000  ParentCid: 0198
    DirBase: 263d2000  ObjectTable: fffff880014e74e0  HandleCount: 527.
    Image: csrss.exe

PROCESS fffffa800244dc10
    SessionId: 0  Cid: 01c8    Peb: 7fffffde000  ParentCid: 0198
    DirBase: 25159000  ObjectTable: fffff880015989a0  HandleCount:  99.
    Image: wininit.exe

PROCESS fffffa8002453c10
    SessionId: 1  Cid: 01dc    Peb: 7fffffde000  ParentCid: 01d4
    DirBase: 24c71000  ObjectTable: fffff8800159b610  HandleCount: 356.
    Image: csrss.exe

PROCESS fffffa800245fc10
    SessionId: 1  Cid: 020c    Peb: 7fffffd5000  ParentCid: 01d4
    DirBase: 23778000  ObjectTable: fffff880015acd10  HandleCount: 128.
    Image: winlogon.exe

PROCESS fffffa80024ad920
    SessionId: 0  Cid: 022c    Peb: 7fffffd3000  ParentCid: 01c8
    DirBase: 22d5f000  ObjectTable: fffff880015fc6b0  HandleCount: 232.
    Image: services.exe

PROCESS fffffa80024d7c10
    SessionId: 0  Cid: 0248    Peb: 7fffffdd000  ParentCid: 01c8
    DirBase: 2289e000  ObjectTable: fffff8800162b390  HandleCount: 612.
    Image: lsass.exe

PROCESS fffffa80024dbc10
    SessionId: 0  Cid: 0250    Peb: 7fffffdc000  ParentCid: 01c8
    DirBase: 22a26000  ObjectTable: fffff8800162afa0  HandleCount: 158.
    Image: lsm.exe

PROCESS fffffa800349e9d0
    SessionId: 0  Cid: 02d8    Peb: 7fffffd3000  ParentCid: 022c
    DirBase: 18703000  ObjectTable: fffff880008edae0  HandleCount: 311.
    Image: svchost.exe

PROCESS fffffa800209f880
    SessionId: 0  Cid: 0310    Peb: 7fffffd3000  ParentCid: 022c
    DirBase: 17293000  ObjectTable: fffff88001693ad0  HandleCount: 297.
    Image: svchost.exe
```

```
PROCESS fffffa8002090c10
    SessionId: 0  Cid: 0330    Peb: 7fffffd6000  ParentCid: 022c
    DirBase: 156c1000  ObjectTable: fffff880017d8c00  HandleCount: 320.
    Image: svchost.exe

PROCESS fffffa8002f10970
    SessionId: 0  Cid: 0398    Peb: 7fffffd5000  ParentCid: 022c
    DirBase: 12eed000  ObjectTable: fffff880016c5c80  HandleCount: 394.
    Image: svchost.exe

PROCESS fffffa80031c54f0
    SessionId: 0  Cid: 03b4    Peb: 7fffffd7000  ParentCid: 022c
    DirBase: 116b3000  ObjectTable: fffff88001885580  HandleCount: 386.
    Image: svchost.exe

PROCESS fffffa8003325540
    SessionId: 0  Cid: 03c8    Peb: 7fffffd7000  ParentCid: 022c
    DirBase: 10e79000  ObjectTable: fffff880018b26e0  HandleCount: 1091.
    Image: svchost.exe

PROCESS fffffa800335f040
    SessionId: 0  Cid: 016c    Peb: 7fffffda000  ParentCid: 0398
    DirBase: 0d691000  ObjectTable: fffff8800167f590  HandleCount: 113.
    Image: audiodg.exe

PROCESS fffffa80033902b0
    SessionId: 0  Cid: 0180    Peb: 7fffffdc000  ParentCid: 022c
    DirBase: 0b916000  ObjectTable: fffff8800188c920  HandleCount:  70.
    Image: SLsvc.exe

PROCESS fffffa8003424ae0
    SessionId: 0  Cid: 0374    Peb: 7fffffda000  ParentCid: 022c
    DirBase: 0a6ec000  ObjectTable: fffff8800191b900  HandleCount: 554.
    Image: svchost.exe

PROCESS fffffa8003475840
    SessionId: 0  Cid: 0428    Peb: 7fffffda000  ParentCid: 022c
    DirBase: 078b8000  ObjectTable: fffff88001973f00  HandleCount: 477.
    Image: svchost.exe

PROCESS fffffa80035db8e0
    SessionId: 0  Cid: 04d0    Peb: 7fffffdf000  ParentCid: 022c
    DirBase: 07e87000  ObjectTable: fffff88001986cb0  HandleCount: 329.
    Image: spoolsv.exe

PROCESS fffffa80035edae0
    SessionId: 0  Cid: 04ec    Peb: 7fffffd5000  ParentCid: 022c
    DirBase: 07515000  ObjectTable: fffff88001978ee0  HandleCount: 283.
    Image: svchost.exe

PROCESS fffffa80038ee9b0
    SessionId: 0  Cid: 0620    Peb: 7fffffd7000  ParentCid: 022c
    DirBase: 05763000  ObjectTable: fffff88001a6a870  HandleCount: 107.
    Image: svchost.exe

PROCESS fffffa800392c2e0
    SessionId: 0  Cid: 0640    Peb: 7fffffd5000  ParentCid: 022c
    DirBase: 049aa000  ObjectTable: fffff880009bad80  HandleCount: 242.
    Image: vmtoolsd.exe
```

```
PROCESS fffffa80039a2940
    SessionId: 1  Cid: 0728    Peb: 7fffffd8000  ParentCid: 03b4
    DirBase: 27e56000  ObjectTable: fffff88001b53c40  HandleCount:  92.
    Image: dwm.exe

PROCESS fffffa80039bac10
    SessionId: 1  Cid: 0734    Peb: 7fffffde000  ParentCid: 0720
    DirBase: 2d6c9000  ObjectTable: fffff8800180cec0  HandleCount: 824.
    Image: explorer.exe

PROCESS fffffa80039f5040
    SessionId: 0  Cid: 076c    Peb: 7fffffdf000  ParentCid: 022c
    DirBase: 282cb000  ObjectTable: fffff88001a3b110  HandleCount:  88.
    Image: svchost.exe

PROCESS fffffa80039fd040
    SessionId: 0  Cid: 0780    Peb: 7fffffdd000  ParentCid: 022c
    DirBase: 26e92000  ObjectTable: fffff88001a35dd0  HandleCount: 703.
    Image: SearchIndexer.exe

PROCESS fffffa8003bac760
    SessionId: 0  Cid: 07cc    Peb: 7fffffde000  ParentCid: 022c
    DirBase: 278c7000  ObjectTable: fffff88001bc9fa0  HandleCount:  90.
    Image: VMUpgradeHelper.exe

PROCESS fffffa8003b500a0
    SessionId: 1  Cid: 061c    Peb: 7fffffdf000  ParentCid: 03c8
    DirBase: 0f1ea000  ObjectTable: fffff880018296c0  HandleCount: 302.
    Image: taskeng.exe

PROCESS fffffa8003b9ac10
    SessionId: 0  Cid: 0710    Peb: 7fffffdb000  ParentCid: 022c
    DirBase: 1a50e000  ObjectTable: fffff88001c370b0  HandleCount: 127.
    Image: TPAutoConnSvc.exe

PROCESS fffffa80039f1c10
    SessionId: 0  Cid: 01d8    Peb: 7fffffd9000  ParentCid: 03c8
    DirBase: 20a3c000  ObjectTable: fffff88001cc0710  HandleCount:  84.
    Image: taskeng.exe

PROCESS fffffa8004039040
    SessionId: 1  Cid: 08f4    Peb: 7fffffdb000  ParentCid: 0710
    DirBase: 193d7000  ObjectTable: fffff88001b6e4d0  HandleCount: 125.
    Image: TPAutoConnect.exe

PROCESS fffffa80040a3410
    SessionId: 0  Cid: 093c    Peb: 7fffffdb000  ParentCid: 022c
    DirBase: 16561000  ObjectTable: fffff88001e495d0  HandleCount: 245.
    Image: dllhost.exe

PROCESS fffffa80040fba50
    SessionId: 1  Cid: 09f4    Peb: 7fffffde000  ParentCid: 0734
    DirBase: 0b54f000  ObjectTable: fffff88001ec95c0  HandleCount: 382.
    Image: MSASCui.exe

PROCESS fffffa80040cc280
    SessionId: 1  Cid: 0a00    Peb: 7fffffd3000  ParentCid: 0734
    DirBase: 06bda000  ObjectTable: fffff88001a93920  HandleCount:  67.
    Image: VMwareTray.exe
```

```
PROCESS fffffa80020a1c10
    SessionId: 1  Cid: 0a08    Peb: 7fffffdf000  ParentCid: 0734
    DirBase: 0c19f000  ObjectTable: fffff88001ee97b0  HandleCount: 208.
    Image: VMwareUser.exe

PROCESS fffffa8003994990
    SessionId: 1  Cid: 0a1c    Peb: 7fffffde000  ParentCid: 0734
    DirBase: 1d9ec000  ObjectTable: fffff88001e5f4f0  HandleCount: 428.
    Image: sidebar.exe

PROCESS fffffa80040e1ae0
    SessionId: 0  Cid: 0a2c    Peb: 7fffffd5000  ParentCid: 022c
    DirBase: 1d37b000  ObjectTable: fffff88001814f00  HandleCount: 162.
    Image: msdtc.exe

PROCESS fffffa8001361040
    SessionId: 0  Cid: 09ec    Peb: 7fffffde000  ParentCid: 02d8
    DirBase: 37fa4000  ObjectTable: fffff880018e70b0  HandleCount: 108.
    Image: WmiPrvSE.exe

PROCESS fffffa8001519040
    SessionId: 0  Cid: 08e8    Peb: 7fffffd7000  ParentCid: 02d8
    DirBase: 137c1000  ObjectTable: fffff88002e788d0  HandleCount: 162.
    Image: WmiPrvSE.exe

PROCESS fffffa80014f0040
    SessionId: 1  Cid: 0370    Peb: 7efdf000  ParentCid: 05f0
    DirBase: 1b3d8000  ObjectTable: fffff88001689350  HandleCount: 238.
    Image: ieuser.exe

PROCESS fffffa80040d2040
    SessionId: 1  Cid: 05b0    Peb: 7efdf000  ParentCid: 05f0
    DirBase: 03d42000  ObjectTable: fffff88002740010  HandleCount: 336.
    Image: iexplore.exe

PROCESS fffffa8001571040
    SessionId: 0  Cid: 0590    Peb: 7fffffd4000  ParentCid: 0780
    DirBase: 316ee000  ObjectTable: fffff88002d819f0  HandleCount: 246.
    Image: SearchProtocolHost.exe

PROCESS fffffa80014ce2f0
    SessionId: 0  Cid: 071c    Peb: 7fffffd7000  ParentCid: 0780
    DirBase: 23ab9000  ObjectTable: fffff88002c220b0  HandleCount:  90.
    Image: SearchFilterHost.exe

PROCESS fffffa8001579040
    SessionId: 1  Cid: 0948    Peb: 7fffffde000  ParentCid: 0734
    DirBase: 2863d000  ObjectTable: fffff880017bc580  HandleCount:  48.
    Image: notepad.exe

PROCESS fffffa800159fb40
    SessionId: 1  Cid: 07c8    Peb: 7fffffd7000  ParentCid: 02d8
    DirBase: 3228c000  ObjectTable: fffff8800259fda0  HandleCount:  83.
    Image: dllhost.exe

PROCESS fffffa8001579c10
    SessionId: 0  Cid: 08c8    Peb: 7fffffd9000  ParentCid: 02d8
    DirBase: 1ef31000  ObjectTable: fffff88002702900  HandleCount:  79.
    Image: dllhost.exe
```

```
PROCESS fffffa8001412040
    SessionId: 1  Cid: 03bc    Peb: 7fffffd4000  ParentCid: 0734
    DirBase: 16e27000  ObjectTable: fffff8800327b5e0  HandleCount:  49.
    Image: NotMyfault.exe
```

We check IE process **Stack Trace Collection** (we use 3f flags to have the process context, the correct physical to virtual translation, established during execution of **!process** command and at the same time to load the needed symbol files for user space module address ranges):

```
1: kd> !process fffffa80040d2040 3f
PROCESS fffffa80040d2040
    SessionId: 1  Cid: 05b0    Peb: 7efdf000  ParentCid: 05f0
    DirBase: 03d42000  ObjectTable: fffff88002740010  HandleCount: 336.
    Image: iexplore.exe
    VadRoot fffffa80013f4970 Vads 275 Clone 0 Private 1536. Modified 56. Locked 0.
    DeviceMap fffff88001697690
    Token                             fffff88002dd0a70
    ElapsedTime                       00:00:28.052
    UserTime                          00:00:00.156
    KernelTime                        00:00:00.265
    QuotaPoolUsage[PagedPool]         205248
    QuotaPoolUsage[NonPagedPool]      28032
    Working Set Sizes (now,min,max)  (5635, 50, 345) (22540KB, 200KB, 1380KB)
    PeakWorkingSetSize                5694
    VirtualSize                       113 Mb
    PeakVirtualSize                   128 Mb
    PageFaultCount                    6778
    MemoryPriority                    BACKGROUND
    BasePriority                      8
    CommitCharge                      3462

    PEB at 000000007efdf000
    InheritedAddressSpace:    No
    ReadImageFileExecOptions: No
    BeingDebugged:            No
    ImageBaseAddress:         0000000000e00000
    Ldr                       00000000777af980
    Ldr.Initialized:          Yes
    Ldr.InInitializationOrderModuleList: 00000000000826e0 . 0000000000082a40
    Ldr.InLoadOrderModuleList:           00000000000825f0 . 0000000000082ba0
    Ldr.InMemoryOrderModuleList:         0000000000082600 . 0000000000082bb0
            Base TimeStamp                     Module
          e00000 4549b133 Nov 02 08:49:55 2006 C:\Program Files (x86)\Internet Explorer\iexplore.exe
        776a0000 4549d372 Nov 02 11:16:02 2006 C:\Windows\system32\ntdll.dll
        74fb0000 4549d371 Nov 02 11:16:01 2006 C:\Windows\system32\wow64.dll
        75580000 4549d374 Nov 02 11:16:04 2006 C:\Windows\system32\wow64win.dll
        759e0000 4549d372 Nov 02 11:16:02 2006 C:\Windows\system32\wow64cpu.dll
    SubSystemData:     0000000000000000
    ProcessHeap:       0000000000080000
    ProcessParameters: 0000000000081d00
    CurrentDirectory:  'C:\Windows\system32\'
    WindowTitle:  'C:\Program Files (x86)\Internet Explorer\iexplore.exe'
    ImageFile:    'C:\Program Files (x86)\Internet Explorer\iexplore.exe'
    CommandLine:  '"C:\Program Files (x86)\Internet Explorer\iexplore.exe" '
    DllPath:      'C:\Program Files (x86)\Internet
Explorer;C:\Windows\system32;C:\Windows\system;C:\Windows;.;C:\Program Files\Internet
Explorer;;C:\Windows\system32;C:\Windows;C:\Windows\System32\Wbem'
    Environment:  0000000000081310
        =::=::\
        ALLUSERSPROFILE=C:\ProgramData
        APPDATA=C:\Users\Training\AppData\Roaming
        CommonProgramFiles=C:\Program Files\Common Files
        CommonProgramFiles(x86)=C:\Program Files (x86)\Common Files
        COMPUTERNAME=LH-UZIYU07F029O
        ComSpec=C:\Windows\system32\cmd.exe
        FP_NO_HOST_CHECK=NO
        HKCU_S=\REGISTRY\CUSER\Software
        HKLM_S=\REGISTRY\MACHINE\Software
        HOMEDRIVE=C:
        HOMEPATH=\Users\Training
        LOCALAPPDATA=C:\Users\Training\AppData\Local
        LOGONSERVER=\\LH-UZIYU07F029O
```

```
        NUMBER_OF_PROCESSORS=2
        OS=Windows_NT
        Path=C:\Program Files\Internet Explorer;;C:\Windows\system32;C:\Windows;C:\Windows\System32\Wbem
        PATHEXT=.COM;.EXE;.BAT;.CMD;.VBS;.VBE;.JS;.JSE;.WSF;.WSH;.MSC
        PROCESSOR_ARCHITECTURE=AMD64
        PROCESSOR_IDENTIFIER=EM64T Family 6 Model 15 Stepping 11, GenuineIntel
        PROCESSOR_LEVEL=6
        PROCESSOR_REVISION=0f0b
        ProgramData=C:\ProgramData
        ProgramFiles=C:\Program Files
        ProgramFiles(x86)=C:\Program Files (x86)
        PUBLIC=C:\Users\Public
        SESSIONNAME=Console
        SystemDrive=C:
        SystemRoot=C:\Windows
        TEMP=C:\Users\Training\AppData\Local\Temp
        TMP=C:\Users\Training\AppData\Local\Temp
        USERDOMAIN=LH-UZIYU07F029O
        USERNAME=Training
        USERPROFILE=C:\Users\Training
        windir=C:\Windows


        THREAD fffffa800141dbb0  Cid 05b0.0890  Teb: 000000007efdb000 Win32Thread: fffff900c228d1d0 WAIT:
(UserRequest) UserMode Non-Alertable
            fffffa80040d2490  SynchronizationEvent
            fffffa800121c180  SynchronizationEvent
        Not impersonating
        DeviceMap                 fffff88001697690
        Owning Process            fffffa80040d2040       Image:         iexplore.exe
        Attached Process          N/A            Image:         N/A
        Wait Start TickCount      41157          Ticks: 1301 (0:00:00:20.328)
        Context Switch Count      2106           IdealProcessor: 1                 LargeStack
        UserTime                  00:00:00.359
        KernelTime                00:00:01.375
        Win32 Start Address iexplore!wWinMainCRTStartup (0x0000000000e02d61)
        Stack Init fffff9800db54db0 Current fffff9800db54260
        Base fffff9800db55000 Limit fffff9800db4a000 Call 0
        Priority 10 BasePriority 8 PriorityDecrement 0 IoPriority 2 PagePriority 5
*** ERROR: Module load completed but symbols could not be loaded for myfault.sys
        Child-SP          RetAddr           Call Site
        fffff980`0db542a0 fffff800`0185d695 nt!KiSwapContext+0x84
        fffff980`0db543e0 fffff800`0185ad2f nt!KiSwapThread+0x125
        fffff980`0db54440 fffff800`01ac1813 nt!KeWaitForMultipleObjects+0x703
        fffff980`0db544b0 fffff800`01ba477a nt!ObpWaitForMultipleObjects+0x216
        fffff980`0db54960 fffff800`0184dcf3 nt!NtWaitForMultipleObjects32+0xd9
        fffff980`0db54bb0 00000000`759e373f nt!KiSystemServiceCopyEnd+0x13 (TrapFrame @ fffff980`0db54c20)
        00000000`0022ea18 00000000`74fbabfe wow64cpu!WaitForMultipleObjects32+0x3a
        00000000`0022eac0 00000000`74fba202 wow64!RunCpuSimulation+0xa
        00000000`0022eaf0 00000000`776de23d wow64!Wow64LdrpInitialize+0x492
        00000000`0022f050 00000000`7774e974 ntdll!LdrpInitializeProcess+0x1333
        00000000`0022f2e0 00000000`776ec4ee ntdll! ?? ::FNODOBFM::`string'+0x1d641
        00000000`0022f380 00000000`00000000 ntdll!LdrInitializeThunk+0xe

        THREAD fffffa80015ce800  Cid 05b0.0bd8  Teb: 000000007efd5000 Win32Thread: 0000000000000000 WAIT: (WrQueue)
UserMode Non-Alertable
            fffffa8003421b00  QueueObject
            fffffa80015ce8b8  NotificationTimer
        Not impersonating
        DeviceMap                 fffff88001697690
        Owning Process            fffffa80040d2040       Image:         iexplore.exe
        Attached Process          N/A            Image:         N/A
        Wait Start TickCount      40912          Ticks: 1546 (0:00:00:24.156)
        Context Switch Count      64             IdealProcessor: 1
        UserTime                  00:00:00.000
        KernelTime                00:00:00.000
        Win32 Start Address 0x0000000076de3242
        Stack Init fffff980133ffdb0 Current fffff980133ff810
        Base fffff98013400000 Limit fffff980133fa000 Call 0
        Priority 8 BasePriority 8 PriorityDecrement 0 IoPriority 2 PagePriority 5
        Child-SP          RetAddr           Call Site
        fffff980`133ff850 fffff800`0185d695 nt!KiSwapContext+0x84
        fffff980`133ff990 fffff800`01868d10 nt!KiSwapThread+0x125
        fffff980`133ff9f0 fffff800`01a94647 nt!KeRemoveQueueEx+0x848
        fffff980`133ffa80 fffff800`01ac1b7d nt!IoRemoveIoCompletion+0x47
        fffff980`133ffb00 fffff800`0184dcf3 nt!NtRemoveIoCompletion+0x13d
```

```
        fffff980`133ffbb0 00000000`759e39a2 nt!KiSystemServiceCopyEnd+0x13 (TrapFrame @ fffff980`133ffc20)
        00000000`0110ef18 00000000`74fbabfe wow64cpu!RemoveIoCompletionFault+0x41
        00000000`0110eff0 00000000`74fba202 wow64!RunCpuSimulation+0xa
        00000000`0110f020 00000000`776c894c wow64!Wow64LdrpInitialize+0x492
        00000000`0110f580 00000000`776ec4ee ntdll! ?? ::FNODOBFM::`string'+0x1d777
        00000000`0110f620 00000000`00000000 ntdll!LdrInitializeThunk+0xe

        THREAD fffffa80017dfbb0  Cid 05b0.012c  Teb: 000000007efad000 Win32Thread: 0000000000000000 WAIT:
(UserRequest) UserMode Alertable
            fffffa80015b4d10  SynchronizationTimer
            fffffa800128c100  SynchronizationEvent
        Not impersonating
        DeviceMap                 fffff88001697690
        Owning Process            fffffa80040d2040       Image:         iexplore.exe
        Attached Process          N/A            Image:         N/A
        Wait Start TickCount      40710          Ticks: 1748 (0:00:00:27.312)
        Context Switch Count      1              IdealProcessor: 0
        UserTime                  00:00:00.000
        KernelTime                00:00:00.000
        Win32 Start Address 0x0000000077916235
        Stack Init fffff980049b2db0 Current fffff980049b2260
        Base fffff980049b3000 Limit fffff980049ad000 Call 0
        Priority 8 BasePriority 8 PriorityDecrement 0 IoPriority 2 PagePriority 5
        Child-SP          RetAddr           Call Site
        fffff980`049b22a0 fffff800`0185d695 nt!KiSwapContext+0x84
        fffff980`049b23e0 fffff800`0185ad2f nt!KiSwapThread+0x125
        fffff980`049b2440 fffff800`01ac1813 nt!KeWaitForMultipleObjects+0x703
        fffff980`049b24b0 fffff800`01ba477a nt!ObpWaitForMultipleObjects+0x216
        fffff980`049b2960 fffff800`0184dcf3 nt!NtWaitForMultipleObjects32+0xd9
        fffff980`049b2bb0 00000000`759e373f nt!KiSystemServiceCopyEnd+0x13 (TrapFrame @ fffff980`049b2c20)
        00000000`02a9ecc8 00000000`74fbabfe wow64cpu!WaitForMultipleObjects32+0x3a
        00000000`02a9ed70 00000000`74fba202 wow64!RunCpuSimulation+0xa
        00000000`02a9eda0 00000000`776c894c wow64!Wow64LdrpInitialize+0x492
        00000000`02a9f300 00000000`776ec4ee ntdll! ?? ::FNODOBFM::`string'+0x1d777
        00000000`02a9f3a0 00000000`00000000 ntdll!LdrInitializeThunk+0xe

        THREAD fffffa800155ebb0  Cid 05b0.0ab4  Teb: 000000007efaa000 Win32Thread: 0000000000000000 WAIT:
(DelayExecution) UserMode Non-Alertable
            fffffa800155ec68  NotificationTimer
        Not impersonating
        DeviceMap                 fffff88001697690
        Owning Process            fffffa80040d2040       Image:         iexplore.exe
        Attached Process          N/A            Image:         N/A
        Wait Start TickCount      40716          Ticks: 1742 (0:00:00:27.218)
        Context Switch Count      6              IdealProcessor: 1
        UserTime                  00:00:00.000
        KernelTime                00:00:00.000
        Win32 Start Address 0x0000000075bffc53
        Stack Init fffff9800e3d2db0 Current fffff9800e3d2990
        Base fffff9800e3d3000 Limit fffff9800e3cd000 Call 0
        Priority 11 BasePriority 8 PriorityDecrement 3 IoPriority 2 PagePriority 5
        Child-SP          RetAddr           Call Site
        fffff980`0e3d29d0 fffff800`0185d695 nt!KiSwapContext+0x84
        fffff980`0e3d2b10 fffff800`0185bbe9 nt!KiSwapThread+0x125
        fffff980`0e3d2b70 fffff800`01a8b1cd nt!KeDelayExecutionThread+0x339
        fffff980`0e3d2bf0 fffff800`0184dcf3 nt!NtDelayExecution+0x5c
        fffff980`0e3d2c20 00000000`759e3cf9 nt!KiSystemServiceCopyEnd+0x13 (TrapFrame @ fffff980`0e3d2c20)
        00000000`00a5ec18 00000000`759e3bad wow64cpu!CpupSyscallStub+0x9
        00000000`00a5ec20 00000000`74fbabfe wow64cpu!Thunk2ArgNSpNSpReloadState+0x21
        00000000`00a5ec90 00000000`74fba202 wow64!RunCpuSimulation+0xa
        00000000`00a5ecc0 00000000`776c894c wow64!Wow64LdrpInitialize+0x492
        00000000`00a5f220 00000000`776ec4ee ntdll! ?? ::FNODOBFM::`string'+0x1d777
        00000000`00a5f2c0 00000000`00000000 ntdll!LdrInitializeThunk+0xe

        THREAD fffffa8001573bb0  Cid 05b0.0998  Teb: 000000007efa7000 Win32Thread: fffff900c220f330 WAIT:
(UserRequest) UserMode Non-Alertable
            fffffa8003939660  SynchronizationEvent
            fffffa8001521be0  SynchronizationEvent
        Not impersonating
        DeviceMap                 fffff88001697690
        Owning Process            fffffa80040d2040       Image:         iexplore.exe
        Attached Process          N/A            Image:         N/A
        Wait Start TickCount      40917          Ticks: 1541 (0:00:00:24.078)
        Context Switch Count      10             IdealProcessor: 0                 LargeStack
        UserTime                  00:00:00.000
        KernelTime                00:00:00.000
```

```
        Win32 Start Address 0x0000000076a5639b
        Stack Init fffff9801038ddb0 Current fffff9801038d260
        Base fffff9801038e000 Limit fffff98010387000 Call 0
        Priority 9 BasePriority 8 PriorityDecrement 0 IoPriority 2 PagePriority 5
        Child-SP          RetAddr           Call Site
        fffff980`1038d2a0 fffff800`0185d695 nt!KiSwapContext+0x84
        fffff980`1038d3e0 fffff800`0185ad2f nt!KiSwapThread+0x125
        fffff980`1038d440 fffff800`01ac1813 nt!KeWaitForMultipleObjects+0x703
        fffff980`1038d4b0 fffff800`01ba477a nt!ObpWaitForMultipleObjects+0x216
        fffff980`1038d960 fffff800`0184dcf3 nt!NtWaitForMultipleObjects32+0xd9
        fffff980`1038dbb0 00000000`759e373f nt!KiSystemServiceCopyEnd+0x13 (TrapFrame @ fffff980`1038dc20)
        00000000`0327ebf8 00000000`74fbabfe wow64cpu!WaitForMultipleObjects32+0x3a
        00000000`0327eca0 00000000`74fba202 wow64!RunCpuSimulation+0xa
        00000000`0327ecd0 00000000`776c894c wow64!Wow64LdrpInitialize+0x492
        00000000`0327f230 00000000`776ec4ee ntdll! ?? ::FNODOBFM::`string'+0x1d777
        00000000`0327f2d0 00000000`00000000 ntdll!LdrInitializeThunk+0xe

        THREAD fffffa8001565bb0  Cid 05b0.06c8  Teb: 000000007efa4000 Win32Thread: fffff900c3239b20 WAIT:
(WrUserRequest) UserMode Non-Alertable
            fffffa8003b49950  SynchronizationEvent
        Not impersonating
        DeviceMap                 fffff88001697690
        Owning Process            fffffa80040d2040       Image:         iexplore.exe
        Attached Process          N/A            Image:         N/A
        Wait Start TickCount      41157          Ticks: 1301 (0:00:00:20.328)
        Context Switch Count      1321           IdealProcessor: 1             LargeStack
        UserTime                  00:00:00.296
        KernelTime                00:00:00.921
        Win32 Start Address 0x000000007306e3a4
        Stack Init fffff98015af5db0 Current fffff98015af58c0
        Base fffff98015af6000 Limit fffff98015aec000 Call 0
        Priority 12 BasePriority 8 PriorityDecrement 2 IoPriority 2 PagePriority 5

        Child-SP          RetAddr           Call Site
        fffff980`15af5900 fffff800`0185d695 nt!KiSwapContext+0x84
        fffff980`15af5a40 fffff800`0185d3dd nt!KiSwapThread+0x125
        fffff980`15af5aa0 fffff960`000c95f8 nt!KeWaitForSingleObject+0x5f5
        fffff980`15af5b20 fffff960`000c9686 win32k!xxxRealSleepThread+0x278
        fffff980`15af5bc0 fffff960`000dbf57 win32k!xxxSleepThread+0x56
        fffff980`15af5bf0 fffff800`0184dcf3 win32k!NtUserWaitMessage+0x37
        fffff980`15af5c20 00000000`759e3cf9 nt!KiSystemServiceCopyEnd+0x13 (TrapFrame @ fffff980`15af5c20)
        00000000`0390ee88 00000000`759e3cb5 wow64cpu!CpupSyscallStub+0x9
        00000000`0390ee90 00000000`74fbabfe wow64cpu!Thunk0Arg+0x5
        00000000`0390ef00 00000000`74fba202 wow64!RunCpuSimulation+0xa
        00000000`0390ef30 00000000`776c894c wow64!Wow64LdrpInitialize+0x492
        00000000`0390f490 00000000`776ec4ee ntdll! ?? ::FNODOBFM::`string'+0x1d777
        00000000`0390f530 00000000`00000000 ntdll!LdrInitializeThunk+0xe

        THREAD fffffa80015cbbb0  Cid 05b0.083c  Teb: 000000007efa1000 Win32Thread: 0000000000000000 WAIT:
(UserRequest) UserMode Alertable
            fffffa8004197190  NotificationEvent
            fffffa80015cbc68  NotificationTimer
        IRP List:
            fffffa80015b8010: (0006,01f0) Flags: 00060070  Mdl: 00000000
        Not impersonating
        DeviceMap                 fffff88001697690
        Owning Process            fffffa80040d2040       Image:         iexplore.exe
        Attached Process          N/A            Image:         N/A
        Wait Start TickCount      41484          Ticks: 974 (0:00:00:15.218)
        Context Switch Count      12             IdealProcessor: 0
        UserTime                  00:00:00.000
        KernelTime                00:00:00.031
        Win32 Start Address 0x0000000076c22a6b
        Stack Init fffff9800df1cdb0 Current fffff9800df1c960
        Base fffff9800df1d000 Limit fffff9800df17000 Call 0
        Priority 12 BasePriority 8 PriorityDecrement 2 IoPriority 2 PagePriority 5
        Child-SP          RetAddr           Call Site
        fffff980`0df1c9a0 fffff800`0185d695 nt!KiSwapContext+0x84
        fffff980`0df1cae0 fffff800`0185d3dd nt!KiSwapThread+0x125
        fffff980`0df1cb40 fffff800`01a8b27b nt!KeWaitForSingleObject+0x5f5
        fffff980`0df1cbc0 fffff800`0184dcf3 nt!NtWaitForSingleObject+0x9b
        fffff980`0df1cc20 00000000`759e3cf9 nt!KiSystemServiceCopyEnd+0x13 (TrapFrame @ fffff980`0df1cc20)
        00000000`0370ed28 00000000`759e3af6 wow64cpu!CpupSyscallStub+0x9
        00000000`0370ed30 00000000`74fbabfe wow64cpu!Thunk0ArgReloadState+0x1a
        00000000`0370eda0 00000000`74fba202 wow64!RunCpuSimulation+0xa
        00000000`0370edd0 00000000`776c894c wow64!Wow64LdrpInitialize+0x492
```

```
        00000000`0370f330 00000000`776ec4ee ntdll! ?? ::FNODOBFM::`string'+0x1d777
        00000000`0370f3d0 00000000`00000000 ntdll!LdrInitializeThunk+0xe

        THREAD fffffa800159e060  Cid 05b0.0a60  Teb: 000000007ef9b000 Win32Thread: fffff900c315f2e0 WAIT:
(UserRequest) UserMode Non-Alertable
            fffffa8003b2aad0  SynchronizationEvent
            fffffa800159e118  NotificationTimer
        Not impersonating
        DeviceMap                 fffff88001697690
        Owning Process            fffffa80040d2040       Image:         iexplore.exe
        Attached Process          N/A            Image:         N/A
        Wait Start TickCount      40919          Ticks: 1539 (0:00:00:24.046)
        Context Switch Count      5              IdealProcessor: 0                 LargeStack
        UserTime                  00:00:00.000
        KernelTime                00:00:00.000
        Win32 Start Address 0x000000007230dacf
        Stack Init fffff98011db3db0 Current fffff98011db3960
        Base fffff98011db4000 Limit fffff98011dad000 Call 0
        Priority 9 BasePriority 8 PriorityDecrement 0 IoPriority 2 PagePriority 5
        Child-SP          RetAddr           Call Site
        fffff980`11db39a0 fffff800`0185d695 nt!KiSwapContext+0x84
        fffff980`11db3ae0 fffff800`0185d3dd nt!KiSwapThread+0x125
        fffff980`11db3b40 fffff800`01a8b27b nt!KeWaitForSingleObject+0x5f5
        fffff980`11db3bc0 fffff800`0184dcf3 nt!NtWaitForSingleObject+0x9b
        fffff980`11db3c20 00000000`759e3cf9 nt!KiSystemServiceCopyEnd+0x13 (TrapFrame @ fffff980`11db3c20)
        00000000`03c4ea68 00000000`759e3af6 wow64cpu!CpupSyscallStub+0x9
        00000000`03c4ea70 00000000`74fbabfe wow64cpu!Thunk0ArgReloadState+0x1a
        00000000`03c4eae0 00000000`74fba202 wow64!RunCpuSimulation+0xa
        00000000`03c4eb10 00000000`776c894c wow64!Wow64LdrpInitialize+0x492
        00000000`03c4f070 00000000`776ec4ee ntdll! ?? ::FNODOBFM::`string'+0x1d777
        00000000`03c4f110 00000000`00000000 ntdll!LdrInitializeThunk+0xe

        THREAD fffffa80012b7bb0  Cid 05b0.086c  Teb: 000000007ef98000 Win32Thread: fffff900c30c7ad0 WAIT:
(UserRequest) UserMode Non-Alertable
            fffffa80039c6dc0  SynchronizationEvent
            fffffa80012b7c68  NotificationTimer
        Not impersonating
        DeviceMap                 fffff88001697690
        Owning Process            fffffa80040d2040       Image:         iexplore.exe
        Attached Process          N/A            Image:         N/A
        Wait Start TickCount      40954          Ticks: 1504 (0:00:00:23.500)
        Context Switch Count      83             IdealProcessor: 1                 LargeStack
        UserTime                  00:00:00.093
        KernelTime                00:00:00.062
        Win32 Start Address 0x000000007230dacf
        Stack Init fffff98010367db0 Current fffff98010367960
        Base fffff98010368000 Limit fffff98010360000 Call 0
        Priority 8 BasePriority 8 PriorityDecrement 0 IoPriority 2 PagePriority 5
        Child-SP          RetAddr           Call Site
        fffff980`103679a0 fffff800`0185d695 nt!KiSwapContext+0x84
        fffff980`10367ae0 fffff800`0185d3dd nt!KiSwapThread+0x125
        fffff980`10367b40 fffff800`01a8b27b nt!KeWaitForSingleObject+0x5f5
        fffff980`10367bc0 fffff800`0184dcf3 nt!NtWaitForSingleObject+0x9b
        fffff980`10367c20 00000000`759e3cf9 nt!KiSystemServiceCopyEnd+0x13 (TrapFrame @ fffff980`10367c20)
        00000000`0374e9b8 00000000`759e3af6 wow64cpu!CpupSyscallStub+0x9
        00000000`0374e9c0 00000000`74fbabfe wow64cpu!Thunk0ArgReloadState+0x1a
        00000000`0374ea30 00000000`74fba202 wow64!RunCpuSimulation+0xa
        00000000`0374ea60 00000000`776c894c wow64!Wow64LdrpInitialize+0x492
        00000000`0374efc0 00000000`776ec4ee ntdll! ?? ::FNODOBFM::`string'+0x1d777
        00000000`0374f060 00000000`00000000 ntdll!LdrInitializeThunk+0xe
```

We see WOW64 modules on all thread stack traces (**Virtualized Process**). We need to load WOW64 debugging extension and then to switch to one of the threads in x86 mode. After that we are able to check 32-bit modules, disassemble functions, etc.

```
1: kd> .load wow64exts

1: kd> .thread /w fffffa80012b7bb0
Implicit thread is now fffffa80`012b7bb0
WARNING: WOW context retrieval requires
switching to the thread's process context.
Use .process /p fffffa80`01412040 to switch back.
Implicit process is now fffffa80`040d2040
The context is partially valid. Only x86 user-mode context is available.
x86 context set

1: kd:x86> .reload
Loading Kernel Symbols
...............................................................
................................................................
.........
Loading User Symbols
.....
Loading unloaded module list
.........Unable to enumerate user-mode unloaded modules, NTSTATUS 0xC0000147
Loading Wow64 Symbols
................................................................
.......................

1: kd:x86> kv
  *** Stack trace for last set context - .thread/.cxr resets it
ChildEBP          RetAddr           Args to Child
043bf9e0 76af1220 00000550 00000000 043bfa28 ntdll_77850000!NtWaitForSingleObject+0x15 (FPO: [3,0,0])
043bfa50 76af1188 00000550 000927c0 00000000 kernel32!WaitForSingleObjectEx+0xbe (FPO: [Non-Fpo])
043bfa64 7238f57d 00000550 000927c0 722f0000 kernel32!WaitForSingleObject+0x12 (FPO: [Non-Fpo])
043bfa7c 72386c92 00000000 00000000 7230dadc mshtml!CDwnTaskExec::ThreadExec+0x127 (FPO: [0,0,4])
043bfa88 7230dadc 043bfa9c 76b619f1 03d85e88 mshtml!CExecFT::ThreadProc+0x3c (FPO: [0,0,0])
043bfa90 76b619f1 03d85e88 043bfadc 778cd109 mshtml!CExecFT::StaticThreadProc+0xd (FPO: [Non-Fpo])
043bfa9c 778cd109 03d85e88 043bdb05 00000000 kernel32!BaseThreadInitThunk+0xe (FPO: [Non-Fpo])
043bfadc 00000000 7230dacf 03d85e88 00000000 ntdll_77850000!_RtlUserThreadStart+0x23 (FPO: [Non-Fpo])

1: kd:x86> lmtu
start             end                 module name
00000000`00e00000 00000000`00e9a000   iexplore  Thu Nov 02 08:49:55 2006 (4549B133)
00000000`722f0000 00000000`7265f000   mshtml    Thu Nov 02 09:42:13 2006 (4549BD75)
00000000`72710000 00000000`72787000   mshtmled  Thu Nov 02 09:42:14 2006 (4549BD76)
00000000`72810000 00000000`72888000   jscript   Thu Nov 02 09:39:46 2006 (4549BCE2)
00000000`72900000 00000000`7290e000   pngfilt   Thu Nov 02 09:43:21 2006 (4549BDB9)
00000000`72910000 00000000`72970000   ieapfltr  Thu Nov 02 09:40:04 2006 (4549BCF4)
00000000`72980000 00000000`72991000   SAMLIB    Thu Nov 02 09:43:04 2006 (4549BDA8)
00000000`729a0000 00000000`729c1000   NTMARTA   Thu Nov 02 09:43:55 2006 (4549BDDB)
00000000`729d0000 00000000`72a87000   PROPSYS   Thu Nov 02 09:42:46 2006 (4549BD96)
00000000`72b10000 00000000`72b6f000   SXS       Thu Nov 02 09:43:46 2006 (4549BDD2)
00000000`72b70000 00000000`72d1a000   gdiplus   Thu Nov 02 09:38:55 2006 (4549BCAF)
00000000`72d20000 00000000`72d49000   msls31    Thu Nov 02 09:42:48 2006 (4549BD98)
00000000`72d50000 00000000`72db0000   tiptsf    Thu Nov 02 09:44:19 2006 (4549BDF3)
00000000`72db0000 00000000`72e62000   WindowsCodecs  Thu Nov 02 09:44:51 2006 (4549BE13)
00000000`72e70000 00000000`72e92000   xmllite   Thu Nov 02 09:44:37 2006 (4549BE05)
00000000`72ea0000 00000000`72ed0000   MLANG     Thu Nov 02 09:40:07 2006 (4549BCF7)
00000000`72ed0000 00000000`72f0b000   mswsock   Thu Nov 02 09:42:01 2006 (4549BD69)
00000000`72f10000 00000000`72f63000   actxprxy  Thu Nov 02 09:39:11 2006 (4549BCBF)
00000000`72f70000 00000000`72f7b000   msimtf    Thu Nov 02 09:42:44 2006 (4549BD94)
00000000`72f80000 00000000`72faf000   IEUI      Thu Nov 02 09:40:14 2006 (4549BCFE)
00000000`72fb0000 00000000`72fc2000   pnrpnsp   Thu Nov 02 09:43:28 2006 (4549BDC0)
00000000`72fd0000 00000000`7359a000   IEFRAME   Thu Nov 02 09:40:08 2006 (4549BCF8)
00000000`735a0000 00000000`735a6000   rasadhlp  Thu Nov 02 09:42:58 2006 (4549BDA2)
00000000`735b0000 00000000`735db000   DNSAPI    Thu Nov 02 09:40:01 2006 (4549BCF1)
00000000`735e0000 00000000`73615000   dhcpcsvc  Thu Nov 02 09:39:18 2006 (4549BCC6)
00000000`73620000 00000000`73665000   schannel  Thu Nov 02 09:43:16 2006 (4549BDB4)
00000000`73670000 00000000`73690000   dhcpcsvc6  Thu Nov 02 09:39:19 2006 (4549BCC7)
00000000`73690000 00000000`736a9000   IPHLPAPI  Thu Nov 02 09:41:19 2006 (4549BD3F)
00000000`736b0000 00000000`736bf000   NLAapi    Thu Nov 02 09:42:03 2006 (4549BD6B)
```

```
00000000`736c0000 00000000`736c7000   credssp   Thu Nov 02 09:40:48 2006 (4549BD20)
00000000`736d0000 00000000`73708000   OLEACC    Thu Nov 02 09:42:43 2006 (4549BD93)
00000000`73710000 00000000`73743000   WINMM     Thu Nov 02 09:45:01 2006 (4549BE1D)
00000000`73750000 00000000`737ba000   NETAPI32  Thu Nov 02 09:41:39 2006 (4549BD53)
00000000`737c0000 00000000`738b1000   CRYPT32   Thu Nov 02 09:40:52 2006 (4549BD24)
00000000`738c0000 00000000`73a54000   comctl32  Thu Nov 02 09:40:25 2006 (4549BD09)
00000000`73a60000 00000000`73a67000   WINNSI    Thu Nov 02 09:45:02 2006 (4549BE1E)
00000000`73a70000 00000000`73a76000   sensapi   Thu Nov 02 09:43:50 2006 (4549BDD6)
00000000`73a80000 00000000`73ab1000   TAPI32    Thu Nov 02 09:43:45 2006 (4549BDD1)
00000000`73ac0000 00000000`73b07000   RASAPI32  Thu Nov 02 09:42:59 2006 (4549BDA3)
00000000`73b10000 00000000`73b90000   UxTheme   Thu Nov 02 09:44:25 2006 (4549BDF9)
00000000`73b90000 00000000`73bc8000   rsaenh    Thu Nov 02 09:43:10 2006 (4549BDAE)
00000000`73bd0000 00000000`73bfd000   WINTRUST  Thu Nov 02 09:45:19 2006 (4549BE2F)
00000000`73c00000 00000000`73c87000   AcLayers  Thu Nov 02 09:38:59 2006 (4549BCB3)
00000000`73c90000 00000000`73ca4000   rasman    Thu Nov 02 09:43:07 2006 (4549BDAB)
00000000`73cb0000 00000000`73cc2000   MSASN1    Thu Nov 02 09:41:21 2006 (4549BD41)
00000000`73cd0000 00000000`73d11000   WINSPOOL  Thu Nov 02 09:45:14 2006 (4549BE2A)
00000000`73d20000 00000000`73d5e000   AcRedir   Thu Nov 02 09:39:04 2006 (4549BCB8)
00000000`74f10000 00000000`74f1c000   rtutils   Thu Nov 02 09:43:22 2006 (4549BDBA)
00000000`74f20000 00000000`74f25000   MSIMG32   Thu Nov 02 09:42:42 2006 (4549BD92)
00000000`74f30000 00000000`74f36000   wship6    Thu Nov 02 09:45:05 2006 (4549BE21)
00000000`74f40000 00000000`74f46000   wshtcpip  Thu Nov 02 09:45:11 2006 (4549BE27)
00000000`74f50000 00000000`74f7c000   apphelp   Thu Nov 02 09:38:55 2006 (4549BCAF)
00000000`74f80000 00000000`74f8f000   napinsp   Thu Nov 02 09:41:15 2006 (4549BD3B)
00000000`74f90000 00000000`74f98000   winrnr    Thu Nov 02 09:45:03 2006 (4549BE1F)
00000000`74fa0000 00000000`74fac000   ImgUtil   Thu Nov 02 09:40:55 2006 (4549BD27)
00000000`74fb0000 00000000`74ff5000   wow64     Thu Nov 02 11:16:01 2006 (4549D371)
00000000`75560000 00000000`7557e000   USERENV   Thu Nov 02 09:44:02 2006 (4549BDE2)
00000000`75580000 00000000`755ca000   wow64win  Thu Nov 02 11:16:04 2006 (4549D374)
00000000`75700000 00000000`75714000   MPR       Thu Nov 02 09:40:36 2006 (4549BD14)
00000000`75720000 00000000`7573e000   ShimEng   Thu Nov 02 09:43:19 2006 (4549BDB7)
00000000`759b0000 00000000`759bf000   iebrshim  Thu Nov 02 09:40:05 2006 (4549BCF5)
00000000`759c0000 00000000`759c8000   VERSION   Thu Nov 02 09:44:04 2006 (4549BDE4)
00000000`759e0000 00000000`759e9000   wow64cpu  Thu Nov 02 11:16:02 2006 (4549D372)
00000000`75a50000 00000000`75ab0000   Secur32   Thu Nov 02 09:44:25 2006 (4549BDF9)
00000000`75ab0000 00000000`75b3c000   OLEAUT32  Thu Nov 02 09:42:45 2006 (4549BD95)
00000000`75bc0000 00000000`75d04000   ole32     Thu Nov 02 09:42:42 2006 (4549BD92)
00000000`75d10000 00000000`75d70000   IMM32     Thu Nov 02 09:44:24 2006 (4549BDF8)
00000000`75d70000 00000000`75d79000   LPK       Thu Nov 02 09:44:24 2006 (4549BDF8)
00000000`75d80000 00000000`7684e000   SHELL32   Thu Nov 02 09:43:16 2006 (4549BDB4)
00000000`76850000 00000000`76879000   imagehlp  Thu Nov 02 09:40:47 2006 (4549BD1F)
00000000`76880000 00000000`768ad000   ws2_32    Thu Nov 02 09:44:46 2006 (4549BE0E)
00000000`768b0000 00000000`768f9000   WLDAP32   Thu Nov 02 09:45:40 2006 (4549BE44)
00000000`76900000 00000000`76a24000   urlmon    Thu Nov 02 09:43:55 2006 (4549BDDB)
00000000`76a30000 00000000`76ada000   msvcrt    Thu Nov 02 09:41:53 2006 (4549BD61)
00000000`76ae0000 00000000`76bf0000   kernel32  Thu Nov 02 09:47:00 2006 (4549BE94)
00000000`76bf0000 00000000`76bf7000   PSAPI     Thu Nov 02 09:42:49 2006 (4549BD99)
00000000`76c00000 00000000`76ccf000   WININET   Thu Nov 02 09:44:57 2006 (4549BE19)
00000000`76cd0000 00000000`76d25000   SHLWAPI   Thu Nov 02 09:43:21 2006 (4549BDB9)
00000000`76dc0000 00000000`76eb0000   RPCRT4    Thu Nov 02 09:44:24 2006 (4549BDF8)
00000000`76eb0000 00000000`76f34000   CLBCatQ   Thu Nov 02 09:39:53 2006 (4549BCE9)
00000000`76f40000 00000000`770c8000   SETUPAPI  Thu Nov 02 09:43:12 2006 (4549BDB0)
00000000`770d0000 00000000`771a0000   USER32    Thu Nov 02 09:44:25 2006 (4549BDF9)
00000000`771a0000 00000000`77230000   GDI32     Thu Nov 02 09:44:24 2006 (4549BDF8)
00000000`77230000 00000000`772ef000   ADVAPI32  Thu Nov 02 09:39:30 2006 (4549BCD2)
00000000`772f0000 00000000`773b7000   MSCTF     Thu Nov 02 09:41:30 2006 (4549BD4A)
00000000`773c0000 00000000`77405000   iertutil  Thu Nov 02 09:40:11 2006 (4549BCFB)
00000000`77410000 00000000`7748d000   USP10     Thu Nov 02 09:44:03 2006 (4549BDE3)
00000000`776a0000 00000000`7781a000   ntdll     Thu Nov 02 11:16:02 2006 (4549D372)
00000000`77820000 00000000`77823000   Normaliz  Thu Nov 02 08:33:06 2006 (4549AD42)
00000000`77830000 00000000`77836000   NSI       Thu Nov 02 09:43:35 2006 (4549BDC7)
00000000`77850000 00000000`779a0000   ntdll_77850000  Thu Nov 02 09:44:24 2006 (4549BDF8)

1: kd:x86> !chkimg -d ntdll_77850000
0 errors : ntdll_77850000
```

```
1: kd:x86> !dh ntdll_77850000

File Type: DLL
FILE HEADER VALUES
     14C machine (i386)
       5 number of sections
4549BDF8 time date stamp Thu Nov 02 09:44:24 2006

       0 file pointer to symbol table
       0 number of symbols
      E0 size of optional header
    2102 characteristics
            Executable
            32 bit word machine
            DLL

OPTIONAL HEADER VALUES
     10B magic #
    8.00 linker version
   BF600 size of code
   57C00 size of initialized data
       0 size of uninitialized data
       0 address of entry point
   10000 base of code
         ----- new -----
0000000077850000 image base
   10000 section alignment
     200 file alignment
       3 subsystem (Windows CUI)
    6.00 operating system version
    6.00 image version
    6.00 subsystem version
  150000 size of image
     400 size of headers
  124F8D checksum
0000000000040000 size of stack reserve
0000000000001000 size of stack commit
0000000000100000 size of heap reserve
0000000000001000 size of heap commit
     140  DLL characteristics
            Dynamic base
            NX compatible
   10008 [    ED50] address [size] of Export Directory
       0 [       0] address [size] of Import Directory
   F0000 [   48BC0] address [size] of Resource Directory
       0 [       0] address [size] of Exception Directory
  114800 [    3340] address [size] of Security Directory
  140000 [    46AC] address [size] of Base Relocation Directory
   CF2A4 [      38] address [size] of Debug Directory
       0 [       0] address [size] of Description Directory
       0 [       0] address [size] of Special Directory
       0 [       0] address [size] of Thread Storage Directory
   6CE60 [      40] address [size] of Load Configuration Directory
       0 [       0] address [size] of Bound Import Directory
       0 [       0] address [size] of Import Address Table Directory
       0 [       0] address [size] of Delay Import Directory
       0 [       0] address [size] of COR20 Header Directory
       0 [       0] address [size] of Reserved Directory


SECTION HEADER #1
   .text name
   BF303 virtual size
   10000 virtual address
   BF400 size of raw data
     400 file pointer to raw data
       0 file pointer to relocation table
```

```
       0 file pointer to line numbers
       0 number of relocations
       0 number of line numbers
60000020 flags
         Code
         (no align specified)
         Execute Read


Debug Directories(2)
      Type       Size     Address  Pointer
Can't read debug dir

SECTION HEADER #2
      RT name
     18C virtual size
   D0000 virtual address
     200 size of raw data
   BF800 file pointer to raw data
       0 file pointer to relocation table
       0 file pointer to line numbers
       0 number of relocations
       0 number of line numbers
60000020 flags
         Code
         (no align specified)
         Execute Read

SECTION HEADER #3
   .data name
    A6FD virtual size
   E0000 virtual address
    7A00 size of raw data
   BFA00 file pointer to raw data
       0 file pointer to relocation table
       0 file pointer to line numbers
       0 number of relocations
       0 number of line numbers
C0000040 flags
         Initialized Data
         (no align specified)
         Read Write

SECTION HEADER #4
   .rsrc name
   48BC0 virtual size
   F0000 virtual address
   48C00 size of raw data
   C7400 file pointer to raw data
       0 file pointer to relocation table
       0 file pointer to line numbers
       0 number of relocations
       0 number of line numbers
40000040 flags
         Initialized Data
         (no align specified)
         Read Only

SECTION HEADER #5
  .reloc name
    46AC virtual size
  140000 virtual address
    4800 size of raw data
  110000 file pointer to raw data
       0 file pointer to relocation table
       0 file pointer to line numbers
       0 number of relocations
```

```
       0 number of line numbers
42000040 flags
         Initialized Data
         Discardable
         (no align specified)
         Read Only
```

Here are some links for further reading about the pattern language approach. In these 2 books a pattern language was systematically introduced for architecture and building in the late 70s.

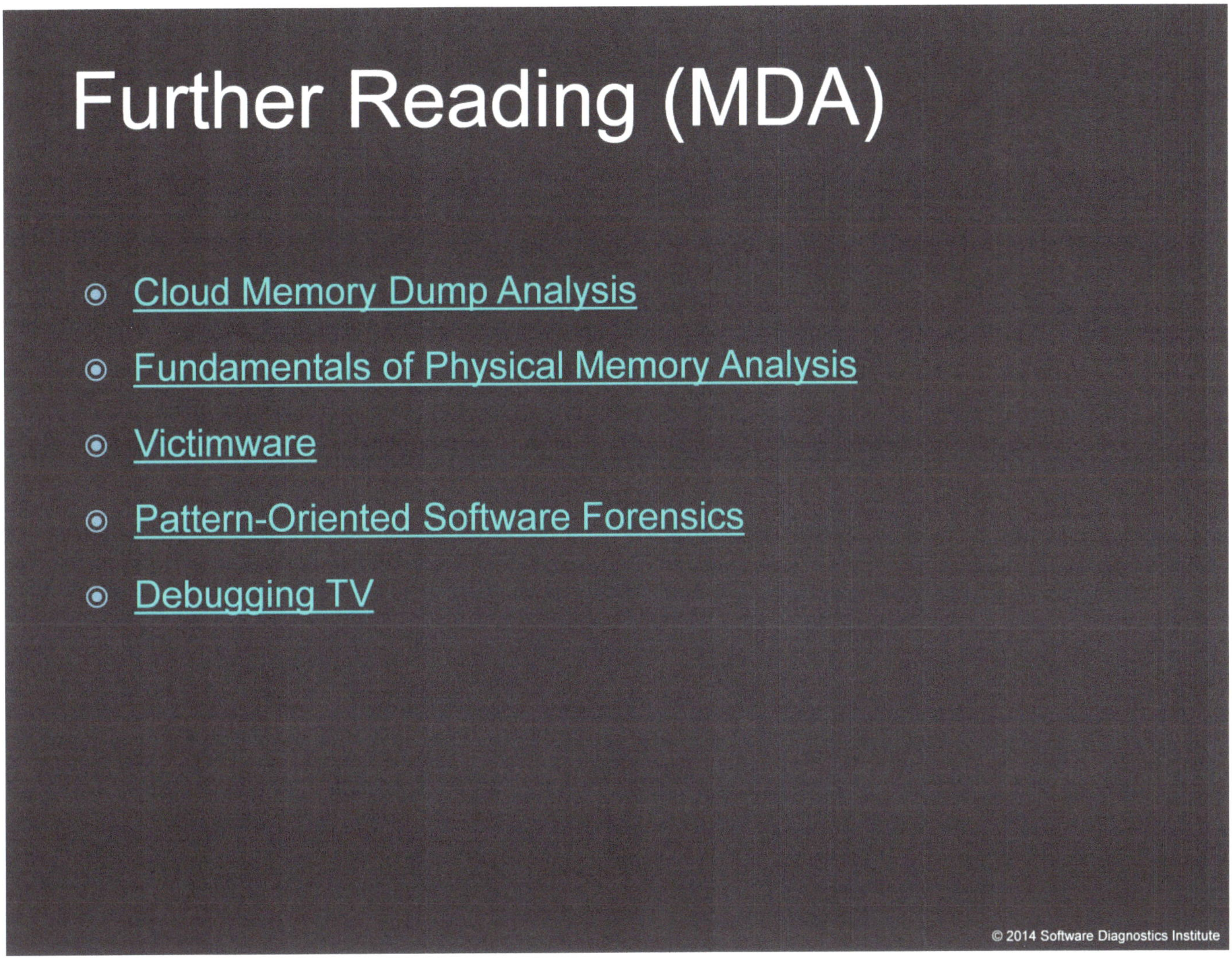

Here are links to memory dump analysis presentations which are also applicable to memory forensics. Many Debugging TV episodes also cover memory analysis and tools such as WinDbg from Debugging Tools for Windows.

Cloud Memory Dump Analysis:
http://www.patterndiagnostics.com/CMDA-materials

Fundamentals of Physical Memory Analysis:
http://www.patterndiagnostics.com/FPMA-materials

Victimware:
http://www.patterndiagnostics.com/Victimware-materials

Pattern-Oriented Software Forensics:
http://www.patterndiagnostics.com/pattern-oriented-software-forensics-materials

Debugging TV:
http://www.debugging.tv/

Further Reading (SD)

- Software Diagnostics Institute
- Pattern-Driven Software Diagnostics
- Systemic Software Diagnostics
- Pattern-Based Software Diagnostics
- Philosophy of Software Diagnostics

Here are some links for further reading about pattern-oriented software diagnostics which can serve as a foundation for pattern-oriented memory forensics. Most of them are presentations with recordings and transcripts published as books.

Software Diagnostics Institute:
http://www.dumpanalysis.org

Pattern-Driven Software Diagnostics:
http://www.patterndiagnostics.com/Introduction-Software-Diagnostics-materials

Systemic Software Diagnostics:
http://www.patterndiagnostics.com/systemic-diagnostics-materials

Pattern-Based Software Diagnostics:
http://www.patterndiagnostics.com/pattern-based-diagnostics-materials

Philosophy of Software Diagnostics:
http://www.patterndiagnostics.com/philosophy-diagnostics-materials

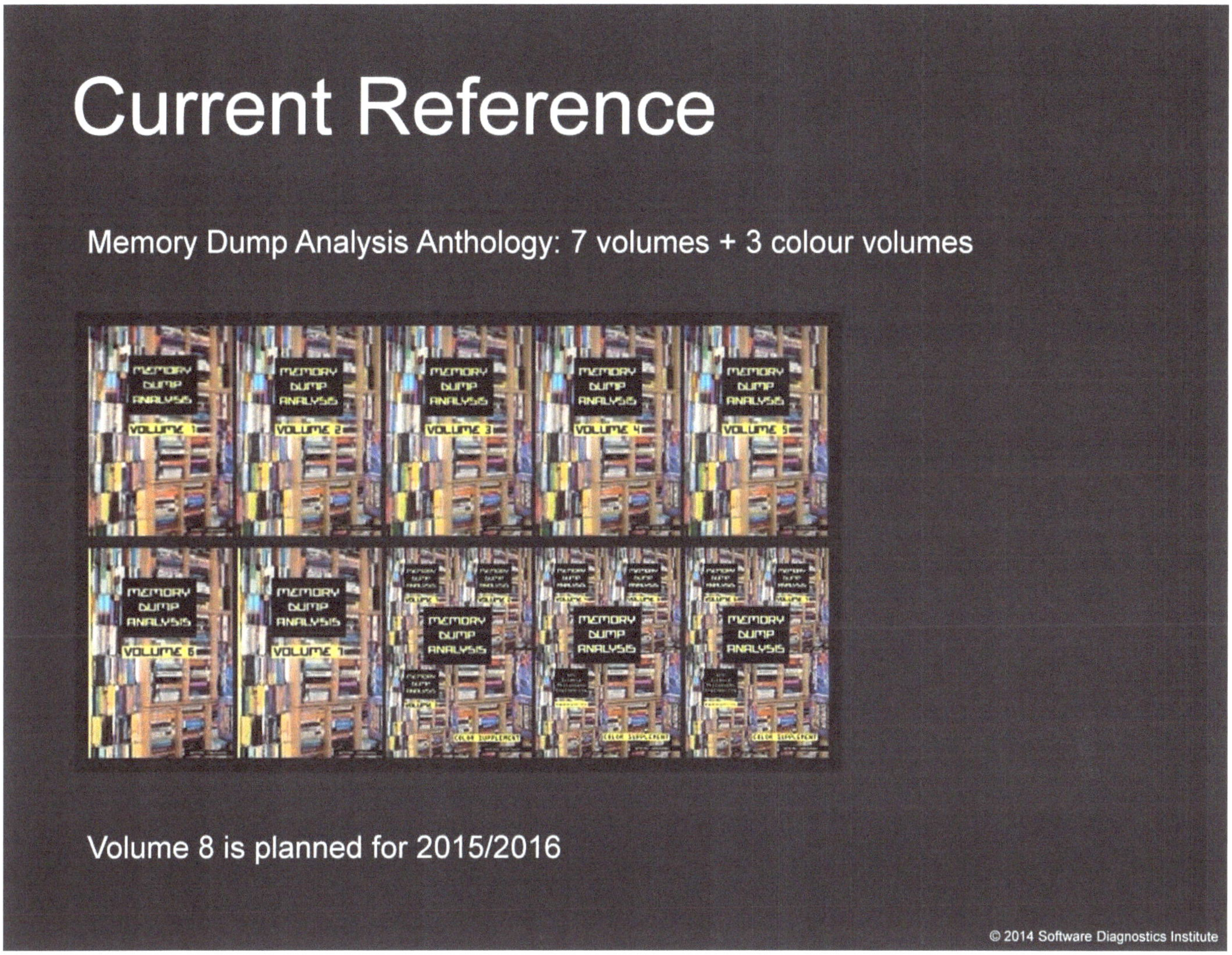

This is a current pattern reference. The 7 volumes have more than 3,000 pages and mostly devoted to memory dump analysis and case studies.

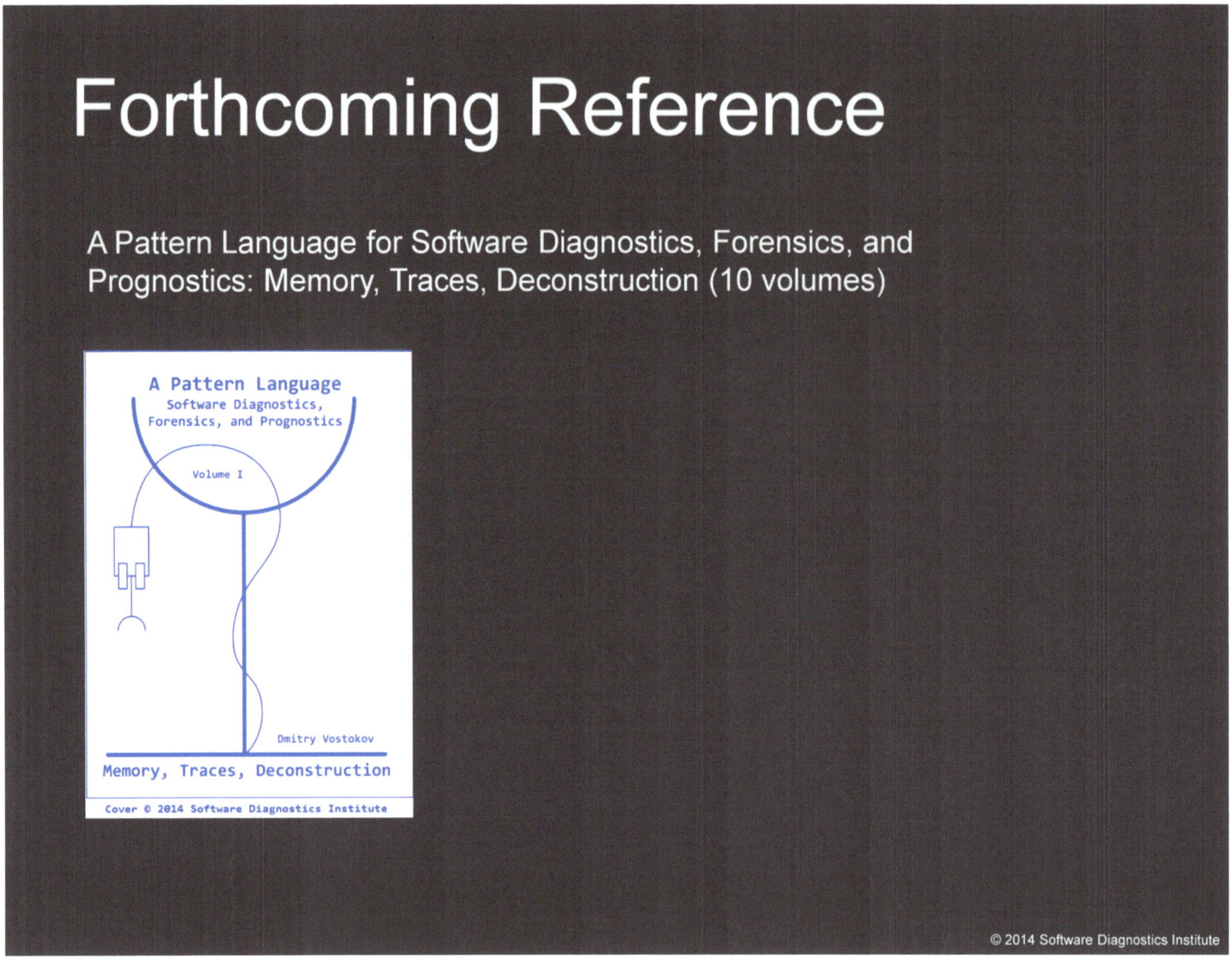

Memory Dump Analysis Anthology is now restructured as a pattern language reference with a title **"A Pattern Language for Software Diagnostics, Forensics, and Prognostics: Memory, Traces, Deconstruction"** with projected 10 volumes.

Mobile Software Diagnostics

Introduction

Version 1.0

Dmitry Vostokov
Software Diagnostics Services

Published by OpenTask, Republic of Ireland

OpenTask books and magazines are available through booksellers and distributors worldwide. For further information or comments send requests to press@opentask.com.

A CIP catalogue record for this book is available from the British Library.

ISBN-l3: 978-1-908043-65-8 (Paperback)

First printing, 2013

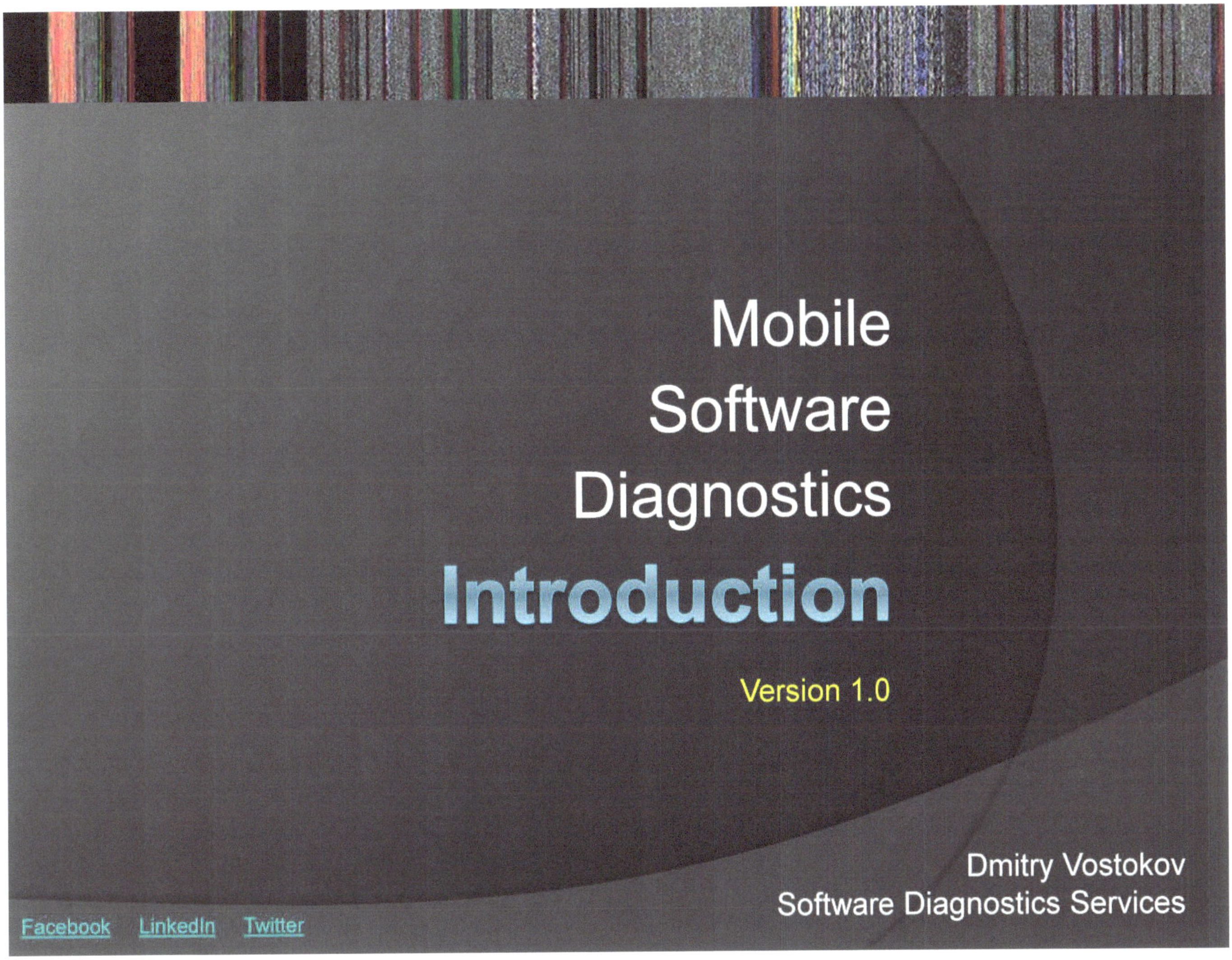

Hello Everyone, my name is Dmitry Vostokov and I introduce pattern-oriented mobile software diagnostics today. I decided to keep this presentation short and as simple as possible. If anything needs to be added or modified in the future I create another version of it.

Facebook:
http://www.facebook.com/SoftwareDiagnosticsServices

Linkedin:
http://www.linkedin.com/company/software-diagnostics-services

Twitter:
http://twitter.com/DumpAnalysis

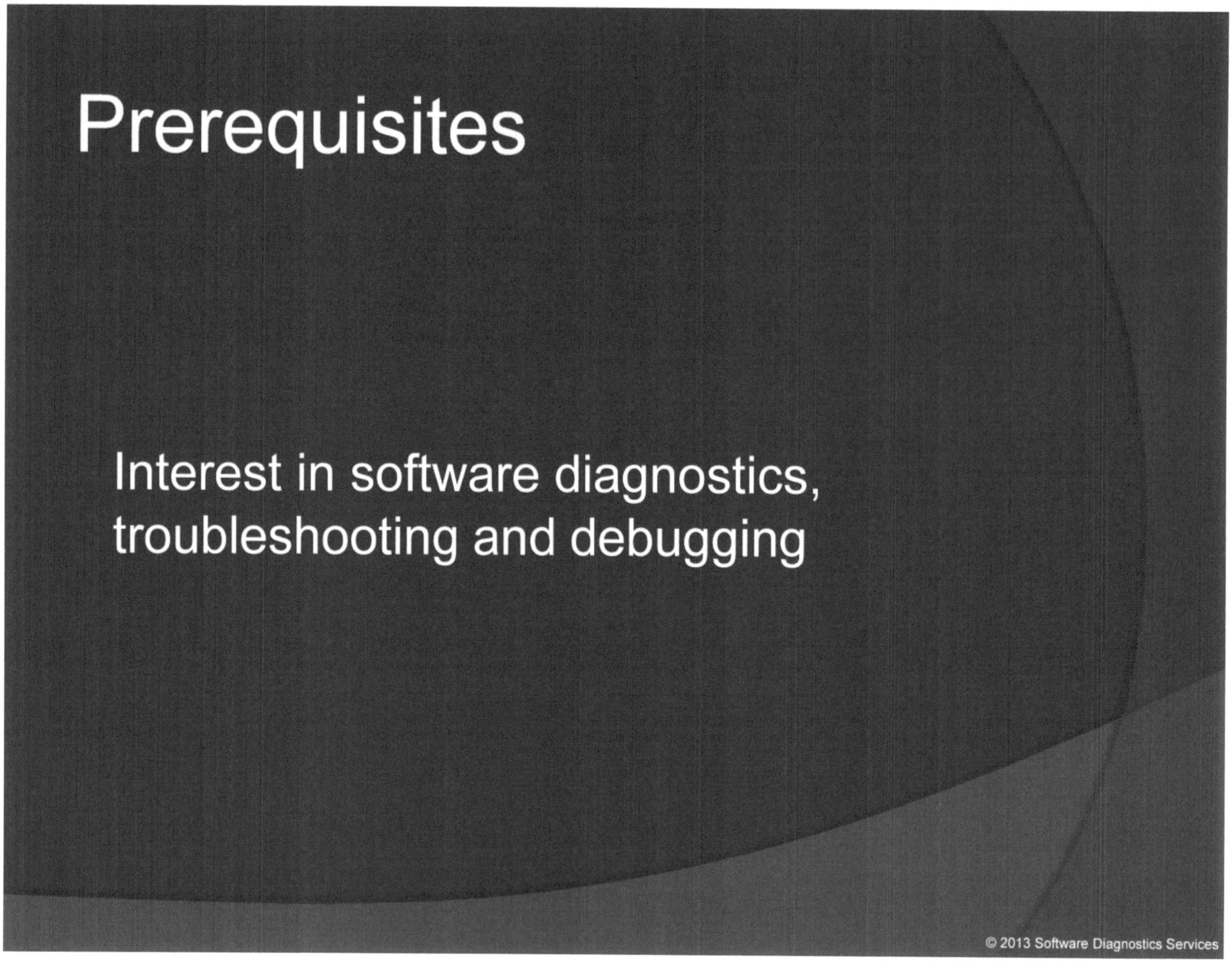

These prerequisites are very simple and I suppose you all like me enjoy diagnosing software problems, troubleshooting and debugging.

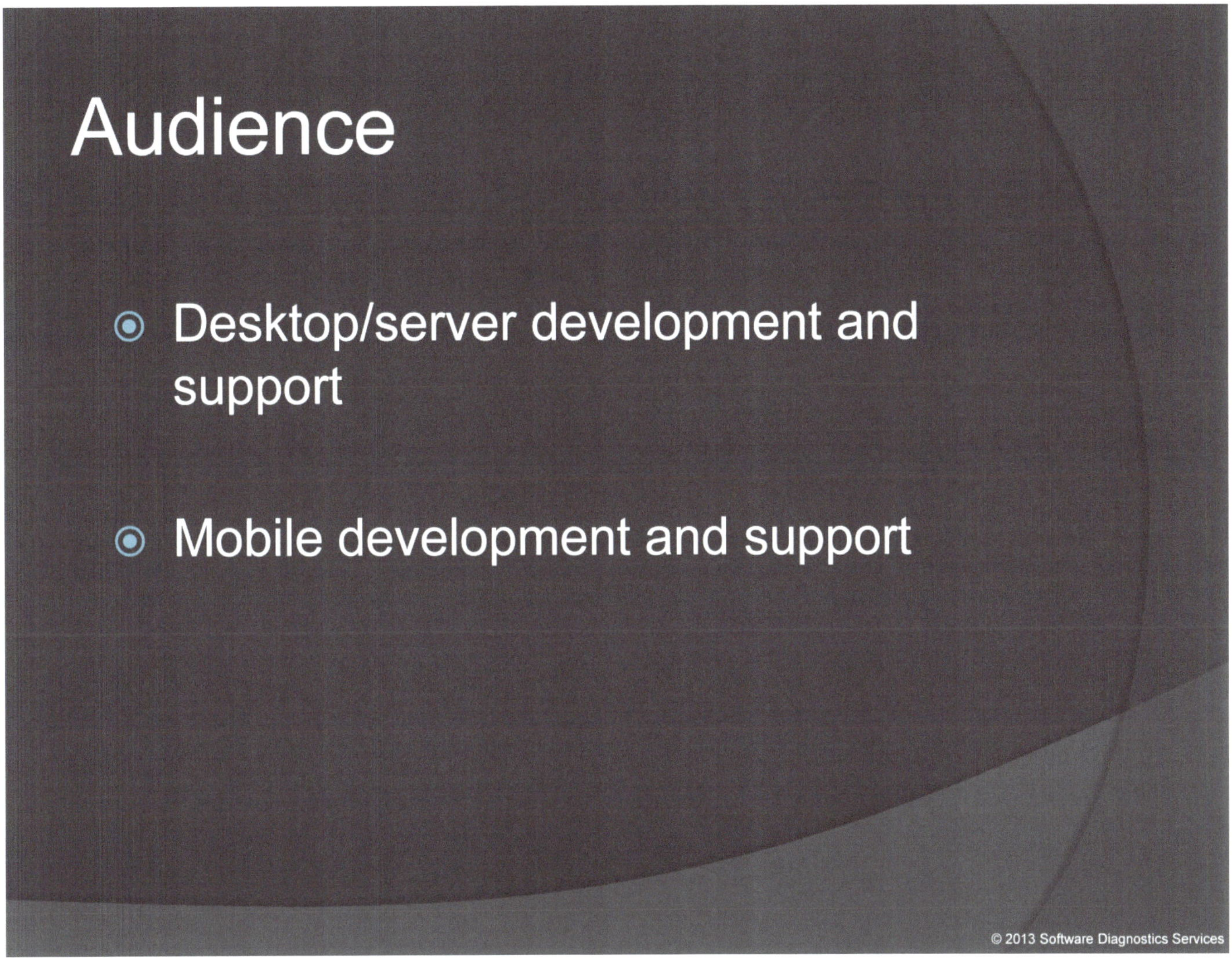

This introductory presentation is either for desktop and server development and support engineers who are moving to mobile development and support and would like to reuse pattern-oriented software diagnostics there, but it is also for mobile development and support who want to learn about recent advances in pattern-oriented software diagnostics methodology originally coming from complex server environments.

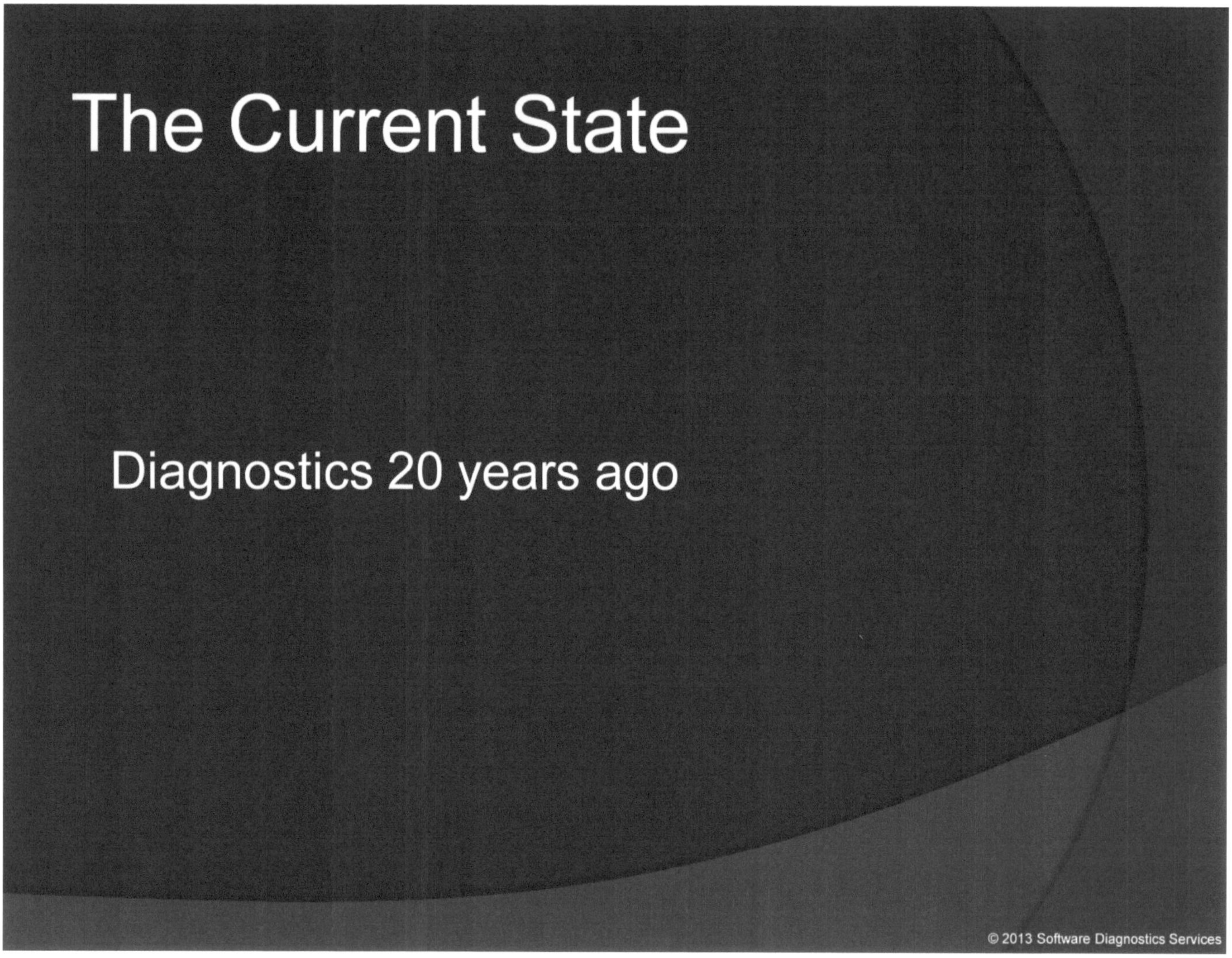

The current state of mobile software diagnostics on some platforms (for example, memory dump analysis) is like desktop diagnostics decades ago.

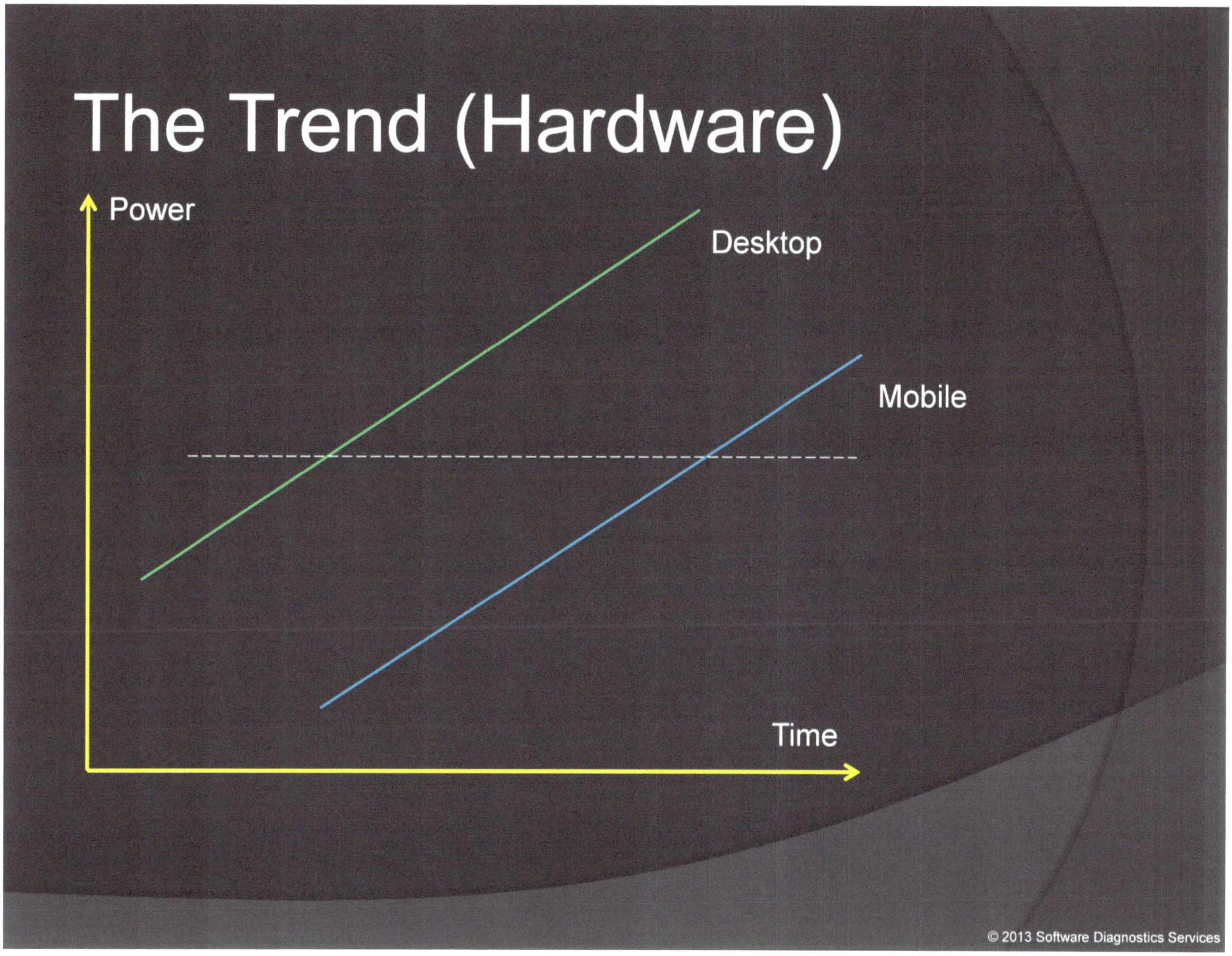

However, all this is rapidly changing and mobile devices now acquire hardware power that was unthinkable some time ago. Such devices might completely displace desktops even for traditional applications because it would be possible to connect mobile devices to large visualization devices to perform traditional desktop work such as editing and designing.

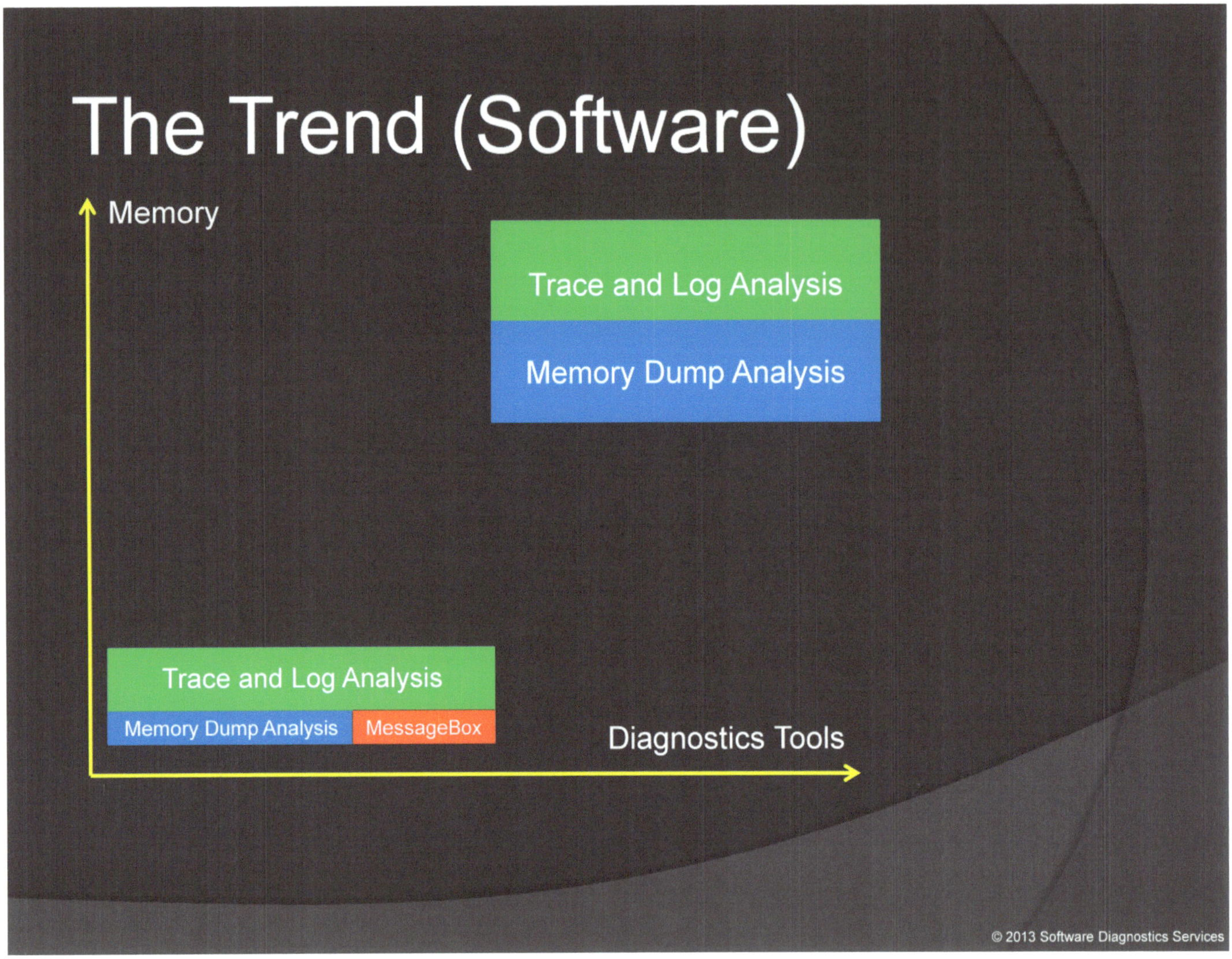

As hardware power increases the traditional desktop and server diagnostics ability also come in. For example, memory analysis role would increase and trace analysis would become more sophisticated on some mobile platforms. For example, the old methods of displaying message boxes for tracking variable values is dying as there is console log and tracing API for JavaScript.

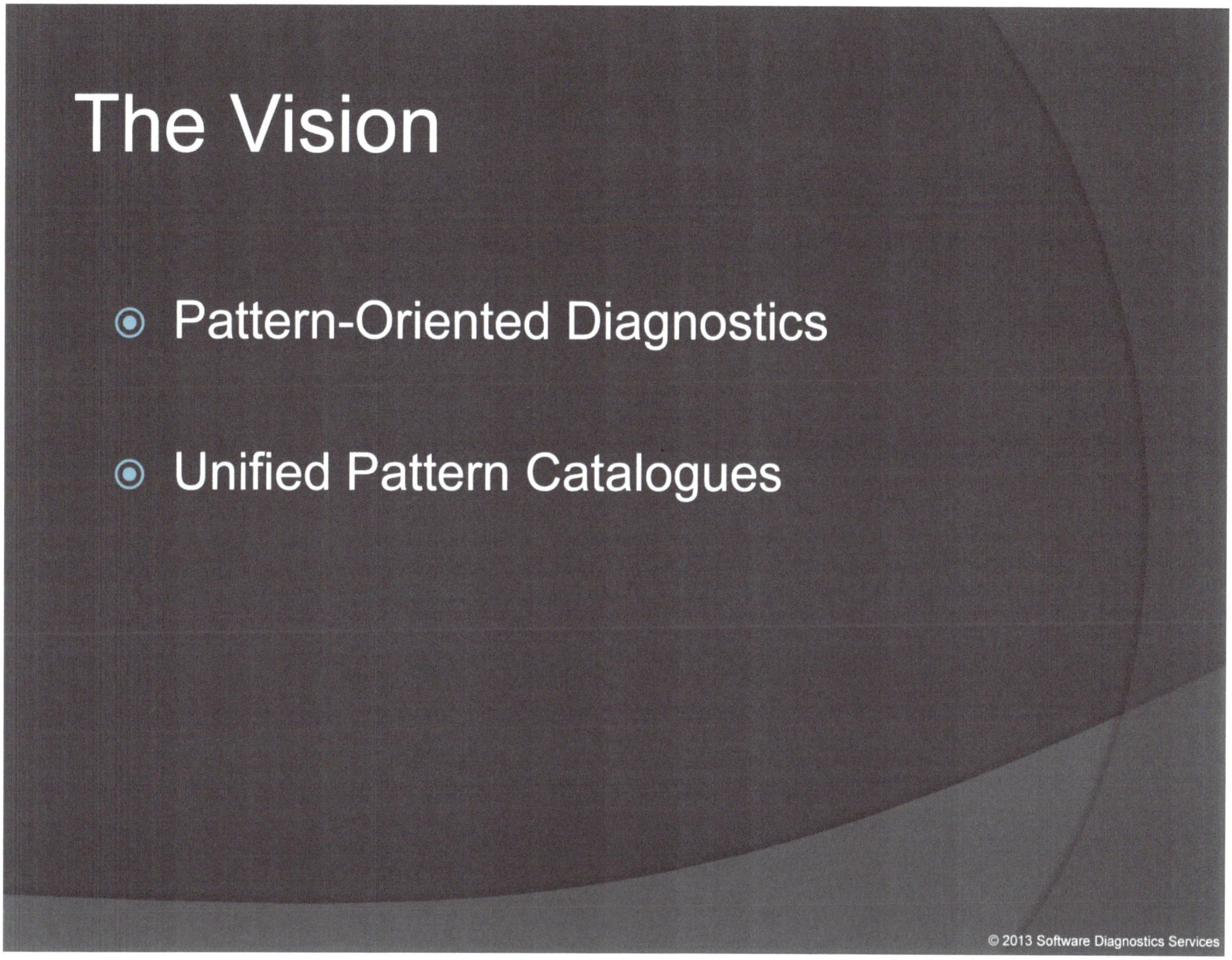

So our vision is reuse of traditional desktop/server diagnostics methods and tools and with this come adoption of pattern-orientation and unification of pattern catalogues and languages. Now I show you some slides from a few previous presentations mainly for those who are unfamiliar with pattern-oriented software diagnostics.

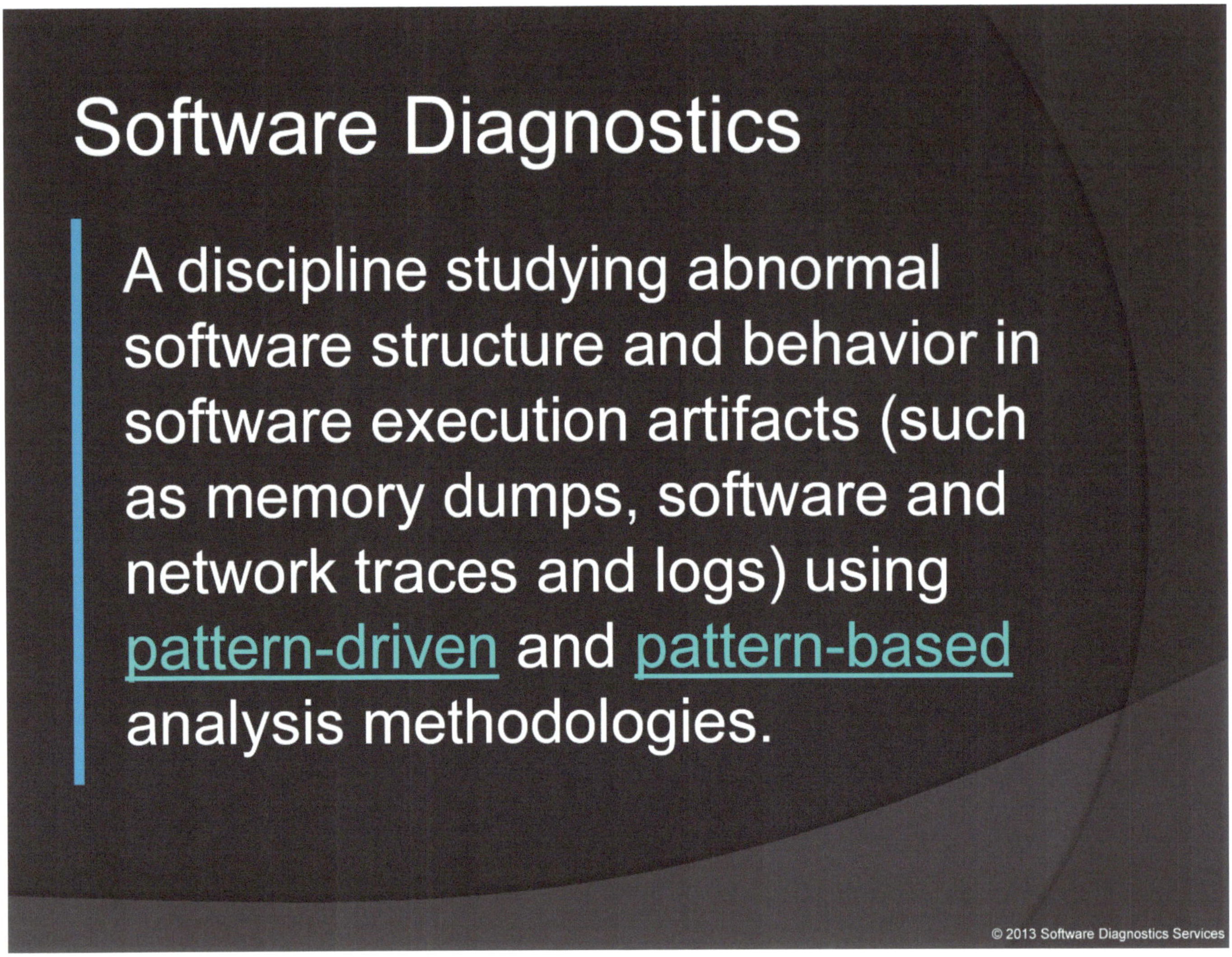

First, I would like to remind you a definition of pattern-oriented software diagnostics as pattern-driven and pattern-based.

Pattern-driven:
http://www.patterndiagnostics.com/Introduction-Software-Diagnostics-materials

Pattern-based:
http://www.patterndiagnostics.com/pattern-based-diagnostics-materials

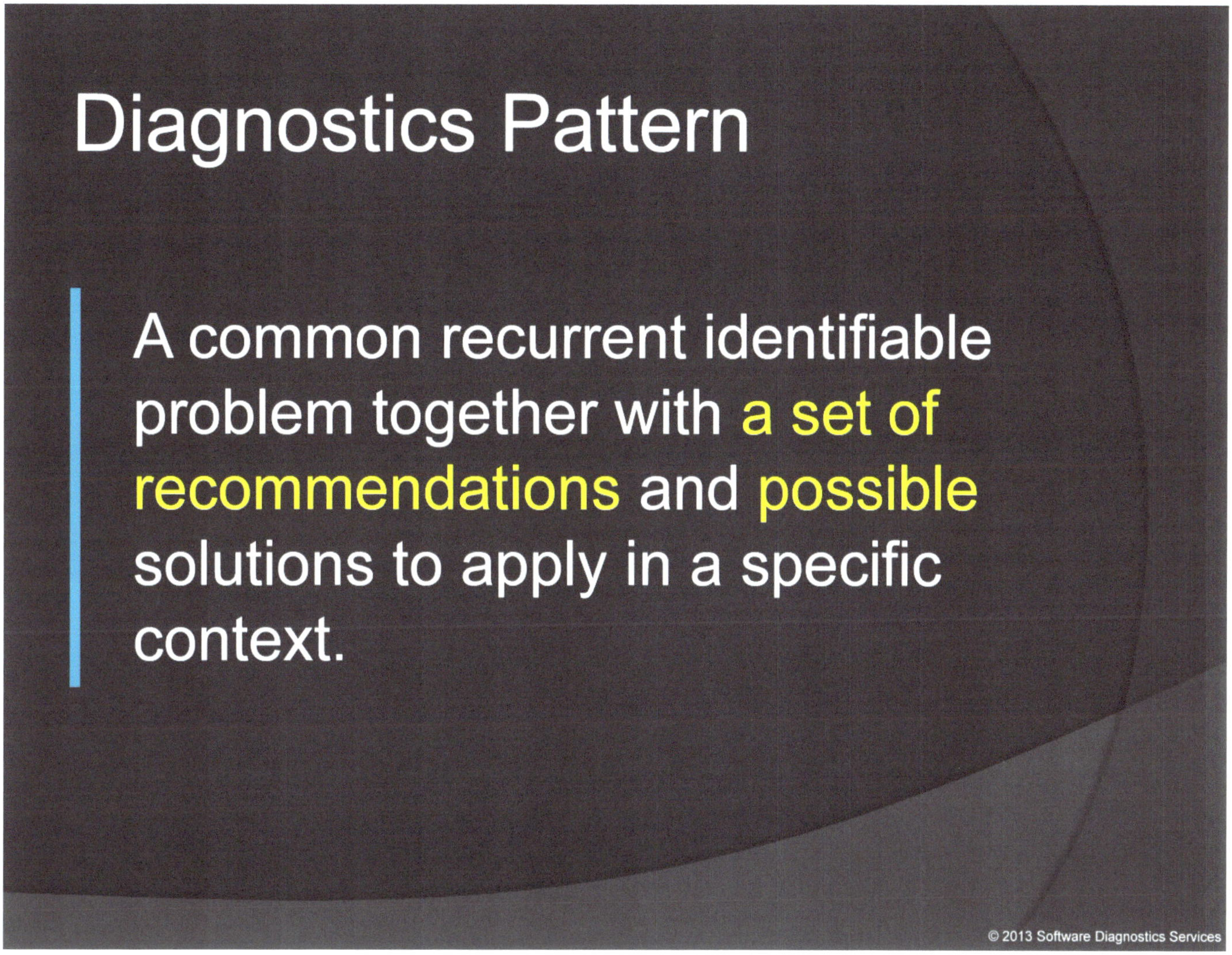

Next, I would like to remind you a definition of a software diagnostics pattern.

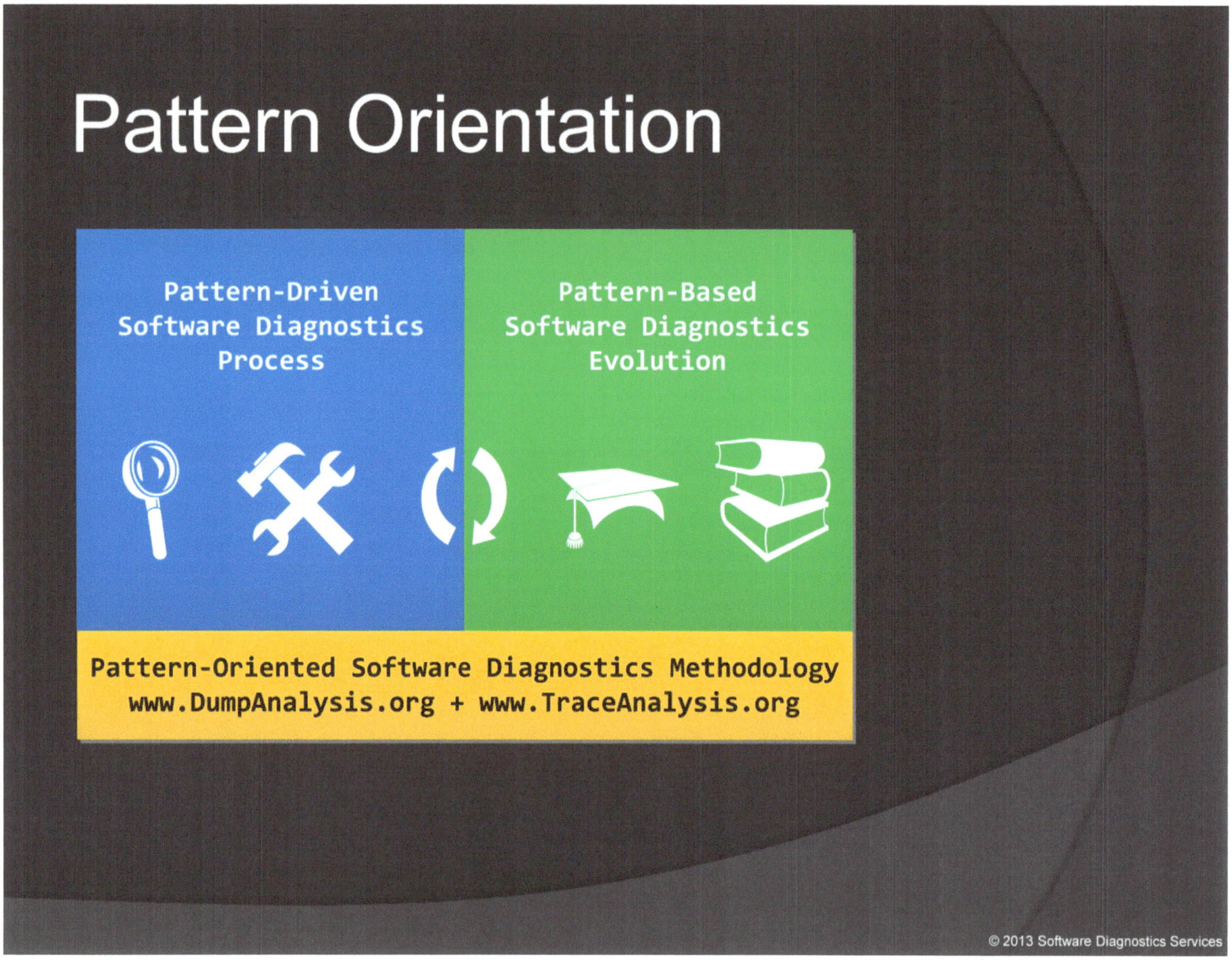

So you see that software diagnostics is about patterns. Pattern-driven part is about diagnostics pattern recognition and pattern-based part is about pattern and pattern catalogue life cycle.

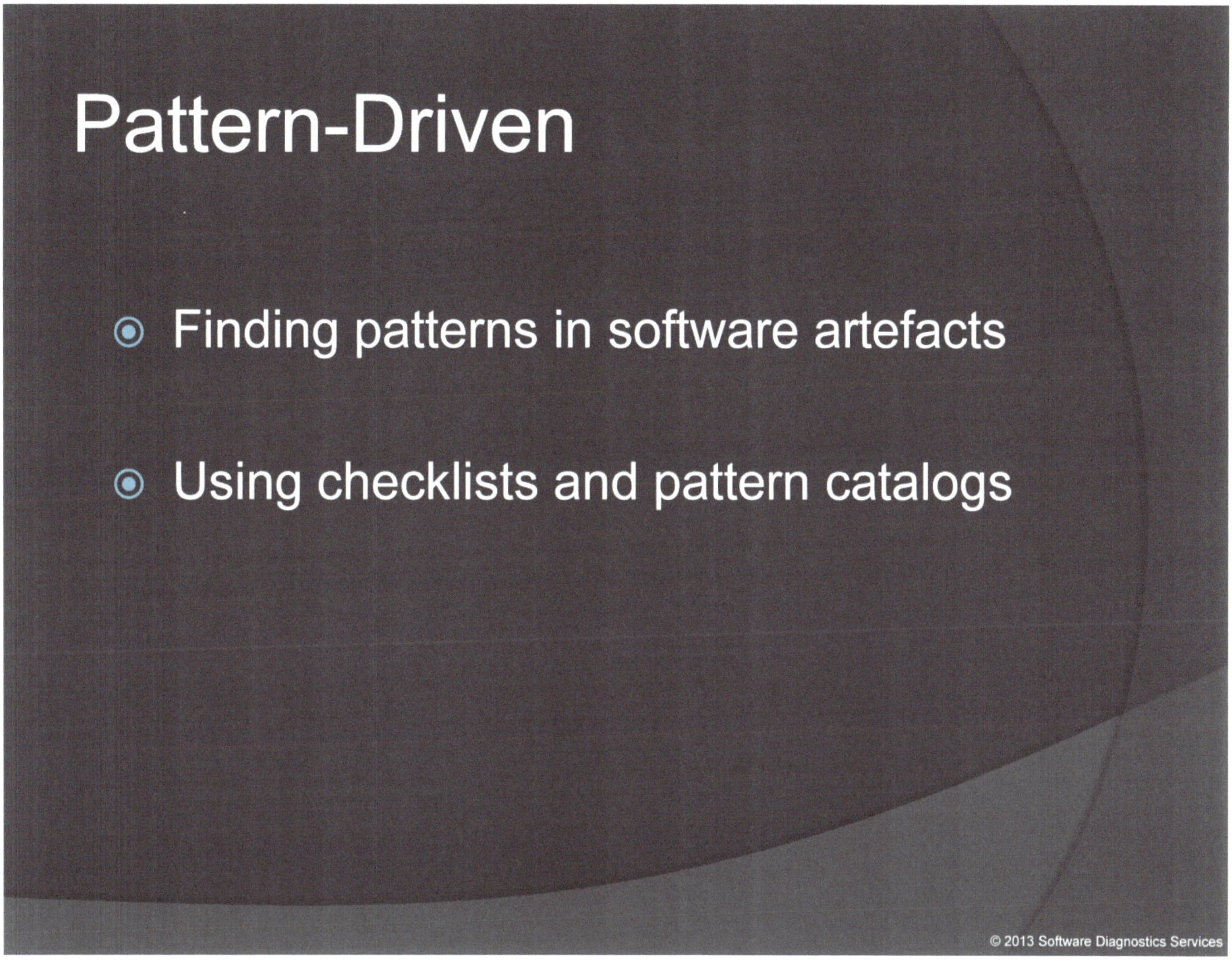

To repeat, pattern-driven means finding patterns of abnormal structure and behavior in software execution artifacts such as memory dumps, software logs and network traces. To help with this there are checklists, pattern catalogs, and tools.

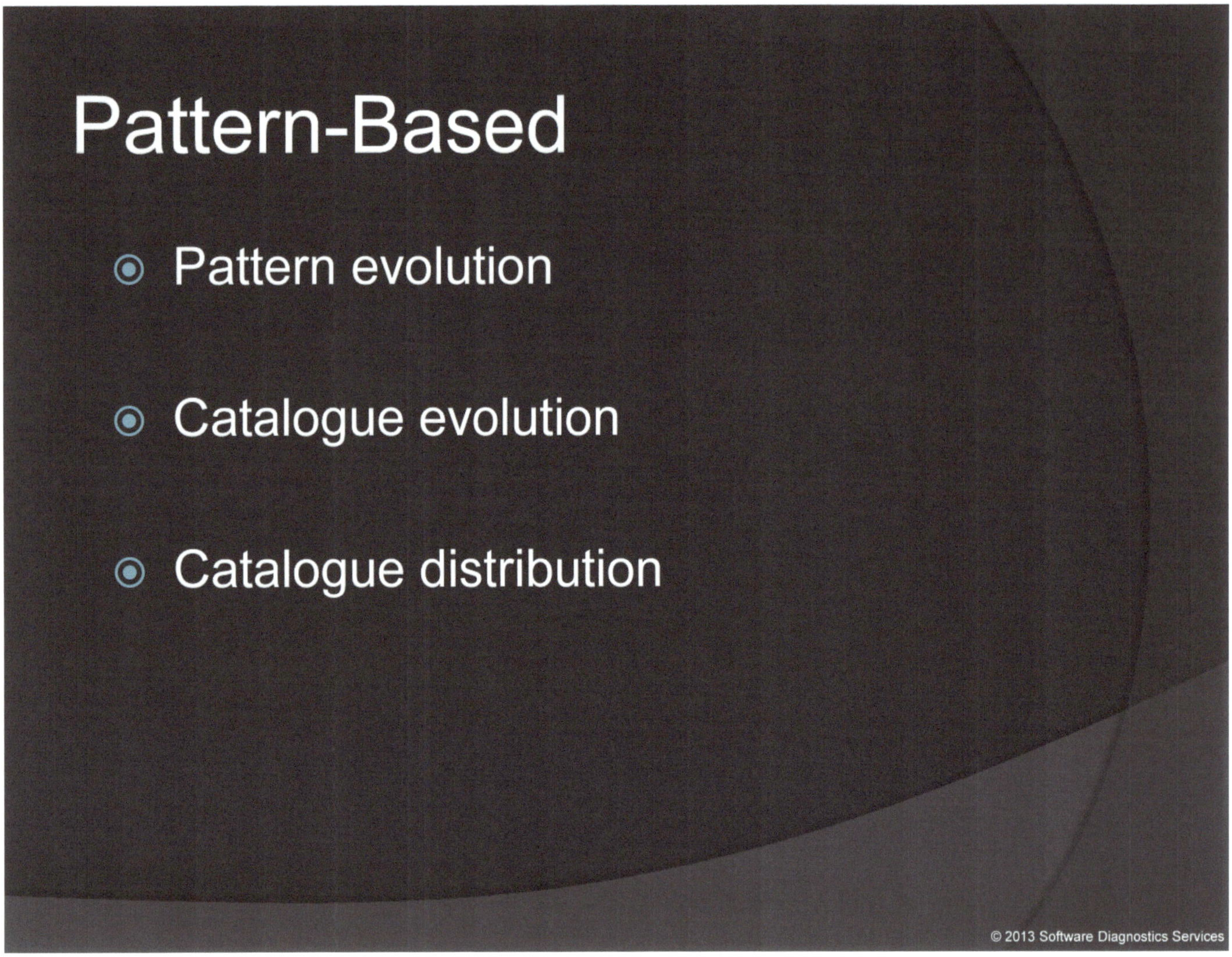

Patten-based part is about evolution and distribution. New patterns are constantly added, old ones are refined, new pattern descriptions for different platforms (we say pattern implementations as would be seen later on) are added. The customers of this technology need to be updated of all changes.

And so the reuse of pattern-oriented software diagnostics brings tangible economic benefits including quantifiable analysis such the number of patterns searched and the number of them identified.

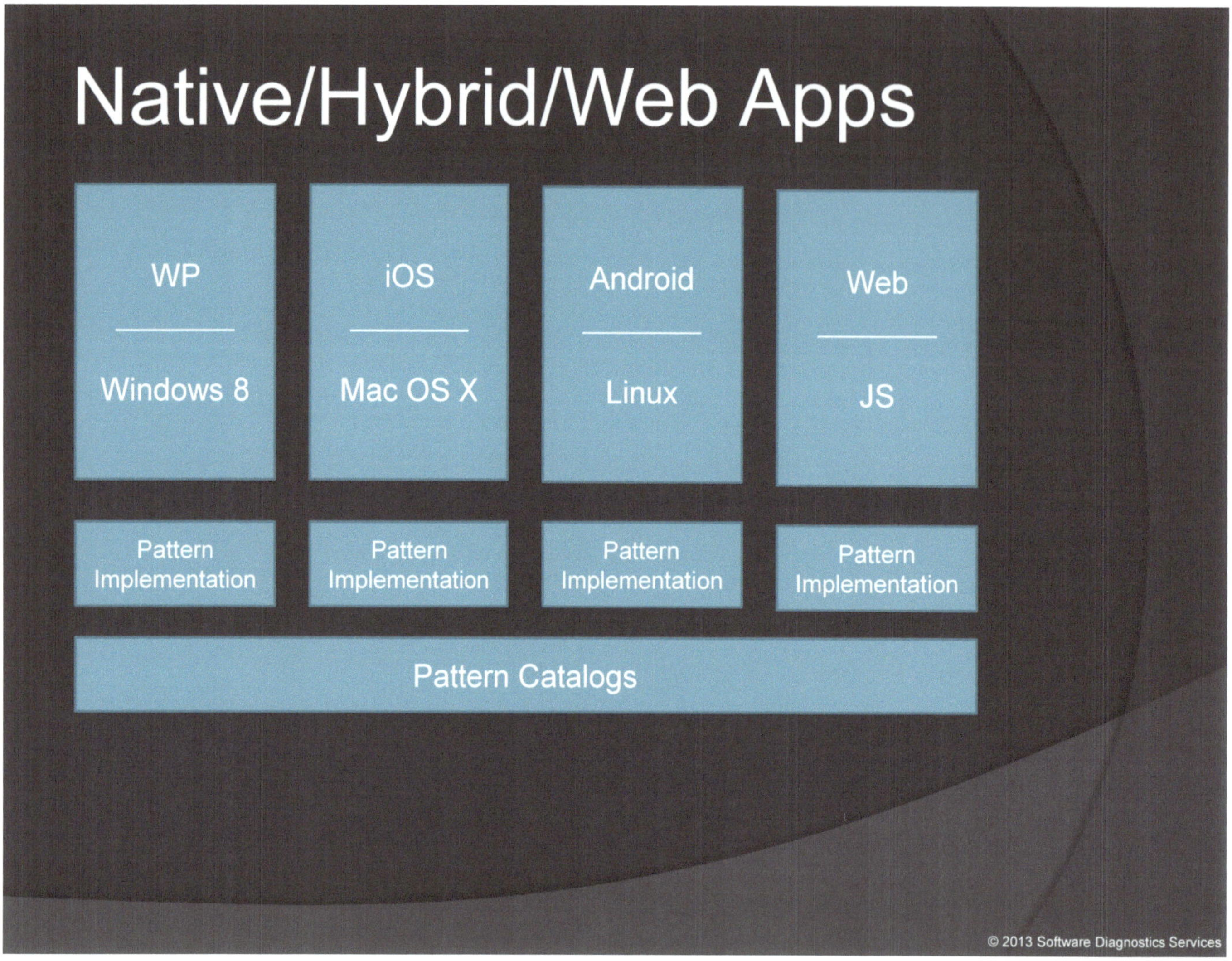

We see the main advantages of pattern-oriented diagnostics on this unification diagram for main mobile platforms. Such modern platforms are based on traditional desktop operating systems and so it is already possible to reuse tracing there. Unified pattern catalogues even allow for pattern prediction if a particular pattern implementation is missing on one platform but available for the other.

One example here we can provide is **Stack Trace Collection** memory analysis pattern. Originally it was discerned on Windows platforms for WinDbg debugger from Debugging Tools for Windows where we can get a collection of stack traces from all threads from a specific process or system including managed .NET stack traces. Later on another implementation was created for Mac OS X / GDB and to some extent it is possible to reuse it on Linux GDB debugger and other platforms that support GDB. Here is an example output from Android / Java platform and it is possible to reuse it for other Java implementations as well. You can see this Java implementation including modelling source code in one of the Debugging TV episodes I provide the link on Further Reading slide.

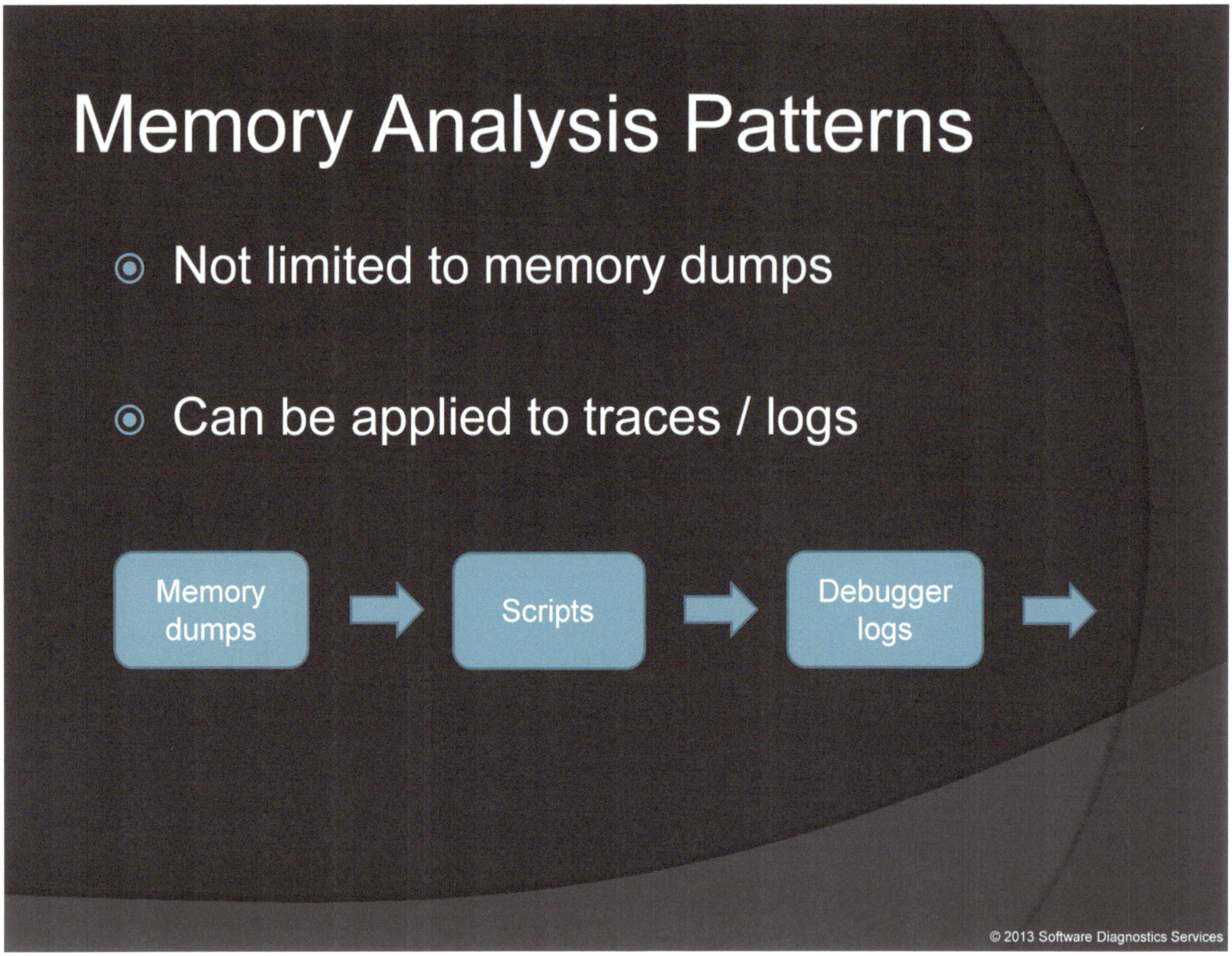

We saw on the previous slide that stack trace collection was taken from a log file. Contrary to common belief memory analysis is not limited to memory dumps or live debugging. It is common in software diagnostics of artefacts from the complex environments to process memory dumps into log files and then recognize patterns there.

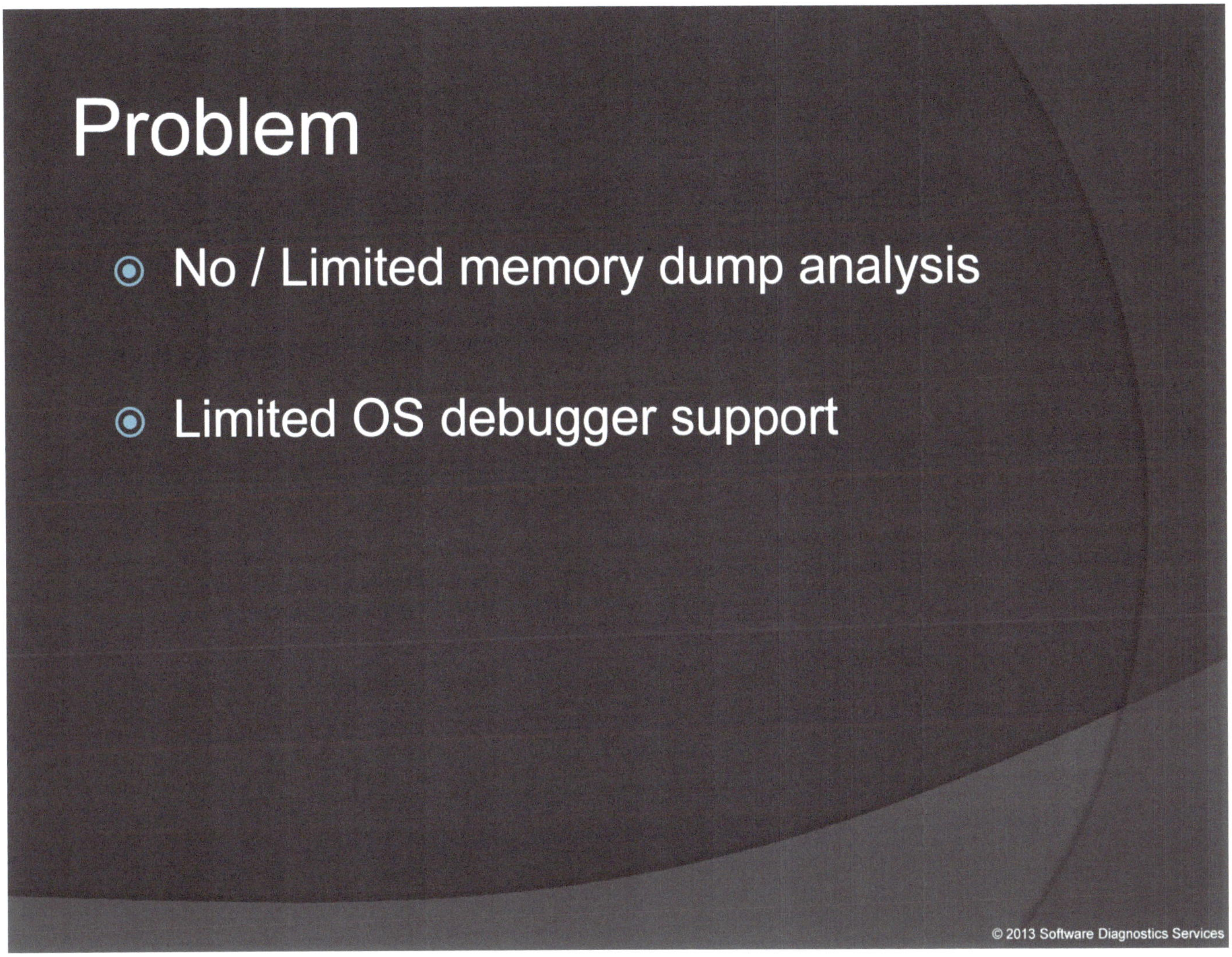

Now a few slides about one problem we found in the current state of mobile software diagnostics on some platforms. There is very limited memory dump analysis and if this is possible there is limited OS support for the platform debugger for postmortem analysis.

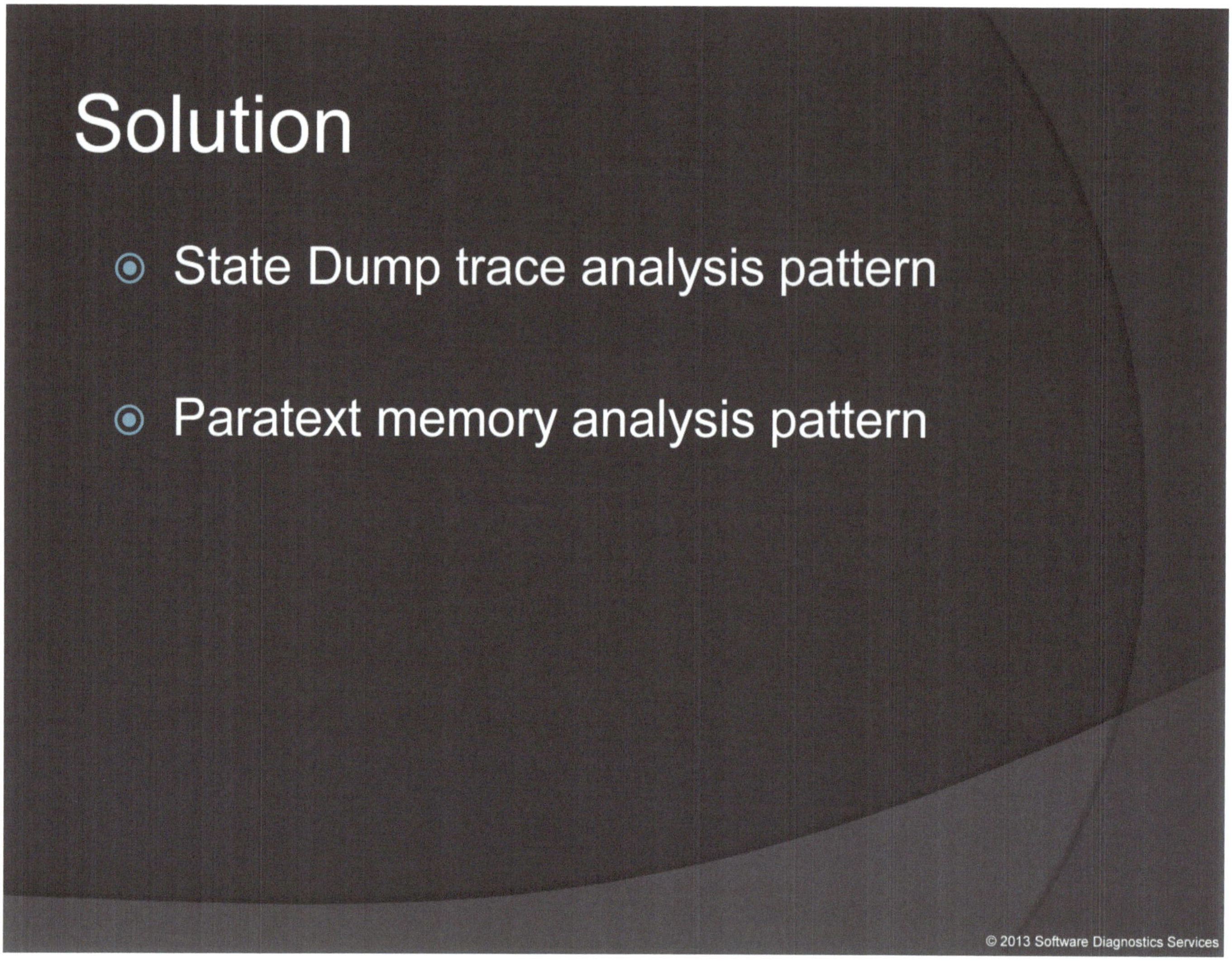

The solution we found for limited memory analysis is to introduce yet another trace analysis pattern that would allow reuse of some memory analysis patterns. It is called **State Dump** pattern and you would see a diagram explaining it on the next slide. For limited OS debugger support we reuse the so called **Paratext** pattern we explain further later on.

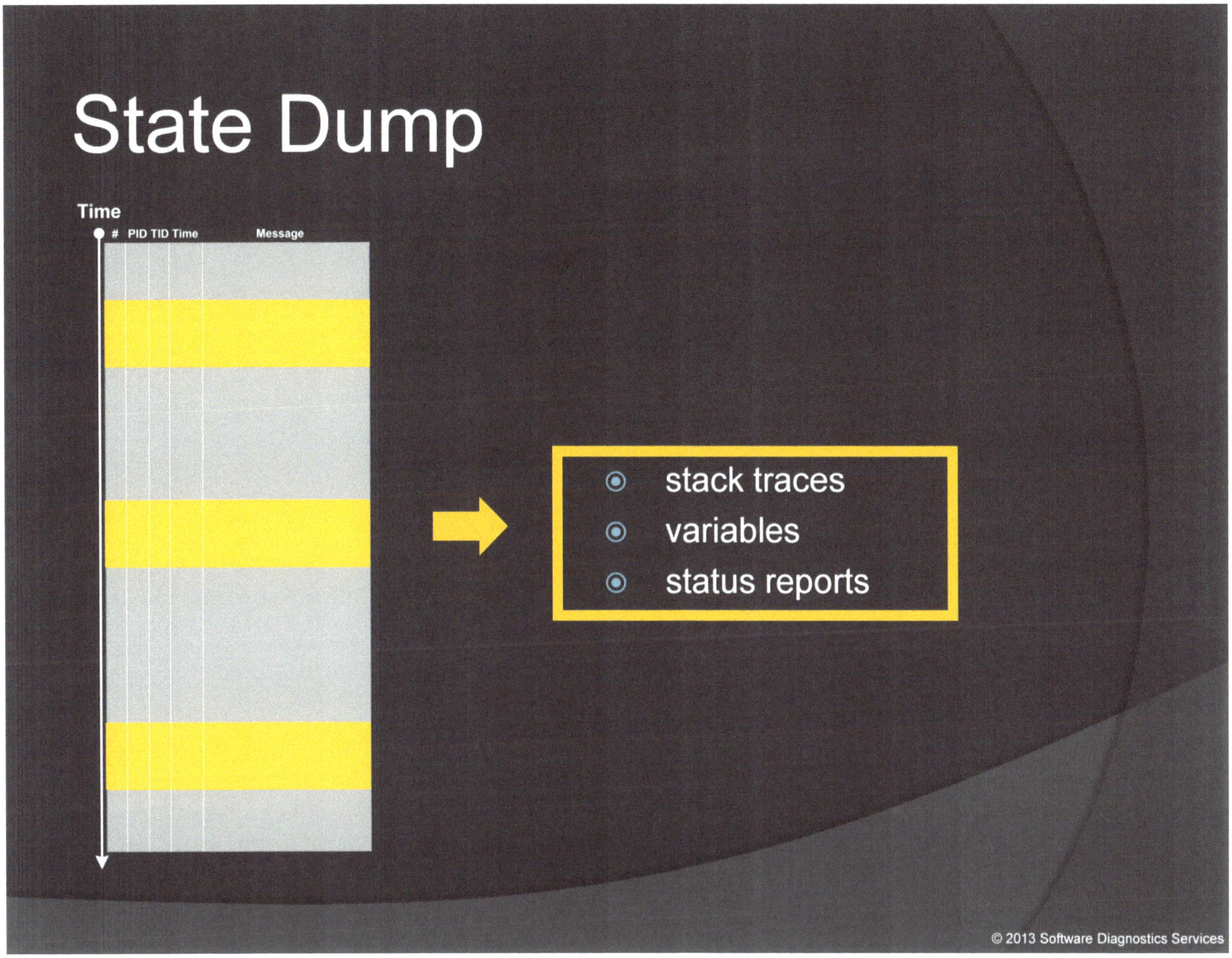

State Dump means periodic logging of stack traces, important variables and status reports.

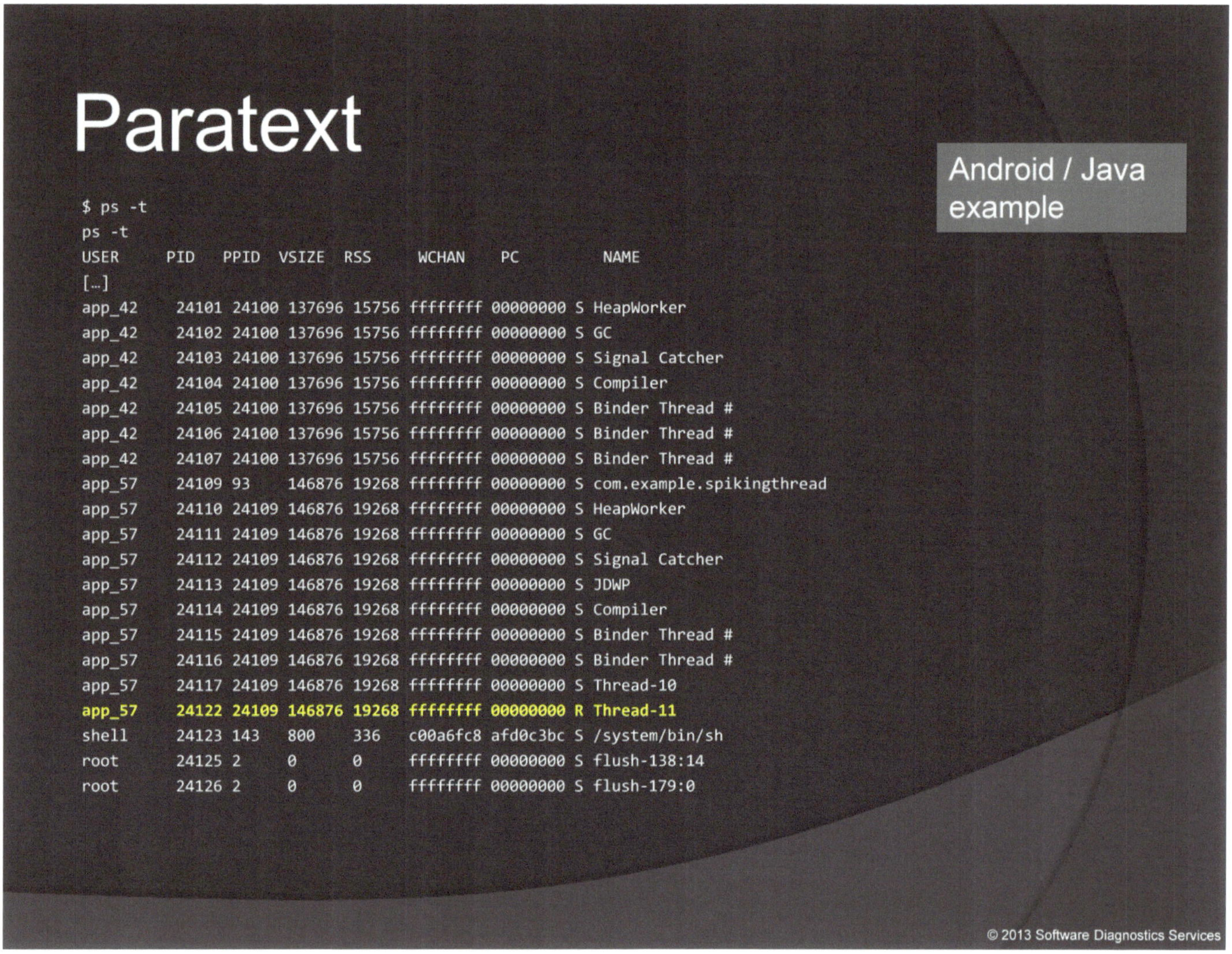

Paratext name originally comes from narratology and means extra information to supplement textual narrative such as notes and text description. Here information from a system collected by OS tools may assist in memory analysis. On this slide we see an indication of a running thread that helps with diagnosing **Spiking Thread** memory analysis pattern.

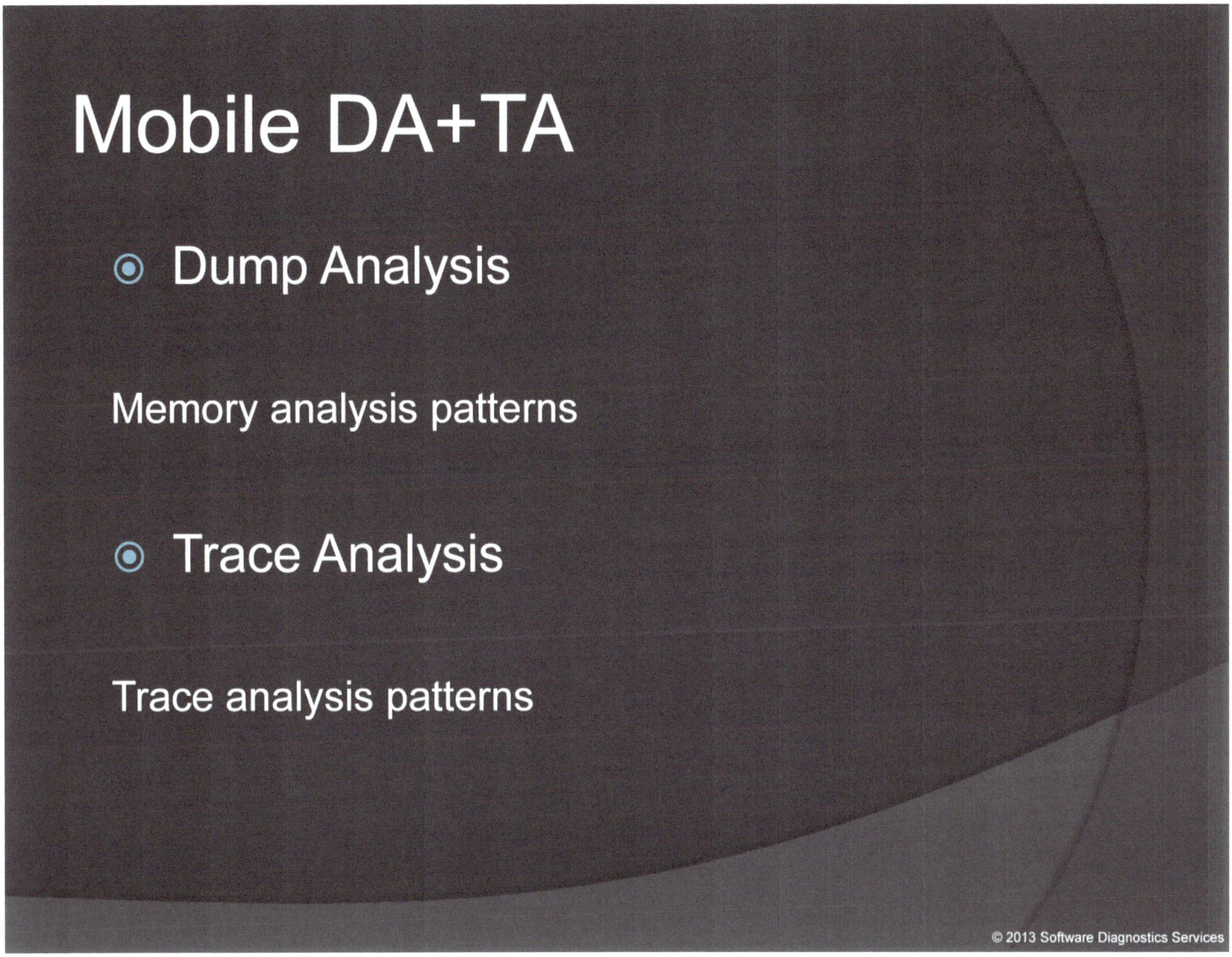

To summarize, it is possible to reuse **D**ump **A**nalysis and **T**race **A**nalysis pattern catalogues: what we call mobile DA+TA.

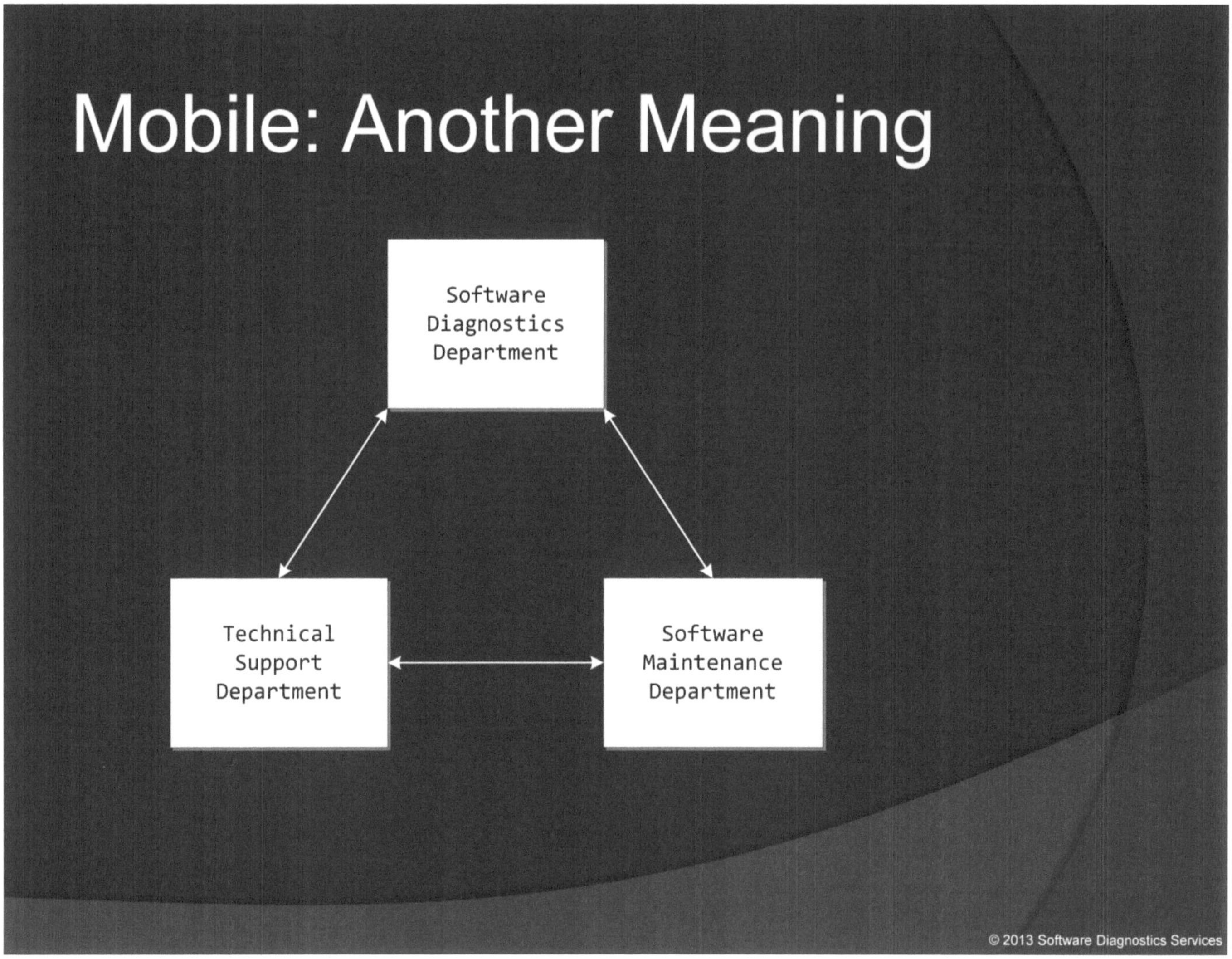

There is another meaning of “mobile” we would like to cover at the end of this presentation. It means flexible software diagnostics independent from support and engineering organizational structure and interaction. This is mainly for big companies of course.

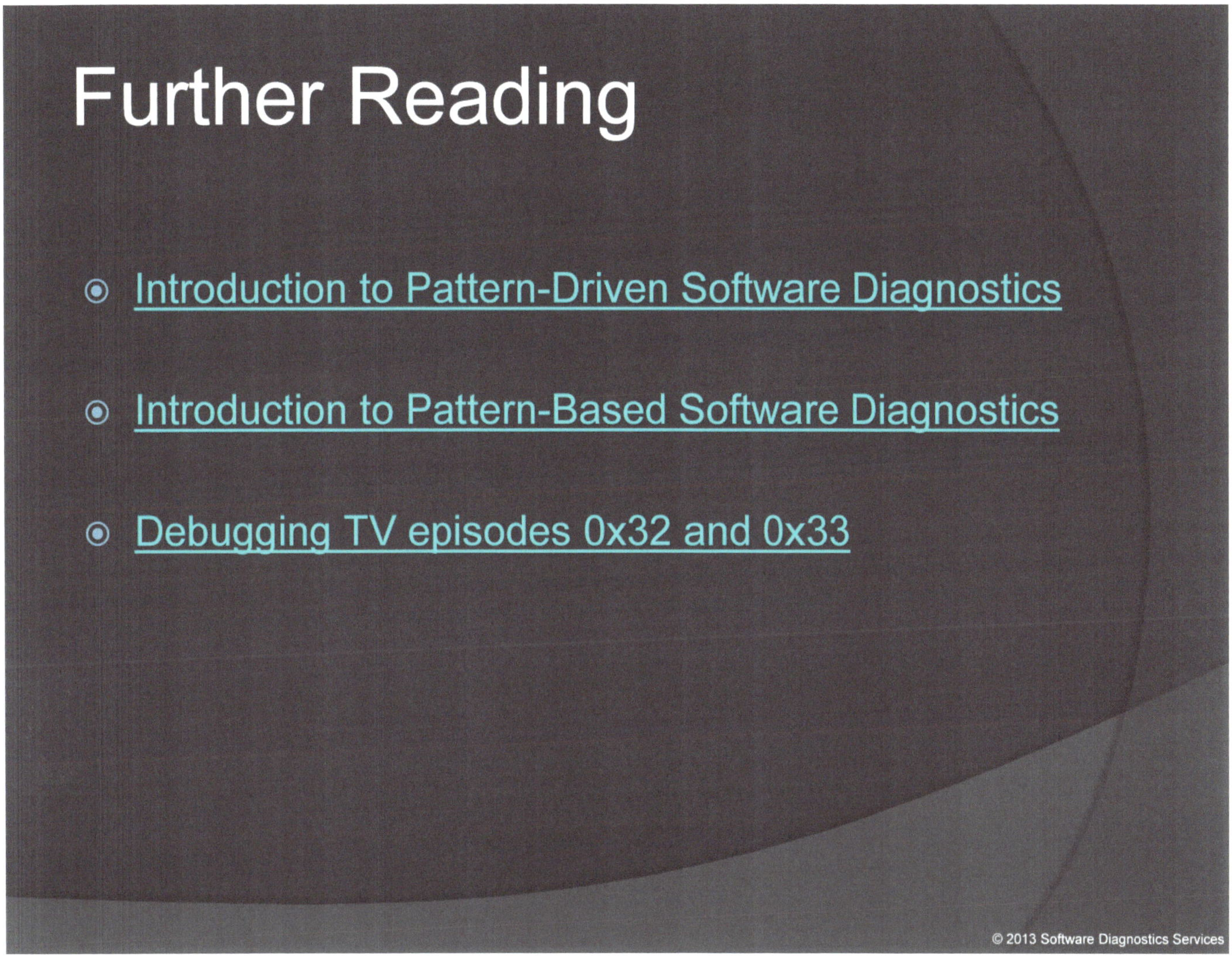

On this slide I included links to relevant past presentations focused on pattern-driven and pattern-based parts where you can find additional references such as for Software Narratology. There are also the recent Debugging TV episodes which provide pattern reuse examples for Android/Java platform I mentioned previously.

Introduction to Pattern-Driven Software Diagnostics:
http://www.patterndiagnostics.com/Introduction-Software-Diagnostics-materials

Introduction to Pattern-Based Software Diagnostics:
http://www.patterndiagnostics.com/pattern-based-diagnostics-materials

Debugging TV episodes 0x32 and 0x33:
http://www.debugging.tv/

www.ingramcontent.com/pod-product-compliance
Ingram Content Group UK Ltd.
Pitfield, Milton Keynes, MK11 3LW, UK
UKHW061545051026
15625UKWH00012B/619
* 9 7 8 1 9 0 6 7 1 7 6 6 7 *